The Depiction of Terrorists in Blockbuster Hollywood Films, 1980–2001

The Depiction of Terrorists in Blockbuster Hollywood Films, 1980–2001

An Analytical Study

HELENA VANHALA

McFarland & Company, Inc., Publishers
Jefferson, North Carolina, and London

Some sections of the book are based on an article published in *Jump Cut* No. 50, spring 2008. *Jump Cut: A Review of Contemporary Media* is available online at http://www.ejumpcut.org.

LIBRARY OF CONGRESS CATALOGUING-IN-PUBLICATION DATA

Vanhala, Helena.
The depiction of terrorists in blockbuster Hollywood films, 1980–2001 : an analytical study / Helena Vanhala.
p. cm.
Includes bibliographical references and index.

ISBN 978-0-7864-3662-0
softcover : 50# alkaline paper ♾

1. Terrorism in motion pictures. 2. Motion pictures — United States — History — 20th century. 3. Motion pictures — Political aspects — United States. I. Title.
PN1995.9.T46V36 2011 791.43'6556 — dc22 2010048308

British Library cataloguing data are available

Front cover image: *Blown Away* (1994, MGM/Photofest); background © 2011 Shutterstock

Manufactured in the United States of America

McFarland & Company, Inc., Publishers
Box 611, Jefferson, North Carolina 28640
www.mcfarlandpub.com

For my parents
Kaija and Teuvo Vanhala

In memory of my brother
Jukka Vanhala

Contents

Acknowledgments

This research grew out of the question of how Hollywood films have portrayed modern international terrorism in an era when we need accurate information about the threats that are confronting the world, in particular international terrorism and its threat to the lives of innocent bystanders. The research has been a long process, and I sincerely want to acknowledge the people who have reviewed my work, and my family and friends whose presence and support have made it possible for me to reach the finish line.

Many thanks go to Janet Wasko, Julia Lesage, H. Leslie Steeves, Steve Ponder and Lars Skålnes at the University of Oregon, who provided thoughtful feedback on the very first version of the manuscript. Also, thanks to Virpi Zuck, Alan G. Stavitsky, Tim Gleason and Petra Hagen for their support, and to the three journalism and communication professors whose courses during my exchange year at the university inspired me to continue my studies at the School of Journalism and Communication at the University of Oregon: Ron Sherriffs, Bill Willingham, and Michael Majdic. Great appreciation goes to Bob Avery at the University of Utah for his friendship and advice to an international scholar in the U.S.

People at the Division of Communication at the University of Wisconsin, Stevens Point, in particular Mark Tolstedt and Rich Ilkka, have not only been colleagues but also family and friends whom I cherish. Also, many thanks for their support to my colleagues at the Media Arts Department at Robert Morris University, and to David Jamison, Barbara Levine and Tim Hadfield for their support for trips to present work in the U.S. and abroad, and for their encouragement. Also, a big round of applause goes to my students at Robert Morris University and the University of Wisconsin, Stevens Point. Their questions and interest in the topic of terrorism and Hollywood portrayals of international terrorism were great motivators for me to finish the research and manuscript, and make the work available to a bigger audience. Also, thanks to a fellow film and James Bond enthusiast, Ken Hartman.

In Finland, the University of Tampere was central in my leap across the Atlantic. Many thanks to Tenho Takalo, Olli Vehviläinen, David Robertson, and the Department of Journalism and Mass Communication, and the Department of English Philology.

Also many thanks to Tom Adamich who was the first to mention my research to my editor, which led to this book.

Thanks also to Linda and Dave Pompel, who were a family away from family during my years in Eugene, and to Grant and Lelia Smith, and Kathryn and Gavin, with whom I first experienced the U.S. as a high school exchange student.

I truly wish to express my sincere thanks and appreciation to my parents, Kaija and Teuvo Vanhala, and the rest of my family in Finland: Jukka, Olga and Aleksandra Vanhala, Anne, Jouko, Toni, Rita and Mari Karttunen, and Eeva, Timo, Venla and Santeri Kääriä, for their always-unwavering support and encouragement. Home is where your family is, and they are always in my heart.

Finally, who knew that a short motorcycle ride on the back of a Harley-Davidson in Las Vegas in the middle of an academic convention could turn into the ride of a lifetime. Many thanks to Tim Hudson for his inspiration, support, and advice, and for being there now and always.

Introduction: Bringing the Terrorist into Frame

Make no mistake, we will hunt down the enemy, we will find the enemy, and we will kill the enemy.

—Actor Bruce Willis as General William Devereaux, *The Siege* (1998), 20th Century Fox

Make no mistake, the United States will hunt down and punish those responsible for these cowardly attacks.

—President George W. Bush, September 11, 2001

Terrorism is a political method for creating spectacles of violence aimed at news media audiences. Both international terrorists and Hollywood filmmakers have understood this. For real-life terrorists the success of their acts equals news media coverage that reaches large audiences around the world, creating fear and chaos in society. Similarly, the commercial film industry measures the success of its film versions of international terrorism in large audiences — that is, in paying audiences. For film producers, big sales at the box office translate into commercial profitability.

On Tuesday morning, September 11, 2001, real-life terrorism caught up with fictional film terrorism and created the largest terrorist media spectacle seen since the 1972 Munich Olympic Games, when Palestinian terrorists took hostage and eventually killed eleven Israeli athletes. Twenty-nine years after the Munich massacre, as it was called, the world's leading news media were broadcasting live images that looked familiar from the movie screen: from plane hijackings, high-rise explosions and suicide attacks, to anti–American hatred. But the story was not over after an exciting two-hour rollercoaster ride, and the "actors" did not get back on their feet after the cameras stopped rolling. The coordinated attacks of 9/11 killed some 3,000 real people and caused real destruction. They also brought to a standstill the part of the media industry whose fictional disasters the real-life events resembled most: the commercial Hollywood film industry. No Hollywood production could match the audience or events of that day. Some film professionals, among them director Robert Altman, even blamed Hollywood for having taught terrorists how to attack America.[1] In the midst of extensive suffering, Hollywood postponed the theatrical releases of films that had terrorism themes, and also shelved terrorism-themed television movies. Two days after the attacks, Hollywood producer John Davis told the *Wall Street Journal*: "Once it becomes reality and not fantasy, it ceases to be entertaining."[2]

While the television networks and cable channels were continuing 24-hour coverage of

General Devereaux (Bruce Willis) brings New York City under a military siege when he declares martial law in *The Siege* (1998, 20th Century Fox) to counter fundamentalist Islamic terrorists. Similarly, after 9/11 the George W. Bush administration considered deploying military force on U.S. soil to combat international terrorism.

the attacks and their aftermath, the commercial film industry was predicting terrorism to be off limits as a movie topic for years to come because the experience of actual terrorism on U.S. soil had so traumatized the nation. Warner Bros. was one of the first major film studios to face the new post-attack world. The studio decided to delay the release of its newest Arnold Schwarzenegger film, *Collateral Damage*, which portrays Colombian terrorism on U.S. soil. The movie studio's caution about the release of its terrorist film did not echo the public reaction to the attacks. The rental of films on terrorism, such as *Die Hard* (1988) and *The Siege* (1998), skyrocketed in the first weeks after the attacks[3] when Americans rushed to see fictional disasters on their home screens, seeking refuge in witnessing how scores of foreign terrorists would die at the hands of American heroes at the end of each film — something that reality failed to provide for shocked audiences on September 11, 2001.

The Hollywood Terrorist: A Loan from the U.S. Foreign Policy Agenda and News Headlines

Acts of international terrorism fit the traditional Hollywood action film genre structure. Action films are traditionally about a conflict between an American hero and a foreign villain.

Politically motivated acts of violence that cross international borders offer screenwriters an opportunity to create a variety of foreign threats which domestic heroes remove after a thrilling two-hour narrative. For Hollywood's action-packed film productions, terrorism has been a creatively productive and financially profitable source of entertainment, in particular for the industry's ultra-high-budget action-adventure film genre, which emerged in Hollywood in the 1980s as an attempt to create larger profits for production and distribution companies.

The American commercial film industry has often borrowed its story ideas from the U.S. foreign policy agenda, at times reinforcing U.S. policies and at other times undermining them, offering alternative interpretations to official policies and news media portrayals. It took a while before Hollywood found international terrorism. Film producers rarely touched the topic in the late 1960s and in the 1970s when the phenomenon was not high on the U.S. foreign policy agenda, in the news headlines or in the American public consciousness. In the 1980s, in the footsteps of the Reagan administration, the commercial film industry found international terrorism a threat to the U.S. and brought terrorist villains to the big screen, eventually making international terrorism a blockbuster film product in the 1990s. Fictional spectacles of terrorism quickly surpassed real-life terrorism in their destructiveness and firepower.

Movie images of international relations and state affairs, including portrayals of international terrorism, may manipulate viewers' understanding of real world events, especially when in-depth international affairs news coverage reaches only a small number of Americans. News media representatives argue that Americans are not interested in foreign news, and then use that argument as an excuse for not covering the rest of the world properly and in depth. For example, in the late 1990s foreign news stories comprised less than two percent of local daily newspapers' content. The papers treated foreign news stories as filler unless the U.S. was heavily involved in a foreign crisis.[4] The situation is not any better in the 21st century when the mainstream news media of the world's only superpower largely ignores the world's almost two hundred other sovereign nations. Typically, mainstream news coverage focuses on a small number of countries, less than a dozen. The focus is on the closest allies and main adversaries. This narrow worldview is also familiar in Hollywood portrayals of the rest of the world.

A culture industry such as Hollywood and its cultural products are central in the creation of consensus and popular mentality in society because they reach vast audiences. Hollywood influence is not only limited to the United States. Hollywood entertainment is the second largest American export after military hardware,[5] with Hollywood films shown in over 150 countries. For the first time the international box office beat the domestic box office revenue numbers in 1993, and it soon took over the main revenue producer position.[6] As a result, the commercial film industry now produces films with the global market in mind. The domestic market alone is often too small to cover the production costs of the biggest films, whose budgets can easily march beyond the $100 million mark in their efforts to produce spectacles that could gain worldwide blockbuster status. Big investments are expected to bring in big profits, after all, Hollywood studios are dependent on the financial success of their films in order to stay in business. The focus on a film's success at the box office has resulted in the repeated use of film formats that have been popular among viewers in the past.

At best, Hollywood films can provide viewers with information about events of which they know little, if anything. But the commercial film industry is not shy about reinventing history if a crudely fictionalized version of real events matches its financial interests and traditional screenwriting formats better than the real story. At worst, Hollywood films can serve as propaganda tools, offering screen stories that distort history and stereotype national, racial, ethnic, cultural and religious groups for the sake of a profit.

Modern International Terrorism, the United States, and the Media

The year 1968 is generally considered to be the starting year of modern international terrorism due to the July 23, 1968, hijacking of an Israeli airliner by the Popular Front for the Liberation of Palestine (PFLP).[7] The attack and the perpetrators of the attack crossed international borders for political motivations and to gain worldwide news media coverage. The U.S. government started to collect annual statistical data on international terrorism that same year. However, the U.S. did not become a prime target of terrorists seekng world media attention until Iranian students overtook the American embassy in Tehran on November 4, 1979. The Iran hostage crisis (1979–1981) truly introduced the topic of international terrorism to the American public. U.S. television networks covered the crisis in detail every single day of the 444-day event. Iran released the fifty-two American hostages who went through the whole ordeal on the day President Ronald Reagan took office in January 1981.

The unprecedented extensive news media coverage of the Iran hostage crisis alerted international terrorists to the potential of U.S. citizens as targets and in attracting the American news media to spread news images of terrorist acts worldwide. The United States became a favorite international terrorist target due to its policies, interests, media, and military presence around the world. Terrorists encountered a conservative Republican president, Ronald Reagan, who was more likely to rely on military power in his policies and responses than was his predecessor, President Carter. Under President Reagan the U.S. took a tough stand on terrorism, interpreting the phenomenon through the prism of the Cold War.

The news media are central in modern international terrorism because terrorists seek international news coverage. Terrorists have learned the news values of the Western mainstream media, which disproportionately focus on violence. The news media also have a central role in the public understanding of terrorism. When modern international terrorism emerged in the late 1960s, the news media and reporters were crucial sources of information because they were the only sources of information on the topic, other than government. For example, research on the topic in academic circles was hindered by a fear that it would be interpreted as support for the perpetrators of terrorist acts.[8]

Previous analysis of the relationship between the media and terrorism has heavily focused on the relationship between the *news* media and terrorism. While the news media and reporters play crucial roles in modern terrorism, today they are not alone in creating a public understanding of the phenomenon. Commercial films on domestic and international terrorism have been spreading a fictionalized Hollywood version of the phenomenon around the world, in particular since the Reagan era. However, only a few of the films have been blockbusters. These films have often found their heroes in white American men, and villains in foreigners or American minorities.

The little research there is on Hollywood portrayals of international terrorism heavily concentrates on the image of Arabs, arguing that Hollywood has stereotyped Arabs as psychopathic terrorists. While that may be partially true, the portrayal is not unique to films that depict Arabs. It follows the action-adventure film tradition which often finds the villain's motivation, no matter what his (rarely her) nationality or ethnic background is, in his insanity. Furthermore, only a few of the films that portray Arab terrorism have been blockbusters. In other words, most of those films have not reached large audiences in movie theaters (which are also the launching pads for home viewing).

While insanity is a familiar characterization of most film terrorists, Hollywood reserves certain stereotypes and characterizations for film terrorists according to their national, cultural, ethnic and religious background. Furthermore, the ways in which Hollywood heroes kill terrorist villains and in what numbers are dependent on the part of the world from which the fictional terrorists come.

The Book's Purpose

The purpose of this book is to offer an understanding of how the commercial film industry's economic interests intertwined with U.S. foreign policy interests have influenced the portrayal of international terrorism in blockbuster Hollywood films. Blockbuster action and action-adventure films' portrayals of terrorist threats and international terrorists parallel the U.S. Department of State's views of international terrorism. However, due to the commercial film industry's reliance on film formats that have been commercially profitable in the past, film portrayals offer more simplified and stereotypical images of terrorists than do the official documents on international terrorism.

While Hollywood has at times been critical of U.S. policies on and interpretation of international terrorism — for example, in Latin America in the 1980s —films critical of the prevailing U.S. foreign policy have not been popular among paying audiences. Filmmakers have acknowledged this. After all, commercial film production is a business: a film that does not return its investment and bring in profits is simply bad business.

Film genres follow the traditional classical Hollywood cinema narrative structure of a hero versus a villain but also respond to prevailing political conditions, as well as to changes in public opinion and audience interests. During specific political eras it is possible to find certain genres, themes and styles which dominate, and which are repeated. When political changes are under way, the previously repeated themes start to change.[9] These trends can be seen in the historical development of commercial films on international terrorism. Hollywood has updated its fictional terrorist threats as real-life terrorist threats have changed. For example, in the 1980s the U.S. State Department and news headlines highlighted Libya and Hezbollah, an Iran-backed Shia organization with headquarters in Lebanon, and a worldwide communist network as terrorist threats that the country was facing. Commercial films also brought these topics to viewers. In the post–Cold War era (the 1990s specifically) Northern Irish terrorists, fundamentalist Islamic terrorists, communist and anti-communist villains, all ripped from the decade's news headlines, made the biggest splash in the North American box office.

Methodology and Study Data

This book analyzes the ideological role of film in society. The mass media, including films, have ideological power to define reality. This includes the ownership of problems in society, such as terrorism and other threats.[10] Culture industries, such as the commercial film industry, and cultural products, including films on terrorism, are central in the creation of consensus and popular mentality because they reach vast audiences. For this particular study the focus is on the larger social construction of one particular problem and threat, modern international terrorism, and its portrayal in Hollywood films.

My study defines a terrorist film as an action or action-adventure film that uses modern international terrorism as the main theme. I have examined terrorist films that were produced, distributed and exhibited in the domestic market between the time period of the first major international terrorist attack against the U.S., the Iran hostage crisis (1979–1981), and the September 11, 2001, simultaneous international terrorist attacks against the United States. The latter, according to President George W. Bush, made international terrorism the first major American war of the 21st century.[11] I analyzed each year's top fifty domestic box office earners, collecting the information from film and entertainment industry publication *Variety*'s online edition, Variety.com, which gathered the information from *Variety* and Nielsen EDI. According to Nielsen EDI, it is "the first centralized source for box office information," and "the film industry's No. 1 provider of reliable, accurate and timely box office information."[12] The company has domestic box office data available from 1982 forward. Variety.com provides data from 1980 forward, relying in its data also on information collected from *Variety.* According to Variety.com:

> Box office receipts are calculated via reports from the studios and from the exhibitors, and are subject to early estimates and later corrections....
>
> Domestic box office totals (weekly and weekend charts) come directly from EDI's database....
>
> On the other hand, the charts in the newspaper are created entirely from *Variety's* internal data in order to meet our production deadlines.
>
> Therefore, the chart on Variety.com and the chart in Variety may not match exactly. Variety includes box office totals from French-speaking Quebec (EDI does not), courtesy of Alex Films, a Quebec box office agency. Also, a distributor may report box office numbers to Variety but not to EDI, or vice versa.
>
> EDI has domestic box office data from 1982 forward. In some cases, it is not possible to calculate a film's final gross by using its weekly box office receipts due to unreported or missing grosses. In most cases, however, the running total displayed on the chart as "Domestic Box Office Total," has been adjusted to reflect the film's box office total through the specified play period.[13]

I compiled and identified films as action or action-adventure and terrorist films from *Variety*, Variety.com, the Internet Movie Database,[14] *Variety Movie Guide 2001, Halliwell's Film and Video Guide 2001*,[15] and by watching hundreds of films for their content to see if they fall under the analysis category. I analyzed the films in a widescreen DVD format, which was available in the analysis time for all but one film. *The Delta Force*'s North American release was available only in a standard format. I viewed each film several times on a large screen, using a video projector.

From 1980 through September 11, 2001, Hollywood produced sixteen films that used international terrorism as the film's central theme, and which were in the annual domestic top fifty box office:

Invasion USA (1985)
Commando (1985)
Iron Eagle (1986)
The Delta Force (1986)
Die Hard (1988)
Die Hard 2: Die Harder (1990)
Patriot Games (1992)
Passenger 57 (1992)
Blown Away (1994)
True Lies (1994)
Die Hard with a Vengeance (1995)
Executive Decision (1996)
Air Force One (1997)
The Jackal (1997)
Ronin (1998)
The Siege (1998)

The sixteen films are action, in particular action-adventure, films. Movies in this genre are the commercial film industry's most popular and profitable products in both the domestic and the foreign market. These sixteen films are the international terrorist films that reached the largest domestic movie theater audiences annually in the years 1980–2001. The films have produced popular cultural images of international terrorism, and therefore have a bearing on the public understanding of the phenomenon.

While Hollywood produced dozens of films in the 1980s that had international terrorism as their central theme, only five of the films broke into the top fifty domestic box office in that decade. When spectacular international terrorist incidents started to claim more space in the American news headlines in the 1990s after the end of the Cold War, spectacular terrorist attacks also started to threaten American citizens in growing numbers in the domestic box office top fifty. Eleven films on international terrorism were among the top fifty annual films in the 1990s. No film that had international terrorism as its central theme cracked the domestic box office top fifty between January 1, 2000, and September 11, 2001.

I chose 1980 as the study's starting year because of the significance of the Iran hostage crisis. The production of a Hollywood film is a long process, which at the very minimum takes several months, but more likely from a year to two.[16] The year 1980 is the study's starting year because the influence of the Tehran hostage crisis on the choice of film themes would not have been seen until 1980 at the very earliest.

As the power changed in the White House in January 1981, also the commercial film industry took notice of the new president's antiterrorism policies. The annual box office data[17] reveal that terrorist films did not truly emerge until in the 1980s when the Reagan administration highlighted international terrorism. The new administration found the main threats in the Middle East and in the Soviet-led worldwide Red Terror Network which, in President Reagan's view, was threatening the U.S., particularly in Latin America. Toward the end of President Reagan's second term the red scare was fast disappearing as the Cold War was crumbling.

The 1980s also saw the emergence of VCRs as a home theater form, which resulted in an increased demand for films among viewers. Due to the increased demand, there was also an increase in the production of films for the growing market.[18] Furthermore, the decade's media mergers further emphasized the commercial nature of films in a business that relies heavily on the success of a few films to cover the losses of the majority of Hollywood releases. As a result, the 1980s saw an unprecedented demand for films, and the gradual emergence of the so-called ultra-high-budget films. These are films that have high budgets for special effects and marketing, aim at high profits, use bankable stars, and repeatedly use storylines that have been financially successful in the past.[19] All this is done in order to reduce the financial risks of film production. The ultra-high-budget films are the backbone of the commercial film business.

International Terrorism in Hollywood Films and U.S. Foreign Policy

The United States government has been collecting statistical data on terrorism since 1968. The U.S. Department of State has been in charge of the publication of the annual report, *Patterns of Global Terrorism,* since 1981. The department released its first two reports under the title *Patterns of International Terrorism,* following in the footsteps of the Central Intelligence Agency (CIA) and its National Foreign Assessment Center. The U.S. State Department is required by law to give Congress an annual report on international terrorism. The annual reports detail each year's, and the past five years', international terror threats to the U.S.

In 2004 the State Department replaced the *Patterns of Global Terrorism* reports with *Country Reports on Terrorism.* The updated documents include data collected by the National Counterterrorism Center (NCTC), created after 9/11. The State Department's main focus is on policy issues. Today the most recent reports can be found on the Internet, on the State Department's website.[20] The annual documents provide the only consistent statistical database on international terrorism in the United States.[21] This study compares the content and

The U.S. Department of State is required by law to give Congress an annual report on international terrorist threats. In 2004 the department replaced its *Patterns of Global Terrorism* reports with *Country Reports on Terrorism*. The most recent reports are available online at the U.S. Department of State website: http://www.state.gov/s/ct/rls/crt/.

portrayals of international terrorism of the sixteen films to the data and definitions provided by the U.S. Department of State, and to the annual documents provided by the CIA before 1981.

Terrorism is hard to define; also the U.S. State Department has struggled with this problem. The department first relied on the definition that the U.S. government had been using since the emergence of modern international terrorism in 1968[22] but updated the long definition slightly in the aftermath of the 1983 Lebanon bombings:

> **Terrorism** is premeditated politically motivated violence perpetrated against noncombatant targets by subnational groups or clandestine state agents.
> **International terrorism** is terrorism involving citizens or territory of more than one country.[23]

The 1983 report also replaced the word "international" with "global" in the report title. In the future, *Patterns of Global Terrorism* documents would continue to use the new definitions. The 1990 report added a particular definition for terrorist groups: "The term terrorist group means any group practicing, or that has significant subgroups that practice, international terrorism."[24]

The difficulty in defining terrorism, even after these guidelines, becomes obvious when analyzing the annual reports. Over the years they have covered a variety of violent activity, for example, different countries' domestic violence, anarchist activity, and violence for political independence. The State Department reports a large variety of activities under the umbrella of terrorism and terror. These include, for example, terrorist and other violent actions by groups with left-wing and right-wing ideologies, as well as with ethnic, religious and fascist motivations. The problem of how to define terrorism also surfaces when analyzing international terrorism in Hollywood films. At times Hollywood films have clearly defined film villains as international terrorists while at other times film antagonists or protagonists who have committed clear terrorist activities have escaped the definition.

My study follows the U.S. Department of State report definitions. That is, if a Hollywood film portrays as its central theme politically motivated violence or activity that falls under any of the State Department definitions of international terrorism, the film is analyzed as a terrorist film. Also, a film is included in the study if its script refers to the film's main antagonist or main protagonist as a terrorist, or if either character belongs to any of the foreign terrorist organizations or represents any of the state sponsors of terrorism, as listed by the State Department. Furthermore, if a fictional terrorist event or act has a counterpart in real life, that is, if it uses a real-life terrorist event or terrorist as its inspiration, the film is included in the study data.

Only the films that have international terrorism as their *central* theme qualify for this study. For example, films such as the *Under Siege* series are not included in the study because they focus on domestic conflicts. These film villains' only connection to international terrorism is the characters' intent purpose to sell stolen weapons to clients outside the U.S. borders, the plan only briefly brought up in the films. Also, films that use science fiction and futuristic medical innovations as a central part of the terrorist plot, such as *Face/Off*, are left out of the analysis. Furthermore, the study only analyzes films that are American productions, or international co-productions that have an American co-producer and distributor.[25] The study leaves out foreign imports, also the ones that have been in the annual top fifty in the North American market because those films do not directly follow Hollywood production principles, practices and screenwriting formats. For example, such U.K. imports as the box office hit *The Crying Game* (1992) and the films of the James Bond series, which are based on a British spy created by Ian Fleming, are omitted from the study.

U.S. Counterterrorism

The U.S. Department of State, which since the 1970s has been defining American counterterrorism, details the four main parts of the U.S. counterterrorism policy as:

- **First**, make no concessions to terrorists and strike no deals.
- **Second**, bring terrorists to justice for their crimes.
- **Third**, isolate and apply pressure on states that sponsor terrorism to force them to change their behavior.
- **Fourth**, bolster the counterterrorist capabilities of those countries that work with the United States and require assistance.[26]

The policies have developed over time as the U.S. has reacted to attacks against its citizens and political interests. When looking at methods of action, the U.S. lists five traditional ways to fight terrorism: diplomacy, sanctions, covert operations, military options and law enforcement actions.

In its annual reports on global terrorism, the U.S. Department of State details a list of countries that are considered to be state supporters of terrorism. The listed countries support international terrorism through a variety of actions, including funding, training and giving safe haven to terrorist organizations. In addition, the State Department has gradually developed a list of foreign terrorist organizations. According to the department, the named groups practice terrorist activity and pose a threat to the United States and its citizens. Since the late 1990s such organizations have been known as Designated Foreign Terrorist Organizations (FTOs). U.S. counterterrorism policy is, in particular, applied to the identified state sponsors of terrorism and to the organizations which are considered a direct threat to the U.S. Both state sponsors of terrorism and FTOs are under sanctions.

Hollywood films have found inspiration in real-life terrorist threats, as listed by the State Department, for both film villains and heroes. For example, references to Libya, Iran, Hezbollah and the Provisional Irish Republican Army (PIRA) are easy to find in several films and the State Department reports on international terrorism.

Terrorists choose their targets carefully and for a clear purpose in order to reach a certain goal.[27] Since the 1980s the most common terrorist targets have been civilians. The U.S. State Department includes in its noncombatant category also off-duty military personnel. The analyzed sixteen films follow this trend, portraying both civilian and off-duty military personnel as targets.

Before 9/11 there were some fifty agencies involved in American counterterrorism. Usually the lead federal agency in managing terrorist events outside the U.S. borders was the U.S. Department of State, within U.S. territory the Department of Justice and under it, the Federal Bureau of Investigation (FBI), and for hijackings the Federal Aviation Administration (FAA). In addition, the Federal Emergency Management Agency (FEMA) was usually in charge of addressing public health matters and recovery in the aftermath of terrorist attacks. The Assistant to the President for National Security Affairs was ultimately in charge of determining what agency would be in charge and what different agencies' responsibilities would be.[28]

The pre–9/11 structure that had dozens of agencies involved in counterterrorism, and a structure of lead agencies that "normally" applied in terrorist crisis situations, had left some confusion over who leads counterterrorism, how, and in which circumstances. Also, *The 9/11 Commission Report* criticizes pre–9/11 U.S. counterterrorism for lacking a clear leadership. That confusion is also reflected in Hollywood productions which portray law enforcement, CIA and FBI agents, U.S. military, and agents of unnamed and fictional federal agencies as the country's counterterrorist weapons.

The sixteen films' heroes are largely representatives of the official power structure. According to Van Dijk, the prevailing ideology uses law to spread hegemonic definitions in society. The prevailing power structure relies on positive self-representation in order to legitimate its own position in society while relying on the use of negative representation of the "other" to undermine threats to the prevailing ideology.[29] The films on international terrorism that have succeeded in the domestic box office very clearly set up official representatives of the U.S. power structure as heroes against evil film terrorists. With an excessive use of violence the heroes kill, with law on their side, foreign threats to the U.S. They are fighting for Western, in particular for U.S., viewers, defending the U.S. against foreign villains.

International Terrorism in the News Media and Hollywood Films

As Stuart Hall points out, language is a site of struggle.[30] He continues by saying that an important tool in hegemony is who gets to define whom. Labeling opponent groups as deviant, criminal, irrational, crazy or psychopathic is an effective use of ideological power.[31] In news coverage of terrorism, the descriptions of terrorists and their acts emphasize the words *insane* and *psychopathic*.[32] This study examines what definitions and terms the films under study use to describe the perpetrators of political violence; for example, political terms such as *terrorist*, *freedom fighter*, *revolutionary*, and *guerrilla*, or labels such as *insane*, *psychotic* and *crazy*. Each of these terms reveals a different approach to understanding terrorism, from condemning and trivializing it to accepting it as a legalized fight for freedom.

The news media are central to the emergence, construction and understanding of modern international terrorism.[33] Critical researchers have argued that the news media only support the official views of terrorism by not providing the historical, political and social context of the phenomenon.[34] The criticism can be echoed when looking at the sixteen films under study. They all focus in their film terrorism on the terrorist act or threat but leave unexplored the context of terrorism and terrorists' motivations. In contrast to real-life terrorists, only some of the films portray terrorists who aim at publicity through their actions. In Hollywood films, the news media are used largely for exposition, for providing necessary plot information through news media reports. Some of the films even trivialize the news media, using them as comedic tools, as do, for example, the first two installments of the *Die Hard* series.

The present work also examines the amplification of violence. Violence and deviant behavior are the most covered news topics both in domestic and foreign news. This is also the trend in action and action-adventure films. *Iron Eagle* (1986) is the only film among those analyzed that has a PG-13 rating, according to which the rated film is deemed suitable for children 13 years of age or older. The remaining fifteen films are all rated R (restricted), which in practice means that anyone under 17 years of age should have a parent or another adult guardian with them when seeing the film in a theater. The further away from the U.S. in cultural, ideological and religious terms, the more brutal film violence is, and the bigger the number of the foreign villains who die. The portrayal is similar to U.S. news media coverage of foreign countries. These sixteen films portray so-called good violence, which supports the prevailing power structure's use of violence against those whom society has defined as the enemy. In contrast, film villains practice bad violence, that is, violence that threatens those in power and the citizens of that country.[35]

International Terrorists and Heroes in Hollywood Films

The most commercially popular terrorist film villains have come from the Middle East in five films. Another five films draw their terrorist theme from the U.K., four of them from Northern Ireland. Two of these films introduce a hero who has a background as a Northern Irish terrorist. Other familiar film villains are plucked from the State Department terrorist listings, among them left-wing European terrorists and the Latin American Red Terror Network. Religion is brought up only if the religion is Islam. In the five films that portray Arabs, an Arab equals a Muslim, but the films largely ignore what that means in practice. *True Lies* (1994) and *Executive Decision* (1996) draw upon violent fundamentalism within Islam for their themes, along with the growing threat of violent Muslim extremists to the West in the 1990s. The films stereotype their Arab villains as enraged and insane fundamentalist Muslim men of undefined countries who hate the U.S. but hardly, if at all, practice their religion. There are 22 Arab and 57 Muslim countries in the world,[36] but Hollywood films seem to refuse to acknowledge their individual existence. A better film commodity is an Arab male from an unspecified country and whose religion is generally Islam. Both the ethnicity and religion make him a cultural "other" in the Western world. In contrast, European villains and their sidekicks have specific nationalities but no religious backgrounds, though the conflict itself may be rooted in religion. The arrival of European villains in Hollywood films coincided with the end of the Cold War. The Hollywood film market was becoming truly globalized in the post–Cold War era, and the foreign film market soon surpassed the domestic one as the main revenue provider.

Each of the sixteen films is analyzed in the context of the action-adventure film genre, in particular in the context of its narrative structure, the classical Hollywood cinema structure, and its traditions and trends, including traditional antagonist and protagonist portrayals. According to previous research, action-adventure film heroes predominantly come from white Anglo-Saxon America while their enemies come from different minority groups or from abroad.[37] Loyal to the action and action-adventure film genres, Hollywood counterterrorism heroes' ethnic and national backgrounds have little variety. Most are Anglo-Saxon American men of the middle or upper middle class. Only two films, both from the 1990s, portray a minority actor as the hero. *Passenger 57* (1992) stars Wesley Snipes, and Denzel Washington saves the country from foreign and domestic threats in *The Siege* (1998).

Previous research has indicated that women's roles in action and action-adventure films are often nonexistent, or female characters are minimal as targets of sexual desire, or they are portrayed as seductive sexpots. However, romance is a primary or secondary plot to almost nine out of ten Hollywood films.[38] In the 1980s, in President Reagan's America, most muscular action heroes avoided topics of romance and love. By the end of the decade, and then in the 1990s, women, and also preteen and teenage daughters, entered the lives of American action and action-adventure heroes.

Book Structure

The book is divided into three parts. Part I discusses modern international terrorism in relation to the news media, the United States, and the commercial Hollywood film industry. Part II analyzes the blockbuster action and action-adventure films on international terrorism that Hollywood released during the Cold War. Part III discusses the action and action-adventure films on international terrorism that were in the annual box office top fifty in their release year in the post–Cold War era, starting with *Die Hard* (1988), which was already moving away from the standard Cold War heroes and welcoming the new world order.

Part I: Modern International Terrorism

I will start with an analysis of the political and social construction of terrorism, and then follow with an analysis of the relationships among terrorism, the media and the state.

"Chapter 1: International Terrorism and the News Media" traces the beginnings of modern international terrorism and the news media's central role in it.

"Chapter 2: International Terrorism and the United States" examines the U.S. relationship with modern international terrorism, and explains the main structures of U.S. counterterrorism in the pre–9/11 era. In addition, the chapter gives a brief overview of the U.S. Department of

State's *Patterns of Global Terrorism* documents, the only continuous statistical database on international terrorism in the United States, used here to indicate the official U.S. interpretation of international terrorism and terrorist threats to the U.S. security.

"Chapter 3: International Terrorism and the Hollywood Film Industry" analyzes the emergence of terrorism as a profitable Hollywood film product, in particular as a product of the action and action-adventure film genres.

Part II: The Hollywood Terrorist and the Cold War Red Terror Network

The second part of the book discusses the films on international terrorism that Hollywood produced and released during the Cold War. Terrorism became a financially successful Hollywood commodity under President Reagan, who made terrorism a central part of his foreign policy, defining it as warfare. During that time the U.S. policymakers were discussing a communist terror network which, according to them, was reaching its threatening arm from the Soviet Union around the world. In the Reagan administration's view, the Soviet communist influence was real in Latin America, from where it was supposedly trying to enter the U.S.

"Chapter 4: International Terrorism in the Americas: 'It's Time to Die'" analyzes two films that echo the Reagan-era fear of communism. *Invasion U.S.A.* (1985) portrays the ultimate American nightmare when Soviet-led communist terrorists invade the country. In *Commando* (1985) U.S. policies in Latin America come to haunt a retired colonel when a former dictator wants to return to power and tries to force the colonel to participate in that attempt.

"Chapter 5: State-Sponsored Middle Eastern Terrorism" analyzes two films that portray anti–U.S. terrorism that was developing in the Middle East. *Iron Eagle* (1986) echoes the strained U.S. relationship with Libya in the 1980s as an American teenager takes destructive action in the Middle East. *The Delta Force* (1986) draws from the events of the 1985 TWA flight 847 hijacking from Athens to Beirut by Hezbollah, an Iran-backed terrorist organization based in Lebanon. The news media followed the seventeen-day TWA hostage event in detail, interviewing the hijackers, the captain and the hostages for the world's media. The Hollywood version of the TWA hijacking both imitates and rewrites history, portraying a celebration of explosives and the deadly power of the film's Delta Force unit. Such success had eluded the real Delta Force in the 1980 American rescue effort of the U.S. hostages in Tehran.

Part III: The Hollywood Terrorist after the Cold War

The last part of the book looks at how the end of the Cold War reshaped the Hollywood terrorist character of the 1980s and introduced a new set of international terrorists in the 1990s. In the new era, screenwriters updated the 1980s one-man war machine to match the new world order: he had fewer muscles, more brain power and, often, a meaningful heterosexual relationship.

"Chapter 6: 'Yippee Ki-yay, Motherfucker': From German Euroterrorists to Heroes of the Past" discusses the first three *Die Hard* films, which star Bruce Willis as John McClane, a New York City police officer. McClane appeared towards the end of the Cold War, in 1988. He saves American lives in *Die Hard* (1988), and in its sequels, *Die Hard: Die Harder* (1990) and *Die Hard with a Vengeance* (1995). While terrorism became a familiar foreign policy and news media topic under President Reagan, terrorism as a film product did not emerge as a true blockbuster product until *Die Hard*, which introduced a new type of hero and a smart and sophisticated villain. The re-creation of the hero's and the villain's prototypes to match the political and cultural conditions of the emerging post–Cold War world opened the door for a new generation of heroes and Hollywood terrorists in the 1990s. In the first post–Cold War years Hollywood sped past the official power structure. The collapse of the communist threat left U.S. policy makers looking for a new enemy, but Hollywood films had already moved on. They had largely abandoned communist villains and were now portraying international terrorists who attack U.S. citizens on their own soil.

"Chapter 7: Euroinvasion: Madmen from Britain and Northern Ireland" examines five 1990s films whose villains or heroes are from the U.K. *Passenger 57* (1992) finds its villain in a British aristocrat. The film's events take place in a closed space, on a hijacked plane. *Passenger 57* introduces a rare minority hero, African American actor Wesley Snipes as a security expert. The other four films draw their theme from the conflict in Northern Ireland. The films are *Patriot Games* (1992), *Blown Away* (1994), *The Jackal* (1997) and *Ronin* (1998). The 1990s was the decade during which the U.S. became actively involved in extensive peace negotiations in Northern Ireland. Both the news media and Hollywood took notice. While the U.S. State Department was listing the Provisional Irish Republican Army (PIRA) as a terrorist organization, the U.S. news media and the commercial film industry were at times quite lenient in their portrayals of the organization. Also, the official view was occasionally a bit shaky. For example, the U.S. and its closest Western ally, the U.K., clashed over the U.S. visits of some members of the Sinn Fein party, the PIRA's political wing. The four films introduce the PIRA and, in particular, PIRA splinter groups. Interestingly enough, none of the four films portrays the PIRA per se or its members as villains.

"Chapter 8: Hollywood's Version of Fundamentalist Islamic Terrorism: Return of the One-Dimensional Evil Arab Muslim" discusses *True Lies* (1994) and *Executive Decision* (1996), which both bring fundamentalist Islamic terrorists to threaten the U.S. mainland. The films reflect the emergence of religiously motivated terrorism in the 1990s, and the threat that was realized on U.S. soil in 1993. Islamic extremists targeted the World Trade Center in New York in February 1993, killing six and injuring a thousand. Later that same year a fundamentalist Islamic group targeted several New York City landmarks, but the FBI was able to preempt the attack plans.

"Chapter 9: Return of the Communist Threat: U.S. President Takes On Russian Communist Terrorists" analyzes *Air Force One* (1997) which thematically draws from the post–Cold War new world order. On a U.S. president's return trip from the new capitalist Russia, a group of Russian ultra-nationalist radicals, who long for the old communist times, hijack the president's plane, which is also carrying his wife and preteen daughter. The president is left to defend physically, in practice, his own "be afraid" message to terrorists that he had just delivered in Russia in a public address.

"Chapter 10: Predicting 9/11: Power of Belief" discusses *The Siege* (1998), which brings terrorism into the heart of New York City. The film takes a much darker approach to terrorism than the other films of this book. It focuses on the aftermath and social consequences of terrorist attacks rather than on a more traditional special effects showcase of Hollywood film explosives. It comes closest to depicting real-life terrorism, touching on the political complexity and development of terrorism and showing that terrorism consists of very systematic, premeditated and calculated acts. Furthermore, the film portrays an educated Palestinian terrorist who was on the CIA payroll in his anti–Saddam Hussein operations, but whom the CIA had abandoned after the Persian Gulf War. He has a political motivation for his anti–U.S. actions, but also draws from his religious beliefs.

Conclusion: Patterns and Themes of the Hollywood Terrorist

The book concludes with a discussion of the major similarities, differences and changes in the portrayal of international terrorists in Hollywood films in the time period from 1980 until September 11, 2001. The chapter reviews how the commercial film industry's portrayal of terrorists and terrorist incidents compares to official U.S. definitions of international terrorism, including specific terrorist threats, and to U.S. counterterrorism, as well as to news media portrayals of international terrorism. The chapter also gives a summary of the film heroes who have saved the U.S. from Hollywood terrorists. I discuss the hero depictions in the context of film genre traditions and by comparing these U.S. counterterrorism weapons to the real-life U.S. counterterrorism structure. In addition, the analysis also shortly addresses how Hollywood has defined the role of women in countering international terrorism. The chapter concludes with a discussion of how the fact that terrorist films are film commodities has affected commercial films' terrorist portrayals.

Part I. Modern International Terrorism

On Tuesday morning, September 11, 2001, modern international terrorism entered U.S. soil and the American public consciousness with a shock. Two hijacked commercial airliners hit the skyscraper twin towers of the World Trade Center in New York City and another hijacked commercial plane crashed into the Pentagon, the military nerve center of the United States. The collapse of the twin towers and the crashing of a fourth hijacked airliner in Shanksville, Pennsylvania, soon followed these events. At first it was estimated that over five thousand people had died in the day's attacks.[1] The number was later lowered to about three thousand. Two days after the attack President George W. Bush announced that the fight against international terrorism is "the first war of the 21st century. It will be the focus of my administration."[2]

The horrendous live images of the coordinated simultaneous terrorist attacks that worldwide television audiences witnessed on September 11, 2001, resembled images that viewers had previously only seen on movie screens. The difference was that now reality was imitating fiction with horrifying results. Real people died, real people were injured, and real destruction was caused by the combined attacks. Furthermore, unlike at the end of a Hollywood action-adventure film, the villain was not caught and killed after a two-hour roller coaster ride of intense action and heroic measures by a white American male hero.

International terrorism in news headlines and fictional Hollywood films had not prepared Americans for the death, suffering and destruction of real-life terrorism. Pre–9/11 Hollywood films and even news coverage had largely simplified international terrorism into a dramatic fight between good (us) and evil (them), not properly addressing the roots of terrorist events or analyzing the phenomenon of international terrorism in its historical, social and political contexts. The mainstream U.S. media had failed their audiences when they had not provided a contextual understanding of international terrorism and what the phenomenon means to the United States and its citizens, and to the rest of the world.

The first part of this book discusses the social and political construction of real-life terrorism and reviews the historical origins of the form of terrorism we are facing in the 21st century—that is, modern international terrorism, which emerged in the late 1960s. The globalization of the world's news media has had a central role in the emergence and development of modern international terrorism. Chapter 1 analyzes in more detail today's symbiotic relationship between the phenomenon of international terrorism and the mainstream news media.

While terrorists aim at gaining news media coverage, their ultimate target is society's prevailing power structure. Economic destruction is a decades-long modern terrorist method but attacks on a target society's noncombatant citizens bring more news headlines through the destruction and suffering of human lives. According to unclassified CIA and State Depart-

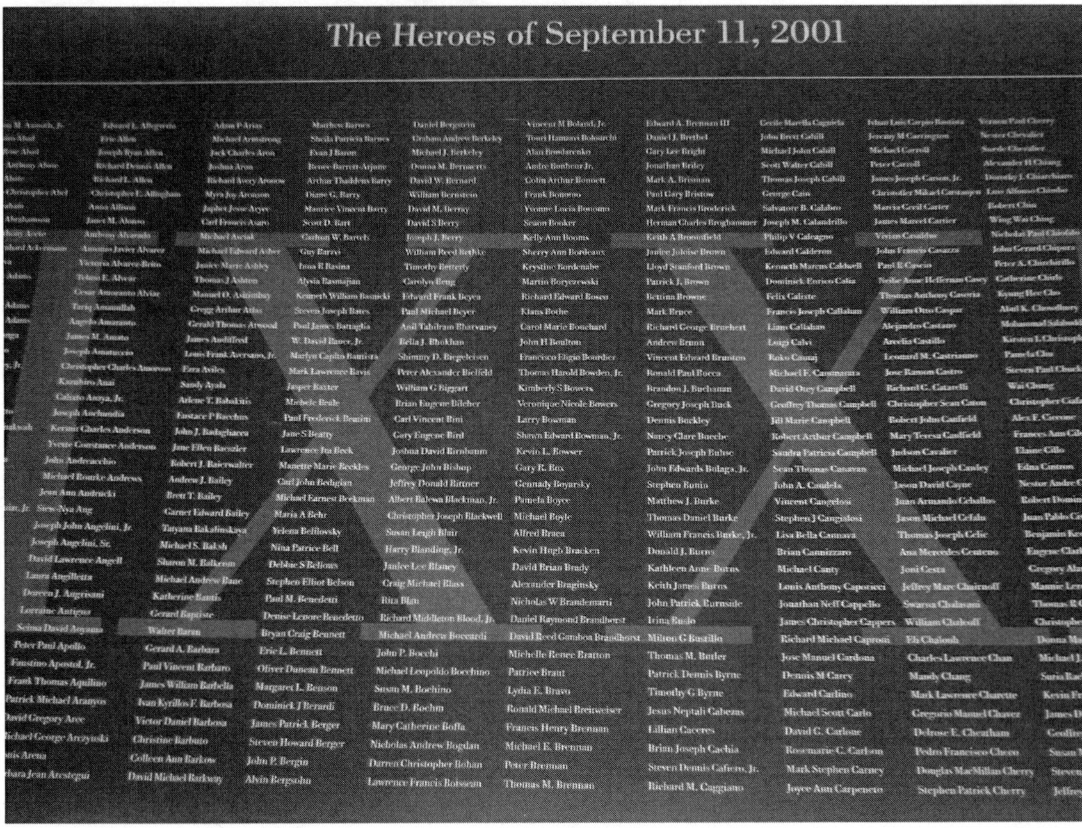

The television images of 9/11 resembled what viewers had seen in Hollywood productions of international terrorism. The media spectacle stopped the nation and the world when al Qaeda murdered some 3,000 people. The 9/11 Memorial in New York City remembers the heroes of that day.

ment reports on international terrorism, the United States, in particular its economic interests, has been the number one target of modern international terrorism since its emergence. American citizens became targets in particular in the aftermath of the Iran hostage crisis (1979–1981), which attracted continuous worldwide media attention for the whole length of the 444-day event. Chapter 2 briefly addresses U.S. experience with modern international terrorism and reviews pre–9/11 American counterterrorism structures. The chapter details the official U.S. interpretation of modern international terrorism, as documented in unclassified CIA documents on international terrorism from the 1970s and the annual *Patterns of International Terrorism* and *Patterns of Global Terrorism* reports by the U.S. Department of State from 1981 till 2001. These documents are the only available consistent unclassified database on international terrorism in the United States.

At the height of the Cold War, international terrorism did not grab big news headlines until the 1972 Munich Olympic Games attack on the Israeli team. The U.S. mainstream film industry tried international terrorism as a major film theme with some delay. *Black Sunday* (1977) was a rare film plotted around an international terrorist spectacle, uncannily predicting today's target fears. The film's Palestinian terrorists, led by a woman, attack the Super Bowl with the help of a disillusioned and bitter American Vietnam War veteran. But unlike in today's films, it is an Israeli, not an American hero, who saves the Super Bowl and the innocence of American society and American lives. Only two years after the film's release, the Iran hostage crisis introduced the phenomenon of international terrorism to large American audiences through news media coverage of the entire 444-day event. The mainstream commercial film industry, which often draws its ideas from international news headlines and U.S. foreign policy, took notice of this opportunity to find new film villains. As the more traditional communist film antagonists gradually started to disappear, new foreign threats arrived to menace the United States. In the 1980s the commercial film industry brought fictional international terrorists to attack the U.S. inside and outside its borders.

Coming to the 1990s Hollywood's terrorist spectacles were larger than life, thanks to the reliance on the latest special effects. Eerily, but unbeknownst to the world, Hollywood's blockbuster action-adventure films on international terrorism were predicting what was to become reality only a few years later. A variety of films introduced to worldwide audiences airplane hijackings and attacks in and against high-rise buildings to the beat of flashing special effects. The images were similar to what viewers witnessed on their television screens as news images on September 11, 2001. Chapter 3 discusses how international terrorism developed into a profit-making subgenre of action-adventure films in the 1980s and gained true blockbuster status a decade later. The chapter reviews the main aspects of commercial film production, which will provide background for examining how the action-adventure film genre emerged as a global media commodity. It borrows from older commercial film genres. In the 1980s it developed into its own popular film genre which targets American and foreign film audiences in its efforts to recoup rising film production costs and to make a profit. After all, Hollywood film business is like any business: it is about making money.

Defining Terrorism: A Political and Violent Site of Conflict

The world has not been able to reach consensus over how to define the term *terrorism*. Any definition includes the definer's own political and moral views of whose fight is legal and justified, and whose fight is outside legal society. The only thing most definitions have in common is that terrorism is a form of *political* violence and action.[3] Mostly, the word *terrorism* is never a neutral descriptive term, but always a subjective and value-loaded one, and a political concept.[4] That makes it impossible to collect objective data on international terrorism or to provide an objective list of the world's terrorist organizations. For example, from the Western perspective the loose al Qaeda network, which is an anti–Western extremist Sunni Islamic militant network, clearly poses a threat to Western security, lives, values and interests, as several anti–Western attacks have manifested. In contrast, for the supporters of the network it is the Western world that sets a threat to their security, interest, lives and values. According to that perspective, al Qaeda is a defender against a foreign threat rather than a terrorist network. Northern Ireland offers another familiar example from news headlines. The Provisional Irish Republican Army's violent anti–British campaign found sympathy and strong support during the years of the Troubles when part of the Catholic population in Northern Ireland saw the PIRA to be fighting and speaking for their interests, values and security, which the British rule in their view was threatening.

When the term *terrorism* is encountered, one should always ask what person or group defined it, what exactly they mean by it, why they use it, and in what circumstances.[5] Each user of the term defines it according to the person's own purposes, values and interests. Hoffman points out that terrorism "is a word with intrinsically negative connotations that is generally applied to one's enemies and opponents, or to those with whom one disagrees and would otherwise prefer to ignore."[6] Due to differences in political interests and in political and moral views, one person's terrorist may be another person's hero. Or, as an old cliché puts it, "One person's terrorist is another person's freedom fighter."

Even the U.S. government acknowledges the difficulty of defining terrorism. For example, the CIA's *International Terrorism in 1976* report points out that different moral perspectives and values determine whose acts are considered to be justifiable and whose illegal.[7] The term in itself is marked by continuous and irresolvable conflict. That can be seen in the U.S. government reports on international terrorism. Already in 1981, after the end of the Iran hostage crisis, the first U.S. experience with a major terrorism media spectacle, the State Department brought a variety of groups and actions under the umbrella of international terrorism. These included, for example, nations promoting their foreign policy or domestic interests, separatist groups, nihilists, left-wing and right-wing groups, anti–U.S. and anti–Soviet groups, environmental and religious groups, and groups that were motivated by ideological, class, cultural or racial conflicts.[8]

Political and legal implications are always included in the use of the term. To define someone as a terrorist means taking a stand on the person's actions, morally judging those actions as illegitimate and therefore defining the person as outside legal society.[9] In contrast, the perpetrators of violent attacks see their fight as a legitimate political struggle against a power they define as illegal.[10] They define themselves as representatives of a legal structure. For example, when Provisional Irish Republican Army (PIRA) prisoners in the U.K. under Prime Minister Margaret Thatcher's rule in the 1980s claimed to be soldiers, not criminals, they declared their loyalty to the community they saw themselves to be representing. In their view the British presence in Northern Ireland was illegal and therefore its rules did not apply to them. For Prime Minister Thatcher, all PIRA activity was criminal activity conducted under the guise of ideological or other motivations. When the U.K. refused to give its PIRA prisoners political prisoner status in 1981, Thatcher amplified the decision by repeating: "A crime is a crime is a crime."[11] However, terrorists are quite different from traditional criminals who commit crimes for their own personal gain. Terrorists commit their acts for the political gain of the group they are representing. One person can terrorize, but he is not a terrorist unless he is part of a group that performs violent acts for political ends. For example, although the Unabomber (Ted Kaczynski) terrorized the United States, he was not a terrorist. He was mentally unstable and acting alone for his own personal agenda. This disqualifies him from a terrorist definition. When he was caught, the terror rampage was over.

The prevailing power structure effectively subverts its opposition when it defines activity that seeks to undermine its power as illegitimate deviant behavior. Positive self-presentation and negative other-presentation are essential parts in these discourse methods of legitimation and delegitimation.[12] It is important who gets to define whom, for example, in news media reports. The news media often rely heavily on official reports as their sources of information on terrorism, which leaves audiences with a limited view of terrorism, derived from one single source. When society has officially defined certain activities as terrorism, it can promote and use harsh methods to counter or preempt the activities of the opposing force without much, if any, reaction or resistance from the public. After all, the society is performing its main responsibility: defending and protecting its citizens.

The term *terrorism* is a powerful political weapon to use against political opponents in both the domestic and international arenas. It can describe real threats, but it can also be used for the describer's own political gain, in extreme cases to attack targets the describer wants to undermine or destroy. For example, soon after the 9/11 attacks, the U.S. attacked Afghanistan, where the Taliban was hosting Osama bin Laden. But the George W. Bush administration also had other attack plans. First it effectively launched a campaign to gain the approval of the American public for its plans to attack Iraq before taking the actual war action in March 2003. The administration connected Iraq to the 9/11 attacks on the U.S. and claimed to have found strong links between al Qaeda and Saddam Hussein's administration. It also claimed that Iraq had weapons of mass destruction. These are all claims *The 9/11 Commission Report*, published in 2004, contradicted. In the post–9/11 era the mainstream news media largely repeated the Bush administration's claims of Iraq as a threat to the U.S. without carefully analyzing or researching these claims. According to "Iraq: The War Card. Orchestrated Deception on the Path to War," a report by Charles Lewis and Mark Reading-Smith for the Fund for Independence in Journalism, President Bush and seven of his administration's top officials made a case for invading Iraq in a careful manner. In its efforts to craft the public opinion favorable for the war, the administration made, according to Lewis and Reading-Smith, "at least 935 false statements in the two years following September 11, 2001, about the national security threat posed by Saddam Hussein's Iraq.... The statements were part of an orchestrated campaign that effectively galvanized public opinion and, in the process, led the nation to war under decidedly false pretenses."[13] Iraq had had a long, adversary and troubled relationship with the U.S., but the two countries had also found common interests in the 1980s during the Iran-Iraq War. Coming to the 1990s, hostilities between the two countries had intensified. After the Persian Gulf War and the Iraqi defeat, Iraqi leader Saddam Hussein tried to have former president George H. W. Bush, George W. Bush's father, assassinated in 1993. Hussein was an old political and personal enemy, but the George W. Bush administration qualified the U.S. attack on Iraq as a defense against other threats, including a supposed link to the 9/11 terrorist attacks.

As political interests change in a country's foreign policy agenda, the definitions of *enemy*, *friend* and *terrorist* also change. It is not uncommon for officials to avoid defining terrorism in detail because that would set limitations on counterterrorism and on defining threats in a constantly changing global community.[14] Alternative terms that media and others have at times used in place of *terrorist* include, for example, guerrilla, commando, freedom fighter, insurgent, militia, and soldier. Ahmad analyzes the definition bluntly: "The terrorist of yesterday is the hero of today, and the hero of yesterday becomes the terrorist of today."[15] Simply by looking at the roots of the 9/11 events we can see how historical and political developments and contexts influence the use of the term *terrorism*. For example, the status of the Afghan and foreign mujahideen fighters has changed over time. Under President Ronald Reagan they received U.S. and Saudi support when they were fighting against the Soviet Union. In 1985 President Reagan welcomed Afghan mujahideen in the White House as freedom fighters. By the late 1990s a group based on mujahideens fighters, and known as al Qaeda, had developed into an enemy, with Osama bin Laden as a leader. In the aftermath of the 1998 bombings of U.S. embassies in Kenya and Tanzania, which were traced back to al Qaeda, President Clinton targeted the group with air strikes in Sudan and Afghanistan. In less than two decades, mujahideen fighters had transformed from friends to foes when their targets and interests had changed. Mujahideens had gone from targeting a common enemy, the Soviet Union, with U.S. assistance, to intra-group fighting and disagreements, and to the emergence of al Qaeda. Eventually al Qaeda, led by Osama bin Laden, turned on its old Cold War–era ally, the United States.

We can see another type of reversal when we look at the reemergence of the state of Israel. In the 1930s and 1940s the Jewish resistance in the British-governed Palestine was considered to be terrorist activity, but this view started to change around 1942 when the world learned about the Holocaust, the killing of six million Jews by Nazi Germany. By 1944 the resistant Zionist groups, previously labeled terrorists, had become freedom fighters in the eyes of the Western world.[16] Their goal of an independent Israeli state had become a generally accepted political goal in the West, leading to the independence of Israel in 1948.

Warfare or Terrorism

How society defines terrorism influences what counterterrorism methods it can use. The military is primarily in charge if a country is waging a war on terrorism. But if terrorism is defined as a crime, then the legal system is primarily in charge of counterterrorism.

In the aftermath of the 9/11 attacks, President Bush declared a war on terror, calling it the country's first war of the 21st century. He was not the first U.S. president to view terrorism as war. Two decades earlier President Ronald Reagan had considered terrorism to be warfare to the point that during his administration the U.S. went after terrorists outside U.S. borders after the country had been targeted by state sponsors of terrorism and by groups that some of the sponsors were supporting. The first such U.S. act took place in 1986. By that year the U.S. had connected Libya to several anti–American terrorist acts. In response, the U.S. launched air strikes against Libya in April 1986. The Reagan administration defined the air strikes as acts of self-defense and therefore legal. In self-defense or in war, Executive Order 11905, signed by President Ford in 1976, and Executive Order 12333, signed by President Reagan in 1981, which ban political assassinations by the U.S., did not apply.[17]

When President Clinton, in response to the 1998 attacks on the U.S. embassies in Kenya and Tanzania, ordered air strikes on suspected terrorist facilities in Afghanistan and Sudan, there was a new addition to the policy of self-defense. The administration was targeting, not the countries that were at the receiving end of the U.S. air strikes, but a network whose leadership and hiding places the U.S. suspected of being in these countries. Under President Clinton the U.S. also targeted Osama bin Laden directly, with the goal of killing him, but air strikes from far away failed to achieve that goal.

Terrorism is not officially warfare, according to traditional definitions of war, since the people resorting to acts of political violence represent small groups which do not form a nation-state, and furthermore, they are not large enough to form a nation-state that would be recognized by the international community.[18] President Bush's familiar post–9/11 slogan "War on Terror" may have helped to bring the nation behind a common cause, the words themselves revealed very little. The term *terror* was not clearly defined, and furthermore, war is a method that is used against another nation-state. If discussing the term in a legal or political context, it is thus impossible to wage war on a phenomenon, especially when that phenomenon cannot even been defined in detail. But the Bush administration used the slogan effectively, for example, when the U.S. invaded Iraq in search of weapons of mass destruction and, from that perspective, to protect itself against the terror of Saddam Hussein.

A country under attack may define terrorism as an act of war, and terrorists themselves may see their violent actions as acts of war, but terrorists do not follow the rules of law. As Hoffman points out, terrorists constantly break the internationally codified rules of law, as stated in the Geneva and Hague Conventions of Warfare (1860s, 1899, 1907, 1949). Terrorists target and kill civilians and military personnel, take hostages, retaliate against innocent civilians, and target diplomatic representatives.[19] For example, in the 1980s the Iran-backed Hezbollah was infamous for keeping Western hostages for years in Lebanon.

Also, some U.S. actions under President George W. Bush, such as the treatment of suspected terrorists at the Guantánamo Bay prison, and revelations of human rights abuses and the use of torture at the Abu Ghraib prison, raised questions about whether the U.S. was following the Geneva and Hague Conventions of Warfare.[20] Although the U.S. generally defines terrorists as criminals, under President Bush that did not mean the suspected terrorists would have the right to due legal process. Even in terms of warfare, the terrorist suspects were not treated as prisoners of war. Soon after taking office, President Barack Obama ordered the Guantánamo Bay prison to be closed and a ban on torture. In January 2011 the prison was still in use.

Terrorism has a greater psychological impact on the public than more traditional criminal activity, warfare or other lethal activity, because terrorists usually target noncombatants. Terrorism also has indirect costs, for example, economic and social effects. In addition, the countermeasures a country takes after it has been targeted by terrorists can influence the function of society.[21] For example, the post–9/11 world saw the negative economic impact of the attack on the U.S., new counterterrorism legislation, changes in air travel regulations, and limitations to civil liberties.

Terrorism as a Method of Communication

The term *terrorism,* as well as violent acts of terrorism, sends out messages in society. The perpetrators of violent acts communicate to the world through their acts that they exist in opposition to the prevailing power structure. When their acts attract media attention, the coverage publicly recognizes the terrorists' existence. The attacked party may oppose and undermine the attackers but cannot ignore them. Violent action gives recognition in the news media and in the social reality the media create. The message of violence is simultaneously aimed at the public and the established power. The goal of terrorists and their attacks is to create shock and fear in society in order to undermine the established authority, and to gain recognition for the views and motivations of the specific group behind the acts.[22] Today's terrorists are especially interested in seeing how their audiences react. These reactions may influence government actions.

Terrorism is very systematic in practice. Acts of terrorism are premeditated and calculated. Terrorism covers a large variety of attack types for political motivations. For example, the U.S. Department of State has listed the following as incidents of international terrorism: kidnappings; barricade-hostage situations; bombings; armed attacks; hijackings of an airplane, ship or other vehicle; assassinations; sabotage; exotic pollution using atomic, chemical, or biological substances to contaminate materials; terrorist threats and hoaxes; thefts and break-ins for funding; sniper shootings; shootouts with police; arms smuggling; and other plots.[23] Terrorist acts carry clear messages of a force that opposes the prevailing power structure, with the goal to undermine it. Terrorism is about power: "the pursuit of power, the acquisition of power, and the use of power to achieve political change."[24] When violent acts receive media coverage, the coverage gives those behind the acts visibility and power in society. Each successful terrorist act not only causes chaos but also brings into question the ability of the established order to protect its citizens.

As Pillar points out, "terrorism is a *method*— a particularly heinous and damaging one — rather than a set of adversaries or the causes they pursue. Terrorism is a problem of what people (or groups, or states) *do,* rather than who they are or what they are trying to achieve."[25] Usually terrorism is a method of those who have very little or nothing, and for whom terrorism can be an outlet of anger or an offer of hope. It is rare, although not unknown, for someone with a good life to get involved in terrorism even if the person agrees with the political views of terrorists.[26] Traditionally terrorism has been a phenomenon of young people, mostly males although, as events in the Middle East have shown in particular after the 2003 U.S. invasion of Iraq, women too have participated in attacks. Terrorist organizations have even used children and mentally disabled people in their acts, for example, in Iraq. Terrorists can take advantage of someone who does not understand what they are asked to do, or terrorists may force civilians to commit acts by holding their loved ones as hostages.

The party that is attacked responds to violence with its own message: it defines the attackers as terrorists and therefore outside legal society. A repeated use of an imprecise and undefined term, in particular through news media, can become a widely accepted truth in the society under attack without a proper analysis of the context of events. As a result, a terrorist becomes the terrifying enemy of everyone in society. This is a way to dehumanize and depoliticize opponents and legitimize all actions taken against them, no matter how violent and illegal these actions at times may be.[27] The term not only effectively defames opposition; it also serves as a qualifier for military actions and the use of weapons,[28] as was seen in the U.S. actions against Iraq in the post–9/11 era. Any society targeted by terrorists will look for methods to defend itself. Counterterrorist activity protects the security and safety of the society under attack, but counterterrorism also serves the *political* interests of that society, including whom it defines as its enemies under the flag of terrorism. In a worst case scenario, acts of counterterrorism can take extreme forms without much question from the public because counterterrorism is officially done only in the name of defense. For example, it took several years before American public opinion started to question the legality of the Guantánamo Bay prison and severe interrogation methods the U.S. had been using on some of the terrorist suspects. These methods raised the uncomfortable question of whether the country, officially a supporter of human rights and democracy, was using torture. As was learned through news reports in the summer of 2008, some of the interrogation methods imitated the methods China had used during the Korean War on American prisoners, which had resulted in faulty confessions.

Terrorists use language as a method of communication and for propaganda. For example, terrorists' own starting point is that they are not choosing to fight but they are *forced* to fight a state or another group that terrorists themselves define as an oppressor.[29] This becomes clear also when we look at any list of terrorist organization names. Terrorists choose their names purposefully to avoid the term *terrorism* and to put a positive spin on the name of their organization and their activities. Hoffman offers examples of groups that draw from

- freedom and liberation (for example the National Liberation Front, the Popular Front for the Liberation of Palestine, Freedom for the Basque Homeland, etc.);
- armies or other military organization structures (for example the National Military Organization, the Popular Liberation Army, the Fifth Battalion of the Liberation Army, etc.);
- actual self-defense movements (for example the Afrikaner Resistance Movement, the Shankhill Defence Association, the Organization for the Defence of the Free People, the Jewish Defense Organization, etc.);
- righteous vengeance (the Organization for the Oppressed on Earth, the Justice Commandos of the Armenian Genocide, the Palestinian Revenge Organization, etc.;

— or else deliberately choose names that are decidedly neutral and therefore bereft of all but the most innocuous suggestions or associations (for example the Shining Path, Front Line, al-Dawa ('The Call'), Alfaro Lives — Damn It!, Kach ('Thus'), al-Gamat al-Islamiya ('The Islamic Organization'), the Lantero Youth Movement, etc.).[30]

Language is central for the creation of a shared conception of the world,[31] as it is also a site of struggle.[32] For example, whether the perpetrators of violent political acts are called terrorists or freedom fighters is usually dependent on an individual country's own political interests, which can also be seen in news media coverage. The closer to one's own turf and interests, the more negative are the terms a country and its media use of the groups that are opposing the prevailing power structure. Also, at the international level a country can try to take advantage of another country's internal struggles. A foreign nation can exploit conflicts between different groups in another country or region by selectively relying on some of the groups in its conquest or attempts to influence the other country.[33] For example, a number of Arab states have selectively supported different Palestinian organizations in the Middle East, according to each country's own political interests. While these states have often defined as freedom fighters the groups they have been supporting, the West has largely classified the same groups as terrorists. Both superpowers got their hands dirty during the Cold War when they got involved in internal struggles in different parts of the world. A face-to-face violent confrontation between the U.S. and the Soviet Union was avoided; the adversaries waged the Cold War by supporting opposing parties in a variety of domestic conflicts around the world in order to support their own international political and economic interests.

Ideological conflicts similar to conflicts in the arenas of culture and language can also be found in science. Science is not value-free but has been used to promote and support many agendas and ideologies in society.[34] For example, scientific theories have been used to justify racism. In the mid–19th century, European imperialist powers relied on a systematic racist ideology to justify slavery and the massacres of indigenous people who were living in colonized areas. Native peoples had no way to resist the white colonialists who used firepower against them from far away with destructive results.[35] The continuation of this is still seen in Hollywood action and action-adventure films in which faceless Third World citizens often die in large numbers, simply being used as props for a variety of creative killings by First World male heroes. For example, the heroes of *Iron Eagle* (1986) and *True Lies* (1994) massacre dozens of faceless Arabs with firepower from far away. In contrast, Hollywood grants Western European terrorist villains individual deaths, for example, in *Die Hard* (1988), *Patriot Games* (1992), and several other films.

Terrorism: A History of Resistance

The interpretation of terrorism is further complicated by the fact that the character of terrorism has changed over time in the methods used, aims of the struggle, as well as in the character, motivations and background of the people who resort to acts of terrorism.[36] Terrorism is relative to the time and place, so to understand terrorism properly, the phenomenon should be evaluated in its historical context.[37]

Terrorism and terrorists, whether considered criminals or fighters for political goals, have a long history in the conflicts of humankind. The use of the term has varied throughout centuries, according to historical, social and political events of different societies. In order to understand the form of terrorism we are facing today, a short historical overview of the use of the term helps us to understand how the term has emerged and how its usage has developed over time.

The origins of the term *terrorism* date back to the Enlightenment and to the French Revolution of 1789.[38] Ideas of enlightenment paved the way to what took place in France in the late 1780s and in the 1790s. The slogan of the revolution, "Liberty, Equality and Fraternity," followed the Enlightenment ideas of universalism and equality, and the concepts of reason and progress.[39] The French Revolution's roots were in a political, social and economic struggle. The revolutionists were men of subordinate classes led by the Paris bourgeoisie. They revolted against a new tax plan which would have put further hardships on the already struggling subordinate classes. The revolutionists wanted to have an equal say in the running of the country and therefore formed their own National Assembly, soon displacing the monarchy and aristocracy in their reach for a just and equal society.[40]

After the revolution, and with the end of feudalism, France adopted the Declaration of the Rights of Man in 1789, which emphasized the Enlightenment ideas of liberty, equality and fraternity. These ideas did not materialize in the conditions of political unrest. Supporters of the monarchy received help from other monarchist powers in Europe. In response, and also against internal struggle, Maximilien Robespierre, the revolutionary leader, resorted to a policy of terror in order to stay in power. Terror was a method of a new revolutionary state. As a result, various civil wars raged in France in 1793, eventually resulting in 1794 to the rule of law being legally suspended. In the years of "*régime de la terreur*,"[41] the Terror (1793–1794), over 200,000 died and some 40,000 met their destiny at the guillotine on different sides of the cause, including eventually, Robespierre.[42] The policy of terror in practice meant the use of violence by the state for political purposes. The policy was called terrorism, a "reign of terror" and "system of terror."[43] Anyone who was practicing terrorism was a terrorist. In other words, terrorists were the ones who resorted to the use of violent action or threat of violent action in order to further their own cause.[44] Terrorism was not a criminal but a legal act. Robespierre and his supporters legally carried out acts of terrorism in order to stay in power. At this point in history the term *terrorism* was a *positive* one. Terror was a method used by the state to establish and maintain order in post-revolution France by intimidation — for example, arranging public executions by guillotine. Terror was a method used to eventually reach a democratic state structure.[45]

Modern terrorism and the terrorism of the Terror regime of the French Revolution share two characteristics. As Hoffman points out, during this era terrorism

> was neither random nor indiscriminate, as terrorism is often portrayed today, but [it] was organized, deliberate and systematic. Second, its goal and its very justification — like that of contemporary terrorism — was the creation of a "new and better society" in place of a fundamentally corrupt and undemocratic political system.[46]

After Robespierre's fall the term *terrorism* "became a term associated with the abuse of office and power" with the idea that the behavior was not legal.[47] The word itself was popularized in the English language by Edmund Burke in his attack on the French Revolution.[48]

Although the term *terrorism* did not emerge until the late eighteenth century, the phenomenon itself is very old. The coercive use of force by individuals and groups which are unsatisfied with the prevailing conditions in society is an old method to intimidate social and political power structures. There is no single definition that would adequately cover all forms of terrorism throughout history. For centuries, since ancient Greece and the writings of Aristotle, attack targets were rulers who were considered tyrants.[49] The first terrorists included Brutus and Wilhelm Tell, who both took action against the tyrants of their own time.[50]

The U.S. State Department's *Patterns of Global Terrorism: 1988* gives a brief history of terrorism, pointing out that a small group of assassins in Persia some 900 years ago, and later in Syria, "recognized that a tiny group of men prepared to die could paralyze a larger foe, and that fear of such attacks could give them power beyond their size."[51] However, according to Karim Karim, the story of "the Assassins" is only a legend which arrived as a popular tale with the Crusaders and Marco Polo in Europe. While assassins are often cited in the West when discussing terrorism, Karim mentions that the story fails to prove their true historical existence.[52] The 1988 State Department report further points out that "[G]iven the persistence of terrorism over centuries, it is unreasonable to expect we can eliminate it completely."[53]

The use of new, destructive weaponry in the 19th century introduced a new, limited form of terrorism. In addition to targeting rulers, the perpetrators of the new form of political violence also targeted individuals who were associated with the power structure that the perpetrators saw as unjust.[54] General population was not a target. Hoffman credits a 19th-century Italian republican extremist, Carlo Pisacane, as the father of the theory and strategy known as "propaganda by deed." For Pisacane, violence was the very method of making people free: "Violence, he argued, was necessary not only to draw attention to, or generate publicity for, a cause, but to inform, educate and ultimately rally the masses behind the revolution."[55]

Terrorism further developed in the 19th century among anarchists who targeted the oppressive state. Their policy followed the original French idea of trying to achieve political goals through violent acts and terror. Anarchists relied on a limited use of violent acts as well as on Pisacane's idea of propaganda by deed. Their policy was to assassinate people in high political positions, in particular the heads of states. This policy was highlighted in 19th-century Russia. A small anti-czarist group of Russian constitutionalists, Narodnaya Volya ("People's Will" or "People's Freedom"), was perhaps the first group to try Carlo Pisacane's "propaganda by deed" tactic in practice. The group was careful to target only those it saw as a hindrance to reforms. Their list included the practitioners of autocratic power. On the top were the highest state representatives, from the czar to the highest government officials. But they were careful not to include innocent bystanders as victims of their attacks. After eight failed plots to assassinate Czar Alexander II, the group finally succeeded in its attempt in 1881. The assassination also brought an end to the group itself when the Russian secret police forcefully went after the group's members.[56]

The Russian anarchists were the first so-called group terrorists. In the pre–World War I era they were followed by other revolutionary groups in different parts of Europe. The U.S. also experienced anarchism and reacted with legislation. In the aftermath of the 1901 assassination of President William McKinley, Congress took action to prevent the entrance of any anarchist in the country. The president's killer was a Hungarian refugee whose actions had been influenced by anarchism. Some ten years later, a member of a European anarchist group, Young Bosnians, set in motion events that led to the First World War. Gavrilo Princip assassinated a symbol of the prevailing power structure, Habsburg Archduke Franz Ferdinand, in Sarajevo on June 28, 1914.[57]

After the destruction in World War I, political violence was highlighted in Germany and Italy. Coming to the 1930s, the meaning of the term *terrorism* changed from referring to revolutionary groups to referring to the violence that totalitarian power structures were practicing against their own citizens.[58] Extreme right-wing groups were relying on the use of violence and terror in their search for political power in Germany and Italy, while in the Soviet Union the country's leader, Joseph Stalin, was relying on terror to implement his version of communism. Nazis in Germany, Fascists in Italy and the Stalinist Soviet Union reached and maintained their power by abusing their position, similar to the way the French Terror regime had done. Hitler's actions in Germany and Mussolini's in Italy brought on a new war in Europe, a war which expanded into World War II.

After the Allied Powers, led by the U.S., the Soviet Union and the U.K., had defeated the Axis Powers, a coalition headed by Germany, Italy and Japan, Europe was separated into the capitalist West and the communist East. The meaning of the term *terrorism* changed once again, now going back to its revolutionary framing, in particular in the developing world. In the 1940s and 1950s groups in the Middle East, Africa and Asia rose to resist their European colonizers. They demanded independence from these countries which had artificially drawn borders according to the colonial powers' own conquests and interests. The term *freedom fighter* emerged during this time period as a popular political description of some of the resistance groups. The term *freedom fighter* was particularly preferred over "terrorist" in the Third World and the communist bloc, which both resisted the influence and domination of Western colonial powers.[59]

Terrorism changed again in the late 1960s and in the 1970s. It was still centrally revolutionary but was no longer limited to anti-colonial struggles. Other ethnic and separatist groups from around the world as well as groups with ideological, usually left-wing, agendas fell under the wide umbrella of terrorism. Nationally motivated minority groups and left-wing groups that drew from Marxism, Leninism and Maoism were terrorizing Western Europe, Latin America and the U.S.[60]

Since the late 18th century terrorism has developed from a tool of French revolutionists, European anarchists, Russian anti–Czar forces, and extreme right- and left-wing forces in Europe into a tool used by groups which understand the power of media images. The development of new communication technologies in the 1960s, in particular satellites and the first U.S. television satellite in 1968, gave new tools for terrorists to use. Satellites and other technological developments, primarily portable television cameras, battery-powered video recorders and the time-base corrector, which eliminated distortion in video signals, made it possible to transmit and broadcast live television images over the airwaves around the world.[61] These technological advancements did not go unnoticed by those who wanted to send violent, politically motivated messages to their opponents and media audiences around the world. Global television audiences were soon to witness the first global message of terrorism.

Modern International Terrorism

The 1960s was a decade of social and political unrest at a global level. Western Europe and the United States experienced domestic terrorist attacks and civil unrest. Latin American countries faced military and domestic agitation. In the communist Eastern Europe there were unsuccessful attempts to resist the Soviet power. But political unrest in the Middle East was the first to grab global media attention.

When politically motivated violent groups realized in the late 1960s that they had within their reach the tools to expand their fight to a global level, a new system of terror started to develop. Technological developments had already been expanding terrorists' weapons arsenal, adding to their traditional bombs and machine guns a new set of weapons, from smaller bombs to chemical, biological, radiological and nuclear weapons. However, another weapon was even more effective in their attempts to take their cause to a worldwide audience: live global television coverage.[62] For example, the participants of a 1976 U.S. Department of State–sponsored conference on terrorism saw the mass media as a root cause for the ability of terrorism as a phenomenon to exist. The media's central role in terrorism was further emphasized by the conference's focus on discussing how the news media could be controlled.[63] This is an issue that has stayed hot and unresolved between governments and journalists, especially in Western democracies in which any attempt to control media coverage would conflict with the principles of media freedom. However, this is not to say that Western governments would not have tried or succeeded in controlling news media.

The emergence of communication satellites and the proliferation of television made possible live international broadcasts. International travel became commonplace thanks to jet aircraft, and terrorists quickly adopted jet planes as part of their "arsenal."[64] Suddenly it was possible to keep hundreds of hostages in a closed space that could easily move anywhere in the world, and do all that in front of millions of television viewers around the globe. Terrorists embraced the new weapons, and soon organized the first incident of terrorism that had international implications, and which not only terrorized but also fascinated live global television audiences.

On July 23, 1968, three members of the Popular Front for the Liberation of Palestine (PFLP) hijacked an Israeli El Al airliner en route from Rome to Tel Aviv to Algeria.[65] The hijacking itself was nothing new. It was actually the twelfth commercial hijacking of the year. What separated this hijacking from the eleven others were its political motivations and implications. The hijackers' goal was to trade their hostages for Palestinian terrorists in Israeli jails. Furthermore, the target was clearly, unlike in the year's previous hijackings, a certain country's national airline. El Al was a well-known and clear symbol of Israel. Also, the hijacking forced Israel directly to negotiate with the hijackers, which violated the Israeli policy of no negotiations with terrorists. The hijackers noticed they had a powerful combination of tools at their hands. They had created a media event which brought them immediate worldwide media attention.[66] Captivating real-life drama was evolving in front of international audiences.

After 40 days of negotiations and news media coverage of the first incident of modern international terrorism, everyone on the plane, including the three hijackers, was released.[67] This hijacking was a starting point for new terrorist tactics. Regular international travel offered terrorists an easy way to cross borders to perform attacks outside their own region. They now targeted innocent civilians of foreign countries in order to receive news media coverage.[68] Terrorists developed their methods by adapting the latest technological advancements. By using global targets, they were able to attract international media coverage and therefore expand local violent and political disputes into topics of world politics. Ahmad accurately points out that "globalization of violence is an aspect of what we call globalization of the economy and culture in the world as a whole. We can't expect everything else to be globalized and violence not to be."[69]

The first to introduce and skillfully use the new terrorist methods were different Palestinian groups under their umbrella organization, the Palestine Liberation Organization (PLO), which was founded in 1964. They exported a local dispute, which had its root in international politics, worldwide. In the first years of international terrorism, Palestinian groups carried out more international terrorist attacks for the Palestinian cause than any other organization in the world.[70] One persecuted ethnic and religious group had regained its independent-nation status as Israel in 1948 after almost two thousand years. Another group, which largely resisted the founding of Israel in the area the group considered its own, was still left struggling for its internationally recognized existence in the Middle East. Some 300,000 Arabs had become refugees when Britain left the region in 1947, and another 400,000 after the independence of Israel in order to avoid the violence that erupted at the rebirth of the new nation.[71] At first Palestinians tried to further their cause through official international organizations but with little success. Terrorism is usually a method chosen by small groups which feel powerless, and that came to be the case with Palestinians. They resorted to violent methods in order to bring worldwide attention to their cause, and they succeeded, as Palestinians themselves have acknowledged. Hoffman cites a 1976 interview of Zehdi Labib Terzi, the PLO's chief UN observer: "The first several hijackings aroused the consciousness of the world and awakened the media and world opinion much more — and more effectively — than 20 years of pleading at the United Nations."[72]

Two years after the first modern international terrorist attack, the PFLP hijacked five airliners to Jordan. In the aftermath of the massive September hijacking, Jordan and Palestinian rebels had an armed confrontation when Jordan expelled the rebel forces from its region in order to improve its relationship with other countries in the region and around the world. For Palestinians the incident became known as the "Black September."[73] A Palestinian group carrying that specific name planned an attack to take place at the 1972 Munich Summer Olympic Games when television audiences around the world, in particular in the West, would be watching. On September 5, 1972, the Black September (which was also suspected of having ties to Fatah, the main organization of the Palestinian movement) attacked the Israeli Olympic team. The terrorists killed two of the athletes and took nine of them as hostages. The attackers had specifically planned the assault to take place when Western audiences would be glued to their television screens as media organizations from all over the world were in West Germany to cover the games.[74]

The violent act in the middle of the games with global media coverage was a terrorist public relations campaign. An international audience of over 800 million followed the event as it unfolded on television screens. The hostage drama and the final shootout between the police and the terrorists left the kidnapped Israeli athletes dead, as well as five terrorists and one policeman. While the attack was not a success to the terrorists in operational terms, the terrorists did reach one of their goals when the unresolved issue of the creation of a Palestinian state became a recognized political issue worldwide.[75] A Palestinian terrorist directly acknowledged the combined power of news media and sports:

> We recognized that sport is the modern religion of the Western world. We knew that the people in England and America would switch their television sets from any program about the plight of the Palestinians if there was a sporting event on another channel. So we decided to use their Olympics, the most sacred ceremony of this religion, to make the world pay attention to us. We offered up human sacrifices to your gods of sport and television. And they answered our prayers. From Munich onwards, nobody could ignore the Palestinians or their cause.[76]

Palestinian organizations were the first to effectively use news media coverage, so much so that their umbrella organization, the PLO, became in the 1970s a recognized political establishment in different countries and an observer at the United Nations. The Palestinian success and news media coverage of Palestinian terrorist acts became a learning ground for emerging terrorist groups. Over time they have learned what types of attacks and targets, and what levels of violence and destruction result in news media coverage, and how the targeted party reacts to attacks. Modern terrorists understand how to attract news media attention, and produce content that gains media coverage. For example, today several different terrorist organizations have their own media personnel who are in charge of press releases and their organization's publicity efforts.

The 1980s started to see a divide in terrorism methods. In 1983 suicide bombings in Beirut highlighted a major change in terrorist methods against Western targets. The U.S. Embassy was targeted in April and the U.S. and French Multinational Forces headquarters in October. These attacks killed over three hundred people, and some two hundred were injured.[77] The goal of indiscriminate mass casualties became a trademark of Middle Eastern–originated terrorism. In contrast, Western European groups, which competed with Middle Eastern terrorists in the number of terrorist acts, largely tried to avoid casualties. Western European terrorist groups would usually give advance warnings, bomb empty facilities at nighttime, or perform clearly targeted murders of individual officials.

Regional groups that have regional goals and targets rarely use a great amount of force in their attacks, because a limitless number of casualties might harm terrorists' long-term goals. They aim at killing *enough* people to make their attacks newsworthy, and to create fear in society.[78] Terrorists know exactly what they are doing: "terrorist groups have one trait in common: none commits actions randomly or senselessly."[79] Many terrorist groups aim at regional or political changes, and some have even succeeded in becoming negotiation partners. This was the case, for example, with the Provisional Irish Republican Army (PIRA) and the Palestine Liberation Organization (PLO). Attacks against the U.S. have been an exception to the rule of a limited number of casualties, in particular since the 1980s. The 1983 attacks against American targets in Beirut, the Oklahoma City bombing in 1995 by domestic extremists, the attacks on American embassies in Kenya and Tanzania in 1998, and the World Trade Center bombings in 1993 and 2001 all gained extensive media coverage but also aimed at a large number of casualties and material destruction.

In the 1980s terrorism also clearly emerged as a method used by weaker states to support their foreign policy interests. These so-called state sponsors of terrorism aided terrorist groups by providing them, for example, with training, funding and weapons, and a safe haven. Due to the absence of a direct confrontation with the targeted states (usually the U.S. and Western European countries), the state-sponsors of terrorism at first had little fear of repercussions. This all changed in 1986 after the U.S. linked Libya to several anti–U.S. attacks which had claimed American casualties. The Reagan administration took aggressive measures in the name of self-defense and launched air strikes against Libya in April 1986.

As a result of terrorists targeting large numbers of innocent bystanders, the lethality of terrorism started to rise in the 1980s, and especially in the 1990s. While the actual number of attacks started to go down, the number of victims started to go up. Attacks are today more destructive than in the first decades of modern international terrorism. One of the highlighted fears post–9/11 has been terrorists gaining access to weapons of mass destruction. However, that discussion is almost as old as the phenomenon itself. In the 1970s the CIA warned of the possibility of nuclear weapons in terrorists' hands but suspected that the likelihood of terrorists seizing "a nuclear weapons storage facility or a nuclear power plant" would be more likely since nuclear weapons are hard to transport and store. Also, terrorists could "exploit the publicity and the bargaining power inherent in the attendant threat of radiological pollution." As a more imminent threat the CIA listed "chemical, biological, and radiological agents of mass destruction." These substances are fairly easy to acquire, and they also "tend to be easy to conceal, easy to transport, and easy to introduce to the target area."[80] But as the U.S. State Department has pointed out, al Qaeda has announced several times that its goal is to acquire weapons of mass destruction.

Other trends that emerged in the 1990s were cyberterror and narcoterrorism. Terrorists can hack into and alter different nations and organizations' telecommunications and computer systems, as well as provoke people to violence via the Internet.[81] What Johnson pointed out at the end of the first decade of modern international terrorism about terrorist targets still holds true today. The interdependent modern world offers terrorists a wide range of targets: "These include large aircraft, supertankers, international power grids and pipelines, transportation hubs, commercial and communications centers, motorcades, offshore oil rigs, liquefied natural gas facilities, nuclear power facilities, and computerized information and management systems."[82] In the age of the Internet, terrorists have kept up with the times and have a strong presence online. In cyberspace they find support, funding and information, and communicate with supporters and their own group members. They know how to use democratic societies' structures to their advantage. Just like anyone else, terrorists can, for example, access public documents that are posted online in order to learn about Western nations' vulnerabilities.

The U.S. Department of State has at times discussed narcotrafficking under the rubric of narcoterrorism, but makes a separation between narcoterrorism and international terrorism.

While drug cartels have gone after and killed official representatives of power in Latin America, their goal has been to prevent government actions that would limit or prevent drug cartel actions. In other words, the cartels' primary goal is profit through criminal activity. For terrorist organizations the primary goal is political change, not profit, through violent activity. Narcotraffickers have at times cooperated with terrorist organizations, but their activities are largely domestic and not primarily for political change unless it helps their criminal activity.[83]

Since the 1990s terrorism has gained even more attention in the news media than it did in the previous decades. In the early 1990s the collapse of the Soviet Union ended the Cold War, creating a political vacuum in international relations. The post–Cold War world structure, combined with the Persian Gulf War (1990–1991), brought major changes in U.S. military theory, doctrine, and organization. The goal of low-level casualty numbers brought high-tech, airpower-oriented war to the front.[84] The new world order also sent the West and, in particular, the world's only remaining superpower, the United States, looking for a new enemy. Terrorism has partially filled that position. Even before the September 11, 2001, attacks, the U.S. State Department had defined international terrorism as one of the country's main security threats. However, it did not top the list. It seems obvious that since 9/11 the extensive media coverage of the day's attacks and their aftermath and, since then, of international terrorism, has heightened Americans' awareness and fear of international terrorism. The media have brought the phenomenon into the public consciousness and have kept it there through their continuous headlines on terrorism.

The terrorism the world is facing today is not far removed from the original French description. The use of violence or threat of violence is still the main operating method for terrorists in their goal to undermine the power structure they oppose. The biggest difference to the old definitions is that terrorism, in particular in the Western world, is defined in terms of legitimate and illegitimate forms of power. It is a *crime,* not a legal political method, as was the case in late 18th century France. Furthermore, as terrorist methods and acts have escalated, some Western leaders, for example, Presidents Ronald Reagan and George W. Bush, have clearly stated that terrorism is warfare, which allows the use of military forces as the country's primary counterterrorism weapon. In the post–9/11 reality some of the American counterterrorism methods that the Bush administration approved, and which were mostly rejected by the Obama administration soon after the new administration took power, even imitated terrorist methods, such as torture.[85] As widely reported in news media, these included, for example, waterboarding, which simulates drowning, forced sleep-deprivation, slamming into the wall, no access to legal representation, and the holding of unaccounted secret prisoners, so-called ghost detainees. Unfortunately, these are not examples of successful counterterrorism but examples of terrorists succeeding in their goal of undermining a legal and democratic society.

While governments publicly like to repeat that terrorism is ineffective, history shows otherwise. For example, Israel, Cyprus and Algeria gained independence through terrorist activities. These regions' anti-colonial groups were the first to understand the value of news media images. They brought local conflicts to worldwide audiences,[86] but with a delay since no live television existed yet. With the arrival of jet aircraft and new technologies that allowed virtually instantaneous live television coverage around the world, Palestinian groups were the first truly to make their fight global. They targeted innocent citizens of other countries, in particular citizens of the Western world, to attract news media attention to their cause. Only after terrorist media spectacles did the PLO find a world which listened to and recognized the unresolved Palestinian political dilemma. However, countless other organizations have failed in which these rare examples succeeded.

Since 1968, international terrorists have been successful in gaining worldwide notice through news media coverage of their attacks. The media are an arena of struggle for access and coverage because one of the fastest ways to get recognition in society is through the mass media. From movie stars, popular singers, American Idol candidates and reality-TV hopefuls to murderers, fame attracts for personal gain. Terrorists also yearn for media coverage, in particular for *news* media coverage, but not for personal fame. They use news coverage as a tool to become recognized by and in society. If the news media cover their acts, the media and society acknowledge their presence in society, and their oppositional stand.

The media define social reality. Consumers receive information about the world outside their immediate personal experience from news media, books, radio, music, films, and the Internet. News media cover events that are extraordinary. Deviant behavior tops the Western news values. Terrorist acts are out of the ordinary and therefore news. For news media not to cover violent terrorist acts would be to ignore its own news values and the media's role in society as providers of information. The next chapter will discuss in more detail this symbiotic but conflicted relationship between the news media and modern international terrorism.

Chapter 1

International Terrorism and the News Media

The hijacking of an Israeli El Al airliner by the Palestinian Popular Front for the Liberation of Palestine (PFLP) introduced modern international terrorism to the world in 1968. The event mixed worldwide publicity and political violence and in so doing created a new political phenomenon. Since then, terrorist groups have targeted the news media as carriers of messages about politically motivated violent acts. The media have also been sources of information to the public about terrorism. Furthermore, current and emerging terrorist groups use news coverage of terrorism as an educational tool. They learn not only about methods of terrorism but also about society's soft and weak target points through media reports. For example, an al Qaeda manual advises its members to follow the news media in order to gather information that would help the organization in the planning of attack operations and finding out about the target's actions.[1]

The news media have a central role in modern international terrorism, including in how the public understands the phenomenon and those who commit violent attacks. When modern international terrorism emerged in the late 1960s, the news media and reporters were crucial sources of information because to the public they were the only sources of information on the topic, other than government. For example, academic research on terrorism was limited due to fear that it would be interpreted as support for terrorists.[2]

This chapter discusses the conflicted relationship between terrorism and the news media. Central in that relationship is the news media's dual role as businesses and as definers of social reality. The media inform and entertain people around the world and shape media consumers' worldview, in particular about issues of which consumers have no firsthand experience. The media are also in the business of making money. For every story on terrorism there has to be a buying audience, which can influence what stories are covered and how.

Similar to media organizations, terrorists have understood the value of live pictures, immediate information and big audiences. Since the emergence of modern international terrorism, terrorists have kept up with the latest technologies and have become media savvy. Through media images of human suffering and disaster, terrorists aim at creating fear and chaos in society, and at undermining the established power whose responsibility it is to protect society and its citizens. Coverage of terrorist acts and terrorist organizations brings recognition to organizations to the point that they may gain support for their organizations or become recognized negotiators, as was the case, for example, with the Palestine Liberation Organization (PLO) and the Provisional Irish Republican Army (PIRA).

Terrorists rely on news media coverage of their acts. Traditionally, as terrorism expert

Usama Bin Ladin

Description

Date of Birth: 1957
Place of Birth: Saudi Arabia
Height: 6'4"-6'6" (193-198 cm)
Weight: 160 lbs (72 kg)
Hair: Brown
Eyes: Brown
Complexion: Olive
Nationality: Saudi Arabian (citizenship revoked)
Scars/Distinguishing Characteristics: Full beard, mustache; walks with cane
Status: Fugitive

This altered photgraph shows what Usama Bin Ladin might look like if he were to wear Western-syle cloting and trim his hair and beard.

Aliases

Usama bin Muhammad bin Ladin, Osama Bin Laden, Shaykh Usama bin Ladin, the Prince, the Emir, Abu Abdallah, Mujahid Shaykh, Hajj, the Director; also known as UBL, OBL

On 9/11 al Qaeda changed the U.S. experience with international terrorism when it achieved two goals in the day's attacks: a massive number of casualties and worldwide media exposure. Al Qaeda leader Osama bin Laden is wanted by several U.S. federal agencies. The National Counterterrorism Center web site shows an altered photograph of bin Laden, portraying how the terrorist leader might look in Western-style clothing with his hair and beard trimmed.

Brian Jenkins has pointed out, terrorists do not want lots of people dead, but they want lots of people *watching*.[3] Terrorists have succeeded extremely well in this policy. The phenomenon of terrorism has been a familiar topic in the U.S. news media since the Iran hostage crisis of 1979–1981. However, for the first decades international terrorism was something that took place outside U.S. borders. Before 9/11 the U.S. had experienced two completed large-scale terrorist acts on U.S. soil. The first attack, the 1993 World Trade Center bombing by Islamic extremists, killed six people and injured a thousand, though the goal had been to kill a quarter million people. In 1995, domestic paramilitary ultra-right-wing terrorists bombed a federal building in Oklahoma City, killing 168 people and wounding over 500.[4]

Tuesday, September 11, 2001, introduced to the general public a new form of international terrorism on U.S. soil. The al Qaeda network aimed not only at extensive worldwide media attention and economic destruction but also at causing mass casualties on U.S. soil. Al Qaeda successfully combined two goals in its attacks: the maximization of international news media coverage and the number of casualties. The 9/11 World Trade Center attacks in New York City took place in front of the world's leading news media organizations, which had the capability to immediately broadcast live news coverage of the attacks around the world. International audiences followed in real time on their television screens the destruction of human lives and symbols of U.S. economic and military power. In a few hours, al Qaeda changed the U.S. experience with international terrorism, bringing fear and chaos directly into American homes and offices, and into Americans' futures.

Media as Part of Mass Culture

The media are part of society's general culture. The United States is often accused of cultural imperialism. Mainstream American culture, it is argued, is expanding globally at the expense of local cultures. American companies' worldwide economic interests push American mass culture to the farthest corners of the world, promoting consumption of American clothing styles, music, news, TV programs and movies. For example, Hollywood films are shown in over 150 countries in the world.[5] Global audiences can watch the films while consuming Coca-Cola or another of that company's over 300 brands.[6] The mainstream mass media are effective in creating a worldwide mass phenomenon. Consumers of American mass culture form a worldview that is shared among consumers in different parts of the world.[7]

In the modern era, mass culture has become an everyday phenomenon. Culture, in particular popular culture, penetrates all parts of society in a variety of forms.[8] For example, the news media and the entertainment media are central parts of people's everyday lives, during free time and at work. Consumption is easy, but gaining access to traditional forms of broadcast or print media as producers of media content or as story subjects requires more effort.

The Western media perform in a capitalist market economy. They are foremost businesses that are driven by market forces just like any other businesses. In that environment, cultural products are produced as any other industrial products: for a profit.[9] Today's media businesses need large financial resources to stay above the water in the constantly changing technological environment. In the competitive market for profits and publicity, Western news media prefer to use what sells, from violence to sex. But at the same time, the mass media industries have a dual role in society. While they are businesses, they also disseminate ideas about society and about its economic and political structures.[10]

Mass Media's Ideological Role in Society

The public is dependent on the news media in order to receive knowledge about what is taking place in the world. That knowledge shapes their understanding of how to see and understand the world, in particular in the case of those issues about which audiences have little or no advance and firsthand knowledge. The more coverage a topic receives, the more likely audiences are to understand the topic to be of importance.[11] People base their decisions of how to act in society on the reality they have constructed from the media. Media representations greatly affect public attitudes and knowledge about current and past affairs in society since the public receives the bulk of their information on matters outside their immediate experience from the media.[12]

The mass media are gatekeepers. They determine what is available to consumers, in what form, and who is allowed to have access to the media as content producer or as subject of a story. The mass media legitimate and reproduce certain political, social and economic structures while they question or deny others by giving the latter negative coverage or no coverage at all.[13] The mass media are central in the creation and maintenance of ideology, in particular in the process of defining opposition — and also when defining opposition away.[14] The media have power to define reality. They draw attention to certain groups and behavior at the expense of those they ignore in their coverage.[15]

One particular media product, news, is a political resource and a contested domain since different groups often seek news media attention in order to advance their interests and to shape public perceptions of them and their issues. Terrorists well understand this and have embraced news media as a methodological tool of action. They plan acts in order to receive and maximize news media coverage, and through that coverage receive recognition for their existence. Terrorists have gradually learned who to attack and how, and where to go for the attention they crave. For example, the coordinated simultaneous 9/11 attacks received much more news coverage around the world than the almost simultaneous 1998 al Qaeda attacks on the U.S. embassies in Kenya and Tanzania. For the dominant Western news media, the mass destruction of Western lives in front of the world's leading news media and at the heart of the world's leading economic, financial and military power was, as cruel as it sounds to say it out loud, a more profitable news commodity than the mass destruction of non–Western lives far away from immediate live news coverage. Even in the case of a developing massacre, such as the Rwandan genocide in 1994 when an estimated 800,000 people were killed in a short period of time, the massive loss of life of Third World citizens was not enough to appeal to large Western news media businesses to grant the horror proper news coverage.

News Commodity and Its Ideological Role in Society

News is not an objective reflection of reality but a manufactured product that is created in a field of financial competition. The news media produce, distribute and exhibit news to make a *profit*. News that is inexpensive to produce and sells well is an ideal product. The news format that brings back the invested money and makes a profit in the financial market is replicated and used over and over again. News is a commodity first; in other words, economic necessities and pressures determine what types of news stories are produced, distributed and sold to consumers. Economic and political interests of news producers and organizations determine what versions of reality are used.[16] For example, the cable news networks CNN, MSNBC and Fox News rarely agree with one another when they are reporting on politics. If news were an objective reflection of reality, we would not be able to distinguish between the news stories presented by these three news networks.

The role of news as a commodity in the West helps to explain why the news media are so central in modern international terrorism, and why the news media and terrorists have a symbiotic relationship that neither can ignore. Terrorists act to become newsworthy and the news media cannot ignore violent events that are news. After all, news is new information about something, especially about something violent.[17] News is something that differs from normal day-to-day routines and the lives of Western societies.[18] This social construction of reality tells the public what is worth their attention. As Fishman puts it, "News organizes our perception of a world outside our firsthand experience.... The media construct something in the society as well as in people's heads."[19]

As we know, news does not emerge straight from reality or portray objective reality.[20] Rather, journalists *create* news.[21] A variety of factors shape news production and content. For example, journalists' own views and values, the news production processes, journalistic routines and values, political connections, political and corporate control, and the availability of material all contribute to the type of news we consume.[22] For example, what the public sees, hears and reads about terrorism in the mass media is "the result of multiple decisions made by cameramen, reporters, producers, copywriters, editors, and managers throughout the news industry."[23] In the fierce competition between different news businesses, technology holds an important role in guaranteeing that those who are covering a story have immediate access not only to what they are covering but also in sending it back to their news outlets. Reporters, photographers and videographers compete to be the first to report on the latest news and developments, but they also have to be able to convince their producers of the importance of each story.

It has become a common practice that the news media follow one another's lead. What one news outlet reports on is often soon covered by other media outlets. In practice, news becomes established as news when journalists report on the same occurrence or theme.[24]

In order to guarantee a profit, news producers prefer to rely on stories which have the lowest common denominator and a high audience appeal. Stories on crime and violence, and preferably involving celebrities, have become today's news.[25] At worst, news stories are news stories only by definition when news organizations go after the latest celebrity story to guarantee an audience for their products. Daily news and updates on the hookups, breakups and partying of entertainment stars and those who want to extend their 15 minutes of fame have become news because these "news" stories are easy and cheap to produce. Furthermore, the constant supply of these stories creates and maintains an audience for them. Infotainment can become social currency in society when it is more important to know the latest celebrity news than to understand the events that truly affect society and people's lives. News is simplified when it becomes what Murdock and Golding call an "entertainment commodity."[26] Television news stories have become spectacles for audiences rather than sources of information which would provide context and explain what is taking place in the world and why, and how local and global events affect us.

The focus on entertainment at the expense of content that has a real bearing on society highlights the fact that to media conglomerates news is first and foremost a commodity, and they treat it as their commodity property. News for broadcast or publication is an expensive product to manufacture, so before an investigation and collection for a story starts, a news business wants to guarantee the story can be used and sold. This practice has put emphasis on deviant behavior and entertainment in news media coverage.

Becoming News through Violence

Marginal groups can become identified in society if they become newsworthy. Acts that are uncommon, new and unexpected are news by the definition of the word. The Western news hierarchy places new information about deviant behavior at the top of its news list. As Gitlin has pointed out, a violent act is news, and violence is a proven method to gain visibility in society.[27] Terrorists use this news fascination with violence and destruction to their advantage in their methods and in their goal to become recognized. When terrorists receive news coverage, the coverage "legitimizes" their existence in the social reality that the news media create. Through news coverage, terrorists become recognized as anti-hegemonic forces in society. The power they are opposing can reject their demands but it cannot deny their existence.

Coverage of crime and violence in the news reaches back in history to the times when portrayals of crime and violence in news ballads and the press were accompanied with coverage of violent and gruesome punishment for the covered crimes.[28] As Foucault points out, the state effectively used stories about deviant behavior and different forms of punishment for crimes as a controlling and deterrent device. The stories gave detailed descriptions of what happens to those who break the rules of society.[29]

Crime and violence as news topics have proved to be profitable to media businesses because they have a great audience appeal. Today's news journalism is still following the 19th-century crime reporting style, in which court reporters directly cited court and police reports, and used colorful language to enliven their stories. This is "drive-by journalism—a ton of anecdotes and graphic detail about individual cases drawn from the police blotter but not an ounce of leavening context to help frame and explain crime."[30] Deviancy is an easy phenomenon to recognize, as well as cheap and easy to report on, because the sources are easily available in the form of police and court reports and other official sources. News on terrorism also relies heavily on official sources and uses graphic details, but still has plenty of work to do when it comes to explaining the phenomenon of terrorism to audiences.

Modern International Terrorism and the News Media

The news media and terrorism have been entangled in a complicated relationship since the emergence of modern, news media-oriented terrorism in the late 1960s. Since then the news media have been bringing terrorism into viewers' living rooms around the world. Airline hijackings, bombings and kidnappings are only a few examples of terrorist activities that are familiar from news headlines. Today it is seemingly impossible to follow the day's news and avoid hearing or reading about terrorism. The phenomenon is covered for the simple fact that it is news in the tradition of what Western societies regard as newsworthy. Terrorist acts are unexpected and irregular events in society. Furthermore, as Laqueur points out, terrorism has media appeal because terrorism "has all the ingredients of a good story—mystery, quick action, tension, drama."[31] And if the cameras and reporters are there to cover the story, it makes the news.

The news media and terrorists have a symbiotic relationship, "each feeding off and exploiting the other for their own purposes."[32] Terrorists use violence and the mass media in order to achieve certain political goals. Hoffman lists five clear objectives that terrorist organizations try to achieve:

1. *Attention.* ... most often from news media coverage.
2. *Acknowledgment.* ... terrorists seek to translate their new-found notoriety into acknowledgment (and perhaps even sympathy and support) of their cause.
3. *Recognition.* ... recognition of their rights (i.e., acceptance of the justification of their cause) and of their particular organization as *the* spokesman of the constituency whom the terrorists purport to, or in some cases actually do, represent.
4. *Authority.* Armed with this recognition, terrorists seek the authority to effect the changes in government and/or society that lie at the heart of their movement's struggle: this may involve a change in government or in the entire state structure, or the re-distribution of wealth, readjustment of geographical boundaries, assertion of minority rights, etc.
5. *Governance.* Having acquired authority, terrorists seek to consolidate their direct and complete control over the state, their homeland and/or their people.[33]

The news media's role is central in these goals because without the first goal, attention, which is most effectively reached through news media coverage, it is hard for a terrorist organization to reach the other four goals. A terrorist attack without public information about the attack is as noticeable as a falling tree in a forest where there is nobody to witness it. The effect of the act is still there, but the lack of publicity keeps the act hidden, using former Israeli prime minster Benjamin Netanyahu's description. For example, in the 1950s Algerian rebels against the country's colonial master, France, transferred their fight from the countryside to the capital, where their victory in the actual fighting was unlikely but where they were sure to gain extensive news coverage. The move guaranteed international publicity for the organization's acts.[34] France tried to secure order by torturing not only terrorists but also those it only suspected of being terrorists. With international media attention on Algeria, the extreme government methods alienated and enraged the locals and the French public.[35] Although France won the military fight, the rebels beat the colonial power in the publicity and political fight to the point that eventually France left Algeria and President de Gaulle granted the country its independence in 1962. The Algerian fighters had calculated their risky move right, as shown by the worldwide audience reaction to the rebels' actions and especially to the overwhelming violent response by France. The latter alienated viewers from the French cause.[36] The Algerian rebels understood the power of the media as a weapon and used it effectively. In the late 1960s Palestinian groups made the weapon global by crossing international borders and targeting civilians of different countries in front of live television audiences.

Terrorists are mainly interested in the audiences who witness their attacks, wanting to see how these audiences react to seeing civilians being killed on the viewers' own television screens.[37] Killing a small number of people is enough to make the news, but the more gruesome and unexpected a terrorist attack is, the more coverage it will receive. Each terrorist group "wants maximum publicity to be generated by its actions and, moreover, aims at intimidation and subjection to attain its objectives."[38] For example, Hezbollah, an Iran-backed terrorist organization, effectively manipulated the American news networks in 1985 when the group hijacked TWA flight 847 on its leg from Athens to Rome. After several stops and hostage releases, there were thirty-nine American men left. The terrorists took the hostages to Beirut and scattered them around the city in order to prevent a U.S. rescue operation. The event lasted seventeen days, attracting over 500 news segments on the three national networks ABC, CBS and NBC, or 28.8 news segments per day. Even when no new developments had taken place, the event was covered.[39] Hoffman sees the incident as a polished public relations campaign. He cites a British journalist who was covering the story. According to the reporter, graduates of American college media studies programs had attended the meetings at which the hijacking plans had been finalized. Furthermore, the terrorists had clearly understood the value of the *American* news media coverage. A British correspondent soon realized that the terrorists were ignoring him and several others; they were interested only in American television journalists.[40]

Research on the News Media and Terrorism

Throughout the history of modern international terrorism, the media have faced a problem in defining terrorism. This problem can also be seen in the research literature on the relationship between the media and terrorism, as it has focused on the relationship between the *news* media and terrorism. Academic research on the topic has largely seen and analyzed news media portrayals of terrorism as closed texts, although the two main views completely disagree on what the portrayal supposedly is. The dominant research perspective, also known as the pro-terrorist literature, claims that the news media provide terrorists with publicity which only encourages more terrorism and sets a threat to society. This perspective sees the news media as pro-terrorist. In contrast, the critical research perspective, also known as the anti-terrorist literature, argues that the media only reproduce the official version on terrorism, which supports military actions against those whom the established power has defined as terrorists. The critical view further argues that the media do not cover terrorism in its political, historical or social contexts but as acts by crazed and irrational groups and individuals.[41] The anti-terrorist literature argues that as a result of this policy, the media are strong supporters and allies of the prevailing power structure. Furthermore, the mass media form a big, unanimous group that acts as a mouthpiece of the power structure, loyally repeating its definitions of terrorism.[42] Both research approaches are very critical of the news media. Neither finds the media do their job well; they see the media as clearly subjective and biased participants in modern international terrorism. Holders of each view just disagree over which party the media are supposedly supporting.

The mainstream paradigm considers the news media to be promoters and allies of terrorists. Researchers who hold this view argue that the media use their freedom of expression irresponsibly when they cover acts of terrorism in the news. These scholars claim that the news media offer terrorists easy access to a powerful propaganda tool and forum of propaganda. According to the pro-terrorist literature, news on terrorism erodes the legitimately chosen order in society and encourages more terrorism.[43]

Some researchers and politicians see the media as the root cause of modern international terrorism. For example, Margaret Thatcher, prime minister of the United Kingdom from 1979 to 1990, argued that the news media offer terrorists publicity, which is the very oxygen of their existence. Her policy was to try to deprive those she labeled as terrorists of that oxygen.[44] Thatcher's policy greatly affected the British news media because the British government was not shy about charging journalists with breaking the Prevention of Terrorism Act if the government did not happen to like news coverage of Republican, that is, Irish nationalist, acts. This resulted in self-censorship in the British media in their coverage of the background and context of terrorism, in particular of PIRA terrorism. The news media learned to agree with the efforts of the British army and accept its versions of violent events. The news media left the actual context and motivation for violent behavior in Northern Ireland unexplored and unquestioned. At its worst, self-censorship led to banning, censoring and delaying the broadcasting of plays and drama productions that had nothing to do with terrorism but whose content was seen as "too Irish" because it drew from Irish culture.[45] The broadcasting corporations felt these programs were politically risky and therefore chose to ban them rather than face the fury of the British government. Terrorists responded to the media war by adjusting their own methods. Attacks or attack warnings took place so close to the start of live broadcasts that there was no time to acquire or receive official government statements on them.

When discussing how terrorism should be covered, some researchers support and propose educational methods, seeing the news media as a public forum which should be used to educate the public and public opinion about terrorism. The U.S. government has analyzed the power of the media as "educators" of public opinion. It has studied, for example, how to use the media in its efforts to position world opinion against the countries and groups that the U.S. defines as terrorist or supportive of terrorism.[46]

Some researchers have argued that the American news media constitute a propaganda forum for the U.S. government. In their view, news media coverage of international events largely reflects U.S. foreign policy interests, which helps the U.S. government to manage the public opinion.[47] When Altheide researched the American television networks' evening newscast coverage of the Iran hostage crisis, he concluded that the newscasts supported official U.S. policy during the hostage event. Altheide analyzed evening newscasts over an eight-month period in 1979–1980. The news reports continued to emphasize the conflict situation and the release of the hostages while they largely ignored the political, historical and social context of the situation and of Iran.[48]

It is not uncommon for a country which defines itself as a target of terrorism to try to limit terrorism news coverage to align with the official views. This is not necessarily done through direct censorship but through a variety of indirect methods. These include, for example, name-calling ("unpatriotic"), limiting journalists' access to government sources, and describing stories critical of counterterrorism as a threat to the country's security.

Terrorist News Commodity

The amount of investment required in today's media industry is so high that only large corporations are capable of raising the needed capital. The economic concentration of the media has led to the emergence of media conglomerates which increasingly produce their media products as they do any other commodity: purely for profit, and to reproduce themselves in the system. In the era of media concentration, a few Western news agencies and corporations have reached the position of being able to control the news production not only in the United States but also on a worldwide scale. They are the gatekeepers which decide what the international news of the day is, how different topics are portrayed, and who gets coverage.

The close relationship between the media and the prevailing power structure is evidenced by the use of institutional sources as news sources. Van Zoonen argues, "Journalists tend to evaluate institutional sources as producing accurate and general information (governmental sources), as being representative (political parties and unions), or as producing disinterested and expert knowledge (universities)."[49] This is typically the case with terrorism coverage too. The practice also helps journalists to shift responsibility for the information they use onto outside, often institutional, sources, especially if the journalists themselves have not properly investigated a story. For example, when CBS, CNN and others covered the Oklahoma City bombing in 1995, they used government representatives and terrorism experts who said the attack matched the signs of Middle Eastern–originated terrorism. Experts' assessments of perpetrators turned out to be wrong. However, journalists are not doing their jobs if they rely on the easy "drive-by" journalism, offering graphic details of terrorist acts and gathering their information mostly from official sources. Without investigating and analyzing terrorism on their own, journalists define terrorism according to official views. This was clearly seen in the mainstream U.S. news media coverage in the months before the U.S. invasion of Iraq. Critical views were largely missing because the news media did not do, or were afraid to do, their jobs at a time when questioning the Bush administration's activities, done in the name of defending the U.S., could have been a disastrous political and business decision, and could have negatively affected the media's profits and access to decision makers.

Terrorism is such a contested topic that journalists do a disservice to a nation if they only repeat definitions and information from official sources. When journalists, researchers and others investigate terrorism in order to understand it better they are not agreeing with terrorism, but they are trying to provide a better understanding of the context of terrorism and its threats. As we witnessed in the U.S. in the pre–9/11 era, spotty and insufficient coverage of terrorism that repeats stereotypes of mad villains leaves the public unprepared for the reality of terrorism.

However, covering terrorism is also a dangerous job for journalists in a variety of ways. Gaining access to terrorists, interviewing terrorists, and producing stories with which terrorists do not agree can be life-threatening. News coverage of terrorism and research for investigative reports on the topic have unfortunately resulted in the death of dozens and dozens of dedicated journalists. Furthermore, journalists can easily become targets of government questioning if they gain access to terrorist sources. Also, ethical and moral questions come into play if a journalist is interviewing sources that are responsible for the killing or the planning of the killing of other people, especially citizens of the journalist's own country.

News Media Coverage of Terrorism

In 1986 NBC News president Lawrence K. Grossman defended news coverage of terrorism at a journalism symposium when discussing how the media should deal with it: "The press cannot treat terrorist kidnappings, murders and bombings as if they have not happened, ... it is better for the people to be informed than to be kept in the dark."[50] When covering news on terrorism, the media see themselves as serving the people's right to know. While terrorists cannot control the type of news coverage they receive, they benefit from publicity. News coverage gives them identity and recognition in public, turning the publicity into political power of acknowledged resistance.

When news defines someone as a terrorist, the story defines the person as an outlawed opponent and therefore a threat to the established order. The news report not only covers a violent act but also tells the public what to think about of the perpetrator of the act. However, terrorists are not after PR stories about their worldview. When their violent acts gain news media coverage, they have already succeeded in the sense that they have become news. That helps them to set the public agenda. Their violent resistance is news. Publicity forces governments to confront the reality of terrorism, because while they can always reject terrorists, they cannot pretend the terrorists do not exist. News media coverage forces a government to take notice of terrorists and their demands.[51] For example, the Western media and governments clearly reject al Qaeda and other anti–Western terrorist networks and organizations, but the media, governments and citizens cannot ignore them, as the post–9/11 era has shown in the U.S. and worldwide. Everyday lives are also affected. For example, we acknowledge terrorism and its impact on our everyday lives every time we take a commercial flight. We cannot board a plane without first going through security checkpoints where we have to remove our shoes, display any small amounts of liquids in transparent plastic bags, take laptops out of briefcases, and agree to the patting and probing of our bodies and private parts at public places at random checks if the security beeper goes off.

If we look at the number of news stories on terrorism, it may seem that media institutions have given terrorism disproportionate significance. Coverage of the phenomenon is greatly out of balance when it is compared to the statistical likelihood of an American falling a victim to terrorism. In comparison to other sources of human death and suffering — for example, car accidents, suicides, murders and meningitis — terrorism is statistically insignificant.[52] For example, Hoffman writes that in 1989 "an American was just as likely to be killed by a dog as by a terrorist."[53] The 1985 hijacking of TWA flight 847 and the extensive news media coverage it received resulted in some 850,000 Americans canceling their foreign and domestic travel reservations and another 200,000 changing their foreign trips into domestic ones because of their fear of terrorism. However, that year the likelihood of an American dying abroad was one in 150,000 and the threat of dying in a terrorist attacks many times smaller.[54]

Coming to the 1990s the number of terrorist attacks decreased while the number of casualties rose. But the statistical likelihood of being a victim of a terrorist attack was still very small. For example, people were more likely to die in a bathtub, crossing the street or falling off a ladder than in a terrorist attack.[55] Even after the September 11, 2001, attacks with their three thousand victims, the statistical likelihood of dying in a terrorist attack remains very small. For example, American highways offer a much greater threat to Americans than does terrorism. In 2001, the year of the 9/11 attacks, over forty thousand people were killed and over three million were injured in traffic accidents.[56] These types of deaths, however, do not have the same impact on a whole nation's psyche as terrorist attacks do. Terrorist violence kills large numbers of civilians simultaneously, and often the event or its aftermath is seen live, in "real time," on TV screens around the world. Furthermore, terrorists purposefully plot to kill civilians.

Over the years the news media have been accused of oversimplifying terrorism in their news coverage. The media have put under the umbrella of terrorism various far-right and far-left intellectual movements, religious and independence movements, as well as revolutionary groups and many others throughout the decades.[57] While the inclusion of a variety of groups under the heading of terrorism is familiar also to the U.S. Department of State, the difference is that the news media represent terrorism as a homogeneous phenomenon even though there are notable differences between the actions and ideologies of different groups. A vague use of the term *terrorism* causes confusion over what the phenomenon truly is. As Laqueur points out, confusion continues when the term

> is used as a synonym for rebellion, street battles, civil strife, insurrection, rural guerrilla war, coups d'etat, and a dozen other things. This indiscriminate use of the term not only inflates the statistics, it makes understanding the specific character of terrorism and how to cope with it more difficult.[58]

News being a commercial business commodity influences how terrorism and terrorist acts are covered. Emphasis is on the human drama of terrorist incidents at the expense of exploring the actual historical or political context and motivation of different incidents: "Immediacy, exclusivity and drama (the more violent or life-threatening the better) thus become the essential 'hooks' with which to reel in viewers and ensure a flow of advertising revenue."[59] As a result, the media provide distorted knowledge about terrorism when they leave contextual understanding of terrorism out.[60] Furthermore, news reports focus on *acts* of terrorism rather than on the phenomenon itself. For example, a 1982 analysis by Plaetz, Fozzard and Ayunian of *New York Times* coverage of the PIRA (Northern Ireland), the Red Brigades (Italy), and Puerto Rico's Fuerzas Armadas de Liberacion Nacional (FALN) from July 1, 1978 until June 30, 1979, found that "70 percent of the stories mentioned neither the cause nor the objectives of terrorists; almost 75 percent mentioned neither the organization nor its supporters; and the 7 percent that did mention names surrounded them with statements by authorities."[61] According to the results of a follow-up study on the American television network news coverage, the latter coverage showed the same tendency. Reports frequently left out causal explanations for terrorist acts. Furthermore, mental instability was the main frame for describing terrorists and their leaders.[62]

The news media have room to improve their terrorism coverage. Over the years the mass media have repeatedly portrayed terrorists as psychopaths who attack without any motives. This type of a portrayal is a familiar theme also in action-adventure films. However, real-life terrorists are very careful. They plan their weapons, targets, and the time and type of each attack in detail. Their acts are not random incidents but based on strategic decisions.[63] For example, the 9/11 targets were very clearly an attack on the U.S. power: the World Trade Center as the heart of the world economy and the Pentagon as the U.S. military nerve center.

Furthermore, the world's leading news media are located in New York City, as well as several countries' foreign correspondents, so the city was the very place to gain immediate worldwide news media coverage. An image of a terrorist as a psychopath may sell well, but it leaves the public unprepared for the reality of terrorism. Stereotypical and uninformed portrayals of terrorism undermine any society's ability to protect itself against terrorist acts.

Terrorism is a special form of violence that aims to intimidate a general population through horrifying acts in order to reach certain political goals. When the news media cover these violent acts, they actually sell the violence to the public. The media divide violence into good and bad violence based on which form they see as a legal form of violence. If the prevailing power structure uses violent force in the name of protecting society, the use of that force is legitimized. The media define threats to the established society as bad violence and therefore illegal activity.[64]

Violent acts of counterterrorism are examples of good violence while terrorists, who function outside legal society, practice bad violence. The media implicitly defines which forms of violence the public understands as a legitimate part of the normal social order, and which acts the public sees as senseless. Violence that is framed as a threat to the public, in particular if it is portrayed out of context, invites audiences to accept counter-violence, which can make them feel safer in society. But extreme use of good violence, familiar from action-adventure films, may in extreme cases result in a higher threat of terrorism or, as is the case with box office hits, in a film sequel.

International News on Terrorism

International news is dominated by a few Western news producers. The Internet age offers a large variety of information sources, but it is still the largest Western media companies that dominate worldwide news business and production on and off the Internet. Expensive technologies such as satellite connections, vast numbers of mini-camcorders and satellite phones demand financial resources that only big corporations can afford. There has to be an audience for every story. Politics or economics as news topics often translate into bad television because they do not offer dynamic footage. Television news footage has to be visually interesting so the whole story is interesting too.[65]

Conflicts are the essence of news.[66] In the portrayal of international events this is seen in the structure of news. The news media present international events from the perspective "us versus them" to emphasize conflicts. News stories are video postcards which offer heroes and villains. They emphasize visible action and what is happening right now. Television news is good drama, reacting to events rather than reflecting or representing reality, or offering in-depth understanding of different events.[67]

Only the largest Western news agencies, large newspapers and CNN have been able to employ dozens to over a hundred foreign correspondents around the world. Satellite connections, portable cameras and laptop computers have made it possible to cover events live from around the world 24/7, but all that is expensive. With its extensive network of foreign correspondents and its global viewership, today in over 200 countries, CNN became in the 1990s the network that largely frames what the international news of the day is. It was a forerunner in the use of new technologies which allowed live news coverage of historical changes, including the collapse of communism. Even world leaders at times rely on CNN to learn the latest on rapidly changing events. The terms "CNN Effect" and "CNN Impact" have been used to describe a situation when live television coverage of an event influences how a country conducts its foreign policy.[68] The U.S. government and military are very aware, just as terrorists are, of the 24/7 live news flow and the power of news media coverage, especially in war conditions.

CNN's success has encouraged other companies to start cable news networks. For example, the News Corp. successfully launched the conservative Fox News Network. However, CNN's competitors have a very limited number of foreign correspondents in comparison to CNN's worldwide network of journalists. The expense of news production, especially the current 24/7 mode, has also been highlighted by the emergence of news "commentators," that is, very opinionated pundits whose programs are cheaply produced in a TV studio and sold to audiences as news. This category includes Bill O'Reilly, Glenn Beck, Keith Olbermann (parted ways with MSNBC in January 2011), and Chris Matthews, among others.

Even as the world has been shrinking, news stories covered by U.S. media still focus on the areas which are in the U.S. foreign policy interests, and on the areas that have similar cultures, religions, and economic and social systems, or are geographically close to the U.S.[69] The rest of the world goes ignored. For example, in the 1990s Russia, the U.K., Israel, Japan and Germany were constant news locales and topics for the mainstream U.S. news media. Few local U.S. newspapers saw a world outside U.S. borders. Foreign stories filled less than two percent of U.S. local newspapers' pages in the late 1990s when the world was becoming more and more globalized.[70] Coverage of the rest of the world shifts according to where the latest crises are taking place.[71] In the 21st century, as China has been rising to a world power status, news coverage on China has been increasing. Crisis stories about Iraq started to dominate the American foreign news stories as the U.S. invasion of Iraq approached and eventually took place.

The American and other Western media have very clear shortcomings in their coverage of the world. In news coverage they have traditionally focused on the West, on bad and negative events, in particular when covering the Third World, on events at the expense of the context, and on the elite and governments of different countries. This has resulted in a distorted picture of the world, emphasizing American and other Western interests and elites while the rest of the world is ignored.[72] Furthermore, international reports in the U.S. news media are often about Americans and American interests rather than purely stories about what is taking place internationally.[73] For example, browsing the headlines in the international news sections of American news websites offers a limited view of the world. It is common for stories to be about U.S. involvement in the world rather than actual foreign news stories. Furthermore, alternative views of world events, as offered, for example, by Al Jazeera, a Qatar-based news network that broadcasts in Arabic and English, do not reach most Western citizens on television.

In addition to the mainstream media, alternative news media have created a web presence. For example, Al Jazeera has found new audiences through its website and video streaming. This news network also gained the attention of the George W. Bush administration, in particular due to its broadcasts of Osama bin Laden videos, and the administration's view that the network has an anti–U.S. bias. According to a leaked British government memo, in 2004 the U.S. president had discussed the possibility of bombing Al Jazeera's Arabic channel's headquarters.[74]

Violence becomes a likely news topic the farther away from the U.S. an event takes place. The farther the locale and deaths are from New York City, the more deaths there have to be for a story to be covered. This cultural determinism in practice means that one dead American and Western European equals in newsworthiness several dead people from other parts of the world. The farther away, the bigger the number of lost lives needs to be for the story to be covered.[75] At worst the Western media may ignore large numbers of deaths in the areas that are not considered to be in the interests of Western news consumers. For example, the Western news media largely ignored the 1994 Rwandan genocide which resulted in the death of some 800,000 people.[76]

Modern terrorists understand the structure of international news. They know that in order to become newsworthy they have to attract the attention of the Western media — in particular the dominant American media. And they know that U.S. media attention is reached through a certain level of violence and by targeting American citizens. For example, after the U.S. invasion of Iraq, American news reporting on casualties detailed the number of American casualties, but left local civilian deaths largely unreported even when the Iraqi casualty numbers were much larger than the American ones. From a terrorist strategic viewpoint, it is no wonder that an anti–U.S. and anti–Western terrorist network targets New York City since it is the center of the world's news media and economy, and a home to millions, including a large international community.

International News Coverage versus Foreign Policy: National Security versus Free Press

News media and governments do not find a common ground on how to cover national security topics, for example, topics such as terrorism or war. There is, and always will be, a conflict between a country's national security and a free press.[77] In free societies the legal restrictions set on a free press mostly find their origin in national security or defense affairs.[78] The media have recognized this conflict when covering foreign policy topics. The *New York Times*, for example, redefined and postponed its article on the CIA and Cuban exiles' plans to invade Cuba in 1961 after the White House contacted the paper.[79] During the first years of the Vietnam War, most foreign desks published articles that used Washington sources rather than reports from their own foreign correspondents because the correspondents' stories contradicted the official version of the war going well for the U.S.[80]

The U.S. government fully acknowledges the power of the media to influence public opinion, which has created conflicts between the free media and the government. For example, in World War I and II, and during the Cold War, the media often found themselves being something that should be silenced or used for propaganda. When a news media outlet or reporter tries to go against official interests, the U.S. government is known to have resorted to a policy of intimidation or censorship. These methods have included, for example, passport and visa denials to reporters, withdrawal of press privileges, requiring preapproval for foreign speakers, and denials of access to cover certain events.[81] The U.S. invasion of Iraq came with restrictions to reporters. In July 2008 the *New York Times* reported that several news photographers had been stripped of their credentials to cover military action because the U.S. military disapproved of images these photographers had taken and published. Limitations on pictures of American deaths in war conditions and on the arrival of U.S. soldiers back home in coffins kept wars sanitized and the public sheltered from the real costs of war. The ban on coffin images was in place from the first Persian Gulf War in 1991 until late February 2009. The new Barack Obama administration reversed the ban, and left it to individual families to decide whether their loved ones' last journey could be photographed and published by the media.

The framing of news stories directly influences how the public understands the covered events and reacts to them, which in turn influences the policy makers' actions and views. For example, during the 1979–1981 Iran hostage crisis, when Iranian students overtook the American embassy in Tehran and kept fifty-two Americans as hostages, the absence of direct and official communication between the two countries was replaced by news media coverage of the events. President Carter's approval rating initially rose from 30 to 61 percent when the American public wanted and expected something to be done fast, and therefore stood behind its president. He became a personification of the country in its efforts to resolve the issue. The continuous news media coverage further added pressure for a fast resolution, which did not happen,[82] and was further complicated by the failed Delta Force rescue effort.

At times the mass media, in particular television, have taken on a diplomatic role. Television can act as the negotiator between a government and, for example, terrorists. While the two sides are not directly communicating with each other, they do that indirectly through television. For example, television coverage became a critical source of information on the hostages' location and condition during the June 1985 TWA flight 847 hijacking. The hijackers also relied on the media to send out their demand to Israel to release Muslim prisoners who had been captured in Israeli-occupied Lebanon. Officials had no access to the hostages or the hijackers, but the media did, and thus the hijacking became a media, in particular a television, event.[83]

The news media have a central role in U.S. foreign policy. For example, according to President George H. W. Bush's press spokesman Marlin Fitzwater, live video images took priority to the State Department and desk officers during international crises during the Bush administration.[84] As Taylor cites, President George H. W. Bush went as far as to say: "I learn more from CNN than I do from the CIA."[85] The Clinton administration also closely followed live news coverage. According to George Stephanopoulos, then part of the Clinton administration: "In the White House ... We have 24 hour news cycles ... CNN assures you that you are forced to react at any time, and that's going to happen throughout the time of the Clinton presidency."[86] Decision makers are well aware of the power of live media coverage, especially since modern technology permits coverage of world events to reach the public and politicians at the same time.

The instantaneous news coverage makes both journalists and politicians' reaction time shorter.[87] As a result, journalistic error can be more likely than before because there is less or no time to wait for background information or confirmation of the facts.[88] Also, in order to cut costs, international news is often covered by so-called parachute journalists who fly in and out of the latest international news location as needed. They lack knowledge of the local language and customs, as well as the full complexity of what they are covering since they may not have followed the event in depth for a long period of time. Parachute journalists are only able to give quick soundbites before they rush to their next crisis area.

Diplomats benefit from the media's lack of interest in foreign affairs because it gives them room to act without publicity. If media coverage does emerge, diplomats can use that as a guide for how to prioritize the handling of different foreign affairs issues.[89] If policymakers are expecting news media coverage to lead the discussion on certain policy issues, they often take an initiative to counter that. For example, President George H. W. Bush had an article in *Newsweek* before the 1991 Persian Gulf War. In the article, titled "Why We Must Break Saddam's Stranglehold," the president made his case for the war.[90]

How the media cover wars and conflicts is very different from real wars which have real destruction and real death, complete with the smells and anguish of what has taken place. The media only *mediate* these events for their mass audiences, and they present sanitized versions of real wars. A media war is only an audiovisual representation of a real war, which, as Taylor puts it, "is about the sound, sight, smell, touch and taste of the nasty, brutal business of people killing people."[91] A media-depicted war can never come close to portraying the reality of war. Furthermore, though a war is always news, American journalists and government both analyze war from the perspective of whether the U.S. is involved in it or not.[92]

The goal of journalism is objective and neutral coverage of events, but that can be hard in conflict areas. It is not uncommon for journalists and news media to take sides in their coverage of foreign policy issues. For example, during the Persian Gulf War, news anchors talked about "our side" and "we" when they discussed the U.S.-led allied forces, and therefore clearly took a side rather than objectively reported on the events. In the Persian Gulf War reporting, the historical context of the war was missing, including the 1980s U.S.-Iraq cooperation, which helped Iraq to build up its military forces and become a regional military powerhouse. While the mainstream U.S. news media was ignoring Kuwait's human rights violations,[93] an American PR company, Hill & Knowlton, was selling the war to the American public in the name of "Citizens for a Free Kuwait," a group primarily financed by the Kuwaiti government.

Just as media coverage and media technology have dehumanized war, the development of high technology weaponry has done the same. High-tech weaponry has been the focus of the American armed forces since the Vietnam War, with the goal of fast and easy victories and few casualties on the American side. The approach was intensified in the post–Cold War era. For example, the Persian Gulf War emphasized the goal of low-level casualty numbers. Post–Cold War methods have preferred high-tech airpower-oriented operations to conventional warfare.[94] The news media largely focus on admiring the effectiveness of the high-tech weaponry, as they did, for example, during the Persian Gulf War when they forgot to verify the effectiveness of the weapons and neglected what happened to the targets of those weapons. Human suffering is lost in the flashy showcase of the latest weapons technology. Colorful flashes make good prime-time TV, which the armed forces also well know.

The military has realized it cannot keep democratic media and journalists from conflict and war areas. Rather, the military has noticed it can work best with journalists by giving them access to these sites.[95] The U.S. government has masterfully limited journalists' access in the two Persian Gulf Wars. During the first Persian Gulf War, journalists' access was granted only to a press pool under the Pentagon command. No reporter was allowed to go anywhere without military escorts, and stories were pre-filed to the military before to the media. News production was in the hands of the military, which did its best to provide only its side of the operation. The media, in particular television, simplified the war, presenting a story between good versus evil while ignoring opposition to the war.[96]

During the U.S invasion of Iraq, embedded journalists traveled with U.S. troops and did not have a full picture of the war or access to alternative sources of information. Furthermore, when an embedded journalist's safety is dependent on the troops with whom she or he is traveling, it is quite natural for the journalist to start feeling comradeship with the troops and see the war as "our" war. For example, in the spring of 2008 I had a discussion with an American journalist who had covered Afghanistan and Iraq in the past. The journalist was very clear about being on the American side, to the point that he mentioned he would relay any information he received about the enemy to American officials.

Taking sides in war coverage is nothing new. For example, during the Cold War journalists clearly took a side in their reporting, although at times they were forced to do so. At the same time, journalists also face other problems when they cover military-related topics because they often lack a clear understanding and knowledge of wars, as well as of military jargon and battles. This has made it easier for the military to manipulate journalists.[97]

The military-versus-media problem arose also in Grenada in 1983 and in Panama in 1989 when the military prevented media access to the conflict sites until the military operations were over. At the other extreme of the media's access to military operations was Operation Hope, in Somalia in 1992, when the news media hit the beach before the Marines did. The arriving troops were met by camera lights when Operation Hope was broadcast live on CNN and the networks.[98]

The news media are not faced only with the government if they are questioning or criticizing government or military actions. The public does not easily waive its support to the officials if the media dare to question the officials or if the media do not support government policies in their news coverage. The public turns its anger on the messenger instead of the officials.[99] This can effectively keep news organizations from reporting on topics that could diminish their profits. For example, in the post–9/11 U.S., the U.S. invasion of Iraq was an easy sell to not only the media and the public but also to politicians who in large numbers supported the invasion. In October 2002 both the U.S. Congress and Senate passed House Joint Resolution 114, Authorization for Use of Military Force Against Iraq Resolution of 2002. The Senate supported the invasion by a vote of 77–23, and Congress by 296–133.[100]

Terrorists and the news media have a symbiotic but conflicted relationship. Terrorists seek the limelight in order to be recognized, and to create fear and chaos in society. The news media cover terrorist acts because the acts are deviant and uncommon events in society, and therefore news according to Western news standards. Furthermore, for the news media, which are corporate entities, terrorism is a commodity which creates a profit due to its ability to sell well. However, while terrorists may succeed in creating media spectacles, they are not in control of how the news media cover them.

International news, which provides information about what is taking place in the world, is not a reflection of reality. It is influenced by commercial interests, journalistic routines and journalists themselves, as well as by foreign-policy interests and foreign-policy makers. The closer to the U.S. a country is in cultural, religious and ideological terms, the more coverage the story receives. The further away a country is from the U.S. in cultural, religious and ideological terms, the more stereotypical the image is — if the country receives any coverage at all. In addition, the further away a country is from the U.S., the larger the act of violence or destruction has to be for it to receive news media coverage in the West.

International terrorists understood the corporate structure of international news early. This was the case especially with the terrorists operating in the Middle East when they started to target U.S. citizens in the 1980s and aim at mass casualties to make themselves and their causes known around the world.

Terrorism is still an umbrella term for many different forms and motivations of political violence. The differences between groups become clear when comparing 1990s attacks against the United States and U.S. interests to attacks in Europe and the Middle East. In the attacks in the latter areas, terrorists have traditionally claimed public responsibility for their violent acts. They have aimed at media recognition which would also bring political recognition and eventually maybe even a seat at a negotiation table. In contrast, the attacks on the U.S. have largely been left unclaimed. In the 21st century new forms of terrorism have brought that trademark to other regions.

In the U.S. it has been the responsibility of law enforcement to find out, for example, what forces were behind the two attacks on the World Trade Center (1993 and 2001), the Oklahoma City bombing (1995), and the attacks against U.S. embassies in Kenya and Tanzania (1998). This is a tactic that demands more time and effort from the party that is attacked. It also has the potential to create more fear and chaos in society when the state and its citizens do not even know who has attacked them. Furthermore, the World Trade Center and Oklahoma City attacks claimed a large number of casualties on U.S. soil. The attacks were similar, although the U.S. traced the World Trade Center attacks to militant Islamic extremists and the Oklahoma City attack to homegrown Fundamentalist Christian right-wing extremists.

According to unclassified CIA and annual U.S. Department of State reports on international terrorism, the U.S. has been the primary target of international terrorism since the emergence of the phenomenon. In the late 1960s, and in the 1970s and 1980s, the majority of the attacks against U.S. interests took place outside U.S. borders, targeting symbols of Western power. In particular, American businesses, businessmen and diplomats were targets, but these attacks rarely resulted in death or extensive material destruction. The U.S. government has had modern international terrorism on its radar since the phenomenon emerged, but the American public did not truly become aware of international terrorism until November 1979 when Iranian students took over the American embassy in Tehran. Daily news coverage of the 444-day hostage drama made international terrorism a visible topic on the U.S. foreign policy agenda, in the American news media and public consciousness, and soon after, also on the big screen. Chapter 2 will discuss how the U.S. became a target of international terrorists, and what the country's counterterrorism structure, in particular in crisis situations, was before the 9/11 attacks.

Chapter 2

International Terrorism and the United States

On September 11, 2001, reality created a larger terrorist spectacle than any Hollywood film about terrorism had ever done. The coordinated attacks reminded viewers of Hollywood fiction but, instead of special effects and actors who could get up after the end of a violent scene, terrorists used real airplanes as weapons and destroyed real lives and property. Reality had not only caught up with fictional terrorism but it had beaten Hollywood in competition for viewers. The events of 9/11 created history's largest terrorist media spectacle to date for immediate worldwide television audiences.

The United States has been following modern international terrorism closely since its emergence, analyzing the threats it poses to U.S. security, interest and citizens. The federal government started to record international terrorist incidents and to collect statistical data on the phenomenon in 1968.[1] In the 1970s presidential directives set the U.S. State Department to lead the country's counterterrorism efforts overseas and the FBI on U.S. soil.[2] In National Security Decision Directive Number 30 (1982), President Reagan detailed the coordination of the country's response to terrorist attacks, and stated that the Interdepartmental Group on Terrorism at the U.S. State Department was to "be responsible for the development of overall US policy on terrorism, including *inter alia*, policy directives, organizational issues, legislative initiatives, and interagency training programs."[3] Later the group was renamed the Interagency Working Group on Counterterrorism (IWGT), and was still housed at the State Department. According to President Reagan's directions, the U.S. Department of State was the federal lead agency for terrorist incidents outside U.S. territory, the Federal Bureau of Investigation (FBI) via the Department of Justice for terrorist incidents on U.S. soil, and the Federal Aviation Administration (FAA) for hijackings. The Federal Emergency Management Agency (FEMA) was to manage post-attack recovery efforts. Over the years new directives from the White House have reconfirmed the general structure of the lead federal agencies, with some minor corrections to it, for example, in how to respond to hijackings.

This chapter briefly discusses the U.S. understanding of international terrorism and U.S. policies on international terrorism, as documented by the U.S. Department of State which is in charge of issuing annual reports on international terrorism. The department issued its first report in July 1982. *Patterns of International Terrorism: 1981* continued in the CIA's footsteps. In that report the State Department listed a large variety of terrorist incident categories, for example, kidnappings, bombings, hijackings and assassinations.[4]

This chapter also addresses the U.S. counterterrorism structure in the pre–9/11 era, with its focus on crisis management — in other words, how to respond to a terrorist incident. This chapter only briefly discusses certain international terrorist threats. A more detailed analysis of a variety of international terrorist incidents and threats is left for the book's film chapters, which analyze and compare fictional and real-life terrorist threats and acts.

The following first gives a short historical overview of how the U.S. became a target of modern international terrorism, then discusses pre–9/11 U.S. counterterrorism. The focus is on the U.S. Department of State which, in addition to providing annual reports on international terrorism, is usually the lead federal agency to respond to terrorist incidents which take place outside U.S. borders. The chapter gives an overview of the department's definition of international terrorism, and where it has found security threats to the U.S. The chapter concludes with a brief look at other agencies that are involved in U.S. counterterrorism, including the Federal Bureau of Investigation, which is normally the lead federal agency under the Department of Justice when a terrorist incident takes place on U.S. soil. In addition, the U.S. counterterrorism contingent includes several other law enforcement agencies, the U.S. Department of Defense and others, which translated into some fifty departments and agencies somehow being involved in U.S. counterterrorism in the pre–9/11 era. While a bureaucratic structure for counterterrorism existed, as discussed below, the vast and confusing counterterrorism structure had left no agency in a clear leadership role in the pre–9/11 era. The U.S. counterterrorism structure was focused on an interagency response because, as Brian Sheridan, Assistant Secretary of Defense for Special Operations and Low-Intensity Conflict, pointed out in 2000: "No single agency possesses the authorities, response mechanisms and capabilities to effectively deter or resolve terrorist incidents."[5]

The United States Becomes a Target

The openness of the U.S. and other democracies and their protection of individual rights and freedoms make them vulnerable to terrorist attacks. Terrorists can move freely in these societies and use the system to their advantage. Terrorism hardly exists in tight dictatorships because the state keeps a close watch on everyone in society and can therefore effectively remove threats to its power.[6]

According to the U.S. State Department, the U.S. has been the number one target of international terrorism in most years since the emergence of the phenomenon. For example, in 1981 the State Department's Bureau of Public Affairs estimated that between 1968 and 1980, over one third of international terrorist attacks targeted Americans.[7] The bureau explained: "The US is a prime target because our official and commercial presence overseas is extensive; our citizens and facilities are accessible to the public, our policies are opposed to the interests of many terrorist groups; and we frequently support governments that terrorists are trying to destabilize."[8]

Due to its worldwide presence the U.S. has attracted terrorists' attention as a representative of Western wealth. For example, in the first decades of terrorism the U.S. experience as a target of terrorism was mostly recorded from attacks against American businesses and business interests in Latin America.[9]

In terms of human lives terrorism poses a lesser threat to the United States than, for example, traffic accidents. But the effects of terrorism cannot be measured only in the number of victims because terrorist acts also influence their target societies in social, political and economic terms, as well as their relationship with other countries. All this we have experienced also in the post–9/11 era.

In the 1960s and 1970s the U.S. experienced on its own soil acts of domestic terrorism, for example, by the Weathermen and the Symbionese Liberation Army. Also several domestic skyjackings, often with the purpose of diverting the flight to another country, made the headlines in the 1970s.[10] In the era of domestic terrorism, civil action and other disturbances, international terrorism was not perceived as a threat on U.S. soil. Outside and inside the U.S. borders communism was seen as the primary threat to the country's security and interests.

Terrorism gradually started to become a more serious worldwide threat in the late 1970s. In 1968, the first year of modern international terrorism, attacks were equally divided between strikes against human life and against property. However, by 1981 four out of five of the year's attacks were against human life.[11] Over 3,600 people died as victims of international terrorism between 1968 and 1980.[12] The phenomenon spread to more and more countries. In 1970, terrorists targeted 48 countries and their citizens; by 1981 the number hit 91. Overall, from 1968 till 1981, citizens of 131 countries were victims of international terrorist attacks. The number of terrorist organizations at this time was 670. Most were Palestinian, Armenian, West German or Central American groups. However, as the State Department pointed out, the number did not reflect real, detailed information in the sense that many groups used several names, and terrorist acts can be claimed by criminals and other people who want publicity but have nothing to do with terrorism or with the terrorist acts they claim.[13]

In the 1970s and 1980s terrorism was largely a phenomenon of regional conflicts, in particular in the Middle East.[14] Examining the State Department's data on international terrorism, three areas come into focus: Western Europe, the Middle East and Latin America. For example, from 1968 until 1981 about three fourths of all terrorist incidents took place in these regions. The spillover of Middle Eastern political violence expanded the region's problems worldwide, especially to Western Europe.[15] The latter was also facing domestic left-wing groups, several of which attacked U.S. and NATO targets.

While Latin American terrorism was largely domestic-based, attacks on American business interests in Latin America comprised most of the anti–U.S. attacks. American diplomats were the second most common targets, and U.S. military targets came in third. However, lethal attacks were rare.

Emergence of the No Concessions Policy

In the late 1960s the United States started to draw up policies on terrorism as a response to international incidents of terrorism, in particular after the U.S. had been directly targeted several times in Latin America. At first the U.S. goal was to guarantee the safe return of its kidnapped citizens. For example, in 1969 a group of Brazilian terrorists took the American ambassador to Brazil as its hostage. The U.S. State Department demanded the safe return of its ambassador and put pressure on the Brazilian government to give in to terrorist demands, which the latter did. The U.S. ambassador was released soon after. A year later the U.S. again successfully pressured a foreign government, this time Guatemala, to give in to terrorist demands in order to guarantee the safe return of a kidnapped U.S. labor attaché. But when another American, a police officer advising the Uruguayan police force on harsh interrogation methods, was kidnapped a few months later in Uruguay, he fell victim to the U.S. and Uruguayan refusal to give in to terrorist demands and was killed by the kidnappers. However, the U.S. decision to give no concessions to terrorists was not an official policy. It was not until an international terrorist media spectacle reached TV viewers worldwide that the superpower started to analyze its response to terrorist kidnappings.[16]

In 1972 the world reacted to what it saw on television. In the spring of that year the

Japanese Red Army, on behalf of the Popular Front for the Liberation of Palestine (PFLP), attacked an airport in Israel. A few months later the Black September, a Palestinian organization, targeted the Israeli team at the summer Olympics in Munich, West Germany. The world and the Olympic Games organizers were unprepared. West Germany struggled in its rescue efforts. For example, only after West German authorities had abandoned a rescue attack in the Olympic Village did they learn that the terrorists had been following live television coverage of the supposedly secret effort. In the final confrontation between the terrorists and West German authorities, all remaining hostages lost their lives. In the aftermath of the attacks, several Western European countries, for example, the U.K. and West Germany, drew up policies on terrorism and created counterterrorist special forces.[17] On the other side of the Atlantic, President Nixon opted to focus on international efforts against terrorism although he did begin to coordinate counterterrorism by creating a cabinet-level committee, which only met once, to be helped by the special Inter-Departmental Working Group on Terrorism.[18] Soon also a small office in the State Department started to coordinate U.S. policies on terrorism.[19] Presidential directives in the 1970s designated the State Department in charge of coordinating the country's counterterrorism outside U.S. territory, while the FBI led on the home turf.[20] Directives by later presidents confirmed these roles. In June 1977 President Carter's Presidential Review Memorandum 30 (PRM-30) updated U.S. counterterrorism with a Special Coordination Committee at the National Security Council to review how the country dealt with terrorist incidents. This committee replaced the Nixon cabinet committee.[21] In November 1977 the U.S. finally founded its first counterterrorist unit, the Delta Force.

The FBI got to test its lead agency role in the 1970s. In cooperation with other agencies it effectively prevented bombings in New York City only a year after the Munich tragedy. The Black September had scheduled attacks to take place during Israeli prime minister Golda Meir's visit to New York. Two bombs were placed along Fifth Avenue, and a third in the El Al cargo terminal at Kennedy Airport. After the National Security Agency (NSA) intercepted a message about the bombings, the NSA, CIA and FBI joined forces and were able to prevent the attacks.[22]

After the Munich drama, the White House approach was that there would be no negotiations with and no concessions to terrorists. However, not all were willing to sign in on the new policies as they feared putting American diplomats' lives at risk.[23] A "wait and see" policy was competing with the unofficial "no concessions" policy. A watershed event was the March 1973 kidnapping of five diplomats, including two Americans, at the Saudi Arabian embassy in Sudan by members of the Black September.[24] The group's demands included "the release of Sirhan Sirhan — the man who assassinated Robert Kennedy — from U.S. prison; the release of Palestinian guerrillas being held in Jordan; Arab women detained in Israel; and Baader-Meinhof Gang terrorists in West German prisons."[25] At a news conference, President Nixon announced, "as far as the United States as a government giving in to blackmail demands, we cannot do so and we will not do so.... We will do everything that we can to get them released, but we will not pay blackmail."[26] The terrorists killed their two American hostages and the Belgian chargé d'affaires. Nixon's response to journalists' questions became an official U.S. policy.

President Nixon's followers supported the new policy. For example, as a reaction to the TWA flight 847 hijacking on June 18, 1985, President Reagan clearly spelled out in a speech the U.S. approach: "America will never make concessions to terrorists — to do so would only invite more terrorism — nor will we ask or pressure any other government to do so."[27] In February 1986 Vice President George H. W. Bush, the chair of the cabinet-level Task Force on Combatting Terrorism, issued a report which addressed U.S. experience with Hezbollah taking

American and other Western hostages in Lebanon. While he supported the no concessions policy, he also left some wiggle room: "The United States has a clear policy on no concessions to terrorists as the best way to protect the greatest number of people. However, the United States Government has always stated that it will talk to anyone and use every available resource to gain the release of Americans held hostage."[28] The task force's report led to the Omnibus Diplomatic Security and Antiterrorism Act of 1986, which strengthened legal methods in combatting terrorism. According to the act, it was "a federal crime for a terrorist to threaten, detain, seize, injure, or kill an American citizen abroad."[29] The act allowed the FBI to extend its arm abroad to bring terrorists to justice in the U.S. Terrorists could not hide anywhere in the world.

The Iran Hostage Crisis (1979–1981)

International terrorism really hit the American public consciousness for the first time in November 1979 when radical Iranian students took over the U.S. embassy in Tehran, Iran, and took almost seventy Americans as their hostages. The event became a continuous televised drama. Although the U.S. media had extensively covered the 1972 Munich Olympic Games attack, the threat of terrorism did not hit home until a large number of American citizens became direct targets of international terrorism.

Iran was a country whose leadership, Shah Mohammed Reza Pahlavi, the U.S. and the U.K. had helped to put back in place in the 1950s. In 1953 the CIA and Britain's Secret Intelligence Service (SIS) arranged a coup against Iran's democratically elected Prime Minister Mohammed Mossadegh, a nationalist and reformist, whose policies were undermining the shah and Western interests. The intent was to counter the nationalization of the Iranian oil industry, in particular the nationalization of the British Petroleum Company. The coup also aimed at preventing the influence of the country's communist party, and through that, the influence of the Soviet Union in the region.[30] In return for U.S. support, the shah guaranteed the U.S. a steady flow of oil. The next eight U.S. presidents supported the shah by economic and military aid.[31]

Dissatisfaction with the shah, who was a modernizer and dictator, came to a peak in the late 1970s to the point the he left Iran in January 1979. As the shah was in exile, anti–Western and anti–Shah views led to an Islamic fundamentalist revolution, led by Shia leader Ayatollah Ruhollah Khomeini, who had returned from exile. After the revolution Iran cut its ties to its ex-ruler's Western allies. Later that same year, on November 4, radical Iranian students seized the U.S. embassy in Tehran and took sixty-six American embassy employees as their hostages while six Americans escaped.[32] Eventually fifty-two of the hostages went through the whole 444-day hostage period. The students demanded that the shah be returned to Iran from the U.S., where he was going through cancer treatment. Khomeini supported the students' actions, calling America "the big Satan."[33]

The hostages became highly publicized in the U.S. and all over the world. For 444 days the American news networks followed the Iran hostage crisis every night in detail.[34] In order to be able to offer U.S. viewers the latest developments just before they went to bed, one of the big networks, ABC, created a late-night news show, *Nightline*.[35] The popularity of the Carter administration rose and fell according to its dealings with the crisis.[36] The Iran hostage crisis gained unprecedented media coverage of a terrorist act. During the 444-day event, the news media focused on the daily drama at the expense of context and the historical turmoil between Iran, the U.S., and the U.K.

The hostage crisis also changed the structure of U.S. counterterrorism leadership. The State Department had to give way to the Carter administration's national security adviser, after which the White House was in charge of coordinating the U.S. counterterrorism policy.[37]

The events in Iran highlighted a change in the U.S. experience with international terrorism. In the previous years Americans had largely been innocent bystander victims of terrorist attacks against other targets. Now they were direct targets. The State Department calls 1980 a watershed year because Americans in growing numbers were targeted for their *nationality*.[38] For the world's terrorists the prolonged media event was a learning tool of the power of news media images, and in particular of the power of American citizens as targets who would attract worldwide news media attention.

Before 1979 was over, the United States faced another setback in the global arena. In December 1979 the Soviet Union invaded Afghanistan. Not only had the United States arrived in the world stage as a target of spectacular attacks of international terrorism, but the country and its special hostage rescue unit, the Delta Force, had failed to rescue the American hostages and resolve the Iran hostage crisis in its 1980 attempt. A further insult to U.S. power and policies was added by the world's other superpower, the communist Soviet Union, which was expanding its ideology and military power into Afghanistan. There was a fear the communist giant would try to expand its power all the way into the oil-rich Persian Gulf region, where the United States had just suffered the humiliation of not only losing its ally the shah of Iran, but was also facing a new anti–American adversary in Ayatollah Khomeini.

The international difficulties of the Carter administration, the bitter internal politics in his executive branch, and the growing opposition to détente in the U.S.-Soviet relationship on the home front did not bode well for President Carter.[39] The failed special forces rescue mission of the hostages and the administration's unsuccessful attempts to resolve the crisis in Tehran added to the Carter administration's problems in the elections. In November 1980 Americans elected Ronald Reagan of the Republican Party as their new president. On the day he took office, Iran released the American hostages. By that time the Iraq-Iran War had started, and the shah had died.

Worldwide Soviet Terrorist Network

The new president's touch soon became evident in the superpower relations. The time of détente, a calmer era in the relationship between the superpowers and limited cooperation that the Nixon administration had initiated, was now over. President Reagan renewed the Cold War in the superpower relations until the war reached its final peak and fast "defrosting" under the same president and Soviet leader Mikhail Gorbachev in the late 1980s.[40]

The Iran hostage crisis and the U.S. presence and interests in the Middle East increased the U.S.'s attraction as a target to the point that the 1980s was the decade when the U.S. truly experienced terrorism abroad. Also, the 1980s was the decade when the U.S. took aggressive steps against those it considered to be terrorists or sponsors of international terrorism. Norwitz points out that the American experience with international terrorism did not truly start until President Reagan took office:

> Upon assuming office, President Reagan was deeply affected by the Carter administration's struggle against international terrorism and, as a result, was determined to deploy the traditional elements of national power to defeat terrorist menace. Economic measures, diplomatic mechanisms, and military force were the tools that supported Reagan's strategy. During the early Reagan years,

terrorism became synonymous with warfare, particularly after 241 Marines and other servicemen were killed in Beirut by a terrorist truck bomb on 23 October 1983.[41]

The newly shaping Middle Eastern–originated terrorism culminated in the 1983 attacks, introducing to the world a new form of terrorism that aimed at mass casualties. The Reagan administration reacted to the large number of American casualties in Lebanon by withdrawing its forces, an act which terrorists — among them al Qaeda — have used as an example of their ability to undermine the U.S. Soon after the withdrawal, the U.S. showcased its military might in the militarily weak Grenada, but the response in Lebanon became an often repeated example among U.S. opponents of the country's inability to tolerate mass casualties. In the aftermath of the Lebanon bombings, the State Department's counterterrorism office gained more status when its head was promoted to an ambassador-at-large who reports to the Secretary of State.

The further the 1980s proceeded, the more the State Department warned about the increase of attacks which aim at mass casualties. The department described 1985 as a "banner year" for international terrorists, and called international terrorism in its 1986 report "a priority item for concern."[42] Also, the president's words were tough. In a July 1985 speech to the American Bar Association, President Reagan announced: "There can be no place on earth left where it is safe for these monsters to rest, to train, or practice their cruel and deadly skills. We must act together, or unilaterally, if necessary to ensure that terrorists have no sanctuary — anywhere."[43]

President Reagan actively sought to defeat international terrorism, which he considered to be a threat to U.S. security. In his administration's view there was a worldwide terrorist network, backed by the communist Soviet Union, which was threatening America's interests and security. Accordingly, the administration saw the country's ideological enemy as a provider of direct and indirect support to terrorist groups in the Middle East and Africa. Soviet ties to Cuba raised concern about Soviet influence in Latin America. The State Department's annual reports under President Reagan lack evidence of any direct Soviet involvement in terrorist attacks against the U.S., but they support the view of a worldwide Soviet terrorist network.[44] In addition to seeing a threat in the Soviet Union and Cuba, the U.S. listed Libya, Iran, South Yemen, Iraq and Syria as providers of indirect or direct support to terrorist groups. These countries avoided direct confrontation with the U.S., but they still promoted anti–U.S. policies and other foreign policy interests by providing support to several terrorist groups that performed anti–Western attacks. Due to their sponsorship of these groups, the supporters could largely control the groups' activities.[45]

Although the Reagan administration saw the Soviet support to its ideological clients as terrorism, the administration viewed its own role in supporting brutal dictatorships — for example, in Latin America — as support for freedom. These U.S. clients were fighting leftist forces, some of them citizens' organizations. For example, the U.S. targeted the leftist Nicaraguan Sandinista regime. It listed Nicaragua as a provider of a safehaven for leftist groups in Central America, and for Palestinian and left-wing Western European groups. Nicaragua also provided safehaven, training, advice and weapons to Latin American insurgent or guerrilla groups such as the Salvadoran FMLN. But in the mid–1980s the Department of State's evidence of Nicaragua's involvement in actual terrorist acts was limited.[46]

For President Reagan terrorism translated into an act of war, in particular after the 1983 bombings in Lebanon. But the Reagan administration also defined terrorism as criminal activity which needed to be punished. Taking that approach to an international level, the administration interpreted punishment as a military action. For example, it took an aggressive approach to a major state sponsor of terrorism, Libya. Investigating the 1986 bombing of a West German discotheque that was frequented by American soldiers, the U.S. connected the bombing to Libya and also suspected Libya of being linked to several other terrorist attacks against U.S. interests. President Reagan took a critical step that changed U.S. response and counterterrorism approach by ordering air strikes against Libya, and targeting areas where its leader, Muammar Qadhafi, was believed to reside.

Executive Order 12333 prohibits assassinations,[47] but the administration considered the attack on Libya in different terms. In its view Libya was a known state sponsor of terrorism and therefore the country should be challenged, especially in this case when it was directly linked to the discotheque bombing. The attack not only highlighted international terrorism as an agenda item for the Western world but "it established a critical precedent that force could and would be used against those who support, plan, or finance terrorism, or who use their sovereign territory to harbor or train terrorists."[48]

President Reagan's approach to terrorism suffered a major setback towards the end of his second term when a major scandal broke out. The administration was caught trying to work around U.S. law in its dealings with what it considered to be terrorism in the Middle East and part of a worldwide Soviet terrorist network's influence in Latin America. The Reagan administration was caught selling arms to Iran which, according to the administration's own definitions, was a state that sponsors terrorism and was therefore under sanctions.[49] The profits from the arms business were used to aid the Nicaraguan anti-communist Contra fighters, who were opposing the prevailing leftist Nicaraguan government.[50] As *The 9/11 Commission Report* points out, military aid to the Contras was illegal, so to use the proceeds of the arms sales to aid the Contras was an attempt to get around U.S. law. The arms business mixed two goals, both of which were outside U.S. law. First, through its arms sales the U.S. was negotiating with Iran in order to gain the latter's assistance in the release of American hostages held in Lebanon by Hezbollah, an Iran-backed terrorist organization. Second, the U.S. intended to forward the profits to the Contras. A U.S. bill had made the latter directly an illegal act.[51] Both the selling of arms to Iran and, through that, the making of concessions to terrorists, in this case either to their primary sponsor or directly to the group holding American hostages, were direct violations of the official counterterrorism policies. Reagan himself had said on June 18, 1985: "America will never make concessions to terrorists — to do so would only invite more terrorism — nor will we ask or pressure any other government to do so."[52]

The Iran-Contra facts surfaced in 1986 and 1987, and several members of the Reagan administration were indicted, such as national security adviser Robert McFarlane, his deputy, Admiral John Poindexter, and their staffer, Marine Lieutenant Colonel Oliver North, who was behind the actual plan. The CIA's Clandestine Service was also tarnished when a special counsel indicted several of its high-ranking officers.[53] The effects of the Iran-Contra scandal were felt globally. In its aftermath, there was a large loss of international support to American counterterrorism efforts.[54] Furthermore, to the American public it seemed that the misuse of power in covert actions that had taken place in the 1970s was now being replayed before its eyes.[55] The repercussions of the Iran-Contra case were also felt in the country's counterterrorism structure.[56] The Iran-Contra scandal made many question the wisdom of having the White House lead the country's counterterrorism.[57] The U.S. reduced its military responses while law enforcement and the court of law once again gained the center stage in the fight against terrorism.

The U.S. Becomes a Target on U.S. Soil

Towards the end of the Cold War, the world saw a drastic drop in the number of terrorist attacks. For example, in 1988 the State Department data showed 176 attacks, but in the following year the number of attacks declined to 58, and in 1990 it declined further, to 54.[58] But new threats were already emerging in the newly shaping world order, waiting for their turn to grab the headlines. The nature of terrorism was changing. State sponsorship of terrorism was declining as groups with other financial backing and without the control of a sponsor started to make waves. The State Department was noticing a rapid increase in attacks by Islamic extremist groups, describing "terrorism in Islamic guise" as a small minority but a threat to the Arab-Israeli peace process and to recognized governments in the Middle East.[59] In the new era, formerly communist countries were soon to encounter their share of terrorist destruction.

The growth of international terrorism as a topic in U.S. foreign policy coincided with the collapse of communism and the Soviet Union. President George H. W. Bush encountered a new world order which left the U.S. as the world's only superpower. His administration relied on international cooperation when it defeated Iraq's attempt to claim Kuwait as a province of Iraq. As part of the Persian Gulf War, the Bush administration also brought American troops to Saudi Arabia, the holy land of Islam, where they stayed after the end of the war. This did not sit well with Islamic fundamentalists, including Osama bin Laden and his al Qaeda terrorist network, which had grown out of the veterans of the Saudi Arabia and CIA-backed mujahideen fighters who had resisted the Soviet occupation of Afghanistan. For them the United States would soon become the target of a new jihad.

Under President Clinton the U.S. experienced several major terrorist attacks, two of them on U.S. soil: the 1993 World Trade Center bombing by radical militant Muslims and the 1995 Oklahoma City bombing by American extremists. On February 26, 1993, a bomb exploded in an underground garage below the two World Trade Center towers. It killed six people and injured over a thousand. The FBI's New York Field Office led the local investigation, quickly arresting several Islamic extremist suspects who had links to the Farouq mosque in Brooklyn and Sheikh Omar Abdel Rahman. His message was that the U.S. was oppressing the Muslim world, and it was a "religious duty to fight against God's enemies."[60]

Another attack was in the works. An informer's tip in June 1993 soon led to arrests through which the FBI was able to preempt a plan to bomb New York City landmarks, including the United Nations building and the Holland and Lincoln tunnels.[61] The FBI was also quick to track down anti-government domestic extremists on April 19, 1995, when it went after the bombers of the Murrah Federal Building in Oklahoma City. The trail soon lead the bureau to Persian Gulf War veteran Timothy McVeigh, and later also to his accomplice, another Persian Gulf War veteran, Terry Nichols.

The 1993 bombing and the Iraqi plot that same year to kill former President George H. W. Bush on his visit to Kuwait, the latter resulting in a retaliatory U.S. military response, brought the Clinton administration to declare: "Global issues are a central focus of the Clinton administration, and international terrorism is one of the deadliest and most persistent.... It is clear that terrorism is an issue that will remain with us for quite some time."[62]

The 1993 World Trade Center attack's planner, Ramzi Yousef, a nephew of the suspected planner of the 9/11 attacks, Khalid Sheikh Mohammed, was captured in Pakistan, and handed over to the U.S. in 1995.[63] The effectiveness of the FBI and the Justice Department left the United States with a false sense of security against international terrorism. The investigation into the World Trade Center bombing and the averted landmark bombings traced the terrorists to a training camp on the Afghanistan-Pakistan border. However, the investigators did not examine this new anti–U.S. threat further in its complexity.

Further attacks against the U.S. took place later that decade outside U.S. borders. In 1998 the U.S. embassies in Tanzania and Kenya were targeted in simultaneous attacks. The U.S. responded with missile attacks against a pharmaceutical plant in Sudan which was suspected of producing VX nerve gas, and against training camps in Afghanistan. However, the U.S. attempts to capture the suspect behind the attacks, Osama bin Laden, failed, as did the later attempts to kill him. Two years later, in October 2000, the bombing of the USS *Cole* killed 17 and wounded 39 in Yemen. This attack was also traced back to the Taliban-controlled camps in Afghanistan. To al Qaeda's astonishment, there was no U.S. retaliation.[64]

Under President Clinton the U.S. defined terrorism as a crime. The president expanded law enforcement and local police funding and gave these bodies more authority over counterterrorism.[65] Primarily the country's counterterrorism was in the hands of law enforcement until September 11, 2001.[66] But the president also emphasized that terrorism is a national security issue, which his Presidential Decision Directives Number 39 (1995) and Number 62 (1998) underlined in emphasizing the role of the National Security Council in coordinating counterterrorism efforts.[67]

Towards September 11, 2001

As was the case with his predecessors, international terrorism was not the number one topic on President George W. Bush's agenda. During its first few months in office, the new administration isolated and alienated itself from the international community and several international agreements by refusing to ratify, sign or support agreements. The list included, for example, "the ABM Treaty; the Comprehensive Nuclear Test Ban Treaty; the Kyoto Protocol on climate change; the International Criminal Court; the Biological Weapons Protocol mechanism."[68]

In the spring of 2001 three former lawmakers, former senators Gary Hart (Colorado) and Warren Rudman (New Hampshire), and former representative Lee Hamilton (Indiana), from the Commission on National Security in the 21st Century, reported to a Senate Judiciary subcommittee in a terrorism hearing that "a possible strike inside the United States is the nation's top security concern." The three recommended that one cabinet-level agency should be formed so the country would be better prepared and would be able to respond in case such an attack ever took place.[69] At that time there was not enough political will in the U.S. for the foundation of such an agency. Had one been founded, it is open to question whether it would have been able to prevent the September 11, 2001, terrorist attack.

According to *The 9/11 Commission Report*, the main planner of the 9/11 attacks was Khalid Sheikh Mohammed, an uncle of Ramzi Yousef, the plotter of the 1993 World Trade Center bombing. Khalid Sheikh Mohammed was a college-educated Afghan war veteran who had studied in North Carolina. In the mid–1990s he met with Osama bin Laden and proposed him a plan which eventually evolved into the 9/11 operation. Khalid Sheikh Mohammed was not originally an al Qaeda member but formally joined the organization in late 1998 or early 1999, after which he received approval for his plan from bin Laden. After that, Khalid Sheikh Mohammed moved to Afghanistan to work on the plan. He also became the leader of al Qaeda's media committee.

According to *The 9/11 Commission Report*, Khalid Sheikh Mohammed's original attack sketch was even larger than what eventually took place on September 11, 2001:

> KSM [Khalid Sheikh Mohammed] describes a grandiose original plan: a total of ten aircraft to be hijacked, nine of which would crash into targets on both coasts — they included those eventually hit on September 11 plus CIA and FBI headquarters, nuclear power plants, and the tallest buildings in California and the state of Washington. KSM himself was to land the tenth plane at a U.S. airport and, after killing all adult male passengers on board and alerting the media, deliver a speech excoriating U.S. support for Israel, the Philippines, and repressive governments in the Arab world. Beyond KSM's rationalizations about targeting the U.S. economy, this vision gives a better glimpse of his true ambitions. This is theater, a spectacle of destruction with KSM as the self-cast star — the superterrorist.[70]

Osama bin Laden wanted to scale down the original plan which, in his view, had too many bombings and targets. In April 1999 Khalid Sheikh Mohammed received al Qaeda's support to his proposal and he started to develop it further with bin Laden and others. The targets that surfaced in these discussions were the two targets that were hit on 9/11: the World Trade Center and the Pentagon. Also, the White House and U.S. Capitol were discussed. The goal was to coordinate the hijackings and crashing into the chosen targets to be simultaneous in order to maximize the combined attacks' psychological influence.[71]

Khalid Sheikh Mohammed and al Qaeda's final plan, which was estimated to have cost $400,000–$500,00, materialized on September 11, 2001. On that Tuesday reality imitated Hollywood action movies. Two hijacked commercial airliners, American Airlines flight 11 and United Airlines flight 175, hit the skyscraper twin towers of the World Trade Center in New York City on a busy morning. Only a moment later another hijacked commercial plane, American Airlines flight 77, crashed into the Pentagon, the military nerve center of the United States. The collapse of the twin towers and the crashing of a fourth hijacked airliner, United Airlines flight 93, in Pennsylvania, soon followed these events.[72] Newscasts first reported that five to six thousand people had died in the attacks.[73] Five months after the attack the official number of casualties was estimated to be about three thousand.

The biggest terrorist act ever against the United States and its interests targeted civilians and also hit symbols of American values: the World Trade Center for the capitalist economic structure, and the Pentagon for the military might. The day's events brought the country to a state of alert. Two days after the attack President George W. Bush announced that the fight against international terrorism is "the first war of the 21st century. It will be the focus of my administration."[74] The international community that the administration had snubbed came behind the U.S. after al Qaeda had turned four hijacked airplanes into weapons of mass destruction.

According to *The 9/11 Commission Report*, the Clinton administration's representatives and Clinton himself, and the incoming Bush administration's representatives and Bush himself, have somewhat different recollections of how the issue of terrorism was covered at the time of the transfer of power. The outgoing administration argued that it had specifically warned about the threat of bin Laden and al Qaeda, but the new administration did not remember that having surfaced as much as issues such as North Korea and the Middle East peace process.[75]

U.S. Counterterrorism

According to the U.S. State Department, there were over 10,000 incidents of international terrorism from 1980 until 2001, the analysis period of this book. Most attacks took place in the 1980s. The decade's peak year was 1987, with 666 attacks,[76] after which the number of attacks largely started to decline. The State Department credited the growing international cooperation among governments in the late 1980s and in the 1990s as one of the main reasons for the success in lowering attack numbers. The State Department also highlighted the United States' leading role in counterterrorism, the country's consistent counterterrorism policy, and a global understanding that terrorism is a threat to the whole world.[77]

In the 1980s terrorists primarily targeted nonofficial targets. Diplomatic targets, businesses, tourists and other civilians were by far the most used targets, and this was true also during the following decade. The weapon of choice throughout both decades was explosives, bombings being very clearly terrorists' most preferred method. Armed attacks, kidnappings, firebombings and arson were the other popular terrorist choices, although bombings often comprised over half of the annual attacks, at times close to two thirds of them. While skyjackings, that is, the hijacking of airplanes, receive extensive news media coverage, they have been rare.[78]

In the spring of 2001 former senators Gary Hart and Warren Rudman, and former representative Lee Hamilton from the Commission on National Security in the 21st Century, spoke at a Senate Judiciary subcommittee terrorist hearing. They pointed out that the American anti-terrorist units are "scattered across 50 agencies, with no chain of command if a terrorist act happens."[79] Over the years several government agencies have been part of American counterterrorism efforts. These include, for example, the Federal Bureau of Investigation (FBI), the Department of State, the Department of Defense, the Central Intelligence Agency (CIA), and the Federal Aviation Administration (FAA). For example, at the press briefing for the *Patterns of Global Terrorism 2000* report, Edmund J. Hull, acting coordinator for counterterrorism, pointed out that although the annual reports are issued by the U.S. Department of State, the counterterrorism successes the reports detail

> by no means are the exclusive responsibility of the State Department. We have very strong partners throughout the US Government, including in the White House, Justice, the FBI, CIA, DOD, Joint Chiefs of Staff, Department of Treasury, and really one of the great strengths of counterterrorism, as it is done by the US Government, is this interagency cooperation and teamwork. Without that, we would not have the kinds of successes that we can report to you today.[80]

The complex phenomenon of international terrorism and its growing threat, in particular in the post–Cold War world, have produced a complex U.S. counterterrorism structure. As *The 9/11 Commission Report* highlights, one of the major problems in American counterterrorism in the pre–9/11 era was that no part of the U.S. government was completely responsible for dealing with international terrorism because dealing with terrorism did not fall under any one part of the U.S. government. The country lacked clearly centralized counterterrorist measures, as well as a clear chain of command which would be fast to implement. Furthermore, several agencies' activities were overlapping and cooperation between different agencies was far from ideal.

An organization chart (see page 64) of the U.S. counterterrorism structure in a 1997 Institute for Defense Analyses report to the President's Commission on Critical Infrastructure Protection gives an excellent overview of the complex hierarchical U.S. counterterrorism framework before 9/11.

The State Department's 2001 report explains the structure and interagency approach in more detail:

> The US Government's international counterterrorism community has long been well integrated by the National Security Council (NSC)–chaired Counterterrorism and Security Group (CSG), an interagency body with representatives from all major US Government national security agencies — State, Defense, Justice, FBI, CIA, and the JCS — as well as key players from Treasury,

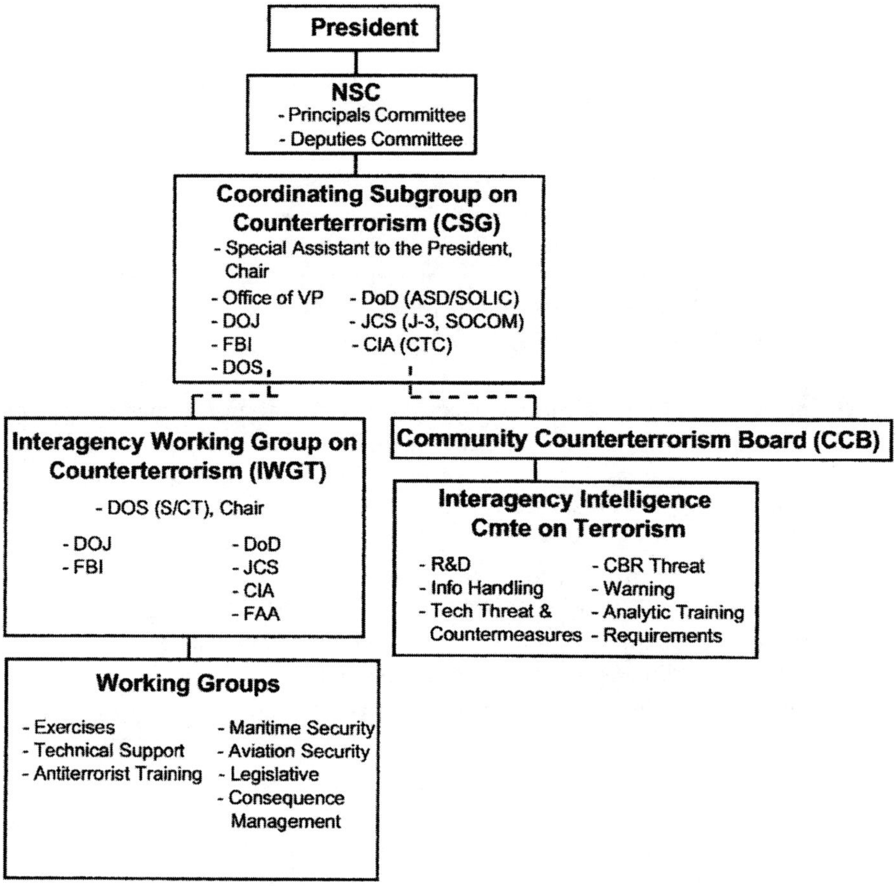

Source: **Figure 1. The Counterterrorism Framework, Institute for Defense Analyses (1997). Federal Structures for Infrastructure Protection. Report to the President's Commission on Critical Infrastructure Protection, p. 5. ASD/SOLIC: Assistant Secretary of Defense for Special Operations/Low Intensity Conflict. JCS (J-3, SOCOM): Joint Chiefs of Staff (Joint Task Force Operations, Special Operations Command). CTC: Counterterrorist Center. CBR: Chemical, Biological, Radiological.**

Transportation, Energy, INS, Customs, and other agencies and services. The CSG's membership meets on a near daily basis to accomplish the US Government's counterterrorism objectives:

- Ensure that each agency understands and can contribute to the overall counterterrorism campaign.
- Coordinate strategic and tactical policy and operational activities against terrorists and their supporters.
- Assess and counter terrorist threats to the citizens and interests of the United States and the international community.
- Respond effectively to attacks against US citizens and interests overseas and bring perpetrators of terrorism to justice.
- Maximize seamless integration of international and domestic counterterrorism efforts.[81]

During his two terms, President Clinton gave several Presidential Decision Directives (PDD) to clarify different agencies and programs' role in counterterrorism. For example, the May 1998 PDD-62 and PDD-63 strengthened the U.S. counterterrorism structure and the protection of the country's critical interconnected infrastructures. PDD-62 also established a new position in the administration, the National Coordinator for Security, Infrastructure Protection, and Counterterrorism.[82] President Clinton also emphasized the U.S. commitment to catch terrorists no matter where in the world they might be, as he did, for example, with the June 1995 PDD-39.

In the complex counterterrorism structure the State Department has a central role. As the Institute for Defense Analyses pointed out in 1997, the Interagency Working Group on Counterterrorism, chaired by the department,

> provides a standing structure for coordinating a wide range of counterterrorism activities. It is responsible for developing policy on terrorism; it addresses organizational issues, proposes legislation, and coordinates interagency exercises and training activities. Membership includes all departments and agencies with responsibilities related to counterterrorism.[83]

Since the 1970s the U.S. presidents have turned to the State Department, asking it to coordinate U.S. counterterrorism activities and policies. But as the chart above shows, the structure is far from simple. For example, one of the conclusions *The 9/11 Commission Report* reached was that the complex pre–9/11 counterterrorism structure had not worked in the country's best interests and defense.

When discussing and practicing counterterrorism, it is also central what definitions of terrorism are being used because these definitions determine whether an act of terrorism is considered to be a crime, in which case it falls under law enforcement, or whether an act of terrorism is defined as war, which falls under military means.[84] This book relies on the definitions that the U.S. State Department uses in the annual *Patterns of Global Terrorism* reports.[85] The department issued its first report on the year 1981 when it continued the CIA's reporting on international terrorism. The early CIA and the State Department reports provide the only publicly available continuous statistical database on international terrorism in the U.S.

Lead Federal Agency for Counterterrorism outside U.S. Territory: The U.S. Department of State

In addition to the complex interagency counterterrorism structure, U.S. presidents have also set up a lead federal agency system that clarifies which agency would usually be in charge when responding to a terrorist incident. Starting with President Reagan's 1982 National Security Decision Directive (NSDD) 30, in the pre–9/11 structure the State Department was the lead agency when responding to incidents outside U.S. territory. When responding to incidents on U.S. territory, the FBI, under the Justice Department, was the lead agency. Starting with the 1981 report on international terrorism, the State Department was also in charge of issuing an annual report on the phenomenon of international terrorism and the threat it poses to the U.S. security and American citizens.

Patterns of Global Terrorism Reports

The United States government has been collecting statistical information on international terrorism since 1968. It started the practice in the aftermath of the July 1968 hijacking of an Israeli El Al airliner by three members of the Palestinian Popular Front for the Liberation of Palestine (PFLP).[86] The State Department issued its first report in 1982 with *Patterns of International Terrorism: 1981,* largely following the format established by the CIA, and in particular the CIA's National Foreign Assessment Center, in their 1970s reports. Two years after its first report, which combined narrative and quantitative data, the State Department slightly changed the report title, replacing "international" with "global" when it issued *Patterns of Global Terrorism: 1983* in the aftermath of the 1983 Lebanon bombings. The department also updated its terrorism definitions, and continued to use the updated version as a basis for its statistical data in the future years.

The U.S. Secretary of State, as required by U.S. law, provides Congress every year with the latest information on terrorism, analyzing the countries and groups that are at the center of international terrorism as targets of or participants in terrorism. The reports cover the previous five years.

In the post–9/11 restructuring of American counterterrorism the State Department replaced *Patterns of Global Terrorism* with *Country Reports on Terrorism* in 2004. The updated documents include data collected by the National Counterterrorism Center (NCTC), established post–9/11; the State Department's main focus is on policy issues. Today the most recent reports can be found on the Internet, on the State Department's website.[87]

As academic terrorism researchers, also the State Department points out that there is no generally accepted universal definition of terrorism. Reports mention that the department uses a definition used by the U.S. government since 1968,[88] although in the aftermath of the 1983 Lebanon bombings the department adjusted its definitions. Its 1981 and 1982 definitions were more restrictive than the updated 1983 one. For example, the 1982 report provides the following definitions:

> **Terrorism:** The threat or use of violence for political purposes by individuals or groups, whether acting for, or in opposition to, established governmental authority, when such actions are intended to influence a target group wider than the immediate victim or victims.
>
> **International Terrorism:** Terrorism conducted with the support of a foreign government or organization and/or directed against foreign nationals, institutions, or governments. International terrorism has involved groups seeking to overthrow specific regimes, to rectify national or group grievances, or to undermine international order as an end in itself.[89]

And a year later, in the aftermath of the Lebanon bombings, the 1983 report stated:

> There are a wide variety of definitions used by experts to describe the phenomenon of terrorism, but no single one has gained universal acceptance. For purposes of recording and coding data on terrorist incidents, we have adhered to definitions that represent a middle ground within the broad range of expert opinion, both foreign and domestic.
>
> **Terrorism** is premeditated politically motivated violence perpetrated against noncombatant targets by subnational groups or clandestine state agents.
>
> **International terrorism** is terrorism involving citizens or territory of more than one country.[90]

Thus more flexibility was provided to define under the term *terrorism* also groups that were more independent in their activities and not necessarily linked to state sponsors. The updated definitions reflected the impact of the 1983 bombings of the U.S. embassy in Beirut and the U.S. and French Multinational Force headquarters, which together killed over three hundred people and injured over two hundred. In addition, the 1983 report had reporting and data changes to match the newer forms of international terrorism. The department continued to use the updated 1983 definition also in its future reports. The 1990 report added a definition for terrorist groups: "The term terrorist group means any group practicing, or that has significant subgroups that practice, international terrorism."[91]

The difficulty of defining terrorism has not been resolved by these official definitions. Different agencies define terrorism according to their own specialty area. The State Department has also addressed the difficulty of separating terrorism from other violent acts:

terrorist acts are part of a larger phenomenon of politically inspired violence, and at times the line between the two can become difficult to draw. To relate terrorist events to the larger context, and to give a feel for the conflicts that spawn violence, this report will discuss terrorist acts as well as other violent incidents that are not necessarily international terrorism.[92]

According to Pillar, the State Department definition has four main parts, each of them separating terrorism from other forms of activities:

> The first, premeditation, means there must be an intent and prior decision to commit an act that would qualify as terrorism under the other criteria.... Terrorism is not a matter of momentary rage or impulse. It is also not a matter of accident....
>
> The second element, political motivation, excludes criminal violence motivated by monetary gain or personal vengeance.... Terrorists' concerns are macroconcerns about changing a larger order, ...
>
> The third element, that the targets are noncombatants, means that terrorists attack people who cannot defend themselves with violence in return....
>
> The fourth element, that the perpetrators are either subnational groups or clandestine agents, is another difference between terrorism and normal military operations. An attack by a government's duly uniformed or otherwise identifiable armed forces is not terrorism; it is war.[93]

Furthermore, terrorism is not just about the acts that have taken place but also about the threat of terrorist attacks now or in the future. Terrorism is cyclical in nature, as the National Foreign Assessment Center at the CIA pointed out in its *International Terrorism in 1977* report. As governments have caught up with the latest forms and methods of terrorism to the point that counterterrorism has succeeded in reducing the number of terrorist attacks and threats, terrorists have adjusted their methods and have emerged with new ones, and with new leaders if their previous ones have been caught or otherwise eliminated. Counterterrorism has then been forced to find new effective methods.[94]

The constantly changing nature of terrorism and the difficulty of properly defining it are reflected in the acts that the annual reports have covered. They have included, for example, acts motivated by left-wing and right-wing ideologies, ethnic and religious motivations, political motivations for independence, anarchist motivations, transnational terrorism, domestic terrorism in different countries around the world, and by active insurgency. At times it has been hard for the State Department to decide once and for all if a certain form of violence is terrorism or not. For example, it has included in reports violence related to narcotics trafficking, at times even calling it narcoterrorism. But in its 1989 report the State Department clearly points out that it ignores narcoterrorist attacks due to their domestic origin, that is, they are not acts of international terrorism.[95] Furthermore, narcotraffickers perform their acts for a profit, not due to political motivations. Edmund J. Hull, acting coordinator for counterterrorism, noted the difference between terrorism and narcotics activity at the briefing for *Patterns of Global Terrorism 2000* in April 2001: "Any time we have a number of groups under consideration for designation as Foreign Terrorist Organizations, it is a very rigorous process; the requirements are laid out by US law. Those requirements do not include narcotics activity per se, but are rather focused on terrorist activity."[96]

It is not only the acts that are difficult to define but also the people behind the acts. For example, the 1987 report made a point of trying to avoid stereotyping any group in any part of the world as a terrorist group. The 1987 report was also the first to detail on its pages the legislative requirement according to which the State Department must give a report to Congress on terrorism every year:

> This report is submitted in compliance with Section 140 of the Foreign Relations Authorization Act, Fiscal Years 1988-1989 [P. L. 100-204], which requires the Department of State to provide

Congress a full and complete annual report on terrorism for those countries and groups meeting the criteria of Section (a) (1) and (2) of the Act.[97]

As required by legislation, the report includes detailed assessments of foreign countries where significant terrorist acts occurred, and countries about which Congress was notified during the preceding five years pursuant to Section 6(j) of the Export Administration Act of 1979 (the so-called "terrorism list" countries that have repeatedly provided support for international terrorism). In addition, the report includes all relevant information about the previous year's activities of terrorist groups, or umbrella groups under which such terrorist groups fall, known to be responsible for the kidnaping or death of any American citizen during the preceding five years, and groups known to be financed by "terrorism list" countries, plus any other international terrorist groups that the Secretary of State determines should be included in this report.

No one definition of terrorism has gained universal acceptance. For the purposes of this report, however, we have chosen the definition commonly used by the US Government for the past 20 years, which also is widely accepted and one which we have used in previous reports.

Accordingly, "terrorism" is premeditated, politically motivated violence perpetrated against noncombatant[98] targets by subnational groups or clandestine state agents, usually intended to influence an audience. "International terrorism" is terrorism involving the citizens or territory of more than one country.

Adverse mention in this report of individual members of any political, social, ethnic, religious, or national group is not meant to imply that all members of that group are terrorists. Indeed, terrorists represent a small minority of dedicated, often fanatical, individuals in most such groups. It is that small group — and their actions — that is the subject of this report.

L. Paul Bremer III

Ambassador-at-Large for Counter-Terrorism[99]

The annual publications began, as the National Foreign Assessment Center called them, as "research papers," only a few pages long. Gradually the reports grew to some sixty or seventy pages, publications which covered the world's hot spots in terms of international terrorism as well as domestic political violence. The 2001 report, which covers the September 11, 2001, terrorist attacks, runs for almost two hundred pages.

Each report gives a short review of a certain year's most important statistics, including the number of international attacks, the number of attacks against American interests, and the number of international and American casualties. Each report also includes a review of the previous year's most important statistical data, for example, the number of overall and anti–U.S. attacks and American victims. The documents give regional overviews, with a focus on the countries which encountered terrorism or domestic violence in the analysis year. They also give updates on the current status of the influence of the previous year's violence. In addition, the documents list, for example, the main types of attacks, the names of the state sponsors of terrorism, as well as the nationality of the known terrorists or terrorist organizations and information on their activities, strength, external aid and areas of operation. The amount of the published statistical information has steadily grown over the years.[100] For example, in the 1990s the reports added more detailed information on the status of international cooperation in fighting terrorism, part of it classified, and information on the extradition of terrorist subjects from abroad to the U.S. In addition, appendices, insets and tables give more detailed statistical information, as well as information on the most recent developments in international terrorism. For example, several insets on the emergence of Osama bin Laden's group were published in the late 1990s.

Since there is no universally accepted or value-free definition of terrorism, there is no consistent and reliable way to produce terrorism statistics. The 1979 report, issued by the National Foreign Assessment Center at the CIA, for example, addresses this very issue. It mentions, for example, that judgmental distinctions, which are not as reliable as enumerative, may at times distort the collected data. Furthermore, attacks that seem to be terrorist attacks on the surface but are actually acts committed by criminals or psychopaths, can contaminate the statistical information. The 1979 report continues to explain that after a testing of different variables,

> Several variables were deleted because of lack of data (for example, purpose of attack, age of terrorists), their unreliable judgmental nature (for example, degree of discrimination in selection of victim), or lack of discriminable (that is, minimal variance) data. The benefits of including some variables did not justify their data collection costs; these variables were also dropped. New variables have been added based on suggestions made by academic and governmental users of the pilot data set (for example, several variables on the legal issues involved in the adjudication of the terrorist incident)....
>
> Intercoder reliability has been substantially improved, because of the nonjudgmental nature of most of the variables, greater care in making coding distinctions explicit in the codebook, and increased supervision by the project director of the coders' work.[101]

The National Foreign Assessment Center explains the method of its data collection and analysis in its 1979 report, but that information is largely missing in the State Department's *Patterns of Global Terrorism* reports.

The State Department has continued the style of its predecessors' reports when it comes to the textual descriptions of different incidents and yearly developments. This is also the case with the representation of quantitative data. The State Department has added statistical information on new categories over the years, and has also at times updated and replaced previous years' data as the department has changed its coding methods. Some of the State Department and CIA reports mention that they have collected data from host governments and international news media, but generally the reports do not address in detail how each year's data have been collected and coded. Both the State Department and the CIA have pointed out in their reports that the data on the U.S. and other Western countries are more complete and overemphasized in comparison to the countries that do not have a visible role in world politics, for example, countries in Asia and Africa. Also, during the Cold War years the Soviet bloc and its area of influence were underreported.[102]

The U.S. State Department database on international terrorism is the most consistent and available database on international terrorism in the world, but as Falkenrath points out, the statistical information on terrorism is influenced by U.S. policy preferences and therefore is not universally useable.[103] The State Department's annual compilation of statistical information on terrorism provides an *official U.S. interpretation* of international terrorism and decides whose fight in the international arena is an act of terrorism and whose an act for freedom, democracy and the free world. For other countries and policy interests the terms and definitions the State Department uses can mean something quite opposite. Even among the different U.S. agencies there can be differences in collecting data, understanding terrorism and how to respond to terrorism. For example, in the summer of 2009 U.S. news media reported that the FBI had not accepted the harsh interrogation methods the CIA had been practicing. The Bush administration did not consider methods such as waterboarding, which simulates drowning, forced sleep-deprivation of ten days or more, repeated slamming of suspects' heads into walls, slapping of suspects in the face and abdomen, and forcing and keeping suspects in boxes for hours or in the dark with insects as torture. However, when some of the harsh methods were revealed in 2009, public discussion intensified about whether the U.S. had been practicing torture under President Bush.

Policy interests change over time, which also affects data. For example, Iraq has been on and off the list of the states which sponsor terrorism. The country's absence from the list of the state sponsors of terrorism coincided with most of the time period when Iraq was waging a war against Iran, a well-known adversary of the United States since 1979. The Iraq-Iran War lasted from 1980 until 1988, and Iraq was absent from the list of state sponsors of terrorism from 1982 until it was again added to the list in 1990. During the war the Reagan administration supported Iraq extensively on the basis "the enemy of my enemy is my friend."[104]

U.S. Counterterrorism Policy

The 1987 report details U.S. counterterrorism policy which has stayed steady over the years:

> The US Government has developed a comprehensive strategy to respond to the problem of international terrorism. The first element of our counterterrorism strategy is firmness toward terrorists. Making concessions of any nature, whether paying ransom, releasing convicted terrorists from prison, or changing our policies to accommodate terrorist demands, only encourages more terrorism. And we vigorously encourage other countries to be firm with terrorists, for a solid international front is essential to overall success.
>
> The second element of our strategy is to make state sponsors of terrorism pay a price for their actions. This policy was most graphically demonstrated by the April 1986 bombing raids on terrorist support facilities in Libya. But there is also a range of peaceful measures that can be crafted to discourage states from persisting in their support of terrorism, These include political, diplomatic, and economic measures, public diplomacy, and sanctions.
>
> Third, the US Government has developed a program of action, based on practical measures. These are designated to bring terrorists to justice, to disrupt their operations, and to destroy their networks. They include aggressive measures, working with our friends and allies, to identify, track, apprehend, prosecute, and publish terrorists. They also include measures designed to protect our citizens abroad by strengthening security, and research to develop equipment to prevent terrorist incidents.
>
> The final element of our counterterrorism policy is the Department of State's Anti-Terrorism Training Assistance Program (ATA), which gives training in antiterrorism techniques to law enforcement officials around the world. Given our country's strong commitment to human rights, ATA promotes a thorough understanding of the importance of human rights in all aspects of law enforcement."[105]

Or, simply put, as the 1999 report does:

> Our policy has four main elements:
>
> - **First**, make no concessions to terrorists and strike no deals.
> - **Second**, bring terrorists to justice for their crimes.
> - **Third**, isolate and apply pressure on states that sponsor terrorism to force them to change their behavior.
> - **Fourth**, bolster the counterterrorist capabilities of those countries that work with the United States and require assistance.[106]

The U.S. uses five traditional ways to counter terrorism: sanctions, international diplomacy, law enforcement, intelligence collection and sharing (including covert operations), and military force.[107] Sanctions against the states that the U.S. considers to be supporters of international terrorism have been the most commonly used U.S. method in the fight against terrorism.

Antiterrorism Training Assistance Program

The U.S. established in 1983 a new program to assist its international antiterrorism efforts, the Antiterrorism Training Assistance Program (ATA), which is housed at the Department of State. The program's main objectives are:

- Enhancing the antiterrorism skills of friendly countries by providing training and equipment to deter and counter the threats of terrorism;
- Strengthening the bilateral ties of the United States with friendly, foreign governments by offering concrete assistance in areas of mutual concern;
- Increasing respect for human rights by sharing with civilian authorities modern, humane and effective antiterrorism techniques.[108]

The program plans its courses according to the latest manifestations of international terrorism, and provides assistance in antiterrorism and advisement in different areas of law enforcement security services. The recipients of this cooperation are "selected friendly foreign governments. Courses cover such areas as airport security, bomb detection, hostage rescue, and crisis management. A recent component of the training targets the financial underpinnings of terrorists and criminal money launderers."[109] In particular the training focuses on "Crisis Prevention, Crisis Management, Crisis Resolution and Investigation."[110] By 2001, 152 countries with 35,000 students had participated in the training provided by the ATA.

In the area of international cooperation, in 1996 Congress also added a requirement that the State Department will annually inform Congress of other countries' level of cooperation with the U.S.

State Sponsors of Terrorism

Some of the most important pieces of information that the State Department provides in its annual documents are the list of the states that are considered to be supporters of international terrorism and the lists of the foreign terrorist organizations that are considered to be security threats to the U.S. and its citizens.

The State Department designates certain countries as state sponsors of terrorism: "After extensive research and intelligence analysis ... in order to enlist a series of sanctions against them for providing support for international terrorism."[111] The goal is to isolate the states listed as state sponsors of terrorism "from the international community, which condemns and rejects the use of terror as a legitimate political tool."[112] At first the department referred to the list as its "terrorism list":

> The "terrorism list" is a list of countries formally designated by the Secretary of State under the US Export Administration Act of 1979 as having repeatedly provided support for acts of international terrorism. Congress must be informed before goods over a certain value are exported to these countries. Iraq is included in the section of the 1987 Patterns of Global Terrorism Report dealing with state support of terrorism because it appeared on the "terrorism list" within the previous five years. Iraq will not be included in future reports unless circumstances warrant inclusion.[113]

The first list was issued in 1979. Ten years later the Anti-Terrorism and Arms Export Control Act of 1989 set guidelines on how a country could be taken off the list. In the post–Contra hearings era Congress was reacting to the Reagan administration's State Department, which had removed Iraq from the list in 1982. Without any input from Congress, the administration had favored Iraq in the war that Iraq had started against a clear U.S. enemy: Iran. The new act "laid out specific criteria and advance notification procedures that had to be followed before a country could be taken off the terrorism list."[114]

According to the State Department, state-sponsored terrorism activities include

> direct involvement, instigation and encouragement, support to terrorist groups through provision of safehaven, financial resources, arms, technical expertise, and documentation.... Some states, although not direct sponsors of terrorist organizations, contribute to the groups' capabilities by giving them unimpeded transit, permitting them to engage in commercial enterprises, allowing groups to recruit members, and carry out other support activities.[115]

In addition:

> Sometimes the state is directly involved, using its own agents or working jointly with international terrorist groups on operations. In other cases, states may provide close support to particular terrorist groups but may not be directly involved in specific operations. A third type of support is more general: logistic, financial, weapons, and training support, as well as allowing terrorists to maintain offices and training camps, permitting safehaven and transit through the state's territory for operations.[116]

The U.S. has seen state sponsorship to be a problem particularly in the Middle East. In the department's view, state sponsorship is what has enabled Middle Eastern groups to conduct attacks outside their own region. For example, throughout the 1980s state support by Syria, Libya and Iran not only helped terrorist groups to export their attacks especially to Western Europe, but their actions also promoted the three countries' foreign policy interests.

The list of state sponsors of terrorism has remained quite unchanged over time. For example, seven countries, Cuba, Iran, Iraq, Libya, North Korea, Sudan[117] and Syria, were on the list uninterrupted from 1993 till 2001, the end year of this analysis. In the 1980s the list included Libya, Iran, Syria and for a while also South Yemen, as well as Cuba, and later also North Korea. According to the State Department, Iran has been by far the most active state sponsor of terrorism. It supports, for example, such terrorist organizations as Hezbollah, HAMAS, and the Palestinian Islamic Jihad (PIJ).[118] In the 1980s it was closely followed by Libya, which was linked to several anti–Western attacks. By the end of the 1980s the State Department held Libya responsible for sponsoring at least 30 international terrorist groups. In addition to Palestinian groups such as Abu Nidal and the Palestinian Islamic Jihad, Libya had also supported the Provisional Irish Republican Army, which had received money, training, and other support from Libya. In 1989 Libya's leader Muammar Qadhafi most likely restricted the activities of Libya's clients in having non–Israeli targets.[119]

Officially the United States has a zero tolerance policy on terrorism. This policy also extends to old acts of terrorism — that is, time will not wash any terrorist's slate clean.[120] In particular, state sponsors of terrorism have experienced this policy. According to the State Department, the removal of states from the state sponsorship list is one of the main U.S. interests in counterterrorism. The State Department advises state sponsors to take certain steps in order to remove themselves from the list.[121]

Foreign Terrorist Organizations

The U.S. faces threats also from groups that engage in terrorism. Some of the groups have a state sponsor which largely controls them. In the 1990s the nature of anti–U.S. terrorist threats started to change. New groups that were independent in their funding and actions were emerging. The State Department provided in its 1987 report for the first time a separate list of terrorist organizations. Titled "Worldwide Overview of Organizations That Engage in Terrorism,"[122] the list provided an overview of the main groups discussed in the report. Future reports followed this model, providing background information on dozens of groups, briefly describing each group, its activities, estimated strength, location and areas of operation, and information on external aid. New legislation, the Antiterrorism and Effective Death Penalty Act of 1996,[123] provided further analysis, now separating the category of terrorist groups to *designated* foreign terrorist organizations and other terrorist groups, the following year's report being the first to use the separation in its listings. Secretary of State Madeleine Albright issued the first list, of 30 designated organizations, in October 1997. The State Department's 1997 report separated the designated foreign terrorist organizations from other major active terrorist groups by an asterisk in its Appendix B, Background Information on Terrorist Groups. The 1999 report was the first to use separate listings for "Designated Foreign Terrorist Organizations (FTOs)" and "Other Terrorist Groups." The State Department describes FTOs as groups "that are foreign, engage in terrorist activity, and threaten the security of US citizens or the national security of the United States."[124] Over the years the organizations that have been highlighted for their anti–American stance and as threats to the U.S. have largely come from the Middle East. These include, for example, the Abu Nidal organization, HAMAS (Islamic Resistance Movement), Hezbollah (Party of God), the Popular Front for the Liberation of Palestine, and other Palestinian groups. Groups from other parts of the world have also made the list, for example, organizations from Latin America and national extremists in European countries. The U.S. secretary of state added al Qaeda on the list in 1999.

The U.S. secretary of state consults with the U.S. attorney general and the secretary of the treasury when designating groups on the foreign terrorist organizations list.[125] The 1996 Antiterrorism and Effective Death Penalty Act also provided additional counterterrorism methods. These included, for example, a ban on any FTO's fundraising activities in the U.S., and required their funds to be blocked by American financial institutions, and to be reported to the Department of the Treasury. The law also updated the methods that help to prevent terrorists from entering the U.S., for example, on a visa, and also the methods of how to deport terrorists.[126] Furthermore, any American who knowingly gives any material support to a terrorist organization commits a crime.[127]

Acting Coordinator for Counterterrorism Edmund J. Hull explained the separation between designated FTOs and other terrorist groups at the briefing for *Patterns of Global Terrorism 2000*. In his words: "We designate Foreign Terrorist Organizations according to a law. It is a very, very rigorous process. It requires a legal basis, because they can be challenged in court."[128] The annual reports lack explanations of these methods. The list of other terrorist groups refers to groups that the U.S. is concerned about, that is, whose activities have brought them to the attention of the U.S. but whose appearance on the list is not based on a legal process.[129]

Rewards for Justice Program

Another central antiterrorism weapon is the Rewards for Justice program, which compensates recipients with monetary rewards if the information they provide prevents terrorist attacks or finds terrorists. The 1984 Act to Combat International Terrorism, Public Law 98-533, included rewards for the conviction of terrorists. The U.S. Department of State's Bureau of Diplomatic Security is in charge of the program.[130]

In 1989 Congress set the highest payable reward to $2 million, an amount that civil aviation organizations matched the following year. That brought the combined reward to $4 million.[131] The reward was raised to $5 million after the 1998 terrorist attacks on the U.S. embassies in Kenya and Tanzania.[132] According to the State Department, the rationale of the rewards program is that

> Civilized people everywhere are outraged by terrorist crimes. The scars are long lasting, and there is no recompense for victims. But terrorists are a small minority, whose crimes, deadly as they are, cannot be allowed to intimidate the forces of peace and democracy. The message to terrorists from Americans and other free people and nations is that we are strong, vigilant, and determined to defeat terrorism.[133]

In the first twenty years of its operation, the Rewards for Terrorism Information Program, aka the Rewards for Justice Program, "paid out over $57 million for information leading to the capture of terrorists or individuals associated with terrorist-friendly regimes."[134] The program has a website which gives more information about reward offers and about terrorists wanted by the U.S.[135] Anyone with access to the Internet can submit a tip to U.S. authorities through the website, which can be read in over twenty languages.

A month and half after 9/11 the USA PATRIOT Act of 2001 became law. It authorized the U.S. secretary of state to reach deeper into the government's pockets and raise the reward if the secretary considered such an act necessary for defending the U.S. For information that would lead to the capture of Osama bin Laden and other central al Qaeda members, Secretary of State Colin Powell raised the reward up to $25 million.[136]

Lead Federal Agency for Counterterrorism on U.S. Territory: The Federal Bureau of Investigation

The Justice Department led the response to terrorism inside the U.S. borders until the Department of Homeland Security was established and took over in 2003. The leading law enforcement organization under the Justice Department at the federal level is the Federal Bureau of Investigation (FBI).[137] National Security Decision Directive Numbers 30 (1982) and 207 (1986) had already named the Justice Department as the lead federal agency when responding to terrorists incidents on U.S. soil, and in particular the FBI as the operational agency. Later pre–9/11 presidential decisions upheld the approach.

The FBI, founded in 1908 as a force of special agents, has a long history of intelligence gathering, reaching back to the 1930s. Before the establishment of the Central Intelligence Agency (CIA) in 1947, the FBI had foreign intelligence duties until the end of World War II. The agency continued to conduct intelligence work in the domestic arena, but also in cooperation with the CIA and Army Intelligence until the 1970s, when it was revealed that some of the FBI's domestic surveillance targets and methods were less than legal.[138]

The FBI defines terrorism as a criminal act that breaks the laws, values and norms of the legitimate power. However, the FBI points out that there is no specific federal law that addresses terrorism per se as a crime. Rather, the handling and prosecution of terrorism follows existing criminal statutes.[139]

Like the State Department, the FBI states that there is no single definition of terrorism, listing the definition it uses according to the *Code of Federal Regulations*: terrorism is "the unlawful use of force and violence against persons or property to intimidate or coerce a government, the civilian population, or any segment thereof, in furtherance of political or social objectives." (28 C.F.R. Section 0.85)."[140] The FBI makes a distinction between domestic and international terrorism, "depending on the origin, base, and objectives of the terrorist organizations."[141]

In detail the FBI defines domestic and international terrorism for reporting purposes in its *Terrorism in the United States* documents as follows:

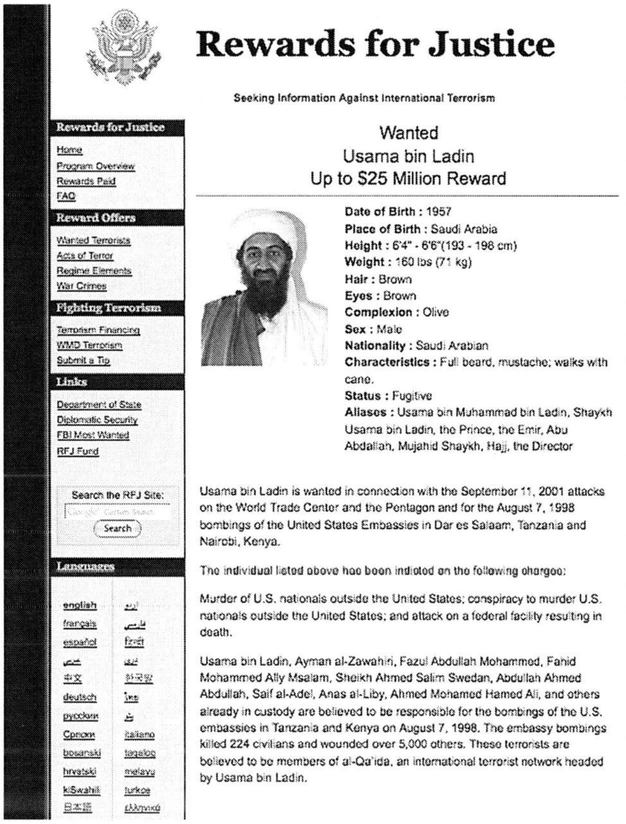

The Rewards for Justice program gives informants monetary awards if the information they provide leads to the capture of terrorists or the prevention of terrorist acts. After 9/11, Secretary of State Colin Powell raised the reward on Osama bin Laden to $25 million. Anyone with access to the Internet can give tips on terrorists and terrorist threats directly to the U.S. government at: http://www.rewardsforjustice.net.

- Domestic terrorism is the unlawful use, or threatened use, of force or violence by a group or individual based and operating entirely within the United States or Puerto Rico without foreign direction committed against persons or property to intimidate or coerce a government, the civilian population, or any segment thereof in furtherance of political or social objectives.
- International terrorism involves violent acts or acts dangerous to human life that are a violation of the criminal laws of the United States or any state, or that would be a criminal violation if committed within the jurisdiction of the United States or any state. These acts appear to be intended to intimidate or coerce a civilian population, influence the policy of a government by intimidation or coercion, or affect the conduct of a government by assassination or kidnapping. International terrorist acts occur outside the United States, *or* transcend national boundaries in terms of the means by which they are accomplished, the persons they appear intended to coerce or intimidate, or the locale in which their perpetrators operate or seek asylum.[142]

The FBI divides international terrorism further into three categories: "the radical international jihad movement, formalized terrorist organizations, and the state sponsors of international terrorism."[143] The bureau also addresses activity that is terrorist-related (italics are original):

- A terrorist *incident* is a violent act or an act dangerous to human life, in violation of the criminal laws of the United States, or of any state, to intimidate or coerce a government, the civilian population, or any segment thereof.
- A *suspected terrorist incident* is a potential act of terrorism to which responsibility cannot be attributed at the time to a known or suspected terrorist group or individual.
- A terrorism *prevention* is a documented instance in which a violent act by a known or suspected terrorist group or individual with the means and a proven propensity for violence is successfully interdicted through investigative activity.[144]

Like the U.S. Department of State, the FBI clarifies that terrorism does not stereotype any certain ethnic, religious or other groups:

> *The FBI investigates terrorism-related matters without regard to race, religion, national origin, or gender. Reference to individual members of any political, ethnic, or religious group in this report is not meant to imply that all members of that group are terrorists. Terrorists represent a small criminal minority in any larger social context.*[145]

The FBI has had a central role in investigating domestic terrorism. In 1980 the U.S. responded to domestic terrorism by creating a Joint Terrorism Task Force (JTTF) in New York City, the FBI's New York City Field Office running the force. The effort to counter domestic terrorist organizations also included the goal of allowing information sharing between federal, state and local law enforcement. The same office became central in international terrorism investigations when in 1993 the World Trade Center attack investigations relied on the use of the task force. In the 1990s several field offices received their own JTTF. By 9/11 there were 34 of them. While not all were functioning properly,[146] the existence of JTTFs allowed federal, state and local law enforcement agencies to exchange information and cooperate.[147] In the post–9/11 era the number of JTTFs grew rapidly, from 35 to 101 across the country by 2009. In addition, a "National JTTF, located just outside Washington, D.C., includes representatives from over 40 agencies, including components of the Department of Homeland Security, Central Intelligence Agency, Department of Defense, and the Department of Energy."[148]

In 2009 the FBI had 56 field offices around the country and Puerto Rico, each headed by a Special Agent in Charge except for the large offices of Los Angeles, New York and Washington, D.C., which are headed by an Assistant Director in Charge. The field offices cover metropolitan areas, and about 400 resident agencies do the rest of the country.[149]

Before the 9/11 attacks the Special Agent in Charge largely determined what her or his local office was investigating and how to assign the personnel for the investigations. Counterterrorism was not high on the field offices' agenda, in particular when resolved crimes rather than counterterrorism intelligence brought career opportunities and field office success. Furthermore, when a certain office started to investigate a crime, the crime and anything related to it more or less became the property of that office, leaving other offices less than interested in investing their efforts in the same crime.[150]

The FBI's success and effective role in the investigation of the 1993 World Trade Center bombing, the summer 1993 revelation of radical Muslim militants' plot to bomb New York City landmarks, and the successful investigation of the 1995 Oklahoma City bombing made the legal approach to analyzing terrorism and terrorist events the norm when dealing with terrorism aimed at mass destruction on U.S. soil. However, the threat of international terrorism was not quite yet understood in the U.S. in the aftermath of the first World Trade Center bombing and the arrest of the participants of the planned New York City landmark bombings. Ramzi Yousef, the first WTC bombing planner, intended to kill a quarter million people. That threat was overshadowed by the public ridicule of one of the terrorists who was caught because he had been demanding back his $400 rental truck deposit. The deposit was for the truck the group had used in the bombing and which the man had reported stolen.[151]

In 1978 Congress passed the Foreign Intelligence Surveillance Act, which regulated the FBI's intelligence activity when investigating foreign threats inside and outside the U.S. borders, and made it difficult to share information between agencies devoted to intelligence gathering and those devoted to criminal prosecution. Information gathered by the CIA and the National Security Agency was lost in the confusion over what information could be shared to the point that accurate threat scenarios could not be put together.[152] In the 1980s Congress expanded the FBI's authority to investigate terrorist attacks that take place abroad and attack American citizens or certain American interests. Acts such as the Comprehensive Crime Control Act of 1984, the Omnibus Diplomatic Security and Antiterrorism Acts of 1986, the Antiterrorism and Effective Death Penalty Act of 1996, and Presidential Decision Directive 39 authorized the bureau to investigate foreign threats to U.S. interests. U.S. legal protection now applied to American citizens abroad. Outside the U.S. borders the FBI worked with the U.S. Department of State and the host governments, coordinating its actions with the local U.S. embassies and the host nations, as required. In 1989 Congress authorized the bureau to make arrests outside the U.S. without the approval of the country in which the arrests would take place.

The expansion of the FBI's authority abroad helped the creation of international offices known as legal attachés. In 2009 the FBI had 62 such offices to help its counterterrorism investigations and international organized crime.[153] In the bureau's own words:

> Today, we have Legal Attaché offices — commonly known as Legats — and smaller sub-offices in 75 key cities around the globe, providing coverage for more than 200 countries, territories, and islands. Each office is established through mutual agreement with the host country and is situated in the U.S. embassy or consulate in that nation.
>
> Our Legal Attaché program is managed by the Office of International Operations at FBI Headquarters in Washington, D.C. This office keeps in close contact with other federal agencies, Interpol, foreign police and security officers in Washington, and national and international law enforcement associations. International liaison and information sharing are conducted in accordance with Executive Orders, laws, treaties, Attorney General Guidelines, FBI policies, and interagency agreements.[154]

There have been attempts to arrange cooperation in counterterrorism between the FBI and the CIA. For example, the terrorist attacks at Rome and Athens airports in Europe in the 1980s were followed by the emergence of the Counterterrorist Center, located at the CIA, but a center at which the CIA, the FBI and also other agencies would cooperate in their counterterrorism efforts. Officially the purpose was

> to unify activities across the Directorate of Operations and the Directorate of Intelligence.... The Center stimulated and coordinated collection of information by CIA stations, compiled the results, and passed selected reports to appropriate stations, the Directorate of Intelligence analysts, other parts of the intelligence community, or to policymakers.[155]

Primarily the center's role was to support operations, not analyze terrorist threats.

Under director Louis Freeh (1993–June 2001), the FBI created a separate Counterterrorism Division in 1999, intended to complement the Counterterrorist Center. The FBI's Counterterrorism Division investigates domestic and international threats on U.S. soil, and supports investigations outside U.S. borders.[156]

While there were attempts at the FBI to emphasize counterterrorism work in the pre-9/11 era, more traditional areas, such as drug enforcement and violent crime, dominated the FBI agenda throughout different levels of the bureau. As *The 9/11 Commission Report* discusses, this was largely due to a lack of funding, resistance within the bureau to focus on a new threat area, the bureau's inefficient system of hiring analysts from within rather than analysts who might actually have been the most qualified for the job, poor intelligence training, a lack of translators, and a lack of a centralized intelligence database containing information collected by different offices. Due to the problems, the FBI never properly estimated before the 9/11 attacks what kind of threat international terrorism posed on U.S. soil.

Other Law Enforcement Agencies Before 9/11

According to *The 9/11 Commission Report,* other law enforcement agencies under the Justice Department which were also involved in counterterrorism before 9/11 were a U.S. Marshals Service, Drug Enforcement Administration (DEA), the Immigration and Naturalization Service (INS), and the department's Consular Affairs Bureau.

Also the Treasury Department and its different branches, among them the Secret Service, the Customs Service, and the Bureau of Alcohol, Tobacco, Firearms, had at times been involved in counterterrorism while it was not their primary role. The different branches cooperated with the FBI or the INS in investigations or if a threat emerged.[157] But as *The 9/11 Commission Report* emphasizes, most of the U.S. law enforcement community was focusing on other issues than terrorism before September 11, 2001. Only one section of the FBI was investigating international terrorism.

The Department of Defense

The Department of Defense's role in counterterrorism is to support the lead federal agencies. It also has a variety of special units ready at all times in case a military action is ordered.[158] The department's role is limited. For example, in domestic situations it may support civilian law enforcement agencies only if it has been requested for support, and still the authority of the operation stays under the law enforcement agencies. However, if the president considers a national emergency to require the deployment of active duty military, for example, to protect the nation and its government when targeted by terrorists, then the president may authorize such military action.[159]

Like the State Department and the FBI, the Defense Department defines terrorism according to its own area of specialty. The United States Army and Air Force *Field Manual 100-20: Military Operations in Low-Intensity Conflict* defined terrorism in 1990 as "[T]he unlawful use of— or threatened use of— force or violence against individuals or property to coerce or intimidate governments or societies, often to achieve political, religious, or ideological objectives."[160]

The 1994 *Department of Defense INSTRUCTION* emphasizes that terrorism is preplanned and aims at fear:

> 3.6. Terrorism. The calculated use of violence or threat of violence to inculcate fear; intended to coerce or to intimidate governments or society in the pursuit of goals that are generally political, religious, or ideological.[161]

The department defines not only terrorism but also antiterrorism, counterterrorism, combatting terrorism, and terrorism targets:

> 3.1. Antiterrorism (AT). Defensive measures used to reduce the vulnerability of individuals and property to terrorist acts, to include limited response and containment by local military forces.
> 3.2. Counterterrorism (CT). Offensive measures taken to prevent, deter, and respond to terrorism.
> 3.3. Combatting Terrorism. Actions, including AT and CT, taken to oppose terrorism throughout the entire threat spectrum.
> 3.4. High-Risk Position. Authorized personnel position (identified and recommended by appropriate authority) that because of grade, assignment, travel itinerary, or symbolic value may make personnel filling it an especially attractive or accessible terrorist target.
> 3.5. High-Risk Personnel. U.S. personnel and their family members whose grade, assignment, travel itinerary, or symbolic value may make them an especially attractive or accessible terrorist target.[162]

When the United States faced modern international terrorism as a worldwide media spectacle for the first time with the Iranian Hostage Crisis, counterterrorism coordination slipped away from the State Department, which by then had been dealing with short-term terrorist events, for example, hostage-takings. Widely publicized international hostage-takings had also drawn the attention of the Department of Defense, a federal agency with civilian and military aspects, and in particular the attention of the Pentagon.[163]

Israel and West Germany, for example, had special forces trained to deal with hostage situations, but the U.S. had not seen a need for such forces. After successful hostage rescue operations in 1976 by an Israeli commando team and in 1977 by a West German special force concerns about the absence of such a U.S. force were raised to the point that the army now created a new force, the first permanent American counterterrorism unit. It was called the Delta Force, the U.S. 1st Special Forces Operational Detachment.[164] The British 22 Special Air Service (SAS) Regiment, which has often been considered to be the world's number one counterterrorism unit, was central in the development of the Delta Force.[165]

The new unit was first tested during the Iran hostage crisis in April 1980, and was a disastrous failure: no hostages were saved. Rescue efforts were abandoned at the early stages of the operation due to mild sandstorms, accidents, and the death of five airmen and three marines. The failure became known as "Desert One," after a site outside Tehran where marine pilots in navy helicopters were to meet Delta Force commandos on air force planes.[166] According to Stoffa, as a result of the disastrous rescue effort, the U.S. created several new counterterrorism establishments:

> This new force has a four-tiered chain of command. At the highest level is the president. At the second level are the Joint Chiefs of Staff. At the third level is the Unified Combatant Command for Special Operations Forces. The final level is the Joint Special Operations Command (JSOC). JSOC counterterrorism assets include Delta Force, SEAL Team Six, and USAF 1st Special Operations Wing.
>
> Each of these units is a highly specialized counterterrorism unit. Missions are designated based on the particular skills of each unit. For example, SEAL Team Six's specialties include countering terrorist attacks on oil rigs and ships.[167]

The hostage rescue teams are not only in charge of the hostage rescue. They are also responsible for preventing extensive media coverage of terrorists. In the 1980s it was actually rare for the hostages of terrorist incidents to die. The main goal of terrorists was publicity and through that the creation or maintenance of support to their cause, or a seat at a negotiation table. If they did take hostages, the odds were 96 percent that hostages would walk out alive.[168] Hostages were taken "for three reasons: attention for their cause, the release of imprisoned comrades, or ransom (profit)."[169]

The Department of Defense has several elite forces from the army, navy, and air force countering terrorism.[170] The Department of Defense put the joint U.S. Special Operations Command (USSOCOM), created in 1987, in charge of counterterrorism.[171] Medd and Goldstein explain:

> Within this structure, forces from the Joint Special Operations Command (JSOC) are typically called on by the National Command Authority (NCA) for special counterterrorist operations. The JSOC was activated at Ft. Bragg in 1981 after the failed Tehran hostage rescue effort. JSOC's mission includes command and control, doctrine, training, and employment of DoD's principal counterterrorist forces. Until 1994, the counterterrorist forces in JSOC included the Army's Delta Force, the Navy's SEAL Team 6, and specialized aviation units of the Air Force's Twenty-third Air Force and the Army's Task Force 160. In 1994 SEAL team 6 was disbanded.... Other forces available within USSOCOM include the Green Berets; the Rangers, experts in psychological warfare

> and civil affairs; Navy SEAL special boat and swimmer delivery units; and Air Force secret infiltration and air-cover units.[172]

The elite forces have been used rarely, at least to public knowledge. Stoffa also brings up the problem of the U.S. breaking international law if it sends a U.S. special forces unit into a foreign country without a direct request from the country's law enforcement officials. He further points out that both civilians and the military are very cautious and distrustful of special forces and their use in counterterrorism.[173]

The Department of Defense's concerns about domestic terrorist attacks, in particular concerns about the use of weapons of mass destruction on U.S. soil, led at the end of the 1990s to the creation of the Joint Forces Command, which "is responsible for military response to domestic emergencies, both natural and man-made."[174] Furthermore, in 1997 the department had started to train respondents for emergencies in the 120 largest U.S. cities. In addition, it created National Guard WMD Civil Support System Teams to be ready to respond to a WMD terrorist attack and to help civilian agencies as commanded by state governors.[175]

While the FBI and the CIA are well-recognized agency names, their operating costs claim only a small portion of American intelligence costs. According to *The 9/11 Commission Report*, the intelligence agencies under the Department of Defense actually claim about 80 percent of the country's total intelligence costs. One of the agencies is the National Security Agency (NSA), an organization "with a national customer base ... which intercepts and analyzes foreign communications and breaks codes."[176] The NSA needs a warrant for collecting information on U.S. citizens or on those in the U.S. It forwards to the FBI information about suspicious activity so the latter can acquire the required warrant.[177]

Other agencies in the Defense Department include the National Geospatial-Intelligence Agency (NGA) and the National Reconnaissance Office. In addition, the "Defense Intelligence Agency supports the secretary of defense, Joint Chiefs of Staff, and military field commanders."[178] More intelligence services can be found in the army, navy, air force, and Marine Corps.

Other Agencies

Outside of the U.S. law enforcement community, other forces involved in counterterrorism can be found in the Federal Aviation Administration (FAA) and the intelligence community. The FAA, housed at the Department of Transportation, was in charge of protecting commercial air transportation against terrorist and criminal acts and threats through intelligence. Its area of responsibility also included passenger prescreening, checkpoint screening, and onboard security.[179] The inefficiency in the sharing of terrorist information was blatant in the case of the FAA and the terrorist watchlist, or in FAA terms, the "no-fly" list. By 9/11 only twelve names of suspected terrorists were on the list, yet the government watchlists had already collected thousands of names of known and suspected terrorists. Furthermore, several tests had suggested that checkpoint screenings performed poorly.

The most recent hijacking of a U.S. commercial airliner before 9/11 took place in 1986. Guidelines for dealing with hijacking, which expected terrorists to have demands in return for ending the hijacking, told "flight crews that the best way to deal with hijackers was to accommodate their demands, get the plane to land safely, and then let law enforcement or the military handle the situation."[180]

Other intelligence components

> include the national security parts of the FBI; the Bureau of Intelligence and Research in the State Department; the intelligence component of the Treasury Department; the Energy Depart-

ment's Office of Intelligence and Counterintelligence, the former of which, through leveraging the expertise of the national laboratory system, has special competence in nuclear weapons; the Office of Intelligence of the Coast Guard, and today, the Directorate of Intelligence Analysis and Infrastructure Protection in the Department of Homeland Security.[181]

The Central Intelligence Agency

An organization whose name raises images of secrecy is the Central Intelligence Agency (CIA). It has at times tested the tolerance of the American public and U.S. law when some of its questionable methods in protecting U.S. security and political interests have become known to the public.

The CIA saw daylight in 1947 after President Truman dissolved the Office of Strategic Services. The new agency, under the Director of Central Intelligence, was in charge of external threats against the U.S. while the FBI had authority inside the U.S. borders. The agency was a Cold War creation, primarily seeing the threat in the Soviet Union and communism, and their expansion around the world.

The CIA's National Foreign Assessment Center defined terrorism in *Patterns of International Terrorism: 1980*:

Terrorism The threat or use of violence for political purposes by individuals or groups, whether acting for, or in opposition to, established governmental authority, when such actions are intended to shock or intimidate a target group wider than the immediate victims.

International terrorism Terrorism conducted with the support of a foreign government or organization and/or directed against foreign nationals, institutions, or governments. Terrorism has involved groups seeking to overthrow specific regimes (for example, Yugoslavia and El Salvador), to rectify national or group grievances (for example, the Palestinians), or to undermine international order as an end in itself (for example, the Japanese Red Army).

These definitions elaborate and clarify the definition of international terrorism used in our previous studies of the phenomenon, but they do not change in any way the criteria used for selecting incidents included in the data base for these studies.[182]

On its website, the Central Intelligence Agency has definitions that directly cite the State Department definitions in the *Patterns of Global Terrorism* documents:

"The Intelligence Community is guided by the definition of terrorism contained in Title 22 of the US Code, Section 2656f(d):

* The term "terrorism" means premeditated, politically motivated violence perpetrated against noncombatant targets by subnational groups or clandestine agents.
* The term "international terrorism" means terrorism involving the territory or the citizens of more than one country.
* The term "terrorist group" means any group that practices, or has significant subgroups that practice, international terrorism."[183]

Comparing the FBI and the CIA in their counterterrorism activities shows that the CIA's guidelines on analyzing foreign terrorist threats are looser because the agency is not investigating U.S. citizens.[184] Also, the two organizations have not always agreed on their counterterrorism methods, as happened, for example, in the post–9/11 era in the case of interrogation methods of suspected terrorists.

The 9/11 Commission Report describes the CIA: "As an independent agency, it collects, analyzes, and disseminates intelligence from all sources. The CIA's number one customer is the President of the United States, who also has the authority to direct it to conduct covert operations."[185] The public understanding of the CIA is largely based on its covert operations, which at times have been controversial but which form only a very small part of its whole budget.

The CIA has engaged in some activities that the U.S. and international public have questioned. These include, for example, the failed Bay of Pigs invasion of Cuba. Later, in the 1980s, some senior officers of the CIA's Clandestine Service were indicted because of their involvement in the agency's questionable covert actions in Central America.[186] In addition to the revelations in the media, and after congressional hearings about the CIA having been involved in planning the assassination of Fidel Castro of Cuba and also some other foreign leaders, the public learned that the agency had been busy also on the home front. The CIA was revealed and further alleged to have illegally spied on American citizens, including some members of the U.S. Congress.[187] The world of espionage and its questionable methods that had the spotlight during the Watergate investigations left the American public and politicians cautious about the agency.

After Watergate, Congress tethered the CIA so the agency's actions would not sidestep U.S. law. The agency was hesitant about this aggressive approach: it had committees overseeing it, covert operations required presidential approval, and the agency had to file a report from the president to Congress on covert operations. Furthermore, post–Cold War budget cuts left the CIA struggling in international coverage and dependent on information from its contacts in foreign countries. Budget cuts combined with demands to invest in the new communication technologies and communication satellites in the post–Cold War era left the CIA and other intelligence agencies to cope by cutting their staff numbers.[188]

New methods of communication and the changing mass media also added to the CIA's troubles. The emergence of the 24/7 news cycle and widening use of the Internet provided decision makers quickly with the latest news events, which undermined the CIA's traditional role of being a producer of in-depth analyses. The information the agency was providing in the new age of communication was scattered and failed to predict events the U.S. saw as important to its safety, such as nuclear weapons testing by India and Pakistan.[189] Political leaders were looking for the latest information from sources that had a wide international network and could produce information in real time. For example, both the Clinton and George H. W. Bush administrations had CNN on in the White House. President George H. W. Bush went as far as to say, "I learn more from CNN than I do from the CIA."[190]

In the post–Cold War era the analysis and investigation of the threat of fundamentalist Islamic terrorism that originated in the Middle East was further complicated in the CIA by the lack of Arabic speakers, and the near impossibility of foreign-born applicants to get clearance and a job at the CIA. The agency was not alone in not knowing Arabic before 9/11; in 2002 there were only six U.S. universities that offered undergraduate degree programs in the Arabic language.[191]

According to *The 9/11 Commission Report*, in the 1990s CIA leaders were cautious about undertaking controversial covert actions, including actions against al Qaeda, even when policy makers were demanding that the agency be more aggressive. The report said that CIA leaders wanted to guarantee that any action taken would have a legal standing and be approved by the president. That approach was a result of the agency's previously revealed and alleged illegal activities.

No Clear Leadership Agency in Practice

One of the biggest problems that American counterterrorism faced in the pre–9/11 era was the fact that the different departments and agencies involved in counterterrorism were not sharing information with each other. Furthermore, there was no clear leader that would have organized all counterterrorist activities into an effective joint action. Neither was there political will in the U.S. to create such an agency before 9/11. For example, former senators Gary Hart and Warren Rudman, and former representative Lee Hamilton from the U.S. Commission on National Security, came under fire in January 2001 when they proposed the creation of a new agency, the National Homeland Security Agency. In their report *Road Map for National Security: Imperative for Change*, they argued that such an agency was needed to counter terrorism. Neither the news media nor politicians were thrilled:

> Americans really don't understand terrorism because it is such a cowardly act, and lawmakers will find it hard to generate enthusiasm in Congress for such a radical reorganization, said Sen. Dianne Feinstein, D–Calif. Plus, a proposed Homeland Security Agency name has a "Third Reich" sound to it, she said.[192]

The former lawmakers warned about attacks in which Americans would die on American soil in large numbers. Hart in particular warned of the use of weapons of mass destruction in high-rise buildings.[193] He defended the committee's idea of the creation of a new agency: "Such an agency will be created because it has to be created, and what it's called will be up to Congress."[194] After the September 11, 2001, terrorist attacks the country was finally ready for the creation of a new agency. In October 2001, as an attempt to rectify the absence of a clear leadership in the country's counterterrorism, and as a response to the September 11, 2001, events, the Bush administration created a new federal office, the Office of Homeland Security. The new agency was to lead the national fight against international terrorism. In the department's words, it was established "to provide the unifying core for the vast national network of organizations and institutions involved in efforts to secure our nation." Its mission is to "lead the unified national effort to secure America. We will prevent and deter terrorist attacks and protect against and respond to threats and hazards to the nation."[195] This was an office which President Bush himself had originally opposed after the 9/11 attacks.

Three years later President Bush established the National Counterterrorism Center (NCTC) on the recommendation of the 9/11 Commission. It superseded the Terrorist Threat Integration Center (TTIC), established in 2003, and had a larger role in combined counterterrorism efforts. The center is part of the Office of the Director of National Intelligence. The center's purpose is to

> serve as the primary organization in the United States Government (USG) for integrating and analyzing all intelligence pertaining to terrorism and counterterrorism (CT) and to conduct strategic operational planning by integrating all instruments of national power.... The NCTC is a multi-agency organization dedicated to eliminating the terrorist threat to US interests at home and abroad.[196]

Under NCTC different counterterrorism agencies work side by side. The center's role is strategic operational planning. It does not perform counterterrorism operations, as those are done by the currently existing agencies.[197]

U.S. counterterrorism efforts influence not only the U.S. but also the country's relationship and standing with other countries, as Pillar discusses:

> First, the possibility of terrorist attacks inhibits, or at least complicates, a wide range of U.S. activities overseas and the maintenance of an official U.S. presence abroad....

Both the Hollywood terrorist and real-life terrorists have found high-rise buildings attractive targets. In January 2001 former senators Gary Hart and Warren Rudman and former representative Lee Hamilton from the U.S. Commission on National Security warned about attacks in which Americans would die on American soil in large numbers. Hart in particular warned of the use of weapons of mass destruction in high-rise buildings.

> A second cost of terrorism in terms of foreign policy is the undermining of peace processes, including ones in which the Unites States has invested heavily and which, absent the disruption of fresh terrorist attacks, might otherwise be ripe for progress....
> Third, terrorism risks enflaming other regional conflicts that are already closer to war than to peace....
> Fourth, the concern of an otherwise friendly government that it will become a target of terrorism may dissuade it from cooperating with the United States....
> And fifth, terrorism can destabilize friendly governments.[198]

Foreign policy is naturally influenced also by political, economic, diplomatic, cultural and other factors, but terrorism, both counterterrorism and being a target of terrorism, is an important part of U.S. foreign policy.[199] The role of terrorism in the U.S. foreign policy agenda became particularly clear after 9/11 when the U.S. required other countries to define their relationship with the U.S. according to their stand on international terrorism and on the September 11, 2001, attacks against the United States. In President George W. Bush's words on September 20, 2001: "Every nation in every region now has a decision to make. Either you are with us, or you are with the terrorists.[200]

The United States reacted to the emergence of modern international terrorism by starting to gather statistical information and researching terrorism trends. When the United States was not the main target of terrorist media spectacles, counterterrorism developed slowly, but the Iran hostage crisis changed that. International terrorists had found American citizens to be attractive subjects to the world's media.

In the 1980s the U.S. truly became a target of destructive terrorist attacks. In that decade President Reagan took steps to confirm and further develop the U.S. counterterrorism structure. As his predecessors had done in the previous decade and his successors would also do, Reagan announced the U.S. State Department as the lead agency in federal responses to terrorist incidents abroad. Inside U.S. borders the FBI had the lead agency role under the Department of Justice. The Department of Defense's role was to support federal efforts but also to have special units ready to be deployed. The usual structure could be changed at the orders of the assistant to the president for National Security Affairs. The presidents following Reagan reconfirmed the lead agency roles of the State Department and the FBI. President Clinton emphasized the CIA's role as an agency that fights terrorism by aggressive intelligence.

As the U.S. became a familiar target of terrorist news media spectacles, Hollywood started to take notice of modern international terrorism. In the late 1960s and in the 1970s the mainstream film industry mostly depicted communists as villains on the big screen. After the Iran hostage crisis and the Reagan administration's focus on terrorism, also Hollywood found terrorist villains. Communist terrorist threats and Middle Eastern terrorists entertained viewers in films in the 1980s before terrorism became a true blockbuster film product in the 1990s with the arrival of fictional Euroterrorists and Islamic militant extremists.

On 9/11 fictional creations met reality when real-life terrorists brought home the horrendous effects of a real terrorist attack. There was no single heroic American male in the style of Sylvester Stallone, Arnold Schwarzenegger, Bruce Willis, Harrison Ford or Denzel Washington to find and punish the terrorists in two hours. However, Hollywood had screenwriters who had received handsome paychecks for creating fictional terrorist attacks against the U.S. They were experts in planning media spectacle attacks against the United States. The White House and U.S. Army intelligence turned for help to Hollywood. In the post–9/11 world, the U.S. Army beat the White House in its reach for the minds that had created spectacular fictional terrorist attacks against the U.S. on its own soil for millions of viewers around the world to consume. In October 2001, intelligence specialists of the U.S. Army met with Hollywood screenwriters and directors to discuss what possible targets terrorists might have on U.S. soil and what methods terrorists might use.[201]

In November 2001, White House political adviser Karl Rove met with Hollywood studio heads and with representatives from the networks and creative guilds to discuss how political and fictional worlds could combine forces to support the U.S. war on terror. The film industry agreed to produce public service announcements and to organize shows for the United Service Organizations (USO), a group dedicated to improving the welfare and helping boost the morale of U.S. troops.[202] The participants announced that film content or propaganda had not been on the agenda, but Rove had introduced several themes that the White House favored and which Rove asked the filmmakers to remember.[203] It would not have been the first time that Hollywood got involved in foreign policy or security topics. For example, some Hollywood filmmakers have in the past relied on the help of the U.S. Department of Defense. The use of expensive military weaponry and American soldiers in films at a reduced cost has come at a price when movie content must be approved in advance by representatives of the U.S. armed forces, in particular to meet the requirement of portraying U.S. forces in a positive light.[204]

Hollywood has been portraying terrorism in films for decades, but in the immediate post–9/11 era Hollywood steered away from terrorist themes, fearing the topic to be too sensitive for American viewers. However, in the weeks following the attacks, American viewers disagreed with Hollywood when they rented in record numbers films on terrorism, including *The Siege* and films of the *Die Hard* series.[205] The intense two-hour rides had comforting endings when American heroes eventually captured and killed the foreign terrorist villains who were threatening the U.S. But post–9/11 life did not fully imitate these fictional terrorist captures and killings. For example, Osama bin Laden, whose organization soon emerged as the suspect behind the 9/11 attacks, eluded the U.S. attempts to capture or kill him.

It is no wonder Hollywood taps into the U.S. foreign policy agenda and news headlines of terrorist threats when searching for new film ideas. When the movie industry portrays threat scenarios with which the public is already familiar from news headlines, each news story on new and old terrorist attacks and threats works as free advertising for films on terrorism. While Hollywood's fictional creations do not always agree with news media and government portrayals of enemy threats, history has taught the commercial film industry that presenting critical views of America's foreign policy can be a very risky business.

While the profit-conscious business side of the film industry determines which films get produced, films are still also cultural products. They reach vast audiences and therefore have power to represent and reproduce social norms and values. Similar to news, Hollywood films are not only commodities but also important ideological and cultural products.[206]

The next chapter analyzes the main steps of the commercial Hollywood film production, and the emergence and effects of the globalized film market on commercial film production. It also examines where the film industry has found its threats and villains over the years, with a focus on Hollywood portrayals of the main ideological, racial and ethnic enemies of the past decades. The chapter concludes with an analysis of the action-adventure film genre and its roots. Violent action is an essential part of the traditional action-adventure film format, so the chapter lastly reviews Hollywood portrayals of violence.

Chapter 3

International Terrorism and the Hollywood Film Industry

Flipping through TV channels on September 11, 2001, brought to the screen eyewitness after eyewitness describing the World Trade Center attacks as being directly from movies. The comparisons are not surprising since the destruction of human life and property has been familiar in commercial action and action-adventure films for decades. Even the 9/11 hijackers' training included the watching of films on hijackings.[1] On September 11, 2001, al Qaeda terrorists made reality imitate Hollywood fiction when they produced the largest terrorist media spectacle ever seen on the small or big screen.

In the midst of extensive real-life human suffering, filmmakers shelved television programs and movies that had terrorist themes. In Hollywood producer John Davis's words: "Once it becomes reality and not fantasy, it ceases to be entertaining."[2] Warner Bros. was one of the first major studios which had to make a decision about the release of a new movie that the studio had already been advertising. Warner Bros. decided to delay the release of *Collateral Damage*, a film completed before 9/11 that starred Arnold Schwarzenegger as a heroic firefighter battling Colombian terrorists on U.S. soil. However, the movie studio may have miscalculated the American public's reaction, for U.S. viewers rushed to rent terrorism-themed films, such as *Die Hard* and *The Siege*, in the first weeks after the attacks.[3] Audiences found comfort in American movie heroes' successful efforts to fight international terrorists on U.S. soil, bringing back law and order and lethally removing foreign threats to American lives. But reality did not mirror Hollywood.

Hollywood films are today seen in over 150 countries.[4] Arabs as well as other foreigners and ethnic minorities are familiar villains from the action-adventure films which have been Hollywood's main domestic and foreign products since the 1980s. Violent action scenes and minimal dialogue easily translate into any culture, and spread around the world a fictional view of violent entertainment, including portrayals of international terrorism. These films, like other Hollywood films, traditionally reduce complex events to conflicts between two people, the hero and the villain.[5] Action-adventure films have usually found their heroes in white American men who serve the country's official power structure as officers, secret agents or in the military, and villains in men who are foreigners or American minorities.[6] Typical film antagonists have been Native Americans, black Africans, African Americans, Russians, Arabs, alien monsters and evil cosmic powers. As a character the villain is typically depicted as a devil, or subhuman, sadistic, anti–American, anti-freedom, anti-capitalist, and/or an adherent of a non–Judeo-Christian religion.[7]

The little research that there is on Hollywood portrayals of international terrorism has heavily concentrated on the image of Arabs, arguing that Hollywood has stereotyped Arabs as insane psychopathic terrorists. While it is true that Hollywood films often portray Arab terrorists as insane and bloodthirsty villains, the film industry does not reserve this type of portrayal only for Arab characters; rather, it is a general characterization for any terrorist villain. The portrayal of an insane terrorist is also familiar from traditional news coverage of terrorism. The villain, whether real or fictional, needs to be a character whose brutal death at the hands of an American hero is justified. However, certain factors do separate Arab terrorists from other international terrorists in Hollywood films, as will be discussed later in this book.

This chapter analyzes the path taken by international terrorism to become a Hollywood action-adventure film product. The following discusses the commercial Hollywood film industry, film production, and the globalization of the film market. All have a bearing on the emergence and development of the action-adventure film genre, which is the main generator of films on international terrorism. As part of the examination of the term *film genre*, and in particular the action-adventure film genre, the chapter also addresses the classical Hollywood cinema screenwriting structure which is the basis of most commercial Hollywood films. The chapter concludes with an analysis of where Hollywood films have found U.S. enemies in the past decades, and how screen violence, an essential ingredient of action-adventure films, has developed as an entertainment-business product.

International Terrorism as a Hollywood Film Theme

The commercial movie industry has traditionally borrowed story ideas from the U.S. foreign policy agenda. For example, during the Cold War years movie villains from the Soviet Union were familiar big-screen characters. Before international terrorist villains could make a name for themselves in Hollywood, they first had to make the U.S. foreign policy agenda in such a way that also the news media and the American public would take notice of them.

In the late 1960s and in the 1970s the majority of international terrorist attacks against U.S. interests took place outside U.S. borders in Latin America, in particular against American business interests. These low-scale attacks received little sensational news media coverage. In the 1970s most of the spectacular attention-grabbing attacks took place in the Middle East and Western Europe, including the 1972 Munich Olympic Games massacre of Israeli athletes by the Black September, a Palestinian group. A few years later *Black Sunday* (1977) introduced a Black September plot to attack the Super Bowl with the help of a disillusioned Vietnam veteran, a former prisoner of war. The film was not a box office success. International terrorism as a central Hollywood film theme barely surfaced in this decade. It was not until the continuous daily news media coverage of the Iran hostage crisis (1979–1981) had familiarized American viewers with international terrorism that Hollywood started slowly to warm up to international terrorism as a central theme in adventure and action-adventure films.

Traditionally, action and action-adventure films are about a conflict between an American hero and an alien villain. Acts of international terrorism are politically motivated acts of violence that cross international borders and therefore easily fit the Hollywood action and action-adventure film genre format of setting up an American hero against an evil foreign villain. In Hollywood films by major studios, the United States has refought several wars and battles of the past with heroic and fictional endings that often distort history.[8]

In the 1980s the commercial film industry created the ultra-high-budget action-adventure film genre in an attempt to reap greater profits for production and distribution companies. Large investments in films were expected to bring in a large return on each investment.[9] In pre–9/11 America, terrorism was a productive and profitable source of entertainment, in particular for the action-adventure film genre. Extensive news and film media coverage of terrorist attacks had created a general fear and awareness of terrorism. However, despite the 1993 World Trade Center and the 1995 Oklahoma City terrorist attacks, the likelihood of a large-scale terrorist attack against the U.S. on its own soil was statistically almost nonexistent in the pre–9/11 world.[10] A threat of a terrorist attack on U.S. soil was not generally conceived to exist in real life, which made fictional terrorist attacks inside the U.S. borders entertaining film products, since they were supposedly far from reality. Even today the statistical likelihood of a terrorist attack taking place on U.S. soil is still small, but 9/11 made the nation realize that even one successful attack can create enormous chaos and destruction in society and have long-lasting effects.

For Hollywood, statistical data was no barrier to introducing evil foreign villains who attack Americans on their own soil. Film producers have interpreted and fictionalized terrorism according to the laws of the commercial movie-making business. The use of bankable stars, special effects, commercial film production policies, and the traditional narrative form of the classical Hollywood cinema, which relies on a conflict between an individual hero and an individual villain, have all shaped Hollywood terrorism and the portrayal of the Hollywood terrorist and American counterterrorism. Large film production budgets, in particular since the 1990s, have added even more destruction and plot twists to films on terrorism.

Research on the relationship between the media and terrorism has heavily focused on the relationship between the *news* media and terrorism. As discussed in Chapter 1, the news media play crucial roles in modern international terrorism but they are not alone in creating a public understanding of the phenomenon. Commercial films that depict international terrorism have spread fictionalized Hollywood versions of the phenomenon worldwide. Popular Hollywood films follow traditional film formats in their portrayal of heroes and villains. The films set up an American hero, most often a white Anglo-Saxon male, against a foreign villain whose skin color is usually darker than the hero's. That applies especially to those films which portray the hero killing not only the foreign male villain but also masses of the latter's faceless accomplices in a variety of brutal ways.

As Gregg has pointed out, traditionally structured depictions influence, even manipulate, viewers' understanding of the world.[11] A Hollywood touch can distort different groups, religions, cultures and minorities. The commercial film industry has, for example, a long history of portraying Native Americans as savages, Latin Americans as greasers, Italians as mobsters, and Arabs as fanatic terrorists.[12]

Several researchers have argued that the traditional Hollywood image of heroic white American men and murderous foreign villains can produce the most insidious propaganda and support for American policy interests.[13] This cinematic propaganda may go unnoticed since film audiences rarely, if at all, analyze how films depict and develop different characters. Viewers rather focus on the film narrative, which propels the story, and on being entertained by the film they are watching. In particular, in the United States where citizens remain poorly informed of international affairs[14] movie images of international relations and state affairs may manipulate the understanding of real-life world events. A 2002 report by the Pew Research Center for the People and the Press found that the events of 9/11 had not really changed American news habits. According to the 2002 survey, 61 percent of Americans pay attention to international news only when something major takes place. The minority that does follow international news, 21 percent very closely and 37 percent consistently, represents a narrow part of the population: the affluent, college graduates and older people. The report details that a major reason Americans do not follow international news is their lack of background information. When surveying the recognition of specific international news items, the 2002 report listed that 48 percent of Americans recognized Yasser Arafat as the leader of the Palestinians and 41 percent knew that Israel was founded in 1948, but only 29 percent knew that Donald Rumsfeld was the U.S. secretary of defense at the time. The report concluded: "People who were born overseas know more about international affairs than those who were born in this country."[15]

Countries and people worldwide are influenced by Hollywood images. Hollywood films are the second-largest American export. In the early 1990s the foreign box office started to give signs of overpowering the domestic one, and finally it did. This continued through the 1990s[16] and beyond. For example, in 2008 international box office comprised two thirds of the worldwide box office figures, bringing in $18.3 billion while the domestic one made $9.8 billion.[17] Action films, and in particular the action-adventure film genre which emerged in the 1980s, reach the largest audiences both in the U.S. and worldwide.[18]

Film genres follow the traditional classical Hollywood cinema narrative structure which sets a protagonist against an antagonist but also responds to the prevailing political environment, as well as to changes in public opinion and audience interests. During specific political eras it is possible to find certain genres, themes and styles which dominate and which are repeated. When political changes are under way, themes start to change.[19] These trends can also be seen in the historical development of the most commercially successful films on international terrorism. Hollywood showed little interest in international terrorism in the 1970s when the topic was not high on the national agenda, but since the Iran hostage crisis of 1979–1981, international terrorists have periodically attacked American interests and American citizens on the big screen.

Hollywood images of heroes and villains are affected by the fact that each mainstream Hollywood film is an expensive business product. The goal of any film is to recuperate its production costs and to make a profit. That shapes what stories producers and studios choose for production, what the plotlines are, and how films portray different events and characters, including the film hero and villain. The following section traces the main steps of producing a Hollywood film, which will help to explain how Hollywood business structures and practices influence the industry's terrorism and counterterrorism film portrayals.

Hollywood

The word *Hollywood* is often used only to refer to the American movie business, but in practice "Hollywood" is a much larger concept. It refers to a set of corporations involved in the entertainment and media businesses that act as production and distribution companies.[20] In addition to the film industry, the corporations are involved in the television, cable, book and record industries, video games, theme parks, and a great variety of merchandising. As large transnational conglomerates, their activities extend from one media industry to another across national and international borders.[21] The best product for a conglomerate is a product that one of its companies has produced, for example, a movie, which can then be sold in the mass market to audiences as a variety of products from toys to clothes.[22] In other words, the best product allows synergy, the marketing and selling of a company product throughout the company's different branches, and therefore the maximization of the product's financial profit to the parent company. Furthermore, in the age of globalization a good film product must sell in any market in the world — it must be able to cross cultural and national barriers in its content and theme.

The traditional Hollywood products, motion pictures, are foremost commodities and have been recognized as such for a long time.[23] Films are like any other mechanically produced products that fit the same model. Similar to cars, the number of differences between models is declining; in Adorno and Horkheimer's words: "for films there are the number of stars, the extravagant use of technology, labor, and equipment, and the introduction of the latest psychological formulas."[24]

Commercial Hollywood Film Production, Distribution and Exhibition

The three main steps of creating a film are production, distribution, and exhibition — in other words, the process of making a product, distributing it for sale, and then selling it.[25] Hollywood distributes and exhibits its films domestically and globally. The domestic market consists of the U.S. and Canada, leaving the rest of the world as the foreign market.[26] Today Hollywood films are seen in over 150 countries.[27] In 2001 Miller, Govil, McMurria and Maxwell stated that "Hollywood owns between 40 percent and 90 percent of the movies shown in most parts of the world."[28]

Hollywood has a central role, not only in the American entertainment and culture industries, but in the whole U.S. economy. Hollywood entertainment, led by commercial films, is second only to military hardware as an export industry in the U.S.[29] And due to their reach across the globe, Hollywood films also form an important part of the global entertainment culture. The same films and film stars are seen and recognized by audiences around the world. The commercial Hollywood film industry's fictional portrayals of the world reach, entertain, enlighten, infuriate, and skew the worldview of hundreds of millions of viewers around the world from the Americas to Europe, Asia, Africa and Australia.

Film Production

While Hollywood is like any industry in the sense that it is in the business of making money, there is one major difference between Hollywood films and products of other industries. As Janet Wasko points out, "each film is a unique product — a different set of circumstances, deals, and players are involved for every film."[30] The film industry's trade organization, the Motion Picture Association of America (MPAA),[31] calls moviemaking "an inherently risky business."[32]

Film production includes several steps, from idea development to the moment a film is seen in movie theaters. The whole process usually takes from one to two years.[33] While each film is a unique product, each one goes through the same three main steps: production, distribution and exhibition. In other words, a film is produced, then sold and rented by distributors to exhibitors, and finally shown to audiences.[34]

Wasko discusses how big studios may receive financing from their parent companies, banks and other financial institutions. Financing may be in the form of loans, or through merchandising, product placement, co-productions, or limited partnerships. Financing is needed in the development stage in order to turn an idea or concept into a script, and later for turning the script into a film. Part of the development process is the hiring of a line producer who oversees the budget. It is divided into above-the-line and below-the-line costs: "Above-the-line costs include major creative costs or participants (writer, director, actors, and producer) as well as script and story development costs. Below-the-line items are technical expenses (equipment, film stock, printing, etc.) and technical labor."[35] If a film hires bankable stars or a bankable director, the above-the-line talent costs may well be half or more of the budget. The rising costs of film production have made it very hard to recoup production costs, especially when big stars and directors, in addition to their multimillion-dollar salaries, often also receive a certain percentage of the gross revenues.[36] Since the 1990s a film budget of $100 million or more has not been unusual.

When a film is approved for production, it enters pre-production. This includes doing the film's final casting, hiring its key production personnel, scouting and choosing the shooting locations, planning the film's final budget, opening an account for it, writing the shooting script, planning the shooting schedule, and renting the equipment needed in the shooting.[37] After these arrangements the film will enter the next step, principal photography. This is the actual shooting of the film, also known simply as production. On average, shooting a film takes from six to twelve weeks. During that time the film's post-production (editing) can be started, although it primarily takes place after the shooting has ended, lasting from four to eight months.[38] Editing also includes, for example, the production and addition of computerized visual special effects, sound effects, and the film's score, as well as the production and addition of the film's automated dialogue replacement (ADR), which in practice means the rerecording of the film's dialogue in a studio environment.[39]

Film Distribution

Usually the film's distributor or financier determines the film's final version. Carrying the financial responsibility, they are concerned about the film's profitability and make decisions based on what they think will sell the best.[40] This is why bankable actors and familiar, tried and true story formulas dominate the business. Wasko points out that film distributors are often "totally in control of a film, but even for other projects, they can influence script and title changes, casting decisions, final edits, marketing strategies, and financing of the film."[41]

The Hollywood Majors

Before audiences can watch a film, the film has to be distributed to theaters. The ultimate goal of any Hollywood film is to gain the largest possible paying audience. Distribution aims at maximizing the film's ability to earn a profit.[42] Distribution companies "form the core of economic power in the commercial film industry. Filmmakers need them to circulate their work; exhibitors need them to supply their screens."[43] In 2008 a familiar film oligopoly of six was dominating the business: Warner Bros., Disney/Buena Vista, 20th Century Fox, Paramount, Sony Pictures Entertainment/Columbia, and Universal Pictures, accompanied by one "minor major," MGM/UA. Each is a subsidiary of a large multinational conglomerate.[44] These distributors' film releases earn up to 95 percent of the ticket sales in the domestic market and over half in the foreign one.[45] When looking at the gross domestic box office at five-year intervals from 1980 till 2000, the majors' releases claimed from 77 percent up to 91 percent of the returns.[46]

Due to the nature of the business, ownership relationships among the distribution companies are in a state of constant change. Below is a review of the ownership structures as they were in early 2009:

Production/distribution company[47]	*Parent company*
Warner Bros.	Time Warner (until 2003 AOL Time Warner)
Walt Disney Pictures/ Buena Vista International	The Walt Disney Company
Twentieth Century Fox	News Corporation Ltd.
Paramount	Viacom, Inc.(since 1994)
Sony Pictures Entertainment (Columbia)	Sony Corp. (Sony purchased Columbia from Coca-Cola in 1989, which had bought Columbia in 1982)
Universal Pictures	General Electric & Vivendi-Universal; in 2003 NBC (GE) and Vivendi Universal Entertainment signed a merger which included Universal Pictures.[48] Universal Pictures is run under NBC Universal which Vivendi Universal Entertainment and NBC created in 2004. At that point GE owned 80 percent, and Vivendi 20 percent of the new company.[49] A new merger in January 2011 gave Comcast 51 percent and GE 49 percent of NBCUniversal, LLS
MGM/UA[50] (both distributing separately under MGM and UA)	Metro-Goldwyn-Mayer, owned by an investor consortium which includes Sony[51]

A smaller force, which also can be counted among the decision makers in Hollywood, has been DreamWorks SKG, a company founded in 1994 by Steven Spielberg, Jeffrey Katzenberg and David Geffen.[52] Twelve years later Dreamworks SKG was sold to Viacom, the parent company of Paramount Pictures. In 2008 the company separated from Paramount with financial backing from Reliance Entertainment. In February 2009 it reached a distribution deal with the Walt Disney Company.[53]

Distribution, which contains the most economic power of the three steps of production, can help a film when it is done right but can also bring a film down if it is done improperly.[54] The distributor is in charge of deciding the release date after the company has licensed the film from its producer. The distributor does the film's market research and marketing, and handles the prints and financial matters with exhibitors.[55] The distribution companies offer films to exhibitors who make a bid on each release in the U.S. In the foreign market, exhibitors are not necessarily allowed to see in advance the films they are bidding for. In addition to this practice, called "blind booking," distributors may conduct in the foreign market a practice which today is illegal in the U.S. In "block booking" the distributor forces a foreign exhibitor also to rent unwanted films as part of the rental package in order for the latter to be able to rent the films it wants.[56]

Film Exhibition

Film exhibition is the part audiences know the most about, the part they experience when they buy a ticket to see a film, or when they rent or watch one on television, at school, or at some other location. Although Hollywood receives most of its revenue from home video, theatrical releases of big Hollywood productions are pertinent for the success of any film.[57] They bring attention to the film and raise interest in it: "Critics review the film, television programs publicize it, and people tell others about it. The theatrical run is the film's launching pad, determining how successful it will be in other markets. Theatrical hits may account for as much as 80 percent of a video store's rentals."[58]

While theatrical releases receive the most advertising and attention, the theaters themselves do not make much money on the films they have leased from distributors and are showing to audiences. Most of the revenue from theatrical releases, known as box office receipts, goes to the distributor. After the exhibitor's expenses are deducted from the box office receipts, the distribution company takes out its rental fee, which can be as much as 90 percent of the sum. Exhibitors rely on other sources to make a profit, the most important being concession sales that form 50 percent to 80 percent of their profits.[59]

In the conglomerate era Hollywood has maximized its way to create a profit, which in practice means that a film's life is far from over when it leaves theaters. The Hollywood film industry has for long been a closed oligopoly of a few major studios, which it uses to its advantage to prolong the life of each film. The major studios not only produce films but also release them, using their distribution companies. They release their films in a certain order to maximize their profits: "theaters, home video, pay-per-view, pay cable and finally, broadcast and basic cable television."[60] Each release forms a separate "window." Hollywood is very careful about squeezing every dollar out of a certain window before it allows the film to be released in the next one.[61] The combined revenue from all of the windows is called "gross receipts."[62]

Producing a film is a multimillion-dollar business. Domestic box office, home video, DVD, television and cable revenue is not enough to recoup the invested money unless the film is a major blockbuster. The Hollywood film industry has found its savior in the foreign market, which surpassed the domestic market as the main revenue producer in the 1990s.[63] The American film industry's global expansion follows the general trend of the U.S. businesses, as Guback points out: "the film industry stands as just another segment of American business that has stretched its operations around the globe, seeking more and more places to market its goods, to return its investments, or to supply it with human and natural resources."[64] The globalization of the film market has not left the Hollywood film industry untouched. A brief historical overview of the development of the foreign market helps to explain how Hollywood became a global film giant, the importance of the foreign market to the American commercial film industry, and some of the main effects the globalized film market has had on the industry.

Hollywood and the Foreign Market

The U.S. film industry has been dominating the global film market since the end of the First World War (1914–1918). To Hollywood's advantage, the U.S. mainland was never a battlefield in World War I or in World War II, in contrast to its competitors in Europe, which experienced both wars on their own soil. While the wars disrupted film production in Europe, Hollywood was able to carry on its film production uninterrupted in the U.S. World War I forced the U.S. film industry to become self-sufficient as a producer since the main European film exporters and producers, such as France, Italy, Denmark and Germany, were focused on the war.[65] After the war the U.S. film industry had a backlog of films that it was able to release in the foreign market while its European competitors were recovering from the war's destruction. (This happened after World War II as well.) Main European film producers from Italy, France, Denmark, Germany and Britain were not able to properly recover from the effects of the war.[66]

The large American domestic market allowed American films to recoup their expenses, which made it possible for the industry to rent U.S. films abroad at an inexpensive price when it was expanding outside North America.[67] The U.S. government helped films, as was the case also with other American goods, to expand their markets. The State Department, the Department of Commerce, and the Foreign Department of the Motion Picture Producers and Distributors of America (MPPDA) all tried to guarantee Hollywood films access into the foreign film market. They did that with such success that Hollywood films have dominated the global market since the First World War.[68] The foreign market thus became essential for Hollywood's ability to produce large spectacles that require high budgets.

U.S. government officials early on had mixed feelings about the stories the motion picture industry was portraying, but at the same time they saw American films as important tools in helping the U.S. to become a global economic hegemony. Films helped to market abroad the acceptance of American products and the American way of life.[69] The value of the films' propaganda was underlined by a Department of Commerce representative: "Only the movies which put America's best foot forward will be sent abroad."[70] Hollywood's insensitive and stereotypical images of foreign countries and cultures, and also of the U.S., were acknowledged aloud by Henry S. Villard, a senior official of the State Department's Office of the Economic Adviser, but at the same time Villard also acknowledged the films' effectiveness as creators of demand for American commodities.[71]

The American film industry had two obvious weapons which helped it to keep the dominance it had earned during World War I: the movie star and film distribution systems.[72] While glamorous film stars intrigued audiences and attracted them to movie theaters, the stars and their films were being marketed internationally by a distribution system that was imitating the system the industry had on its own home turf. The system enforced block booking. Only powerful distributors were able to avoid that if they paid a higher rental fee and used the preferential dates the studios announced.[73] With the international popularity and financial success of American films, American movie stars became international stars who attracted audiences around the globe, a phenomenon on which the industry still relies today. For decades action and adventure stars such as Bruce Willis, Harrison Ford, Arnold Schwarzenegger, Tom Cruise, Denzel Washington, Matt Damon, Will Smith, Vin Diesel and others have been able to sell a film in any market just by their name.

American distribution companies successfully worked to keep foreign distributors from the American film market. They were effective in their efforts to dominate the domestic and foreign film markets. For example, in the U.S. it was American distribution companies that distributed foreign films. Overseas, American companies were able to strengthen their position to the point that they were, for example, the ones releasing European films in the European countries' own market areas.[74]

In 1945 the American film trade association, the Motion Picture Producers and Distributors of America (MPPDA), which was founded in 1922, changed its name to the Motion Picture Association of America (MPAA). The association's Foreign Department changed its name to the Motion Picture Export Association of America (MPEA[A]), and changed it in 1994 to the Motion Picture Association (MPA).[75] While antitrust laws were preventing cartels inside the U.S. borders, the MPEA was a legal cartel for the American film industry's efforts abroad.[76]

The State Department distanced itself from the MPAA in the early post–World War II years.[77] MPEA fast bounced back from its breakup with the State Department and started to see its independent role in negotiations in the foreign market as an advantage. Jack Valenti, MPAA/MPEA president until 2004, was quite proud of the organization's special role: "To my knowledge, the motion picture is the only U.S. enterprise that negotiates on its own with foreign governments."[78] According to the MPAA website, "Since its early days, the MPAA, often referred to now as 'a little State Department,' has expanded to cover a wide range of foreign activities falling in the diplomatic, economic, and political arenas."[79]

Just like other media products, films were part of the U.S. efforts during the Cold War to undermine communism and represent the American system in a positive light to the world. MPAA/MPEA president Eric Johnston wrote in 1950: "Many times I have talked with President Truman about the influence of American films abroad, and he has said he regards American films as 'ambassadors of good will.'"[80]

Effects of the Globalized Film Market

With the growing market and business interests at domestic and global levels, film companies are no longer acting independently; they have become subsidiaries of large conglomerates. This development started in the 1950s, intensified in the 1960s,[81] and really made major changes in the 1980s as foreign companies entered the U.S. market with power purchases. As troubled financial times hit U.S. industries, foreign corporations invaded the American business market through mergers and acquisitions, and by foreign loans. The entertainment market was no exception. For example, from 1985 to 1990 ownership of several of the major studios in Hollywood changed into foreign hands. Rupert Murdoch's News Corporation Ltd. bought Fox, Sony acquired Columbia from Coca-Cola, and another Japanese company, Matsushita Electrical Industrial Company, acquired MCA/Universal (it was later acquired by Canada-based Seagram, which merged with Vivendi and Canal+ in 2000 to form the Paris-based Vivendi Universal). In addition, Pathé Communications, led by an Italian businessman and originally a French company, acquired MGM/UA.[82] As Wasko discusses, the ever-growing consolidation has been due to "Deregulation, privatization, technological developments, and the opening of new international markets."[83]

The incursions of foreign companies into the U.S. and Hollywood coincided with changes in world politics. As Balio describes, this also had an effect on film production:

> During the 1980s, the worldwide demand for films increased at an unprecedented rate, the result of such factors as economic growth in Western Europe, the Pacific Rim, and Latin America, the end of the Cold War, the commercialization of state broadcasting systems, and the development of new distribution technologies. To capitalize on these conditions, Hollywood entered the age of "globalization."[84]

For Hollywood, globalization translated into gaining a major status in the foreign market through vertical and horizontal operations. In other words, the movies studios' operations included horizontal integration. That refers to acquiring "additional units at the same level of production," for example, a media company acquiring ownership of other media forms. In vertical integration a firm acquires "units at different levels," for example, a media company extends its control over different levels of production.[85] The film industry formed alliances and created new partnerships in its efforts to create new sources of financing. These steps started a merger wave in the film industry that still has not seen its end. Furthermore, as a film's ability to earn a profit became even more emphasized than in the past, the industry's answer was to invest in high-budget films with the goal of reaching worldwide blockbuster success. This was done as an attempt to maximize profits at the domestic and foreign box office, as well as in the other release windows.[86]

The Blockbuster Film

The growing popularity of home video created a larger demand for films in the 1980s. While the majors still kept their film production at seventy to eighty films a year, mini-majors and independent production companies started to produce more films, calculating that the important home video market, purchases and rentals, would help them to recoup their production costs. Hollywood went from producing some 350 films in 1983 to nearly 600 films only five years later.[87] Balio calls the majors' answer to the times the "ultra-high-budget film":

> Popularized by Carolco Pictures, the independent production company that invested $100 million in Arnold Schwarzenegger's *Terminator 2: Judgment Day* (1991) to create a vehicle that grossed $204 million domestic and $310 million foreign, ultra-high-budget pictures started a spending spree which boosted average production budgets to new highs.[88]

The new ultra-high-budget films were secure investments for Hollywood majors:

> Containing such elements as high concepts, big-name stars, and visual and special effects, such pictures reduced the risk of financing because (1) they constituted media events; (2) they lent themselves to promotional tie-ins; (3) they became massive engines for profits in ancillary divisions like theme parks and video; (4) they stood to make a profit in foreign markets; and (5) they were easy to distribute.[89]

Ultra-high-budget films brought ultra-high grosses. An important step toward high grosses was a distribution tactic called saturation booking: "the practice of releasing new films simultaneously in every market of the country accompanied by a massive national advertising campaign." The aim of saturation booking was to "recoup production costs quickly."[90] Universal's *Jaws* (1975), directed by Steven Spielberg, was the first film to open simultaneously at some 1,000 U.S. movie theaters. The film's release was accompanied with extensive advertising on network television. The new saturation booking system and extensive advertising became trademarks of the blockbuster phenomenon.[91] *Jaws*, based on a Peter Benchley book by the same name about a great white shark hunting for human flesh, was released in summertime, not traditionally an attractive release time but which since then has become a central one.

The success of the new marketing and release strategy also meant a new approach to film advertising. After the financial success of *Jaws*, the old-style publicity departments at film companies "gradually evolved into 'multi-disciplined' marketing departments, which include specific divisions for publicity, creating advertising, media buying, and promotion (including product placement and tie-in activities)."[92] The latest addition has been Internet promotion. The film's success at the box office also gave birth to *Jaws* sequels, starting the now familiar blockbuster phenomenon. If a film succeeds at the box office, the studio often tries to ride the film's success by producing a sequel. This approach has also brought popular comic book characters to the big screen, generated remakes of old popular films and TV series, and also sequels to films which first saw the daylight ten to twenty years before the latest sequel, as was the case, for example, with *Die Hard* and the Indiana Jones films. The original *Die Hard* was released in 1988, and its sequels in 1990, 1995 and 2007. *Raiders of the Lost Ark* was released in 1981, and its sequels in 1984, 1989, and 2008. Saturation, however, also pushed up the print and advertising costs, adding to the final cost of each film. Claiming up to one third or more of a film's budget, the print and advertising costs were up by the 1990s to $35 million and more per film from the 1980 average figures of $4.3 million of a budget of $13.7 million.[93]

In the 1990s film production costs were still growing rapidly, in particular for films intended to achieve blockbuster status at the box office. The introduction and use of computerized special effects added to the cost, as did the expanded length of movies and the hiring of famous actors with multimillion-dollar salaries and/or a share of the gross receipts. Similarly, expenses from union labor and extensive marketing increased the final cost of films.[94] According to the MPAA, "In 2000, the average major studio film cost $55 million to produce with an extra $27 million to advertise and market, a total cost of over $80 million per film. No other nation in the world risks such immense capital to make, finance, produce and market their films."[95] To put the expensiveness of film entertainment in perspective, we can compare it to the reward the U.S. government offered after 9/11 for tips that would lead to the capture of Osama bin Laden. After the September 11, 2001, terrorist attacks Secretary of State Colin Powell raised the reward to $25 million. In Hollywood the amount is a pittance, not even one third of the average production budget of a major studio film.

Movie studios need big blockbuster films to make up for the financial loss the majority of produced films cause to them. According to the MPAA website, "in actuality, only one in ten films ever retrieves its investment from domestic exhibition. In fact, four out of ten movies never recoup the original investment."[96] Hollywood produces from 400 to 600 films a year, but the profits are brought in by a small number of blockbuster films, making studios very dependent on the financial success of their expensive blockbuster investments.

In addition to changes in world politics and economy, changes in the global media market helped the expansion of American entertainment products worldwide. In Hollywood's most important foreign market, Western Europe, the commercialization of the old strong public broadcasting markets and the spread of cable and satellite services created a new demand for films. New, modern movie theaters, in particular in Western Europe, and expanded television advertising also helped the foreign box office. While movie theaters had traditionally been the main source of profits to American film companies, by 1989 they had fallen behind home video as an overseas revenue producer. Television ranked as the number three revenue producer in the foreign market.[97] In the era of blockbuster films the international market has become a matter of life and death to Hollywood. A film must be able to attract foreign audiences in order to cover its production and marketing costs, and to make a profit. In 2001 Hollywood studios incorporated their foreign revenues in their domestic planning, therefore emphasizing the foreign market's importance.[98]

As a result of Hollywood's media mergers, the movie business has been focusing on profit making even more than before. In the industry's efforts to maximize its profits, it has started to invest in strategies that are most certain to guarantee a profit. In its pursuit of that goal, Hollywood relies on the repetition of old successful movie formulas, only updating them to fit the times as viewers tire of a certain formula. Since it is hard to predict what audiences might like, studios may dismiss new creative ideas simply because they consider them too drastic and not financially attractive. Finally, a movie's release date influences how it is expected to perform at movie theaters.[99]

The business approach to filmmaking is essential to "Hollywood's commercially motivated aim of providing the maximum pleasure for the maximum number, to ensure a maximum profit."[100] The large Hollywood studios are feeling the hand of their large conglomerate masters. Film studios are being run according to typical business practices even more than they were in the era of traditional movie moguls. Market and audience research and investments entered the film industry in force in the 1970s and became essential parts of the business by the 1980s. Today's safe business practices include the repetition of previously popular script content and formats, the production of sequels to financially successful films, and the use of directors and stars with proven box office appeal.[101]

Hollywood's Main Domestic and Foreign Product: The Action-Adventure Film

Historically the most successful Hollywood film exports have been comedies and adventure films.[102] Humor is culture-bound, a fact that movies relying on American humor as their main theme have at times had to face in the new blockbuster era. Although many American comedies have done well financially in both domestic and international box office, foreign audiences have also ignored in large numbers some culture-bound comedies. The "over-the-top" comedy *There's Something About Mary* was a worldwide blockbuster in 1998, yet a domestic blockbuster of the same year, *Waterboy*, about American football, flopped miserably overseas. Differences between cultures and what different cultures find funny may at times make it hard for American comedies, which are based on particular aspects of American culture, to entertain foreign audiences. In addition to American sports films, other aspects that make films hard to sell in the foreign market have been, as Don Groves listed in 1999 in *Variety*, black themes, little-known American stars, and courtroom dramas.[103]

In contrast to humor, violent action combined with a minimum amount of dialogue translates fairly easily into any culture. Action and adventure films have been steadily profitable in the global market but they are not risk-free to produce either. The production of action and adventure films is financially very risky because these films are the most expensive ones to produce. These films are extremely vulnerable to box office reactions since they are all about money. They demand huge budgets for special effects, explosions, car chases, elaborate plot twists, shooting on domestic and international locations, and movie star salaries.[104] A film producer's job is to oversee the making of the film and guarantee its success by casting the right box office magnet, a star such as Matt Damon, Will Smith, Bruce Willis, Tom Cruise, or the latest new star. The director's job is to transform the script into a successful film. It is not uncommon for an action or adventure film to have a budget of over $100 million, as has been estimated, for example, for the respective budgets of *True Lies* (1994) and *Speed 2: Cruise Control* (1997). The first one earned its money back and made a great profit, while the second one flopped in the domestic box office. However, due to the latter's success in the foreign box office, it was still able to recoup its production costs. Hollywood studios have high expectations for the films they invest in and which succeed in the domestic market. The majors expect the success to be repeated in the foreign market as well.[105]

Action films can be separated into two categories: pure action and action-adventure films.[106] Pure action films portray a disaster or catastrophe that threatens the film's main character(s). After a film has introduced its primary threat, it mainly focuses on spectacular special effects. For example, in the action-disaster film *Twister* (1996) tornadoes played the role of the main villain. Another action-disaster film, *Titanic* (1997), made film history with its enormous box office success and production budget, but in general the action-adventure category was the more profitable of the two action film categories in the 1990s. Action-adventure films have complicated plots, colorful characters, heroic main character(s), villains, and plenty of dangerous situations.[107] Heroes of these films can be found in series such as *Lethal Weapon*, *The Terminator*, *Die Hard*, *Mission Impossible*, *Aliens*, *Spiderman*, and the James Bond films.

The action-adventure film is Hollywood's main product in both the domestic and global markets. The genre became popular in the 1980s when Hollywood's target audience was American males between the ages of 14 and 25. For this reason, the decade saw a big number of violent action-adventure films. As Herman and McChesney put it: "Hollywood has established itself as the preeminent producer of 'action' fare."[108] The target audience has not changed much since the 1980s; in the first decade of the 21st century American movie theaters received most of their visits from 12 to 20-year-old Americans.[109]

Today's action-adventure films have long roots in the Hollywood film history. The classical Hollywood narrative structure of three acts and a hero and a villain, profit-consciousness of commercial film production, development of the domestic and, in particular, the foreign market, and several other factors have shaped what we see on the big screen today. Action and adventure films from different decades also reveal something about the past history, fears, celebrations, pride, values and knowledge, as well as lack of knowledge, of a nation.

The Action-Adventure Film Genre

Hollywood films are commodities but also important ideological and cultural products.[110] They have power to represent and reproduce social norms and values. While the commercial side of the film business determines which films get produced, "film is not just an ordinary business, but one vested with social consequences because of its communicative powers. As such, film is a mixture of business and art."[111] In the process of producing pleasure for profit, as Adorno and Horkheimer describe film production, film content is still secondary to profits.[112] In Hollywood history this has taken the shape of standardized film structures. In their search for the biggest possible audience, standardized films have relied on presenting stereotypical images of different groups at home and abroad. Historical accuracy has taken a backseat to profits and entertainment. When films are considered to be entertainment or art, the worldview they represent is hidden under the movie watching experience, which, as some researchers have pointed out, gives them an opportunity to advance the most insidious propaganda.[113] In Walter Lippmann's words, "pictures in our heads" affect how we perceive the world. As Adorno and Horkheimer point out: "Pleasure always means not to think about anything, to forget suffering even where it is shown."[114] Action and adventure films are often about suffering—the suffering and death of the main villain and his accomplices in such ways that audiences celebrate the hero's brutal violence against the foreign villains who are threatening "us." Hollywood paints the villainous characters in terms which invite viewers to support the Hollywood action-adventure hero's use of extreme violence against foreign villains. There is no room for viewers to be horrified by the protagonist's brutality against one-dimensional film antagonists. For example, in *True Lies* (1994) Arnold Schwarzenegger's character kills dozens of nameless and often faceless Arabs in horrific and painful ways. Rather than portraying these Third World characters as human beings, the film uses them as props for a variety of creative and brutally entertaining killings.

Film Genres

Film genres offer one solution to the problem of unpredictable audience viewing tastes. Film genres and the Hollywood star system are the closest things the motion picture industry has to recognizable brand names.[115] An action or adventure film starring Matt Damon, Will Smith, Tobey Maguire, Harrison Ford, Denzel Washington, Bruce Willis or Arnold Schwarzenegger draws a different type of audience than a drama starring Meryl Streep or a romantic comedy starring Kate Hudson, Anne Hathaway, Isla Fisher, Cameron Diaz or Sandra Bullock. Film genres and stars are recognizable and familiar to audiences, so viewers know what to expect when they buy or go to see a film of a certain genre and starring a certain star.

Hollywood advertises and supports genre films and big-name stars in its attempt to protect its investments. Belton puts it accurately when he points out that the foremost purpose of film genres is "to stabilize an otherwise unstable film industry."[116]

The movie industry recognizes a variety of film genres. The word *genre* comes from French, meaning "type" or "kind." The term *genre* is normally used to refer to certain types of commercial Hollywood films, such as western, comedy or horror films.[117] Generic categories can also be listed, for example, by the emotional effect of a film, such as thrillers, or by specific film content, such as science fiction. However, different genres overlap and intersect, as well as change over time. Furthermore, the film industry itself as well as film critics and audiences may all understand genres very differently.[118]

A 1942 survey by the Motion Picture Research Bureau on audiences' genre preferences listed eighteen different genres, from comedies and love stories to adventure and action films.[119] While women preferred love stories and stayed away from films with mystery, horror, war, western and other related topics, male audiences' preferences were the exact opposite. It was the survey's results which most likely influenced Hollywood to come up with a "generic cocktail" to attract bigger audiences. The cocktail was to marry action storylines with love storylines.[120] Heterosexual love found a home in Hollywood films. According to Maltby, "85 percent of Hollywood movies feature heterosexual romance as a main plot device."[121] Male-female relationships with a touch of humor help to keep audiences entertained.[122]

Hollywood has been using a variety of film genres since the industry's emergence but the classifications have changed over time. Films are cyclical in the sense that the genres and films that audiences prefer are imitated until other genres become popular.[123] The deciding factor of what to produce is not a specific genre per se but what is seen to be commercially most profitable. However, a well-established and financially popular film formula enables film producers, screenwriters and directors to calculate in advance the audience demand for a certain type of a storyline,[124] that is, until that specific formula loses its appeal among paying audiences. Today's film sequels and prequels have taken profit-consciousness to the next level. Now production and distribution companies expect ready-made audiences loyally to come back to see the next release in the *Die Hard*, *Bourne* or *Star Wars* series. The longest-running film franchise, the James Bond series, has retained original viewers and created new ones by adapting the familiar Bond film ingredients to match the times by bringing in new actors in the main roles and updating the portrayal of women in the films.

The use of a certain genre to classify a soon-to-be-released film raises audience expectations, especially if something new is added to the old formula.[125] Viewers go to see films expecting a certain familiarity, but they still want to be somehow surprised. However, it is economically more feasible for Hollywood to standardize its film production and only create a limited number of new plot twists rather than create something completely new that has not yet been tested in front of mass audiences. New ideas could cause extensive financial damage to the producer.[126] The majors' most expensive productions usually stay away from new ideas until the box office success of a less expensive production by one of their own companies or an independent production company clears the path for a new idea.

In this process of offering viewers something old and familiar with only minor touches of novelty, genre films make it possible for audiences to stay "brand loyal" as much as possible. The rise and death of new film "brands" takes place at movie theater ticket windows. New genres emerge as a result of a certain film's success at the box office.[127] For example, after 9/11 the box office success of *The Bourne Identity* (2002) broke the ice created by the events of 9/11, clearing a path for sinister films in which one cannot trust the government.

The Classical Hollywood Cinema

Hollywood genre films usually rely on a narrative format that applies to most films. Screenwriters and directors maintain their own unique styles, but when it comes to film content, they all follow one major narrative: the "classical Hollywood style." The "narrative machine," as Belton calls Hollywood, is a master at hiding this from audiences.[128] The machine is so well oiled that audiences hardly notice that they are paying to see films that all follow the same narrative process. As Bordwell and Thompson point out, the classical three-act structure with a main protagonist and a main antagonist is as old as the Hollywood industry itself.[129] The narrative structure starts with an order that is disturbed, after which the film portrays attempts to reestablish order, that finally being done at the film's end.[130]

The classical Hollywood cinema is character-driven. It is the decisions, actions and personality of individual characters, and their other individual characteristics, that move the story forward.[131] The film's protagonist faces a problem she or he has to resolve. Audiences love to worry and identify with the protagonist, so the hero's problem must be worthy of the viewers' worry. Also, the hero must be strong and committed to her or his goal so that audiences know for certain that the character will take them not only for a ride but also to its conclusion.[132] Hollywood action and adventure heroes have traditionally been the last line of U.S. defense, saving the country, American citizens and their own family members. Personal characteristics, "ranging from physical appearance to personality to the nature of his or her character or morality," and the protagonist's human flaws are key to making audiences care about the hero.[133] Belton points out: "The movies tell us that the individual *can* make a difference, even within modern mass society."[134] Central in creating viewer identification with the protagonist is the naming of the hero and other characters because people make assumptions about other people based on their names.[135] For example, in action-adventure films strong traditional male names, such as John, James and Jack reappear time after time as the hero's name, for example, John McClane in the *Die Hard* series, John Matrix in *Commando*, John Cutter in *Passenger 57*, John "Jack" Ryan in *Patriot Games* and other films based on Tom Clancy's novels on Dr. Ryan, Jimmy Dove in *Blown Away*, and James "Jim" Marshall in *Air Force One*.

In order to keep audiences entertained, the classical Hollywood cinema script creates conflict by introducing a counterforce that tries to prevent the protagonist from reaching her or his goal.[136] The counterforce, known as the antagonist or the villain, is often a person but it can also be, for example, a natural force, as in the film *Twister* (1996). After the screenwriter has created the conflicting characters, "the plot becomes a series of struggles, battles, or tugs of war, building from scene to scene, act to act, crisis to crisis, until, finally, the protagonist either reaches the goal or fails — or the goal changes."[137] For audiences to care about the battles, the antagonist character has to be written to have a true commitment to her or his goal, which is opposite to the protagonist's goal. That creates the film's main conflict, which can be an obstacle, disharmony, discord, event, or any turbulent action or inner turbulence that the hero has to overcome in order to restore everything in her or his life.[138]

A full-length film script is on average 110 to 120 pages. One page is approximately equal to one minute of screen time.[139] A traditional Hollywood film follows a classical three-act structure. Act by act, the tension level increases, most often in a linear way.[140] The events of Act II create more havoc than the events of Act I, and Act III tops the first two acts. Each crisis takes the story forward and creates the basis for the next battle and crisis.

The first act, which constitutes about twenty-five percent of the film, sets up the plot and the main storyline in motion by introducing the locale and all major characters, and sets tone. It introduces, visually or in dialogue, the necessary information, called exposition, that audiences need to know in order to be able to follow the film's events.[141] Generally the basis of the film's plot — the conflict — is presented within the first ten minutes of the film. The real story will not start until at the end of Act I after the main characters and background information have been established. The first ten minutes often also introduce an "inciting incident" that starts the main plotline and draws the hero into the conflict, no matter whether it is the protagonist or the antagonist who sets the story in motion. If the antagonist sets the story in motion, the protagonist does not normally want to get involved but is forced to do so because of the antagonist's actions.[142]

The second act, which comprises about half of the film, focuses on the confrontation between the protagonist and the antagonist. It usually introduces the hero as a strong character. Since the first act has started with a bang, the second act usually starts with a lower level of tension before events take off and the tension rises. The two main characters are reacting to each other, and after each confrontation the conflict only escalates.[143] The second act often ends in a setback to the protagonist, making it seem almost impossible for her or him to reach her or his goal. It is a moment when all hope seems to be gone, which will eventually make the protagonist even more determined to reach her or his goal.[144] The second act often also introduces a subplot, which involves one or more of the main characters. It is freer in its narrative structure than the main plot, which usually follows the classical Hollywood cinema structure. The subplot is often more emotional and original in its content. For example, romantic subplots primarily take place in the second act. The subplot can be resolved at any point from the end of Act II till the very end of the film.[145] *True Lies* (1994) is an example of a film whose main story is the protagonist's activities against terrorists, yet the subplot brings in his family, allowing an almost failed family unit to come back together as the film's secondary storyline. By the end of Act II the marriage is back together, but now the wife is in the terrorists' hands. The focus returns to the fight between the hero and the villain, culminating in the hero first saving his wife and eventually his teenage daughter from the terrorists' clutches before he kills the main terrorist.

In the third act, which forms about one quarter of the film, the story reaches its climax. Similar to Act II, Act III starts with a lower level of tension before it introduces the ultimate confrontation between the protagonist and the antagonist. Usually the former defeats the latter and therefore brings the story to its resolution when the conflict has been resolved. The denouement, set in the last few minutes of the film, brings the last pieces of the plot together, although not all films have one.[146] Hollywood screenwriter Larry Ferguson notes that the ending also introduces a transformed protagonist: a typical Hollywood film protagonist grows as a person in the process of reaching for her or his goal. At the film's beginning the character is incapable of doing something, while by the film's end she or he can do it. It can take the form of emotional growth or a physical activity.[147] For example, the film *Executive Decision* (1996) shows the protagonist taking flying lessons during the first minutes of the film, and at the film's end he is forced to rely on his shaky flying skills and land a jet in order to save lives. Ferguson calls the character transformation the protagonist's "prodigal journey." Armer, who uses the term "character arc" for the transformation, explains that due to the pressure the protagonist has experienced, she or he will emerge as a changed person at the film's end.[148]

Most scripts, especially the ones that succeed at the box office, also have a theme which refers to "the underlying *meaning* of a play, the message communicated to audiences not through the speeches of its characters but by its action and content. It is the play's **subtext** realized by the audience in retrospect, perhaps consciously, perhaps subconsciously."[149] A typical theme would be, for example, "crime does not pay" when a crime film shows at the end how criminals are caught. Each good script needs a theme, although sometimes the theme

In the post–Cold War world, romance entered the Hollywood action-adventure hero's life. He defended his wife and daughter first, and his country second. In *True Lies* (1994, 20th Century Fox) agent Harry Tasker (Arnold Schwarzenegger) rekindles his marriage with Helen (Jamie Lee Curtis) and patches up his relationship with his rebellious teenage daughter while preventing a terrorist attack.

does not emerge until the writer has finished her or his script. A film's theme is usually the screenwriter's view of the world. The theme itself is most strongly expressed through the actions of the script's characters rather than directly in dialogue.[150] Some genres can be categorized by their themes: for example, gangster films draw thematically from urban crime, and science fiction films from technology. Thematic films often draw from current or past social phenomena.[151] However, even if a film has a strong thematic content or message, the film's primary goal is still to make a profit.

Emergence of the Action-Adventure Film Genre

Movie producers aim at making a product that plays well all over the world.[152] In action-adventure films, of which many have grown to become worldwide blockbusters, they have found that product. The term *action-adventure* primarily refers to films made since the 1980s that have certain common ingredients, as Neale discusses: "A propensity for spectacular physical action, a narrative structure involving fights, chases and explosions, and in addition to the deployment of state-of-the-art special effects, an emphasis in performance on athletic feats and stunts."[153] The films portray heroes, both men and women, who have hyperbolic bodies.[154]

Usually action, adventure or action-adventure films are high-budget films that only the big studios can afford to produce and distribute in the domestic and foreign markets. In addition, there is a market also for low-budget action films which do not aim at a blockbuster status. Independently produced low-budget action films can skip the domestic distribution companies and find a market and distributor for their films abroad.[155]

The Adventure Film

The fact that Hollywood filmmakers, critics, researchers and viewers may understand film genres very differently is seen, for example, in the simultaneous use of the terms "action film," "adventure film," and "action-adventure film" to describe the films that rely on intense action and adventures for their central content. The following discusses the development of this action-packed genre, starting with adventure films.

There is no clear adventure film genre per se. It actually consists of several film genres, such as war, survival, swashbuckler and safari films, which all have adventures as their main content. The combining factor for these different adventure genres is, as Thomas Sobchack points out, "certain plot formulas, settings, character networks, icons, and conventions of action."[156] Two particular plot structures are common to these films; both clearly focus on adventures. The first consists of adventures of a lone hero who is "marked by his superior intelligence, grace, and fighting skills," but who believes in the equality of all men.[157] The second type presents a protagonist who rises to the occasion when a heroic leader is needed for a group to survive but who in the end returns to being one of the ordinary men. The lone hero films are "swashbuckler films" and the group leader films "survival films."[158]

In swashbuckler films a lone law-abiding hero is forced outside his (rarely her) society. Each film depicts a hero who attempts to bring back order and his own status in a legal society. The hero does not try to change the social structures: "Political stability and the status quo of traditional social structures are prominent values of this genre."[159] For example, the different versions of *The Prisoner of Zenda* (1937, 1952, 1979) and *The Adventures of Robin Hood* (1938) are products of this genre. A romantic subplot is common, normally taking the structure of a romantic comedy: "the male and female meet, hate and distrust each other after an initial attraction, bicker and argue throughout the film, and finally resolve their differences at the end in a marriage or the promise of one."[160] Additionally, depictions include the male hero saving the female character from a physical danger. The heroine, often aristocratic, chooses the hero, who is a defender of democratic values. Only after she has chosen him will she learn that the hero actually comes from the same circles in society as herself. Several directors of swashbucklers have also directed musicals, which reveals similarities in the physical expressiveness of the two genres. In musicals the physical expressiveness comes through in dance numbers; in adventure films it comes through in violent confrontations. Swashbuckler films also portray irony and self-parody, as does, for example, James Bond when he comments on his own actions and adventures.[161]

Sobchack categorizes war films and disaster films as survival adventure films. The swashbuckler film takes place in exotic locations and cultural surroundings, and often in the past. The survival film draws from contemporary events, such as recent wars or terrorists taking hostages — that is, events that can be found in the latest news headlines. *The Dirty Dozen* (1967) and *Escape from Alcatraz* (1978) are representative of such films. The survivor hero leads and fights for a small isolated group that needs his help while the swashbuckler hero often fights for his country and therefore defends his whole society. Sobchack finds the survivor film similar in its structure to romance: "They both emphasize the heroic triumph over obstacles which threaten social order and the reaffirmation of predominant social values such as fair play and respect for merit and cooperation."[162]

War films emphasize the importance of cooperation for the survival of a group. The world of these films is a battlefield where "the laws, beliefs, behavior, and morality of civilization are suspended. It is not merely permitted for one man to kill another; it is imperative for him to do so. War rewrites civil and criminal law."[163] The line between what is right and what is wrong is not as clear as in other films, but certain things are clear: "The good guys (usually us) fight fair and the bad guys (usually them) do not. Our enemies are shown not only torturing captured soldiers but also killing innocent civilians."[164] At times a film shows the good guys breaking the rules of the game, but in such cases "they are generally seen as motivated by either moral outrage, expediency, or compassion."[165] Representatives of the genre include, for example, the Rambo films, starring Sylvester Stallone. Films of the genre portray violence cartoonishly and allow their characters little or no depth. Women have no role or a very limited role in war films. If they do enter the man's world, they are often depicted as targets of desire, an emotion that makes men vulnerable in war conditions. A man's attempt to resist his vulnerability emerges as a repression of his feminine side, making him "a ruthless, unemotional, fighting machine," which is the key to his own and his comrades' survival.[166]

For Parenti, films that rely on intense action are all just different variations of movies about cowboys and Indians. They traditionally portray a white Anglo-Saxon man saving the day in the western wilderness. The hero of action films is a cowboy of the Wild West, outer space, the police world, or a spy.[167] These films replace the Western frontier with space or a dangerous urban or international world. Western films, a uniquely American genre, dominated Hollywood film production until 1967. The genre emerged as the real Wild West was already a thing of the past. Western films drew from the myth of the West and the American frontier. They were stories about civilization, culture and progress confronting wild nature, strange Native American cultures, outlaws, cattlemen, and old times. At the edge of civilization the hero could rely only on himself.[168]

The protagonist of the Western film is a traditional hero, a white loner who is a rugged individualist. He has set his own rules. As a traditional hero his actions are marked, as in swashbuckler films, by his intelligence, resourcefulness, dignity, courage, justice and fair play. He fights only when he is forced to do so. Like the hero of swashbuckler films, the hero of Western films fights for the weak and women. He combines the characteristics of swashbuckler and survival adventure films in the sense that he may act alone or be a group leader. The antagonist is almost the protagonist's mirror image, but the hero always does everything a bit better than the villain. While the hero has a reason for his fight, the motivation of the evil Indian or outlaw is often absent. In the end the protagonist will resolve the conflict and save civilization by killing the villain, scaring him away, or by taking him to jail.[169] There is no place for a minority representative, foreigner or woman in the hero's role in Western films. If a film does show a woman, her role is to be a sexy seducer or someone whom the white hero must protect and save.[170] In typical Western films, a woman's role is minimal. She represents civilization, family and community. She often loses her faith in the hero. In the end the protagonist regains his possible love interest's trust and respect, but he usually does not stay. After having saved one community he mounts his horse and rides away to start his search for another civilization to save.[171]

The Action-Adventure Film

The term *action-adventure* is still quite new in film history, dating only to the 1980s when films with intense action were accorded high budgets with the goal of becoming domestic and global blockbusters.[172] Since then, action-adventure heroes such as those in the *Die Hard* and *Lethal Weapon* series and the Indiana Jones movies have conquered the big screen with financial success. Action-adventure films became especially popular in the 1990s. These high-testosterone entertainments usually have complicated plotlines and are spiced up with lots of dangerous situations. The films also have colorful characters, the main character being a heroic individual.[173] The films' audiences know the traditional formula thoroughly and expect to have "wild but predictable characters, laconic heroes sometimes supported by prop partners, male or female, and designing, inhuman villains motivated by evil intent and a lust for power, always posing a threat to civilization or order."[174] In his (seldom her) attempt to save the day, the hero, who is often muscular and oversized, is faced with "wicked villains, terrorists, mad bombers, anarchists, power-hungry despots, or crime lords."[175]

Action-adventure films typically follow the classical Hollywood cinema narrative structure, having stereotypical characters, formulaic storylines, and a predictable ending between the hero and the villain. Traditionally the protagonist is a white Anglo-Saxon Protestant male who is saving Western civilization from threats to its structures and way of life.[176] Slocum's analysis of the classical period filmmaking (circa 1927 until the late 1960s) still holds true and is very familiar to the action-adventure film genre of today:

> Narrative filmmaking practices during the classical period typically involved strictly linear narratives, centered on individual, white, psychologically well motivated male protagonists, moving through the resolution of public conflicts toward social integration and heterosexual coupling that reaffirmed prevailing ideological currents that were themselves grounded in national cultural myths. These narratives are presented through well-focused compositions, continuity editing, realistic settings, naturalistic lighting, and frequent reliance on generic story forms and recognizable star performers.[177]

As is the case with any Hollywood film, the action-adventure hero must resolve a conflict which usually translates into the killing of the villain since he (seldom she) is the one causing the conflict. It is typical for action-adventure films to justify the killing of the villain by never representing the antagonist as a human being in the same terms as the hero.[178] Parenti, who uses the term *action films*, calls action films "swarthy horde" films because the antagonist is usually a foreigner whose skin color is darker than the white protagonist's. The hero's primary task is to defeat an alien threat that faces the Western world. The latter stands for freedom, capitalism and democracy. The villain poses a threat to Western society and its structures, but viewers know that the hero will fight for them, restore order and effectively deal with the villain by the film's parting shot.[179] The films that portray adventures rely on attracting the viewer to identify with the hero. According to Sobchack,

> During the course of an adventure film, the audience can vicariously live out their fantasies of personal prowess and vigorous action in heightened, emotionally intense, extraordinary situations, and can be moved by images of titanic struggle against the opposing forces which seek disruption — political upheaval, war, disaster — yet the ending, the closure of the adventure, always returns the viewer to the position of social conformity. All the values in the traditional adventure film uphold and reinforce the status quo, the idea of stability and regularity in the workings of the social order.[180]

Although action-adventure as a film genre did not become part of the popular culture until the 1980s, the 1960s had already introduced spectacular nonstop action with the screen arrival of British import James Bond in *Dr. No* in 1962. The Bond films, which at first were considered to be B-films in the U.S., set the standard for big event action-adventure films with their repeated ingredients, including a simplified characterization of villains, usually foreign and at least somewhat insane. The action-packed Bond film also introduced to the world exotic locations and touches of irony and comedic style. At the end of each film the white hero returns the balance of power, the last shot usually showing Bond's departure from the screen with his latest female conquest. The Bond formula appealed to audiences, resulting in launching the world's longest-running film series.

Action-adventure films truly became blockbuster commodities in the 1990s when producers started to invest enormous amounts of money to highlight action and complicated plot twists, including romantic subplots. For example, the estimated budget of the 141-minute *True Lies* (1994) was over $100 million. The film brought in over $146 million in the domestic box-office alone,[181] leaving the film's foreign box office success as in its profit margin. The word *excessive* describes well the action-adventure films of the 1990s. The decade's genre films often had excessive budgets, excessive running times, and were even bigger spectacles than the films of the previous decades.[182]

Two actors from Hong Kong, Jackie Chan and John Woo, reintroduced an old movie method, comic style, after the dominance of the 1980s' one-man war machines.[183] The recycling of old American and new foreign ideas has worked in action-adventure films to the point that some of their one-liners have become part of American cultural history, such as Arnold Schwarzenegger's lines "I'll be back" and "Hasta la vista, baby."

Another major addition in the 1990s, a wife with a career, made the lonely hero a family man. More women started to appear in action-filled movies, albeit in the roles of wives and daughters or other supporters of the male hero and/or the male villain. The invasion of women into male territory hinted at Hollywood studio efforts to attract more female viewers into movie theaters.[184]

Action-adventure films combine classical Hollywood cinema structure with awareness of what is taking place in society. The films are often conservative in content, usually conforming to the prevailing social norms and order in their efforts to alienate the least amount of paying viewers. But when society and its threat scenarios change, films follow suit, movie studios naturally preferring to be at the vanguard. Since the emergence of the commercial film industry, films have found their threats to U.S. security and American citizens in those who are outsiders in American society, and in foreigners, in particular those identified by U.S. foreign policy.

Hollywood's Worldview

Hollywood has traditionally borrowed ideas for its productions from the arena of world politics. Different film themes and portrayals of heroes and enemies have been closely connected to the country's prevailing political, social and economic conditions.[185] In action-adventure movies white American male heroes have found themselves confronted by alien powers, both by foreign and domestic villains who represent different ethnic and minority groups. The commercial film industry has offered stereotypical portrayals of these groups, reproducing and circulating a variety of stereotypes time after time.[186] Hollywood's fictional make-believe world images have a bearing on the public's interpretation of the world, including the public understanding of world politics and of their own country's position in it. Screen images can serve as sources of information but they may also convince viewers of a particular worldview that teaches them whom they should hate, love or fear.[187]

At best, films can add to viewers' understanding and knowledge of current and past international relations, but at worst they can be propaganda tools. Films do not reflect reality but translate abstract concepts of international relations into concrete and dramatized movie ideas.[188] They disproportionally focus on conflict, which follows the traditional dramatic writing structure, the classical Hollywood cinema structure. The film industry's choice of whom to cast as the villain and how to treat him or her in that role can affect how viewers understand groups they know nothing about. Positive and negative stereotypes of different groups in society and outside U.S. borders may be the only experience a U.S. viewer has with a particular group. While these "political entertainment" films draw their content from politics and entertainment, each film's political message gets hidden under the film's entertainment.[189] Since movies are disguised as entertainment, viewers may not notice if the movie industry feeds them propaganda.[190] Media manipulation is at its most effective when it is imperceptible to those who are the target of the manipulation.[191] In particular, when films are considered as nothing but entertainment, they have an opportunity to manipulate audiences into accepting as true fictitious portrayals of different groups and views in society.[192]

Character portrayals are central to each film genre. The Hollywood cinema structure and genre traditions largely determine how a film portrays its hero and villain. The classical Hollywood cinema storyline reveals a state of constant hostility. It sets up the protagonist to fight the antagonist till the end, when the latter is taken out of the game, usually by the hero. The storyline promotes a traditional American view of a strong self-made man who succeeds by going after his goals. He pushes aside everyone who stands in his way. Although this idealized image is distributed globally in American movies, it does not apply to all cultures as an ideal model.[193]

Hollywood films sell American ideologies and products to a global audience. Film genres serve "as formal strategies for renegotiating and reinforcing American ideology."[194] As Stuart Hall sees the media as a site of struggle,[195] Schatz sees the film genre specifically as a site of struggle: the generic film genre structure tends to support the status quo and capitalist values.[196] Films promote American interests and undermine in particular the Third World.[197] For example, in films with action and adventure content the foreign villain's destiny is traditionally a violent death. The further away from the U.S., the bigger the number of the villains the hero faces and kills. This Hollywood policy follows international news portrayals in the U.S. mainstream media which highlight American and Western deaths but rarely find room for reports about deaths in the less developed world.

At best, films can educate viewers, but they are not necessarily reliable when it comes to historical accuracy. Films about international relations mostly portray the world according to the worldview of the realist school of international relations.[198] In other words, films reflect the realist view that there is a state-centric order in the world in which different parties are on a crash course because they all focus on reaching their own goals in the world, and they do that by any means possible. As Gregg points out, in this type of world conflicts are common, just like in films that draw from international relations:

> Films dealing with international relations are disproportionally concerned with war, espionage, revolutionary nationalism, and other forms of conflictual behavior. The participants may vary from large armies to individuals who serve as surrogates for some larger group or interest ... the state and its agents — governments, armies, spies — are conspicuously engaged in doing the state's business, openly or clandestinely, heroically or disreputably, successfully or unsuccessfully.... In other cases, we see the enemies of the state seeking to undermine its authority or even its existence, often with the objective of taking over the government and acquiring state authority in the process.[199]

Furthermore, films simplify international relations by personifying complex ideas into conflicts between individual characters.[200] When analyzing how Hollywood has portrayed conflicts of international relations on the big screen over time, it is possible to find some general trends. To understand how Hollywood portrays domestic and international events, in particular international terrorism, it helps to take a short historical look at how the film industry has and has not reacted on the big screen to different events inside and outside the U.S.

Hollywood Policies

At the early stages of film production, Hollywood approached both domestic and foreign policy topics with caution. Movie producers and studios often chose not to directly confront the prevailing political environment and events. In particular, in the pre–World War I era Hollywood produced racist movies and stereotypes of minority and foreign threats in accordance with the prevailing policy and social lines. As Washington started to show keen interest in Hollywood productions before World War II, and in particular during the war, Hollywood's efforts to stay outside political controversies were doomed.[201]

Hollywood could not ignore World War II, the war-era fear of fascism, and the American involvement in the war. While the U.S. government drafted Hollywood to help in the war effort, it limited how the real horrors of war could be depicted on the big screen, as Slocum explains: "The Office of War Information, the government unit charged with monitoring and collaborating with the studios in order to ensure their contribution to the war effort, was keenly aware of the dangers of presenting war in its full, intense, and graphic reality."[202] The Hollywood version of World War II was sensitized and supportive of the American war effort. Commercial films depicted U.S. foreign policy goals and were antifascist in content. They portrayed the enemy, Nazi Germany, as a great danger to American society and to all of its values. The events of World War II forced Hollywood to produce some pro–Soviet movies and to show how cooperation with the Soviet Union in the war was in the interests of the United States. The wartime cooperation with the government introduced Hollywood to what it was to face hardly a decade later.

In the 1950s the United States and the Soviet Union were waging the Cold War which extended its reach to the U.S. entertainment industry. Fear of the communist ideology culminated in Hollywood in a red scare. Numerous screenwriters, producers and directors were suspected of left-wing connections and were investigated by the House of Un-American Activities Committee (HUAC). Several Hollywood producers, writers and directors were blacklisted because of their alleged communist ties. During this period anticommunist films flourished in Hollywood.[203] The HUAC inspired the movie industry to produce some forty anticommunist movies. All got big distribution but small audiences.[204] The Red Scare on the big screen was bad business. Hollywood had miscalculated audiences' interest in the threat promoted by the government and news media. Viewers avoided the films, and the film industry had to swallow the financially painful lesson.[205]

Hollywood images of the Cold War from the late 1940s until the early 1960s depended on the relationship between the U.S. and the Soviet Union at the time of the production process.[206] Hollywood also tested the official foreign policy and the public opinion by offering comical and satirical images that overemphasized the fear and differences between the two societies. In contrast to straightforward Red Scare films, the combination of fear and comedy proved to be profitable. As the relationship between the two superpowers improved, Hollywood eased off its view of the Soviet Union. Détente in the U.S.-Soviet relations from 1965 till the late 1970s again brought some movies that showed cooperation between the two.[207]

Hollywood finally became openly political in the 1960s in the middle of vocal political protests on the domestic front. Movie studios took notice of the New Left movement, student protests, and the emerging protests against the war in Vietnam.[208] The civil rights movement that had emerged in the 1950s gathered momentum, as did political violence. President John F. Kennedy and later his brother, Senator Robert F. Kennedy, were assassinated, as were African American leaders Martin Luther King, Jr., and Malcolm X. However, Hollywood films ignored the political upheavals, including racism, because the industry was trying to reach a general audience and therefore wanted to avoid insulting or angering anyone.[209]

The 1960s and the early 1970s were the primetime of American film violence. Also, this era was marked by widespread cinematic expression of American countercultures.[210] Films were challenging, for example, the traditional masculine Hollywood hero. At the end of the 1960s Hollywood relaxed its content rules, which resulted in more violent and sexual screen content.

Also in the 1960s, the women's movement helped to legalize abortion, and a reliable oral contraceptive liberated women to have more control over their own lives. Women were entering college and graduating in record numbers, and also entering the workforce, some in positions that had traditionally been held by men. Women became more independent, but their paychecks were lower than men's in spite of demands for equal treatment. Hollywood's reaction was to depict "sexually liberated or aggressive" women who portrayed stereotypical characters: "either madonnas or whores. The only working women are motherly governesses or prostitutes."[211] Hollywood kept working women who held white- and blue-collar jobs hidden until the late 1970s.

Movie audiences divided in the 1960s into a "conservative, middle-aged, middle-class mainstream" and "a younger, more liberal, middle- and lower-class audience."[212] By the 1970s the main audience was Americans between the ages of 12 and 20, who formed almost half of the country's movie audiences. Also, a new generation of directors was emerging. As a result of younger viewers and directors, films were "stylistically youthful and inventive but politically conservative."[213] After the major studios suffered major financial setbacks in the 1980s, studios turned to the young generation. Young directors and youth-oriented themes took over because they could earn money. Coming to the 1990s, the over–40 crowd started to make a comeback. In 1984, it made up 15 percent of the audience. In 1990, it claimed 24 percent. But, as Maltby points out, Hollywood saw its main market in Generation Y, those born between the years 1977 and 1995. Also, in their efforts to bring women and men to see films together, film studios released films such as *Ghost* and *Pretty Woman*. But Hollywood still relied on the old method of a bankable male star in its mainstream productions in the 1990s.[214]

International terrorism made its way to the big screen slowly. At the height of terrorist attacks in Western Europe and the Middle East in the 1970s, hijackings, assassinations, bombings, and hostage-takings became gradually familiar through the news media in the U.S. even though the attacks were occurring far away from U.S. soil. The U.S. did not experience a major attack of international terrorism until 1979, during Democratic president Jimmy Carter's administration when Iranian students took over the American embassy in Tehran. The 444-day hostage crisis was a daily television news story. The event had taken the U.S. by surprise. Even during the period of détente, the U.S. viewed as its main adversaries the Soviet Union and communism. The role of the "political other" had been reserved to the Soviets.[215]

Images of the Iran hostage crisis were broadcast around the world. Real-life terrorist attacks were also taking place in West Germany, Italy, the Middle East and Northern Ireland. It took a few years before fictional terrorists found their way onto television screens, and they gradually also came into Hollywood films. The studios started to introduce international terrorists as villains and originators of conspiracies, for example, in the 1977 release *Black Sunday*. However, the theme did not emerge as a major trend. The decade's film portrayals of terrorism mostly repeated what was already familiar from the news media: movie terrorists were psychotic fighters who had no clear political agenda but were only pursuing revenge.[216] Against that trend *Black Sunday* introduced an Israeli male hero who, while saving the U.S., also understood that every story, including the Israeli-Palestinian conflict, has many sides to it. The film was not a big hit among audiences.

Reaganite Cinema

With the arrival of Republican president Ronald Reagan in the White House in January 1981, the United States returned to conservative values that many felt had been eroded by prior decades' political and social activism. For instance, the women's movement of the 1970s, as well as 1980s feminism, made gains that some Americans found threatening. Thus, a backlash emerged in entertainment, calling for a strong, heroic white male who would restore and reconfirm his dominance and that of conservative values.[217] Violence is closely linked to masculinity,[218] and that is what Hollywood found as its answer to the new times. Violence and white muscled men filled the big screen to reclaim the manliness of the U.S. in the global arena. Views that contradicted the prevailing administration were largely missing in Hollywood films.[219] Movies that reflected conservative themes and values found box office success while the films that resisted them failed, with the exception of Oliver Stone's Vietnam War film *Platoon*.[220] Films of this era became known as "Reaganite cinema"[221] or Reaganite entertainment. It primarily covered the presidency of Republican Ronald Reagan (1981–1988), and, to a lesser extent, the presidency of George H. W. Bush (1989–1992).

The U.S. move to the right also intensified the Cold War. Reagan denounced the Soviet Union as an evil empire, the center of an international terrorist network, and the source of all unrest in the world. The president also found terrorists in Central and South America, where he denounced as communist, and therefore terrorist, the groups that resisted the governments that his administration was supporting. In the name of freedom and liberty against Soviet-led communist terrorism, the U.S. attacked a militarily easy target, tiny Grenada, and influenced the outcome of the civil war in El Salvador.[222] It is worth noting that the U.S. invasion of Grenada, "Operation Urgent Fury," which ended Grenada's socialist rule, took place two days after the bombing of the U.S. marine barracks in Beirut, although the preparations for the operation had been underway before the Beirut bombing. In the Middle East, the U.S. was incapable of controlling the situation with military force, but on the other side of the world it was able to showcase its power and military might against the smallest country in the Western Hemisphere.[223]

The Reaganite entertainment of the 1980s reflected the Reagan administration's emphasis on demonstrating U.S. military power in the international arena. The Reagan-era action and action-adventure films were full of cartoonish violence. The decade's stars, such as Sylvester Stallone and Arnold Schwarzenegger, were hypermasculine Caucasians whose movie actions were often supported by special effects.[224]

In Jeffords's view the era can be analyzed well through the decade's three Rambo films, *First Blood* (1982), *Rambo: First Blood, Part 2* (1985), and *Rambo III* (1988), which span the Reagan era. All three films portray a hard-bodied white Vietnam veteran, John Rambo, played by Sylvester Stallone. Jeffords argues that Stallone and the decade's other muscular hero, Arnold Schwarzenegger, stood "for a type of national character — heroic, aggressive, and determined" as well as for the country.[225] The one-man war machine restores pride in American military forces as well as the power of the white male in American society by his denial of women and sexuality. The movies of the era gave audiences an opportunity to experience the films at a personal and national level, that is, to identify with the hero while his hard body, which stood for the country, defeated the country's enemies.[226]

Belton sees *Rambo: First Blood Part II* (1985), which depicts Rambo on a rescue mission in Southeast Asia, as a messenger of the era. The film

> epitomizes the new conservatism, which is based, in part, on the desire to rewrite the recent past and put a positive face on our nation's more negative experiences.... The plot of the film is a symbolic reworking of the American right wing's perception of the war — Rambo's mission is undermined by political bureaucrats, military brass, and the CIA, who didn't want him to win. If America lost the Vietnam war back in 1975 on both the military and political fronts, Rambo won it for us in the mid–1980s, single-handedly killing hundreds of the enemy and rescuing a chopperful of American MIAs. President Ronald Reagan led the cheering section for the film. After Lebanese terrorists released 39 American hostages, Reagan declared, "I saw *Rambo* last night. I know what to do the next time this happens."[227]

The Rambo series portrayed a maverick soldier who was supporting the Reagan-era policies. For example, in *Rambo III* the hero first turns down his Vietnam War commanding officer's request to help mujahideen fighters in their battle against the invading Soviet Union in Afghanistan. When the Soviets capture the officer, Rambo travels to Afghanistan to release him with the assistance of local heroic mujahideen fighters. As Rambo and his commanding officer leave the mujahideen camp at the film's end, the film emphasizes its Reagan policy message with the text that appears on the screen: "This film is dedicated to the gallant people of Afghanistan."

The heroes of *Rocky*, *Rambo*, *Terminator*, *Crocodile Dundee*, *Die Hard*, *Beverly Hills Cop* and *Lethal Weapon* uphold mainstream values: "They promote law and order, interracial harmony, police camaraderie, and a celebration of the family."[228] The films of the era depicted a patriarchal country and families with strong father-son relationships — that is, if families were portrayed. For example, in the *Star Wars* trilogy, father Darth Vader and son Luke reconcile as Luke helps his father to return to the good side of the Force before his father's death.

In Reaganite cinema films that depict events on foreign soil, Hollywood was not shy to rewrite history and cast the U.S. as a hero even if history remembered the events differently. Under the leadership of Hollywood's one-man war machine, Rambo, the white Hollywood hero, refought, revenged and resolved American minds about the Vietnam War by distorting facts to the advantage of the U.S.[229] The Reaganite cinema films crudely altered history and introduced heroes who reached salvation through individualistic acts of heroism and massive applications of violence. The historical roles of the aggressor and defender were reversed so that, for example, in movies on the Vietnam War, the United States and its representatives became innocent heroes while Vietnam, target of foreign invaders, became a simplified sadistic aggressor and oppressor. Targets of President Reagan's foreign policy, such as Cuba, Nicaragua and the Soviet Union, were also soon attacking the U.S. in Hollywood productions.[230]

During the Cold War, the U.S. and the Soviet Union were literally waging a war, not directly between themselves but mentally and often physically in some of the Third World countries. Hollywood was not immune, especially to the U.S. attempts to counter the suspected Soviet influence in Latin America. The U.S. involvement in Latin American politics inspired Hollywood to produce "innocent abroad" stories in which ordinary citizens, often journalists, found themselves faced with death squads of various Latin American governments.[231] Some of the movies, such as *Salvador* (1986), *Under Fire* (1983) and *The Year of Living Dangerously*

(1983), undermined the official American explanation of the situation. Their message was that reality was being manipulated for political reasons.[232] Gregg lists as the most famous films of the era the movies which addressed the U.S. interventions in Nicaragua (*Under Fire*, directed by Roger Spottiswoode), in El Salvador (*Salvador*, by Oliver Stone), and in Chile (*Missing*, by Costa-Gavras). Each film introduced a journalist who was covering the country's events in politically uncertain times.[233] Nicaragua's leader was a right-wing anticommunist dictator, Anastasio Somoza, whom the U.S. was supporting. In Salvador the U.S. was supporting a conservative anticommunist regime in its effort to keep leftists from taking power, while in Chile the U.S. was giving its support to a new right-wing regime that had claimed power from a leftist government. Costa-Gavras was also behind another film which criticized the U.S. policies and involvement in Latin America. His *State of Siege* (1972) sympathized with the 1970s left-wing rebels in Uruguay who killed an American government adviser,[234] a trainer in counterintersurgency methods, including torture.

While some Hollywood producers and directors based their films on true events in Latin America and countered the official U.S. foreign policy, their films still followed the traditional Hollywood narrative structure. The foreign locations were portrayed as locations of violence. The films starred traditional white Western protagonists while nameless non–Western locals were used as props of humanitarian and political abuses.[235] Some of these films won critical acclaim but not box office success.

Terrorism and drug trafficking became targets of the Reagan administration in the 1980s in the changing international and domestic arenas. In that decade the Israel-Palestine conflict kept tensions high in the Middle East. Also, the Iran hostage crisis had only been the beginning of anti–American attacks by different Middle Eastern groups which opposed U.S. policies. The 1980s saw, for example, the U.S. servicemen's club bombing in West Germany, the TWA flight hijacking from Athens, the *Achille Lauro* cruise ship hijacking in Greece, and the Pan Am airliner bombing over Scotland. All incidents had American casualties. The largest number of casualties was caused by the October 1983 suicide bombing attack on the U.S. marine barracks in Beirut, which killed 241 American marines and other personnel.

Hollywood took notice of the new threats that President Reagan was drawing attention to. Hostage-takings and terrorism became a boom industry for Hollywood films and television in the Reagan era. The fictional anti–American and evil terrorists largely lacked political motivations. They filled their shoes in movies so that white American heroes could kill them, highlighting the efficiency of American weapons and prowess. According to Parenti, the films of the era that portrayed terrorism shared certain common characteristics:

> The antiterrorist films, if that's what they really are, have all the ingredients of the swarthy hordes flicks: 1) White humanity is threatened by barbaric forces; 2) the White heroes use superior intelligence, technology, and limitless bravery to rescue their own from alien clutches; and 3) in doing so, they kill large numbers of Third World savages, thus demonstrating that force and violence are the necessary solution. Violence serves as the main vehicle for plot development (such as it is) and plot resolution. Far from being "antiterrorist," these productions are celebrations of state-sponsored terrorism, helping to set the stage for such events as the real-life, high-tech military destruction of Iraq in 1991.[236]

These signs are easy to find in the Reaganite films.

Towards the end of the Reagan presidency, and under the leadership of Mikhail Gorbachev in the Soviet Union, communism declined as a threat. By the decade's end the Red Scare was old news. Threats to American interests in the Middle East and the Third World were emerging as the U.S. was starting to clear its head of the Cold War stupor and look for a new enemy.

The swan song of the Cold War sent the outdated Soviet communist villain and the heroic American one-man war machine packing. The arrival of the 20th Century Fox film *Die Hard* in 1988 brought to the front a white man with modest muscles. New York City police officer John McClane, played by Bruce Willis, was married to a wife who had a successful career. McClane's opponents were smart Euroterrorists who had abandoned their leftist ideology and arrived in the U.S.—country of the capitalist dream—to have their own version of a capitalist success story. The film mixed Reaganite cinema ingredients with post–Cold War themes. Its box office success helped to bury the strict Reaganite cinema action-adventure stories.

President Reagan was succeeded in the White House by another conservative Republican, George H. W. Bush, in January 1989. His presidency was affected by the collapse of the Soviet Union and communism. The end of the Cold War created a deep political, social and intellectual crisis in the West.[237] With the disappearance of the threat of communism, the Western countries, in particular the U.S., faced a moral and political vacuum during the Bush era. In foreign relations, President Bush found the biggest threat to American interests in Iraq and in the person of its leader, Saddam Hussein. Kellner argues that the 1980s films on Arab terrorism and their commercial success helped President Bush to dehumanize Iraqi leader Saddam Hussein and to promote a war that the administration argued to be a rightful war. Hollywood had mostly been depicting a negative view of the Arab world, and of Arabs as barbaric and anti–American crazed fanatics. With that hegemonic image of the Arab world, a true U.S. patriot was expected to support the war against Iraq.[238] In 1991 President Bush launched the Persian Gulf War as a response to Iraq's invasion of the oil-rich Kuwait.

Clinton-Era Cinema

In November 1992, after twelve years of a Republican White House, Democrat Bill Clinton was elected to the presidency; he would serve two terms. The U.S. moved more to the center in its political views. Women's movements celebrated a president who was more liberal in his views than his two predecessors.

In the 1990s, profit-consciousness affected the Hollywood film business to the extent that commercial interests took priority at all times.[239] The newest technologies, and the majors and their business policies, drove film production more than ever before. This was seen in the production, distribution and marketing of films, as well as in film content, structures and themes. Due to higher and higher production expenses, films became expensive commodities that investors sought to protect at all costs. Commercial interests were only intensified by the fact that in the 1990s the foreign market took over the domestic market as the primary revenue producer. The first year to witness that development was 1993. The domestic market briefly returned to the top two years later, but the following year the foreign box office grabbed back its lead and kept it.[240] Films now had to appeal to worldwide audiences in order to earn the best possible return on each investment.

The films of the previous decades, while still commercial products, had often also had a subtext that had tried to address some of the prevailing social issues and also prompt public discussion. In the 1990s genre films started to offer overly simplified characters with little or no backstory. They were characterized by little more than costumes and hairstyle. The films of the decade largely became purely entertainment, escapist stories that were made visually perfect with digital effects and post-production doctoring, but this was all at the expense of the story.[241] *Godzilla* (1998), *The Phantom Menace* (1999) and *Armageddon* (1998) were among the movies that highlighted new technological inventions. The major studios' blockbuster productions mixed genres in their efforts to bring something new and entertaining to the large nonspecified target audience.[242] For example, films released in this decade mixed action-adventure with comedy, romance, drama or science fiction, or anything that would keep mass audiences entertained.

In its pursuit of profit, the film industry looked for success in the profitable films of the past decades.[243] As a result, Hollywood still drew on the familiar basic thematic structures, plots and formulas. Genres were popular in the 1990s, just as they are today. Genre films continue to "answer, within structured fantasy, social, historical, psychological, or cultural issues within the culture that produces and consumes them."[244]

Hollywood waved good-bye to the Reaganite cinema denial of women and sexuality in action and action-adventure films. In President Clinton's America, the profit-conscious Hollywood producers responded to the changing gender roles. The movie industry incorporated the genre of melodrama — generally perceived as female-oriented — into action and action-adventure films in order to attract female viewers.[245] The financial success of the films that were testing the waters, in particular the success of *Die Hard* in the domestic and foreign market, kept a wife and children in the life of the action hero. The fight was now primarily personal and only secondarily for his country. As in the previous decades, the heroic male figure still championed the American capitalist system and ideology. The main female character was no longer just a sex object but a new, strong career woman. Yet even though strong, she still needed rescuing if she were the hero's romantic partner. Strong women also started to surface in films in their own right. *Aliens* had introduced a rare strong female lead in 1986 in Sigourney Weaver, and some strong female characters emerged also in the 1990s, for example, Sandra Bullock in the surprise hit *Speed* (1994). However, the main story still concerned the male hero in the post–Cold War world. Sons were absent in the films.[246] The father was the savior of his wife and his preteen and teenage daughters, rejecting the appeal and dangers of the outside world to these daughters. No son would compete with him for the role of man of the family.

The 1990s turned out to be the decade when terrorism hit the United States on its own soil. In 1993 the bombing of the World Trade Center by Islamic fundamentalist terrorists killed six and injured over a thousand. Two years later, 168 Americans died in Oklahoma City in a federal building bombing. The man behind the act was an American, Timothy McVeigh, a Persian Gulf war veteran. Immediately after the bombing, the news media focused on Arabs, America's favorite terrorists in media portrayals, as presumptive perpetrators of the act.[247] These highly publicized terrorist attacks on the U.S. mainland that caused civilian casualties and material destruction brought the fear of terrorism close to home, but the topic itself still did not top the foreign policy agenda.

Hollywood was not afraid to try to profit from fear and knowledge of terrorism as a threat to the U.S. that extensive news media coverage of the attacks had created. As the U.S. had struggled with not having a clear enemy since the end of the Cold War, the film industry had faced the same problem in its creation of believable screen villains. After terrorist attacks on U.S soil had brought the fear of terrorism inside the U.S. borders, Hollywood was able to capitalize on real world events in its productions. The industry continued its production of films on terrorism but now updated its villains and heroes to better reflect the domestic and international arena of the 1990s. Several terrorist-themed films of the decade, such as *True Lies* (1994), *Air Force One* (1997), and *Face/Off* (1997), were among the decade's highest-grossing blockbusters.

Hollywood Villains

Conflicts make good stories, but abstract political concepts such as hegemony, deterrence, balance of power, sovereignty and nationalism do not.[248] Hollywood knows that a conflict, in the world of international relations or in everyday life, is exciting and can be turned into a profitable commodity if it is packaged right. The mainstream movie industry has translated conflicts between governments, opposing groups, armies and nations into conflicts between individual protagonists and antagonists. These screen conflicts invite viewers to identify with the characters who have to face these tense and exciting situations.[249] The conflicts of international relations have become Hollywood commodities that sell audiences stories about power battles. When looking at Hollywood depictions of domestic and international conflicts, the issues of race, ethnicity, gender and ideology come to focus. The Hollywood Other — the Hollywood outsider and enemy — is traditionally an outsider on the basis of race, ethnicity or gender, while the traditional political Hollywood enemy can be found in the ideological circles of communism and fascism. Both groups present values different from those held by the traditional protagonist: the white male Christian Anglo-Saxon American.

Hollywood's close ally, the State Department, criticized early on stereotyping by Hollywood. According to Trumpbour, although the State Department was content with the advertising of American products that Hollywood films effectively did around the world, at the same time foreign critics' concerns did not go unnoticed. Trumpbour cites a 1929 comment by "Henry S. Villard, a senior figure in the State Department's Office of the Economic Adviser":

> The French are resentful that their nationals are so often pictured as immoral, the Spanish and Italians that they are so frequently villains, the English that they are snobs, etc. The sensitiveness of the Latin temperament to constant tactless allusions of this kind has found vigorous expression on several occasions in Spain, Brazil, Mexico, and Costa Rica. The latter country in fact has deemed it necessary to legislate against the exhibition of films which might give rise to demonstrations or outbursts of national feeling.[250]

Villard himself was not convinced that the global distribution of American films was good for the country's image. He saw it possible that Hollywood's gangster and crime films might damage America's reputation. In his view, film producers were completely unaware of the false propaganda they were spreading because their only concern was the financial success of their films.[251]

One of the countries to complain about Hollywood images of its citizens was Mexico. Hollywood borrowed from popular literature and editorial cartoons an image known as "the greaser" when the film industry started to depict Latin Americans, in particular Mexicans, in films for the first time. The greaser was a Latino who would rob, rape and kill. When Mexico protested this negative portrayal and threatened a film boycott, Hollywood did not want to lose a market. Instead, it sent the greaser packing. Furthermore, the U.S. needed all the help possible in World War II, so the country could not bear to alienate potential allies. As a result, Hollywood introduced a new educated Latin American, a more sympathetic character to its big northern neighbor.[252] Although the negative greaser stereotype disappeared, another negative Latino portrayal emerged in the 1980s. Latino violence and drug dealers found their way onto the big screen to compete with the number-one screen immigrant criminals, Italian-Americans. *The Godfather* series and other Mafia movies met competition from Latino criminals.[253]

On the domestic front Hollywood did not perform any better. A large domestic minority, African Americans, got harsh treatment from filmmakers. In the pre–World War II era of segregation and racism, Hollywood portrayed African Americans as simple-minded, lazy, fun-loving and ignorant Sambos. In the depictions of the old South, patriarchal white plantation owners and southern belles were accompanied by their loyal, ignorant slaves. In the 1930s Hollywood started to tone down the portrayal of the simple-minded Sambo, who disappeared by the World War II years when the country was trying to pull together for the war effort. The participation of African Americans in the war, revelations of Hitler's atrocities, demands to end racism and segregation, and the shift towards civil rights after World War II in America denied Hollywood the return to a crude black stereotype.[254] However, even in later commercial films that portray slavery, the norm has been to show reassuring images of loyal and servile blacks who are dependent on their white masters.[255] As American society tackled the issue of racism, black Americans, mainly men, started to find work in Hollywood in strong roles that addressed the issues of racism, inequality and prejudices.[256] Sidney Poitier, for example, starred in big-production films in the late 1960s and in the 1970s. He appealed to both black and white audiences, but the main roles still went primarily to white actors.

In the late 1960s and early 1970s Hollywood was convinced by audience statistics that there was a paying black audience for films starring African American actors. The film industry began to produce inexpensive action films starring black actors. The films targeted lower- and middle-class African American viewers in urban areas. Although these films mostly targeted African Americans, at times even touching upon the concerns of the target group, they were still primarily only a black rewrite of the traditional white stories, plots and characters. The films were exploiting an era in American history and thus became known as "blaxploitation" films.[257]

History shows that Hollywood has largely avoided casting African American and other minority actors as protagonists in big-production films. It is still hard for non-white actors to land a starring role in a Hollywood production due to "[C]ommercial potential, image and institutional racism."[258] Tom Long explains that actors of color find starring roles inaccessible due to producers' perception that they are not bankable stars (posing financial risks to the studio), as well as due to film decision-makers' own white world and the suspicion that the largely white American majority is not receptive to non-white actors in serious drama. African Americans, Asian Americans, Latinos and other non-white actors succeed easier in the music business in which the primary content is sound. On the big screen they have succeeded best in comedy.[259] Todd Boyd, a critical studies professor at the University of Southern California, argues in an interview with Long that "[T]here's a long tradition of African Americans performing for the amusement of white audiences.... Comedies are much less threatening. It's easy to laugh at something. By laughing at it, you potentially minimize it. Drama represents the opposite of that."[260] For example, one of the biggest African American stars of the early 21st century, Will Smith, made it eventually to the big commercial film productions through his commercial success in music and TV comedy. His high TV ratings and box office accomplishments in comedy and action films gave him true film star status, finally allowing him also to star in big-production drama films. In 2008 the movie exhibitors voted him in the 77th annual Quigley Publishing Company's poll as the star who made the most money at the box office. He was only the second African American actor to claim the top spot, after Sidney Poitier's historical top position exactly forty years earlier.

Native Americans are even more lacking in screen representations than are African Americans. For most viewers Native Americans are mostly familiar from Western films, although Native Americans did not usually play themselves on the big screen — white actors filled these roles. Native Americans were typically stereotyped in the Western film genre as evil and sadistic characters. Some rare Hollywood films have depicted Native Americans as noble savages but a much more common Hollywood image has been the bloodthirsty and crazed Indian chief.[261]

Also the new immigrants of the early 20th century became targets in Hollywood. Immigrants from Eastern and Southern Europe, Asia and Latin America worried white Anglo-Saxon Americans because of their skin color and, in some cases, their unfamiliar religion. Film images of European immigrants who had similar skin tones to those of white Anglo-Saxon Americans were mostly positive while Latin American characters, as mentioned above, were depicted as criminals. While pride in cultural pluralism in the U.S. has improved the image of different ethnic and racial groups since the 1960s, crime has stayed an essential content ingredient in the movies which depict Italian-Americans, Latinos and Asian Americans. Asian immigrants faced deep suspicion in American society to the point that they experienced racial discrimination which was regulated by laws at the beginning of the 20th century and later, during World War II.[262]

One of the most vilified and stereotyped groups in Hollywood is Arabs.[263] Gregg points out that "Western popular culture has, on the whole and over many years, done much to demonize Arabs and Islam."[264] In Shaheen's view the Hollywood image of Arabs is similar to the depiction of Jews in Nazi propaganda films in Nazi Germany. In his study of over 900 Hollywood films that depict Arabs, Shaheen concludes that the Hollywood portrayal of Arabs has been distorted, and the industry has been dehumanizing Arabs since the emergence of film:

> Seen through Hollywood's distorted lenses, Arabs look different and threatening. Projected along racial and religious lines, the stereotypes are deeply ingrained in American cinema. From 1896 until today, filmmakers have collectively indicted all Arabs as Public Enemy #1—brutal, heartless, uncivilized religious fanatics and money-mad cultural "others" bent on terrorizing civilized Westerners, especially Christians and Jews.... What is an Arab? In countless films, Hollywood alleges the answer: Arabs are brute murderers, sleazy rapists, religious fanatics, oil-rich dimwits, and abusers of women.[265]

Islam is the fastest growing religion in the U.S. Shaheen estimated the U.S. Muslim population to be between six and eight million. The Pew Forum on Religion & Public Life estimated the number to be 2.6 million in 2010, and reach 6.2 million by 2030.[266] Shaheen points out that it is typical for Hollywood films to mistreat the religion of Islam. Films often show Arabs praying and then quickly cut to Arabs shooting and killing Americans and other Westerners. Further misunderstanding is added by filmmakers' lack of knowledge of Arabic. Shaheen explains that the world *Allah* is an Arabic word that refers to god of *any* religion, including Christianity. In Hollywood films the word *Allah* is used to refer only to the Islamic god. Furthermore, as Karim Karim points out, not all Arabs are Muslims, and not all Muslims are Arabs.[267] There are 22 Arab and 57 Muslim countries in the world,[268] but Hollywood films have had a hard time identifying any singular Arab or Muslim country. Rather, mainstream commercial films throw the Arab and Muslim words together, and by that action add to the lack of knowledge in the Western world of the Arab world, Muslim countries and different branches of Islam.

According to a *New York Times* article by Rick Lyman, published soon after the September 11, 2001, attacks, Hollywood had tried to be sensitive in its portrayal of villains in the pre-9/11 era. For some fifteen years before the 9/11 terrorist attacks the film industry had consciously tried to avoid negative stereotyping of any ethnic or racial group. As a response to accusations of bias and stereotyping, Hollywood has at times drawn the hero's sidekick from the same ethnic group as the enemies.[269] However, while Hollywood may have occasionally granted the protagonist a sidekick from an American minority or even a foreigner, a more common Hollywood tradition has been to make the sidekick give his or her life for the American hero.[270] Lyman's article quotes Robert Sklar, a film historian at New York University, explaining:

> People are so much more attuned to issues of racism today than they were after Pearl Harbor.... That's why one of the big questions about movies and television in recent years has been, because

> of race, How do you represent the villains? ... Bad guys in movies in recent years have been evil white guys, suggesting a kind of turncoat or traitor figure, as opposed to an enemy from outside.[271]

The September 11, 2001, attacks posed a dilemma to Hollywood. The industry had to ponder whether it could use in a fictional film an Islamic fundamentalist Arab terrorist drawn from real life scenarios while somehow avoiding the stereotyping of a whole ethnic or religious group.[272] At the same time, Hollywood could not escape international events and politics if it were to stay current or ahead of the times in its film portrayals.

While the events of September 11, 2001, were a shock to the world, the images were still somehow familiar to film audiences from Hollywood film creations. Action and action-adventure films have brought to film viewers high-rise explosions, airline hijackings and bombings. Hollywood films imitate reality and draw ideas from real events, but ironically, those who aim to destroy or hurt the U.S. have used fictional films as training. For example, *The 9/11 Commission Report* tells that the training of some of the 9/11 terrorists included the watching of films that portray hijackings.

The Hollywood film industry has long been expert in the creation of fictional destruction, violence and loss of life. The U.S. has an entertainment industry which makes its consumers experts on violence and makes violence as American as apple pie. The Federal Communications Commission (FCC) estimates that by the time an American child leaves elementary school, the child's television viewing has exposed her or him, on average, to some 8,000 murders and 100,000 acts of violence.[273] Violence is an essential ingredient of action-adventure films. With the arrival of special effects, a violent death in most gruesome and creative ways has become an inescapable part of action-adventure movies. A brief overview of the history of screen violence helps us to understand how violence is portrayed in the films this book analyzes.

Screen Violence

Watching violence on movie screens and on television has been a popular form of entertainment in American culture since the emergence of film.[274] As Stephen Prince puts it: "popular film and culture, in general, exhibit a fascination with the spectacle and pleasure of violence."[275] That fascination has long roots. Violence has been a topic in films for well over a hundred years. One of the first violent film sequences was an 1895 film, *The Execution of Mary, Queen of Scots*, that depicted the beheading of Mary, Queen of Scots.[276] In the United States one of the first films, *The Great Train Robbery* (1903), portrays a person being thrown out of a moving train and later climaxes in the killing of the train robbers.

Hollywood has endured growing pains while learning how to portray violent film content and how to kill on the big screen in such a way that American viewers would not question the content. Domestic film audiences and courts have disagreed with Hollywood's view of what is acceptable on the big screen. In 1915 the U.S. Supreme Court ruled that freedom of speech does not apply to movies, and therefore censorship of movie content was allowed in the United States. The constitutional protection of the First Amendment was not applied to films until 1952, when the Court extended the umbrella of freedom of expression to films.[277]

In the 1910s and 1920s American audiences protested against movie violence. A variety of groups, from citizens' committees to state agencies, wanted to censor films with violent content.[278] Film producers took quick defensive steps as a reaction to several early 1920s Hollywood scandals: accusations of murder and rape leveled at comedy star Fatty Arbuckle, the drug overdose death of actor Wallace Reid, and the murder of director William Desmond

Taylor. In order to prevent external efforts to regulate Hollywood, the film industry created a self-regulatory organization, the Motion Picture Producers and Distributors of America (MPPDA) in 1922. The man they chose to run the organization was William H. Hays, "Warren Harding's Postmaster General and former Chairman of the Republican National Committee."[279] In 1927 the Hays office, in cooperation with movie studio representatives, introduced a list of "The Don'ts and Be Carefuls," which gave Hollywood producers thirty-six guidelines on what kinds of films they could produce.[280] But the movie industry did not enforce The Don'ts and Be Carefuls, which eventually led to a backlash from audiences, in particular from religious organizations.

The 1930 Production Code

The movie industry reacted in self-defense to protests against movie violence. In 1930 it passed the Production Code which in detail listed the type of movie content that would be allowed in Hollywood productions.[281] the Code had its roots in the Catholic Church doctrine, which greatly influenced how the Code approached the topic of showing violent and sexual content on the screen. In general, the Code regulated that the industry should "enforce a strict morality and healthy-mindedness in the movies."[282] The Production Code, created by the Association of Motion Picture Producers, Inc., and the Motion Picture Producers and Distributors of America, Inc., dictated in detail how, for example, crimes, sexual behavior, profanity, religion, and repellent subjects could be portrayed. Receiving special attention were crimes, evil, sins, and any other type of wrongdoing. Films were to portray these topics in such a way that viewers would not sympathize with them or imitate them.[283] As for crime and violence, the Code detailed that "brutal killings must not be shown in detail" and "murder must not be glamorized so as to inspire imitation."[284] Furthermore, the Code directed the use of firearms to be kept to the minimum, a regulation whose limits especially gangster films often tried to stretch.[285] The Code had both followers as well as sidesteppers in Hollywood.[286]

In the early 1930s the effects of brutal and vicious film violence were studied for the first time systematically, using social science methodologies. These studies, by the Payne Fund Institute, examined delinquency and sexuality, and the effects of such film content on children and the youth. Although gangster films did not portray violence or sexual content in graphic detail, their violent content was under a microscope. The studies were inconclusive and suggested only limited effects, but they still manifested the fear that existed in society about the influence of screen violence on viewers'—in particular on younger viewers'—behavior.[287]

As a response to the gangster films and sex comedies that did challenge or ignore the Code but were popular among audiences, the Catholic Bishops of the United States created in 1934 the Legion of Decency, an organization to counter what they viewed as indecency in Hollywood films. The organization declared it would launch a national boycott of films if Hollywood did not clean up its productions.[288] That same year the film industry founded the Production Code Administration (PCA), to ensure that the studios would follow the Code in detail. In the new code era Hollywood studios were to give their scripts and finished films to the agency for its approval. If necessary, the studios would make changes in order to receive the PCA's approval. As a result of these steps, movies with violent, criminal and sexual themes were under strict control until the late 1960s.[289] In Prince's view the Production Code and its strict hold on the American screen was the reason why extreme portrayals of violence, in his words, "ultraviolence," did not gain a footing in Hollywood productions.[290]

The 1968 Movie Ratings Classification System

The first to push against the Code's restrictions were some independent film productions in the 1950s. The majors would not follow the example until a decade later. In the late 1960s several films by Hollywood's major studios eroded the strict Production Code, which eventually lead to its dismantlement. The 1966 Warner Bros. film *Who's Afraid of Virginia Woolf*, starring Elizabeth Taylor and Richard Burton, introduced vulgar language that mainstream Hollywood films had not scripted in decades. The actors' lines included words such as "*goddam, son of a bitch, bastard, screw you*, and *up yours*."[291] Instead of disapproving the film that clearly tried the Code's limits, the PCA revised the Code by adding a new film category: "Suggested for Mature Audiences." Also revised that year were the Production Code's recommendations on how to portray murders and other killings on the big screen. The new recommendation to filmmakers was to "exercise discretion in showing the taking of human life."[292]

In late 1968 the old, strict Production Code was buried with the arrival of a new ratings system that the Motion Picture Association of America administered with the National Association of Theater Owners. Films were rated according to the suitability of the content to different age groups.[293] The new system reflected the liberal views and social movements of the time as well as changes in culture. General atmosphere in society was now more tolerant also of film content.[294] Belton explains that a film with a G rating meant that the "film was suitable for general audiences of all ages; an "M" (which was subsequently changed to "PG") identified a film as suitable for mature audiences (that is, adults), and subject to parental guidance for children's viewing. R-rated films were for adult audiences, "children younger than the age of sixteen (later changed to seventeen) were admitted only if accompanied by an adult."[295] The films that got an X rating were restricted without exception to audiences over sixteen (the age limit later changed to seventeen). A new category was added in 1984 with the release of *Indiana Jones and the Temple of Doom*. The film's violent content was considered too extreme for children under thirteen years of age, and therefore the film got the new PG-13 rating, distinct from the "general audiences" PG rating. The most recent addition, NC-17 (no children under 17), was made six years later, to help audiences to "distinguish 'serious' films with mature themes from X-rated pornographic films."[296] Today the Motion Picture Association of America lists the classification scheme as

G General Audiences — all ages admitted

PG Parental Guidance Suggested — some material may not be suitable for children

PG-13 Parents Strongly Cautioned — some material may be inappropriate for children under 13

R Restricted — under 17 requires accompanying parent or adult guardian

NC-17 — No one 17 and Under Admitted[297]

Reemergence of Violent Film Content

Since the relaxation of the Production Code in 1966 and the arrival of the 1968 ratings classification, violence has become a persistent theme in Hollywood films. The MPAA strongly encouraged studios to catch up with the times by making films that would be relevant in the modern era and not just portray old-fashioned Production Code views as American films had done since the 1930s. Now that studios were able to produce films specifically for adult audiences, they could depict extreme violence, sexual content and profanity. Hollywood was also trying hard to keep up with the values and views of Americans from 16 to 24 years old, who were responsible for 48 percent of the ticket sales in the country. Furthermore, the ongoing televised war in Vietnam was bringing brutal images directly into American living rooms, as were domestic political murders and violence. Hollywood had to beat the images the real world was producing if the industry wanted to be able to offer something new to American viewers.[298]

The year 1967 proved to be the year to do exactly that. United Artists distributed that year Sergio Leone's *Dollars* trilogy of Westerns made in Italy. Two American films, Robert Aldrich's *The Dirty Dozen* and Arthur Penn's *Bonnie and Clyde*, accompanied Leone's films. These films portrayed extreme violence, brutality and lots of blood. Each film was a box office hit, *The Dirty Dozen* being the year's top film.[299] MPAA President Jack Valenti defended the new violent Hollywood images. When speaking before the National Commission on the Causes and Prevention of Violence in 1968 he stated that films should be free of constraints but responsible in their content. He stressed that

> the essential point becomes not the inclusion of violence or the quantity of it or the nature of it but really how it is treated, how it is handled.
>
> I don't have to tell you — I think it's almost a cliché to say — that throughout the whole history of drama, violence is a common ingredient. That goes without saying. The very nature of drama is conflict. New plays and old plays, ancient chants, litanies, the epic poems, and traditional literature of practically every country and civilization that you can name are rooted in violence because man's whole existence has been a story of conflict.
>
> And I might add that we know, even to this very hour, that all civilizations have been alternately horrified and fascinated by death and violence. I didn't make it that way. That's the way it is.[300]

Prince credits Arthur Penn as a pioneer of the new Hollywood violence. Penn borrowed filming techniques from Akira Kurosawa's 1954 *Seven Samurai*, introducing to the American film production the use of several cameras simultaneously, the new method contrasting the traditional one camera filming. Penn also used montage editing, that is, the use of several short shots, as well as slow motion and so-called squibs. It was Penn's 1967 bloody *Bonnie and Clyde* that introduced a new way of showing on the screen how bullets hit human flesh. The squibs, which became an industry standard, "were condoms filled with fake blood, concealed within an actor's clothing, and wired to detonate so as to simulate bullet strikes and blood sprays."[301] They changed the film history of screen violence, which until 1967 had been clean and unreal, but now became graphic in showing the bloodbath of killings. Penn, and Sam Peckinpah with his *The Wild Bunch* (1969), were among the first to set stylistic standards for ultraviolent films. They used montage effectively, "making violence balletic, a dance of death."[302] Penn and Peckinpah used violence as social critique and for the purpose of deglamorizing it. Their followers have too often been guilty of exaggerating violent content to the point of making it extremely graphic, for example, by using special effects and makeup, but without a message or purpose for that ultraviolence.[303]

Devin McKinney considers the James Bond films as the origin of "disconnected, uncommitted movie mayhem ... that came of age with the sociopathic crime dramas of the early 1970s and served the reactionary agenda of the 1980s."[304] In his view this development reflected the modern era of violence at a global level. The Bond films introduced screen violence that existed only for the sake of violence, not for taking the plot forward. While the Bond films often combine violence with comedy, today's screen violence is more brutal, even if it adds comedy to the mix. Movie violence has become so common that it is now understood as a screen norm.[305]

Hollywood is a master at understanding the prevailing values in American society. In the late 1960s the MPAA encouraged filmmakers to push the limits in the name of new American values, but in the 1980s, with the return to more conservative values, the organization gave in to government and watchdog groups' pressure to limit film violence. The MPAA's Jack Valenti commented on the organization's new stand: "The political climate in this country is shifting to the right, and that means more conservative attitudes toward sex and violence. But a lot of creative people are still living in the world of revolution."[306] However, if one looks at the content of 1980s action-adventure films, the limitations seem to have largely ignored violence against the Third World and U.S. enemies.

Today's Hollywood has come a long way from the first big studio films with violent content. The technological advances since the 1980s have made it possible to kill movie villains and victims in hundreds of different ways and with lots of blood. Digital expansion and computerized special effects have become everyday tools, offering viewers explosions, decapitations, shootings, and even atomic explosions, often killing hundreds, if not thousands, of people in a single film.

Weak Violence versus Strong Violence

European and American films approach the portrayal of violence quite differently. European films are more likely to depict violence in terms that make the viewer understand the finality of death. In contrast, American films tend to reduce a victim of fatal violence to a thing that has to be cleared out of the way, or which moves the plot forward but does not raise deep feelings among audience members. The viewer does not become emotionally involved with the victims of film violence.[307] McKinney calls violence that exists only to move the plot forward but makes no connection with the viewer "weak violence." In contrast, "strong violence" succeeds in delivering the true mortality of death. Viewers feel for the victims.[308]

Film viewers are usually left with little choice to interpret the deaths and violence they see on the screen in any other way but how the film they are watching portrays it. Films that effectively portray violence and death invite viewers to identify with the film characters by letting viewers learn more about these characters, and by having a meaning for the portrayed violence. For example, in Neil Jordan's *The Crying Game* (1992),[309] "the bloodshed has subtext, [it] carries the weight of fear and mystery, and is piercing enough to shoot past the crap violence we all drink like beer."[310] Strong film violence leaves viewers touched, thinking about what they have seen, and even possibly changes their moral positions, while weak violence is only a film device to which viewers will not give a second thought after they have seen it on the screen. In McKinney's words, "without emotional response, film violence trades flesh and blood for hamburger and ketchup."[311] The films that depict weak violence take an easy way out because they do not commit to portraying the reality of death and violence. Instead of delivering that reality to their audiences "they want to look at horror, but they don't want to feel it, smell it, take the chance of getting sick from it. By insuring itself in this way, a violent film can't help but resist a viewer's emotional investment, which, frustrated, displaces itself onto an academic admiration of style."[312]

One trademark of today's violence is the lack of guilt when film characters kill.[313] This applies in particular to action-adventure films. While a film hero is growing the pile of the people he has killed, viewers rarely, if ever, get to see the pain or suffering of the victims who are at the receiving end of the hero's violent acts. This is not far from news images of war, especially if the U.S. is involved in aggressive military actions. TV presents images of U.S. military weapons but rarely of the targets of those weapons. Local citizens or American soldiers who have been killed or injured, and the pain of those left behind, would create images that would remind viewers of the nasty business of people killing people, and therefore negatively affect advertising profits. This approach was familiar, for example, during the Persian Gulf War and the later U.S. invasion of Iraq.

Films and news media sanitize war and violence for viewers' consumption. Violence is a sanitized corporate media commodity that is distributed for a profit. A commodity that could make a viewer to stop to think about violence and its impact might make the viewer not want to buy similar products in the future. That would simply be bad business. However, extraordinary events such as the 9/11 attacks can boost profits but also affect them negatively. For example, TV networks dropped advertising when covering the 9/11 terrorist attacks and therefore lost advertising revenue, yet newspapers sold out on the following day.

It has now become more important for films to have violent content per se than for that violence to stand for something. Today's film violence is too often senseless, without a narrative purpose.[314] Screen violence has become such a routine, in particular in action and action-adventure films, that it lacks any social commentary. The film industry treats violence as a special effect, a tool that is a shortcut to success at the box office.[315] While violence is an effective form of art, the industry uses it commercially, "as a spectacle, an easy way to get to the viewer emotionally and to solve narrative issues."[316]

Screen violence in action and action-adventure films since the 1980s has often been weak violence. Films use violence as a special effect for the sole purpose of entertainment. Hollywood has often placed foreigners or ethnic and ideological minorities as the targets of that firepower. Screen violence has thrived as a profitable action-adventure film ingredient, but simultaneous, massively violent real-life attacks put it on hold on September 11, 2001, when TV news images of real violence became strong violence. News audiences around the world felt the emotional impact of the victims' deaths and suffering. Although international terrorist attacks were familiar from news headlines and Hollywood films, the phenomenon of terrorism itself, as well as terrorist attacks, had been covered only superficially and sensationally, leaving audiences unprepared for the reality of international terrorism, in particular international terrorism on U.S. soil.

Like news, Hollywood films are products that the industry manufactures for a profit. American films dominate the global film market for political, economic and historical reasons. In the aftermath of the First World War, American film studios were able to gain the upper hand in the world market with the help of the U.S. government. Films were not only to create a profit for the industry but also to create goodwill for the U.S., be bearers of the American flag, and create new markets for U.S. commodities. With the end of the Cold War the global market burst open to Hollywood films, creating new markets that the industry eagerly embraced. In the 1990s the foreign market started to create more revenue than the domestic one.

The big production and distribution companies, the so-called majors that dominate the film business, have tried to protect their investments by producing films that would be most certain to recoup the costs and earn a profit in the global market. As a result, Hollywood saw the birth of blockbuster films, that is, films with high budgets, high marketing and advertising costs, and with bankable actors and directors. The commercial success of the first such film, Universal's *Jaws* (1975), directed by Steven Spielberg, convinced the film industry to produce more films that would be released simultaneously across the country and have a nationwide advertising campaign. As a result of the industry's constant search for the highest profit, Hollywood has produced films that repeat the formulas of earlier films, and have offered audiences predictable storylines and sequels as studios have tried to repeat the financial success of their previous box office hits. Film genres with their traditional and repeated formats have traditionally conformed to the prevailing social norms and order, and supported the status quo. An essential part of each film genre is the classical Hollywood cinema blockbusters, which divides a film into a three-act structure and focuses on a conflict between the film's protagonist and antagonist. Action-adventure films, which emerged in the 1980s as blockbusters, follow the classical three-act structure, as well as the genre's own traditions and formats, when seeking success at the box office.

Throughout history Hollywood films, including action-adventure films, have drawn story ideas from reality. In its search for a profitable film commodity, Hollywood has over the years distorted history, supported and undermined U.S. policies, as well as stereotyped different national, racial, ethnic and religious groups in its films. Violence and destruction are familiar Hollywood film ingredients. The industry set self-imposed limits on film content, including screen violence, in the 1930s with the arrival of the Production Code. It changed course quickly in the late 1960s as society's norms became more flexible. The movie industry introduced a new ratings classification system which categorized films according to their content, as well as according to their perceived suitability to different audiences.

Violence is a familiar film ingredient, especially in action-adventure films. Villains in these films are usually targets of weak film violence, which leaves the viewer cheering for the death of the villain rather than mourning his brutal death. In contrast, strong violence makes the viewer think about the reality of suffering of those who are victims of violence. Action-adventure films offer spectacular violence with the help of special effects, but the deaths they portray are full of weak violence, unless the target of violence is the hero or someone on his side.

Like film violence, terrorism is about creating violent spectacles for large audiences. The next two parts of this book address both real-life and film terrorism. Part II discusses films that were released before the end of the Cold War. As communism started to collapse in Europe, new U.S. foreign policy and film threats started to emerge. Part III analyzes Hollywood films from the last moments of the Cold War era until the 9/11 terrorist attacks against the United States. Each of the sixteen films discussed has international terrorism as the film's major theme and was in the annual top fifty domestic box office the year the film was released. Only films that portray events that could take place in real life are included; science fiction films and films that rely on possible medical inventions of the future are not included in the data. Also, any film that only refers to international terrorism but does not draw the film's central conflict from it is excluded.

Part II. The Hollywood Terrorist and the Cold War Red Terror Network

In the 1980s international terrorism threatened the U.S. outside the country's borders. Hollywood was the first to bring large international terrorist media spectacles onto U.S. soil. Each news headline about real-life terrorist incidents acted as free advertising for the movies on the topic. News stories were promises of what film stories could provide in the comfort and safety of movie and home theaters: thrilling rides, but with happy Hollywood endings. The American hero would always catch the foreign villains and usually kill them in a brutal manner. It was safe for Hollywood to bring fictional terrorism to the U.S. since the real international terrorism that killed and mutilated people and destroyed property was taking place far away from the U.S. Viewers of fictional terrorism could safely munch on popcorn and sip soft drinks in movie theaters while "witnessing" the latest attack on the U.S. and the hero's successful rescue mission that restores order.

The Reagan Years: Middle Eastern and Soviet Communist Threats

Middle Eastern terrorism received extensive media coverage after the Iran hostage crisis, but according to the State Department's annual reports on international terrorism, most anti–U.S. attacks took place in Latin America. Throughout the 1980s about half of all anti–U.S. attacks took place in that region, often targeting American business interests. The incidents rarely had human casualties. They were often a spillover from different countries' internal political conflicts. The acts provided little exciting television news footage, in contrast to attacks in Western Europe and the Middle East which were the regions with the biggest number of destructive acts of international terrorism.

In Hollywood the Reagan era was the decade of muscled one-man war machines whose physique alone seemed enough to beat a much larger enemy. These limited-vocabulary heroes such as Sylvester Stallone, Arnold Schwarzenegger, Chuck Norris and others practiced on the big screen what President Reagan was preaching in the White House. The use of extensive power was the answer to the country's adversaries' actions. Negotiations were for sissies, whether the U.S. was dealing with terrorists or the world's other superpower. It was time to flex some muscle both in Washington and on the big screen. Action and the emerging ultra-high-budget action-adventure films of the Reaganite cinema era, namely the film years under President Reagan and also some under President George H. W. Bush, focused on patriotic themes, on the portrayal of muscular men and interracial harmony, and on close son-father relationships while women were often conspicuous only by their absence.[1]

The Cold War was based on the fear that the country's national security was under a constant threat. Stressing this message to the citizens, the government was able to build a large military establishment.[2] The country's overall defense costs rose drastically under Reagan.[3] Critical views were silenced in the climate of a constantly hovering security threat.

The CIA had an important role in the fight against perceived threats. The agency was considered to be a paramilitary arm of the U.S. government, "entrusted with a non-accountable budget and a mandate to conduct 'covert operations.' These undertakings often involved terrorism of the most primitive sort — assassination plots against foreign leaders or support for violent takeovers of constitutional governments."[4] The CIA also had a role in failed counterterrorism efforts, caused by its inefficient intelligence gathering. In addition, in the 1970s and the 1980s the CIA's questionable recruiting methods and actions caused a public expression of anger against the intelligence agency. As a result, the CIA changed its recruiting to the point that agents could no longer recruit sources whose backgrounds raised questions, a practice which directly influenced the agency's counterterrorism efforts and activities.[5] While the American public did not always agree with the CIA's harsh methods, viewers accepted and even expected brutal methods on the big screen.

Dozens of films on international terrorism saw the daylight in the 1980s. Hollywood was following the times, emphasizing the Reagan policy of peace through strength with a large weapons arsenal. Fictional films drew their plotlines from the hot spots of real-life international terrorism in the Middle East, Latin America and Western Europe. In particular, developments in the Middle East, specifically in Lebanon, gave material to Hollywood scriptwriters. The Israeli invasion of Lebanon, strong Hezbollah presence in the country with the support of Iran, and Hezbollah kidnappings, hijackings and bombings of Western, in particular American, targets were a creative ground for movie ideas. Also, the presence of an international peace force in Lebanon, and the withdrawal of U.S. forces from Lebanon after the 1983 car bombing of the U.S. marine barracks, brought the torn country onto the big screen. In addition, the unresolved issue of Palestine made news headlines and provided script material to Hollywood in the 1980s.

The U.S. government had brought American domestic terrorist organizations largely under control by the 1980s, but this was not the case in Western Europe. In the 1970s and early 1980s, active Western European organizations included the Red Brigades (Italy), Direct Action (France), the Red Army Faction aka the Baader-Meinhof Group (West Germany), and the Provisional Irish Republican Army aka PIRA (the U.K., in particular Northern Ireland). Several of these organizations, particularly those with leftist agendas in West Germany, France, Belgium, Spain, Portugal and Greece, combined their forces in 1984 and had a common set of targets related to NATO that they attacked.[6] Another form of cooperation was taking place in the Middle East where the PLO was offering training to guerrilla movements from around the world at camps in Jordan, Lebanon, and Yemen from the late 1960s at least until the early 1980s, if not longer. Some of the participants included terrorists from the Baader-Meinhof Group, the PIRA, and the Japanese Red Army.[7]

Reaganite Cinema Films on International Terrorism

Nighthawks (1981) was an early example of Euroterrorist films. The film stars Sylvester Stallone as a New York City detective and Rutger Hauer as Wulfgar, an extreme left-wing

The Hollywood terrorist and real-life terrorists have found a target in the United Nations. In *Nighthawks* (1981, Universal) an extremist left-wing Euroterrorist arrived in New York City to target the organization, as did real-life fundamentalist Islamic terrorists twelve years later. On a tip from an informer in June 1993 the FBI was able to preempt attacks on New York City landmarks, including the United Nations building, shown here.

Euroterrorist. The film's terrorism expert voices what al Qaeda realized twenty years later: terrorists come to New York City to obtain worldwide publicity. Furthermore, Wulfgar was ahead of his time in targeting the United States, Wall Street, and the United Nations. Terrorists with fundamentalist militant views of Islam found New York City landmarks as targets in the 1990s. *Nighthawks* portrayed a mixture of methods that terrorists were using in Western Europe, for example, department store and other limited bombings with advance warnings. In comparison to his one-man war machine roles later in the decade, Stallone plays in *Nighthawks* a more human hero who even has an important romantic relationship. The film borrowed ideas from reality and even predicted some targets, but it still reduced the terrorist's end fight to a traditional personal fight between the hero and the foreign terrorist. The film lost out in the box office to films that offered world politics to audiences in a more simplified and stereotyped propagandistic manner.

While the number of films on international terrorism was plenty, most of them did not reach the top fifty in domestic box office. It was not until the second Reagan administration that films about international terrorism started to climb to the top fifty list in the North American market. Under President Reagan five films which had international terrorism as their central theme made the top fifty.

The year 1985 provided the first two films on the list. *Invasion USA* (1985: #49) stars Chuck Norris as the protagonist, and portrays a direct Soviet communist threat in the United States. *Commando* (1985: #22), starring Arnold Schwarzenegger, depicts a former Central American dictator's attempt to force the hero to return him to power since the hero had been instrumental to the dictator's removal. The following year added to the list two more films, *Iron Eagle* (1986: #39) and *The Delta Force* (1986: #49), both drawing from Middle East–originated terrorist threats, in particular from state sponsorship of terrorism. In *Iron Eagle* an American high school student, played by Jason Gedrick, takes on a Libya-like fictional country, "Bilyad," a near anagram of Libya. *The Delta Force* introduces a heroic special forces unit which saves American hostages in Lebanon. Several other films of the decade that had terrorism themes also drew from Middle Eastern terrorism, for example, *Death Before Dishonor* (1987) and *The Little Drummer Girl* (1984), but with meager box office results. Films critical of the American anti-terrorism and anti-communism policies in Latin America, such as *Salvador* (1986) and *Missing* (1982), failed to attract large audiences.

The last top fifty film of the Reagan era, *Die Hard* (1988: #7), was already waving an eager good-bye to the disappearing Cold War, mostly leaving behind the Reagan-era fears. The film, starring Bruce Willis, took the fight into urban America and introduced to viewers a strong female character in the hero's wife, whom the hero saves from Euroterrorists' clutches.

The Reagan administration's threat scenarios and policies, including the focus on building a large weapons arsenal and using overpowering strength, are very much present in the first four films that made the top fifty list. *Invasion USA* as well as *Iron Eagle* and *The Delta Force* are picture-perfect examples of the Reaganite cinema films. *Commando* was a bit ahead of its times in mixing Reaganite cinema themes and portrayals with what became trademarks of 1990s action-adventure films: the hero's one-liners, a young daughter, and a romantic subplot with a strong female character. *Commando* showcases the Reaganite idea of the use of power and weapons at the expense of faceless Central American human targets but the film has more of a James Bond–style comedic approach than the other Reaganite cinema films.

The decade's last top fifty international-terrorism-themed film, *Die Hard*, reflected the changing times in the international arena and American society. The film took the fight into urban America, bringing to the center Euroterrorism, which Western European governments had successfully been able to reduce in real life by the end of the decade from the high mid–1980s attack numbers. Also, the foreign terrorist villain and the white Anglo-Saxon hero received makeovers, leaving in the dust the 1980s one-dimensional muscled war-machine heroes and the one-dimensional villains who were full of hatred for the hero and the United States. *Die Hard*'s hero, John McClane, was an updated version of Rambo as well as of the "mismatched pair" stars, such as in the *Lethal Weapon* series, which had emerged in the 1980s. Only echoes of the Cold War and the Reaganite cinema were present in *Die Hard*, which later received three sequels, the last one to date in the post–9/11 era.

The Cold War Red Terror Network

The U.S. understanding of international terrorism under President Reagan was formed according to the ideological framework of the Cold War. In addition to the threat of Middle Eastern organizations and state sponsors of terrorism, one of the most important incidents that influenced the U.S. understanding of and policies on international terrorism was the Soviet invasion of Afghanistan in 1979. It was accompanied by a fear that the Soviet Union would expand its communist reach into the Persian Gulf. In President Reagan's view his predecessors, who had trusted the Soviet Union and promoted détente, had put the national security at risk. For him the Soviet Union was the center of all unrest in the world. Reagan's policies reflected his views on the matter.[8]

For President Reagan communism was at the heart of international terrorism. The U.S. saw terrorism approaching the U.S. from Latin America with Soviet and Cuban assistance, and in the Middle East, moving towards the Persian Gulf from Afghanistan, with Soviet assistance. The State Department directly addressed the fear in its reports, seeing communist-linked terrorism emerging from Eastern Europe and having ties to the Middle East and Latin America. The U.S. and the communist Eastern bloc were similar in their approach to the help they gave to the groups that furthered their own interests. Both camps assisted in secret regimes that supported their political interests. The help was not public in order to avoid an international incident.[9]

Conservative forces in the country described the biggest terrorist threat to be a Soviet-led worldwide Red Terror Network. According to these thinkers, including Claire Sterling, the author of the 1981 *The Terror Network: The Secret War of International Terrorism*, the Soviet Union and its allies were either directly or indirectly supporting an international terrorist network.[10] Sterling's book promoted conservative policies in Latin America and the rest of the Third World. The Reagan administration's policies very much reflected these ideas. As a result of this fear, the U.S. government labeled groups as terrorists if they expressed any social or communist platforms.[11] This took place especially in Latin America in the case of the groups which were opposing the authoritarian governments that the U.S. was supporting. The U.S. saw insurgency and domestic and international terrorism problems especially in El Salvador, Guatemala, Chile, and Peru. The trend seemed unlikely to go away, given the region's unstable social, economic and political conditions. According to the State Department, most terrorist activity in the area showed links to Nicaragua and Cuba, and it appeared to target governments which were somehow connected to the U.S. The targets included, for example, private American businesses, American officials, and U.S. government installations.[12]

Further State Department documents produced under President Reagan supported the view of a Red Terror Network. In its 1986 *Patterns of Global Terrorism* report the State Department mentions, for example, that several Warsaw Pact countries "continued to provide weapons, training, and other support for a variety of terrorist groups."[13] The report continued:

> The Soviets and various East European states provide arms and training to a broad spectrum of anti–Western groups and "national liberation movements," many of whose members commit terrorist acts. Although the Soviet Union and its allies have sold arms directly to some groups, mostly Palestinians, most Soviet weapons sold or given to terrorist groups are provided by Third World Soviet clients, such as Libya.[14]

Furthermore, in the State Department's view, although the Soviet Union preferred to support groups that promoted revolutionary views, the communist giant did not really care what terrorists did as long as the country itself was not a target.

Edward S. Herman interprets the Reagan administration's Red Scare of the early 1980s as the administration's response to the heightened civil activism in America in the 1960s and 1970s.[15] In the 1980s, the U.S. was, for example, influencing the outcome of the civil war in El Salvador, where the Reagan administration fiercely supported the country's right-wing military junta, which governed with the help of death squads. According to Herman, the world saw the U.S. differently with the arrival of a new tenant in the White House:

> Claiming a new dedication to fighting "terrorism," this administration [the first Reagan administration] has rushed to the support of the world's leading terrorists, including the rulers of the most torture prone NSSs [National Security States] and assorted other right-wing governments with a marked proclivity to violence. In their turn, governments of Argentina, Chile, El Salvador, Guatemala, Israel and South Africa (among others), greeted the arrival of Reagan with enthusiasm. For some reason they felt that with his team in place any prior constraints on violence were no longer operative.[16]

Another thorn in the side of the Reagan administration was Nicaragua. In Reagan's view the Sandinista regime was trying to destabilize non–Marxist regimes in Central America by providing them with training, advice, and channels of arms and ammunition. In the 1980s Nicaragua was highlighted in State Department documents as a supporter of international terrorism. Nicaragua had been a safe haven not only to Central American but also to some Western European terrorists, such as the leftist Italian Red Brigades and separatist Spanish Basque ETA.[17] While the department documents paint Nicaragua as a center for Latin American guerrilla and terrorist groups, at the same time the 1985 report points out that it has only limited evidence that Nicaragua was directly involved in certain terrorist incidents.

In the 1980s the State Department emphasized that violence in Central America was largely due to social, economic and political turmoil. Both leftist and rightist groups relied on violence in order to gain ground in the political arena. Guatemala, Honduras, El Salvador, Colombia, Peru, Chile, Ecuador and Nicaragua had insurgents whose activities also threatened American interests at times, but with minor damage and casualties. The U.S. would be targeted as a protest against its political and commercial influence in the region, and also to garner international media coverage to local disputes.[18] However, while in the 1980s most of the world's anti–U.S. attacks took place in Latin America, the region's political violence was largely domestic in nature and not focused on the U.S.

The State Department saw the biggest threat in a possible ideological spillover. Cuba was a threat throughout the decade, listed annually by the State Department as a supporter of leftist revolutionaries and terrorists in Latin America. According to the department, Cuba provided a safe haven, training, guns, and funding to groups in, for example, El Salvador, Honduras and Colombia. The Cuban efforts were further promoted by the Soviet Union, which the State Department saw as a supporter of revolutionary violence and terrorist groups in Latin America in the communist giant's efforts to establish Soviet-friendly regimes. For example, the State Department's 1984 report points out that "[T]he Soviet Union clearly supports international terrorism, although — in contrast to Iran, Syria, and Libya — we have no evidence of the Soviets directly planning or orchestrating terrorist acts by Middle Eastern, West European, or Latin American groups."[19] The report continues to discuss the Soviet role in international terrorism, for example, to describe how the Soviet Union has a long history as a supporter of groups that the department has linked to terrorism. Over the years that support had extended from political support to funding and providing conventional weapons and military training. Also, some Soviet bloc countries, such as Bulgaria and Czechoslovakia, and a more independent Yugoslavia, are mentioned in the State Department's reports as having links to terrorist organizations and being providers of weapons and/or a safe haven.

Middle Eastern Spillover

Middle Eastern, in particular Palestinian, political violence emerged in the 1960s but the roots of the modern forms of that violence were in the creation of the independent Jewish state of Israel in 1948. Jewish groups had relied on violent acts in their opposition to the British rule and in their goal to establish an independent state of Israel in the area of Palestine. They succeeded in forcing Britain to hand over the issue of Palestine to the United Nations soon after the world organization's emergence. The UN divided the area into two future independent states, Israel and Palestine, but there were disagreements among different interested parties to the dispute about whether the plan was fair.

The creation of the sovereign Jewish state of Israel partially fulfilled the UN plan for the region: Palestinians were still without their own country after 1948. It is estimated that some 700,000 Palestinian refugees were forced out of Israel or left Israel on their own during the period 1947–1948. Israel and its neighboring Arab countries experienced the unresolved issue of Palestinian refugees and the absence of an independent Palestinian state in the form of violent acts by different Palestinian groups. The groups shared a common goal: the establishment of an independent state of Palestine and the erasure of Israel from the world map. Palestinians were not the only ones angered by the creation of the state of Israel. Its neighboring Arab states attacked the newly founded state, which successfully defended its independence. The success was largely due to the military support Israel had received and continued to receive from the U.S.[20]

The Arab nations founded the Palestine Liberation Organization (PLO) in 1964 at the Palestinian Congress in Cairo in order to have an umbrella organization for different Palestinian groups. The primary goal of the organization was the creation of an independent state of Palestine. The PLO considered Israel as a primary obstacle towards that goal.[21] After the 1967 Arab-Israeli War, militant groups took over the organization, bringing Yasser Arafat's Fatah organization and Arafat himself to the front. The PLO targeted Israel and Western states, as well as Arab states in the Middle East. As the organization's supporters the State Department listed countries such as Saudi Arabia, Kuwait, Jordan, the USSR, China, North Korea, some Eastern European countries, and some moderate Persian Gulf states. After severe international pressure, the PLO announced by the mid–1970s that it would limit its attacks in the future to attacks on Israel and the occupied territories. In the late 1980s the organization made a commitment to denouncing terrorism, which Arafat officially and publicly did in 1993.[22] The United States removed the PLO from its list of terrorist groups in 1996.

In the 1980s the spillover of Middle Eastern terrorism continued to grow. For example, in 1985 Western citizens were targeted in Western Europe. About half of the attacks took place in Greece, Cyprus and Italy, but others occurred in Belgium, Denmark, Malta, Sweden and Switzerland. A new trend in terrorism methods was emerging, whereby Middle Eastern terrorists in growing numbers identified unprotected targets in public places and innocent bystanders.[23] Western European countries were a favorite target because some had jailed Middle Eastern terrorists, and therefore terrorists would use their attacks to try to force governments to release them. Also in Western Europe, large Middle Eastern communities of students, expatriates and guest workers attracted terrorist recruiters. Immigrant neighborhoods could provide shelter, but they were also targets of repressive governments' attacks against their opponents. In the Middle East, Western targets are protected, but in the West that is not the case. Travel and access are easy in the West, which makes it easy to find public targets and gain big news headlines if an attack succeeds.[24] When the Middle East peace initiative that the PLO and Jordan had been promoting fell through, there was a clear drop in the number of terrorist attacks in Western Europe in 1986 when the forces against the initiative were less active.[25]

There were several spectacular attacks in the 1980s that grabbed media attention and highlighted the spillover of Middle Eastern terrorism. They included the 1985 hijacking of the Italian cruise ship *Achille Lauro* as it departed Alexandria, Egypt, by the Palestine Liberation

Front; the 1985 hijacking of an Egyptian jetliner from Athens to Malta; the late December 1985 machine gun and grenade attacks at the Rome and Vienna airports; the 1986 U.S. servicemen's club bombing in West Germany by Libya; and the 1988 Pan Am airliner bombing over Scotland, which was linked to Libya.[26] Each of the incidents had American casualties and each of them was linked to the Middle East. In 1985 the State Department declared Middle Eastern terrorist organizations the deadliest in the world. The department categorized the organizations' targets into three main groups: first Israel, then Western governments and citizens led by the U.S. and France, and last, Arab governments and officials that terrorists considered a hindrance to their cause. The targeted Middle Eastern countries included Jordan, Egypt, Kuwait, Saudi Arabia and Iraq. Even the mainstream PLO was a target to the more radical organizations.[27] Familiar names were on the list of the state sponsors of terrorism, the department listing Libya, Iran and Syria as the main threats in the mid–1980s.[28]

From Policy Topics to the Big Screen

Towards the end of President Reagan's second term the administration undermined its own policies on terrorism when it ignored its own legislation and negotiated with Iran, a country which the U.S. had named as a state sponsor of terrorism. The effects of the Iran-Contra scandal were felt globally. In its aftermath there was a large loss of international support to American counterterrorism efforts.[29] On the domestic front the scandal affected the United States' counterterrorism coordination. The presidential staff, which had been in charge of terrorism during the first Reagan administration, had to give way to a high-level interagency committee which was chaired by the deputy national security adviser.[30]

The repercussions of the Iran-Contra case were also felt in the country's counterterrorism structure. The U.S. reduced its military responses while law enforcement and the courts once again gained the center stage in the fight against terrorism. The dominant view defined terrorism as a crime.[31] This was soon also seen in popular film portrayals of terrorism. Warfare in movies had to give way to more individually focused portrayals of international terrorists who started to invade the U.S. from Europe. They encountered law enforcement officials as American counterterrorism experts. But just as the federal government itself did not have any one agency in charge of American counterterrorism, films, too, put different agencies in different films in charge, and also showed them fighting among one another over counterterrorism responsibilities.

The following two chapters analyze four Cold War–era films that draw their central theme from international terrorism. Chapter 4 discusses two 1985 films, *Invasion USA* and *Commando. Invasion USA* introduces Chuck Norris as the film's hero and Richard Lynch as a Soviet terrorist. *Commando* stars Arnold Schwarzenegger as the American hero, Dan Hedaya as a former Latin American dictator who is using terrorist threats, and Vernon Wells as his American associate. Both films introduce U.S. soil as the target of international terrorism attacks. In *Invasion USA* the whole U.S. society is under attack, while in *Commando* the attack is more personal but has links to U.S. activities and policies in Latin America.

Chapter 5 discusses *Iron Eagle* and *The Delta Force*, both released in 1986 and both portraying Middle Eastern threats. *Iron Eagle* introduces unknown teenage actor Jason Gedrick as the hero and David Suchet as the minister of defense of a Middle Eastern country which is a state sponsor of terrorism. In *The Delta Force* a successful operation brings pride to the country's special forces when Chuck Norris rises to the occasion under Lee Marvin to face terrorists from Palestine and Lebanon.

Chapter 4

International Terrorism in the Americas: "It's Time to Die"

Invasion USA (1985); *Commando* (1985)

The U.S. Department of State described 1985 as a "banner year" of international terrorists. That year claimed the highest number of civilian casualties ever to that date, and the news media duly reported them. The publicity-grabbing and tourist-scaring events included, for example, the June hijacking of a TWA jetliner en route from Athens to Rome, the hijackings of the Italian cruise ship *Achille Lauro* and an Egyptian airliner, and the almost concurrent attacks by terrorists armed with machine guns and grenades at the Rome and Vienna airports in December.[1] The year also saw a record number of civilians, "innocent bystanders," as targets, pinpointing the shift in international terrorism from official targets to unprotected and indiscriminate targets, as would largely be true in future years.

The year 1985 was a benchmark year also for the film industry. It was the first year for films that have international terrorism as their central theme to enter the top fifty North American box office. *Invasion USA* and *Commando* brought terrorism to U.S. soil from Latin America, drawing on President Reagan's policies and the Reaganite cinema style. President Reagan had clear goals. For him and his administration détente had been a failure. The new administration did not believe in negotiations but saw the use of strength as the method towards peace. The administration felt that U.S. power had been undermined in the world during the Carter years, and therefore it should now be reasserted effectively. The Reagan Doctrine, as Jentleson points out, "developed as the basis not only for taking a harder line on global containment, but going further than every [ever] before toward rollback — i.e., ousting communists who had come to power."[2] Furthermore, as *The 9/11 Commission Report* discusses, President Reagan described terrorism as "an act of war."[3] In his view the U.S. would go after terrorists no matter where they were hiding. International cooperation was an important part of the effort to find terrorists. *Invasion USA* and *Commando*, and the following year's *Iron Eagle* and *The Delta Force,* paid attention to President Ronald Reagan's view of the world.

Invasion USA (1985: #49)

Distributor: Cannon Group
Production company: Golan-Globus[4]
Producers: Menahem Golan and Yoram Globus

Director:	Joseph Zito
Screenplay:	James Bruner and Chuck Norris
Story:	Aaron Norris and James Bruner
MPAA rating:	R
Release date:	September 27, 1985[5]
DVD (WS) running time:	110 minutes
Box office:	$17,227,874.00[6]

Invasion USA presents to movie audiences an ultimate Reagan-era nightmare. The film fictionalizes on the big screen the State Department's and Reagan administration's fears of a Soviet-led communist invasion of the U.S. With the help of Cuba, the invaders enter the U.S. from the South, landing their boats on a lonely Florida beach. The Russian- and Spanish-speaking terrorists start small attacks on unsuspecting Americans. As the attacks spread terror and chaos, they pose a threat to the American way of capitalist life. The mastermind of the anti–U.S. communist terrorists is a Russian, Mikhail Rostov, played by Richard Lynch. He has a personal vendetta against the film's hero, U.S. agent Matt Hunter, played by Chuck Norris. The hero is a white one-man Rambo-style killing machine. Only Hunter can save the country from a communist "Red Terror Network" invasion.

The film starts with a shot of a barely seaworthy boat full of exhausted and dehydrated Cubans trying to reach Florida. The boat is adrift with a broken motor, but the refugees' hopes are raised when a white, shiny Coast Guard boat with a proudly flying American flag appears and its captain, speaking Spanish, welcomes the refugees to America. The camera looks up at the captain, in white clothing, with whitish blond hair, while eerie music plays in the background. As the captain reaches to welcome an elderly Cuban onto his boat, with his free hand he shoots the man in the head without any hesitation, a cold smile on his face. That starts a bloodbath as his men shoot dead everyone in the Cuban boat, then collect from the boat a large stash of drugs which are to finance their future weapons purchase. We have met the film's villain, Mikhail Rostov, a cold-blooded killer who was merely impersonating a U.S. Coast Guard officer.

After the opening credits the film cuts to introduce the hero, Matt Hunter (Chuck Norris), camera shooting upward, showing him in an airboat in the Everglades with his blond hair flowing behind him. While the villain prefers to wear suit pants and shirts or full suits, the all–American white hero is a jeans man. Tight blue jeans and a denim shirt, at times unbuttoned, are his uniform throughout the film. He enjoys his simple life, joking and catching alligators with his Native American friend John Eagle in typical Reaganite cinema interracial harmony. Quick shots reveal him driving his airboat and tenderly smiling at his armadillo pet. When "the Company" comes calling, asking for his help to track down the man behind the killing of a Coast Guard crew (they suspect Rostov), the name Rostov stops the hero short but he still refuses: "You should have let me kill him when I had the chance. Now he's your problem." Through a Rostov's nightmare sequence we learn that Hunter had stopped Rostov from killing a high-ranking U.S. official on a foreign visit. In the nightmare Hunter delivers his catchphrase, "It's time to die," as he points his gun at Rostov's forehead. But instead of pulling the trigger, he kicks his communist counterpart. The film has now set up the protagonist and the antagonist with a personal hatred for each other, reducing a greater political issue into a personal conflict between two men who represent different sides of the Iron Curtain.

Red Terror Network on U.S. Soil

Following the 1980s official terrorist threat scenarios, the international communist group is led by two Soviets and supported by Cubans and other Spanish-speaking comrades. The attack is reminiscent of the Reagan administration's Red Terror Network fear, bringing the international center of the supposed network, the Soviet Union, to attack the U.S. through Florida and with Cuban help. The State Department was highlighting in its reports the Soviet Union as a supporter of international terrorism, and Cuba as a state sponsor of international terrorism. The early 1980s State Department documents discussed Cuba's support to leftist revolutionaries and terrorists in the form of guns, training, funding and a safe haven.[7] Cuba gave help to local insurgents, for example, in Colombia, El Salvador and Honduras.[8] According to the State Department, Cuba's own benefactor, the Soviet Union, was trying to establish sympathetic regimes in Latin America.[9] The decade's Red Terror Network scenario feared that the Soviet Union would be expanding communism to the U.S. through the latter's own back door. While the State Department's annual reports were confident about reporting on long-term Soviet support of international terrorism, several of the reports also mentioned that the department had no evidence of direct Soviet responsibility for planning or organizing terrorist attacks by Middle Eastern, West European, or Latin American groups.[10]

In this film it is the communist devil itself targeting the U.S. on its own soil with Spanish-speaking accomplices. However, the screen communists do not reveal any clear political motivation for their attack; rather, the film expects viewers to tap into the decade's communist paranoia and believe that the enemy wants to take over the U.S. In the main antagonist's words to his partner, Nikko (Alexander Zale): "Tonight we make history, Nikko. America has not been invaded by a foreign enemy for almost two hundred years. Look at them, soft.... They don't even understand the nature of their freedom.... They are their own worst enemy but they don't know it." The film leaves the Russian communist's anti-freedom and anti–U.S. stand to explain why he would lead an attack against the U.S. The film does not directly address his ideology, but any viewer aware of the U.S. foreign policy or news headlines under President Reagan can easily recognize the communist threat. However, unlike in another extreme Reaganite nightmare, *Red Dawn* (1984), that also featured Soviet and Cuban communists, the communists of *Invasion USA* enter in small groups and do not succeed in overtaking the country and imposing communism. They only pose a terrorist communist threat.

The film's plot falls under the State Department's definitions of international terrorism. Foreign communists, led by Soviets, are attacking unsuspecting American civilians across the country at Christmastime, shooting them and blowing up their homes with portable rocket launchers. The attackers form an international, Soviet-led group that practices premeditated, politically motivated, anti freedom, anti-capitalism and anti–U.S. violence against civilians. During the Cold War being a communist in a Hollywood film qualified the villain and his accomplices to be politically motivated in the sense that they were from the wrong side of the Iron Curtain. In traditions of villain portrayals *Invasion USA* leaves the antagonist's ideological and political motivations unexplored. His hatred of the capitalist U.S. and Matt Hunter are his motivation.

The film's terrorists hide in civilian clothing, bandanas and berets, as well as in police and National Guard uniforms, and wear mirrored sunglasses. When the hundreds of terrorists land on a Florida beach, they tote heavy weapons and wear dark clothing, an allusion to old Western films in which the bad guys typically wore black. They leave in trucks, vans and other big cars for cities around the country, to Chicago, Las Vegas and New York City. However, the attack is not war due to the limited number of the villains, the absence of an official uniform, and the attacks targeting innocent bystanders. The attackers' unexpected violent actions receive media coverage and terrify citizens. However, while the film draws from the Red Terror Network fear of a major communist invasion, the film also undermines that fear. While the film's foreign invaders succeed in creating terror and chaos, their threat is only temporary, not a real threat to the U.S. security and way of life, especially since one heroic man can bring them down.

Vengeful Russian Terrorist Meets a Reaganite Cinema Hero

Hunter and Rostov are distorted, one-dimensional cartoonish mirror images of each other, following traditional portrayals of a Western hero and his villainous counterpart. As is typical of the Western and later action-adventure films, the hero does everything a bit better than the villain. While Rostov does set a threat to the U.S., he does not usually act alone but has from one to several supporters at his sides. In contrast, Matt Hunter's task in *Invasion USA*, in the Reaganite cinema style, is to be a one-man war machine who kills only for a reason but always effectively. He is a traditional lonely swashbuckler hero who carries the burden of saving America on his shoulders when the FBI, as the lead agency in charge of counterterrorism on U.S. soil, the police, and his own "Company," as the CIA is often called, are helpless.

The film never properly explains Rostov or Hunter's backgrounds except to note that both were in the service of secret agencies. The hero has served at some point in South America. The two have had past encounters, which sets up the film's personal conflict and the villain's traditional vendetta against the hero.

Following the traditions of Western and action-adventure films, reluctant protagonist Hunter gets involved only after the antagonist makes the decision for him. Rostov wants his revenge against Hunter and also wants him out of the way before he starts his group's main invasion of the United States. With a dozen supporters armed with powerful Uzis and rocket launchers, Rostov and his men attack Hunter at his simple home in the Everglades swamp, killing his Native American friend John Eagle and severely injuring his pet armadillo. The Native American friend is there to warn the hero of the attack so the hero can survive. It is the friend's film duty to give his life for the white hero, loyally following the genre traditions, in particular when the sidekick is from an American minority. Now the fight is also personal. The protagonist accepts the secret mission to bring down Rostov and his network: "I'll take the assignment but remember, I work alone." Naturally the Company would deny him if the secret mission were to see the daylight. Only Matt Hunter can do the job when he, as his name already reveals, becomes a hunter of the communist villain. In contrast, the villain is not capable of doing his job alone, and even with his group he fails. Thinking that they had killed Hunter in his house with their rocket launchers, the terrorists leave, only later to find out that one man alone can stop their invasion.

The villain performs the most killings in the film. Rostov is a cold-blooded antagonist who kills without hesitation, often smiling as he carries out his vicious acts. He shoots unarmed Cuban refugees, and shoots at men's groins. He throws a woman through a window to her death, and eagerly uses a rocket launcher to torch and explode American suburban homes. His men rely on bombs, shooting and rocket launchers in their attacks, using the favorite methods of real-life terrorism. Nothing is safe from them: children, churches and Christmas are targets. Godless men are trying to bring their godless ideology to the U.S. as the God-loving country is celebrating one of its holiest holidays. The weak plotline reinforces ideological enemy stereotypes and supports the Reagan era's foreign policy.

In the traditions of Western and action films, Rostov's brutality is extreme, while the protagonist relies on violence only for a reason, although he too can be brutal if his mission requires it. Hunter pins a man's already injured hand onto a table with a sharp knife to force him to tell where Rostov is. His parting gift to the man is a grenade which he places in the latter's hand just as it is about to explode. Hunter gives the man his trademark one-liner as his message to Rostov: "If you live through this, tell Rostov it's time to die." As a killer, Hunter is a patriot who is defending the U.S., and doing it honorably, unlike the villain. But as the genre traditions allow, the hero can be brutal if his task to defend the U.S. demands that. For example, when Matt Hunter receives no answer from a terrorist to his question "You like talking?" while pointing a gun at his head, his response to the terrorist's silence is "I didn't think so" as he shoots the man dead.

Matt Hunter (Chuck Norris), dressed in his all-American uniform of tight blue jeans and a denim shirt, rescues the United States from a communist terrorist invasion in *Invasion USA* (1985, Cannon Group). Cold-blooded Soviet killer Mikhail Rostov (Richard Lynch) learns from the American hero that "it's time to die."

Like another 1980s hero and loner, Rambo, Hunter gives long menacing looks that signal his determination to bring the case to its end. Minimal dialogue emphasizes Hunter's overpowering action. He easily defeats muscle men, for example, by crushing the hand of a man who is holding a glass bottle. The protagonist miraculously always manages, as any hero should, to avoid villains' bullets while himself being a good shot. Instead of riding a horse like a cowboy in a Western, the hero drives a truck and carries with him a variety of weapons, from a knife and gun to a portable rocket launcher, a bazooka. A smile does not appear on his face when he is on his mission, but he does deliver dry one-liners in Rambo style, poorly imitating old Western stars and James Bond films. When an old contact tells him "See you in hell," the hero's response is "Send me a postcard."

Rostov sees no humor in anything, but enjoys killing defenseless, unsuspecting people. His mental state starts to unravel when he realizes Hunter is still alive and coming after him. This only reinforces an old media stereotype of terrorists being insane people. In contrast, nothing fazes the hero; he stays focused on catching the country's communist enemy. For Hunter the assignment is just a job, while Rostov is obsessed with his vendetta against Hunter. After his nightmare about the American hero, Rostov is sweaty and full of rage towards Hunter: "We have to kill that bastard before we start the operation." Rostov's partner Nikko does not understand the rage but fears that the operation's success is at risk if Rostov goes after Hunter: "He's one man. Alone. What can he do? You're obsessed."

As in real-life terrorism, the news media have a role also in the film. Exposition, in the form of TV news reports, reveals stories of unexpected violence across the country. According to the media and the police, the wave of violence is turning Americans against each other and authority when the citizens do not know who the enemy is. Rostov follows in his hotel room the big three networks' newscasts of the fear his group has created, and enjoys the chaotic scenes. An American viewer accurately points out that terrorists have been blowing up the rest of the world for years, so the only surprise is that it took them that long to get to the U.S. Real-life terrorists took notice of that with some delay.

A victim wonders about the attackers whom the news media call terrorists: "Why? There has to be a reason." But the film fails to answer the question properly. *Invasion USA* relies on the easy and simple answer that several real-life news media outlets and politicians used to explain the 9/11 attacks: they hate our freedoms. Rostov bombs and kills because Americans do not understand their own freedoms. The statement is merely a simple slogan. Follow-up questions to those who use the slogan could include, for example: What exactly is it about American freedoms that terrorists hate?; What is it about those freedoms that motivates terrorists to kill and injure civilians?; What do terrorists expect to gain through human suffering and destruction? In reality terrorists choose their targets carefully to gain the fullest impact and to reach certain goals. In order to counter terrorism effectively, society must abandon simple slogans that explain nothing, leaving terrorism an unexplainable and fearsome phenomenon. Rather, the news media, officials, researchers, and even scriptwriters, should help the public by getting inside the terrorist mindset, and explain the threat rationally.

Following the Reaganite cinema traditions, the hero does not have time for a romance. However, it is hard to completely ignore women's existence even in a 1980s action-adventure film. The female role is filled by a loud, spunky white photographer-reporter, McGuire (Melissa Prophet). She regularly appears at attack sites, and she and Hunter exchange short greetings and looks. She loyally fills her role as a woman who needs to be rescued by the hero. Rostov's accomplice Nikko grabs McGuire as she is taking photographs of an angry crowd protesting a food shortage. Suddenly the crowd becomes a terrorist target. True to the genre, the hero arrives to the rescue. Hunter takes Nikko out of the game, forcing Nikko to shoot himself with his own gun. But there is no promise of a coupling for Hunter and the photographer.

The film relies on good and strong violence in its portrayals of the characters who die. The foreign villains are props for Hunter to kill. Their deaths are for entertainment value. None of the villains' deaths makes the viewer think about the finality of death of these cartoonish characters. In contrast, the film introduces civilian targets briefly before terrorists target them, which creates a connection with the viewer. We see a glimpse of a brother and sister fighting over who gets to put the last Christmas ornament on the tree, a teenage couple kissing in a car, children playing football — all these wholesome activities interrupted when Rostov and Nikko take action. Rostov wants to be the one using a bazooka. With a smile on his face, he blows up house after house, leaving horror and destruction behind, blaming the targets: "They make it easy, don't they, Nikko?"

Another terrorist couple targets a South American community center in Miami. Disguised as members of the local police force, the two leave death, destruction and rage against authority behind. Others of the group attach a bomb on a school bus that is taking children to safety. The hero drives to the rescue, succeeding not only in removing the bomb from the side of the bus but also in catching up to the terrorists and throwing the bomb in their car. Another bomb goes off at a mall but the hero is again there to blow up the terrorists after a car chase.

Mikhail Rostov's obsession with Hunter only grows as the film proceeds. In the third act he grows mad to the point that he easily walks into a trap set up by Hunter, even when warned by an assistant. The news media are central in setting up the final confrontation. Hunter is presented to the media as a vigilante going on his own after the terrorists. When vigilante Hunter is interviewed on TV, his message through television news to the antagonist is that killing "Nikko was easy. Now it's your turn. One night you're gonna close your eyes and when they open, I'll be there. It'll be time to die." This brings Rostov and his whole remaining group to attack the counterterrorism headquarters in downtown Atlanta, only to find the headquarters building empty and the whole setup a trap.

Following the U.S. structure of conflict response to terrorist incidents on U.S. soil, actually Matt Hunter is a vigilante because the FBI, under the Justice Department, is in charge of response on U.S. soil. *Invasion USA* does portray the FBI in charge, but, against the country's counterterrorism structure, the film also sends the CIA to go after the main terrorist in a covert operation on U.S. soil. The repeated terrorist attacks are eventually so successful that the National Guard is called in to protect the citizens, who are warned to stay off the streets. Curfew and checkpoints limit ordinary life. Tanks eventually roll in to keep and restore order. The film does not explain the arrangement and chain of command of these extreme measures.

In the third act's setup for the final confrontation between the villain and the hero, the U.S. Army and the National Guard surround Rostov and his group in downtown Atlanta. Helicopters, tanks, explosions and shootings fill up the screen when the film crosscuts between the mass fight, in which men on both sides die, and the final confrontation between the hero and the villain in the empty headquarters building. While *Invasion USA* is loyal to the genre traditions, it does break the rules in a very clear way: the villain and his group succeed in killing Americans. In addition, Americans also die in the mass fight between faceless terrorists and faceless U.S. Army and National Guard soldiers.

In the footsteps of older films, according to which the villain would wear black, Rostov is in black as the final confrontation approaches. The terrorist succeeds in scratching Hunter in their one-on-one fight. The two men from different sides of the Iron Curtain rely on automatic weapons, knives, kicking, and their fists. Eventually Hunter destroys the mad communist Russian with a portable rocket launcher and utters his trademark line: "It's time to die." The antagonist disappears when the communist-hunter blows him and the wall behind him up. The hero does not ride off into the sunset in his truck or with the film's female character, but is left standing facing the camera in the film's final shot. This is reminiscent of Western films in which the lonely hero often had a love interest but did not end his lonely journey with a heterosexual coupling.[11]

The film has no denouement that would tie up any loose ends; the killing of Rostov and the stopping of the invasion are the end of the story. The one-dimensional character portrayal offers the hero no prodigal journey. No personal growth takes place. The only thing coming close to the hero's growth is the completion of his mission to kill Rostov. The beginning of the film shows a flashback in which Matt Hunter's agency did not allow him to kill the communist adversary. At the film's end he finally does that. A simple gun is not enough for the awaited moment: Hunter uses a rocket launcher to blow Rostov and half of a wall away.

The film is a celebration of American firepower. Ammunition, firepower and a big weapons arsenal save the country, reflecting the Reagan-era approach of reaching peace through power. The main terrorist group surrenders only when it is met by overpowering weapons and manpower. The film's end credits list military technical advisers and thanks a captain, majors, a lieutenant colonel, major general, and the Georgia Army National Guard. Though the film's fictional hero was capable of taking on the terrorist threat largely on his own, getting help from the armed forces only towards the film's end, in creating the fictional story the filmmakers used assistance from the real-life official power structure. However, the filmmakers take shortcuts in bringing in the National Guard and U.S. Army. Terrorism becomes warfare, as President Reagan saw it, but the film ignores the complex structure of command for using armed forces and the National Guard on U.S. soil. An easier and visually more interesting story was simply to portray them in the film as action intensifies.

The violence Hunter practices in the film is "good violence," done in the name of saving the country. As is traditional of action-adventure films, the film upholds and reinforces the status quo when the hero removes a threat to the existing order and restores power.[12]

Commando (1985: #22)

Distributor:	20th Century Fox
Production company:	Silver Pictures
Producer:	Joel Silver
Director:	Mark L. Lester
Screenplay:	Steven E. de Souza
Story:	Joseph Loeb III, Matthew Weisman, and Steven E. de Souza
MPAA rating:	R
Release date:	October 4, 1985[13]
DVD (WS) running time:	90 minutes
Box office:	$35,100,000[14]

Commando introduces Arius (Dan Hedaya), former dictator of a fictional Central American country, Val Verde.[15] Arius has hired American ex-soldiers to help him in his plan to return to power in Val Verde. His right hand in the attempt is Captain Bennett, played by Vernon Wells, formerly of the U.S. Army. Arius's target is Colonel John Matrix, played by Arnold Schwarzenegger, who had been central in the U.S. actions to remove the dictator from power. Arius's plan includes the killing of some of the men from the retired colonel's unit in order to make the army believe that the colonel's life is at risk. Several villains follow army representatives as they travel to the colonel's secret location to inform him of the threat on his life. Having found the hideaway, Arius's men attack and kidnap Colonel Matrix's preteen daughter. Now the ex-dictator can implement the last step of his plan: in return for his daughter's life, the caring father is to take a plane to Val Verde and kill the current president who knows Colonel Matrix and therefore would allow him access. The assassination would return the former dictator in power.

The film starts with short clips of the murders of some of Matrix's men before cutting to introducing the muscled white hero. Colonel John Matrix has a superior physique, which the film celebrates in the Reaganite cinema style. During the opening credits the movie introduces the hero in a montage of shots that show him doing physical labor, starting with close-up shots of his boots, then moving up to his bulging muscles before cutting to a close-up of his face. Later in the film, the camera again embraces the hero's muscular form with a shot of him in his tight swimming trunks when he is arriving on the island where his daughter is being held hostage.

The foreign villain and his hired American associates are cardboard cutouts who barely fill their task as villains. Arius, a Central American ex-dictator with a darker skin color than the hero and a foreign accent, is a traditional villain who is anti-freedom in his resistance to U.S. policies that took him out of power. His threat is personal to the hero but connected to U.S. foreign policy. In exposition we learn that as dictator, Arius had killed and tortured his country's citizens. Matrix's unit had been in Val Verde to help to bring down Arius and to support the new U.S.-friendly head of state. Arius and Bennett both want revenge against the film's hero because he brought them both down. However, the film does not explain, for example, how Arius has managed to bring a heavily armed Central American military force to an island just off Los Angeles and to put American ex-soldiers on his payroll. The film expects the viewer to take the bad blood between Bennett and Matrix for granted after film dialogue briefly reveals that Matrix had had Bennett thrown out of his unit. The man whose superior, Matrix, thought he enjoyed killing too much now wants revenge. As Bennett points out to Matrix, his skills and actions were due to the training he had received from Matrix.

Like *Invasion USA*, *Commando* follows a traditional setup of the villain forcing the hero to become involved in the events. *Commando*'s Colonel Matrix has retired to lead a simple life with his preteen daughter Jenny, played by Alyssa Milano. He is a loving father, which is revealed in a montage of the two happily eating ice cream, feeding a deer, swimming, fishing, and doing martial arts together while the film's opening credits are running. This white U.S. army specialist, originally from communist East Germany, has disbanded his own unit.

Matrix's ex-supervisor, General Kirby of the U.S. Army, arrives in a helicopter to warn

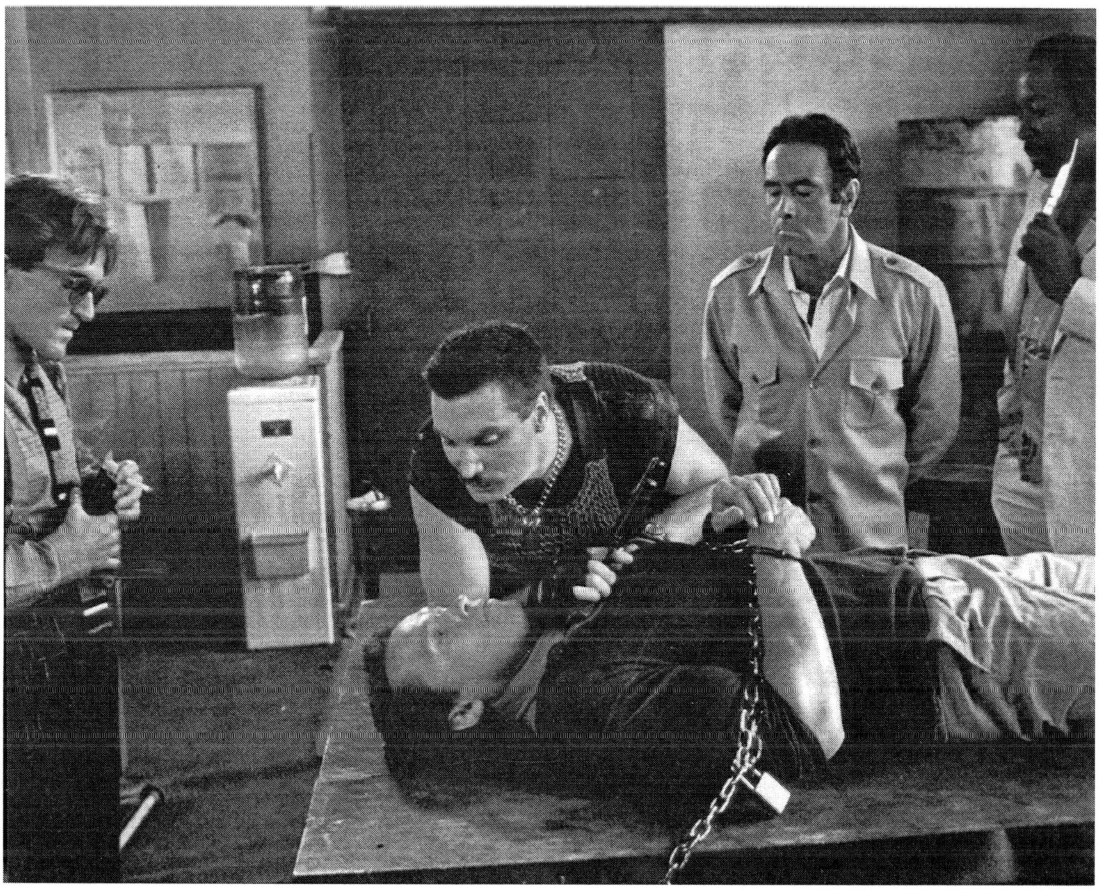

Former Central American dictator General Arius (Dan Hedaya) and former U.S. special forces men who have sold their loyalties try to force Colonel Matrix (Arnold Schwarzenegger) to return the dictator to power in *Commando* (1985, 20th Century Fox). Colonel Matrix's domestic nemesis is Captain Bennett (Vernon Wells), who tries to kill the hero's preteen daughter.

him that he may be a target since several men in his old unit have been murdered. The hero acknowledges the unidentified outside threat, which could be anyone since, in the general's words, "You've made enemies all over the world." The general's list of the possible suspects draws directly from the 1980s U.S. foreign policy agenda: Syrians, South Americans, Russians, or terrorists.

The film raises the hero's personal stakes from the more typical 1980s action-adventure films in a style that became common in the 1990s. The script awards him a preteen daughter, Jenny, although the film avoids any explanation for the absence of the daughter's mother. As General Kirby arrives, Jenny looks up to her daddy: "You said you weren't going to go away again. You said you were through." The threat is even more personal than just between the protagonist and the foreign and the domestic villain. Not only is Colonel Matrix defending the policies of his country in Central America, but he is also protecting his daughter. The film reduces a larger political issue into a fight between individual characters.

Following the genre traditions, the hero wants only to lead a peaceful life, but the villain's actions force him back in the game. When the film's villains attack him at his home in a remote area, just as happened to the hero in *Invasion USA*, the professional fight becomes a personal one. The protagonist cannot avoid meeting the antagonist who has his daughter as a hostage. The hero's past conflicted relationship with the villain affects the latter's actions and is the root cause of the new conflict.

Latin American Terrorists Attack Noncombatant U.S. Targets

Commando falls under the State Department's definitions of international terrorism. The ex-dictator's group consists of his supporters from his native Val Verde as well as of American supporters and hires. They arrive in the U.S. from abroad to attack a noncombatant target. In 1985 the State Department had not yet clarified in its terrorism definitions that attacks on military personnel who are not on duty are also included in its terrorism data, but, for example, in 1985 it included in its terrorism data the killing of four off-duty U.S. embassy marine guards in El Salvador. The 1990 report was the first to make the clarification, further defining the word *noncombatant*: "For the purposes of this definition, the term noncombatant target is interpreted to include, in addition to civilians, military personnel who at the time of the incident are unarmed and/or not on duty."[16]

The group led by Arius involves citizens of more than one country and has political motivations. Their goal is to return to power the man whom the hero had helped to bring down in Central America. The film's theme does reflect the U.S. involvement in Latin America in the 1980s, for example, in El Salvador and Nicaragua, but the movie does not address the villains' political or ideological motivations or background after it has introduced the ex-dictator's wish to return to power.

While the American and some of the Latin American hires wear civilian clothing and therefore can hide among civilian population, General Arius has his own little military base just off the L.A. shore on a small island. The dozens of faceless Val Verde soldiers wear a uniform, and therefore could be defined as guerrilla fighters since they are a military unit that is still loyal to the ex-dictator. However, in the film they attack only when they come under the hero's attack, so in that sense they form Arius's security force although they are a foreign military unit on U.S. soil. But the unit is not large enough to constitute a warlike threat, and the men are not attacking the U.S. directly. Arius is only going after a certain unit in the U.S., having former U.S. soldiers doing the dirty work of going after the hero on U.S. soil.

The American villains have individual roles while the film's Spanish-speaking troops exist only as human props for a variety of the brutal killings the hero performs. The unofficial military base has a large weapons arsenal that contains explosives, tanks and guns, but naturally none of that can match John Matrix's one-man army when he finally arrives to rescue his daughter and even the score with his adversaries.

Commando borrows from old Western and thriller films the use of time pressure. The hero's flight to Val Verde takes 11 hours. When he breaks the neck of the villain who is taking him to Val Verde, and sets him up as a sleeping passenger, the protagonist has 11 hours before the opponent would learn that he has escaped the plane. Until then his daughter is safe. Close-ups of Matrix's watch throughout the film emphasize the urgency and explain why he has to go in with brutal power without waiting for help. While at first the hero is forced to make concessions to terrorists when his daughter is a hostage, he fast breaks free from the situation, and goes after the terrorists with massive firepower to bring them to the only film justice he and Hollywood knows: death. But Colonel Matrix also breaks the rules of the game in his one-man war approach. In real cases of terrorism on U.S. soil, the FBI is in charge, but not in this film. After Matrix's spree of violence, the army arrives to do the clean-up job. The film again takes liberties when it allows armed military forces on U.S. soil in action without any clear explanation of their authorization or as being a supportive force to U.S. law enforcement officials.

Action-Adventure Marries Romantic Comedy

Against the trend in other mainstream action-adventure films of the 1980s, there is room for a woman in this plot. After Matrix has escaped from the Val Verde plane, he avoids any detection at the airport and finds Sully, one of the men who had seen him off. The man harasses an off-duty flight attendant, Cindy, played by Rae Dawn Chong. She is an attractive woman with a mixed racial and ethnic background. Romance enters as a subplot when the hero and the romantic interest at first do not get along, as is typical of romantic comedies. Matrix gets into Cindy's car and orders her to follow Sully's car. As a romantic subplot requires, the conflicted relationship between the two is based on miscommunication before it can start to develop into something more. At this point Matrix is a kidnapper who forces the flight attendant to follow a man into a mall with him. When Cindy is supposed to go to seduce Sully in order to help Matrix, she alerts the mall security, who, as the genre traditions require, go after the wrong guy. The guards describe the hero as a 6' 2" man with brown hair, a "gigantic motherfucker." Sully and another terrorist start to shoot, at which point the guards return fire. As Cindy notices Matrix is everyone's target, she switches sides and prevents a security guard from shooting the hero. Now the actual story can start.

Like his physical appearance, also Matrix's physical movements are superior. He has no trouble jumping to freedom from the Val Verde plane's cargo area. He is run over by a car, shot at hundreds of times, but nothing touches him. Killing has been his business and he is good at it. In the style of James Bond and old Western heroes, he delivers short sentences, often with a comical touch or a taunting comment to his opponents. As Sully is seeing Matrix off to Val Verde, he gives Matrix money telling him to have some beers in Val Verde so the group would have more time with his daughter. Matrix's response is simple: "You are a funny guy, Sully. I like you. That's why I'm going to kill you last." When, inevitably, the time comes to kill Sully, Matrix continues the line: "Remember when I told you I'd kill you last? I lied." When a Green Beret–trained villain attacks Matrix, his response is, "I eat Green Berets for breakfast. Right now, I'm very hungry."

More comedy is added by flight attendant Cindy as she comments on events and Matrix.

For example, Matrix explains his urgency to go after Sully by saying, "A guy I've known for years wants me dead." Cindy's response is "Understandable. I've only known you for five minutes and I want you dead, too." While Cindy supports the hero in his mission, she is still filling a traditional female role as a scared woman who screams during a car chase. The film also provides her with lines that mock the action-adventure role of heroic men. For example, when the hero is engaged in a fistfight with an ex–Green Beret villain, Cindy's response to the violence is: "I can't believe this macho bullshit. These guys eat too much red meat."

The film is refreshing when it awards the hero with a minority female sidekick in Cindy. While she is at times scared, she does not need rescuing, as was the case in most 1980s action-adventure films, that is, if they even portrayed women. Supposedly independent women, for example, in the Indiana Jones films, were still dependent on the hero to rescue them. Cindy was ahead of her time in the Reaganite cinema era. When John Matrix raids a weapons store for rocket launchers, rifles, hand grenades and other weapons that are enough for a small army, he is arrested. Cindy follows the police truck, fires a rocket launcher and frees Matrix. Also, Cindy is a beginning pilot who flies an amphibian plane to take the hero to the island where Jenny is kept. After that she sits and waits for the hero to do his job: confront his adversaries and rescue his daughter.

Latin Americans: Props for Spectacular Killings

The hero is responsible for the majority of the killings in *Commando*. After the initial attacks on Colonel Matrix, his men and his daughter, the film's villains respond only to the violence initiated by the hero. This trend is not broken until the main American antagonist, Captain Bennett, goes after Matrix's daughter in order to kill her. As would occur in *True Lies* two decades later, Schwarzenegger's character performs several spectacular killings. He breaks necks, cuts throats, stabs, throws knives, shoots with automatic weapons, sets up bombs, kills with a rocket launcher, throws hand grenades, spears with farming equipment, scalps with a thrown saw blade, and cuts a villain's arm off with a scimitar. His face stays expressionless throughout this killing spree, which the film qualifies by showing large numbers of villains coming after him when he enters their premises and attacks them in order to save his daughter.

Foreign villains try to shoot the protagonist but fail miserably every time. The film could be titled "How to Kill Central Americans in Spectacular Ways," similar to 1994's *True Lies* with a different set of Third World citizens as the targets of the hero's massive power: "How to Kill Arabs in Spectacular Ways." A Third World human life is cheap: both films use several dozens of unidentifiable characters as props for the hero's spectacular and extremely brutal killings. As is the case with news coverage, the number of deaths of people from the Third World must be high before media businesses offer the story to their Western audiences. In contrast, *Commando*'s American villains have individual deaths at the hero's hands.

The film further dehumanizes the villains by offering only a rare glimpse of any recognizable Latin American characters apart from General Arius. They have short lines in the film, emphasizing their stereotypical image as legal targets of brutal violence by the hero. As one of Arius's men is playing with a long sharp knife, he says to Bennett: "Slitting a little girl's throat is like cutting warm butter."

The inhuman-villain portrayal reaches its height when Arius learns the plane has landed in Val Verde and Matrix is not on it. He orders Bennett to kill Jenny. She is very much her father's daughter. She has not been afraid to tell the ex-dictator that she will enjoy the moment when her father smashes the general's face. By the time Bennett comes to execute her, she has escaped the room where she was held prisoner, making the domestic villain grunt: "Little bitch, I'll kill her." A big man who has sold his country goes after a little girl with a big knife. In the traditions of the action and action-adventure genre, the script has portrayed the foreign and the domestic villain in such despicable terms that the film has by now qualified their unavoidable deaths at the hero's hands.

"We Fight for Love"

Colonel Matrix has two one-on-one final confrontations in the film. The hero first engages in an armed confrontation with the foreign villain, the brains of the operation, before the primary confrontation between the American villain, the muscle of the operation. To Matrix the killing of the ex-dictator just before the film's climax is simply a matter of business. After a one-on-one gunfight, the hero eventually shoots the dictator from dozens of yards away, and the latter falls over a balcony rail.

In the Reaganite cinema era it was time to flex some muscle in Washington and on the big screen. One-man war machine Colonel John Matrix (Arnold Schwarzenegger) used Reaganite firepower on the screen when he supported U.S. policies in Latin America and saved his preteen daughter in *Commando* (1985, 20th Century Fox).

The film's final confrontation sets up the former East German — from the wrong side of the Iron Curtain but now an American hero — against an American who has sold his loyalties to a Central American ex-dictator. After a cat-and-mouse search John Matrix finds Bennett. The domestic villain, loyal to the genre format, is presented as visibly insane. Even with his reliance on a gun, knife and his fists, Bennett is no match to John Matrix, who has brutally killed dozens of men to reach his daughter. The fight is personal for both men. Bennett is trying to even the score for some past abuse while Colonel Matrix is fighting the man who was just about to kill his daughter. A prolonged fist and knife fight ends when Matrix throws Bennett against a hot air pipe which pierces the villain: "Let off some steam, Bennett."

The film's denouement brings the U.S. Army general and his men to clean up the mess of bodies. The lonely one-man war machine took care of what a large unit was prepared to do. In contrast to *Invasion USA*, in *Commando* the hero's prodigal journey is very clear. It is his improved relationship with his daughter. As she saw an army helicopter arriving at the beginning of the film, she loudly complained to her father that he had promised not to go away anymore. In the end Jenny's smile is big when her daddy tells his supervisor that there is "no chance" he would get his unit back together and come back. Matrix, Jenny and Cindy leave the scene with their arms around each other. He saves his daughter, kills the bad guy and gets the girl. Their plane takes off as the credits roll to the beat of "We Fight for Love" by Power Station. The general has no chance against love.

Commando introduces themes that became central in the popular 1990s action-adventure films. Women and family are present in the film. The hero has a conflict both in the main plotline and the subplot. The first is the conflict between the villain and the hero, and the secondary conflict rises from his family situation, which also offers the hero an opportunity for a prodigal journey. His daughter is clearly against her daddy's involvement, but by the film's end the father restores the family harmony, and adds to the mix his new romantic interest.

Arnold Schwarzenegger plays a hero who borrows a famous line from a character he played in the previous year's *Terminator*. Colonel Matrix delivers the "I'll be back" line to Bennett as a threatening promise before he is taken to catch a flight to Val Verde. In *True Lies* he again plays a likable family man who is in the business of killing Third World citizens in most unimaginable and brutal ways. In *Commando* John Matrix is primarily fighting for his family and only secondarily for his country. This approach became a major trend in the 1990s action-adventure films. The character was also ahead of the times with his comical style, which emerged in a more developed form in the late 1980s and in Schwarzenegger's *True Lies* (1994).

Invasion USA and *Commando* draw from Reagan-era fears, but only on the surface. The communist, Latin American, and American villains arrive in the U.S. to counter the country's anti-communist stand and its policies and actions in Latin America, but the films' conflicts are reduced to individual protagonist-antagonist fights. Both movies focus on the villain's personal agenda against the hero rather than on any villain's political or ideological motivations. While the fear of communism and U.S. involvement in Latin America draw from the decade's U.S. foreign policy and news headlines, the topics only provide cartoonish political themes for the films' backstory. They fail to give any clear context or depth.

Invasion USA and *Commando* are representatives of Reaganite cinema. Brutal violence and patriotic pride in the efficiency of one man to beat terrorist threats underline the Reagan approach of peace through military power. The heroes' bodies are hard and muscular. The men fit the description Jeffords gave of the 1980s heroes: they are aggressive and determined, standing for the country.[17] Both Chuck Norris and Arnold Schwarzenegger are traditional heroes. They are white men who save Western civilization from threats to its structures and way of life. In Schwarzenegger the viewer meets a white foreigner whose accent does not reduce him to a villain, but whose white muscles are large enough to promote him to an all–American hero. By the end of the films, both heroes have restored order. Interracial harmony adds to the mix another Reaganite cinema spice. Matt Hunter's Native American friend dies to give Hunter a personal motivation to take the job, and Colonel Matrix, ahead of his time, has a promise of a romance with an American minority woman.

Norris's Hunter is a hero in a swashbuckler film tradition: he is a lone law-abiding citizen who has been living outside society in the Florida Everglades with only a few friends. Schwarzenegger's Colonel Matrix is an updated version of the typical Reaganite hero. Also he has chosen to live in a faraway area outside society but he has a preteen daughter, and soon also a romantic interest. While Hunter can rely only on himself, Cindy supports Matrix at the beginning stages of his operation. Hunter has no one to return to, but Matrix has his daughter and the new possible love interest who will guide him back to civilization.

Both heroes follow the traditional film formula, according to which the villain forces a reluctant hero to become involved in events. That also qualifies the hero's actions; after all, the villain forced the protagonist to fight, so he only gets what he deserves: death in the film's end at the hero's hands. In contrast to the U.S. counterterrorism objective of bringing terrorists to justice, the two movies offer action-adventure film justice: death at the hands of the film's muscled American hero. In action-adventure style the films portray constant hostility, promoting a mainstream traditional view of a strong self-made man who succeeds by going after his goals and pushing everything aside that is in his way.[18]

Invasion USA largely denies in war film style the existence of women while *Commando* not only portrays a female sidekick with a mixed racial background but also allows her to save the hero from the clutches of American officials. She has a traditional role borrowed from romantic comedies in that she and John Matrix at first bicker until by the end of the film there is a promise of a romance.

Both films are traditional also in their portrayal of the villains. Neither film portrays its foreign or domestic villains, Rostov in *Invasion USA*, and Arius and Bennett of *Commando*, in human terms, but simply draws them as cartoon characters whose main role is to be killed by the film's end in such a way that entertains the viewer. While sadistic Russian Rostov is white, he is a typical Red Terror Network villain. He is anti-American, someone who threatens American freedoms and its Judeo-Christian religions with his godless ideology. Arius stands for Latin American leaders whose interests contradicted U.S. interests, the threat from the U.S. perspective usually being communism or socialism. However, neither film *directly* mentions communism as either villain's background. *Invasion USA* hints at the Cold War with the villain's Russian accent and past activities and hostilities with the hero. *Commando* leaves Arius only as a cartoon figure who is not even important enough to grow mad towards the film's end; the main villain's traditional character development is given to the domestic villain, who is part of the international plot.

As the improving relationship between the two superpowers started to thaw the Cold War, the fear of the Red Terror Network started to be replaced by another fear that was claiming space in the latest news headlines: violent activities of Middle Eastern terrorist groups. Car bombings, skyjackings, the goal of mass casualties, and Lebanon hostage-takings would soon also be at the heart of Hollywood terrorism. Chuck Norris returned as a hero with his unit in 1986 to save American hijacking hostages in Lebanon in *The Delta Force*. Earlier that same year *Iron Eagle* brought to the big screen a new teenage heartthrob in Jason Gedrick. To the beat of popular 1980s music, the high school senior saves his father from an evil Middle Eastern country which is reminiscent of Libya, a 1980s U.S. enemy in the Middle East.

Chapter 5

State Sponsored Middle Eastern Terrorism

Iron Eagle (1986); *The Delta Force* (1986)

According to the U.S. State Department, in 1985 over half of all international terrorist incidents originated in the Middle East. A bit less than half (45 percent) took place in that region.[1] The threat of Middle Eastern–originated terrorism found its way to the big screen too but at first with only lukewarm box office success. The films which explored terrorism as more than only a cardboard cutout form of evil, for example, *The Little Drummer Girl* (1984), failed to attract viewers to the same extent as movie portrayals that loyally followed the 1980s official U.S. views and news portrayals. Traditional Reaganite cinema depictions simplified film villains to the point that viewers cheered for the massacre of those who were threatening American citizens and interests in fictional portrayals of international terrorism. Two such films, *Iron Eagle* and *The Delta Force*, made the annual top fifty box office in 1986 in the aftermath of attacks and threats that were linked to Palestinian organizations, Iran-backed Hezbollah, and Libya, a state sponsor of terrorism.

Iron Eagle (1986: #39)

Distributor:	Tri-Star Pictures
Production company:	Falcons Flight, Inc.
Producers:	Ron Samuels and Joe Wizan
Director:	Sidney J. Furie
Screenplay:	Kevin Elders and Sidney J. Furie
Executive producer:	Kevin Elders
MPAA rating:	PG-13
Release date:	January 17, 1986
DVD (WS) running time:	117 minutes
Box office:	$24,159,872[2]

Iron Eagle is a story about a U.S. Air Force Academy reject and fresh high school graduate, Doug Masters, played by Jason Gedrick, who rushes to action to save his father, U.S. Air Force colonel Ted Masters, played by Tim Thomerson. A Middle Eastern country has shot down Colonel Masters's plane over the Mediterranean. A retired Air Force colonel, Charles "Chappy" Sinclair, played by Louis Gossett, Jr., and a group of teenagers from an American air force base help the young Masters in his rescue efforts.

The film opens with two American F-16 fighter planes doing a Freedom of Navigation exercise, flying through clouds and entering disputed territory of a country called Bilyad. This is reminiscent of the American Freedom of Navigation exercises, done in the 1980s close to the Libyan coast, and a constant cause of friction between the U.S. and Libya. The latter's name is almost an acronym of "Bilyad." Several MiG fighter planes, the Soviet model used by Libya, threaten the two U.S. planes, announcing: "Attention, American invader, you're violating territorial airspace." In video game style, the planes engage in a firefight, the American fighters locking in their targets on monitors before shooting. But they are defenseless in front of a larger enemy. One of the American planes is hit but manages to escape, and Colonel Masters stays to fight, only to suffer a turbine failure and capture by the enemy.

Next the camera cuts to the film's longhaired hero, Colonel Masters's son, Doug Masters. The hero is a rule-breaking teenager who idolizes his father. The young man has a habit of sneaking in to use, on Air Force trainers' and his father's approval, a F-16 combat simulator, and secretly with his father, a real F-16 plane. But his short temper and poor grades make him a U.S. Air Force Academy reject. However, it is left to this young man to rescue his father from Bilyad when the State Department stays idle.

Fiction Reflects Reality ... and Reality Reflects Fiction

The film takes its main conflict from mid–1980s news headlines and U.S. foreign policy. The film's threat scenario is based on the real, conflicted relationship between the U.S. and Libya before the wings of film fiction fly the story to new heights, setting up the teenage hero to massacre dozens of faceless soldiers of Bilyad.

Throughout the 1980s the U.S. identified Libya, Iran and Syria as the main state sponsors of terrorism. The secretary of state had designated Libya under the U.S. Export Administration Act of 1979 as a state sponsor of international terrorism due to its support of several international terrorist organizations. The support included training, financial aid and weapons. According to the State Department, Libya was using international terrorism as a central tool in promoting its foreign policy interests.[3] Due to Libya's leader Muammar Qadhafi's anti–Western and revolutionary views and actions, the department defined him as a world leader in supporting international terrorism.[4]

Tension between the U.S. and Libya had been brewing for over a decade. In response to the U.S. resupplying Israel in the Yom Kippur War, Libya had announced in October 1973 that the Gulf of Sidra is within Libyan territorial waters, which the U.S. saw as a violation of international law. In 1981 President Reagan started to challenge the Libyan claim by ordering occasional Freedom of Navigation flights in the disputed area. Outside the Gulf of Sidra, Libya was supporting terrorist groups that targeted Americans and other Westerners. Furthermore, in the 1980s, as a reaction to Libya and also Syria's connection to major terrorist events in Western Europe, the U.S., Canada and several Western European countries had declared military, political and economic sanctions against the two countries.[5]

Around the film's release time the U.S. was linking Libya to several anti–U.S. terrorist acts, among them the December 1985 Abu Nidal attacks at the Rome and Vienna airports which killed twenty people, including five U.S. citizens. The attack planner found a safe haven in Libya. Soon after the attacks the U.S. started to analyze whether Article 51 of the United Nations Charter, the right of self-defense, would apply to attacks outside U.S. borders.[6]

In response to the U.S. conducting a Freedom of Navigation exercise in March, 1986, Libya attacked U.S. forces, which returned fire.[7] At a UN Security Council meeting the U.S. defended its response. Ambassador Vernon A. Walters, the U.S. permanent representative to the United Nations, pointed out that the U.S. had reacted to Libya's missiles: "In accordance with Article 51 of the Charter of the United Nations, I wish, on behalf of my government, to report that United States forces have exercised their right of self-defense by responding to hostile Libyan military attacks in international waters in the Gulf of Sidra."[8]

The analysis of self-defense as a response to terrorist attacks started to become more serious when Abu Nidal bombed a TWA flight heading from Rome to Athens, the attack killing four Americans.[9] Two days later on April 5, 1986, a bomb exploded at a West Berlin discotheque that was often frequented by off-duty U.S. service personnel. Three died, two of them American soldiers. Of the over 200 wounded, 79 were American troops.[10] In 1986 the U.S. linked Libya to at least 19 incidents of international terrorism.[11] Ten days after the discotheque bombing, and after having found evidence supporting Libya's involvement, the U.S., with U.K. assistance, launched two air strikes against Libya, targeting Tripoli and Benghazi. W. Hays Parks, who was involved in addressing the legality of the air strikes, said of the U.S. attack: "It was a limited act of self-defense against a continuing threat for the purpose of deterring Libya's continued reliance upon illegal acts of terrorism as a foreign policy tool."[12] In Parks's view Qadhafi's death would not have violated Executive Order 12333, which prohibits assassinations. He points out that the attack had several effects:

> First, it established a critical precedent that force could and would be used against those who support, plan, or finance terrorism, or who use their sovereign territory to harbor or train terrorists. Second, as British Prime Minister Thatcher acknowledged, it placed terrorism on the international agenda of Western governments. Finally, while alliances in responding to terrorism and other acts by rogue regimes may be nice, they are not critical. U.S. actions on the night of April 15, 1986, indicated to others that their timidity to respond to terrorism would not restrain the United States where action was necessary.[13]

Reflecting the 1980s U.S.-Libya conflict over airspace close to Libya, U.S. authorities in *Iron Eagle* argue that the routine flight took place in an international airspace. In contrast, Bilyad claims that the colonel was flying in its airspace. The film exposition repeats references which are familiar from real U.S. actions against Libya in the 1980s. For example, it reveals that the U.S. has no diplomatic relations with the film's fictional country. Like Libya, Bilyad is a pariah nation under a trade embargo, and, as one character speculates, it is trying to get the embargo lifted by taking Colonel Masters, a uniformed U.S. soldier, as a prisoner. The negotiations proceed slowly, the event actually following the policy of no concessions to terrorists, although the film never has Bilyad demand anything officially. To young Doug Masters's frustration, the U.S. government soon decides to do nothing to save his father. Bilyad shortly finds Colonel Masters guilty of crimes against the country. When he refuses to sign a confession, Bilyad sentences him to death in three days by hanging. The familiar action-adventure ticking clock is now in motion — there is a time limit within which the rescue must take place.

The film's terrorism falls under the State Department definitions of international terrorism. The capture of the American colonel crosses borders, at least from the U.S. perspective, and is politically motivated to undermine Bilyad's enemy, the U.S. The captive is not a civilian or an off-duty military representative but in active service. His captor country's description and the film's events refer to Libya's position on the State Department list of the state sponsors of terrorism. *Iron Eagle* crudely establishes Bilyad as a Muslim country by quick establishing shots which portray minarets and veiled women in a marketplace before cutting to shots of the prisoner and the film's antagonist. To further link the fictional Bilyad to Libya, Bilyad has a Soviet-manufactured weapons arsenal just as its real-life counterpart did. In particular, the film highlights Bilyad's military aircraft, the Soviet-manufactured MiG fighter planes. According to the State Department, Libya was a major Soviet weapons buyer and reseller in the Middle East in the 1980s.[14]

For the teenage hero the big government machinery, led by the State Department in events that take place abroad, is a domestic villain because it refuses to help his father. The film then departs from real U.S. counterterrorism policies when the State Department starts to negotiate with a country it defines as a state sponsor of terrorism. Interestingly enough, the seeds of the Iran-Contra scandal were sowed the year the film was in production. During the Iran-Iraq War, Iran had turned to the U.S. in secret for a weapons purchase, which the U.S. had used as an opening for possibly helping American hostages in Lebanon. The film and real life were both breaking official U.S. counterterrorism policies. Eventually the film's State Department follows the policies when it stops negotiations and does not give anything to the country which has a U.S. hostage.

The film's United States also avoids a physical confrontation, which forces the young white man into action with results that draw attention to the capability and power of American airpower. The film predicted what was to happen in real life only three months after the film's release. In the teenage hero's description, nobody has the "balls" to do something about the "shitty little country." However, President Reagan's aggressive approach on international terrorism was already radically changing U.S. policy on terrorism. In April 1986, after the U.S. had found Libya linked to several anti–American attacks, the U.S. launched two air strikes against Libya, going after the man the U.S. State Department had defined as a world leader of terrorism. However, a hotheaded American teenager got there first.

Iron Eagle, like *The Delta Force*, refers to the Iran hostage crisis. When waiting to hear news about his father and the U.S. government's response, Masters's African American friend encourages him:

> "Those studs won't mess with us. The Air Force will kick ass if they do."
> "Like in Iran, right?"
> "That was different. Mr. Peanut was in charge back then. Now we have got this guy in the Oval Office who don't take shit from no gimpy little countries. Why do you think they call him Ronnie Ray Gun?"

But as Masters finds out, while Ronnie Ray Gun was getting tough on international terrorism in the real world, in the film the State Department and the White House do not lift a finger to help his father. The case is quite the opposite in *The Delta Force*, which celebrates the resolution of a hijacking and hostage crisis with American firepower, and with a success unlike in Tehran.

Interracial harmony and a strong father-son relationship are at the heart of *Iron Eagle* (1986, Tri-Star Pictures) when an American teenager (Jason Gedrick) and his mentor, Air Force colonel Charles "Chappy" Sinclair (Louis Gossett, Jr.), go after Bilyad, a Libya-like country, to save the teenager's father.

Mad and Evil Arab Colonel

During his rescue mission, young Masters meets his foreign antagonist, Colonel Akir Nakesh (played by David Suchet), who is minister of defense of the "shitty little country," as Masters describes Bilyad. He is dressed in a uniform similar to that of Libyan leader Qadhafi. The foreign antagonist has a darker skin color than the American teenager and speaks with an accent. Like the hero and his father, the villain is a pilot. Only Colonel Nakesh is recognizable out of the mass of Arab villains that the film portrays. The rest of the Arab characters serve as targets for a variety of deaths. They are simply film props, as were the Third World citizens of the previous year's *Commando*. They play dead bodies which fly around after each exploding strike by the hero.

The film gives an overly simplified portrayal of Colonel Nakesh. His only role is to fill the boots of a villain whom the viewer can hate. He is brutal not only towards Masters's father but also towards his own men. Like Masters and the film's viewers, he sees his men only as a big, faceless mass. Their singular lives do not matter. Colonel Nakesh forces his men to attack the American invaders through flames, as he mistakes young Masters's attacks for a larger attack. The men's only choice is to risk their own lives either because of the flames or for not following the orders: "The Americans must die or none of you will live to regret your mistakes." The minister of defense is so simplified and one-dimensional as an evil Arab villain that the viewer has no choice but to cheer with the hero and his father when the inevitable moment comes when Masters blows the villain into pieces, the wooden plane model the film is using splintering into pieces.

"We're Not Gonna Take It Anymore"

In the traditions of the war film, the teenager rises to the occasion when a hero is needed. He leads a group of his peers, which include an African American, a nerd, his little brother, and some teenage girls, including his girlfriend. They together prepare the rescue mission that Masters and Chappy Sinclair are to perform. Air Force colonel "Chappy" Sinclair, Masters's sidekick and mentor in the rescue operation, is an African American Vietnam War veteran, now a reservist. The film pulls from the Reaganite cinema building blocks the depiction of interracial harmony and a strong father-son relationship. For Masters, Chappy is a secondary father figure who shapes up the young man for his rescue mission. In Chappy's words, the father has been tough on Doug Masters because "he's just trying to make a man out of you."

Masters is faced with a traditional second act setback when his mentor's plane is hit at the early stages of their rescue mission. He is now left alone to save his father. However, Chappy had anticipated the event and made a recording which helps the young hero to continue the rescue mission on his own.

While *The Delta Force* reinforces the Reagan administration's re-establishment of U.S. military might, *Iron Eagle* both undermines and supports it. The film portrays the State Department as a wimpy negotiator whose negotiations go nowhere because "we don't even have diplomatic relations with the bastards." Furthermore, the air force base has an "open door" policy: Masters and his group of teenagers easily gains access to secret information, troop locations, intelligence, missiles, as well as to the computer system which schedules F-16 flights and work orders. The group even makes a work order to have Masters's F-16 carry a powerful bomb. But the film's ending does give clear support to the view of the U.S. as a military powerhouse. With a spectacular showcase of the might of U.S. weaponry, the young Masters easily completes the task of saving his father. To the beat of loud music, he takes out the enemy MiGs as easily as in a video game, and as he had secretly practiced in the F-16 simulator. An oil refinery, airport, various cars and planes, and buildings are left smoking and in ruins at Masters's hands. The pile of villains is high by the time Masters has successfully saved his father, rescuing him from the airport where the villain was keeping him. The hero succeeds in killing a large number of Arabs, while the villain and his country only succeed in shooting down one American plane at the beginning of the film, capturing Masters's father, and shooting down Chappy.

As the action and action-adventure film tradition requires, the villain is an untrustworthy, dishonorable person. He orders a sharpshooter to kill the American prisoner as the hero lands his plane to pick up the hostage. The son-father duo escapes and are soon followed by the minister of defense himself. Instead of a fistfight or gunfight or car chase, the final one-on-one confrontation between the protagonist and the antagonist takes place in the air. An American F-16 meets a Soviet-manufactured MiG. The villain pilot takes on young Masters, a rookie pilot, while his wounded father cheers him on. It is time for the teenager who once hung out at the air force base's Eagle teenage club to prove that he is an *Iron* Eagle, an Eagle who deserves to be flying that F-16 plane. Masters's father warns him, "This guy is an ace, he knows what he is doing." The villain's angry and determined stare accompanies his promise of a death sentence: "Time to die, Iron Eagle." The teenage Masters's parting words to the evil Arab villain in his Soviet MiG are: "So long, asshole."

The denouement brings the father-son duo to Ramstein Air Force base in West Germany. There they learn that — unusually for a minority sidekick character — the African American sidekick has survived.[15] Chappy's hit was not fatal, and he had been picked up by an Egyptian freighter, that is, by a U.S.-friendly nation in the Arab world.

Masters's prodigal journey takes him from his boyhood and teenage angst into manhood. No longer does his father need to ask him, as in a flashback in the film: "When will you show responsibility? At some point you got to grow up, son." Having grown as a person, he is awarded a place at the Air Force Academy at the film's end. Also, Chappy lets him keep the wings he had given the young man for the mission: "Keep them, you've earned them."

When Masters and his father land in the U.S., the media are completely clueless about how the rescue mission took place. The reporters exist in the film only to highlight how inefficient everyone was, except Masters and his group.

The film both contradicts and supports U.S. counterterrorism policies. One of the main policies and objectives is that state sponsors of terrorism pay a price for their actions and for their support of international terrorism. Instead of the U.S. directly doing that, the film portrays a teenage boy who has a close relationship with his father, and shows him proving to the father that he is a man now and he can do a man's job. In the traditions of the 1980s films, the young man takes matters into his own hands and pushes everything else aside when he saves his father and brings the Arab villain to film justice: to his death. Although the "bombing back to the stone age" approach might seem to be an extreme creation of film fiction, three months after the film's release the U.S. used a similar approach when it attacked Libya with air strikes to punish the country for its anti–U.S. activity. The film's music track also predicts the toughening U.S. policies: Queen's song "One Vision" keeps the young man focused, bringing the eventual message loud and clear from Twisted Sister: "We're not gonna take it, we're not gonna take it anymore." The film and its soundtrack helped to pave the way to the acceptance of tough military acts against Libya and its leader Qadhafi.

Overall the film is almost a caricature of action-adventure films, largely ignoring any character development except for that of its hero. Doug Masters's character arc — growing from a boy to a man under his father's admiring eyes — directly targets and appeals to young male audiences, who can imagine themselves on the seat of that F-16 to the beat of 1980s hit songs. *Iron Eagle* offers serious competition to *Invasion USA* in simplifying a storyline with its facile plot, cardboard characters, and a brutal and unexplainably mad foreign antagonist, but the script does not forget the classical Hollywood narrative structure and action and action-adventure film traditions. An evil foreign villain's actions force a white Anglo-Saxon protagonist to take defensive measures, that is, to apply massive amounts of violence and destroy a large number of Third World lives in spectacular ways. The portrayal of religion is as superficial as possible: the film introduces Bilyad through a few location establishing shots which show veiled women and minarets. The seed of a foreign, non–Judeo-Christian religion has been planted and after that the film forgets the topic.

As Gregg has pointed out, films simplify international events by turning complex ideas into conflicts between individual film characters.[16] In this case the film *over*simplifies. *Iron Eagle* stretches even the boundaries of the classical Hollywood film narrative, which promotes an American ideal of a strong self-made man who succeeds by pushing everything else aside in order to reach his goal.[17] In this case, the young hero pushes aside all rules and U.S. foreign policy in dealing with terrorists to become a real American hero and man. His actions break international laws and undermine U.S. efforts. While in real life the State Department was in charge of negotiations, the FBI was starting to take charge of dealing with American hostages in foreign countries. Also, the U.S. military would have had a stake due to the hostage being an American in uniform — but not in *Iron Eagle.* The film defines terrorism as an act of war when a soldier becomes a hostage, but it is a war that an individual fights, not the U.S. In the Reaganite cinema style, *Iron Eagle* interprets the film's act of terrorism as an incident of war, which qualifies the teenage hero's actions. A month after the film's release, Cannon Films brought grown men to fight terrorism in the Middle East in *The Delta Force.*

The Delta Force (1986: #49)

Distributor:	Cannon Group
Production company:	Golan-Globus
Producers:	Menahem Golan and Yoram Globus
Director:	Menahem Golan
Screenplay:	James Bruner and Menahem Golan
MPAA rating:	R
Release date:	February 14, 1986[18]
DVD (standard) running time:	128 minutes
Box office:	$17,768,900[19]

Golan-Globus, part of the Cannon group, did not look too far for *The Delta Force*'s storyline. The June 1985 hijacking of TWA flight 847 by two Hezbollah terrorists, and the prolonged hostage and hijacking media event after the initial hijacking, were still fresh in the minds of viewers when the film came out. *The Delta Force* replays several parts of the real hijacking until the story takes off and rewrites history in favor of the use of explosives and lethal heroic power by the Delta Force.

The film's hero is Major Scott McCoy, played by Chuck Norris, who lives in a remote area. Unlike Norris's role as a lonely hero in *Invasion USA*, Major McCoy is a member of a group. It is his interracial Delta Force unit, not him alone, which rescues the film's American hostages. In contrast to the film's nationalistic heroism, real events left little for the U.S.

military to celebrate when Syria, a state sponsor of terrorism that was linked to the group the hostage-takers represented, stepped in to obtain the release of the last 39 hostages of the TWA flight 847 hijacking in Beirut.[20] The film ignores the historical record, ending with typical genre violence — and echoing President Reagan's comments on how to resolve a similar crisis in the future. Belton quoted Reagan as saying after the 39 U.S. hostages were let go by their Lebanese captors: "I saw *Rambo* last night. I know what to do the next time this happens."[21] The film's Shia radicals have no chance against the U.S.-Israeli cooperation in locating the prisoners, nor against the American firepower wielded by the Delta Force.

From Iran to Lebanon

The Delta Force starts with fictionalized shots of the failed 1980 Delta Force rescue mission of the American hostages in Tehran, Iran. The film's white hero, Captain (later Major) Scott McCoy, rushes to help Pete, a team member who is stuck in a burning aircraft, even though his superior, Colonel Nick Alexander, played by Lee Marvin, is ready to leave the man and McCoy behind. McCoy rescues Pete, and at the last minute McCoy and Pete make it to the plane. Exposition through news media reports tells that eight died and thirteen were injured in the failed rescue effort of the army's top secret anti-terrorist task force in Iran.

The film next jumps to July 1985 to portray the hijacking of an American ATW passenger plane en route from Athens to New York City via Rome, dating the events only a month later than the real hijacking and only slightly changing the letter order of the real airline, TWA, to ATW. The film introduces Jewish passengers at the airport, for example, a couple celebrating their silver wedding anniversary, the woman showing to another Jewish couple her ring, bought in Jerusalem, that says in Hebrew "the song of songs." In contrast to happy and carefree Jewish passengers, the film shows two solemn-looking but sweaty Arab passengers. As in the real incident, a third Arab passenger, who was to be the third hijacker, has a standby ticket and gets agitated when he is bumped to the next flight. His actions lead to his arrest.[22]

The two Arabic- and English-speaking terrorists, relying on pistols and grenades smuggled in earlier by an airport maintenance worker, hijack the plane soon after takeoff. They are members of the New World Revolution, which in the words of the film's main antagonist, Abdul Rafai, played by Robert Forster, has "declared war against the American imperialists, Zionist terrorists and all other anti-socialist atrocities." However, while the film gives the terrorists an organization which mirrors the 1980s left-wing ideology fears, as well as Hezbollah's anti–American and anti–Israeli stand, the film terrorists have no clear demands, as would be usual of hijackings. During the real-life TWA hijacking the Hezbollah hijackers clearly demanded the release of over 700 Shia prisoners from Lebanon in Israeli prisons. They also condemned American and Israeli actions in the Middle East, in particular the Israeli military presence and activity in southern Lebanon, an area where Hezbollah was operating.

The Delta Force plot matches the U.S. State Department definitions of international terrorism. International terrorist target American civilians, and cross international borders to commit the act. The story's background can easily be dug up in the State Department's documents on international terrorism, in particular those relating to Lebanon.

In the 1980s the Lebanon crisis created new threats to the U.S. and also brought the Reagan administration one of its setbacks in the Middle East. Israel invaded Lebanon in 1982 in the middle of the Lebanese civil war, citing an assassination attack on its ambassador by an operative of the Black June Organization as a justification for the attack. Israel claimed to be aiming at the destruction of the PLO infrastructure, but the organization that had attacked its ambassador was not affiliated with the PLO.[23] However, the PLO had relocated to Lebanon from Jordan, and was attacking Israel across the border. As a response to the Israeli invasion, attacks against Americans and moderate Arab countries and citizens grew. American troops entered Lebanon as part of a multilateral peacekeeping force in a country where a civil war was in progress. The U.S. became a clear target, in particular due to its close relationship with Israel.

In April 1983 the American embassy in Beirut, Lebanon, was targeted by a 400-pound truck-bomb suicide attack. The attack killed sixty-three people and injured 120. Later that same year, in October, simultaneous suicide bombing attacks on American and French compounds in Beirut brought the death toll higher. The 12,000-pound truck-bomb at the U.S. Marine Corps barracks killed 241 marines and other personnel. The 400-pound bomb at the French base killed 58 French troops.[24] It was not immediately clear which group was behind the attack, but Islamic Jihad claimed credit.[25] The group is a front organization of the radical Shia terrorist organization Hezbollah, which is backed by Iran. Towards the end of the decade the State Department repeated its suspicions of the Islamic Jihad's responsibility, and it confirmed in the 1990s the organization's role in the attack.[26]

Soon after the October 1983 attack the Reagan administration pulled American troops out of Lebanon. While "redeployment offshore" was mentioned as the official reason, the U.S. changed its policies on military commitments after the Lebanon failure.[27] Defense Secretary Weinberger set new ground rules for future U.S. military involvement, detailing that any future military commitment undertaken by the U.S. must have clear objectives, and that force would be used only as the last resort in the national interest and only if it had the support of the American public.[28] For those anti–U.S. forces who were observing American military presence in the Middle East and the superpower's unwillingness to suffer human casualties, the American pullout taught a lesson they were to use later. The American response revealed to them how to hurt the superpower. From their perspective, an anti–American attack that causes mass casualties is an effective method. Furthermore, the 1983 attacks brought no American counter-action.

The U.S. State Department saw Iran as having a direct link to the ongoing crisis in Lebanon. The 1984 report on international terrorism states:

> Currently the world's leading supporter of terrorism, Iran has been most active in Lebanon. All the same, Tehran still intends to punish the United States for its support of the late Shah and France for its role in helping Iraq's war effort. Iran's fundamentalist regime, which ultimately hopes to drive US and Western influence from the Islamic world, has championed some of the most viciously anti–Western groups in the region — such as the Hizballah in Lebanon.[29]

The report further drew attention to Lebanon as the area with the most terrorist attacks three years in a row, having witnessed 82 attacks in 1984. The following year would bring the region once again to the news headlines, and soon also to the big screen.

Hezbollah — the Party of God

In 1985 the hijacking of the TWA flight from Athens to Lebanon, and the *Achille Lauro* ship hijacking in the Mediterranean Sea made big news headlines in the U.S. The hijackers behind the TWA attack were from Hezbollah. The *Achille Lauro* attackers were from the Abu Abbas–led faction of the Palestine Liberation Front. Each of the anti–American attacks claimed American casualties.[30]

Hezbollah, the Party of God, is a Middle Eastern group that has been highlighted in the State Department reports. It is a radical, Shia Muslim organization in close cooperation with

Iran. Hezbollah, or as the Statement Department spells the name, Hizballah, emerged in Lebanon in the early 1980s with Iranian support. Its main goals are the removal of non-Islamic influences from Lebanon and the foundation of a Shia Muslim Lebanon. As a model for its structures and governance, the new Lebanon would follow Iran, a Shia Muslim country. Hezbollah is anti-West and anti-Israel. In the mid-1980s it targeted in particular the U.S. and France.[31] Hezbollah has used several names over the years, including Islamic Jihad, Revolutionary Justice Organization, Organization of the Oppressed on Earth, and Islamic Jihad for the Liberation of Palestine. The group has targeted the U.S. several times. In addition to the 1983 suicide bombings in Lebanon, the U.S. embassy annex bombing in 1984 was linked to Hezbollah.[32] In its 1984 report, the State Department described the organization:

> Hizballah, or the Party of God, is the generic name used by the Iranians and their supporters to distinguish their movement from other Muslim groups in Lebanon. Small groups of terrorists within the Hizballah movement — some little more than street gangs in West Beirut — were responsible for many of the numerous attacks last year. Many of these Hizballah elements continue to receive political indoctrination, training, and financial and material support from Iranian Revolutionary Guardsmen based in the Syrian-controlled al Biqa (Bekaa) Valley of eastern Lebanon. While this Iranian assistance has been instrumental in the continuing success of Hizballah terrorists, the radical Shia forces have become strong enough to operate independently in many cases. In fact, increasingly they have developed into a highly structured, cooperative network.[33]

Hezbollah has Iranian support and its activities have supported Iran's policy goals, but the State Department has suspected for decades that Hezbollah has also conducted acts not approved by Iran. In 1987 the State Department estimated the organization's strength to be several thousand.[34] Its areas of operation have been the southern suburbs of Beirut, southern Lebanon and the Bekaa Valley. In the 1980s the State Department suspected that Hezbollah was creating cells around the world. Later years' annual reports listed established cells in Europe, Africa, Asia, and South and North America.[35]

Hezbollah did not stay idle after the 1983 attacks but extended its methods. The organization started to kidnap citizens of its main targets: the U.S. and other Western countries. It kidnapped for example, American journalists, educators, diplomats and businesspeople. The organization made clear in its public statements that Iran would have a central role in any hostage negotiations.[36] West Lebanon proved to be such a kidnapping center in the 1980s that newsmakers and filmmakers took notice.

The Reagan administration responded to the terrorist kidnappings and the UN convention on hostage-takings by the 1984 Act for the Prevention and Punishment of the Crime of Hostage-Taking (18 USC 1203). The new act extended the hand of U.S. law outside U.S. borders, declaring that

> seizure of a US citizen as a hostage anywhere in the world is a crime, as is any hostage-taking action in which the US Government is a target or the hostage taker is a US national. Such acts are, therefore, subject to investigation by the Federal Bureau of Investigation and to prosecution by US authorities.[37]

The TWA Flight 847 Hijacking in June 1985 and the ATW 282 Hijacking in *The Delta Force*

The June 14, 1985, hijacking of TWA flight 847 was the first hijacking of an American airliner in the Middle East since 1970. Two Shia Muslim gunmen hijacked the plane carrying 153 passengers and crew, mostly Americans, soon after its takeoff from Athens.[38] The plane was forced to fly to Beirut where the two hijackers separated thirty-nine male Americans and the crew from the over one hundred passengers. The plane stayed in Beirut for the rest of the seventeen-day event. The terrorists scattered their hostages around the city in order to prevent an American rescue mission, turning 35 of the hostages over to Hezbollah and four to Ahi'a Amal militia. They also beat up and killed one of the hostages, an American naval enlisted man.[39] Hezbollah demanded the release of 700 Shia prisoners in Israeli prisons. While the official U.S. counterterrorism policy dictates that the country gives no concessions to terrorists, makes no deals with them, and will not force any other country to do so, according to Weimann and Winn, the U.S. urged Israel to comply with the demand, which it did.[40] According to the State Department's 1985 report, Israel released 31 prisoners during the hijacking. However, a 2004 report, which gives a brief chronology of terrorist incidents, on the State Department website details that after Israel had released 435 Lebanese and Palestinian prisoners, the hijacked plane returned one more time to Beirut.[41] The crisis was not resolved until Syria, a country on the list of state sponsors of terrorism that had ties to Hezbollah, became involved and helped to release the hostages, who had been scattered around Beirut at various safehouses.[42]

The news media followed the seventeen-day TWA hostage event in detail. Reporters even interviewed the hijackers, the captain and the hostages for the world media. Furthermore, the media played a diplomatic role, passing messages through media reports from the hijackers to the U.S. and Israel, and vice versa. They covered in detail the plane's flights from Athens and back and forth between Beirut and Algiers, finally staying in Beirut. The three American television networks produced over 500 news segments on the event until the hostages were released after their ordeal. During that time each of the three networks dedicated almost two-thirds of their nightly news broadcasts to the hijacking.[43] Hezbollah was in control of the media coverage, arranging press conferences and meetings and holding interviews. The organization even edited American news footage. For example, it deleted the hostage comments it did not approve of. Only after news footage had been re-edited to meet the organization's approval would Hezbollah allow the broadcasting of the re-edited tapes via a satellite link.[44]

The real-life events are present in *The Delta Force* as the basis for the story although the film has an end disclaimer stating that the characters and events are fictional, and any similarities to real people are "purely coincidental." The TWA flight 847 hijacking is clearly the film's inspiration, but business interests take over when the film recreates history and brings to viewers American military heroism that reality had denied. Real-life terrorists had been more creative than Hollywood terrorists were a year later. They had anticipated an American rescue effort, and therefore had pre-empted it by scattering the hostages around Beirut in such ways that hindered serious rescue efforts.

The film makes a concession to its American audience. The real hijackers spoke practically no English, but one of them communicated in German with the flight purser. In the film, the hijackers as well as the other terrorists speak English fluently, although with an accent. Also, the film's hero is multilingual. Major McCoy can pass as a French-speaking employee of a Canadian TV station, and he also understands terrorists who are conversing in Arabic.

The film portrays a heroic flight purser, Ingrid (Hanna Schygulla), based on Uli Derickson, the TWA flight attendant who was credited for saving lives during the hijacking. Imitating real events of the hijacking, the film's two terrorists ask the flight purser to collect passports and identify the passengers who have Jewish-sounding names.[45] Derickson told the terrorists that the passports do not identify religions, and she also hid some of the names. Nevertheless, the hijackers separated five passengers, as the film does too.

Abdul Rafai, a commander in the New World Revolution, and his sidekick, Mustafa,

During a hijacking in *The Delta Force* (1986, Cannon Group) terrorist leader Abdul Rafai (Robert Forster) forces flight purser Ingrid (Hanna Schygulla) to collect passports and identify the passengers whose names "sound Jewish." The film's events resemble the real-life Hezbollah hijacking of TWA flight 847 in June 1985. However, in real life it was not a Delta Force unit which obtained the release of the American hostages in Beirut but Syria, a state sponsor of terrorism and supporter of Hezbollah.

played by David Menahem, separate Jewish men from the rest of the passengers at the beginning of the hijacking. When Ingrid, the German flight purser, attempts to placate them by calling them freedom fighters and pointing out they would not like to be associated with the Nazis, who killed six million Jews, the terrorists respond that the Nazis did not kill enough Jews. They should still be targeted because "the Jews stole Palestine, they took our lands."

When the terrorists are about to hijack the plane, one of them praises God in Arabic. "God be praised," as do other terrorists when the final confrontation starts. The film portrays the terrorists' religion as Islam but does not focus on it as the motivation. As discussed in Chapter 3, setting up the film villain against a Judeo-Christian worldview is a typical characterization in films that portray threats to the U.S. and its way of life. While the film villains are not explicitly motivated by their religion, it does depict a conflict between Islam and Christianity, and Islam and Judaism. For example, when an Israeli undercover agent, a Greek Orthodox priest in Lebanon, becomes a target of Rafai's suspicions, the terrorist comments that he does not trust this Christian while another terrorist had just identified the priest as a friend whom they cannot hurt. When Rafai catches the priest giving information to Israel and prepares to kill him, the priest delivers a fatherly Christian message: "Yes, my son. God will forgive you." Furthermore, a heroic Catholic priest, Father William O'Malley (George Kennedy), joins the separated Jewish male hostages. One of them has a concentration camp number tattooed on his arm, which further emphasizes the terrorists', and also the world's, persecution of Jews. Father O'Malley joins the group of Jews, believing it his Judeo-Christian duty: "You called me, for all the Jews. I'm Jewish, just like Jesus Christ. You take one of us, you'd better take us all." The film depicts a non–Judeo-Christian religion as a threat.

In addition to the few separated passengers, the hijackers also separate three navy divers, as was the case with the real hijacking. Mustafa is enraged to realize the plane is carrying three members of the U.S. Navy: "American Marines kill many of my friends when they bomb Beirut." When Father O'Malley argues that Americans never bombed Beirut, Mustafa hits him. The film traditionally portrays the villain's violence as an act of rage, or without a base against an American. When the enraged Mustafa hits this defenseless churchman, the film violence is strong because it is bound to make the viewer identify with the victim and target of that violence, thus against the aggressor.

The Delta Force's Definitions of Terrorism

The Delta Force plot matches the State Department's definitions of terrorism. While the film fails clearly to spell out what the terrorists are trying to gain with their hijacking in political terms, the act itself is politically motivated. Also, the unstated goal of an independent Palestine can be read between the lines by anyone who had been following the decade's news. The film's terrorists several times refer to their anti–American stand and their goal of gaining media publicity. Their intended audience is the American television audience, just as the case was with the 1985 TWA hijacking. Furthermore, the terrorists have noncombatant targets and cross international borders to commit their act. By the film's release time, the FBI was in charge of American hostages abroad. However, the film defines terrorism as warfare and deploys a uniformed military unit. Action is set in motion when the secretary of state, on the president's command, orders the Pentagon to send in a Delta Force unit to perform an emergency rescue operation. In accordance with U.S. policies on international cooperation, the unit does have the approval of the countries where it is operating except for Lebanon. The film contrasts U.S. policies of the mid–1980s, as Parks describes when discussing the use of military force by other countries outside their borders when countering terrorism:

> Extraterritorial military force had been used in the past, generally, however, only to rescue hostages during an on-going incident.[46] Actions by Israel outside its borders in response to terrorism were generally condemned — in all probability for political as much as legal reasons — and had not been supported by the United States.[47]

Even the real 1985 hijackers did not believe that, and therefore in order to prevent an American rescue operation in Lebanon, they scattered the American hostages around Beirut. Furthermore, the Delta Force had once before tried a rescue in another country: in Iran in 1980. The unit was founded to be deployed in terrorist incidents.

The terrorists call themselves freedom fighters who are fighting for their brothers, following real-life terrorists' positive view of themselves as fighters for a real cause. The film also brings up the mythical view the general public may have of terrorists as freedom fighters. As the hijackers are releasing the women and children hostages, they seize their valuables and money. A young nun asks: "Why are you behaving like common bandits? You're freedom fighters, aren't you?" The terrorist's response is to reach for her cross necklace but he pulls his hand back when the nun puts her hand on the cross to protect her religion. He allows her to have her religion and its symbol. He also returns to a Jewish woman her ring with Hebrew writing on it, but not until after having licked it when taking it off his finger. Male Jews receive no mercy from him as they are his enemies due to their religion, ethnicity and gender.

While Chuck Norris's Matt Hunter in *Invasion USA* was a Rambo-style one-man army, in *The Delta Force* his character, Major McCoy, a five-year Vietnam War veteran, is a man who, in typical war film tradition, rises to the occasion when a group leader is needed. He is a determined man on a mission who would do anything for his men and country. Retired at his remote horse ranch, he learns of the hijacking through TV news media reports, and is again ready for action. This is his chance to redo the failed 1980 hostage rescue attempt in Iran.

Like the teenage protagonist of *Iron Eagle*, the adult heroes of *The Delta Force* have trouble trusting the State Department and the White House. The failed rescue mission of 1980 haunts McCoy and his superior, Colonel Nick Alexander, throughout the film. McCoy puts the blame on the officials who did not understand the situation and gave unsuitable orders to men who knew better but had to follow the orders anyway. This time around, things seem the same at first. The president does not want to risk any lives, so first the U.S. tries to negotiate, which puts the Delta Force on hold. When the negotiations fail, Major McCoy and his men still have a hard time fully trusting the government officials. Just before an anticipated Delta Force attack on the hijacked plane is to take place, one of McCoy's men asks Colonel Alexander, "We're *going* to go for it this time, right, Colonel?" to which the colonel responds, "Damn right." When the time for the attack draws close, after the release of women and children, the Delta Force is still on hold. McCoy says with passion, "Let's not screw this one up." The film was reflecting the Reagan administration's view of the Carter administration and its perceived inability to take on international terrorism. But the film's attack is canceled as the colonel learns from the released Ingrid that new terrorists have joined the hijackers.

More Islamic militiamen boarded the plane of the real-life hijacking in Beirut before the plane took off again.[48] Borrowing from that, the film shows a dozen fighters joining the hijackers in Beirut. These include the hijacker who had missed the original flight due to his standby ticket, again imitating real events. During the TWA hijacking event the third hijacker joined the other hijackers in Beirut after Greece had released him in return for the release of eight Greek passengers, a matter that did not go well down with the U.S.

As terrorists in real life argue that their opponents force them to take action,[49] the film's main villain blames the opponent for their brutal actions. The abandoned rescue effort leads to a firefight between the Delta Force unit and the terrorists whose plane is trying to depart the airport. Mustafa shows no hesitation when he tortures a young U.S. Navy diver by hitting him senseless with an armrest. As Rafai learns of the Delta Force and Algerian commandos' planned rescue effort, he shoots dead the navy diver and drops his body to the tarmac, a scene that also borrows from real events. The real-life hijackers had bound navy diver Robert Stethem and beaten him severely, and eventually shot him and dumped his body on the tarmac. Two other American military personnel received beatings. In the film, as Rafai leaves behind the murdered U.S. Navy diver, his message to the U.S. is: "Look what you have done. Look here, America, look. Now the American president will know we are serious. Here's a present for him and the American people. One Marine killer."

Arab Terrorists

In contrast to *Iron Eagle*'s portrayal of Arabs simply as targets of the hero's firepower, *The Delta Force* introduces four individual members of the terrorist group, and shows other members of the group and Lebanese officials who have short lines in the film. While the real hijackers of the TWA plane were Lebanese Hezbollah terrorists, the film does not clearly spell out the hijackers' background. Rather, they refer to events in ways implying they are Palestinians who are working with Hezbollah. It is less likely for them to be Hezbollah terrorists who are sympathetic to the Palestinian cause due to the hijackers' intense emotional opposition and reactions to Jews and Israel. Either role imitates the real-life Hezbollah sympathies as well as the development of the PLO after Jordan had expelled the organization from its area. The PLO found refuge in Lebanon. Israel suffered several Palestinian attacks across the border, and eventually invaded Lebanon to go after the PLO.

The film's terrorists have their headquarters in Beirut, Lebanon, the city where Hezbollah has its headquarters. The film links the hijacking to Hezbollah in several ways, such as by showing pictures of the Ayatollah Khomeini, the leader of Iran, Hezbollah's state sponsor. Several posters of Khomeini hang on the walls of the terrorists' headquarters as well as around Beirut. Furthermore, later in the film one of the terrorists gets a message saying, "Khomeini, the Ayatollah, will welcome you and your hostages" via Syria, another Hezbollah supporter. As discussed in Chapter 2, according to the State Department, the states that sponsor terrorism often provide a safe haven to foreign terrorist organizations, just as Iran offers to do in this film. While the film does not portray Khomeini in person, in the middle of the fighting American firepower not only kills villains but also destroys images of Khomeini, reflecting the adversarial U.S. relationship with Iran.

The American heroes finally destroy the villains of *The Delta Force*, but before their deaths the film very briefly allows the two hijackers a human touch. While Rafai and Mustafa do not hesitate to hit men and women who resist them in any way, or just to make their message clear, at times they do show some compassion. For example, Mustafa allows a six-year-old Jewish girl to fetch her doll when passengers are moved to the back of the plane. He tells her that his daughter is of the same age. Later he moves a pregnant woman to a more comfortable seat and helps her to settle down, even asking her if she is comfortable.

The hijackers are very determined in their actions and dedicated to their unspecified cause. The film imitates mainstream news media portrayals of terrorism, which largely focus on the act as it is happening but fails to explore the motivations and background of terrorist organizations. Terrorism stays an incomprehensible and fearsome phenomenon when viewers do not know what it actually is. A superficial portrayal of terrorism can, at worst, allow counterterrorism to rely on methods which most legal societies usually do not allow. The film's terrorists stay fearsome and, in film terms, earn their deaths through their brutal anti–American and anti–Judeo-Christian behavior, and by the threats they make against the United States and its citizens. Following action film traditions, they force the heroes to react to their violence and threats. While the film never allows its terrorists to clearly articulate their goals, it still draws their model from real life, and gives the hijackers' group a further 1980s touch. The organization's leftist agenda, as stated in its name, and origin directly draw from the Reagan-era experiences with and policies on terrorism: from an international communist and terrorist network, and from Middle Eastern groups' terrorist attacks against the U.S. The film highlights the terrorists' anti–American stand but leaves it as a mythical, unexplainable hatred that viewers cannot understand, and which the film does not explain to viewers. This is the case, for example, in a scene between Mustafa and two American hostages in Beirut when one of them looks at Mustafa, obviously scared of him:

> MUSTAFA: Why are you looking at me like that? You hate me, huh? It's your government we fight, not you. It is your White House. One day I will go there. I will drive a truck, and the truck, it will blow.
>
> HOSTAGE 1: That will be suicide, you know that.
>
> MUSTAFA: I know how to die.
>
> HOSTAGE 1: The White House is a very big place. You'll need a lot of explosives.

HOSTAGE 2: You'll never get to the place. Don't kid yourself.
MUSTAFA: You think we don't have friends in America? You'll be surprised. One day, one day.

That "one day" arrived fifteen years later. Al Qaeda had friends in America. Some of the 9/11 attackers had entered the United States legally and attended school in the country.

Imitating the real hijacking in 1985, the terrorists of *The Delta Force* place their hostages at different locations in Beirut. In the film version the three separate locations do not prevent a U.S. rescue mission. And in the film there is no need for Israel to release prisoners as a concession to terrorists, as happened in 1985.[50] Instead, with the help of Israeli agents, including from Mossad, the Israeli intelligence agency agents in Lebanon, the Delta Force locates the hostages and proceeds to rescue them. The special unit trains at an Israeli air force base and at a naval base for their mission. When the Delta Force team leaves for Beirut from the Israeli naval base, the colonel's answer to an Israeli colleague's wish to join them is: "Well, you boys have done it before. Now it's our turn." In the end the rescued hostages and the Delta Force land safely in Israel, "America's best friend in the Middle East," as a U.S. government official states in the film. The cooperation the film portrays between the U.S. and Algeria, and the U.S. and Israel, reflects one of the main policies of American counterterrorism: international cooperation in counterterrorism.

The Delta Force unit's attack on the terrorist headquarters resembles Masters's destructive actions against *Iron Eagle*'s Bilyad. To the beat of heroic music, the Delta Force lands at an isolated Beirut beach in a scene reminiscent of the arrival of Soviet and Latin American communists in the U.S. in *Invasion USA*. Putting their American flag patches on their shoulders, the Delta Force unit members start their rescue mission to save the hostages who are scattered at three different locations in Beirut. Inefficient terrorist guards dutifully fill their roles as dumb villains: they roll the dice, chat, and nod off, and completely fail to notice the arrival of the Delta Force as the three coordinated simultaneous attacks start. As is typical of the genre, the heroes easily kill villains by spraying bullets from their automatic weapons and using explosives. The several dozen villains whom the heroes encounter have difficulty hitting any of the heroes, no matter how close they are to their targets. The film is a celebration of Reagan-era American power. It promotes official army representatives as American heroes. The film's end credits thank an army consultant, army liaison, and aviation consultant.

Explosions light up the sky as the American heroes' rocket launchers and automatic weapons kill terrorists and burn Beirut. However, one terrorist detail, holding as hostages the Jewish group, two navy divers and Father O'Malley, escapes and is on its way to Iran via Syria. In the third act Major McCoy's actions resemble those of Matt Hunter in *Invasion USA*. The film is a traditional action and action-adventure film which leaves it to the hero to make the primary killings. McCoy finds Mustafa hiding under a mattress in an empty office and easily shoots him between the eyes, saying "Sleep tight, sucker." The terrorist's bullets do not find him. Riding a motorcycle that is armed with rocket launchers, McCoy next takes on a car convoy of terrorists on their way to Ayatollah Khomeini. When the cars stop, Rafai yells, "You stopped because of one man on a motorcycle?! Move on!" The man on a motorcycle spreads fear when he blows up one car after another with his motorcycle's rocket launcher. When the terrorists attempt to turn back to Beirut, the rest of the Delta Force comes to finish the fight. While the hero is engaged in a prolonged fistfight with a terrorist driver, Rafai seriously wounds Pete, McCoy's protégé, in their firefight. Rafai escapes to be followed by McCoy. The protagonist rides his motorcycle to the final one-on-one hero-villain confrontation. After a fistfight and a knife fight, McCoy takes Rafai out of the game, just as Matt Hunter did in *Invasion USA*: with a rocket launcher.

To the beat of heroic music, in a scene that borrows from the film's beginning, McCoy barely makes it to the plane that the Delta Force has recaptured at the Beirut airport. He easily blows up the terrorists who are trying to prevent the takeoff, leaving behind their bodies on the runway tarmac. As the released hostages celebrate, singing "America the Beautiful," sober Delta Force members witness Pete taking his last breath. This individual death touches the viewer, yet the dozens of enemy killings rarely merit an identifiable body. Father O'Malley blesses Pete in the name of the Father, the Son and the Holy Spirit, which further contrasts the *other* religion that in the film's view begets violence but which the film avoids portraying in any other form but by remarks to God when violent action starts. The images of the dying Pete and his mourning team members are examples of strong violence that brings viewers on the side of the Western victims of violence. In contrast, the killings of the Arab Muslim terrorists are clinical, showcasing American firepower, and therefore never allow viewers to identify with the brutal villains.

As the plane arrives in Israel, music emphasizes the Delta Force's hollow victory. Sounds of the celebrating families, crew and passengers are in the background as sad music emphasizes the price of counterterrorism. The camera follows the Delta Force unit carrying a black body-bag to their plane. The manly man, McCoy, is on the brink of tears. His prodigal journey

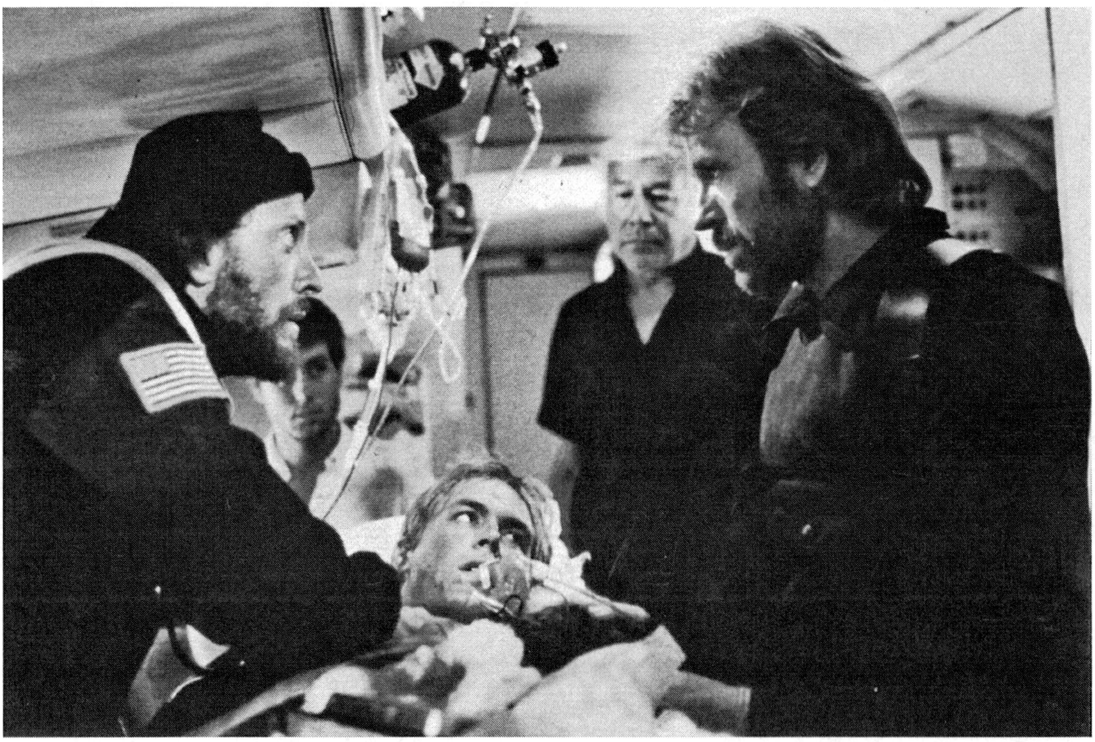

Imitating the events of the TWA flight 847 hijacking in June 1985, *The Delta Force* (1986, Cannon Group) brings to the screen threats against the U.S. in Lebanon. In contrast to the real-life hijacking, during which the terrorists spread their hostages around Beirut in order to prevent an American rescue effort, the fictional terrorists cannot avoid a Delta Force raid. In the traditions of Reaganite cinema, *The Delta Force* portrays interracial harmony and male bonding when Major Scott McCoy (Chuck Norris, far right) rescues the remaining American hostages with his unit. Father William O'Malley (George Kennedy, second from right) blesses a dying member of the unit in the name of the Father, the Son and the Holy Spirit.

teaches him to show his emotions, but only for a fallen comrade of his unit. Furthermore, this time he completes the mission, unlike in Tehran in 1980 when the hostage rescue effort failed almost before it started. But counterterrorism and life go on. Upbeat music begins as the plane takes off and the credits start to roll.

At times the news media play the role of negotiator between government officials and terrorists.[51] That was the case in the 1985 TWA hijacking, as well as in the fictional ATW hijacking a year later. The terrorists of *The Delta Force* arrange an international press conference at the Beirut airport, allowing reporters to shout questions at the captain and the hijackers. This is reminiscent of Hezbollah's controlled press conferences and interviews that took place during the real hijacking in 1985. One of the terrorists, Rafai's commander Jamil, voices the media's role to Rafai: "Now we need the sympathy of the world. Now we need the American public opinion. Now it's time to be united. Release women and children, then the Americans will talk." Also the Delta Force acknowledges the importance of media attention to the film's terrorists: "Now that [they] have world's attention, [they] want to manipulate the press." The motivation follows the general terrorist trend in the 1980s. Terrorists' main goal was to gain publicity in order to create and maintain support for their cause, and possibly become a negotiation partner. As Howard has pointed out, in hostage situations the odds were 96 percent that hostages would walk out alive. He continues, noting that hostages were taken "for three reasons: attention for their cause, the release of imprisoned comrades, or ransom (profit)."[52] In the film, the terrorists try to gain media attention, particularly that of the U.S. media, but the film does not explain their cause or allow them to make demands. The Delta Force also uses the media, relying on a method that has posed a threat to journalists: hero McCoy crosses borders pretending to be a French-speaking journalist, working for a Canadian TV station, CBC-TV.

Iron Eagle and *The Delta Force* draw on the Reagan-era pride in American military power. For example, characters in both films greet the U.S. forces that come to their rescue with pride and relief. Masters excitedly yells to his father: "They are ours, dad! They are Americans!" when his F-16 is met by four other U.S. Air Force F-16 planes when he cannot outrun the enemy MiGs on his tail. Also, one of the navy hostages in *The Delta Force* excitedly announces to the other hostages that Americans are here to rescue them when he sees members of the Delta Force unit. Furthermore, both films celebrate U.S. weaponry. The villains have no recourse in either film after the hero starts using his weapons. In these films it is the heroes who perform the most killings. In both films the heroes kill dozens of Arab enemies. In *Iron Eagle* Americans lose no one, and in *The Delta Force* they lose one member of the unit and one hostage.

The films are representative of the Reaganite cinema era. Interracial harmony, strong father-son relationships, male bonding, and the absence of women, spiced up with an abundant use of violence against Reagan-era enemies, characterize the films. Scott McCoy and young Doug Masters are leaders who rise to the occasion to lead an interracial group of professionals and teenagers, respectively. The teenage hero explores his father-son relationship with his real father and African American surrogate, Colonel Chappy Sinclair, who helps him in his mission. He easily leaves his girlfriend and his mother, who relies on him, at home when his father needs him. McCoy's closest relationships are with his colonel, an African American Delta Force unit member, and especially a young soldier whom he saves at the beginning of the film in Iran and who dies in the end.

Dutifully following war film traditions, neither film has any role for women who could weaken the male bondage and heroism. The films' American male heroes save Western hostages from brutal Arab enemies whom audiences barely get to know. In particular *Iron Eagle* is guilty of portraying an extremely simplified character in the minister of defense. The film all but stamps "mad" and "evil" on his forehead, and it is only a matter of time until the hero can kill him. While *The Delta Force* is also guilty of stereotyping and simplifying its villains, the film provides the antagonists with more dialogue among themselves but still does not directly explain why they are taking hostages and what they are doing in Lebanon. However, against genre traditions they are not mad but rational in their actions otherwise. Both films' foreign antagonists are action and action-adventure film stereotypes: The dark-skinned foreign villains are brutal, anti–U.S., anti-freedom and representatives of anti–Judeo-Christian religions.[53]

After *Iron Eagle* and *The Delta Force* the commercial film industry said good-bye in its popular terrorist films to the manly man who has no room for women in his life. Due to the crumbling of the Cold War and changing values in American society, Hollywood invested in a new type of a hero and a villain, although the film industry still did not completely discard the characteristics of its past heroes. John McClane, a wise guy married to a career woman, entered the stage in 1988 in *Die Hard*. The film's hero meets a real match in the film's left-wing German terrorist, Hans Gruber.

PART III. THE HOLLYWOOD TERRORIST AFTER THE COLD WAR

As the Cold War was drawing to an end in the late 1980s, the U.S. was losing its decades-old communist enemy and with it an easy way to divide the world into communist enemies and capitalist friends. At the same time international terrorism was truly becoming global. According to the 1987 State Department report: "No region, no country, no people are unaffected or completely immune from terrorist violence."[1] The Iran-Iraq War, Israel-Palestine conflict, state sponsorship of terrorism, rising Islamic fundamentalism, the aftermath of the Soviet withdrawal from Afghanistan, and internal violence in Latin America kept international terrorism alive as a threat in the world.[2] However, the threat was not of the same magnitude as it had been with the ideological superpower enemy, the Soviet Union.

According to the State Department data, in the early 1990s the number of international terrorist incidents was much lower than in the previous decade. For example, in 1992 the department recorded 361 incidents, the smallest number of attacks since 1975. The year 1992 also had the lowest U.S. casualty number ever: two killed and one wounded.[3] The calm was shattered soon after the turn of the year. On February 26, 1993, a yellow rental van carrying a massive bomb was left in an underground parking garage below the World Trade Center (WTC). The bombing shook the towers and New York City, killing six Americans and injuring about one thousand. The terrorists' goal had been to kill a quarter million people. The FBI fast tracked down the bombers, a group of Islamic fundamentalists. A few months later the FBI successfully prevented the bombing plans of Islamic extremists who had links to the WTC group. They had selected landmark bombing targets in New York City, including the United Nations building and the Holland and Lincoln tunnels.[4]

In the changing times the lonely Reaganite cinema war-machine hero's time was running out. Commercial movie budgets were going up. Hollywood had to rejuvenate its film threats as well as its action heroes and villains in order to stay above the water. Terrorism, drug lords and governments hostile to U.S. policies and interests emerged as the country's primary threats on the big screen. International terrorism had potential as a commercial and fictional threat scenario in Hollywood action-adventure films. Bickering, mismatched interracial action-adventure heroes, for example, in the *Lethal Weapon* and *Beverly Hills Cop* films, attracted viewers. New York City police officer John McClane, played by Bruce Willis, joined the camp of new heroes in 1988 in the Gordon Company/Silver Pictures production *Die Hard*, which was released by 20th Century Fox. He faced a group of international terrorists on U.S. soil. This film about a New York City police officer, married to a woman with an impressive career, made over $80 million at the domestic box office in its release year, climbing to the #7 spot in the North American box office.[5] *Die Hard* also revitalized the film villain portrayal when it introduced left-wing Euroterrorists who were losing their bearing in the emerging world order wherein the Soviet Union was on its deathbed. Dreams of capitalist prosperity bring the film's Euroterrorists onto U.S. soil to look for their version of the American dream.

The 1990s largely abandoned the formula of a lonely hero who has a limited vocabulary and big muscles. Wives and preteen daughters entered the hero's life. His fight was more personal now than ever before. While the Reaganite cinema era had highlighted father-son relationships, in the new decade sons were absent just as women and daughters had largely been absent during the sons' heyday. Now the father alone was the ultimate savior of the family. The wife might be a strong career woman, or the hero might have a professional female partner or secondary female antagonist, but only the male hero could save his family and the U.S.

The box office success of *Die Hard* brought police officer John McClane back to try his hand at new threat scenarios. *Die Hard 2: Die Harder* (1990: #7) introduced anti-communist fighters as villains two years after the release of the original film. A few years later, *Die Hard with a Vengeance* (1995: #7) returned to the theme of left-wing Euroterrorists who are looking for their place in the new world. Fear of the communists also lurks in *Air Force One* (1997: #4), in which Russian nationalist and communist supporters try to bring back the old times when they attack the highest U.S. authority.

The decade's most popular theme of international terrorism arrived from the U.K. with five films. Wesley Snipes, the first African American hero to appear in a box office top 50 film on international terrorism, tries his wit and muscles in *Passenger 57* (1992: #35) against a British terrorist and his group who create havoc as they hijack an American airliner. Four films find their inspiration in the conflict in Northern Ireland, which made headlines throughout the decade when the U.S. was actively involved in trying to broker a peace agreement between the different parties. The four movies depict the Provisional Irish Republican Army (PIRA) and extremist PIRA splinter groups. *Patriot Games* (1992: #11), *Blown Away* (1994: #45) and *The Jackal* (1997: #34) reduce world politics to a personal conflict between the film's hero and villain. *Ronin* (1998: #46) mixes action, thriller and film noir ingredients when a CIA covert operative goes after a rogue terrorist who is a threat to the Northern Irish peace process.

The 1992 *Patriot Games* continued the adventures of author Tom Clancy's character Jack Ryan, a former CIA agent. (Ryan was also the protagonist of a previous Hollywood film, *The Hunt for Red October* (1990: #5), which was not about terrorism.) In 1994 Ryan reappeared on the big screen in *Clear and Present Danger*, in which he examined narcotrafficking at a time when the Medellín cartel was making headlines as it gradually was destroyed, with its leader on the run. This film is not included in the data since the topic is narcotrafficking and drugs. While the *Patterns of Global Terrorism* reports do discuss narcotrafficking, they regularly separate it from international terrorism even though it can have similarities to terrorism when the drug cartels target politicians, the police and other representatives of the power structure. However, the main operating motivation is profit, not a new and, from the terrorists' viewpoint, a better society for them and their supporters, as is the political goal of terrorists. The State Department's annual reports on international terrorism have rarely used the word *narcoterrorist* but primarily discuss "narcotraffickers."

In the 1990s terrorists were adapting to the post–Cold War world and new terrorist threats were emerging. In its 1993 report the State Department warned: "In the coming decade we will certainly face serious challenges from terrorism growing out of ethnic, religious, and xenophobic tensions around the world."[6] While the number of terrorist incidents had declined, particularly Islamic extremist groups had stepped up their actions. They opposed the peace process in the Middle East, and the U.S.[7] The WTC bombing and the plot to bomb New

York City landmarks made the State Department acknowledge the country's vulnerability in its 1992 report, issued after the February 1993 bombing:

> Until recently, terrorism had receded from the attention of most Americans. Terrorism is now back in the headlines, and we see ominous signs that the problem will escalate, compounded by the resurgence of regional and ethnic conflicts around the world. Since the new year, we have had the bombing of the World Trade Center, the killing of two CIA employees outside CIA Headquarters, and several airplane hijackings. These incidents remind us of our vulnerability to violent attacks.[8]

Hollywood films paid attention to the changing times and new threat scenarios. Three films in the 1990s tapped into the threat that was raising its head in that decade. *True Lies* (1994: #3) and *Executive Decision* (1996: #24) brought to the screen Islamic extremists who drew from real-life terrorist methods: the film's terrorists aim at mass casualties on U.S. soil. In *The Siege* (1998: #48) old U.S. policies came back to haunt the country when disillusioned former allies from the Middle East enter the U.S. to attack New York City. *The Siege* is a sobering film in comparison to *True Lies* and *Executive Decision*. The latter two hardly remember that non–Western and non–Christian people are human beings too. In *The Siege*, the terrorist attacks and threats, and extreme government responses to them, eerily predicted some of the events that took place after 9/11.

End of the Cold War

The Soviet Union announced in 1988 that it would pull its troops out of Afghanistan the following year. However, that did not end the conflict in Afghanistan, as different local groups continued their fight over the governance of the country, and foreign fighters sought their role in the new political environment. A new group that emerged from the Afghan veterans was founded and supported by a Saudi millionaire by the name of Osama bin Laden. He and a cleric named Azzam created in 1988 a group based on their mujahideen fighters. The new group, al Qaeda, Arabic for "the base" or "the foundation," was to maintain a trained mujahideen military force in case such a force would ever be needed in the future.[9] As the superpowers were preparing for a new world order, al Qaeda was able to brew quite undisturbed. Communism was fading from the U.S. foreign policy agenda and being replaced by the growing threats against American interests in the Middle East and the Third World. Nevertheless, Afghanistan no longer attracted U.S. attention. In Europe the Berlin Wall came down, and several Eastern European countries took steps to abandon communism, move away from the Soviet Union, and open up their borders in the revolutionary year of 1989.

As the action-adventure hero mantle was passed on from solitary and muscled 1980s stars to family men towards the decade's end, the White House also received a new master. Conservative Republican George H. W. Bush succeeded President Reagan in 1989. The world was now witnessing a rapidly changing global political and economic landscape as communism was bowing out and making room for capitalism in Eastern Europe. The collapse of the Berlin Wall and the disbanding of the Soviet Union two years later left the U.S. as the only superpower in the world in military, cultural, political and economic terms. The Cold War had peacefully ended under U.S. president George H. W. Bush and Soviet president Mikhail Gorbachev, but the West now had a problem. With the disappearance of the bipolar world structure, the Western countries, in particular the United States, faced a deep moral and political vacuum, and a social/intellectual crisis in the absence of a well-defined enemy.[10] In this era of uncertainty, President Bush found the biggest threat to U.S. interests in Iraq and its leader, Saddam Hussein.

The Persian Gulf War and the Emergence of al Qaeda

The Iran-Iraq War was over by 1988 with heavy losses on both sides. One of the biggest adversaries of the United States, the religious leader of Iran, Ayatollah Khomeini, died in June 1989. However, this did not change Iran's anti–American policies. Before his death Ayatollah Khomeini had denounced British-Indian author Salman Rushdie's *The Satanic Verses* and called for his death, which resulted in a number of attacks against bookstores and publishers related to the novel across Europe, the U.S., and Asia. Furthermore, in May 1989 the Speaker of the Iranian Parliament, Rafsanjani, who became the president later that year, strongly advised "Palestinians to kill Americans and other Westerners in order to avenge those Palestinians killed during the uprising in the occupied West Bank and Gaza. Rafsanjani also publicly encouraged the hijacking of airplanes and the blowing up of factories."[11] Iran also targeted dissidents and Saudi Arabia. It recruited, supported and trained Shia radicals for attacks against Saudi Arabia. Iran also maintained its support for Hezbollah.

After the end of the Iran-Iraq War, Iraq did not enjoy for long its absence from the U.S. State Department list of the state sponsors of terrorism. By 1990 Iraq was back on the list.[12] That same year Saddam Hussein's Iraq invaded Kuwait, Iraq's militarily and politically weak neighbor, and declared Kuwait an Iraqi province. In the matter of how to deal with Iraq, President Bush first acquired from the United Nations Security Council an authorization for an international coalition to force Iraq out of Kuwait. Congress passed a similar resolution, although President Bush felt he was authorized to act on Iraq even if the resolution had not been passed in Congress.[13] Operation Desert Storm started the war on Iraq on January 16, 1991. The coalition forces, led by the United States, fast succeeded in driving the Iraqi forces out of Kuwait. Stereotypical entertainment-media images of the Middle East, and news media reporting that lacked serious, in-depth coverage of Iraq and Kuwait, and of Iraq's relationship with the U.S. over the past decades, left Iraq and its dictator described in simplified terms to American audiences. Hollywood had traditionally portrayed Arabs as barbaric, anti–American crazed fanatics. With that negative, hegemonic image of the Arab world, a true U.S. patriot was expected to support the war against Iraq and Arabs.[14] Kuwait got a free pass on its human rights violations. Congress and the public were duped by stories that American public relations (PR) firm Hill and Knowlton brought in order to sell the war. The PR campaign was primarily financed by the Kuwaiti royal family.

Osama bin Laden's response to the Iraqi invasion was an offer to the Saudi monarchy. He proposed he would call for a jihad and have his mujahideen fighters retake Kuwait. Saudi Arabia refused the offer and, instead, joined the U.S.-led international coalition.[15] Ahmad points out that Osama bin Laden was a U.S. ally until 1990, when the U.S. military were the first foreign military forces to enter Saudi Arabia. For bin Laden, their continued stay in Saudi Arabia after the end of the Persian Gulf War was not acceptable, in particular since "Saudi Arabia is the holy place of Muslims, home of Mecca and Medina."[16] Bin Laden and his group had succeeded in driving the Soviet Union out of Afghanistan, so for them to take on another superpower was nothing new. Bin Laden now started a new jihad with the goal of driving the U.S. military forces out of Saudi Arabia. Ahmad argues that it is important to note that bin Laden's code of ethics is determined by his background:

> he comes from a tribal people. Being a millionaire doesn't matter. His code of ethics is tribal. The tribal code of ethics consists of two words: loyalty and revenge. You are my friend. You keep your word. I am loyal to you. You break your word, I go on my path of revenge. For him, America has broken its word. The loyal friend has betrayed him. Now they're going to go for you.[17]

Furthermore, bin Laden and his group had taken notice of failed U.S. counterterrorism efforts. Even more notorious cases than the abandoned Delta Force rescue mission in 1980 occurred in 1983 and 1993, and terrorists have publicly declared both cases as signs of U.S. weakness and proof of their own power. When a Hezbollah suicide bombing of the U.S. marine barracks in Beirut killed 241 Americans, President Reagan's response was to pull the U.S. forces from Lebanon. Ten years later U.S. military forces were unprepared for Somalia's tribal warfare when President Bush sent them to help to protect the international humanitarian relief efforts in Somalia. The effort by the U.S. military to capture the warlord who was considered to be the main force behind the problems the U.S. troops encountered did not succeed but resulted in the death of eighteen U.S. soldiers. Television images of an American soldier's corpse being dragged through the streets of the Somali capital, Mogadishu, spread around the world. When pressured by Congress, President Clinton ordered the U.S. forces to leave Somalia.[18]

The year 1991 finally brought an end to the era of Lebanon kidnappings for the U.S. when Hezbollah released nine long-held Western hostages, including the last six Americans. The last two Western hostages, two Germans, were released the following year. The 1991 State Department report credits UN Secretary-General Javier Pérez de Cuéllar and his special envoy for the releases. The report highlights that the U.S. gave no concessions to terrorists and therefore the releases could be considered as a sign of success of the government's policy of refusing to bargain with terrorists.[19]

New Forms of International Terrorism

With the end of communism, the face and threat of terrorism started to change. Left-wing terrorism was declining. For example, Germany's Red Army Faction renounced terrorism in 1992, and although it returned to terrorist activity two years later it did not reach the same level of activity as in the 1980s. Ethnic and separatist groups stayed active. After the collapse of communism the State Department warned that ethnic conflicts might be highlighted in the new order and that might result in further acts of terrorism. A new fear was realized in violent right-wing acts by skinheads and neo–Nazis against foreigners in Western Europe.[20]

In the late 1980s state sponsorship of terrorism started to decline. A new trend was emerging that came to the forefront in the 1990s: individual and group-sponsored terrorism, often in the name of fundamentalist views of Islam, and having global implications. While state sponsors of terrorism often can control the activities of the groups they are sponsoring, the new groups were relying on their own financing and therefore were free to act as they saw fit to attain their goals, not the goals of a sponsor. According to the State Department's 1995 report,

> These transnational terrorists benefit from modern communications and transportation, have global sources of funding, are knowledgeable about modern explosives and weapons, and are more difficult to track and apprehend than members of the old established groups or those sponsored by states. Many of these transnational terrorists were trained in militant camps in Afghanistan or are veterans of the Afghan war. In 1995 a conspiracy discovered in the Philippines to bomb US airliners over the Pacific and led by the suspected mastermind of the World Trade Center bombing, exemplified this kind of transnational terrorism.[21]

As the State Department pointed out, many of the new terrorists had their background in Afghanistan. The U.S. fear of the expansion of the Soviet power and ideology had been at its height in Afghanistan during the Soviet invasion. Despite the CIA's difficulties, the agency had maintained an active agenda in Afghanistan under President Reagan. The Reagan administration was not going to let the country slip into Soviet hands. *The 9/11 Commission Report* discusses how Saudi Arabia and the U.S. gave billions of dollars in secret to Afghan fighters to support their fight against the Soviet Union. Jentleson describes that the U.S. assistance included "extensive military aid, weapons, and covert action for the Afghan mujahideen fighting against the Soviets and the puppet government they set up in the Afghan capital, Kabul."[22]

According to Ahmad, the Soviet intervention in Afghanistan brought an opportunity to bring back jihad in its international sense, something that had not happened in the previous four hundred years. He explains that to translate jihad as "holy war," an often used translation in the West, is not exactly right:

> *Jihad* in Arabic means "to struggle." It could be struggle by violence or by non-violent means. There are two forms, the small *jihad* and the big *jihad*. The small *jihad* involves external violence. The big *jihad* involves a struggle within oneself.... In Islamic history, *jihad* as an international violent phenomenon had for all practical purposes disappeared in the last four hundred years. It was revived suddenly with American help in the 1980s.[23]

Ahmad notes that for the U.S. this was

> a God-sent opportunity to mobilize one billion Muslims against what Reagan called the Evil Empire. Money started pouring in. CIA agents starting going all over the Muslim world recruiting people to fight in the great *jihad*. Bin Laden was one of the early prize recruits. He was not only an Arab, he was a Saudi multimillionaire willing to put his own money into the matter.[24]

According to *The 9/11 Commission Report* and the CIA website, bin Laden, who had arrived in Afghanistan in 1980, and his supporters received little or no financial support from the U.S.

Osama bin Laden and the U.S. were on the same side in Afghanistan during the Soviet invasion, which brings into focus the fact that terrorism is a flexible, confusing and changing concept. It is used for a specific purpose, that is, whatever political needs happen to be at a specific point in history.[25] Ahmad explains that when terrorism definitions are vague, the approach allows the government to avoid a commitment to certain definitions of terrorism. He cites Secretary of State George Shultz's 1984 speech on terrorism at the Park Avenue Synagogue in New York City to point out the lack of a clear definition of what terrorism is and where it takes place: "There is no question about our ability to use force where and when it is needed to counter terrorism.... We know the difference between terrorists and freedom fighters and as we look around, we have no trouble telling one from the other."[26] Ahmad continues: "Only Osama bin Laden doesn't know that he was an ally one day and an enemy another. That's very confusing for Osama bin Laden."[27]

The U.S. was soon to experience the new era of international terrorism in practice. When Osama bin Laden failed to drive American forces out of the Middle East, his network started to attack American and other Western targets around the world, and eventually on their own soil. His policy was also to wait for an enemy counterattack which would bring more American and Western targets to the Middle East.

Islamic radicals were not the only religious extremists in the new era of terrorism. For example, Israeli prime minister Yitzhak Rabin became a victim of a Jewish Israeli extremist who was against the ongoing Arab-Israel peace process. Prime Minister Rabin had been a strong promoter of the peace process in the Middle East. The extremist assassinated Rabin at a pro-peace rally in Tel Aviv in 1995.[28]

The First World Trade Center Bombing

In the 1990s, after twelve years of a Republican White House, Democrat Bill Clinton was twice elected to the White House. Middle Eastern terrorism, participation in the peace negotiations in Northern Ireland, and domestic terrorism dominated the agenda on terrorism although terrorism itself was not topping the foreign policy agenda. But the 1990s turned out to be the decade when terrorism hit the United States on its own turf. The year 1993 was one of terrorism's deadliest and most destructive years. The year's most important terrorist incidents according to the State Department's 1993 report were the World Trade Center bombing in February, the foiled Iraqi attempt to assassinate former President George H. W. Bush in Kuwait in April, and the Kurdistan Workers Party's several coordinated attacks in June and November against Turkish diplomatic and commercial facilities in Europe.[29] The year's "spectacular" attack, as the 1993 report calls it, was undoubtedly the bombing of the World Trade Center on February 26 in New York City:

> The massive explosion left a 30 × 30-meter (100 × 100-foot) opening in the underground parking garage, scattered debris throughout an adjacent subway station, and filled all 110 floors of the north tower with smoke. The effects of the blast and the ensuing fire and smoke caused six deaths and 1,000 injuries....
>
> The WTC bombing is considered an act of international terrorism because of the political motivations that spurred the attack and because most of the suspects who have been arrested are foreign nationals. However, the FBI has not found evidence that a foreign government was responsible for the bombing.[30]

The WTC bombing was the year's only international attack that had American casualties. All of the six victims who died were Americans. The main culprits behind the attack were Umar Abd al-Rahman, an Egyptian cleric living in New Jersey and known as the "Blind Shaykh," and some of his followers. The actual bomb's planter was Ramzi Ahmed Yousef, whom Pakistan turned over to the U.S. in 1995. Three years later he was sentenced to 240 years in solitary confinement.[31] If not for an informant's tip, the number of deaths in New York City in 1993 might have been higher. The informant's tip led to a revelation of a plot to target the United Nations building and the Holland and Lincoln Tunnels in New York City. The suspects had links to the WTC bombing suspects. Further investigations revealed, as the 1995 report discusses, that one of the World Trade Center terrorists, Abd al-Rahman, had been leading an organization which had been aiming to fight an urban "holy war" against the U.S., which the organization considered to be an enemy of Islam.[32]

Ramzi Yousef's goal had been to kill at least 250,000 people in the WTC bombing. *The 9/11 Commission Report* criticizes the media for having undermined the threat of terrorism and having neglected to report on how close Yousef came to achieving his goal. Instead, the news media focused on repeating the story of how the FBI caught one of the terrorists because he had reported as stolen the truck which had been used in the bombing. He had kept on calling the rental company, asking to get back his $400 deposit. The description of the van and the repeated calls made the agency report the man to the FBI.[33]

Iraq's most notable anti–U.S. activity was the April 1993 attempt on former President Bush's life. According to the State Department's 1993 report, Kuwaiti officials were successful in preventing the planned car bomb attack when they revealed the plot just before the former president's visit. President Clinton responded with a military act to make it clear to Saddam Hussein's Iraq that the U.S. would not tolerate the country's terrorist acts.[34] After 1993 Iraq still continued to sponsor and support terrorist organizations, but gave up on anti–Western terrorist attacks.[35]

Two years after the World Trade Center bombing, on April 19, 1995, the two-year anniversary of the federal attack on a religious commune in Waco, Texas, a federal building was bombed in Oklahoma City. The bombing killed 168 Americans. News media reports focused on Arab suspects immediately after the attack.[36] However, soon the FBI traced the attack to Timothy McVeigh, an American Persian Gulf War veteran.

The World Trade Center and the Oklahoma City bombings were highly publicized terrorist attacks on U.S. soil. They caused extensive civilian casualties and material destruction, which brought the fear of terrorism close to home to the administration and the public. President Clinton was coordinating counterterrorism from the White House. After the World Trade Center attack and Oklahoma City bombing in the U.S., and the Aum Shinrikyo cult's sarin nerve gas attack in Tokyo, Clinton issued a classified directive, Presidential Decision Directive 39, which called for strong actions against terrorism. Furthermore,

> The directive called terrorism both a matter of national security and a crime, and it assigned responsibilities to various agencies. Alarmed by the incident in Tokyo, President Clinton made it the very highest priority for his own staff and for all agencies to prepare to detect and respond to terrorism that involved chemical, biological, or nuclear weapons.[37]

On the advice of his national security adviser, President Clinton also created a new post, a national coordinator for security, infrastructure protection, and counterterrorism. In particular, weapons of mass destruction in the hands of the countries hostile to U.S. interests were a concern to the Clinton administration. However, terrorism was not the administration's top concern. The top spot was reserved for the country's military operations and commitments around the world.

During the Clinton presidency the State Department kept on emphasizing the country's no concessions to terrorists policy, and continued putting pressure of the state sponsors of terrorism. It also stressed the treatment of terrorists as criminals and that they should be brought to justice.[38] Under Clinton the U.S. also started a practice which allowed another country to hand over terrorists to a third country at the request of the U.S. According to the 2001 report the number of extraditions and renditions of terrorists to the U.S. was 14 between 1993 and 2001.The 2001 report says that 14 terrorists were extradited to the United States between 1993 and 2001.[39] The increase in extraditions was part of American counterterrorist efforts. Also, the U.S. was blocking the assets of any organization that was trying to prevent the Middle East peace process. Furthermore, President Clinton and Secretary of State Warren Christopher both addressed international terrorism and the extreme importance of counterterrorism at the 50th United Nations General Assembly in 1995.[40]

Al Qaeda Targets the U.S.

During President Clinton's second term, the threat of terrorism, in particular Osama bin Laden's group, became more real. In August 1998, the American embassies in Nairobi, Kenya, and Dar es Salaam, Tanzania, were targets of bomb attacks that together killed 301 people, injured about 5,000 people, and caused great material damages. The federal government held Osama bin Laden responsible for the attacks and launched counterattacks against bin Laden's alleged training camp areas in Afghanistan. In Sudan, U.S. air strikes targeted a pharmaceutical plant suspected of producing VX nerve gas. After the attacks President Clinton's Executive Order 12947 acknowledged the threat of Osama bin Laden to the U.S. security and interests. Bin Laden was now added to the official list of terrorists. This also applied to his key associates. The measure prohibited bin Laden from having any property or financial transactions in the

U.S.[41] The U.S. policy on terrorism toughened in the aftermath of the Kenya and Tanzania attacks. After the U.S. air strikes Secretary of State Madeleine Albright voiced the U.S. determination to go after terrorists and to catch them: "The terrorists should have no illusion: Old Glory will continue to fly wherever we have interests to defend. We will meet our commitments. We will strive to protect our people. And we will wage the struggle against terror on every front, on every continent, with every tool, every day."[42] The Clinton administration gave the Taliban, which was in power in Afghanistan, a clear message that the U.S. held the Taliban responsible for the actions of its guest Osama bin Laden. The U.S. set financial sanctions against Taliban-run Afghanistan and demanded the country hand to over Osama bin Laden. In July 1999 President Clinton officially declared the Taliban to be a state sponsor of terrorism.

In the aftermath of the Kenya and Tanzania terrorist attacks and the U.S. counterattacks, President Clinton spoke at the United Nations asking all nations to put the fight against terrorism at the top of their agendas.[43] The Clinton administration further defended the U.S. actions in Sudan and Afghanistan at the end of October by declaring that the country has a legal right to kill those it defines as terrorist leaders.[44] According to *The 9/11 Commission Report*, President Clinton moved gradually in Osama bin Laden's case, starting with the goal of capture and moving to the possibility of killing him, but only if no innocent bystanders would be killed. Eventually Clinton toughened the policy to the point that bin Laden could be killed even if it also meant the killing of innocent bystanders. In the Clinton administration's view the killing of bin Laden translated into self-defense, not into an assassination. President Ford had issued Executive Order 11905 in 1976 in response to press revelations of the CIA's assassination attempts, including on Cuban president Castro's life. The order clearly prohibits assassinations. Later presidents had upheld the ban on political assassinations. Presidents Carter and Reagan both issued executive orders that reconfirmed the ban, Executive Orders 12306 and 12333 respectively.[45] However, presidents Reagan and Clinton interpreted that (foreign) political opponents' deaths are not political assassinations, but acts of war, if they take place when the U.S. is acting in self-defense. Furthermore, soon after 9/11 President George W. Bush signed an intelligence finding which encouraged the CIA to use "lethal covert operations" when going after al Qaeda and its leader.[46] This continued the Clinton administration's approach. For example, under President Clinton, CIA-backed covert operations targeted Saddam Hussein and Osama bin Laden, the latter with the help of Pakistani commandos whom the CIA had trained. Had the covert operations — not assassination plots — succeeded, they most likely would have killed their targets.[47]

In the late 1990s the State Department addressed the growing role of the new form of international terrorism. State sponsorship had been declining in the 1990s when well-financed independent groups had started to emerge. They neither needed nor wanted state sponsorship because it would have meant following the restrictions set by the state sponsor. In its 1999 report the State Department pointed out

> the shift from well-organized, localized groups supported by state sponsors to loosely organized, international networks of terrorists.... With the decrease of state funding, these loosely networked individuals and groups have turned increasingly to other sources of funding, including private sponsorship, narcotrafficking, crime, and illegal trade. This shift parallels a change from primarily politically motivated terrorism to terrorism that is more religiously or ideologically motivated. Another trend is the shift eastward of the locus of terrorism from the Middle East to South Asia, specifically Afghanistan. As most Middle Eastern governments have strengthened their counterterrorist response, terrorists and their organizations have sought safehaven in areas where they can operate with impunity.[48]

The report continued, stating that the new terrorists were hiding in "'swamps' where government control is weak or governments are sympathetic. We seek to drain these swamps."[49] The report emphasized that international cooperation was the key to achieving that goal.

Close to the end of Clinton's presidency there was an attack against the USS *Cole* in the Yemeni port of Aden. Nineteen American citizens were killed, seventeen of them sailors. The State Department's 2000 report stated that there were no definite or proved links to bin Laden; the Yemeni authorities investigating the attack argued it could be traced to veterans of the Afghan training camps.[50]

Osama bin Laden

Osama bin Laden arrived in Afghanistan in 1980 to fight a jihad against the Soviet invaders. When the Soviet Union pulled its forces from Afghanistan, it was a victory to the mujahideen fighters who had received funding from Saudi Arabia and the CIA.

In 1989 bin Laden moved his operations to Sudan where he received support from the leader of the National Islamic Front, Hassan al Turabi. His party was part of a coalition that was now in power in Sudan. While bin Laden helped Turabi against African Christian separatists and in road building, in return he was able to prepare for a jihad in Sudan and continue his business affairs there while he himself moved from Afghanistan to Saudi Arabia.

The year 1990 was the turning point for Osama bin Laden and his supporters in their relationship with the United States. That year Saudi Arabia refused al Qaeda's offer of help against Iraq. Instead, Saudi Arabia turned to the U.S. for help, and allowed the entrance of American troops in Saudi Arabia. For Osama bin Laden, a Sunni fundamentalist, the presence of Western troops in a country that is holy to Muslims was an extreme insult. Osama bin Laden then turned against the U.S. and also against those who disagreed with his extremist interpretations of Islam.

After Saudi Arabia rejected bin Laden's offer to help the country against Iraq, bin Laden vocalized his opposition to the U.S. forces in Saudi Arabia. His opinion did not sit well with the Saudi monarchy. Bin Laden escaped efforts to silence him, and moved to Sudan in 1991 to lead his global business and terrorism affairs from there. Three years later Saudi Arabia revoked his citizenship and put a freeze on his financial assets. In Sudan, bin Laden started an extensive expansion of his organization and network.[51]

The 9/11 Commission Report details how Osama bin Laden had been targeting the U.S. since 1992. Publicly he had announced the U.S. as his main target several times. In 1992 al Qaeda issued a fatwa, an Islamic legal opinion, encouraging a jihad to drive the Western powers, in particular the U.S., from Islamic lands. In 1996 Bin Laden himself urged Muslims to drive Americans out of Saudi Arabia. In 1998 he and Ayman al Zawahiri, a fugitive Egyptian physician, declared a fatwa against America in an Arabic newspaper published in London. The commission report points out that neither man was authorized to issue a fatwa; only scholars of Islamic law can issue fatwa as interpretations of the law. The report continues: "Claiming that America had declared war against God and his messenger, they called for the murder of any American, anywhere on earth, as the 'individual duty for every Muslim who can do it in any country in which it is possible to do it.'"[52] Only three months later, bin Laden argued in an ABC-TV interview that "it was more important for Muslims to kill Americans than to kill other infidels. It is far better for anyone to kill a single American soldier than to squander his efforts on other activities." Asked whether he approved of terrorism and of attacks on civilians, bin Laden replied: "We believe that the worst thieves in the world today and the worst terrorists are the Americans. Nothing could stop you except perhaps retaliation in kind. We do not have to differentiate between military or civilian. As far as we are concerned, they are all targets."[53]

A more traditional U.S. adversary from the list of the state sponsors of terrorism, Iran, had a different view on the matter of targeting noncombatants. In a January 1998 interview with CNN, Iranian president Khatami condemned attacks against noncombatants. And even though there has been no love lost between Iran and Israel, he also condemned attacks on Israeli women and children.[54]

During the ABC-TV interview, bin Laden expressed confidence in his fight against Americans. As proofs of his group's past successes he mentioned the Soviet withdrawal from Afghanistan and the U.S. withdrawal from Somalia.[55] For discontented citizens in the Arab world, he was a symbol of the power that had forced the Soviet Union to withdraw from Afghanistan. He was also becoming a powerful symbol of resistance against the West, particularly against the U.S.

Unlike fictional film terrorists, bin Laden has stated his goals and motivations quite clearly. For example, the February 23, 1998, statement titled "Jihad Against Jews and Crusaders" by bin Laden and his associates, known as the "World Islamic Front," discusses the group's motivations to target the U.S.:

> First, for over seven years the United States has been occupying the lands of Islam in the holiest of places, the Arabian peninsula, plundering its riches, dictating to its rulers, humiliating its people, terrorizing its neighbors, and turning its bases in the peninsula into a spearhead through which to fight the neighboring Muslim peoples.[56]

The statement further "reminds" everyone of "the crusader–Zionist alliance" against Iraq which resulted in the death of over one million, and American efforts "to repeat the horrific massacres."[57] According to the statement, the U.S. is humiliating Muslims. It continues: "Third, if the Americans' aims behind these wars are religious and economic, the aim is also to serve the Jews' petty state and divert attention from its occupation of Jerusalem and murder of Muslims there."[58] For bin Laden, U.S. actions have their basis in a U.S. attack on Muslims: "All these crimes and sins committed by the Americans are a clear declaration of war on Allah, his Messenger, and Muslims. And ulema [Muslim legal scholars] have throughout Islamic history unanimously agreed that the jihad is an individual duty if the enemy destroys the Muslim countries."[59]

Bin Laden wants to implement his extremist version of Sunni Islam, and to prevent the influence of Western countries in the Middle East, and to suppress those who oppose his views and policies, including Muslim countries. The State Department's 1998 report states:

> Bin Ladin seeks to aid those who support his primary goal — driving US forces from the Arabian Peninsula, removing the Saudi ruling family from power, and "liberating Palestine" or his secondary goals of removing Western military forces and overthrowing what he calls corrupt, Western-oriented governments in predominantly Muslim countries.[60]

Additionally, in al Qaeda's view the U.S. should "convert to Islam, and end the immorality and godlessness of its society and culture."[61]

As *The 9/11 Commission Report* points out, it took a while before the United States understood Osama bin Laden's role in new terrorism. In its 1993 report the State Department mentions for the first time the mujahideen training camps in Afghanistan:

> Afghanistan's eastern and northern provinces are sites for mujahedin camps in which Muslim militants from around the world receive paramilitary training. Members of Egyptian, Algerian, and

Kashmiri militant organizations have been trained in these camps, as have members of many other Middle Eastern and Asian groups.[62]

The report further addresses Afghan veterans:

Between 1979 and 1992, several thousand non–Afghan Muslims volunteered to fight alongside the Afghan mujahedin in their ultimately successful war against the Soviet Union and its client government in Kabul. Most of these non–Afghan Muslims fought with the fundamentalist mujahedin groups and received religious indoctrination, paramilitary training, and combat experience. A list of the countries from which these Islamic volunteers hailed includes Egypt, Turkey, Jordan, Sudan, India, Algeria, Malaysia, several European and North American states, Kuwait, Saudi Arabia, and Pakistan. Since the defeat of the Communist regime in Kabul in April 1992, many of these non–Afghan mujahedin have returned home, and some have become active in indigenous insurgent movements. To date, the Afghan veterans have been most prominent in antiregime violence in Algeria and Egypt, and some are reportedly serving as trainers and fighters for Muslim forces in Bosnia.[63]

For the next few years the State Department's *Patterns of Global Terrorism* reports repeatedly mentioned Afghanistan as a training area for terrorists from around the world. Graduates of these camps were taking part in acts worldwide, including the 1993 World Trade Center bombing and Egyptian president Hosni Mubarak's assassination attempt. They were also involved in wars and insurgencies around the world, for example, in Bosnia and Chechnya. Most Afghan political factions, which were competing for power, were maintaining their own training camps. This was that case, for example, with the Kabul government as well as the main Afghan opposition movement, the Taliban.[64]

In 1996 bin Laden left Sudan for Afghanistan. A top secret State Department document from July 18, 1996, titled "Terrorism/Usama bin Ladin: Who's Chasing Whom," unclassified in July 2005 as part of a Freedom of Information Act request by the conservative group Judicial Watch, warned that his move to Afghanistan might turn out to be more dangerous to the U.S. than his stay in Sudan since he could continue to run his activities from there.[65] That same year, in 1996, the CIA set up a new unit whose focus was on Osama bin Laden. By the following year the unit's employees noticed that bin Laden was much more than just a financier of terrorism:

They learned that al Qaeda had a military committee that was planning operations against U.S. interests worldwide and was actively trying to obtain nuclear material. Analysts assigned to the station looked at the information it had gathered and "found connections everywhere," including links to the attacks on US troops in Aden and Somalia in 1992 and 1993 and to the Manila air plot in the Philippines in 1994–1995.[66]

The CIA still had contacts in Afghanistan although the U.S. had largely ignored the country after the Soviet Union had pulled out.

Several different U.S. agencies were working in 1997 and 1998 on plans to bring bin Laden to justice in the U.S. For example, according to *The 9/11 Commission Report*, "The CIA's Counterterrorist Center was developing a plan to capture and remove him from Afghanistan. Parts of the Justice Department were moving toward indicting Bin Ladin, making possible a criminal trial in New York court."[67] In June 1999 the FBI added bin Laden to its Ten Most Wanted Fugitives list. The Department of State bumped up its reward to $5 million for information that would lead to the arrest or conviction of wanted terrorist suspects.[68]

In the 1990s South Asia became the center of anti–American terrorist activity. The State Department's 2000 report saw especially the Taliban as a provider of a safe haven for terrorist leaders and organizations, Osama bin Laden leading the list. That year the U.S. made it very

MURDER OF U.S. NATIONALS OUTSIDE THE UNITED STATES; CONSPIRACY TO MURDER U.S. NATIONALS OUTSIDE THE UNITED STATES; ATTACK ON A FEDERAL FACILITY RESULTING IN DEATH

USAMA BIN LADEN

Aliases: Usama Bin Muhammad Bin Ladin, Shaykh Usama Bin Ladin, The Prince, The Emir, Abu Abdallah, Mujahid Shaykh, Hajj, The Director

DESCRIPTION

Date of Birth Used:	1957	**Hair:**	Brown
Place of Birth:	Saudi Arabia	**Eyes:**	Brown
Height:	6'4" to 6'6"	**Sex:**	Male
Weight:	Approximately 160 pounds	**Complexion:**	Olive
Build:	Thin	**Citizenship:**	Saudi Arabian
Language:	Arabic (probably Pashtu)		
Scars and Marks:	None known		
Remarks:	Bin Laden is left-handed and walks with a cane.		

CAUTION

Usama Bin Laden is wanted in connection with the August 7, 1998, bombings of the United States Embassies in Dar es Salaam, Tanzania, and Nairobi, Kenya. These attacks killed over 200 people. In addition, Bin Laden is a suspect in other terrorist attacks throughout the world.

REWARD

The Rewards For Justice Program, United States Department of State, is offering a reward of up to $25 million for information leading directly to the apprehension or conviction of Usama Bin Laden. An additional $2 million is being offered through a program developed and funded by the Airline Pilots Association and the Air Transport Association.

SHOULD BE CONSIDERED ARMED AND DANGEROUS

In June 1999 the FBI added bin Laden to its Ten Most Wanted Fugitives list. The Department of State increased its reward to $25 million for information that would lead to the arrest or conviction of bin Laden. In October 2001 he appeared on the first Most Wanted Terrorists list.

clear to the Taliban on several occasions that the U.S. would hold the Taliban responsible for any attack by its guest bin Laden.[69] The growing threat of the Afghan veterans can be seen in the State Department's *Patterns of Global Terrorism* reports in the 1990s and especially after the 1998 attacks on the U.S. embassies in Kenya and Tanzania. For example, the introduction to the 2000 report credits the UN for its actions, which show the understanding

> that Taliban-controlled Afghanistan remains a primary hub for terrorists and a home or transit point for the loosely organized network of "Afghan alumni," a web of informally linked individuals and groups that were trained and fought in the Afghan war. Afghan alumni have been involved in most major terrorist plots or attacks against the United States in the past 15 years and now engage in international militant and terrorist acts throughout the world. The leaders of some of the most dangerous terrorist groups to emerge in the past decade have headquarters or major offices in Afghanistan, and their associates threaten stability in many real and potential trouble spots around the globe — from the Philippines to the Balkans, Central Asia to the Persian Gulf, Western China to Somalia, and Western Europe to South Asia. This is why the Taliban's continued support for these groups is now recognized by the international community as a growing threat to all countries.[70]

Like other U.S. agencies, the State Department was waking up slowly to the threat of Osama bin Laden and the al Qaeda network. As the 1990s was drawing to an end, the department added more and more information on bin Laden, the 17th son of a Saudi construction magnate. The 1999 report mentions that bin Laden

> *played a significant role in financing, recruiting, transporting, and training Arab nationals who volunteered to fight in Afghanistan. During the war, Bin Ladin founded al-Qaida (the Base) to serve as an operational hub for like-minded extremists.... Using the ties al-Qaida has developed, Bin Ladin believes he can call upon individuals and groups virtually worldwide to conduct terrorist attacks.*[71]

Although the State Department's annual reports on terrorism did address the threat of Afghan vets and Osama bin Laden, they were not the department's top priorities. Rather, the State Department was focusing its efforts in the region on reducing the area's nuclear tensions, bringing an end to the Afghan civil war, and on improving the Taliban's track record on human rights.[72]

The almost simultaneous attacks on the U.S. embassies in Nairobi, Kenya, and Dar es Salaam, Tanzania, on August 7, 1998, showcased al Qaeda's ability to strike against the U.S. and other Western countries. According to the State Department, bin Laden said that he "instigated" the bombings in Tanzania and Kenya but was not involved in them. In his interviews, bin Laden called for further attacks on U.S. citizens around the world as a punishment for U.S. attacks on Iraq.[73] After the embassy attacks, the U.S. had intelligence suggesting that terrorist leaders were to meet in Afghanistan. The U.S. planned to target the meeting and kill bin Laden, who was expected to be present. The U.S. cruise missiles largely hit their targets according to the plan but missed bin Laden because he had already left the area.[74]

The 1998 attacks and counterattacks highlighted the threat of terrorism, in particular the threat of bin Laden against U.S. interests. The December 4, 1998, Presidential Daily Brief included a CIA warning titled, "Bin Ladin Preparing to Hijack US Aircraft and Other Attacks."[75] The following year more reports came in, warning about bin Laden's possible attacks against the U.S. The warnings continued under President George W. Bush. For example, the August 6, 2001, Presidential Daily Brief titled "Bin Ladin Determined To Strike in US" brought attention to suspicious activity in the U.S., noted by the FBI, which was "consistent with preparations for hijackings or other types of attacks, including federal buildings in New York."[76] The Bush administration's focus was on developing missile defense to protect the U.S. Al Qaeda and Islamic extremists were far from the top of the agenda. Rather, the Bush administration saw terrorist threats in Iraq and other rogue states.[77]

New Terrorism and New Threats

A new form of terrorism emerged with Osama bin Laden and al Qaeda. Howard warns that the new terrorism practiced by bin Laden and his network poses a bigger threat to the U.S. than the more traditional enemies. Past U.S. presidents had a direct personal line to Soviet leaders, but with bin Laden there is no such contact or diplomatic relationship. It is hard to anticipate his and al Qaeda's actions because these actors are outside the traditional structures of power and international relationships.[78] *The 9/11 Commission Report* also points out that during the Cold War the opponent's actions could be predicted to an extent but that has not been the case in the post–Cold War world.

Howard lists six distinguishable differences between the old and new terrorism:

1. The "new terrorism" is more violent. Under the old paradigm, terrorists wanted attention, not mass casualties. Now they want both.
2. Unlike their Cold War counterparts, who were primarily sub-state actors trying to effect change in local politics, today's terrorists are transnational, non-state actors who operate globally and want to destroy the West and all Islamic secular state systems.
3. The "new terrorists" are much better financed than their predecessors....
4. Today's terrorists are better trained in the arts of war and the black arts than those in past decades....
5. This generation's terrorists, particularly the religious extremists, are more difficult to penetrate than terrorists of previous generations. The networked, cellular structure used by al Qaeda and its allies is especially difficult to penetrate, especially for a hierarchical security apparatus like that in the United States. While bribes and sex traps could help catch terrorists for prosecution and information in the old days, now it is difficult to "turn" religious extremists using the same methods....

> 6. Most insidious is the availability of weapons of mass destruction (WMD).... Today, the concern is about nuclear, radiological, chemical, and biological weapons — all of which are potentially catastrophic, with mass killing potential.[79]

Howard describes al Qaeda, a representative of new terrorism, as a global network with a global target. He continues by noting that the organization's members are well trained in paramilitary operations, their training drawing from the special operations of the U.S., the U.K., Russia and other countries. The training also teaches current politics and Islamic studies. Al Qaeda's structure resembles Western and Russian military structures in the sense that the network relies not only on military power but also on intelligence gathering. Attacks are carefully planned out and can take a long time to prepare. The organization's goal is to cause mass casualties. The groups that are part of the al Qaeda network are hard to penetrate due to their organizational structure in which independent cells up to fifteen members have no contact with other cells. To catch one cell does not pose a threat to the other cells.

Essential for al Qaeda's operations has been a continuous flow of available cash. Osama bin Laden's personal wealth has been estimated to be somewhere between $18 million and $200 million.[80] *The 9/11 Commission Report* estimates al Qaeda's annual budget at $30 million, which largely comes from a fund-raising network. Most of the money is spent on "salaries for jihadists, training camps, airfields, vehicles, arms, and the development of training manuals," while actual terrorist operations claim very little of the annual budget.[81] For example, according to the report, the planning and execution of the combined September 11, 2001, attacks cost from $400,000 to $500,000. To put that into perspective in Hollywood terms, an action-adventure film producer would be very lucky if she or he were able to purchase a script for a price equal to the budget of the 9/11 attacks. But the money would not even start a production on that script in the world where $100 million as an action-adventure film budget does not raise eyebrows.

New terrorists, just like anyone else in society, have grown with the latest technologies and use them in their everyday life. They are modern, technologically skilled opponents who communicate, organize themselves, and plan and arrange their attacks by relying on the latest communication technologies:

> With globalization and the telecommunications revolution, and with loosely affiliated but networked adversaries using commercial devices and encryption, the technical impediments to signals grew at a geometric rate.... Modern adversaries are skilled users of communications technologies.[82]

According to the State Department's 2000 report, terrorists

> *embrace IT* [information technology] *for several reasons: it improves communication and aids organization, allows members to coordinate quickly with large numbers of followers, and provides a platform for propaganda. The Internet also allows terrorists to reach a wide audience of potential donors and recruits who may be located over a large geographic area.*[83]

The report also mentions that computer hacking is becoming a new terrorist weapon whose appeal may increase simply due to the news media's trend to sensationalize hacking.

Another modern threat was realized for the first time in international terrorism in 1995 when the Japanese Aum Shinrikyo cult attacked the Tokyo subway with poisonous gas. Twelve people died in the attack and 5,500 were injured, two of them Americans. This was the first major terrorist attack that relied on the use of chemical weapons.[84] According to the State Department's 1999 report, terrorist organizations have either used or have tried to acquire chemical, biological, radiological, or nuclear (CBRN) weapons for a variety of reasons:

Increased publicity highlighted the vulnerability of civilian targets to CBRN attacks. Such attacks could cause lasting disruption and generate significant psychological impact on a population and its infrastructure. As of yearend, the largest attack involving chemical weapons against civilians was Aum Shinrikyo's sarin nerve agent attack on the Tokyo subway system in March 1995.

Some groups, especially those motivated by distorted religious and cultural ideologies, had demonstrated a willingness to inflict greater numbers of indiscriminate casualties. Other less predictable but potentially dangerous groups also had emerged. Those groups may not adhere to traditional targeting constraints.

CBRN materials, information, and technology became more widely available, especially from the Internet and the former Soviet Union.[85]

The 2000 report defines weapons of mass destruction (WMD) as "*chemical, biological, radiological, nuclear (CBRN), or large explosive weapons.*"[86] In addition, the report says that while most terrorists use conventional methods, there are also groups, for example, Osama bin Laden and his followers, which could pose a real threat as users of CBRN weapons if they succeed in getting access to them. Bin Laden has not been hiding his desire to acquire WMD. According to the State Department's 1999 report, bin Laden considers it a religious duty to acquire WMD.[87] Howard sees al Qaeda's determination to use WMD as the biggest threat to the United States. He points out that since al Qaeda does not rely on a state sponsor, it is easier for the organization to use weapons of mass destruction. In the past, a state-sponsored terrorist organization would have essentially committed suicide, bringing the wrath of the U.S. on its state sponsor had they used WMD against the U.S. Al Qaeda, however, not only works independently but also globally. It is free to plan its strategy without being restrained by a state sponsor. It can follow its own policies and interests without others' restraints.[88]

Hollywood Reaction to 9/11

On Tuesday morning, September 11, 2001, al Qaeda executed a plan that had been in the works for several years. Its executors were 19 hijackers who had been training for their mission at camps, at American flight schools, by taking cross-continental flights to see what they could get through security and which are the best seats for a hijacking, and even by watching films on hijackings.[89] Television networks and cable channels broadcast 24-hour coverage of the 9/11 attacks and their aftermath while the commercial film industry stopped its production of films with terrorist themes. Reality had outdone Hollywood in the creation of a spectacular terrorist attack. The difference was that this attack truly killed people and caused real destruction and suffering.

One of the majors, Warner Bros., delayed the release of the new Arnold Schwarzenegger film, *Collateral Damage*, which portrays Colombian terrorism. Ten days after the attacks, some still expected the film to be released by Christmas 2001.[90] The movie studio's caution about the release of its newest terrorist movie did not echo the public reaction to the attacks. According to the Video Software Dealers Association (VSDA), world prophecies and terrorism were popular movie themes among audiences in the weeks following the attacks. VSDA's Vid-Trac, which reports the number of actual rental transactions, found several 1990s terrorist movies re-entering the top 1,000 list. For example, the VHS version of *The Siege* (1998) finished in the top 200 the week following the attack and was still in the top 250 a week later. Also the movie's DVD version attracted renters.[91] But not everyone believed that viewers wanted to watch terrorist-themed films. The video-rental chain Blockbuster announced in the end of September that it would identify new video releases about terrorism with a warning label.[92]

But terrorist films still attracted audiences. When Arnold Schwarzenegger finally emerged on movie theater screens in February 2002 as a firefighter going after the Colombian terrorists who had killed his family, *Collateral Damage* was the top rated movie of the weekend. However, the film did not turn out to be a blockbuster; its cumulative North American box office numbers barely reached $40 million.[93]

Two months after the attack, Harold Evans asserted in *Columbia Journalism Review* that the attack itself was not a surprise. Rather, the surprise was created by the mainstream media's choice to ignore government reports and documents on terrorism.[94] It was not considered hard news in the pre–9/11 U.S. Evans wrote that the editorial boards of *The New York Times, The Wall Street Journal,* and *The Washington Post* each had received a visit from members of the Commission on National Security in the 21st Century. They provided the newspapers with a detailed press kit summarizing the report's main points, including the threat of a terrorist attack on U.S. soil, but the visits brought little success. Evans includes network television news, the serious evening news on public television, *The New York Times* and *The Wall Street Journal* on his list of the news media that ignored the report. In his observation, *The Washington Post, The Los Angeles Times, USA Today* and CNN fully covered the report. Smaller and regional newspapers relied on information from Reuters and the Associated Press. Only *The Los Angeles Times* considered the topic to be important enough to follow up and discuss it in an editorial or op-ed piece. *The New York Times* even rejected an op-ed article on the topic from the co-chairs of the bipartisan commission, former senators Gary Hart and Warren Rudman. In Evans's view, the failure of *The New York Times* was further emphasized by the paper's October 9, 2001, report on the nomination of Tom Ridge to head the new agency on homeland security: "Tom Ridge was sworn in today as the first director of homeland security, *a position the country's leaders never felt was needed before September 11.*"[95] The newspaper failed to notice that Hart, Rudman, and former representative Lee Hamilton from the Commission on National Security in the 21st Century, had proposed the creation of such an agency in the spring of 2001, and had provided the newspaper with a copy of the report.

As the melting Cold War was leaving the U.S. without its communist enemy in the late 1980s, the film industry was already moving on and finding new threat scenarios. The big production and distribution companies brought to viewers a diverse group of foreign terrorists, almost all somehow familiar from the news headlines and the State Department's annual documents on international terrorism.

The following chapters analyze the film terrorists and American heroes of the post–Cold War era until 9/11. "Chapter 6, 'Yippee Ki-yay, Motherfucker': From German Euroterrorists to Heroes of the Past," discusses the first of the heroes, police officer John McClane, played by Bruce Willis, who started his career in the final years of the Cold War, in 1988. He returned to the big screen when communism was nothing but a bad dream in American minds. The *Die Hard* series introduced villains, both ex-communists and anti-communist fighters, whom the Cold War had replaced, to try their luck in the U.S. Left-wing terrorists, including the German Hans Gruber in the first film and his brother, Simon Gruber, in the third film, threatened the American hero with their brain power and analytical approach to the business of killing. In the second *Die Hard* film an American colonel longs for the Cold War and executes a rescue operation for a former Latin American dictator in a plot that echoes General Noriega's experience with the U.S.

In the 1990s five popular films found their inspiration in the United Kingdom, four of them in Northern Ireland. "Chapter 7, Euroinvasion: Madmen from Britain and Northern Ireland," first addresses an aristocratic British terrorist's madness in *Passenger 57* (1992) before analyzing how Hollywood married action-adventure film genre traditions with film themes that found their inspiration in a real conflict. The films that draw from "the Troubles" in Northern Ireland and from the Provisional Irish Republican Army (PIRA) and its splinter groups are *Patriot Games* (1992), *Blown Away* (1994), *The Jackal* (1997), and *Ronin* (1998). In contrast to 1980s films, which starred little-known actors as antagonists, bankable movie stars Tommy Lee Jones and Bruce Willis tried on the villain's coat in *Blown Away* and *The Jackal*, respectively.

"Chapter 8, Hollywood Version of Fundamentalist Islamic Terrorism: Return of the One-Dimensional Evil Arab Muslim" examines angry fundamentalist Islamic terrorists who plan to bring mass destruction onto U.S. soil. Their efforts are defused in *True Lies* (1994) by Arnold Schwarzenegger, and in *Executive Decision* (1996) by Kurt Russell and a politically correct multi-ethnic special forces unit.

Air Force One brought back communist and ultranationalist fears in 1997. "Chapter 9, Return of the Communist Threat: U.S. President Takes On Russian Communist Terrorists" discusses a threat to the ultimate U.S. authority, the U.S. president. In this film, Russian nationalists, who consider capitalism to be a nightmare which has brought chaos, criminals and prostitutes onto the streets of Moscow and other cities, go after the president in their efforts to turn back time.

"Chapter 10, Predicting 9/11: Power of Belief" analyzes the book's darkest film, *The Siege* (1998). The film portrays terrorist attacks and threats in New York City by former U.S. allies from the Middle East, and addresses government responses to terrorism, including harsh ones. Several real-life post–9/11 responses may have seemed familiar to those who had seen this film.

Chapter 6

"Yippee Ki-yay, Motherfucker": From German Euroterrorists to Heroes of the Past

Die Hard (1988); *Die Hard 2: Die Harder* (1990); *Die Hard with a Vengeance* (1995)

As the communist Soviet giant and its influence in the world were fading out, the commercial film industry reacted faster than the official power structure. Hollywood left one-dimensional communist villains in the dust of history. In its efforts to bring new heroes and villains to audiences, the commercial film industry also paid attention to the fact that it had been ignoring a certain part of film audiences in its action and action-adventure film formats. The new male hero prototype gained a meaningful relationship with a representative of the opposite sex while a new generation of terrorist villains came to threaten the U.S. from both sides of the old Iron Curtain, arriving in North America from Europe and the Americas.

The first three *Die Hard* films are examples of a changing world order. The films introduce left-wing Euroterrorists and North and South American communist hunters who threaten the private and public sphere. They threaten the white Anglo-Saxon hero's personal life and U.S. interests. Bruce Willis starred as New York City police lieutenant John McClane in *Die Hard* at a time when the communist bloc in Europe was beginning to crumble. The film was released nationwide on July 20, 1988. The movie's wise guy hero and intelligent villain appealed to viewers, with such success at the box office that the production and distribution companies combined forces again for a sequel, *Die Hard 2: Die Harder*, directed by Renny Harlin. In 1995, seven years after the first *Die Hard* film, John McTiernan returned to direct the second sequel: *Die Hard with a Vengeance*. The fourth installment of John McClane's adventures, *Live Free or Die Hard*, was added in 2007. This chapter examines only the first three *Die Hard* films, which were all released before 9/11.

Die Hard (1988: #7)

Distributor: 20th Century Fox
Production company: Gordon Company/Silver Pictures
Producers: Lawrence Gordon and Joel Silver
Director: John McTiernan

Screenplay:	Jeb Stuart and Steven E. de Souza
Screenplay based:	on the novel *Nothing Lasts Forever* by Roderick Thorp
Executive producer:	Charles Gordon
MPAA rating:	R
Release date:	July 20, 1988.[1]
DVD (WS) running time:	132 minutes
Box office:	$80,029,086, cumulative total: $83,008,852[2]

Die Hard 2: Die Harder (1990: #7)

Distributor:	20th Century Fox
Production company:	Gordon Company/Silver Pictures
Producers:	Lawrence Gordon, Joel Silver, and Charles Gordon
Director:	Renny Harlin
Screenplay:	Steven E. de Souza and Doug Richardson
Screenplay based:	on the novel *58 Minutes* by Walter Wager
Co-producer:	Steve Perry
Executive producers:	Lloyd Levin and Michael Levy
MPAA rating:	R
Release date:	July 4, 1990[3]
DVD (WS) running time:	124 minutes
Box office:	$115,294,526, cumulative total: $117,540,947[4]

Die Hard with a Vengeance (1995: #7)

Distributor:	20th Century Fox
Production company:	Cinergi
Producers:	John McTiernan and Michael Tadross
Director:	John McTiernan
Screenplay:	Jonathan Hensleigh,[5] certain original characters by Roderick Thorp
Executive producers:	Andrew G. Vajna, Buzz Feitshans, and Robert Lawrence
Co-producers:	Carmine Zozzora
MPAA rating:	R
Release date:	May 19, 1995[6]
DVD (WS) running time:	131 minutes
Box office:	$100,012,499[7]

Die Hard steps away from the action-adventure film format of the previous decades. It still stars a white middle-class hero but this time he is married to a strong woman who has an impressive career and a large role in the film. The hero's task is to save his wife and her colleagues from international terrorists. The film transforms the Reaganite cinema hero from a monosyllabic muscleman to a wiseguy who gets on the terrorists' nerves. The film's biggest innovation is the introduction of a smart and sophisticated villain in Hans Gruber, played by Alan Rickman. He is a match to the hero and keeps him on the edge. The smart German villain, whose intellectual power at times seems to overpower the American hero's, separates the film from the Reagan-era movies with their one-dimensional villains.

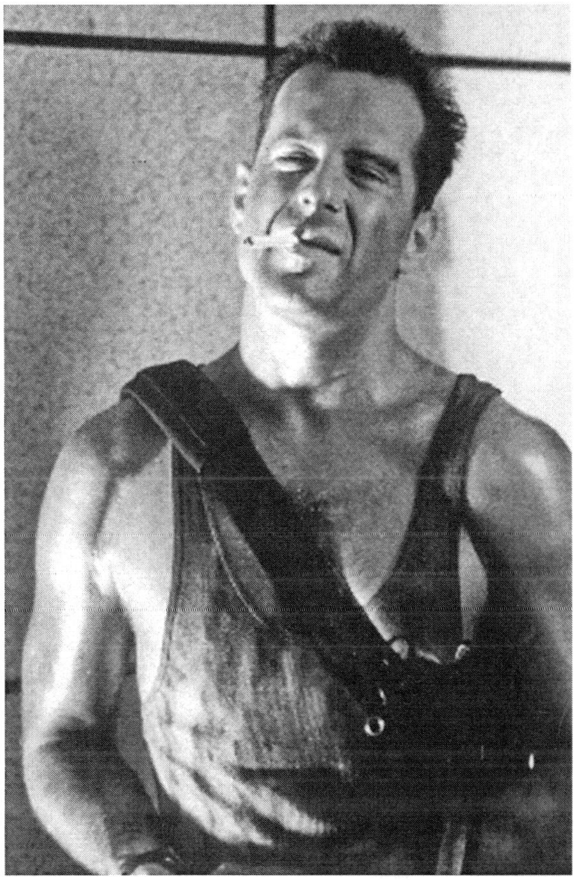

In 1988 *Die Hard* (20th Century Fox) introduced Bruce Willis as John McClane, a New York City police officer who had modest muscles, a sarcastic sense of humor, and a wife who had an impressive career. The film made Willis a major star and rejuvenated the action-adventure hero to meet the post-Cold War world.

The filmmakers saw the comical character as a new type of a hero.[8] However, several heroes of the classic action dramas, such as John Wayne, Clint Eastwood and Chuck Norris, also combined humor and action.[9] James Bond married action and comedy in the early 1960s, and the still-running James Bond series also includes a wide range of foreign locations, foreign villains, and beautiful but dangerous women. Arnold Schwarzenegger toyed with the combination of action and humor in *Commando*, and that film added to the mix a preteen daughter. These ingredients became repeated characteristics of the 1990s action-adventure films. Ahead of the times, *Commando* had also introduced a female sidekick who delivered comical lines but did not see much action.

Comic violence is an old film tool, dating back to the earliest slapstick comedies, but the arrival of *Die Hard*'s heroic cop, John McClane, rejuvenated the action-adventure genre, which helped the film to gain financial success at the box office. A sarcastic hero, the combination of humor and action, and the addition of a family, or at least a supporting female role as a romantic interest, became central in the action-adventure film genre. *Die Hard*'s fast-moving script keeps viewers on the edge of their seats when the white German Euroterrorist forces John McClane to rely on his intellect and muscles, although his muscles do not match the hypermuscles of the big 1980s heroes like Sylvester Stallone and Arnold Schwarzenegger.

Two years after the success of *Die Hard*, the film's first sequel hit movie theaters. *Die Hard 2: Die Harder* echoes the U.S. Cold War experience of supporting Latin American dictators and military leaders opposed to left-wing and communist views. An American colonel with men from U.S. special forces units express their loyalty to a Central American military leader who is being extradited to the U.S. to face drug charges. Their attempt to release the leader is complicated by John McClane, who just happens to be picking up his wife from the very airport which is central to the film terrorists' plans. The villains take over the airport tower and gain control of all air traffic. The script is based on *58 Minutes*, a novel by Walter Wager about terrorists taking over an airport.

The third installment of the series, *Die Hard with a Vengeance*, released in 1995, was not intended as a *Die Hard* but meant for a Brandon Lee movie. After Lee's death, Jonathan Hensleigh's original script, *Simon Says*, eventually became the basis for *Die Hard with a*

Vengeance.[10] Unfortunately it is quite obvious the script was meant to be something else. The film drastically moves away from the *Die Hard* formula: Christmastime events, the hero's relationship with his wife who has an impressive career, his conflicted relationship with official representatives of power, his heroic and largely individual confrontations with the villains, eavesdropping on the villain's internal communications, and his sarcastic comments. Furthermore, instead of locating most of the action at one primary location in a big city, the third installment sends the hero and his African American sidekick on a wild goose chase around another metropolitan area, New York City. The film does keep one successful ingredient from the first two films: a smart terrorist villain who constantly calls the shots in the game and forces McClane, and this time also his sidekick, to try to keep up with the terrorist's game. In 1988, *Die Hard* had rejuvenated the action-adventure film genre, but seven years later *Die Hard with a Vengeance* was behind the times. *Lethal Weapon*, *Beverly Hills Cop* and other films had already portrayed bickering interracial action-adventure partners. The film did not distinguish itself as a *Die Hard* film when it stepped away from the formula of the first two films and imitated films of other series. However, loyal *Die Hard* fans arrived in droves to witness John McClane's latest adventures, and the movie followed the box office success of its predecessors.

The *Die Hard* trilogy stayed buried until 2007 when McClane reemerged in *Live Free or Die Hard*. This time he was hunting for a villain who was shutting down the U.S. infrastructure. McClane's daughter is grown up and generates the family conflict. The villain threatens her, which motivates her father. The prodigal journey portrays the father and daughter patching up their relationship. The fourth installment of the series followed the Hollywood trend of investing in previously tested "brand films" that had ready-made audiences. Popular film series heroes such as Indiana Jones and John McClane reappeared on the big screen. Also, popular comic book characters and TV heroes gained success in the box office.

Updated Hero Meets Left-Wing and Anti-Communist Threats

The casting of Bruce Willis as the hero of *Die Hard* was a risky business decision since Willis had no credentials as a big action-adventure star. At that time he was known for his role in the hit television series *Moonlighting* and was only starting out his movie career. When a Los Angeles film audience laughed at a trailer which showed Willis as the film's hero, the movie studio and distributors removed Willis's name and image from the film's advertising and posters.[11] The trick worked. When the film opened in July 1988, audiences loved the sarcastic hero cop who was fighting for his family and country. Bruce Willis had arrived as a superstar.

Unlike the heroes of the decade's other terrorist films, McClane's physique and weapons are not overpowering forces in *Die Hard* or in its sequels. He is more human than the typical lonely 1980s hero with bulging muscles. John McClane bleeds and gets hurt in his fights. He fails in love, only to regain an understanding of his love and the relationship by the film's end. Naturally he still follows some of the most essential genre traditions and emerges as the winner at the end, but only after a suspenseful rollercoaster ride that his smart opponent, the Euroterrorist Hans Gruber, forces him to take. Throughout the film the hero is an underdog who has to strain his physical and mental capabilities in order to stay in the game started by Gruber and his group. Furthermore, this time the hero's fight is more personal when the villain's actions put his wife's life at risk.

The film starts with a New York City police officer arriving in Los Angeles for Christmas to meet his wife, Holly Gennaro (played by Bonnie Bedelia), and their small children. The marriage is strained because Holly Gennaro has made a career move to Los Angeles for a job at a Japanese company, Nakatomi. Soon after McClane's arrival, Hans Gruber and his associates take over the Japanese company's LA building and seize some thirty employees as their hostages, including Holly Gennaro. Gruber's associates are largely German stereotypes: tall, blond, muscular and effective, though eventually not a match for McClane. Hans Gruber is the brains of the operation, and the muscle force is led by tall Karl, who has a long blonde hair. Different members of the Gruber group succeed in wounding McClane throughout the film while the hero is taking European terrorists out of the game one by one. But Hans Gruber, the master villain, forces the hero to run and hide, and to try to catch up with him almost until the last moments of the film.

Die Hard introduces one of the smartest Hollywood terrorist villains in Hans Gruber, played by Alan Rickman. He is a well-educated, worldly, intelligent, multilingual, arrogant and stylish German. This white villain was originally a member of a West German leftist radical domestic terrorist group, the Volksfrei movement, but the group expelled him. He is an articulate speaker and fast thinker. For example, when he runs into an armed John McClane in the building, he pretends to be one of the hostages by instantly "stealing" a name from a wall directory, even shortening the name William to Bill, and easily losing his foreign accent. He is also a calculating, cold-blooded killer. Without any hesitation, he shoots in the head the company's Japanese manager and an arrogant American employee who promises to deliver McClane but who cannot do that.

In *Die Hard* (1988, 20th Century Fox) dreams of capitalist prosperity bring Euroterrorists onto U.S. soil to look for their version of the capitalist American dream. Hans Gruber (Alan Rickman), a rare Hollywood terrorist because he is smart and educated, knows how U.S. counterterrorism works in a crisis situation and uses that knowledge to his advantage.

As is typical of terrorist hostage situations, Gruber makes demands. In his statement he demands "comrades in arms around world languishing in prison" to be released: "U.S. State Department enjoys to rattle its saber for itself. Now it can rattle it for me." Gruber's demands include the release of imprisoned members of the New Provo Front 7 (Northern Ireland), Libértie de Québec (Canada), and the Asian Dawn (Sri Lanka), all groups he had learned about in *Time* magazine, as he tells one of his associates. But the political demands are only a ruse to bring in the FBI, the federal agency in charge of responding to terrorist crisis situations on U.S. soil. Gruber needs the FBI at the hostage site in order to use it to his group's advantage in its plan to rob the Japanese company. He knows the FBI's manual on hostage situations, and has planned his actions according to that.

Die Hard 2: Die Harder introduces in the first act two antagonists, the American colonel Stuart (played by William Sadler), and General Ramon Esperanza of the fictitious Central American country Val Verde,[12] played by Franco Nero. Colonel Stuart is a loyal ally of General Esperanza. Through news media reports the film exposition reveals that General Esperanza, the former commander in chief of Val Verde, is being extradited to the U.S. He is a former U.S. ally who led his own country's army against communist insurgents but who got involved in drug trafficking. His story echoes news headlines around the film's production and release time. General Manuel Noriega of Panama, a longtime CIA ally in countering communism in Central America who reportedly had a close relationship with Presidents Reagan and George H. W. Bush, had run afoul of the U.S. by the late 1980s. Like the film's General Esperanza, Noriega was a military figure. Although never officially a political leader, as the head of the Panama Defense Forces General Noriega ran the country from 1983 until 1989. He had attended the United States Army School of the Americas, which is a U.S. Army training facility meant mostly for Spanish-speaking Latin American cadets and officers. Noriega was one of the ten Latin American leaders who had attended the school.[13]

Noriega's involvement in drug trafficking, racketeering, and his political move closer to Libya, and to a lesser extent also to Iran, North Korea and Cuba, did not sit well with the U.S. After a freeze in U.S. military and economic aid to Panama in 1987, U.S. sanctions on Panama, accusations of human rights violations and an annulment of elections, President George H. W. Bush took action.[14] In December 1989 U.S. military entered Panama "to protect U.S. lives and property, to fulfill U.S. treaty responsibilities to operate and defend the Canal, to assist the Panamanian people in restoring democracy, and to bring Noriega to justice."[15] Operation Just Cause was over fast, but Noriega was able to seek "refuge in the Vatican diplomatic mission in Panama City. American troops played deafening pop and heavy metal music day and night outside the building to flush him out."[16] On January 3, 1990, Noriega surrendered. Since his capture was a result of a military invasion, he became a prisoner of war (POW), which gained him a better status in comparison to an average prisoner. He was convicted of drug trafficking, racketeering and money laundering in the U.S. for which he eventually served 17 years of a 40-year sentence in the U.S.[17]

The story of Noriega, the U.S. invasion of Panama, and drug trafficking in the news headlines made the film's events timely when it was released on the fourth of July, 1990. *Die Hard 2: Die Harder* could have been reporting on Noriega. The film's foreign villain is a general, a former U.S. ally who became involved in drug trafficking as his relationship with the U.S. soured and he needed alternative resources of financing. When the U.S. cut its assistance to the fictional General Esperanza, he found his new funding in cocaine smuggling, which echoes Noriega's experiences and actions. In the film, the U.S. Justice Department brings charges against the foreign film villain for cocaine smuggling, racketeering and bribing. Like Noriega, General Esperanza turned from a friend to a foe. His past political usefulness does not matter; he is now an enemy in the U.S. war on cocaine. Film exposition also reveals that General Esperanza's forces violated the neutrality of his neighboring countries. The Noriega-like story also brings back memories of the Iran-Contra scandal and illegal weapons trade. In the film, the news media reports reveal that high-ranking Pentagon officials were charged with supplying the general with weapons despite of a congressional ban.

The film's main American antagonist, Colonel Stuart, sees it as his patriotic duty to support General Esperanza. He defends his views to John McClane: "I think Cardinal Richelieu said it best: 'Treason is merely a matter of dates.' This country has got to learn that it can't keep cutting the legs off of men like General Esperanza, men who have the guts to stand up against communist aggression." Later, Colonel Stuart commends his men and the general for having "won a victory for our way of life."

The communist-hunter Matt Hunter of *Invasion USA* was a hero in the Reagan era, but by 1990 his position had become outdated. Hunter's post–Cold War counterpart, Colonel Stuart, does not even qualify for the role of the action-adventure hero anymore. This hunter of communists becomes the hunted himself when he puts the hero's wife at risk with his attempt to release the general. Colonel Stuart is a disciplined special forces man. The film

The communist hunter's time was running out at the end of the Cold War. In *Die Hard 2: Die Harder* (1990, 20th Century Fox). Colonel Stuart (William Sadler) is in charge of arranging the escape of General Ramon Esperanza (Franco Nero) when the general is being extradited to the U.S. Echoing the news stories about real-life General Noriega of Panama at the time of the film's production, the fictional General Esperanza is a former U.S. ally in countering communism but is now being extradited to the U.S. for cocaine smuggling, racketeering and bribing.

introduces him as he is following a news story about General Esperanza's extradition. The colonel is exercising in the nude. His body is muscled and lean, without a drop of fat. He is in control of himself and his environment.

The third installment of the series, *Die Hard with a Vengeance*, starts with an explosion in a department store in Manhattan. An anonymous caller demands to talk with John McClane. Film audiences are soon introduced to Lieutenant McClane, who is suspended from his job, estranged from his wife, and close to being an alcoholic. The wisecracking cop has become a loudmouth whose lines lack the entertaining sarcastic tone his character had in the first two films of the series.

The anonymous caller turns out to be Hans Gruber's brother Simon Gruber (played by Jeremy Irons), who makes McClane an essential part of his plans. Because the villain forces McClane to become involved in his actions, McClane is again granted his badge. If McClane does not find the bombs Gruber has hidden around the city, they will go off. In this game of "Simon Says," the antagonist gives clues to the bombs' locations only to McClane and his involuntary sidekick, Harlem shopkeeper Zeus, played by Samuel L. Jackson. Zeus unwillingly joins McClane after he has rescued the latter from an angry mob in Harlem. Simon had ordered McClane to parade through wearing only his underwear and a sign proclaiming "I hate niggers." Zeus's attitude and mouth match McClane's. After a subway bomb explosion close to Wall Street, which McClane succeeds in minimizing, Simon raises the stakes when he announces that there is another bomb, this time in a city school. His only demand is for McClane and his sidekick to play the game. In order to find the bomb, they must be able to solve the riddles which Simon has placed around the city.

Simon Gruber and his main associate have terrorist backgrounds, but their backgrounds also echo the 1980s fear of communism, as does the second part of the series. Simon Gruber served as a colonel in the East German army, running an infiltration unit. By the time we meet him in the film, he has become a mercenary. His associate, briefly portrayed, is Hungarian, a former army officer who is an explosives expert and whose background includes freelance terrorist activity by contract, Iran being a client of his. In real life the U.S. State Department has for decades considered Iran to be the number-one state sponsor of terrorism. In the film the Hungarian associate's female partner betrays and kills him, and then joins Simon Gruber.

Loyal to the classical Hollywood narrative structure, the antagonist's actions force the hero to become involved in each of the three films. In *Die Hard* the terrorists take over the very LA office building and company that McClane is visiting during his wife's company's Christmas party. He must save his wife and her colleagues before the terrorists destroy the building and escape. In *Die Hard 2: Die Harder*, which also takes place at Christmastime, McClane, now living in LA, is at Dulles Airport in Washington, D.C., to pick up his wife for their Christmas visit with her parents when terrorists shut down the air traffic control system, leaving airplanes and their passengers, including Holly McClane, at their mercy. The film relies more directly than the first film on an old Hollywood method of creating suspense: a limited time structure. Holly McClane's plane has sufficient fuel for only a limited time, so John McClane is racing against the clock in his effort to save his wife and the passengers of several other planes. The third film also relies on the old method of limited time. It sends McClane and Zeus, as well as the NYPD and the FBI, on a wild goose chase through New York City to find a bomb in a school building. The terrorist villain keeps his opponents on their toes, threatening that if any school is evacuated or the media alerted to the threat, the bomb will go off.

Each of the three films introduces smart, calculating and cold-blooded antagonists. Their commitment is to their mission. Anything that stands in the way of the mission is to be destroyed. The hero just happens to be in the way of business and therefore must die. The villains of the three films are intelligent professionals who anticipate events and take advantage of the knowledge of how counterterrorism works in the U.S. McClane's role becomes pivotal in each film because it is he who surprises and upsets the terrorists' well-rehearsed plans. Representatives of the official power structure advise McClane to let the pros handle the situation in the first two films. However, only McClane can save the day since the terrorists know what to expect from the officials and use the anticipated counterterrorist moves to their advantage.

Old World Terrorists with Capitalist Dreams

The *Die Hard* films are advertised and known as terrorist-themed films. It is true that the first three films' villains target and terrorize civilians due to their declared political motivation and therefore each film's threat initially matches official descriptions of terrorism. Furthermore, each film portrays international threats: the first and third film bring German-led Euroterrorists onto U.S. soil, and the second one introduces members of American special forces who are attacking the U.S. due to their commitment to a Central American former military leader who is an ex-ally of the U.S.

On the surface, the first and third film fall under the State Department definitions of international terrorism until it turns out that the terrorists are actually after money and only pretend to be terrorists. The two antagonists and their associates' threats against civilians emerge from their plans to commit large robberies, not from political goals or motivations, as they pretend. However, since the other film characters are not initially privy to the information, they respond to the acts as if they were international terrorist threats and attacks on U.S. soil. Both Gruber brothers do have terrorist backgrounds and have planned their acts to imitate terrorist threats and attacks. In the first film Hans Gruber is well aware that the FBI is in charge of responding to terrorist crises on U.S. soil, and of how the FBI responds to such situations. The villain has actually planned his robbery to take advantage of such response: the robbers gain entrance to their robbery site because of a major electronic shutdown ordered by the FBI. Also Hans's brother, Simon Gruber, has planned his robbery with knowledge of how officials would respond to a terrorist threat against a school in New York City. That clears the way for him and his group to rob the Federal Reserve Bank of New York City when the local police and the FBI are hunting for a 2,400-pound bomb in one of the 1,446 schools in the greater New York City area, as Simon Gruber describes the bomb which is timed to go off at 3:00 P.M. on the afternoon of his call.

In the first and third film, even soldiers of the old communist military structure and left-wing Euroterrorism have discarded the communist ideology and embraced capitalism. Hans Gruber arrives with his associates to commit robbery. Simon Gruber and his associate are soldiers for hire, but try to release themselves from the power of others by stealing money for themselves. After their successful robbery they are at the top of the capitalist world. Simon Gruber describes the moment to his group: "Yesterday we were an army with no country. Tomorrow we have to decide which country we want to buy." Not only are foreign businesses, like the Japanese company for which McClane's wife is working, invading the U.S. and Hollywood, but also international terrorists want their share of the profits. The new world order has corrupted even old leftist terrorists, winning them over to the power of capitalism. These Euroterrorists have turned their backs on their left-wing pasts.

Only the second film of the series, *Die Hard 2: Die Harder*, actually matches the State Department definitions of international terrorism. Colonel Stuart and his American military associates take over the Dulles Airport control tower and keep civilian passengers as hostages in the planes circling the airport. They run their operation from a close-by abandoned church. The group's goal is to free General Esperanza, a former dictator of Val Verde, as he is being extradited to the U.S. due to his involvement in a drug trade. The violent act and threats of violence are politically motivated and target noncombatants, in this film, airline passengers. Because the group includes U.S. and Central American citizens, it is an international coalition that is threatening U.S. citizens on their own soil. As is typical for terrorists in hostage situations, the film terrorists make demands: no one can meet the general's plane and no plane lands until the general's plane has arrived, and the group is to get a fully fueled plane. Colonel Stuart's primary goal is to support a loyal anti-communist ally and rescue him from the claws of the U.S. of the new world order. But Colonel Stuart is late; by 1990 communism was old news, and the U.S. no longer needed partners in a global push against communism. Just as with real-life terrorism, a matter of dates can make a difference to a film terrorist. In the new world order, a former hero becomes a new, threatening terrorist. In 1985 Matt Hunter of *Invasion USA* was a hero who saved the U.S. from communists, but by 1990 the world had left him in the frost of the Cold War. His counterparts in *Die Hard 2: Die Harder* are fighting ghosts of the past while reaching for their share of the capitalist world for which they had fought, but which had failed them.

Colonel Stuart is a true terrorist: he threatens and kills innocent bystanders in order to reach his political goal. When the control tower personnel try to find alternative communication methods with the support of a SWAT team, Colonel Stuart crashes a civilian airliner to make the point that he is serious. The crash kills all 230 people on the plane. He is committed to the Cold War time when communism was the ultimate foreign policy monster, even when it meant supporting dictators and brutal military leaders in Latin America and elsewhere. Colonel Stuart's loyalty to the old world makes him a terrorist who believes his cause justifies the killing of innocent American civilians. The colonel's cold-blooded approach to killing is not reserved only for bystanders. When one of his men fails his mission, the colonel puts a gun on the man's face and pulls the trigger. The chamber is empty, but his words sting: "You fail me again and the chamber won't be empty." The words echo the words of *Iron Eagle*'s minister of defense to his men when they failed to capture the film's teenage hero.

General Esperanza's approach to the mission is similar to his supporters'. He kills in cold blood everyone on the plane that is transferring him to the U.S. The film's third recognizable villain is Major Grant (John Amos), the film's special army counterterrorist team's leader, but he soon turns out to be in on the scheme with Colonel Stuart and General Esperanza. Grant, an African American antagonist, adds to the interracial harmony of the film's white and Latino villains. He brutally cuts the throat of a young soldier who was not part of his original loyal unit which had served in Grenada. These military men are in the business of killing, and do it effectively. Trained by the Department of Defense and the CIA, the men are veterans of conflicts and special missions in Afghanistan, Saudi Arabia, Grenada, Honduras, Cambodia, Laos and Thailand.

Just like their North and Central American counterparts, the German antagonists lack human emotions when completing their missions. Brothers Hans and Simon Gruber show no pleasure or sadness when they kill. For them there is no need to become emotional at those moments when the business requires the killing of someone who is in the way of their capitalist missions.

While the antagonists of the three films are all smart and cold-blooded, there is a certain difference between the two German antagonists and the American colonel. Hans and Simon Gruber do not kill women or children. Hans Gruber, like Mustafa in *The Delta Force,* even allows a pregnant woman to make herself more comfortable. Simon Gruber's bomb in a New York City school turns out to be made of pancake syrup: "I'm a soldier, not a monster, even though I sometimes work for monsters." This terrorist-robber considers himself, as real-life terrorists do, a soldier. Although he has become a traditional criminal who is motivated by his own greed, he still sees only men as his targets. His motivation to send the police to look for a bomb in a school is to get them out of the way so his group can have an easy access to the robbery site. Even his German associates, dressed as American police, will not leave a bomb on a street because, as one of them points out, a child might find it. Furthermore, the approach follows the methods of Western European left-wing terrorists who, while attacking representatives of capitalist power structures, tried to avoid innocent-bystander casualties.

When it dawns on the Japanese manager in *Die Hard* that Hans Gruber's group is after $640 million, locked in the company's vault and behind seven vault safeguards, he is stunned: "You want money? What kind of terrorists are you?" Hans Gruber laughs and asks, "Who said we were terrorists?" Then he shoots the manager, who had not told him how to access the vault. As was typical of terrorist hostage situations in the 1970s and 1980s, Gruber demands that the FBI arrange the release of several foreign terrorists. However, he smiles at a member of his group and comments that he read about them in *Time* magazine. He could not care less about these terrorists. He is only *pretending* to be a terrorist who is demanding the release of his comrades. He has calculated that the FBI would be called to the site. The FBI is in charge of terrorist threats that take place in the U.S. In this particular film, the villain is relying on that information. He knows that in order to break the last of the seven vault safeguards, he needs to have the power cut off in the whole building, a method he knows the FBI will use in hostage situations. His plan relies on his knowledge of American counterterrorism structures and methods.

The disappointment of the terrorists not being terrorists after all is also revealed in the hero's wife's words: "You're nothing but a common thief," which Hans Gruber answers with a smile: "An exceptional thief." When McClane tries to prevent the explosion of the office building, an action that the fake terrorists are planning to use as their exit, he does not comprehend why the hostage-takers would need to "nuke the whole building" when it is only "a fucking robbery." The exit strategy is repeated in the third film when Simon Gruber imitates Hans's plan to make it look like the perpetrators of the act have died in an explosion. Like his brother, Simon Gruber claims political motivations in order to cover up his robbery of the Federal Reserve Bank of New York and his escape. He claims that he is blowing up the stolen $140 billion in gold and himself because the West has conspired to steal the wealth of the rest of the world. According to that claim, destroying the money in an explosion on a ship in New York would help to even the score:

> This is a communiqué from the CRF. For too long the West has conspired to steal the wealth of the world consigning the balance of humanity to economic starvation. Today we will level the playing field. In a few minutes the contents of the Federal Reserve Bank, the gold your economies are built on, will be redistributed by explosive across the bottom of the Long Island Sound. If you're not in gridlock, I invite you to come and watch.

Married Hero Meets Sane Villains with Echoes of the Past in the Post–Cold War World

Die Hard is often credited for having started a new trend in action-adventure films. The hero is funny and sarcastic, a family man, and more than just muscles. Even his clothing is missing the 1980s heroic camouflage outfit, uniform, or tight jeans. This hero is not afraid to wear a warm sweater when saving his wife and planes full of Christmastime passengers. However, an even bigger innovation in the *Die Hard* films was to portray smart antagonists who offer McClane an opportunity to be a hero who, instead of just firepower and muscles, also has to use his *head*. In addition, while the more traditional white Anglo-Saxon Protestant male heroes faced foreign villains whose skin color was darker than theirs, and who were anti–American, anti-freedom, anti-capitalism and of an anti–Judeo-Christian religion,[18] this hero fights mostly white villains who want their share of America's capitalist goods. The *Die Hard* films replace traditional Third World villains, often portrayed as faceless barbaric masses, with white Western villains who are intelligent and educated, and who speak English fluently but still with a foreign accent. Even the villain from Central America is a former U.S. ally who speaks English fluently, although with a foreign accent. But he has no Third World accomplices to be targets of mass destruction at the hero's hands. Furthermore, the hero does not use superior intelligence or technology to beat the villains; rather, each film's main villain almost beats the hero because it is the villain who possesses these qualities.

In the first and third film the Euroterrorists of the new world order have discarded their leftist ideologies and are embracing capitalism. In the second film Colonel Stuart and General Esperanza are frozen in the Cold War mentality and want to make sure that ideology is followed in the post–Cold War world. They also want to harvest their capitalist rewards in that world. The second film especially contradicts the Reaganite cinema ingredient of taking great pride in U.S. military forces. Rather, the film underlines how extreme policies in the Reagan era may have produced monsters, such as the film's former U.S. ally and the domestic villains who are all special forces soldiers. Unlike in the Reagan-era *Commando*, there is no heroic military man saving the day and returning the pride.

The three films' villains are worthy opponents to McClane, who is actually outsmarted by each of these terrorists. It is not enough for the hero just to spray bullets around, because these terrorists use their heads and require the hero to do the same. Furthermore, these villains with their Western and Eastern European accomplices die individually at the hero's hands, or in a small group in an airplane or helicopter, but in such a way that the viewer knows the characters. As villains they all are individuals, which largely contrasts the portrayal of the more traditional villains who in the 1980s arrived from the less developed world. For example, the villains of *Commando* and *Iron Eagle*, and to some extent also of *The Delta Force* and *Invasion USA*, die in large numbers. As is the case with cultural determinism in news coverage, the farther away the dead are from the U.S. geographically, culturally, or in religious and economic terms, the bigger the number of the deaths must be for the deaths to be portrayed on the big screen. Furthermore, the more brutal the death is at the hands of the hero, the more likely it is that the victim of the hero's violence is a citizen of the less developed world. This is the case, for example, in *Commando* and *True Lies*, both starring Arnold Schwarzenegger. However, it does not matter whom the hero kills or how; each death is full of weak violence. The films qualify the hero's killings by portraying the villains in such terms that the viewer does not identify with them. The villains are cold, intelligent and brutal, a threat to everyone in society so their deaths at the hands of John McClane are justifiable. As a police officer, he is a representative of the official power structure who fights for all of us. His use of violence is good violence since he is protecting society, even if he is doing it as a maverick. The villains' violence is bad violence because it disrupts society.

The three *Die Hard* films use violence for the purpose of entertainment. They do not stop the viewer to think about the finality of death. *Die Hard 2: Die Harder* creates lukewarm strong violence before the plane crash that kills 230 people. Just before the crash the film cuts to the inside of the plane, familiarizing the viewer with some of the people on the plane, for example, the plane's pilot and co-pilot, and a steward talking to different passengers. When the viewer "knows" some of those killed, even if briefly, the viewer is more likely to feel the impact of the killings at some level and accept, and even want and cheer for, the killing of the villain at the end of the movie. *Invasion USA* used the same tactic when it briefly first introduced some of the victims that the film's terrorists were targeting before showing on the screen the destructive terrorist attacks. The killing of the villains is weak violence in each film because those portrayals will not make the viewer think about the reality of the killing of a human being.

Although the three films' antagonists die at the hero's hands as the genre traditions require, they are also rare antagonists: in addition to being Western, they are *sane*. Hans Gruber, Colonel Stuart and even Simon Gruber are smart white antagonists who are professionals; specifically, professionals in the field of killing. General Esperanza from Central America is also a smart, cold and sane villain. The third film is inconsistent in its description of Simon Gruber. At the film's beginning a police psychiatrist describes the anonymous caller as "nuts," with a megalomaniac personality and possibly a paranoid schizophrenic. Furthermore, he describes the caller as "sitting on anger," wanting to see McClane crumble and die under pressure while knowing who is doing that to him. However, the film poorly portrays Simon Gruber exhibiting any of these signs in other ways, except for bursts of anger. In contrast, he is very much in charge and having fun at McClane's expense while executing a well-planned robbery. For

British actor Jeremy Irons (right) played the main villain in *Die Hard with a Vengeance* (1995, 20th Century Fox). As Simon Gruber he is a former left-wing terrorist from East Germany who, like his brother in *Die Hard*, camouflages his robbery attempt as a terrorist attack. His associate in the attack is freelance terrorist Targo (Nick Wyman), a former army officer from Hungary.

Simon Gruber, revenge on McClane for killing his brother is only gravy to his robbery plans. He has no problem when his Hungarian associate asks him to stop toying with McClane and simply get rid of him. For Simon Gruber his game with McClane has been a little bonus; after all, he did not even like his brother.

In the three films, McClane is completely overpowered by the terrorists' weapons arsenal. They are the ones with rocket launchers, explosives, machine guns, handguns and knives. In the first two films McClane has to rely on his intellect as much as on his physical prowess to even the score. In the third one, he is mostly following the antagonist's lead until the very end when he finally overpowers the antagonist, taking down his helicopter by cutting off a wire with a precise shot. McClane sends Simon Gruber to his death accompanied with the line "Say hello to your brother." The cut wire hits the villain's helicopter and takes it down to McClane's familiar yell from the first two films: "Yippee Ki-yay, motherfucker." The hero is finally back at the top of his game.

In *Die Hard*, the final confrontation ends when Hans Gruber falls out of a window after a physical skirmish and gunfight with McClane. In *Die Hard 2: Die Harder*, McClane first has a one-on-one confrontation with his third antagonist, Major Grant, which ends when the major is cut to pieces by the escape plane's propellers. Trying to prevent the colonel, the general and their supporters from leaving the Dulles airport, McClane opens the escape plane's fuel tank. When the main antagonist, Colonel Stuart, armed with a knife, kicks McClane off the plane's wing after their one-on-one fistfight, McClane lights up the fuel trail which is dripping from the plane. The fire catches up to the plane, which explodes as McClane lets go his trademark yell: "Yippee Ki-yay, motherfucker." To the beat of Jean Sibelius's "Finlandia," the still burning fuel serves as a landing light and runway for the planes which have been circling the airport for hours.

In the three films the death count of villains is largely reduced in comparison to the terrorist films of the 1980s. For example, in contrast to Arnold Schwarzenegger's cartoonlike hero character in *Commando*, who commits his mass killings by spraying unidentifiable foreign villains with machine guns and automatic assault weapons, McClane mostly works one-on-one when fighting his European and American opponents, including lesser characters. In *Die Hard* each of his foreign opponents dies. The only survivor of the German group is its African American technology partner, whom a minor African American character on the hero's side knocks unconscious. For the rest, McClane's parting words are "Yippee Ki-yay, motherfucker." Mostly he relies on his gun, but he also breaks necks and, in *Die Hard 2*, stabs one of his opponents in the eye with an icicle. He taunts the terrorists, especially in the first film. After he has killed a terrorist he sends him down in an elevator to the floor where the rest of the terrorists and the hostages are. A sign on the man's chest announces: "Now I have a machine gun. Ho-ho-ho." Hans Gruber calls the protagonist Mr. Cowboy, "just another American who saw too many movies as a child," and who thinks that he is John Wayne or Rambo. Similarly, McClane's adversary in the official power structure, Captain Lorenzo (Dennis Franz), in *Die Hard 2: Die Harder*, accuses him of playing John Wayne. McClane also follows a traditional hero model. Just as Major McCoy's (Chuck Norris) main terrorist villain in *The Delta Force* voiced disbelief when his men were afraid of one man, General Esperanza spits to his men when McClane is causing problems: "Two months of planning and you can't anticipate one policeman?"

Unlike his predecessors in the 1980s, the hero of *Die Hard* is a talker, which is a change from the lonely, quiet hero. While past heroes have entertained viewers with comical one-liner comments, as did, for example, Colonel Matrix in *Commando*, McClane is a constant talker and wise guy. He has a comment, most often a sarcastic one, on most of his own activities throughout the film: "Why did you shoot, John? Because you'd have been shot, asshole." The second film relies on the first film's formula and repeats the protagonist's sarcastic take on the world:

> Another basement, another elevator. How can the same shit happen to the same guy twice? ...
>
> Just once, I'd like a regular normal Christmas, eggnog, a fucking Christmas tree, a little turkey ... but no, I got to crawl around in this motherfucking tin can....
>
> Oh, we're just up to our ass in terrorists again, John.

The hero entertains the viewer, but he also guides the viewer through the films, at times providing exposition through sarcastic comments in order to give the viewer necessary information.

The hero's wisecracks entertain throughout the first and the second film but run out in the third one. The James Bond films of the 1960s had already combined action and adventure with a comical style and exotic locations. The first two installments of the *Die Hard* series successfully borrowed from that formula but kept the action on home turf and introduced a wisecracking man who is married. However, *Die Hard with a Vengeance* changed the formula and featured a mouthy and mismatched interracial pair whose bickering is reminiscent of the *Lethal Weapon* style. The bickering, at times somewhat racist, fails to entertain in the manner of the first two films.

From Heterosexual Coupling back to Reaganite Cinema Male Bonding

Unlike the heroes of the 1980s, the hero of the modern post–Cold War world is not afraid to express his love. The first two *Die Hard* films portray a man who loves his wife and is not afraid to show or say it. The films replace a Reaganite cinema feature, a strong father-son relationship, with a strong husband-wife relationship. In the first film the McClane couple patches up their marriage, and in the second one, they are very much in love. In the first film McClane tells his sidekick Sergeant Powell that it took him a while to figure out what a jerk he had been by not supporting his wife's career. He asks Powell to tell his wife Holly that he is sorry and that Holly was the best thing that ever happened to him. At the end of the second film the couple declare their love for each other and the fear of not seeing each other ever again. McClane is fighting for his family first. As a reward, his wife, who is an independent and strong career woman, comes through to support the old action-adventure film traditions. As her husband saves her in *Die Hard*, she discards her maiden name at the film's end, and proudly introduces herself as Holly McClane, restoring the patriarchal order of the action-adventure film genre. Furthermore, her great reward for a big business deal, a valuable Rolex watch, almost gets her killed. When Hans Gruber falls through an office window, he manages to get hold of the Rolex on her wrist, almost pulling her down with him. The only way to save her is to release the Rolex, the symbol of her status as a successful career woman. Her successful career is her accomplishment but also a threat to her life and to their marriage.

By the third film McClane's marriage is in trouble and neither his wife nor children are seen. They are mentioned only very briefly. He has not been in contact with his wife since they fought over the phone a year ago, and he just never called back. Zeus makes him think about his current life. As a result, McClane makes a call to Holly but cuts the call short just when she gets on the line because his job is more important and just happens to take over exactly at that moment. He is in a manly world where his job, with his mismatched partner Zeus Carver, is to save New York City and catch Simon Gruber. The third film leaves no room for an admiring wife who would discard her maiden name at the film's end or run to the hero's arms after he has rescued her. Rather, this is reminiscent of the 1980s Reaganite cinema films which portrayed interracial harmony (at least among Americans), and comradeship and loyalty between men. There is no room for a romantic heterosexual subplot. The relationship between McClane and Zeus follows the storyline of a traditional romantic coupling, just leaving out the actual coupling. At first they dislike each other, but, forced together by circumstances, they finally turn those feelings around, and by the film's end they have earned each other's respect. With the end credits starting, John McClane remembers the outside world as he notices he left Holly hanging. The hero starts to make another call to his estranged wife.

In *Die Hard* the hero's prodigal journey is from a troubled marriage to a saved marriage. McClane's sidekick is also granted a prodigal journey. Sergeant Powell has not been able to use his gun for years, since he shot an unarmed teenager. At the end of the film he is the only one to react when German terrorist Karl, mistaken for dead, suddenly targets McClane. In slow motion Sergeant Powell takes his gun out and shoots the tall, vengeful German whose brother McClane had killed.

In the last two films McClane's prodigal journeys are in his relationships with those he is forced to work with. His bickering with the airport security head, Captain Lorenzo, in the second film and with Harlem storeowner Carver in the third both end when the parties earn each other's respect. The third film's ending also leaves hope of McClane salvaging his marriage.

Traces of the Reaganite Cinema

While the three films do offer an updated version of the action-adventure hero, each of the films is also reminiscent of the Reaganite cinema style. Each film pairs McClane with an African American sidekick, drawing from the Reaganite cinema's interracial harmony and also from the popular late 1980s and early 1990s "mismatched pair" films. In the *Die Hard* series, that approach culminated in the third film which paired John McClane with another loud-mouth in Zeus Carver.

In the first two movies the hero primarily works alone, only getting some support from his African American supporter. Although the minority sidekick often traditionally dies, the three African American sidekicks, L.A. cop Al Powell (Reginald VelJohnson) in *Die Hard*, lesser sidekick airport chief engineer Leslie Barnes (Art Evans) in *Die Hard 2: Die Harder*, and Harlem store owner Zeus Carver (Samuel L. Jackson) in *Die Hard with a Vengeance*, all survive in the end. These men are smart and independent characters on whom McClane relies. As is the case with the hero, they are forced to take part in the events. The characters with significant sidekick roles, Powell and Carver, become involved because of the hero's activities, because of the hero's response to the villain. To counterbalance these partnerships, the hero is in conflict with official representatives of power who do not know how to do the job of counterterrorism. John McClane is a traditional hero in the sense that he is a strong self-made man who pushes everything else aside to reach his goals.[19]

As is the case with *Iron Eagle* and *The Delta Force*, the first three *Die Hard* films do not present a particularly positive image of the official power structure, even when the hero himself is a law enforcement officer. Conflict is at the heart of drama,[20] which the first two films use effectively when they set the hero against not only the terrorists but also official representatives of power. In *Die Hard* the inefficient L.A. police and FBI are in charge. In *Die Hard 2: Die Harder* the FBI, in real life the country's primary force in counterterrorism on U.S. soil, is nowhere to be seen when the going gets tough. Avoiding an explanation of the complex chain of command required to use military forces on U.S. soil, the film takes a shortcut and has the U.S. government send in a special army counterterrorist team to resolve the crisis, but this turns out to be part of the terrorist plot. As in *Die Hard*, the villains of the second film know what counterterrorism measures to expect, and rely on that in their plans. These soldiers are veterans of several wars who follow Colonel Stuart who, in return, is loyal to General Esperanza. While McClane comes under fire several times, none of the dozens of soldiers who fire shots, real and blank ones, at him, succeed. Only McClane's aim is good enough to kill.

The first film celebrates the ineffectiveness and dumbness of the FBI and L.A. police department in their counterterrorism efforts. They are used as props to provide comical and frustrating moments. FBI agents Johnson and Johnson are one-dimensional and arrogant: they would be happy with their performance even if they lost up to one-fourth of the hostages. When the two Johnsons' helicopter explodes, the L.A. Deputy Chief of Police remarks, dead-pan, that it looks like the agency will need new agents. The arrogant and angry deputy chief wants McClane to stay out of the way and let the professionals take care of the situation. The film's official representatives of power who are on a crash course with John McClane are largely caricatures of incompetent police and FBI agents. McClane gets his help from lower-level official power representatives. In *Die Hard* only McClane's sidekick, Sergeant Powell, supports him via their radio contacts. In *Die Hard 2: Die Harder*, McClane's antagonist in the official power structure is the head of airport security, Captain Lorenzo, who does not understand the situation as well as McClane, and does not take the terrorist threat seriously until it is almost too late.

Even as the films take a stab at the FBI and law enforcement, they also criticize the media while using it for exposition and comical relief. The first two films introduce an overeager television reporter in Richard Thornburg (William Atherton), who has no ethical standards. In the first film Hans Gruber learns from Thornburg's story about McClane's children that Holly Gennaro is actually McClane's wife, allowing him to grab her as a personal hostage to smoke McClane out of his hiding place. The reporter is one more person to provide laughs under strained conditions. When McClane's wife hits him in the face after the hostage crisis because he endangered her family and children, Thornburg eagerly asks his videographer if he got the punch on tape. In the second film the reporter, who now has a restraining order against Holly McClane, is stuck on the same plane with her due to overbooking. He creates chaos at Dulles Airport when his live report from the plane reveals to viewers that the airport delays are not due to a snowstorm but a terrorist attack, and that terrorists have already crashed one plane. (Illogically, Thornburg knows the events because a news team member has a receiver that can pick up the radio frequency that is discussing the events.) Holly McClane interrupts Thornburg's report with a Taser. In the second film John McClane relies on help from a female reporter whom Colonel Stuart calls a "pinko bitch," which reflects a conservative view of seeing the media as liberal. The female reporter gives McClane a ride in a news helicopter that allows him to catch up with the terrorists' plane just as it is leaving.

The films' reporters are pushy in trying to get the latest scoop, not stopping to think about the impact of the stories. This approach goes back to the question about how to cover terrorism in news stories. Terrorist acts are news but news coverage of them can add to the chaos, as happens in *Die Hard 2: Die Harder* when Thornburg's report scares everyone at the airport.

Die Hard introduced humor and women to the action-adventure film genre as successful ingredients. While comical style had been used in other films too, for example, in Westerns, James Bond films, and in films starring Arnold Schwarzenegger and Chuck Norris, *Die Hard* made the hero's sarcastic comments an essential part of the character even when he was only talking to himself. The film also revivified the role of the villain by introducing a smart Western villain and his group who keep McClane at a disadvantage throughout the film almost until the very end. Furthermore, the hero is not an overpowering figure with massive muscles and weapons arsenal but one who takes the terrorist robbers out of the game one by one while also getting hurt himself.

Die Hard 2: Die Harder continued the first film's formula with a Christmastime terrorist incident in a closed area. The hero is still a wisecracking married police officer whose wife has a central role in the film as a strong woman whose life is at risk and who needs to be saved by her husband. Lieutenant McClane is still in conflict with bad-tempered official representatives of power and intelligent terrorists. He is only one man, as his terrorist opponents point out, but he also has help. As in the first film, he receives assistance from an African American man. In addition, a janitor provides him with a receiver he can use to listen in on and communicate with the terrorists, just as he did in the first film. The film ends with the minor sidekick, janitor Marvin, driving the McClanes out of the airport in an open airport vehicle, maintaining the formula of the first film which ended with John McClane's driver driving the couple away from the attack site in a beaten-up limo.

The third film loses the touch of the first two films, largely abandoning the formula and using as its script a screenplay that would have better fitted the *Lethal Weapon* series. Three strong actors, Bruce Willis, Samuel L. Jackson and Jeremy Irons, are left with little to work with in the overdrawn film that sets up a white and an African American man to bicker, at times in racist terms, while trying to find bombs set and hidden by the villain. Due to their constant bickering matches and attempts to solve the antagonist's riddles, which would lead to the bombs, they almost miss his big robbery. In the first two films the viewer meets several of the villain's associates, who are recognizable to the point that the viewer can form a clear dislike for them, but the third film leaves the role of two villainous associates very brief.

The first *Die Hard* films emphasized the collapse of communism and left-wing ideologies in the post–Cold War world. The first and third installment of the series brought left-wing Euroterrorists to the U.S. to try their hand at capitalism while abandoning their left-wing policies to the altar of money, and making them common criminals. The second film closed the door to U.S. policies of supporting dictators and military leaders who had been waging a Cold War in the American backyard. In contrast to anti-communist fighter Matt Hunter in *Invasion USA* in 1985, five years later the world had changed to the point that Colonel Stuart, another anti-communist fighter, had now graduated to a role of an anti–American terrorist villain due to his loyalty to the past.

German left-wing terrorists were not the only ones to travel across the Atlantic from Europe. Terrorists from the United Kingdom, a British aristocrat in *Passenger 57* (1992), and terrorists from Northern Ireland in *Patriot Games* (1992), *Blown Away* (1994), *The Jackal* (1997), and *Ronin* (1998) came to threaten and also to defend the U.S. in the 1990s with box office success.

CHAPTER 7

Euroinvasion: Madmen from Britain and Northern Ireland

Passenger 57 (1992); *Patriot Games* (1992); *Blown Away* (1994); *The Jackal* (1997); *Ronin* (1998)

The United Kingdom has given the Middle East serious competition as the origin of film terrorists among the annual highest-grossing films in the domestic box office from 1980 until September 11, 2001. The five films that draw from terrorism originating in Northern Ireland and Britain equal the number of the movies that portray Middle Eastern terrorism.

This chapter analyzes the five films that draw their content from the United Kingdom. *Passenger 57* was in 1992 the first of the sixteen terrorist films in the annual top fifty box office from 1980 till 9/11 to portray an African American hero. The film's storyline is the most fictional of the sixteen films in terrorist terms, having no parallel in its storyline in real-life terrorist threats. The other four films all draw from terrorism in Northern Ireland, in particular from the Provisional Irish Republican Army (PIRA) and its splinter groups. Three of the films, *Patriot Games* (1992), *Blown Away* (1994) and *Ronin* (1998), find their villains in terrorists who are too extreme for the PIRA. *The Jackal* (1997) introduces in Bruce Willis an international terrorist-assassin for hire. Two of the films cast their heroes from Northern Irish terrorists. In *Blown Away* a former Republican terrorist from Northern Ireland has escaped to the U.S. and has created a new respectable life. *The Jackal* (1997) promotes a jailed PIRA terrorist to its hero role. Even the fifth U.K. terrorism-themed film, *Passenger 57* (1992), very briefly refers to Northern Ireland in the aristocratic British terrorist's background.

Passenger 57 (1992: #35)

Distributor: Warner Bros. Pictures
Production company: Lee Rich Productions
Producers: Lee Rich, Dan Paulson, and Dylan Sellers
Director: Kevin Hooks
Screenplay: David Loughery and Dan Gordon
Screenplay based: on story by Stewart Raffill and Dan Gordon
Executive producer: Jonathan Sheinberg

Co-producer:	Robert J. Anderson
MPAA rating:	R
Release date:	November 6, 1992[1]
DVD (WS) running time:	84 minutes
Domestic box-office:	$41,677,708 (1992), cumulative box office $44,065,653[2]

Passenger 57 starts with credits running on top of images of airport security, baggage and a passport. The film's title appears on a person's head before the camera cuts to a close-up of the person's eyes. We have met the film's mad terrorist, Charles Rane, played by Bruce Payne. Next the camera cuts to introduce Rane in person, a white man with golden curls, in a plastic-surgeon's chair. The camera pulls out from a close-up of his eyes. The white man with a high-class British accent refuses anesthesia. The film crosscuts between shots of a SWAT team ready to attack, and the surgery room, the doctor in the room nervously checking the wall clock. But the surgery never takes place: Rane cuts the doctor's throat and runs out of the room. He jumps through a third-floor window onto a street. After a chase, the FBI catches and arrests him.

The film next introduces its protagonist. An African American man armed with a gun is hijacking a plane when the flight attendant whom he grabs stomps on his foot and stops the situation. The viewer learns the event is only an airline training security session on how to handle hijackings. The trainer, John Cutter, played by Wesley Snipes, is a former security specialist. His pride hurt, he verbally abuses the attractive light-skinned African American flight attendant Marti Slayton (Alex Datcher) for endangering her own and the passengers' lives by not following the hijacker's orders.

Passenger 57 was brave to test the waters with an African American actor as its hero. The action-adventure genre has since its emergence been the white man's playground. From a distributor and producer's viewpoint it was risky business to cast an African American actor as the protagonist of an action-adventure film. The question was whether the U.S. was ready for an American hero with a darker skin tone. Hollywood had long considered such casting a financial risk to the point that until the early 1990s it was hard to find successful action-adventure films that starred actors from minority groups in roles besides the film villain, the hero or villain's accomplice, or, at times, the romantic female interest. In contrast, a white foreigner with an accent and muscles which did not find a match in the U.S. had qualified Arnold Schwarzenegger to star as the protagonist in several successful films in the 1980s and 1990s.

The film's script pokes some fun at Snipes's starring role, by overdone "brother" comments from other film characters. Also, Cutter gives the white terrorist a piece of roulette advice: "Always bet black." Otherwise the screenplay gives Snipes's character, John Cutter, a role that is largely written like that of any other action-adventure character, no matter his background. The antagonist forces the hero to become involved because the villain and his supporters hijack the very plane John Cutter is taking. The protagonist and the antagonist are counterparts, both intelligent men who use their muscles and brains in this terrorist match.

White Aristocratic British Madman Faces an African American Hero

The film's antagonist Charles Rane is a sophisticated British aristocrat better known internationally as the "Rane of Terror." His operation method is the most commonly used terrorist weapon: bombings. His list of accomplishments includes several airliner, train and

Wesley Snipes as John Cutter (left) was the first minority actor to make it as the hero in the most popular action-adventure films on international terrorism. In *Passenger 57* (1992, Warner Bros.) he faces Charles Rane, the "Rane of Terror" (Bruce Payne), an insane British terrorist. The film distorts terrorism in its portrayal of an insane criminal as its international terrorist. According to the CIA and the U.S. State Department, including acts of insane people in terrorism data contaminates the data because those acts are not done for political motivations, as is the case with terrorism.

other bombings in London, Ireland and Northern Ireland. He has close ties to the Middle East. However, the film never explains any motivation for any of his terrorist acts. The bombings he is linked to hint at a link to Northern Irish Republican Catholic rather than loyalist Protestant activities. The Provisional Irish Republican Army was largely in charge of anti–British attacks in different parts of Europe, in particular in London and Northern Ireland. But Rane's proper British accent and limited background information leave unclear what ideology or policies he is supporting with his activities. If the filmmakers had done their homework properly, they would have been able to write a more convincing background for the terrorist and his group, easily finding models in real life. Even the Euroterrorism of the early 1990s had several active groups to pick from, such as the Kurdish Workers' Party (PKK), several Corsican nationalist groups, Basque Fatherland and Liberty (ETA) in Spain, German (Red Army Faction) RAF, and groups operating in the former Soviet area, not to mention a variety of groups in Northern Ireland.[3]

Charles Rane is a Russian Rostov look-alike, an insane cold-blooded blond man with piercing cold eyes and a cold smile, and wearing a suite. Similar to Hans Gruber, he is stylish, educated and arrogant. Rane does not give second chances. His barrel is not empty as Colonel Stuart's was in *Die Hard 2: Die Harder*. When one of his group's members fails his part of the mission when John Cutter unarms him, Rane shoots his underling, commenting: "I loathe incompetence." To Cutter's earlier threat to shoot the man whom he calls Rane's friend, Rane's response is "I have no friends." Rane forces Cutter to surrender by threatening to kill a passenger, asking the man's name and if he has any children, and then without hesitation shooting the man in the head. The screenplay also makes him inconsistent: when another of his men fails when John Cutter catches the man and ties him up, Rane in no way reacts to this accomplice's incompetence.

The antagonist sees himself in John Cutter: "We share the same hunger. We're both killers. I know the breed." Rane values his opponent: "You've been a worthy adversary." John Cutter, a jeans and leather jacket man, is a highly regarded security specialist. He is a troubled man who blames himself for his wife's death. A flashback reveals she died when he tried to prevent a convenience store robbery. His Italian-American friend, Sly Delvecchio (Tom Sizemore) of Atlantic International Airline, tells him to move on, and arranges for Cutter to be hired to head the company's counterterrorism unit. It just happens that on his way to a meeting with his new employer Cutter is on the very plane the terrorists hijack. The film's romantic subplot adds to the story Marti Slayton, the flight attendant with whom he bickered at the film's beginning. As Slayton is taking a passenger headcount, she notices, with distaste, John Cutter. He is passenger number 57. As is customary with romantic plotlines, the conflicted relationship turns into romantic interest by the film's end.

Two FBI agents arrive at the very last minute to board the plane with Charles Rane to take him to Los Angeles, where he will stand trial for bombings. Their arrival is a surprise to the airline. Rane had told his lawyer to notify his people that he will be moved to L.A., but the lawyer does not know when and how, so it is against all logic that Rane's supporters could have arranged to be on the plane with a plan, ready to kill the agents and hijack the plane in order to release their leader.

Terrorist Film That Distorts International Terrorism

The film only partially matches the U.S. State Department definitions of international terrorism. It is lacking the main requirement, an act or threat for political motivations. However, the movie does portray a villain whom it characterizes as a recognized international terrorist. His comrades cross international borders to commit an act which terrorizes and threatens American civilians. The terrorists of *Passenger 57* use a rare but usually highly publicized method of international terrorism: a hijacking. This draws from the terrorist methods of the 1980s. As Howard points out, in the 1980s terrorists hijacked planes for three reasons: for media attention, for profit by demanding a ransom, and to release their comrades.[4] In this particular case, the terrorist's associates mysteriously know in advance a last-minute FBI plan to transfer their prisoner to Los Angeles. The terrorist group's motivation is to release their leader, Charles Rane, but they have no political motivations. In contrast to real terrorist hijackings and this book's other films on hijackings, the news media are not present and terrorists do not request news media coverage.

The film does get something right in its portrayal of international terrorism. As in real life, in *Passenger 57* the FBI is in charge of crisis response to terrorism on U.S. soil. It is the FBI which catches and transfers Charles Rane, and it is the FBI which takes over from the local authorities in remote Louisiana, where the plane is forced to land when it runs out of fuel. Also, as John Cutter advises during a hijacking simulation, pre–9/11 guidelines on hijackings advised personnel to follow hijackers' demands.[5] However, in contrast to real-life hijackings, the Federal Aviation Administration (FAA) has no role to play in the film.

The screenplay draws from the traditional weak news media image of terrorists: madness. That is an oversimplification of a complex political phenomenon. It creates a false sense of security because terrorism can be explained away if its perpetrators are insane and have no rational and strategic background. Unfortunately the real phenomenon is not that easy. We may disagree with those who oppose us with violent methods, but that does not prevent their actions even if we label our opponents as insane. Real efforts to analyze terrorist methods and the terrorist mindset are better methods of defense. As a profiler of serial killers tries to get inside the head of such killers in order to catch the predators and prevent future attacks, efforts to understand the terrorist mindset, which does not mean to agree with it, are more likely to aid counterterrorism than are simple labels such as "mad" and "insane."

While several of the foreign antagonists of the other films in this study grow mad gradually, usually becoming more or less completely insane and enraged by the final confrontation, this film's antagonist already knows at the beginning of the film not only his intellect but also his insanity. It is obviously a sore spot for him. When Rane's attorney in the early stages of the film proposes an insanity defense to him because of "his childhood," which, according to the attorney, would obviously support it, Rane immediately physically attacks the attorney. Slamming the attorney's head onto a table, Rane points out: "It's the nature of man to confuse genius with insanity." He forces the attorney to repeat several times: "Charles Rane is not insane, Charles Rane is not insane," at which point the viewer knows the opposite to be true. Rane is also suspected of having killed his own father, who had mistreated him as a child. While he is a smart and arrogant villain, similar in that sense to *Die Hard*'s Hans Gruber, unfortunately this villain is reduced by his simplistic characterization to only a simplified version of Hans Gruber and the latter's quick reading of situations. For example, when Gruber came face to face with John McClane the first time, he pretended to be an escaped hostage. Gruber's actions and reactions confirmed that he is smart. In contrast, in *Passenger 57* Charles Rane's behavior and actions fall far behind Hans Gruber's intellect. Exposition reveals Rane's background as an educated British aristocrat, but his actions do not support the assumed characterization as an intellectual and as a smart terrorist.

It is no wonder the filmmakers get terrorism wrong because they already get the definition of terrorism wrong. The film's additional DVD material explains that there are three different types of terrorists: criminals, terrorists for political motivations, and crazies. However, definitions of terrorism throughout decades have only agreed on one thing: terrorists have political motivations. The State Department has clearly argued against including criminals and insane people in any terrorism data because that inclusion would contaminate the data. The 1983 *Patterns of Global Terrorism* report makes this explicit when discussing airline hijackings:

> Our statistics on international terrorist incidents include skyjackings only when they are demonstrably terrorist in nature — that is, when they are politically motivated and are either the work of clandestine state agents or are intended to have a violent demonstrational effect on a target audience other than just the crew and passengers on the plane. Skyjackings, however, are frequently no more than criminal acts, often the work of persons who are mentally deranged, intent on extortion or simply seeking rapid transportation across national boundaries that would be otherwise closed to them.[6]

According to the DVD material, which lists three definitions of terrorists, the terrorist of *Passenger 57* is two out of the three: a criminal and a "crazie." With that comment alone the film undermines its own content when it calls Rane a terrorist but denies him of any political motivations. As the State Department emphasized in the 1980s, a hijacking by a mentally deranged person is a criminal act, not a terrorist criminal act due to the person's lack of political motivations. Several other films on international terrorism have painted their terrorists as insane, but these film terrorists have been granted a clearer political background, if not a motivation, for their acts. The *Passenger 57* script serves a cocktail which mixes fictional international terrorism with the action-adventure film traditions of an insane villain, and comes up with a bad hangover which offers a complete distortion of international terrorism even in fictional Hollywood terms.

Passenger 57 is a watered-down version of *Die Hard.* Even the hero's first name is the same. Cutter is caught in the plane's bathroom, just as John McClane is in his wife's office bathroom when the hostage drama starts. As in *Die Hard, Passenger 57* relies on Cutter's sarcastic comments and on a combination of his intellect and physical prowess. Cutter alerts the airline company with a call from the plane's bathroom, gets caught, and then escapes with Marti Slayton to the plane's avionics area. The hero starts to empty the plane of fuel, guaranteeing to Marti that he knows what he is doing because he "is the best." One of the hijackers manages to pull the flight attendant back to the plane and to kick Cutter off the plane just as the plane is landing in a remote area in Louisiana to refuel. Now the protagonist has an opportunity to redeem himself, and not only to save the situation but also to save this attractive African American flight attendant. Slayton also draws Rane's attention. He lusts after her during the hijacking. Rane moves his gun slowly over her breasts and down her body. Rude and insensitive in the tradition of action-adventure villains, Rane asks, "Did the hero get into your little tight place?"

This terrorist's escape strategy is similar to the Gruber brothers' methods. Interpol reveals that Rane escapes by creating distractions that allow him to get away unnoticed. This time he plans to escape the plane while half of the passengers are released. Later, *Passenger 57* echoes a famous film from Hollywood's past. Rane's escape takes him and two of his accomplices to an amusement park. The physical confrontation between Rane and Cutter brings to mind Alfred Hitchcock's famous *Strangers on a Train* fight between tennis star Guy Haines and psychotic villain Bruno Anthony on a merry-go-round when the police are after the wrong person.

Echoing John McClane's experiences with authorities, *Passenger 57* sets up the protagonist against local authorities when incompetent southern police cannot figure out whether the man is a terrorist or on their side, and therefore treat him as a suspect. In contrast to *Die Hard,* this time the FBI, which comes to the rescue in Louisiana, is portrayed as an efficient organization. Its agent in charge, played by the director's father, Robert Hooks, highly values the lonely fighter's skills and expertise, and even lets him take over at certain parts of the mission — something the real-life FBI would not allow.

Female Accomplices

Passenger 57 introduces a refreshing exception to the general film portrayal of international terrorism. Rane's sidekick, Sabrina Ritchie, is an attractive white Briton whom the film introduces as a friendly flight attendant who is very sweet and attentive to passengers. But the flight attendant, played by Elizabeth Hurley, is as cold as Rane. She even jokes with Marti Slayton that her accent makes her sound cold and heartless. As Ritchie takes Rane's order for his steak dinner, she asks how he wants it cooked. Rane's answer — "bloody" — is followed by her shooting Rane's guards, two FBI agents, in the head without any hesitation or warning.

The only other of the sixteen films to portray female terrorists who participate in the villain's actions and believe in the cause (unlike Juno Skinner in *True Lies,* whose motivation is money), are *Ronin, Patriot Games* and *Die Hard with a Vengeance. Patriot Games* introduces another competent and cold-blooded British female terrorist, a member of a PIRA splinter group, who dies at the film's end. In *Ronin* the contact between the hero and the villain is a female PIRA terrorist who hires and oversees an international group of shady men, and who simply vanishes in the end. In *Die Hard with a Vengeance,* the girlfriend of Simon Gruber's

Hungarian accomplice is briefly shown killing her lover in cold blood towards the film's end before she joins Gruber as his new accomplice and sexual partner. She dies with Simon Gruber when their helicopter crashes. In *Passenger 57* Cutter knocks the attractive female terrorist unconscious with the comment "What a waste."

Largely following the film traditions of the 1980s — as in, for example, *Invasion USA*— the film's violence is for entertainment purposes only. This movie uses strong violence by briefly introducing the first two FBI agents and one passenger before the terrorists shoot them in the head. Otherwise the passengers are a faceless mass of people. Terrorists shoot several of them before the hostage drama is over.

As became an action-adventure film trademark in the 1990s, Euroterrorists deserve individual deaths, and that is the case with this film too. John Cutter uses his fists and kicks to win individual physical fights. The film's traditional final one-on-one confrontation between the protagonist and the antagonist takes place after Rane is back on the plane and Cutter climbs onto the airliner. As Rane shoots at the hero, plane windows break, and the loss of air pressure results in one of the plane's doors bursting out. After a short physical fight Cutter kicks Rane through the missing door into his death.

Passenger 57 portrays a traditional heterosexual coupling which is also the protagonist's prodigal journey. Cutter no longer blames himself for his wife's death. Now his slate is clean after he has saved his new love interest, and also most of the passengers on the plane. The film traditionally creates a conflict between the protagonist and his romantic interest at the film's beginning. When the hijacking is real, the bickering female character follows Cutter and helps him. In the end they leave the scene together, Cutter's arm around her shoulders. The film is reminiscent of *Commando* and *Executive Decision. Commando* also portrayed a single and wisecracking hero, although a white one, with an attractive minority woman, this time Afro-Asian, on his side. Four years after *Passenger 57*, in 1996's *Executive Decision*, Dr. Grant, a white researcher, relies on the help of a light-skinned African American flight attendant, played by Halle Berry. All three films end with a promise of a possible happy heterosexual coupling when the hero and his new love interest leave the scene together. However, Hollywood films only dared to pair people in romantic relationships from the same racial background, or a white man with a minority female, but not a minority male actor with a white female.

Northern Irish Terrorism

For the United Kingdom the threat of terrorism until the late 1990s was primarily in the activities of Republican and Loyalist groups in Northern Ireland, in particular in the activities of the Provisional Irish Republican Army (PIRA), a Republican group. The death toll from sectarian violence, which started in 1969, reached over 3,000 in Northern Ireland in the 1990s. The U.S. State Department acknowledged the threat posed by the PIRA. In its 1993 report the department directly addressed the organization's activities and threat level:

> The PIRA remains by far the most active and lethal terrorist group in Western Europe. In April, following the British election, it exploded a van bomb — the largest ever detonated on the British mainland — in London's financial district, killing three people and wounding more than 90 others, including one American. The amount of property damage caused by this single attack is estimated to be $1.5 billion. The PIRA launched a bombing spree in London against train stations, hotels, and shopping areas in the autumn of 1992 —16 attacks in October alone — that resembled its terror campaign of the mid–1970s. The latest round would have been even more devastating had police not found and defused three bombs loaded in abandoned vans; two of the three contained over 1 ton of explosives each. British insurance companies announced at the end of the year

that terrorism riders on building insurance would be dropped because of the large costs of bomb damage.[7]

The conflict in Northern Ireland has long historical roots, reaching back to the 12th century and the British invasion and rule of Ireland. Centuries later, in 1916 the Easter Rising eventually led to a civil war. As a result, the southern part of the island, 26 counties, became the independent Irish Free State in December 1921. Six counties, Northern Ireland, remained part of the U.K. In 1949 Ireland withdrew from the British Commonwealth.

Violence erupted in Northern Ireland in the mid–1960s as the region's Catholics started to demand equal civil rights. The dominant Protestant Unionists, in whose view Northern Ireland should remain part of the U.K., discriminated against the Catholic minority in politics, voting rights, and housing, among other areas. By 1969 both the Catholics and the Protestants had paramilitary groups defending their areas and targeting the opposition. Differences in religion and views of what the destiny of Northern Ireland should be sharply divided the region. The Irish Republican Army (IRA) re-emerged from dormancy in 1969. It had been founded in 1913 as the Irish Volunteer Force but became known as the Irish Republican Army a few years later, after some internal developments. The IRA split into two in 1969 due to internal conflicts. The more militant Provisional Irish Republican Army (PIRA) took up armed struggle. The Marxist-oriented faction, the Official Irish Republican Army (OIRA), gave up militant activities at the beginning of the 1970s and soon faded away.[8]

The PIRA violently opposed the British presence in Northern Ireland, wanted a unified Ireland and equal civil rights. The organization, often simply known as the IRA, targeted representatives of the official British power structure, Protestant paramilitary groups, and also defended what it saw as its own Catholic areas. The PIRA was running strong during the three decades of violence in Northern Ireland, known as the Troubles. Its methods included, as the U.S. State Department has listed: "Bombings, assassinations, kidnappings, punishment beatings, extortion, smuggling, and robberies."[9] In the 1980s the PIRA targeted, for example, parks and department stores in London, security forces in Northern Ireland, and businesses and individuals who provided services to them. Its primary operating areas were Northern Ireland, Great Britain, and continental Europe.[10] One of its most spectacular attacks was the bombing of the hotel at which Prime Minister Margaret Thatcher and her cabinet were staying during the Conservative Party conference in 1984. Most of the human targets were able to escape.[11]

In the early 1990s, when *Patriot Games*, the first large-scale Hollywood film drawing from Northern Irish terrorism, was released, the State Department estimated the PIRA to have several hundred active members and a few thousand supporters.[12] According to the department, the organization had ties to the PLO and Libya. It had cooperated with the PLO, for example, in training. From Libya the PIRA had received aid including training and arms. Over the years authorities found evidence of Libyan support. For example, in 1987 French authorities intercepted a Libya-supplied shipment to Northern Irish terrorists, and in 1991 the Irish authorities found Libya-supplied guns and ammunition in Ireland.[13]

The violent era of civil disturbances and terrorism continued until the late 1990s, with several failed attempts to reach a lasting peace and political solution in Northern Ireland. In 1985 Ireland and the U.K. signed the Anglo-Irish Agreement, according to which the six northern counties would remain part of the U.K. until that was what the majority wanted. This did not go down well with those who opposed the idea of two Irelands, in particular the PIRA. In the early 1990s the State Department pointed out that the PIRA had become "increasingly indiscriminate in its spectacular bombing attacks."[14] For example, in 1991 its target list included No. 10 Downing Street, railway stations in London, and malls.[15] A year later the organization launched a bombing campaign similar to those of its heyday in the 1970s. Also, the PIRA's splinter groups targeted the official British power structure. While the PIRA received the most headlines abroad, the violence of Loyalist and Unionist paramilitary groups' attacks on Northern Irish Catholics at times surpassed the PIRA violence. For example, in 1992 they performed for the first time more violent attacks than the PIRA.[16]

The United States actively supported the peace process in Northern Ireland in the 1990s. Peace discussions in Northern Ireland brought the PIRA to announce a cease-fire on September 1, 1994. Three major Loyalist paramilitary groups followed suit. PIRA splinter groups also ceased their attacks.[17] According to the U.S. State Department's 1995 report, the country's close relationship with the U.K. and Ireland enabled the U.S. to facilitate new developments in Northern Ireland. The year-long peace process of the mid–1990s was headed by an international committee under the leadership of former U.S. senator George Mitchell. The PIRA participated in several cease-fires from 1994 until 1996. Due to these cease-fires, small militant splinter groups abandoned the organization. These included, for example, the Real IRA (RIRA, 1997/1998) and the Continuity Irish Republican Army (CIRA, 1994), the military wing of the Republican Sinn Fein.[18] In February 1996, the PIRA broke its 17-month cease-fire. The hardcore CIRA, also known as the Continuity Army Council (CAC), joined the PIRA in a new cycle of violence.[19]

In July 1997, after the May election victory of the British Labor Party and its preliminary talks with Sinn Fein, the PIRA's political wing, the PIRA announced an unequivocal cease-fire. Sinn Fein committed to nonviolence, as proposed by George Mitchell. These developments allowed Sinn Fein to return to the negotiation table in the Northern Irish peace process. The multiparty effort had May 1998 as the deadline for an agreement.

In response to Sinn Fein and the PIRA's commitment to a peaceful solution to the Northern Irish power-sharing, some PIRA members left the organization. Also, some of the splinter groups, such as the CAC and the Irish National Liberation Army (INLA), which had been formed in 1975 as the military wing of the Irish Republican Socialist Party (which had left the Official IRA because of its commitment to the 1972 cease fire), turned up the heat in their violent campaigns. Loyalist splinter groups also opposed the multiparty peace talks and heightened their violent activities.[20]

Negotiations and ceasefires eventually led to the Good Friday Agreement in April 1998 which aimed to bring a lasting peace. The agreement included a power-sharing assembly, decommissioning of the paramilitary groups' weapons on both sides, and the Republic of Ireland admitting it had no claim to Northern Ireland.[21] As a result of the PIRA and Sinn Fein's progress, the U.S. removed the PIRA from the State Department's list of *designated* foreign terrorist organizations when the U.S. Secretary of State announced the list in October 1997. However, the department still defined the PIRA as a foreign terrorist organization.[22] In its 1999 report the State Department proudly announced:

> Washington's ties to London and Dublin played a key role in facilitating historic political developments in the Northern Ireland peace process that resulted in a significant decline in terrorist activity. Following a year of intense negotiations and a review of the entire peace process by former US Senator George Mitchell, Britain devolved power to Ulster, and Ireland, gave up its constitutional claim to Northern Ireland; the Catholic and Protestant parties agreed to govern Ulster together in a joint Executive, which held its inaugural meeting on 13 December. Much of the contention between parties was, and remains, about how to address the implementation of the Good Friday Agreement, including the issue of decommissioning paramilitary weapons.[23]

After years of international negotiations and peace efforts in the 1990s and the early 21st century, the PIRA officially declared its armed campaign ended on July 28, 2005. Three months later the Independent International Commission on Decommissioning (IICD) confirmed that the PIRA no longer had weapons.[24] A power-sharing government emerged in May 2007 when the PIRA's political wing, Sinn Fein, took seats at the Northern Ireland Executive, which also has Unionist and other nationalist representatives.[25]

From the U.S. perspective the PIRA was never a serious threat to the U.S. since the group was targeting the U.K. In Europe the U.S. faced terrorist attacks and threats from several anti–U.S. and anti–NATO Euroterrorist groups, such as the Red Army Faction in West Germany, the French Action Direct, and the Italian Red Brigades. However, Hollywood producers did not run after these threats as intensely as the threats related to Ireland and Northern Ireland. In the 1990 U.S. census almost 39 million Americans claimed Irish ancestry. Ten years later the number had dropped to 30.5 million, a decrease from 15.6 percent to 10.8 percent. Ireland is the second most often claimed ancestry for Americans. Germany takes the number one spot.[26]

In the 1990s Hollywood majors brought to movie theaters four action-filled films which drew their theme from the conflict in Northern Ireland. The films were *Patriot Games* (1992), *Blown Away* (1994), *The Jackal* (1997), and *Ronin* (1998).

Patriot Games (1992: #11)

Distributor:	Paramount Pictures
Production company:	Mace Neufeld and Robert Rehme Productions
Producers:	Mace Neufeld and Robert Rehme
Director:	Phillip Noyce
Screenplay:	W. Peter Iliff and Donald Stewart
Screenplay based:	on the novel *Patriot Games* by Tom Clancy
Executive producer:	Charles H. Maguire
MPAA Rating:	R
Release date:	June 5, 1992[27]
DVD (WS) running time:	116 minutes
Domestic box office:	$82,880,259, cumulative total $83,351,587[28]

Patriot Games is representative of the 1990s action-adventure films which combined action with the hero's family life. It is a family-centered film, as is also another terrorist film starring Harrison Ford, *Air Force One*. Both films portray a middle-aged man with a preteen daughter and loving wife. Terrorist attacks make the fight personal when they threaten the domestic bliss. The hero must save his family. There is no son to compete for the hero's limelight.

Patriot Games sets Dr. John "Jack" Ryan (Harrison Ford), a former CIA agent, up against a PIRA terrorist, Sean Miller (Sean Bean). While on a visit to London with his wife Caroline "Cathy" (Anne Archer), a doctor, and preteen daughter Sally (Thora Birch), Ryan interrupts a terrorist attack. As he is rejoining his family after an academic presentation, a small group of terrorists attacks a member of the royal family, Lord William Holmes (James Fox), the minister of state for Northern Ireland, and his family in a car. The attack takes place right next to Ryan's wife and daughter. Ryan attacks the terrorists, snatching a gun from the ski-masked terrorists and shooting one. One of the other terrorists pleads with him to help the badly wounded terrorist: "Help the boy." Ryan removes the ski mask of the terrorist whom he had just shot to find a dying teenager.

In the 1990s action heroes got a wife who has an impressive career and a preteen daughter. In *Patriot Games* (1992, Paramount Pictures) John "Jack" Ryan (Harrison Ford) protects his wife Cathy (Anne Archer) and daughter Sally (Thora Birch) in an attack by a PIRA fringe group. He kills a young terrorist whose brother, Sean Miller (Sean Bean), soon takes his revenge on Ryan's family.

The film's small PIRA group has failed in its attack. Jack Ryan becomes the hero of the day, and the target of the dead terrorist's brother, Sean Miller. Following the action-adventure film traditions, the film introduces two characters who share a hostile moment which lays the ground for a personal conflict between the hero and the villain. Sean Miller, the teenager's brother, wants revenge. Again, loyally following the genre traditions, the hero is forced to become involved because of the villain's actions. In Dr. Jack Ryan's own words at court about Sean Miller, who is caught in the attack: "I didn't make this happen. He did."

Sean Miller's backstory describes him as a boy who lost his father at an early age when he was killed by the RUC (Royal Ulster Constabulary) in Belfast, Northern Ireland. A family friend, Kevin O'Donnell (Patrick Bergin), a longtime PIRA strategist, took in Sean and his younger brother. Miller is an angry PIRA member who is eager to kill, and he had also recruited his teenage brother to join the PIRA. Miller's shot list includes, for example, a parish priest whom he thought to be helping the British, and a non military associate. The film shows him shooting, execution style, an unarmed British (originally Irish) police inspector and other British police officers in the back of their head when he escapes.

The film draws from the U.S. State Department list of terrorist organizations as it introduces the Provisional Irish Republican Army. Drawing from the PIRA's list of targets, in *Patriot Games* the fictional terrorists target a royal family member who is also the minister of state for Northern Ireland. He is a symbol of the prevailing power structure that stands against the independence of Northern Ireland from the United Kingdom. News media in the film provide exposition, telling viewers that no group has claimed responsibility for the attack on

Lord William Holmes, the Queen Mother's cousin, but PIRA involvement is suspected. CNN also brings the news to CIA headquarters as it credits "John Patrick Ryan, an American tourist, an author and professor at the United States Naval Academy in Annapolis, Maryland, former Marine Lieutenant" for the rescue.

While the film provides its terrorists with a target based on real-life PIRA targets, it fails to explain the terrorists' motivation until late in the film when O'Donnell clarifies to Miller that they want the target for a ransom. However, the film expects the viewer to have the background political knowledge to know why the PIRA would target a representative of the official British power structure. After Miller's capture the film even provides one of the detectives with lines that tell how he understands the hatred, but the film still does not explain the historical or political context that has led to Miller's hatred. The only context is his *personal* tragedy of losing at a young age his father, killed by the British power structure.

The story fast moves beyond the PIRA to portray what became a trademark of those who did not agree with the PIRA ceasefires later that decade, such as the CIRA and RIRA: extremists who leave the PIRA. O'Donnell, Miller, and an Englishwoman, Annette (Polly Walker), form a small fringe group in their efforts to radicalize the PIRA. The group, led by O'Donnell, demands that the organization take more aggressive action. *Patriot Games* introduces the group in words similar to what the world heard almost ten years later on September 20, 2001, from a more official source, the president of the United States. When O'Donnell is discussing with a PIRA brigade commander his group's unauthorized attack on a member of the royal family,

In *Patriot Games*, former PIRA terrorists leave the organization to form an ultra-radical group, reflecting the PIRA's real internal struggles in the 1990s. Following the action-adventure film genre traditions, Sean Miller (Sean Bean, front), the insane villain of *Patriot Games* (1992, Paramount Pictures), targets the Ryan family. When his terrorist associates, Kevin O'Donnell (Patrick Bergin) and English Annette (Polly Walker), eventually get in the way of his revenge, they meet their destiny at his hands.

he curses the organization for not being more effective and extreme. The PIRA leader's response is, "You are either with us or you are against us, Jimmy boy. Make up your mind." Nine years later President George W. Bush announced to the world after the 9/11 attacks: "Every nation in every region now has a decision to make. Either you are with us, or you are with the terrorists."[29] For the film's fringe group the decision is easy: they kill their local PIRA competition and continue their own ultraviolent activity. Later the group takes pleasure in the news that the British are going after the PIRA, tearing Belfast apart. One notes that soon "only us will be left standing."

The film links the PIRA splinter group to two real-life state sponsors of terrorism, Libya and Syria. The group escapes the PIRA and the British and U.S. authorities, fleeing to North Africa on a Syrian freighter that is known to have carried arms to client states, including Libya. Also, some of the group's guns are traced to Libyan leader Qadhafi's arms dealer. Furthermore, in North Africa their safe haven is a terrorist training camp, echoing the State Department's discussions of PIRA training at PLO and Libyan terrorist training camps. In the film the CIA identifies close to two hundred training camps in the region by its satellite images. The CIA says that the groups training at these camps include the PLO, the Red Brigades, the French Action Direct, the West German Red Army Faction, and Peru's Shining Path. The groups all appear on the State Department's list of foreign terrorist organizations, and several were linked to North African training facilities in the department's 1980s reports.

Patriot Games simplifies the case of the film's PIRA splinter group into a personal fight between a vengeful and cold-blooded terrorist and an American hero. Sean Miller's personal vendetta surpasses his political ideology. As an international terrorist he crosses borders to commit an attack, not for political but for personal motivations. Not only does he come after Ryan but he particularly targets his pregnant wife and young daughter. Miller almost succeeds in killing Ryan's wife and daughter before he leaves for North Africa. His shots fail to hit them, but he does cause their car to crash, which results in serious injuries to Ryan's young daughter, Sally.

References to the PIRA and its political wing Sinn Fein are sprinkled throughout the film. For example, it portrays Paddy O'Neill (Richard Harris), a Sinn Fein representative who is on a funding trip to the U.S. O'Neill claims in front of TV cameras that Sinn Fein is outraged by the attack, as are most Irish Catholics. In his words the PIRA admits to its campaigns proudly, and had nothing to do with the attack on the Ryan family. O'Neill later comes to Ryan's help, unwillingly passing him information on the unidentified female terrorist with red hair, English Annette.

Dr. Jack Ryan returns to the CIA, to terrorism assessment and the CIA's Patriot Files. Ryan's wife's distaste for his past CIA job is overcome when the antagonist calls their home and taunts Dr. Ryan for not having prevented the villain's attack on his wife and daughter:

> SEAN MILLER:
> — How's the family, Ryan? You nearly lost them, didn't you? It's easy to get at them. You should look after your family better, you know. Are you there? Yeah.
> I understand your little girl's feeling better, eh? Lost her spleen, yeah? Pity. That makes it mighty tough on her to fight off infection, eh, Jackie?
>
> JACK RYAN:
> — You sick son of a bitch.

His wife overhears the conversation. Her words are liberating to him: "He's never going to leave us alone. You get him, Jack. I don't care what you have to do, just get him."

On the day Sally Ryan is released from the hospital, Lord Holmes visits the family at their house to present Dr. Ryan with the honor of knighthood, a Knight Commander of the Victorian Order. That is also the moment when the film's PIRA splinter group renews its attack, coming after their target in the U.S., and with that act breaking away from their real-life counterparts. The Republican groups did not bring their attacks onto U.S. soil. Their activities and attacks took place against representatives of the British authority in Northern Ireland, Britain, Ireland and other parts of Western Europe. Furthermore, attacks in the U.S. would have endangered fundraising activities in the country where, for example, in 1990 some fifteen percent of the population claimed Irish ancestry. In the U.S. the Republican cause could at times find a sympathetic ear and funding.

While Miller's comrades are targeting the visiting member of the royal family, vengeance completely takes over Miller. His only mission is to kill Ryan, and the terrorist group commits the ultimate insult when it attacks the protagonist and his family at their own home. As was the case with Rostov in *Invasion USA*, in this film, too, the villain's focus becomes his revenge on the hero. Without any hesitation Miller kills his own comrades who do not care about Jack Ryan but only want to kidnap Lord Holmes.

One of the film's weakest points is the setup for the final attempt on Lord Holmes, which leads to the final confrontation between the hero and the villain. The principal private secretary to Lord Holmes, Geoffrey Watkins (Hugh Fraser), provides the extremists with the lord's whereabouts and schedule, which is against all logic because the film provides no motivation, political, ideological or financial, for that action. *Air Force One* repeated the same failure five years later when one of the president's Secret Service agents, without any motivation, betrays him and aids the terrorists, and even tries to kill the president.

Dr. Ryan receives some help from the CIA and from a colleague at the Naval Academy, Robby Jackson (Samuel L. Jackson), but primarily relies on himself. The protagonist's intelligence and eventually his muscles help him to defeat the threat to his family. The terrorists' threat to the U.K., a U.S. ally, is of secondary interest.

The film's final confrontation takes place on a boat in the middle of a storm. During a one-on-one fight Ryan punches Miller, who falls and is pierced by an anchor. Ryan jumps off the boat as it explodes. The hero's love for his family makes him so determined that he emerges as the winner over the villain who is motivated by revenge and love for his brother. Both characters draw their strength from their family. Ryan's love for his wife, daughter and unborn child is matched by Miller's love for his brother. However, the simplified characterization of Miller as an enraged, brutal villain prevents the viewer from sharing his sorrow for his brother's death. Loyal to its genre, the film leaves strong violence to the man on the right side of the action. For example, the film effectively portrays Jack and Cathy Ryan's personal grief and worry over their daughter's survival after the terrorist attack on Cathy and Sally. The film allows the viewer to join the couple's pain but does not grant Sean Miller the same privilege. Cinematic strong violence is only for the hero's side.

When Ryan's supervisor is satisfied with Ryan's estimate of the terrorists being at a certain camp in North Africa, the supervisor comments that one cannot be absolutely certain of anything. To this, Ryan's response is: "There's one thing you can be absolutely certain about: my daughter's love." Furthermore, the villain is a brutal killer, yet in contrast, Ryan supposedly feels remorse over the loss of any human life. Due to his suspicions of the fringe group being at a certain camp in North Africa, the CIA and the British Special Air Service (SAS) cooperate. This follows the real-life approach to terrorism. As the State Department's 1994 report points out, "US intelligence and law enforcement agencies have an active network of cooperative relations with counterparts in scores of friendly countries."[30] The camera follows as emotions play over Ryan's face during the live satellite feed of an SAS attack on the camp and their "neutralization" of all targets. The hero's distaste for the killings is obvious, but he is ready to go to any length to save his family. Jack Ryan's prodigal journey is his understanding that his family is his number one priority always, and that he is ready to do anything to protect what is his.

The heroic portrayal of the protagonist as a professor of the U.S. Naval Academy and as a CIA employee shows up in the film's end credits which thank some very powerful supporters. These include, for example, the Department of Defense, Department of Navy, United States Naval Academy, the Brigade of Midshipmen, U.S. Department of the Interior Bureau of Land Management, and also CNN.

Blown Away (1994: #45)

Distributor:	Metro-Goldwyn-Mayer (MGM/UA)
Production company:	Trilogy Entertainment Group
Producers:	John Watson, Pen Densham, and Richard Lewis
Director:	Stephen Hopkins
Screenplay:	Joe Batteer and John Rice
Screenplay based:	on a story by John Rice, Joe Batteer, and M. Jay Roach
Co-producer:	Dean O'Brien
Executive producer:	Lloyd Segan
MPAA rating:	R
Release date:	July 1, 1994[31]
DVD (WS) running time:	121 minutes
Domestic box office:	$30,150,498 (1994), cumulative total: $30,156,002[32]

As the film title, *Blown Away*, suggests, the film is a celebration of explosives and visual effects, but with a storyline that stretches Hollywood fiction to its limits. The weak plot draws from the most often used terrorist method—bombings—but tells of a madman's revenge rather than terrorism. The film barely finished in the annual top fifty domestic box office, being #45 in its release year, and making just over $30 million in the domestic box office.

The film's opening takes the viewer to the coast of Northern Ireland. Thunder and waves hit the rocks to the beat of Irish folk music as the film introduces its villain, long-haired Ryan Gaerity, played by Tommy Lee Jones. The movie leaves him in his Castle Gleigh Prison cell mixing explosives as it cuts to the other side of the Atlantic, to Boston and the film's hero, James "Jimmy" Dove (Jeff Bridges), who is arriving on a motorcycle at his girlfriend's daughter's birthday party. Soon after his arrival his beeper goes off and he rushes off to defuse a bomb at an MIT computer lab. As he is saving others, flashbacks reveal that he is a conflicted man, troubled by memories of a bombing victim lying on the street and calling for him: "Liam, help me."

Jimmy Dove is a former Northern Irish terrorist who has started a new life in the U.S. He is hiding his past and his real name, Liam McGivney. Already his new name reveals how the man of violence has changed. The dove is traditionally a symbol of peace and opposition to war and confrontation. Dove's story is similar to Sean Miller's backstory in *Patriot Games*. He lost his father at a young age in the Troubles. Ryan Gaerity, the film's mad terrorist, took him in. Gaerity taught the hero everything there is to know about explosives. Dove later uses that knowledge to become a hero of the Boston bomb squad. Only his uncle Max, who had helped Dove to find a place in the U.S., knows his violent past, but urges him that he has

In *Blown Away* (1994, MGM) Tommy Lee Jones played Ryan Gaerity, another mad Northern Irish terrorist who is too extreme for the PIRA. Gaerity takes his personal revenge on Jimmy Dove (Jeff Bridges), an Americanized former Northern Irish terrorist who has become a hero in the United States.

done his penance. Dove retires from the force and marries his girlfriend, single mom Kate (Suzy Amis) who has a preteen daughter, Lizzy (Stephi Lineburg). Dove's past comes to haunt him when his past mentor, the bombing specialist Gaerity, escapes to the U.S. and just happens to see one of Dove's rescues on television. He tracks him down, and Gaerity soon forces Dove back to work when he comes after Dove's colleagues and family in revenge for a bombing in Northern Ireland. In traditional heroic terms, even an ex-bomber can be salvaged to become a hero: Dove tried to prevent the bombing because in his view innocent people would have died, and therefore it was not right. And as the hero explains to the villain, he never killed anybody. The event, which killed Dove's then-girlfriend, haunts him. It is also the catalyst for Gaerity's revenge: he was caught because of that incident, and his sister was Dove's girlfriend, the woman killed in the bombing.

The film portrays a heroic bomb squad. The production received cooperation from various authorities — for example, the end credits thank the Los Angeles and Boston Police Departments, the L.A. County Sheriff's Department, the L.A. bomb squad, the Boston Fire Department, and a bomb squad lieutenant. The film is dedicated to the memory of a Boston bomb squad member and certified bomb technicians around the world.

While *Blown Away* looked for help in real-life bomb squad work, the movie tries the viewer's tolerance for film fiction. In the film the U.S. authorities, Interpol and Dove's colleagues have not been able to find out the hero's true identity, but the villain only needs a glimpse of him on a television screen and he immediately recognizes his old protégé. Furthermore, Dove's African American replacement on the bomb squad, Anthony Franklin (Forest Whitaker), does not have much difficulty finding out the protagonist's true identity. The new man wants to prove that he is as good as or better than his predecessor, so he sets out to find out what truly is going on when a madman starts to target Dove's old unit and Dove seems to know a bit more than he shares with others. Franklin easily finds out in the Interpol database that only one of Gaerity's accomplices is still alive: a man by the name of Liam McGivney, an "expert in the manufacturing of all types of explosive devices." The British authorities and Scotland Yard want him for questioning about several bombings. No photo is on file of McGivney, who is at large. However, the file lists Maxwell O'Bannon (Lloyd Bridges), an uncle in Boston, as his only living relative. Dove's colleagues know this uncle very well.

The antagonist of *Blown Away* threatens American civilians, but his motivation is pure personal revenge. That disqualifies him from the State Department's terrorism definitions although the film itself presents the villain as a terrorist who, after his escape from a prison in Northern Ireland, has been a freelancer for the Red Brigades and for Libya, both named on the State Department's list of state sponsors of terrorism and foreign terrorist organizations. Furthermore, in the past he had political motivations for his acts, making him a terrorist by the State Department definitions, although, as the film's protagonist describes, he was "too crazy for the IRA." In the 1990s the State Department defined the Provisional Irish Republican Army and several of its fringe groups as terrorist organizations.

The film borrows some aspects of what was going on in Northern Ireland during the Troubles but then stretches truth for the sake of violent entertainment. The film villain is based on figures from violent Republican fringe groups. The IRA split into the Official Irish Republican Army (OIRA), which avoided violence and had a Marxist approach, and into the Provisional Irish Republican Army (PIRA), which relied on violence in order to reach its political goals, in 1969. Before the OIRA faded away, the organization further split in the early 1970s. Around the turn of the year of 1975 a violent Marxist offshoot, the Irish National Liberation Army (INLA), emerged as the military wing of a competing political group.[33] Several other lesser-known Republican organizations have also violently opposed the British presence in Northern Ireland. In the 1990s Republican extremists did not welcome PIRA ceasefires, and as a result, new violent fringe groups emerged, such as the Continuity Army Council (CAC), aka the Irish Continuity Army Council, in 1994.[34] They continued armed resistance and violent bombings, just like the film's villain.

Blown Away gets right a PIRA trademark, the use of dual bombings. The second device would explode a few minutes after the first bomb, and was often set in the path of the bombing victims escaping the first device.[35] The first of Dove's friends to die is an African American colleague, continuing a 1980s plot device whereby the hero would become committed to a cause after the villain has killed his minority friend. Soon after, two more colleagues die in a dual-bomb attack, which the hero had suspected too late. This time the film disposes of a female and Latino male colleague, both minorities in the white male action-adventure film world. A burned woman haunts Dove again in a flashback, begging him: "Liam, help me."

Dove receives a call from Gaerity at the explosion site. Amazingly, his hearing is intact after a major explosion only a few yards away from him, unlike in *The Siege* when the hero's hearing is impaired by a large explosion. Dove proceeds to have a discussion with Gaerity, who taunts him: "I have come here to create a new country called chaos and a new government, anarchy. All for you." He proceeds to accuse his ex-protégé of having disobeyed an order and betrayed the cause. Gaerity points out that they were at war and that civilians die in war. The film is quite traditional in its portrayal of the villain, in that it avoids clarifying what the mad bomber's cause is. Only close to the final confrontation does the viewer hear the villain raving about Ireland being one nation again, but the film provides no background information about the divided Ireland or the Troubles. Furthermore, the hero's response to the villain's accusations is that the villain had never cared about the cause. However, it is up to the viewer to figure out what the supposed cause is.

Only after the villain sets bombs at the hero's home and kills the family dog does Dove reveal his terrorist background to his wife. He was born and raised in Belfast, where he was taught to hate the English. He says he learned bomb-making from Gaerity. He was a soldier in a war. As Hoffman points out, terrorists do not define themselves as terrorists but as defenders of a system that they see as just and which they want to create; that is, in their own view they are waging a war against a power structure which they define as unjust.[36] However, in Hollywood films only terrorists and ex-terrorists for the Irish cause have the luxury of explaining their violence in terms that may allow the viewer to understand where their actions come from. Even in the 1997 *Devil's Own*, starring Harrison Ford as heroic police sergeant Tom O'Meara and Brad Pitt as PIRA terrorist Frankie McGuire who is hiding in Ford's house, the hero understands his cause and even states it in the film. The film even explains why McGuire has become involved in terrorist acts against the British and why he feels so strongly about the cause. However, since he has killed, the hero's task is still to prevent the terrorist from smuggling missiles to Northern Ireland, which he can only do if he kills McGuire.

As Jimmy Dove (Jeff Bridges, left) has done his penance for his past terrorist acts in *Blown Away* (1994, MGM), a new hero emerges in Anthony Franklin (Forest Whitaker). Franklin saves Dove from madman Gaerity's clutches. Against the action-adventure film genre traditions, the villain dies as a result of his own handiwork in an explosion, not at the hero's hands.

The second act of *Blown Away* ends traditionally, with a setback to the protagonist. The villain beats up Dove's uncle and wraps him up with explosives. After Uncle Max explodes himself, hope is lost for the hero, as the genre traditions require. Kate returns home to the drunk Dove's rescue. The film offers a simple motivation for Dove to get back on track:

> DOVE (to Kate): "You don't know what I have done."
>
> KATE: "I do know you and you're not like him. I love you, Jimmy."

The Fourth of July highlights the film's final confrontation. Dove, spied on and followed by his replacement Anthony Franklin, finds Gaerity at an abandoned ship, where Gaerity sets the bomb's timer. Their physical one-on-one confrontation leaves Dove stuck, waiting only for the explosion, until Franklin sets him free and forces him out of the doomed ship. With his hands up, Ryan

Gaerity burns in the explosion. The man of peace, Jimmy Dove, does not kill the villain. Gaerity dies by his own hand in his own explosion. To finalize his revenge, Gaerity has planted a bomb in Kate's car which is to go off as she leaves her job. Dove, the old hero, and Franklin, the new emerging hero, rush to disarm the bomb and save Kate and Lizzy.

The hero's prodigal journey partially draws from his relationship with his new wife. He gave up his job when he married Kate, telling her: "No regrets, Katie." But he broke his word and returned to the job when the villain started targeting his colleagues, who were called to the villain's first bombing directly from Dove's wedding. But by the film's end he is done, and he willingly lets his replacement Anthony Franklin take the credit and be the hero. Dove turns in his badge. His bomb squad career was about doing his penance for his past terrorist acts, and he can finally rest when he has saved his new family. He is ready to move on with his life and leave the bomb squad behind. The little girl is also finally truly granted her birthday wish of having Jimmy Dove as her father.

The film also grants Dove's replacement a prodigal journey. Anthony Franklin wants to be the new name of the day: "Everybody loves a hero. I am a hero." Before the torch was passed on, Dove first had to save Franklin when Gaerity had succeeded in entrapping the emerging hero by setting a bomb in his headphones. At the end the protégé outsmarts the master, just as Dove had done to Gaerity. Franklin saves Dove from Gaerity's clutches, and helps him to save Dove's family. Anthony Franklin is the new hero. Dove has finally done his penance, and he has earned his adopted name of peace.

The Jackal (1997: #34)

Distributors:	Universal Pictures and Mutual Film Company
Production company:	Alphaville
Producers:	James Jacks, Sean Daniel, Michael Caton-Jones, and Kevin Jarre
Director:	Michael Caton-Jones
Screenplay and screen story:	Chuck Pfarrer
Screenplay and screen story based:	on the motion picture screenplay *The Day of the Jackal* by Kenneth Ross
Executive producers:	Terence Clegg, Hal Lieberman, Gary Levinsohn, and Mark Gordon
MPAA rating:	R
Release date:	November 14, 1997[37]
DVD (WS) running time:	125 minutes
Box office:	$53,250,220, cumulative total: $54,930,280[38]

The Jackal draws from a 1962 attempt on French president Charles de Gaulle's life, one of many, which was also the topic of a 1971 spy novel by Frederick Forsyth, on which the film *The Day of the Jackal* (1973) was based. De Gaulle's attackers claimed they were only trying to kidnap him when they opened fire on his car in 1962. Angered by President de Gaulle granting Algeria independence from France, the attackers, led by Georges Henri Watin, also known as the Jackal, wanted to try de Gaulle for high treason.[39]

The 1990s version has received a post–Cold War wrapping, including the updating of the film's villain to another famous Jackal in the business of assassinations. *The Jackal* opened in the U.S. on November 14, 1997,[40] three years after French agents had captured in Sudan, on Sudanese approval, one of the most famous terrorist assassins, Ilich Ramírez Sánchez, a Venezuelan better known to the world as Carlos the Jackal.

The film briefly introduces the Cold War and its ending in its opening credits, accompanied by Russian music. The film runs clips of Lenin, Stalin, communist October marches, Hitler, the tearing down of the Berlin Wall, and Boris Yeltsin. The opening credits end with news clips which describe a new threat that Russia and the world are facing: the Russian mafia and its global network. The film action starts with a joint FBI-Russian police operation against the mafia in Moscow. The attack at a mafia club introduces the film's sidekick as well as its protagonist's romantic interest, Russian major Valentina Koslova (Diane Venore). She saves the life of FBI deputy director Charles Preston (Sidney Poitier) when she kills his attacker, a mafia boss's brother. As a result, the Russian mafia boss hires an internationally known assassin, an American known only as the Jackal, to avenge his brother's death. In the mafia boss's words: "The FBI declares war on us? War it is." His plan is a big, public political statement to the U.S.

In *The Jackal* both the hero and the villain are terrorists. The film casts action star Bruce Willis as the Jackal, an international terrorist/assassin for hire. In the past he had been on the payroll of the KGB, the Soviet Union security agency, among others. This echoes the background of the real-life Carlos the Jackal, who committed several terror attacks, including assassinations, bombings, kidnappings, and at least one hijacking, mostly in Western Europe, in particular in the U.K. and France, during the Cold War in the 1970s and 1980s. One of his most spectacular acts took place in December 1975 in Vienna, Austria, when Vienna was hosting a ministerial-level OPEC conference. He kidnapped almost all of the conference delegates.[41] Carlos was suspected of having committed some 80 killings in the name of revolutionary, and anti–American causes, but also for his personal agenda. A communist revolutionary, he had ties to, for example, the Popular Front for the Liberation of Palestine and several communist-bloc secret services. He was able to operate freely from some Eastern European communist capitals. On a tip from the CIA, and through an understanding with the Sudanese authorities, French agents finally captured Carlos the Jackal in Sudan in August 1994 and took him to France in a sack. Three years later a French court sentenced the Jackal to life in prison for his crimes.[42]

As Carlos the Jackal was elusive for decades, the film's Jackal is elusive to the point that only a few people know what he looks like. One of them is a Northern Irish terrorist in a U.S. prison, Declan Mulqueen, played by Richard Gere. *The Jackal* is the only film of these four that thematically draws from Northern Irish Republican terrorism and clearly introduces a loyal member of the PIRA. In contrast to the extremists that the other three films portray as film villains, *The Jackal* places the PIRA terrorist in the role of the hero. In *Blown Away*, former terrorist Jimmy Dove was also a hero, but his background and connection with the PIRA were left murky. In *The Jackal* only the imprisoned Declan Mulqueen and his ex-girlfriend, a former Basque terrorist now with a new life in the U.S., can recognize the Jackal. The FBI makes a deal with Mulqueen: in return for his help in locating and capturing the Jackal he will be released to a minimum security prison. The film's setup clearly violates the U.S. policies on international terrorism, including the policy of not making concessions to terrorists, which includes not releasing them from prison. For example, the State Department's 1988 report addresses several ways of how the U.S. will *not* respond to terrorism:

> The US Government has developed a comprehensive strategy to respond to the problem of international terrorism. The first element of our counterterrorism policy is that we do not make concessions of any kind to terrorists. We do not pay ransom, release convicted terrorists from prison, or change our policies to accommodate terrorist demands — such actions would only lead to more

> terrorism. And we vigorously encourage other countries to be firm with terrorists, for a solid international front is essential to overall success.[43]

The film's hero is not released as a result of a terrorist demand, but as an effort to find another terrorist. However, his release and the FBI's promise to relocate him to another prison are concessions and results of a negotiation. He receives the privileges — in other words, concessions — in return for his services.

The film reduces an international assassination story to a personal fight between the hero and the villain. The two share the typical history of hostility, which sets the hero against the villain at a personal level. The conflict between the antagonist and the protagonist has its roots in an arms deal in Libya that the Jackal had set up for Mulqueen. The backstory draws from the PIRA's real-life connections. According to the State Department, the organization received help from Libya, at least in the 1980s.[44] The film exposition reveals that the Libyan arms deal turned out to be a trap. Mulqueen was wounded and his girlfriend, Isabella, a Basque terrorist who was pregnant with the couple's child, lost their baby in the trap.

Mulqueen is a terrorist protagonist with the values of a hero. Even as a PIRA terrorist, he had never targeted civilians in his war against the British. As a traditional hero, he keeps his word, is smart and fights only when he is attacked. He is a more developed version of Jimmy Dove of *Blown Away*, another hero with a Republican terrorist background. Even as a PIRA terrorist, Mulqueen is a likeable character, someone with whom the viewer can identify. The other three films portray angry and cold-blooded terrorists of PIRA splinter groups, the main antagonists being motivated by mad hatred and vengeance.

The terrorism in *The Jackal* matches the State Department definitions of international terrorism, as well as some of the U.S. methods of counterterrorism. The film's hero is a fictional terrorist taken from the department's real terrorist groups list. The villain is an international terrorist assassin for hire in the tradition of the real-life Jackal from Venezuela. The film Jackal's links to the Cold War–era Soviet Union mirror the State Department's documents from the 1980s which point the finger at the communist bloc for aiding international terrorists.

The Jackal is a hired killing machine. His approach to killing is similar to Hans Gruber's: he does it because his business requires it. The Jackal, an American whose true name is never learned in the film, uses poison, handguns and automatic weapons. He is a master of disguise, assuming personas from fit to overweight, from straight to gay, from young to middle-aged. He easily shakes off anyone on his tail, moving around the globe from Russia to Finland, England, Canada and the U.S. He crosses borders to assassinate an American political figure. In the State Department's definition, terrorism "means premeditated, politically motivated violence perpetrated against noncombatant targets by subnational or clandestine agents, usually intended to influence an audience."[45] The mafia boss's motivation is to send a political message, "a statement public and brutal," to the U.S. by killing someone high up in the American power structure in order to prevent future American-Russian cooperation. In the style of terrorists, he wants to create fear in the American public, but his act is a traditional crime, for his personal gain, rather than a clearly politically motivated act.

In *The Jackal* the officials undermine the antagonist with words that are similar to those used in *Invasion USA* and *The Delta Force*. The FBI director, who is assumed to be the Jackal's target, describes the Jackal as "just one guy" and does not really see him as a threat. Mulqueen's response to that is: "You think it's he against us? It's the other way around."

Reflecting the growing international cooperation in counterterrorism and crime in the post–Cold War world, the film packages together Russian and American efforts to counter crime and terrorism with the help of a Northern Irish terrorist. Following the real-life structure,

The Jackal (Bruce Willis), an international terrorist for hire, targets the First Lady in *The Jackal* (1997, Universal Pictures and Mutual Film Company). His character drew from two real-life terrorist Jackals: Georges Henri Watin, the man behind a 1962 attempt on French president Charles de Gaulle, which was the basis of a 1971 book by Frederick Forsyth and a 1973 film, and international terrorist Ilich Ramírez Sánchez, originally from Venezuela and better known to the world as Carlos the Jackal.

the FBI leads the U.S. effort on U.S soil, and also abroad when the targets are American citizens. International cooperation in counterterrorism has been an important cornerstone of U.S. counterterrorism. The U.S. Department of State houses the Antiterrorism Assistance Program, founded in 1983, which promotes international antiterrorism efforts. The program is aimed at friendly governments. In the 1990s the State Department credited the growing international cooperation among governments in the late 1980s and in the 1990s as one of the main reasons for the declining attack numbers. Cooperation between different countries was strengthened by the international community's widely held view that terrorism is a threat to the whole world. According to the State Department's 1992 report: "We have succeeded in focusing attention on three aspects of the issue that are critical to success: the ending of state sponsorship, the strengthening of the rule of law, and the refusal to reward terrorists through concessions."[46] In the State Department's view, all this was achieved due to a strong U.S. leadership, namely due to the country's consistent counterterrorism policy, and strong support and commitment to international cooperation.

While *The Jackal* depicts American-Russian cooperation and a strong, likeable, trustworthy and fearless Russian woman, the film is still suspicious of the new Russia. Major Koslova is the only identifiable Russian; the other Russian characters only get a line or two. It turns out the Jackal was an old KGB asset. This is information that the Russian side gets through a drug-assisted interrogation, during which a mafia prisoner dies. Furthermore, an informer to the Jackal turns out to be a member of the Russian task force.

The Jackal portrays an untraditional protagonist with untraditional sidekicks, as did *The Siege* a year later. Neither film has a middle-class white male American in the film's primary heroic role. In *The Siege*, an African American male hero has a strong white woman and an Arab immigrant as his sidekicks, and in *The Jackal*, a white Northern Irish PIRA terrorist has a strong Russian woman and an African American man as his sidekicks. Both films find an antagonist in the same actor, Bruce Willis as the Jackal in *The Jackal*, and as General Devereaux in *The Siege*.

Valentina Koslova's character is similar to *The Siege*'s female CIA operative. Both are strong and smart women in a man's world. They both take part in physical action and they share the same destiny. A touch of romance is in the air between the protagonist and the female sidekick in both films, but neither film lets that develop further. Instead, the strong women are killed by the films' antagonists. Traditionally it was the destiny of the minority sidekick to die for the hero — that is, if a minority character was even portrayed in a film.[47] In the 1990s the strong female of law enforcement stole the minority role, giving their lives for the hero in popular action-adventure films on international terrorism. The other 1990s female characters, even the wives who had their own careers but not in law enforcement, still needed the hero to save them. These include, for example, the heroes' wives in the *Die Hard* and *True Lies* films, and the flight attendants in *Executive Decision* and *Passenger 57*.

Against the genre traditions, Bruce Willis as an international terrorist does not graduate to be a madman in *The Jackal*. He commits acts for other people's political and criminal motives, but his motive is greed. During the final confrontation, he takes pleasure in terrorizing a female hostage and taunting the protagonist, the act accompanied with a laugh that could be interpreted as manic, but that is only temporary. He becomes somewhat unraveled, which undermines his character portrayal in the sense that until then the film had portrayed him as an extremely professional, cold-blooded and unemotional character who is touched or moved by nothing. For example, when he shoots Major Koslova, he softly draws a heart on her cheek in her blood while she is bleeding to death. He gives her a message to deliver to Mulqueen, which she uses as her dying words to the protagonist: "You cannot protect your women." These words later make the hero realize that the assassination target is the First Lady.

The hero and his African American sidekick, the FBI deputy director, succeed in preventing the assassination of the First Lady. The Jackal escapes into the Washington, D.C., subway system with Mulqueen on his heels. The latter alerts his ex-lover Isabella to the chase, wishing to avenge the past injustice when the couple had lost their unborn child. The film's good hearted PIRA terrorist gives up his gun at the threat of the Jackal killing an innocent female hostage. Isabella arrives to rescue. Her shots save the hero, but Mulqueen is the one who delivers the final killing shot. With his last strength the Jackal tries to shoot Isabella, but now Mulqueen protects his woman. This is part of his prodigal journey. Although he was not able to protect his women in the past nor Major Koslova, the film's romantic interest, he finally succeeds when he kills the villain. The larger part of his prodigal journey transforms him from a PIRA terrorist into a man who earns the FBI deputy director's trust and respect. In the end the deputy director allows the former terrorist to go free. Mulqueen is a man who has let go of his terrorist past. In contrast to the State Department's declared policies on terrorism, this Hollywood film washes a terrorist's slate clean.

Ronin (1998: #46)

Distributor:	United Artists Pictures (MGM/UA)
Production Company:	FGM Entertainment
Producer:	Frank Mancuso, Jr.
Director:	John Frankenheimer
Screenplay:	J. D. Zeik, David Mamet (as Richard Weisz)
Story:	J. D. Zeik
Executive producer:	Paul Kelmenson
MPAA Rating:	R
Release date:	September 25, 1998[48]
DVD (WS) running time:	121 minutes
Box office:	$41,565,875 (1998), cumulative total: $41,616,262[49]

Ronin opens with a gathering of shady men at a shady bar in Paris, France. One of them, Sam (Robert De Niro), arrives cautiously at the bar to meet Deirdre (Natascha McElhone), an Irish woman who is hiring five men who all have questionable pasts. Each man has a certain skill that will help the group in the job the woman has for them: to steal a case. In the tradition of the Hitchcockian MacGuffin method, the film never reveals the case's contents. The story itself is more important than to reveal what exactly it is that everyone is after.

The film is an exception to the popular 1990s format of a hero with a family, and in particular the overused preteen or teenage daughter who needs her daddy to save her. Mixing thriller and film noir ingredients with action-adventure genre traditions, and with a hint of a romantic subplot, *Ronin* introduces old hired guns who have no masters, and who go from one paid job to another until death or retirement releases them from the world of espionage.

The film's hero, Sam, supposedly a former CIA agent down on his luck, is in charge of planning how to steal the case. He is accompanied by Vincent (Jean Reno), a Frenchman whose background hints at intelligence work, and who is in charge of getting what the group needs for its actions. German Gregor (Stellan Skarsgård), an ex–KGB agent, is the group's technology guru, American Larry (Skipp Sudduth) its driver, and British military vet Spence (Sean Bean) its weapons expert. After an attack on the group during their weapons purchase by the Seine, Sam realizes the gun-crazy Spence is only a bad-ass wannabe who cracks under pressure and lacks the credentials he claims. Deirdre pays off Spence and lets him go. After that, Spence is out of the picture.

On the surface the film is about the theft of the case. The supervisor of Deirdre's Irish group wants to acquire the case before Russians can buy or steal it. However, the film cheats both its characters and viewers, the two audiences learning only towards the end what the film is truly about. Sam has never left the CIA but is doing a covert assignment. His mission is to catch Deirdre's contact, Seamus O'Rourke (Jonathan Pryce), a rogue terrorist who is denounced by the PIRA and who stands in the way of the latest round of peace negotiations in Northern Ireland. Since O'Rourke is a wanted man, his assistant Deirdre hires the men to steal the case. While the film was in production, in April 1988 the main parties to the real-life conflict had finally signed the Good Friday Agreement. However, some PIRA splinter groups rejected it. The film reflects truthfully the real-life dissonance among the Irish Republican paramilitary groups, but it simplifies its character portrayal of Seamus. The villain, according to the genre traditions, is a madman, but the film provides him with no motivation for his aggressive pursuit of the case.

The film depicts the 1990s political developments in Northern Ireland, and the U.S.

In *Ronin* (1998, United Artists Pictures) undercover CIA agent Sam (Robert De Niro, second from right) tracks down a Northern Irish terrorist who is a threat to the ongoing peace process in Northern Ireland. As part of his undercover work, he cooperates with old hired guns, including Vincent (Jean Reno, second from left) and German Gregor (Stellan Skarsgård, far left) when the terrorist's representative, Deirdre (Natascha McElhone, far right), hires them for a shady job.

interest and involvement in the region. After the PIRA's ceasefires the U.S. Secretary of State removed the organization from the designated foreign terrorist organizations list in October 1997, although the PIRA was still listed as a terrorist group to which the U.S. should pay attention. The Clinton administration was actively supporting the peace process in Northern Ireland. A three-person international committee, which was helping to broker a peace agreement, was chaired by George Mitchell, a former U.S. senator. A threat to the process in the film is a rogue terrorist whom the PIRA has denounced. As in the film, in real life the PIRA denounced the groups that split from the organization due to its compliance with the ceasefires that the peace negotiations required.[50] To remove the threat, the film's U.S. relies on one of the five traditional U.S. counterterrorism methods: a covert operation.

Ronin is the only one of the sixteen films in which the threat is not directly against the U.S. or the hero. However, the rogue terrorist is a threat to international cooperation against terrorism, which is one of the cornerstones of American counterterrorism. *Ronin* is also the only one of the sixteen films whose events all take place abroad, in the French cities of Paris, Arles and Nice. The movie does not reveal on whose authority the American agent is working, but in real life the permission for a covert operation to capture, or even kill, a target, comes from the sitting U.S. president. When discussing the CIA's plans to capture Osama bin Laden in 1998 with the help of tribal groups, *The 9/11 Commission Report* points out that while a presidential finding from 1986 "had authorized worldwide covert actions against terrorism and probably provided adequate authority,"[51] the CIA still also requested a legal document which authorized the capture, and proved the agency was not working independently. While the film never reveals on whose authorization Sam is working, the fictional story still follows real-life models. The covert operation outside U.S. borders falls under the CIA's aegis when the protagonist is not investigating American nationals, the events take place abroad, and the threat is in the country's policy interests. The film focuses on the world of suspicion and men who cannot break free from that world. *Ronin* depicts less violence than most of the other films discussed in the book.

Ronin introduces two villains. The primary villain is Seamus O'Rourke and the secondary villain is Gregor, who betrays the group and steals the case from the group after a successful ambush and gunfight to steal it. Gregor's character borrows from the post–Cold War uncertainty of espionage, and the selling of one's old life and professional pride to the highest bidder in the new world order. This ex–KGB agent only wants money in return for the case. Soon Seamus O'Rourke, with Deirdre, the Russians, and Sam's group, are pursuing him. Gregor's greed brings him to his death when the Russian boss kills him. The main villain's role is to die last after a one-on-one fight with the hero. However, in this film it is not the hero who performs the final killing. Sam saves his French accomplice Vincent's life during a firefight with Russians, and at the end of the film Vincent repays him. Seamus O'Rourke has wounded Vincent but the Frenchman still follows Sam, who is pursuing the terrorist rogue. Just as the terrorist is about to shoot Sam, Vincent takes action and kills the Northern Irish madman.

The film's title, *Ronin*, refers to a Japanese story about 47 masterless ex-samurai warriors called ronin. Similar to the 47 ronin, the new world order has made the professionals of the Cold War and the Troubles masterless. They have nothing left but to try to earn a living and stay alive until retirement. But unlike in the Japanese story, these warriors do not commit seppuku, the ritual suicide of honored warriors. In this film those who do not fight with honor, such as Gregor and O'Rourke, die for their disgrace while Sam and Vincent stay alive

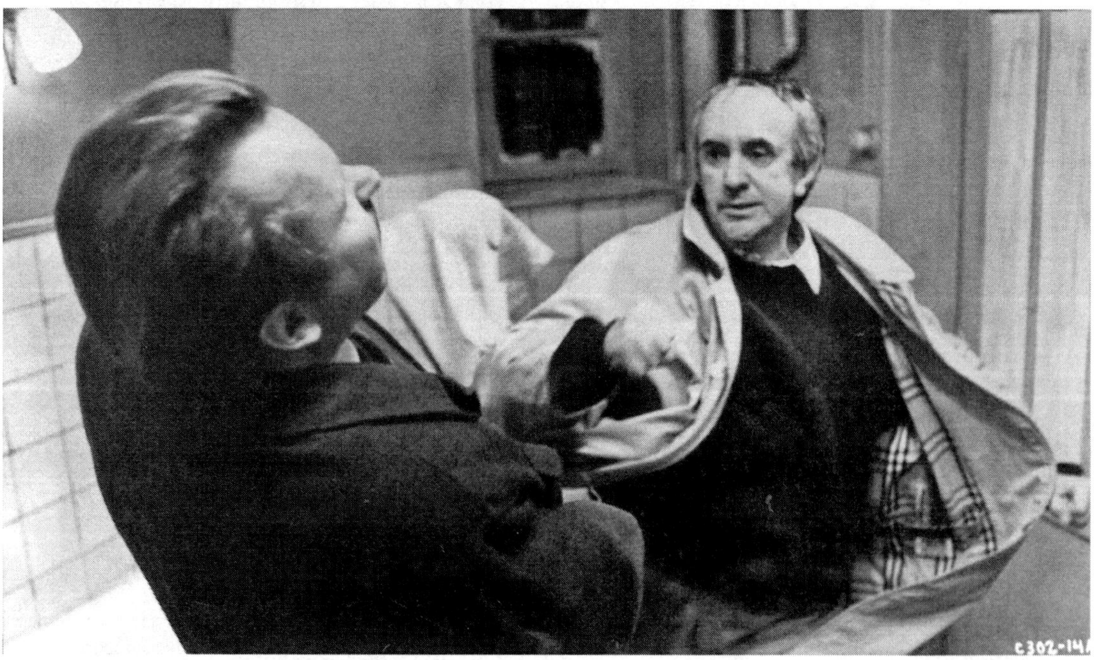

Seamus O'Rourke (Jonathan Pryce, right) plays in *Ronin* (1998, United Artists Pictures) another mad Northern Irish extremist. O'Rourke goes after Gregor (Stellan Skarsgård) when the latter hinders O'Rourke's plans.

another day. Unfortunately, each of the film's characters lacks depth. They are secretive men close to retirement and a woman of dark shadows. All have lost their place in the world, to the point that even the viewer does not get to know them well, not even the last names of most of the film's characters.

Ronin draws from old film genre traditions. Two long car chase scenes are reminiscent of horse chases. A romantic subplot shows Sam falling for Deirdre. They share an intimate moment when keeping watch on the group that has the case. Romance eventually gets in the way of Sam's job. Deirdre is Seamus O'Rourke's driver. Sam has a chance to catch the terrorist villain, but only if he shoots Deirdre and stops their escape car. Deirdre takes advantage of Sam's weak moment and escapes. When Sam and Vincent are again closing in on Seamus O'Rourke, Sam reveals his mission to Deirdre when he sees her waiting for the antagonist once again in a car. Now Deirdre takes Sam's advice and leaves the scene. In film noir style the protagonist cannot trust Deirdre, but he still falls for her. And as the film noir traditions require, while the rugged and shady hero completes his assignment, a heterosexual coupling eludes him.

The film's denouement forces the protagonist to acknowledge his prodigal journey. The movie returns to the shady bar where everything started. As Sam and Vincent sit in the bar, newscasts in the background announce a successful ending to the last round of peace negotiations in Northern Ireland. According to the reports, the result was largely due to the killing of Seamus O'Rourke, a rogue terrorist. Sam completed his assignment, but his hope to see Deirdre again does not come true. As a covert agent he cannot get the girl and the bad guy. Unlike in western films, the choice is not the hero's but the woman's. He wants a heterosexual coupling but the woman disappears, leaving him alone. He has to face the fact that he is a CIA agent in a world of covert actions where there is no place for true love. This film noir–style couple will never have their Paris, only one brief moment in a car during a stake-out.

The commercial film industry's fascination with Northern Irish terrorism soon disappeared as the region took a step in April 1998 toward peace after three decades of violence with the signing of the Good Friday Accord by the Catholic and Protestant parties and the U.K. and Ireland. The State Department highlighted the achievement in its 1998 report:

> This historic agreement outlined a comprehensive power-sharing arrangement between both communities in a multiparty administration of Northern Ireland. For the first time the Irish Republican Army's political wing, Sinn Fein, was allowed to join the new administration, as long as its leaders remained committed to "exclusively peaceful means."[52]

Similar to terrorism originating in the Middle East, these films embrace mad terrorists, except in the case of the professional terrorist assassin in *The Jackal*. His portrayal draws from *The Day of the Jackal* film and novel, and the famous real-life Jackal who evaded capture for years. In contrast to Arab terrorists whom Hollywood films portray as Muslims, although usually forgetting to show them practicing their religion, Hollywood leaves out religion in its portrayals of Northern Irish terrorism, neglecting the context of the region's struggles between the Catholic Republicans and the Protestant Unionists. The films also fail to explain political ideologies and motivations. Only the PIRA terrorist characters are permitted to explain their actions, and in *The Jackal* and *Blown Away*, they are even cleared of their deeds although the latter film does not clearly spell out the hero's group in Northern Ireland but strongly points to the PIRA. The members of PIRA splinter groups do not fare as well: they die for their crimes in Hollywood fiction. In contrast to the State Department documents on international terrorism, PIRA members are not truly terrorists in these Hollywood films. *The Jackal* promotes a full-fledged and jailed PIRA member to the role of the hero. In addition, Jimmy Dove of *Blown Away*, whose background is also reminiscent of the PIRA, is an American hero.

The Northern Irish peace process eventually progressed when on July 28, 2005, the PIRA declared an end to its armed campaign. Two months later, on September 26, the Independent International Commission on Decommissioning confirmed that the PIRA had followed its declaration in practice. However, hardline PIRA splinter groups, such as the Real Irish Republican Army (RIRA) and the Continuity Irish Republican Army (CIRA) did not follow PIRA's decommissioning of weapons, although their level of violence has not approached the lethal numbers reached during the Troubles.[53]

The new world order and the end of the Troubles forced Hollywood to look for new terrorist ideas in the chaos of the dismantled former Soviet Union, and the U.S. involvement in the Middle East. Paramount Pictures had released *Patriot Games* in 1992, the year when the State Department had recorded the lowest number of terrorist attacks since 1975.[54] With the rise of fundamentalist Islamic militants in the 1990s, the commercial film industry started to tap into the threat of mass casualties. In 1994, 20th Century Fox brought to the big screen *True Lies*, which finished as the year's third highest ranking film in the domestic box office. Two years later Warner Bros. distributed *Executive Decision*, in which the U.S. president must give an order to shoot down a civilian airliner to protect the country from a terrorist attack, just as took place five years later in real life. After *True Lies* and *Executive Decision* another film that drew on fundamentalist views of Islam took a more complicated look at terrorism that originates in the Middle East. In 1998, 20th Century Fox released *The Siege*. This film's terrorists had in the past received U.S. support until there was a shift in policy interests. The film gave a dark portrayal of international terrorism on U.S. soil and of the country's overzealous counterterrorism methods but it failed to attract large audiences. In the immediate post–9/11 weeks the film found an audience when some of the haunting similarities of the film to the reality of 9/11 and the day's aftermath made it a popular rental. The next chapter discusses *True Lies* and *Executive Decision*, and Chapter 10 analyzes *The Siege*.

CHAPTER 8

Hollywood's Version of Fundamentalist Islamic Terrorism: Return of the One-Dimensional Evil Arab Muslim

True Lies (1994); *Executive Decision* (1996)

The 1993 World Trade Center attack brought Middle Eastern terrorism as a threat on U.S. soil into American news headlines. Although six American lost their lives, massive destruction of human life and property was just barely avoided. However, this took a backseat when news media reports focused on how one of the terrorists was caught because he was demanding back his $400 deposit for a rental van that his group had used in the bombing. The FBI had been able to figure out the color and make of the van, as well as the rental agency, from what was left of it. FBI agents were waiting for the man when he came to claim the deposit, arguing that the van had been stolen.

In the immediate post–9/11 era Hollywood took steps to avoid terrorism in films, but the limited destruction caused by the first World Trade Center attack, in 1993, did not send Hollywood seeking cover. Quite the opposite — the largely failed attack and the capture of some of the attackers worked as free advertising for Hollywood creations of international terrorism on U.S. soil. The threat was real, but the limited destruction and the prevented attacks of summer 1993 left unreal the potential of actual severe destruction. Soon fictional Middle Eastern terrorists were attempting mass murder on U.S. soil in Hollywood films. Western and ex-communist villains became second-class threats with their limited attack scenarios. The assembly line of make-believe was following the real-life threats of international terrorism.

Hollywood has produced dozens of films that portray Arabs as terrorist villains, but not many of these films have been box office hits. In the 1990s three films with Islamic Arab terrorists made their way into the annual top fifty films. The first of the films was *True Lies* (1994), starring Arnold Schwarzenegger. *Executive Decision*, starring Kurt Russell and Steven Seagal, followed two years later. The last pre–9/11 film that portrayed Arab Muslim villains and finished in the domestic top fifty box office was *The Siege* (1998), starring Denzel Washington. The film eerily predicted some of the events of 9/11 and post–9/11. When 20th Century Fox released the film in 1998, it was not a big box office draw. However, in the immediate weeks after 9/11, audiences found the film, making it a popular rental. Chapter 10 discusses *The Siege* and its similarities and differences to real-life terrorism.

This chapter analyzes *True Lies* and *Executive Decision*. Both films borrow their villains from the rising 1990s Middle Eastern terrorist threats which had their anti–U.S. and anti–Western motivation in extremist militant views of Sunni and Shia Islam, and in opposition to the U.S. and Western presence and influence in the Middle East. The film industry brought to viewers Arab Muslim terrorist antagonists who did not have a recognizable home country and who barely, if at all, practiced onscreen the religion, Islam, that the films claimed they followed. The antagonists of *True Lies* and *Executive Decision* are traditional political Hollywood enemies: they are outsiders on the basis of their ethnicity, skin color and religion. The films' Middle Eastern villains are full of rage to the point of insanity. They take out their anger on the United States and its citizens. *True Lies* and *Executive Decision* also echo the unknown destiny of Soviet nuclear weapons in the post–Cold War era. The State Department reports were warning about the possibility of some of the nuclear weapons ending up in terrorist hands.

Islam Defined in U.S. Government Documents

The U.S. Department of State's annual documents discuss Islamic Sunni and Shia extremists but do not provide background information on the two main branches of Islam. When addressing Osama bin Laden's interpretation of Islam and his appeal among his followers, *The 9/11 Commission Report* provides a brief review of Islam and the Sunni and Shia sects. According to the report,

> Islam (a word that literally means "surrender to the will of God") arose in Arabia with what Muslims believe are a series of revelations to the Prophet Mohammed from the one and only God, the God of Abraham and of Jesus. These revelations, conveyed by the angel Gabriel, are recorded in the Qur'an. Muslims believe that these revelations, given to the greatest and last of a chain of prophets stretching from Abraham through Jesus, complete God's message to humanity. The Hadith, which recount Mohammed's sayings and deeds as recorded by his contemporaries, are another fundamental source. A third key element is the Sharia, the code of law derived from the Qur'an and the Hadith.[1]

Prophet Mohammed died in A.D. 632, which led to disagreements in the Muslim community over who should succeed him and what that leadership should be like.[2] According to the Shia, only a direct descendant of the Prophet can be a religious leader, caliph, in the Muslim community, Ummah. The Sunni do not require a direct lineage, as long as "the candidate met other standards of faith and knowledge."[3] The Shia supported the leadership of the Prophet's cousin, Ali ibn Abi Talib, who was also his son-in-law. A 2006 congressional report explains:

> Those who supported Ali's ascendancy became later known as "Shi'a," a word stemming from the term "*shi'at* Ali," meaning "supporters" or "helpers of Ali." Others respected and accepted the legitimacy of his caliphate but opposed political succession based on bloodline to the Prophet. This group, who constituted the majority of Muslims, came to be known in time as "Sunni," meaning "followers of [the Prophet's] customs [*sunna*]."[4]

Violent clashes between the followers of the two different interpretations took place over centuries. Islam spread around the world from the Middle East with Sunni as its dominant branch. According to *The 9/11 Commission Report*, "The Caliphate — the institutionalized leadership of the Ummah — thus was a Sunni institution that continued until 1924, first under Arab and eventually under Ottoman Turkish control."[5] Extremists such as Osama bin Laden long for the days of the Caliphate, a return, as they see it, to the true path of Islam. Osama bin Laden has announced the reestablishment of the Muslim state as his goal.[6] In that world there is no room for the U.S. and other Western non-believers of Islam, or those Muslims who do not share bin Laden's interpretation of Islam.

The Sunnis and Shias share certain aspects of Islam:

> The concepts of piety, striving for goodness, and social justice are fundamental to Islamic belief and practice. Additionally, all Muslims are expected to live in accordance with the five pillars of Islam: (1) *shahada*—recital of the creed "There is no God but Allah, and Muhammad is His Prophet": (2) *salat*—five obligatory prayers in a day; (3) *zakat*—giving alms to the poor; (4) *sawm*—fasting from sunrise to sunset during the month of Ramadan; and (5) *haji*—making a pilgrimage to Mecca once during a lifetime if one is physically and financially able.[7]

Today Islam is estimated to have from 1.3 to 1.8 billion followers, the majority of them Sunnis and about 10–15 percent of them Shias. The latter can be found, for example, in Iran.

True Lies (1994: #3)

Distributor:	20th Century Fox
Production company:	Lightstorm Entertainment
Producers:	James Cameron and Stephanie Austin
Director:	James Cameron
Screenplay:	James Cameron
Screenplay based:	upon French screenplay *La Totale* by Claude Zidi, Simon Michael, and Didier Kaminka
Executive producers:	Rae Sanchini, Robert Shriver, and Lawrence Kasanoff
MPAA rating:	R
Release date:	July 15, 1994[8]
DVD (WS) running time:	141 minutes
Box office:	$146,282,411[9]

True Lies introduces Arab Muslim villains, a physically fit and intelligent federal spy—Harry Tasker, played by Arnold Schwarzenegger—a marriage in trouble, a wild teenage daughter, action, adventure, romance, comedy and visual effects. The mixing of action-adventure with comedy and romance worked, making the film the third highest rated film in the domestic box office in 1994. The movie was also nominated for several awards for its visual effects and sound. Jamie Lee Curtis, the actress playing the hero's wife Helen Tasker, was also nominated for several awards, winning the 1994 American Comedy Award for Funniest Actress in a Motion Picture and the 1994 Golden Globe Award in the category for Best Actress in Musical or Comedy.[10] The film's domestic box office success alone covered the estimated $100 million budget, bringing in $146,282,411.[11] James Cameron wrote and directed the film.

True Lies borrows from the James Bond film series an exciting action-filled opening that introduces the film's main character, Harry Tasker. In this spectacular action sequence, set in Switzerland, a diver cuts a hole in ice from underneath the icy lake surface, sheds his diving gear, and enters a fashionable, high-class private party wearing a tuxedo and aftershave that he somehow had with him in a diving bag. This is our undercover hero, now known as Harry Renquist. He easily distracts the armed guards and dogs, and steals, via a modem, computer files which his two accomplices in a van outside the gated party area copy. He dances a sensual tango with a beautiful exotic woman and then escapes the party. The protagonist easily kills dozens of anonymous Nazi-like guards who go after him. The film loyally repeats the old genre tradition according to which the hero escapes without a scratch.

The beginning sequence sets the film's tone for action and comedy. One-liners fly between Harry Tasker and his two associates. The primary sidekick is Albert "Gib" Gibson, played by Tom Arnold, a white man like Tasker. The secondary sidekick is Faisil (Grant Heslov), who looks like an Arab, has an American accent and long hair. Faisil's character follows the newer genre trend of using a sidekick who is from the same ethnic group as the villains. He is a minority representative as an Arab-American, but unlike in the typical Reaganite cinema films, his duty is not to give his life for the hero. As a true patriotic American he kills three foreign Arabs towards the film's end. He is a good Arab-American with an American accent who protects the U.S. against evil foreign Arabs.

Protagonist Harry Tasker lives in a suburb of Washington, D.C., and is a spy for a federal agency known as the Omega Sector, "the Last Line of Defense." Although physically fit and intelligent, fluent in English, French, German and Arabic, he is not so talented in keeping his marriage afloat. His wife of seventeen years Helen, a legal secretary, thinks Harry Tasker is a boring computer sales representative who is rarely at home. Then there is Harry's 14-year-old daughter Dana (Eliza Dushku), who, like her mother, has little in common with Harry. Dana is a rebellious daughter who lies, cheats and wears dark, unattractive clothing. Mousy Helen, who wears big glasses and unflattering, ill-fitting suits, is looking for excitement and attention. She finds it in a sleazy used car salesman, Simon (Bill Paxton). Simon pretends to be a spy but is a coward in real life. His over-the-top portrayal and cowardly behavior provide laughs throughout the film, as do the film's tongue-in-cheek dialogue and action which at times draws from slapstick comedy. For Simon, "fear is not an option" when he pretends to be a spy, but he eagerly tells Harry and Gib that he is "nothing" when they are scaring him with a fake interrogation at the top of a tall building. As he urinates on himself, Simon loudly claims: "I'm nothing. I'm navel lint. I got a little dick. It's pathetic."

The film's antagonist is Salim Abu Aziz, played by Art Malik. He is from the Middle East, an Arab, but the film does not detail his exact nationality. Aziz is an angry, fanatical man with black longish hair combed back. He wears a wild-eyed expression to emphasize his insane anger towards the U.S. In Gib's words, "This guy is really hardcore, highly fanatical. The man is a real psycho." Harry Tasker calls the terrorist and his comrades "raving psychotics," echoing the traditional news portrayal of terrorists as insane people. Aziz's background includes an arrest for the possession of narcotics, and he has been linked to dozens of car bombings, including the bombing of a café in Rome and a passenger plane out of Lisbon. He is now the commander of his own splinter terrorist group, Crimson Jihad, and is known as the Sand Spider. The film exposition reveals that Aziz had founded the organization because other organizations were not extreme enough for him, but the film does not explain exactly how extreme: in views, actions or something else. While the film refers to Islam via jihad, "holy war," in the group's name and as the terrorists' background, the film never portrays any of the supposed militant Islamic fighters as actually practicing their religion. *True Lies* does further damage to the understanding of the Arab world and Islam in their real contexts when it packages the two together as inseparable and irrational. This follows a traditional Hollywood portrayal of Arabs as the ultimate threat to the West.[12] In *True Lies* an Arab equals a Muslim. The combination presents a dark-skinned face that is distorted by insanity and anger. There is no distinction between extremist and moderate views of the religion or different branches because there is no portrayal of religion in any other form but in the organization's name. Ahmad has criticized the simplification and translation of the term "jihad" in the West to mean a militant Islamic holy war on the believers of other religions, which is exactly what *True Lies* does. In contrast to the film's interpretation of the term, outside the realms of the Hollywood's make-believe machine, the term primarily refers to a person's internal struggle, and rarely to a struggle with non–Muslims.[13] However, that has not prevented extremists from using the word in a violent context.

Aziz has a female accomplice, Juno Skinner (Tia Carrera) with whom Harry Tasker/Renquist tangoes in the opening sequence. She is an art and antiques dealer who, in her own words, does not care about the group's or Harry's cause, only about the money she earns. Aziz and Skinner are connected through Middle Eastern billionaire Jamal Khaled, the financer of Aziz's operation in the U.S. The film only briefly introduces Khaled at the Swiss party and in intelligence briefs. He is a suspected arms dealer involved in terrorism. His money transfers connect him to a bank which is suspected of handling international transfers to finance terrorism. Omega Sector, the agency for which Harry Tasker works, now suspects that Khaled's recent $100 million transfer has funded the purchases of four former Soviet MIRV-6 (multiple independently targeted reentry vehicle) nuclear warheads from the Republic of Kazakhstan that Aziz's group is smuggling to the U.S., using Juno Skinner's large antique sculptures as their hiding place.

While in *Die Hard* the villain was an equal match to the hero, or even more, *True Lies* returns to a simplified and stereotypical Reaganite cinema portrayal of the villain. There is no moral confusion over who is the bad guy and who should be killed at the film's end. Aziz is not an equal match to Harry Tasker, the federal spy fighting for the U.S. and his family. Tasker is an updated 1980s Reaganite cinema hero: his individualistic acts of heroism still require him to use brutal violence, but now he is a married man with a family which is present in the film (in *Commando* he only had a daughter). In the 1980s action and action-adventure films, heroism highlighted father-son relationships[14] while the rest of the family was in the background, if they were portrayed at all. In the style of the 1990s films, the protagonist's wife and teenage daughter are central to his life and happiness in *True Lies*.

The Arab antagonist is inferior to the protagonist in every possible way. As Harry Tasker is polite, Aziz is rude and unfriendly. The first confrontation between the two takes them through city streets, a mall and a hotel. Aziz, riding a motorcycle, angrily yells to bystanders "Out of the way! Move! Move! Move!" In contrast, Tasker, who, like a cowboy in a western film, is chasing the villain on a horse, finds the time to say "I'm sorry" and "Excuse me" when his and Aziz's fight inconveniences other people. Even when Harry is angry with his wife when he believes her to be cheating on him, he does not take that out on her but takes steps to save their marriage. His Middle Eastern counterpart has no respect for his female accomplice Juno Skinner. Skinner flirts with Harry Tasker/Renquist while he pretends to shop for antiques. He is really trying to find out if she is connected to the nuclear weapons terrorist threat. Aziz, acting as a meek employee of Skinner, comes to see his boss. As the door to her office closes after Tasker's departure, Aziz hits Skinner twice, calling her a "stupid, undisciplined bitch" and a "whore." He reminds her that "we do not tolerate mistakes." He has no respect for a woman. Aziz is rude and brutal in all of his actions, and usually has a crazy look in his eyes.

The film portrays the rest of the Arab terrorists as a mass of brutal fighters who are dressed casually and often wear headscarfs. Beyond Aziz and Juno, only a few of Aziz's group members are very briefly recognizable in the film. Samir, a torturer, has big, bulging eyes, not unlike Aziz's. Close-up shots of the torturer and his sharp tools emphasize his inhuman nature. When another Arab is filming Aziz's demands for a media release, the man starts to sweat and becomes scared because he is afraid of telling the crazy Aziz that the battery has run out. This is the only human feeling, except for anger and madness, the film assigns to the villains. The scene of a member of Aziz's own group being terrified of the leader's reactions also effectively takes the attention away from the message Aziz is delivering, which is actually very similar to

Osama bin Laden's declarations and demands for the U.S. to withdraw from the Persian Gulf area. Aziz delivers his lines with passionate anger:

> You have killed our women and our children, bombed our cities from afar like cowards, and you dare to call us terrorists!
>
> Now the oppressed have been given a mighty sword with which to strike back at their enemies. Unless you, America, pulls all military forces out of the Persian Gulf area immediately and forever, Crimson Jihad will rain fire on one major U.S. city each week until our demands are met. First we will detonate one weapon on this uninhabited island as a demonstration of our power and Crimson Jihad's willingness to be humanitarian. However, if these demands are not met, Crimson Jihad will rain on one major city each week.

Imitating and Ignoring Real-Life Fundamentalist Islamic Extremists

The film's terrorist threat matches the U.S. State Department's descriptions. The terrorist attack is premeditated and politically motivated, targeting noncombatants. The foreign terrorists have crossed international borders to come to commit a terrorist act in the U.S. The group's leader and financer are known international terrorists. The method of terrorism is both modern and old-fashioned at the same time. In the 1990s the State Department started to warn about the threat of nuclear weapons in terrorists' hands. And since the early 1980s the trademark of anti–American terrorists from the Middle East has been mass casualties. But the film also steps away from fundamentalist Islamic terrorism. *True Lies* draws from 1970s airplane hijackings when terrorists made demands, often demanding the release of their comrades in return for hostages. In this case the demand is for the U.S. to withdraw from the Persian Gulf in order for the terrorists not to go through with their bombings of major U.S. cities. While the film terrorists' demand echoes al Qaeda, the real-life organization has made its demands separate from its attacks, of which it gives no clear advance warnings.

True Lies does not follow official counterterrorism structures. In real life, an act of terrorism on U.S. soil falls under the jurisdiction of the FBI, but not in the film. Instead, the film gives Harry Tasker the fictional Omega Agency. Although fictional, its methods include traditional ways to counter terrorism: sanctions, international diplomacy, law enforcement, intelligence collection and sharing (including covert operations) and military force. At the film's end, terrorism clearly becomes warfare when the protagonist receives military help and takes a fighter plane to finish the job. Taking shortcuts, the film omits the need for authorization of such actions.

The film is confused about terrorism that originates in the Middle East and in extremist interpretations of Islam. *True Lies* does portray a publicly recognized threat scenario, but in the portrayal of the terrorists it relies on a simplified stereotype of an evil Middle Eastern group. Coming to the 1990s, state sponsorship of international terrorism was deeply declining and a new type of terrorism was raising its head, al Qaeda being a prime example. The film borrows from the handbook of new terrorism. Older, state-sponsored terrorist groups were largely under the thumb of their sponsors, which used the groups to further their own political goals and interests in the international arena. The sponsors also made sure the attacks were limited, in order not to provoke a full-blown war. The emerging groups were freer in their actions because they were financing and training themselves, which left them in charge of their own actions.[15] New independent militant cells operated underground and were more violent in their actions.[16] The movie's Crimson Jihad applies an independent group's methods when it attacks the U.S. on its own soil with WMD. The film also remembers to bring in a central aspect of modern international terrorism: the terrorist groups' desire for publicity. Aziz prepares angry video releases to condemn and threaten the U.S., but for a man who leads a group that is waging a "holy war," as the film implies and as is an often-used translation of jihad in the West, he sure is a lousy follower of his religion. *True Lies* draws from the scare of anti–Western fundamentalist Islamists, but the film fails to bring such a threat to the screen. Instead, it repeats old stereotypes of mad villains, lazily tattooing the film's mad antagonist with an Arab Muslim extremist label. However, it does not show a character who would act accordingly and practice his extremist interpretation of his religion.

Hero of a Patriarchal Western World

True Lies is a true representative of the blockbuster action-adventure genre. It is excessive in its running time and storyline. The film runs for 141 minutes and actually tells two separate, vaguely linked stories. The film sets up in the first act the main characters and the story, and then focuses in the first part of the second act on the romantic subplot before the main story picks up again. Romance is gone from the Tasker marriage. The best way for Helen Tasker to fall asleep is to ask her husband to tell her about his workday. When Harry Tasker suspects his wife of having an affair, he spies on her with the help of his comedic sidekick Gib and with the help of advanced spy technology. He secretly sets up a fake spy job for his wife to provide some real excitement in her life. Harry's plan to finally reveal his own secret identity to his wife at the end of her fake spy job comes to an abrupt end when the real film villains storm into the hotel room where Helen has danced in her underwear for Harry, who is concealed in shadows. Crimson Jihad kidnaps Harry and Helen. Aziz wants Tasker to prove to the world in a taped media message that his organization, Crimson Jihad, has four nuclear weapons and is ready to use them against the U.S. unless his demands are met.

The film's narrative follows the traditional action and action-adventure film structure. Agent Tasker is in the business of counterterrorism. As the genre tradition goes, his character is forced to get involved in the film events by the villain's actions. Aziz brings a threat onto U.S. soil. Terrorism consists of very systematic, premeditated and calculated acts, just like Crimson Jihad's nuclear weapons plans. Terrorist Aziz has planned his acts carefully in advance but as Harry Tasker gets involved, the terrorist's plans and state of mind start to unravel.

The film also relies on the old method of a limited time threat. Crimson Jihad's first MIRV is set to explode in 90 minutes. As the clock is ticking, the protagonist and his accomplices must destroy the weapon or detour it to a location where it cannot destroy any lives. Naturally the hero succeeds in doing that, that is, after several exciting action scenes.

True Lies is a representative of the traditional action and action-adventure films in which a white middle-class male hero defeats the barbaric alien threat to the Western world through his superior intelligence and bravery.[17] As in *Commando*, and in previous films on Middle Eastern terrorism, Third World citizens, in this case Arabs, serve as targets of the hero's destruction of human life in large numbers. Tasker's weaponry overpowers his opponents' arsenal. The protagonist has access to rocket launchers, automatic rifles, and a fighter plane, and he is not afraid to use them. He is also skilled at breaking necks, stabbing opponents from chest to eye with a variety of weapons, and torching villains to death. He kills because, as he explains to his wife: "They were all bad." The hero kills for a reason while the villain kills because he is a psychopath who is blinded by his jihad and his need for senseless revenge on the United States. He is ready to kill a large number of innocent Americans, including Tasker, his wife and his daughter. Despite his scary looks and threats, Aziz is a very inefficient terrorist. He stays a threat that is never truly realized. He succeeds in killing only one person in the film, and even that is one of his own men. He is aiming at Tasker but does not care that one of his own men is in the line of fire. He misses Tasker and kills his own supporter. The killing of his own man does not affect him in any way. In contrast to this failed fanatical Middle Eastern terrorist, his Western counterpart Harry Tasker succeeds in the killing of the antagonist and dozens of his comrades in a variety of creative and at times brutal ways. This is very similar to Schwarzenegger's role in *Commando*, only now Arabs replace Latin Americans as human props whose film role is to offer spectacular deaths of Third World citizens at the hands of a Western hero. Even an unmanned automatic weapon is smarter and more accurate than the film's Arab villains. When Helen tries to shoot an automatic weapon to save her husband, she drops the weapon which then spirals downstairs, killing some ten armed Arabs.

The second act ends traditionally, in a setback to the hero, when the terrorists escape with the nuclear warheads and Tasker's wife. The terrorists and Helen believe Harry has died after being attacked by Aziz with a portable missile. Juno Skinner gives her acid condolences to Helen, the new widow, whom she mockingly calls Suzy the Homemaker. After the terrorists have left, in a scene echoing Cameron's *Terminator*, Harry Tasker walks through fire unharmed and ready for action. Assisted by the firepower of the American armed forces, Harry and his supporters kill several terrorists and destroy all but one of the nuclear warheads.

True Lies **(1994, 20th Century Fox), starring Arnold Schwarzenegger as Harry Tasker, gives little value to the lives of Third World citizens when the hero confronts the film's mad Arab Muslim villain and his accomplices. The film's Arab Muslim terrorists threaten the U.S. with weapons of mass destruction, a method that the State Department started to mention in the annual *Patterns of Global Terrorism* documents as a growing threat the longer the 1990s proceeded.**

In the escape limo Helen becomes a strong woman when she knocks Juno senseless with a bottle of champagne. But she still needs to be rescued by her husband. As the car and Juno dive into their destruction in the sea, Harry, hanging from a helicopter, grabs his wife from the limo.

The final one-on-one confrontation between the protagonist and the antagonist takes place high above the ground. Aziz has kidnapped Tasker's teenage daughter Dana, who manages to escape as Aziz is giving the media a message threatening the lives of two million Americans with his nuclear weapon. As her mother grew to become a respectable and sexy wife, Dana becomes a worthwhile daughter. She steals the key to the nuclear weapon's launching pad and escapes to the top of a high-rise building in downtown Miami. Aziz runs after Dana with a madman's determination. His anger and eyes grow big when she calls him a wacko as she climbs to the top of a crane on an unfinished building and threatens to drop the key. Enter her father in a fighter plane to the rescue. Dana's pleas for her daddy's help bring results. Tasker saves his daughter when she and Aziz fall on his fighter plane. In front of his teenage daughter's admiring eyes, Tasker launches the missile onto which Aziz has fallen. The missile flies through a destroyed high-rise building and hits a helicopter which is full of terrorists of Aziz's group. The hero's parting words to the villain are, "You are fired." The hero has succeeded in defeating terrorists, preventing the explosion of a nuclear bomb in a city area, and in restoring family harmony with his wife and teenage daughter. The film ends with shots of the happy, attractive family a year later, spending quality time together. When a call comes in, now the job is for both Harry and Helen. The ending draws from the beginning: there is another high-class party, but this time a happy couple tangoes together while their accomplices wait outside in a van.

After an intense roller coaster ride of fast action and danger, Harry and Helen Tasker are in love again, and their rebellious teenage daughter is once again daddy's little girl. Although Helen Tasker has quite a big role in the film, her portrayal is still quite traditional. Tasker saves his wife's life several times, to which Helen admiringly comments: "I married Rambo." She is still mostly a decorative addition who takes part in action dressed in a skimpy little dress, and is there to be saved by the hero. In the end, her husband re-seduces her and she graduates to become a beautiful and confident woman who will be allowed to join her husband in his future missions. Her prodigal journey is to find her confidence and beauty with the help of her husband. Without those qualities the marriage was not working. The film does portray a strong woman in Juno Skinner, but her destiny is to die. In the masculine action-adventure film genre, echoing the Reaganite cinema era, action is a man's world. If a woman enters it, she can be a romantic interest or a child who is about to become a woman, but both still need the man of the family to protect them and teach them how to be physically attractive. Idealized, he is a husband, daddy and Rambo in the same package.

Action-Adventure Marries Romantic Comedy

True Lies pushes the boundaries of the action-adventure genre with its comedic approach and long romantic subplot. The film expands beyond one-liners and John McClane's sarcastic take on life and tight situations. *True Lies* successfully uses several methods of the comedy film genre. Sprinkled throughout are purposefully exaggerated acting and running gags. Harry and Helen Tasker, Gib and Simon, all overact in such a way that it is obvious to the viewer that they are combining comedy and action-adventure in their roles. The exaggerated action-adventure roles become comedic through running gags, repetition and character reactions to film events. For example, at the film's beginning Harry Tasker/Renquist greets by name people who do not know him and who are baffled by his greeting at the high-class Swiss party. At the film's end his wife does the same before she and Harry tango, another action he had done at the film's beginning, but with the film's female villain. We also again meet Simon, a comic relief character, at the film's end when he is working as a waiter at the high class party the Tasker spy couple is attending. He is back to his old tricks of pretending to be a spy. As Simon is trying his spy lines on a beautiful woman, the now-confident and attractive Helen Tasker repeats to him his own line, "Fear is not an option," as she threatens him with a lipstick case. Simon once again urinates on himself. One-liners between Harry Tasker and Gib fly constantly. They are at their best when Gib comments on Helen possibly cheating on Harry with Simon, the fake spy. For example, when Gib and Harry hear Simon taking credit for their work, Gib says "I'm starting to like this guy." A look at Harry's reaction makes him continue in a hurry: "We still have to kill him, that's a given."

The comedy of an automatic weapon alone killing villains is a visual joke that brings laughs, as do several other visual jokes. They effectively take attention away from the film's negative stereotyping of Arabs as evil Muslims. The jokes and stereotyping undermine the film's violence, in particular the dozens of brutal killings the hero commits. The screenplay portrays its villains as caricatures, props for the protagonist's creative killings. The violence is weak because the viewer has no emotional attachment to any of the villains. The film does not portray the villains in human terms, as human beings. The killing of these sadistic villains, who have a foreign religion, accents and dark skin color, at the hands of Harry Tasker, an official representative of the federal U.S. government, is acceptable violence since it is done in the name of protecting society. Agent Tasker kills for the U.S. government and for everyone in the U.S. and the West. After all, the terrorists force the protagonist to kill them in order to prevent their nuclear threat to the U.S. The film supports the Reagan-era policy of reaching peace through military power. It highlights effective modern technology, the use of a large weapons arsenal to support the U.S., and a patriotic pride in the men who do all this. It is no wonder the film received assistance from the armed forces. It lists in its end credits: "We gratefully acknowledge the cooperation of the Department of Defense and the United States Marine Corps." The film additionally thanks two individual Marine Corps attack squadrons, two Marine Corps air stations and a naval air station.

Aziz's character is a caricature of action-adventure film antagonists, which fits the film's comedic approach because it helps to simplify the fight between the good and the evil. However, the portrayal of Aziz as a fundamentalist militant Arab Muslim miserably fails. The stereotype offers only a negative, insulting, and ignorant portrayal of another culture, religion and ethnic group, and simplifies and reduces the threat of militant terrorism that draws from radical views of Islam into something that counterterrorism can easily counter and erase. An entertaining film can manipulate viewers to accept negative and positive stereotypes when the propaganda is disguised as an entertaining film experience.[18] The propaganda of *True Lies* is effectively disguised in its entertaining approach to international terrorism, to the brutal killings of villains, and to the use of massive firepower to prevent the threat. Unfortunately there was no Harry Tasker in a fighter jet to prevent the 9/11 attacks. Unlike Aziz, the 9/11 masterminds succeeded in carrying out their mission. In the post–9/11 era the U.S. went after the guilty party in Afghanistan but also used the attack as an excuse to invade an old enemy, Iraq. The real-life story of fundamentalist Islamic terrorists on U.S. soil and actions of U.S. counterterrorism were far more complicated and dangerous than what the entertaining, and financially very profitable, images of *True Lies* told to audiences.

Executive Decision (1996: #24)

Distributor:	Warner Bros.
Production company:	Silver Pictures
Producer:	Joel Silver
Director:	Stuart Baird
Screenplay:	Jim Thomas and John Thomas
Co-producer:	Karyn Fields
Executive producer:	Steve Perry
MPAA rating:	R
Release date:	March 15, 1996[19]
DVD (WS) running time:	133 minutes
Box office:	$56,569,216[20]

Post–Cold War nuclear weapons fears and a Middle Eastern threat surfaced again in movie theaters when Warner Bros. released *Executive Decision* in March 1996. Like *True Lies*, *Executive Decision* starts with an action sequence while fading in and out the opening credits. We see a map of Europe focused on the boot of Italy, and the story begins with a U.S. Army Special Forces Counterterrorist Strike Team fifteen miles outside Trieste. Lieutenant Colonel Austin Travis, played by Steven Seagal, and his team are hunting for a stolen Soviet nerve toxin, DZ-5, at a suspected Chechen mob safe house. The American team kills several people by cutting their throats or shooting them dead. The unit also loses one of its own but comes up empty-handed in its search for the nerve toxin. Next the film cuts to an inexperienced flying student, Dr. David Grant, played by Kurt Russell, as he is trying to land a small aircraft in Maryland. Dr. Grant is a Beckings Research Institute consultant to the U.S. Army Intelligence, and an academic expert on terrorism. The film crosscuts between his flying and a Middle Eastern wedding, shooting, and the kidnapping of the bride's father. As a result of these events, one of Dr. Grant's colleagues rushes him back to his office where exposition through a CNN newscast reveals that "perhaps the most feared and wanted terrorist" El Sayed Jaffa has been abducted and is to be handed over to the U.S. in the Mediterranean. A suicide bombing at a hotel in London and the hijacking of a plane en route from Athens, Greece, to the U.S. by Middle Eastern men soon follow the abduction. The hijackers, a Middle Eastern group called Al Tha'r, demand the release of their leader, Jaffa, and $50 million in gold bullion. At an emergency meeting that is attended by government and military representatives, including Lieutenant Colonel Travis and Dr. Grant. The caller's recorded voice is matched to Nagi Hassan, Jaffa's deputy director and an "extremist in every sense."

Animosity between Lieutenant Colonel Travis and Dr. Grant is obvious. Lieutenant Colonel Travis holds Dr. Grant responsible for a wild goose chase for the stolen nerve toxic while the latter holds Travis responsible for not having acted early enough to capture the nerve toxin. The man in uniform clearly does not regard highly the bespectacled civilian who arrives at the emergency meeting directly from a cocktail party, dressed in a tuxedo. Dr. Grant, who has studied Nagi Hassan, suspects the extremist is behind the nerve gas disappearance. He believes that Hassan now has it on board the hijacked plane and plans to use it as a "poor man's bomb" in Washington, D.C. In the interests of national security, the U.S. secretary of defense agrees to a proposal to use a space-program-based plane that the Air Force has used to transfer bomber crews at altitude. Lieutenant Colonel Travis and his unit are to board in midair the hijacked 747 that is carrying 406 passengers and the plane's crew. An engineer from ARPA, the Defense Department's Advanced Research Projects Agency,[21] and Dr. Grant are to accompany the unit until its transfer to the hijacked plane. The engineer is to supervise the link-up to the passenger plane, and Dr. Grant is to provide background information on the suspected terrorist and his group. The film uses an old method of limited time in its plot setup. The team has to make it on board and defuse the situation before the plane reaches U.S. airspace.

Towards the end of act one, when finalizing the plot setup, *Executive Decision* refreshingly breaks action-adventure genre traditions. The film's beginning sequence introduced Steven Seagal, a well-known action-adventure hero, in the role of the film's special forces team leader. By the end of act one he becomes a casualty of the rescue efforts, which forces the film's real protagonist, Dr. Grant, to become involved in the conflict. Dr. Grant goes to help an injured team member who is stuck in the wind tunnel between the planes. As the link-up starts to break apart, the engineer and Grant are forced to enter the hijacked plane. Lieutenant Colonel Travis knowingly gives his life to the mission and his rescue team when he seals the hatch to the passenger plane from the wind tunnel as it breaks away and throws him into the sky

A politically correct multiracial unit and Dr. David Grant (Kurt Russell) save the day in *Executive Decision* (1996, Warner Bros.). From left, B. D. Wong, Kurt Russell, Whip Hubley and John Leguizamo. The film's main Arab Muslim terrorist plans to turn a passenger plane into a weapon of mass destruction on U.S. soil. Five years later, real-life terrorists hijacked four airliners and turned them into missiles on 9/11. Part of the terrorists' training for the 9/11 attacks included watching films about hijackings.

without a chance of survival. The expected hero gone, the film introduces a traditional storyline in the sense that the new hero is forced to become involved because of unexpected circumstances. The terrorist's actions first force both Lieutenant Colonel Travis and Dr. Grant become involved. When the original hero is gone, a new one must emerge: Dr. Grant. This academic with no combat experience is an unlikely action-adventure protagonist. When the members of Travis's small special forces unit see Dr. Grant still in his tuxedo, one of them sneers, "Who's this, 007?" Now it is up to the unlikely hero to rise to the occasion.

The U.S. Army Special Forces Counterterrorist Strike Team members who made it to the plane form a politically correct unit. It consists of Rat, a Latino (played by John Leguizamo); Cappy, an African American (played by Joe Morton); Louie, an Asian American (played by B.D. Wong); and Baker, a Caucasian American (played by Whip Hubley). They are accompanied by Cahill (Oliver Platt), the ARPA engineer who is a computer geek. Rat becomes the new team leader, but ultimately Dr. Grant becomes the brains and unifying force behind the rescue mission. He is untested in battle but he rises to the occasion when he is needed. This follows a traditional survival-film formula in the action-adventure genre. When the task is completed, he returns to being one of the ordinary men.[22] When the main antagonist asks Dr. Grant during the final confrontation, "Who are you?" Dr. Grant's response is: "No one." The film also draws from war film traditions. The team's cooperation is essential for its survival.[23] But unlike *The Delta Force* of the Reaganite cinema era, which ignored the existence of women in war and focused on male comradeship, *Executive Decision* bravely meets the

1990s and portrays an attractive female flight attendant, Jean (played by Halle Berry), who assists the hero at a risk to her own life.

The Film's Fundamentalist Islamic Threat

David Suchet, better known throughout the world as Hercule Poirot on TV, returns to play an Arab villain, now Nagi Hassan. The antagonist's role has changed from a 1980s state sponsor of terrorism in *Iron Eagle* to a 1990s leader of an independent terrorist group, following real life. In the 1990s, state sponsorship of terrorism declined, as reported by the State Department. Hassan, a smart terrorist, is a worthy opponent to Dr. Grant and the film's special strike team. He comes from an unspecified Arab country. Like Aziz, he is blinded by his hatred for the U.S. His polite and calm behavior can suddenly turn deadly. The U.S. State Department's fear of terrorist organizations gaining access to weapons of mass destruction, including weapons from the former Soviet Union, is realized in *Executive Decision*. Nagi Hassan has acquired the very nerve toxin the U.S. had earlier tried to acquire. Its origin is Chechnya, a former Soviet republic. He is now bringing the toxin onto U.S. soil with the intention of killing hundreds of thousands of people — a goal similar to the 1993 World Trade Center casualty target number. He manipulates, cheats and lies to achieve his goal.

Executive Decision falls under the State Department definitions of international terrorism. Foreign nationals, Arabs from unspecified Middle Eastern countries, are threatening the security of the U.S. and American citizens. They are crossing international borders to perform politically motivated attacks. The original plan is to release their leader, but Hassan's final plan is to explode a bomb in Washington, D.C. The film fictionalizes U.S. response to terrorist demands for the sake of its story. U.S. policies on terrorism clearly spell out that the country will never make any concessions to or deals with terrorists. The film plainly violates these policies. The U.S. agrees to the terrorist demands to release the group's leader, Jaffa, who is by now in U.S. custody, in return for the safety of the passengers of the hijacked plane. Arranging a phone call to Jaffa on the plane, the U.S. officials ask him to persuade Hassan to give up his bombing plan.

As in *True Lies*, *Executive Decision* also was following the times when it drew from the rising fear of fundamentalist Islamic terrorism that the State Department highlighted during the 1990s. But Nagi Hassan does not convince us as a fundamentalist Islamic villain because the character is a stereotypical villain. The film portrays him ranting about Allah while otherwise his religion and, in particular, his practice of his religion, is almost non-existent. *Executive Decision* portrays Hassan referring to Allah, and praying once on board. While the film depicts him as a smart opponent, his motivation draws from his madness when it comes to his religion. He says, "Allah has chosen for us a task far greater than Jaffa's freedom. We are true soldiers of Islam. Our destiny is to deliver the vengeance of Allah into the belly of the infidel." His second-in-command signs his own immediate death sentence when he argues that the mission ends after Jaffa's release: "This has nothing to do with Islam. This is not Allah's will. You're blinded by hatred and I'll have nothing to do with your plan. Our mission was to free Abu Jaffa. He is our leader, not you."

Through the words of Hassan's second-in-command the film points out that Hassan is blinded by his rage against the U.S. and his extremist view of Islam, which the rest of the group does not share. However, the movie follows what Shaheen has observed: Hollywood Arabs may speak English, but it is the word Allah in their dialogue that points out their foreign religion. However, Allah in Arabic simply means "god," referring to a god of any religion.[24]

Hollywood has been accused of portraying villains who come from outside Judaism and

British actor David Suchet returns as an Arab terrorist in *Executive Decision* (1996, Warner Bros.) ten years after his role as the evil minister of defense in *Iron Eagle.* Ignoring his own group's plans, Nagi Hassan, a fundamentalist Muslim, declares himself a soldier of Islam who is delivering the vengeance of Allah on the U.S. Flight attendant Jean (Halle Berry) helps the film's hero Dr. David Grant (Kurt Russell) at a risk to her own life.

Christianity negatively.[25] In this film the confrontation between Islam and Christianity is very much present but is almost hidden in the film's action. The rescue plane's code name is "Hail Mary." The team uses that code name to notify the officials that they are on the plane. Scattered throughout the film in large numbers are Christian utterances, such as "Jesus," "Jesus Christ," and "God" as the American film characters' most often used response to the militant Islamic threat. The *True Lies* and *Die Hard* screenplays did this too, but on a smaller scale. The threat of Islam is further emphasized when Jaffa contacts Hassan and he ends the call with "Allah has blessed us." But instead of ending the hostage drama, Hassan promises a glorious victory on Jaffa's behalf: "All the people of Islam will embrace you as its chosen leader. I'm the flame, the sword of Allah and with it I'll strike deep into the heart of the infidel."

When Hassan is about to shoot Dr. Grant, he yells "Allah Akbar," God is great, and raises his hands, only to be killed by the wounded Rat of the counterterrorist unit. In contrast to his terrorist counterpart, Dr. Grant is not a killer. Hassan's actions *force* the protagonist to use weapons and violence, and even then he does it unwillingly but rises to the occasion. The purpose of Hassan's character is to provoke distaste, anger and maybe even hatred in the viewer, so his death at American hands becomes good violence: when an American soldier kills him, the soldier kills the terrorist for the good of society. In cinematic terms, the hero and his associates can kill bad guys and their supporters, but the film first must point out who the bad guys are. Even the overdone Middle Eastern terrorist Aziz of *True Lies* briefly declared a political motivation for his hatred and goal of killing a massive number of Americans: to avenge American actions against his people and to drive the U.S. out of the Persian Gulf area. Nagi Hassan in *Executive Decision* has no such luxury. He simply wants to be a tool of the vengeance of Allah against the infidels. Even his organization, Al Tha'r, reflects his mission; Dr. Grant translates it to mean "revenge" in ancient Arabic. But this is a madman talking; even his second-in-command denies the attack has anything to do with Islam. It is unfortunate the film only superficially brings up religious differences between the two men and does not use the opportunity to explore fundamentalist and moderate views of Islam. The simplified mad Muslim terrorist distorts Islam and undermines the true threat of fundamentalist groups which have political motivations for their actions. For example, for al Qaeda and Hezbollah certain religious beliefs are central, as well as their opposition to Western influences, but their violent and political actions have clear political motivations and goals.

In *Executive Decision*, Hassan plays a cat-and-mouse game with a U.S. senator on board the plane. He is polite to the senator, letting the politician believe his position protects him and that this is a political opportunity for him. In the senator's assistant's words, it is an opportunity to make up for not having a war record. The senator repeats the U.S. policy of no deals with terrorists, especially in hostage situations, but in return promises money, a safe passage back to the Middle East and media exposure. Hassan understands the senator's political aspirations and the man's belief that his role as a savior will help: "We both understand dramatic statements to the world. Rest assured, when the times comes, I'll call upon you." But for Hassan the senator is only a pawn in the game in which he needs a person whose death will draw the opponent's full attention. As the plane approaches U.S. airspace, it is surrounded by four F-14 fighter jets. Hassan asks the senator to come to the cockpit to negotiate with the U.S. secretary of defense and other government officials to help to end the hostage drama, but that is only a ruse. Hassan needs an important victim for his influential audience, so he shoots the senator in the face without hesitation when he is in contact with U.S. government officials. Hassan is a time bomb; he has planned his action in detail to the point that he has cheated even his own group, which only wants the release of their leader.

The Executive Decision to Shoot Down a Commercial Airliner in *Executive Decision* and on 9/11

The film's name draws from the executive decision that the president of the United States must make. The film's secretary of defense calls for an executive decision from the president about whether to shoot the passenger plane down. This horrific scenario would have political implications, but it would be too risky to wait for the plane's arrival in case it did carry a bomb that could kill hundreds of thousands of people. The event was eerily replayed five and a half years after the film's release. In *Executive Decision* an unseen and unheard president is out of the country, but the viewer learns the president's decision when the National Command Authority just outside the U.S. airspace gives an order to destroy the plane. On Tuesday, September 11, 2001, U.S. president George W. Bush was whisked to safety after the first attacks but he was also asked to authorize an order to shoot down a commercial airliner, United Airlines flight 93, if necessary.

The film was ahead of its time. The real-life pre–9/11 threat scenarios had anticipated domestic events, and had not expected international terrorists to use a hijacked airliner to attack the U.S. on its own soil. Similar to the film's events, on September 11, 2001, United flight 93 was suspected of carrying a bomb, and it was heading towards Washington, D.C. At 9:46 A.M. it was 29 minutes away from the capital. *The 9/11 Commission Report* discusses in detail the day's chaotic events. Counterterrorism expert Richard Clarke, a special assistant to the president, conducted a video conference from the White House Situation Room that was attended by representatives from the FBI, the Departments of State, Justice, and Defense, and the White House shelter. The conference started at 9:25 A.M. The CIA and the FAA joined it at 9:40 A.M. Clarke reported to the 9/11 Commission that they had asked the president to authorize an order to shoot down the commercial airliner. A confirmation of the authority to do so, if necessary, came at 10:25 A.M. President Bush himself told the commission that he had authorized the order to shoot down the hijacked plane. His press secretary, Ari Fleischer, wrote down that the president told him of the authorization at 10:20 A.M. A military aide had also asked Vice President Cheney for permission to engage the plane that was fast approaching Washington, D.C. Based on an earlier discussion with the president, Cheney gave the authorization twice between 10:10 A.M. and 10:18 A.M. When the authorizations were given, it was not yet known that the plane's passengers had attacked the terrorists and the plane had crashed at 10:03 A.M. in Pennsylvania. Had the passengers not attacked, the plane would have reached Washington before President Bush's authorization, between 10:13 and 10:23 A.M., which would not have left enough time for the shoot-down order to have been issued and have reached the pilots via the chain of command. However, in the day's chaos and uncertainty, the order was never even given to any pilots. Reality did not imitate film fiction in the real-life U.S. chain of command. In contrast, *Executive Decision* gets it right, having the fictional and unseen president issue the order to the secretary of defense. Next in the chain of command is the combatant commander.[26] In the film, pilots do get the order to shoot down the plane.

A hijacking alone is not officially warfare, but turning an airliner into a weapon of mass destruction brings up the threat level. *Executive Decision* directly puts the military in charge of counterterrorism, cutting out the lead federal agency on U.S. soil when countering terrorism, that is, the FBI. Also, FAA is absent. When responding to terrorist crises, the Department of Defense supports other agencies' and departments' efforts. The Posse Comitatus Act, 18 U.S.C. Section 1385, prohibits "[M]ilitary involvement in direct law enforcement activities ... unless otherwise specifically authorized under the Constitution or Act of Congress." The U.S. military can provide "passive" assistance, which includes "logistical support, technical advice, facilities, training, and other forms of assistance to civilian law enforcement agencies." Some of the activities may actually aid the prohibited ones, such as arrests, searches and crime investigations.[27] *Executive Decision* keeps law enforcement and their regulations out of the way when it introduces a hijacking, a very particular terrorist event, and turns the hijacking into a warlike attack on the U.S. when the airliner carries a bomb. The film raises the threat level and U.S. response when the Secretary of Defense puts a special forces unit in charge of defusing the danger and saving the passengers. In the pre–9/11 real-life federal structure, the Federal Aviation Administration's role in confirmed hijackings was to request military assistance from NORAD, a U.S.-Canadian command which protects the North American airspace, but which had never before 9/11 conceived the idea of a terrorist hijacking for the purposes of turning the hijacked planes into missiles. But as *The 9/11 Commission Report* points out, the chain of command and approvals from different officials required several levels in the pre–9/11 structure. These included, for example, asking for military escort aircraft from the Pentagon's National Military Command Center (NMCC), which in return would have asked the Office of the Secretary of Defense for its approval for military assistance. The film shortens the long chain of command when it puts its special forces unit to work at a special meeting led by the Secretary of Defense.

The film's second act setback of the executive order to shoot down the passenger plane turns into hope when the rescue unit succeeds in flashing with the plane's taillights a Morse code message that spells "Hail Mary" and asking for ten minutes. Chaos breaks out when Dr. Grant, behind flight attendant Jean, wrongly identifies a man as having the remote control to the bomb which Cahill, with the help of badly injured but mobilized Cappy, has not yet defused. Bullets hit windows; the plane loses air pressure and is soon out of control in the middle of a gunfight. The military unit succeeds in killing the terrorists, Rat delivering the killing shot against Hassan. Grant, the academic brain of the drama, does not kill, but the film leaves it to him to take the remaining passengers, crew, and the unit to safety. Dr. Grant one more time rises to the occasion when he lands the plane with the help of Jean. The hero is more human than Harry Tasker, and makes mistakes. He misses the main airport and has to land at his small training airport. The academic brings the plane down roughly, in pieces and with destruction to other planes at the small airport.

The 1980s and 1990s U.S. investment in high technology weapons has a supporter in this film. A fictional high technology plane and gear make it possible for the group to defuse the hidden bomb and rescue the hostages. The film portrays military efficiency through a politically correct special unit that saves the U.S. However, the unit's ethnic diversity and skin color rainbow misses gender and religion. The film's competent military men are in charge of the killings. Against the action-adventure genre tradition, it is not the hero who does the final killing. This further underlines the protagonist's background as an academic adviser rather than a trained killer. The heroic role that the film gives to U.S. military counterterrorism can also be seen in the end credits with their long list of military advisers: "We gratefully acknowledge the cooperation of The Department of Defense, The Department of the Army, The Department of the Navy, The National Guard Bureau." In addition the film gives its special thanks to, among others, Army Public Affairs; Los Angeles, California National Guard; U.S. Army 63rd Regional Support; several Naval Air Forces commanders; and several fighter squadrons. But the use of expensive military weaponry and even soldiers in films comes at a price. Movie content and scripts have to be approved in advance by representatives of the U.S. military forces, in particular to meet the requirement of portraying U.S. military forces in a positive light.[28] The film's production notes also refer to that, pointing out that when receiving assistance from the Department of Defense, the government is very strict about what it allows and what it does not allow to take place.

Dr. Grant's prodigal journey is twofold. The film's beginning shows him taking flying lessons, while at the film's end he lands a jumbo jet because the antagonist has killed the pilots. In addition, he earns the respect of the counterterrorism unit. At the beginning of the mission they ridicule him. He gradually gains the respect and trust of everyone but Rat, the mission leader. But at the end it is Rat who calls his team and they respectfully salute Dr. Grant. The protagonist's prodigal journey takes him, like the teenage hero of *Iron Eagle,* from a boy to a man in combat terms. The film barely takes a stab at a traditional romantic subplot in the middle of action. After order has been restored, Jean (Halle Berry), the African American flight attendant who was helping Dr. Grant throughout the mission, leaves the scene with him, with a promise of a heterosexual coupling.

True Lies and *Executive Decision* highlight the effectiveness of a special federal agency and a special military unit in American counterterrorism. *True Lies* is truly lies about American counterterrorism. A fictional government agency expands the rules and allows its agents to run amok. The U.S. military is well represented in *True Lies.* The hero of a secret federal agency uses a U.S. Air Force fighter plane to kill the terrorist. *True Lies* and *Executive Decision* portray effective U.S. counterterrorist measures, repeating a Reaganite cinema approach of reconfirming the status of the armed forces as the country's saviors. They heroically bring the terrorists to Hollywood justice, that is, to their deaths, and not to justice in the U.S. as the State Department describes one of the main goals of American counterterrorism. Furthermore, both films fail to portray the full and complicated chain of command when military takes over to counter a terrorist threat on U.S. soil.

In the 1980s films that have Arab villains, the religion of Islam seems almost an afterthought addition to the terrorist character, even in *The Delta Force* which brings up Islam as the religion of the terrorists in contrast to "our" side's Christianity and Judaism. This chapter's two 1990s films show that action-adventure screenwriters and producers were following the times when they portrayed Islam as the terrorists' religion. However, the Hollywood filmmakers did not do their homework properly. It would have been good for them to read the State Department's caveat that the activity of one small group does not mean that everyone with the same ethnic, national or religious background is guilty:

> Adverse mention in this report of individual members of any political, social, ethnic, religious, or national group is not meant to imply that all members of that group are terrorists. Indeed, terrorists represent a small minority of dedicated, often fanatical, individuals in most such groups. It is that small group — and their actions — that is the subject of this report.[29]

Aziz of *True Lies* and Nagi Hassan of *Executive Decision* are fanatical and the films briefly refer to their religion, Islam. However, both films fail to portray *fundamentalist* Islamic views. The religion of Islam is simplified in short references by madly angry terrorists, and Islam in general becomes the guilty party. It would be comparable to portray members of racist hate organizations that claim to be Christian as sole representatives of Christian views. Radical views of any religion pose a threat to any democracy and civilian life.

In one sense *Executive Decision* shows "progress" in the portrayal of Arabs. Instead of killing dozens of faceless Arabs in brutal ways, the film follows the 1990s trend in the portrayal of European terrorists: the viewer gets to see individual Arab villains who die individual deaths. Also, at one point the film does have a terrorist sidekick separate himself from the main villain's hatred for the U.S. But the main villain is still insane, which follows the genre traditions.

In cinematic terms, the two 1990s films and *Iron Eagle* are missing an important ingredient. These films focus on action and special effects when they portray threats and counteraction, but they fail to create any connection with any of the victims. All violence in *True Lies* is weak, and this is mostly also true in *Executive Decision*. Even Lieutenant Colonel Travis is written in such terms that the viewer does not identify with him; thus his death does not affect the viewer emotionally. The film briefly introduces a flight attendant whom one of the terrorists kills, but otherwise the story is so focused on the military unit that it leaves no room for viewers to identify with the passengers who are facing the threat. The film would more effectively reach viewers if they could identify with the passengers and believe the unit is there for them.

True Lies and *Executive Decision* bring central 1990s terrorist threats onto U.S. soil but oversimplify international terrorism. Terrorism and the cinematic threats of terrorism are purely *violent entertainment* in these films, which undermines the reality of terrorism and leaves audiences with a distorted understanding of terrorism and what counterterrorism can do. The films are fictional business products. Unfortunately a good (profitable) film commodity can be bad for society and add to media misrepresentations of terrorism, and leave media audiences unprepared for the real thing.

A bit over a year after the release of *Executive Decision* Columbia Pictures, part of Sony, entered the race for terrorist movie spectacles when it released *Air Force One* in July 1997. Russian ultranationalists' desire for old communist times and their attack on the U.S. president attracted a large number of viewers to movie theaters, making the film one of the most successful terrorist movies ever. The next chapter discusses the return of the communist threat in *Air Force One*.

CHAPTER 9

Return of the Communist Threat: U.S. President Takes On Russian Communist Terrorists

Air Force One (1997)

Summer 1997 brought to the big screen one of the most successful terrorist films ever, *Air Force One*, which draws from the post–Cold War new world order. The movie finds its villains in radical Russian nationalists who pine for the bygone communist era. The setup was an easy sell after the long Cold War, in which Westerners had been told for decades that communists were the number-one enemy. More complicated story structures, such DreamWorks' first release in September 1997, *The Peacemaker,* had a harder time finding viewers. The film, which starred Nicole Kidman and George Clooney, drew its storyline from the end of the Cold War and the conflict in the former Yugoslavia. A Bosnian man who wants revenge on the West for the death of his family uses a nuclear warhead to threaten New York City during a United Nations conference. The film tried to bring the decade's news headlines of a complicated conflict to the big screen but met with meager box office success. In contrast, *Air Force One* offers a simple storyline of an American hero who protects his family and country. This chapter analyzes the film's take on the post–Cold War world.

Air Force One (1997: #4)

Distributor:	Columbia Pictures (Sony)
Production company:	Beacon Pictures, Radiant Productions, Columbia Pictures
Producers:	Armyan Bernstein, Wolfgang Petersen, Gail Katz, and Jon Shestack
Director:	Wolfgang Petersen
Screenplay:	Andrew W. Marlowe
Executive producers:	Thomas A. Bliss, Marc Abraham and David Lester
MPAA rating:	R
Release date:	July 25, 1997[1]
DVD (WS) running time:	125 minutes
Box office:	$172,215,909, cumulative total: $172,956,409[2]

The film starts with presidential music and long opening credits before cutting to the Presidential Palace of Kazakhstan, a former Soviet republic. Russian and American special forces kidnap General Radek (Jurgen Prochnow), a Kazakh rebel leader, in an international effort to counter terrorism. For the film's U.S. and Russia, Radek and his nationalist communist polices and nuclear arsenal are seeds for a possible new Cold War. Next the film cuts to Moscow, Russia, three weeks later. The film's protagonist, U.S. president James Marshall, played by Harrison Ford, is about to give a speech in Moscow that changes his administration's approach to international terrorism. He declares the new U.S. policy, which emphasizes that the U.S. is tough on terrorists: "Your day is over. We will never negotiate. We will no longer tolerate and we will no longer be afraid. It is your turn to be afraid." President Marshall's national security adviser is unhappy with the speech, which the president defends by saying that the new policy is "the right thing to do." The hero is a morally responsible man whose change of policy is the result of a visit to Red Cross refugee camps that are housing refugees from Kazakhstan where 200,000 people had been murdered under General Radek. The leader of the free world is morally outraged that the world just stood by and allowed such an atrocity to take place. Now he refuses to hide behind diplomatic rhetoric.

President Marshall's speech echoes President Clinton's counterterrorism policies and tough-on-terrorism speeches. The State Department's annual reports on global terrorism highlighted under the Clinton administration U.S.'s zero-tolerance policy on international terrorism in the 1990s. For example, in 1994 at a memorial dedication to the 1988 Pan Am flight 103 bombing victims, President Clinton stated: "Today, America is more determined than ever to stand against terrorism, to fight it, to bring terrorists to answer for their crimes."[3]

A year later President Clinton addressed international terrorism and the importance of counterterrorism at the 50th United Nations General Assembly. In April 1996 he again emphasized his administration's stand on terrorism, in words very similar to what the film's fictional President Marshall used the following year. President Clinton declared in April: "We will never surrender to terror. America will never tolerate terrorism. America will never abide terrorists. Wherever they come from, wherever they go, we will go after them. We will not rest until we have brought them all to justice."[4]

The fictional President Marshall must find out whether he committed political suicide with his speech, as his advisers warn, or if he personally has the guts to back up the speech. Soon after Air Force One departs Moscow, the plane becomes a target of a terrorist attack. Six Russian terrorists, loyal to General Radek, board Air Force One, posing as a television crew whose members they have killed. Against logic, the film expects viewers to accept that the terrorist group has been able to kill the original crew and replace its personal information, including fingerprints, in the Air Force One database in a very short period of time. The president is now faced with international terrorists whom he had just condemned. He must now act according to his "tough on terrorists" policy or eat his words.

The film is weak in setting up the hijacking. Soon after the plane's departure, the secret service agent in charge, Gibbs (Xander Berkeley), shoots several of his colleagues dead and unlocks an Air Force One gun cabinet for the Russian terrorists. After that he still pretends to be serving the president. The film provides Gibbs with no motivation for his actions, which seriously undermines the script. Director Wolfgang Petersen tells in the DVD's additional material that Gibbs's motivation was originally in the script, but it was finally left out because it was felt that his lines explaining his motivation, brought to the screen in the final confrontation between Agent Gibbs and the president, interrupted the film's pacing. Unfortunately, that decision undermines the film when the catalyst that starts the events is not explained.

Originally the script was written for Kevin Costner but when he could not make it, the actor suggested Harrison Ford. The hero of *Patriot Games* plays in *Air Force One* a role very similar to his role as Dr. Ryan. A white middle-aged man with a wife and preteen daughter faces a personal threat to his family from terrorists whose actions in the film have wider international ramifications. The film promotes Harrison Ford to the highest office in the U.S., which makes the terrorist threat against him the ultimate insult against the country. At an individual level he is a family man who loves his wife Grace Marshall (Wendy Crewson) and 12-year-old daughter Alice (Liesel Matthews), who is in a hurry to grow up. The fight is first for his family, and secondarily for his country.

The Russian group easily overtakes the plane. Miraculously, no windows break in the shootout, which saves the plane for the two-hour film ride before sending the presidential air carrier to the bottom of the sea to its destruction. As the terrorist hijacking starts, the president's security team swipes him to safety, forcing him into an escape pod which launches just as terrorists are getting to it. The heroic Air Force One pilots' attempt to land the plane at Ramstein Air Force Base fails, and they pay for the attempt with their lives. A Russian pilot takes over. The group threatens to execute hostages, one every half hour, until General Radek is released.

Veterans of Lost Wars as the Hero and the Villain

The film is *Die Hard* meets *Patriot Games*. Viewers soon find out that the hero naturally would not leave his family and others on Air Force One only to save his own skin. He now faces terrorists in a closed space. President Marshall hides in the plane's cargo area, very much like the special unit in *Executive Decision*, and similar to John McClane hiding in a hijacked high-rise building in *Die Hard*. This medal of honor winner is an ex–Marine Vietnam War veteran who flew more rescue missions than anyone else. He is a one-man solution to the problem. Like John McClane, this hero takes terrorists out of the game one by one. The script makes sure viewers appreciate the president's heroism. One of the hostages tells him: "It makes me so proud, Mr. President, that you stuck with us."

The film's main villain is Ivan Korshunov, played by Gary Oldman. He is an enraged mirror image of the protagonist. Similar to President Marshall, Korshunov is a veteran of a lost war. He fought in the Soviets' own Vietnam, in Afghanistan. A traditional terrorist, he accuses others for his and his group's actions: "This is all your doing; this infection you call freedom without the meaning or purpose. You have given my country to gangsters and prostitutes, you have taken everything. There's nothing left." He resents the changes capitalism and democracy have brought after the collapse of the Soviet Union. He longs for the old communist times when the structure was clear for everyone in society. He would do anything for Mother Russia. In his efforts to return to the past communist glory, his group demands the release of General Radek, the kidnapped Kazakhstan leader, whom the U.S.-Russian team had brought to justice at the beginning of the film.

Air Force One falls under the State Department definitions of international terrorism. The act of the Russian pro-communist and ultranationalist terrorists is premeditated and politically motivated, and has noncombatant targets, in this case everyone on Air Force One. The group is from outside the U.S. borders, targeting American citizens, and crossing international borders on the plane. Participants of an emergency cabinet meeting, led by Vice President Kathryn Bennett (Glenn Close), suspect that the plane might be on its way to Iraq, Libya or Algeria. The first two states are on the State Department's list of the state sponsors of terrorism. A federal briefing on Korshunov's group describes the group members as Russian ultranationalist radicals.

The film reduces American counterterrorism to one person, combining 1980s Reaganite

Air Force One **(1997, Columbia Pictures [Sony]) pitches two veterans of lost wars against each other: U.S. president James Marshall (Harrison Ford), a veteran of the Vietnam War, and Ivan Korshunov (Gary Oldman, left), a veteran of the war in Afghanistan.**

cinema hero portrayals of one-man war machines and the updated 1980s hero of *Die Hard*'s John McClane. Ineffective meetings led by the vice president, which are attended by different representatives of American counterterrorism, emphasize the role of the heroic president who alone can salvage the situation. He is a 1990s modern Rambo in a suit, and with a family and good social skills. He receives some help from U.S. Air Force planes following and eventually rescuing him and his family, but he alone removes the threat of terrorists. The film portrays a form of international terrorism that is merely temporary, a threat which an American hero can easily defeat. This approach worked at the box office with a major success, but the film misrepresents the real threat of international terrorism, and in particular how to counter international terrorism.

In the post–Cold War world, several former Soviet republics had internal conflicts, such as Georgia and Tajikistan. For example, in 1996 and 1997 international organizations' employees and Russian servicemen were targets of renegade Tajik warlords and unidentified assailants. Kazakhstan hardly registered in the State Department reports. In 1998, a year after the film's release, the U.S. and Kazakhstan governments signed a joint statement in which they agreed to combat terrorism. However, the agreement opposed not communism but possible Iranian spies. The film's events actually have similarities in the Russian conflict with Chechen separatists over several years in the 1990s.[5]

Korshunov is a traditional villain who kills in cold blood while the hero only kills for a reason. Korshunov executes hostages without a second thought to make the severity of the terrorist threat clear to the vice president. Like Colonel Stuart in *Die Hard 2: Die Harder* and the minister of defense in *Iron Eagle*, he is tough on his own group too. When the group finds one of their own dead and realizes that there is an unknown person on board, Korshunov's words to his group are: "Find out who killed him or you lie down next to him." Hollywood undermines terrorists' comradeship to emphasize the brutality of the unsavory characters. The film barely touches on the villain's motivation in addition to his goal to force the release of General Radek. When the vice president asks Ivan Korshunov what his group wants, the agitated terrorist responds:

> What arrogance to think that you could ever understand my intentions.... What I want.... When Mother Russia becomes one great nation again, when the capitalists are dragged from the Kremlin and shot in the street. When our enemies run and hide in fear at the mention of our name and America begs our forgiveness, on that great day of deliverance you will know what I want.

The terrorist has deep passion for Mother Russia, but the script does not bother to explore what goals a communist terrorist would have.

Concessions to Terrorists

Through the words of the First Lady and the president's national security adviser, *Air Force One* reminds viewers of one of the four main elements of U.S. counterterrorism: the country makes no concessions to terrorists and it makes no deals with terrorists. Korshunov responds to the national security adviser's statement by executing the man and pointing out that he has just bought another half hour of negotiation time for the U.S. Korshunov's comment to Grace Marshall about why the U.S. should negotiate with him and his group is the film's core. The terrorist points out to the First Lady that no man could live with himself, not to mention that it would be bad politics, if he did not negotiate when his wife and daughter's lives are at stake.

The film portrays the secretary of defense, who tries to follow the official U.S. policy, as a cold man who wants to grab power during the hijacking. Secretary of Defense Walter Dean (Dean Stockwell) reminds the official power structure that the U.S. presidency is more than one man. In his view the lives of fifty people on Air Force One are little to pay for the country to follow its policies. He points out that the policy has been a cornerstone of U.S. counterterrorism for twenty-five years. To step away from that would mean that U.S. opponents around the world would have an open season on the U.S.

Like others of its genre, the film reduces a matter of politics and policies to an individual level, and forces the president to violate the policy in return for his daughter's life. As his vice president does, President Marshall asks his Russian counterpart to order the release of General Radek from prison, which directly violates U.S. counterterrorism policies. For example, the 1988 report clearly states that the U.S. does not release terrorists from prison.[6] But as in the film, also in real life some of the stated counterterrorism policies have been violated, to help hostages or to gain political opportunities. For example, President Ronald Reagan violated the stated policies in the 1980s. His administration traded prevailing policies to new political opportunities when it tried to gain Iran's help in the release of American hostages in Lebanon. The package deal included concessions to terrorists when the Reagan administration, in its effort to gain Iran's help, sold weapons to Iran, a country which the U.S. had officially declared to be a state sponsor of terrorism. The administration forwarded the profits of the arms deal to the Contras, an anticommunist group in Nicaragua fighting against the prevailing leftist Nicaraguan government. A U.S. bill had made military aid to the Contras illegal, so the administration was in several ways trying to get around U.S. laws. President Reagan had himself pointed out in June 1985 that "America will never make concessions to terrorists — to do so would only invite more terrorism — nor will we ask or pressure any other government to do so."[7]

The heroic American president of *Air Force One* succeeds in dumping the plane's fuel, which forces the hijackers to ask for refueling. That gives the hostages and the U.S. an opportunity when an American plane arrives to do the midair refueling. As the plane is refueling, President Marshall leads a rescue effort. Through one-on-one fights he has killed several terrorists and made his way to the room where the hostages are kept. He now leads the group to enter a ramp from where the hostages can start parachuting to safety. But he must stay behind because the terrorists have separated his family from the rest of the hostages. While most of the hostages escape, the terrorists notice the open parachute ramp and arrive to catch the president, which gives him a traditional second act setback.

The film's villain has no moral values, which further emphasizes his contrast to the heroic protagonist. Korshunov does not keep his word, and he attacks the hero when he is defenseless. Korshunov is even willing to kill the president's wife and daughter if the president does not comply with the group's demands. President Marshall begs Korshunov to leave his family alone, pointing out that this is not war and the fight is between him and Korshunov. The angry terrorist tells Marshall not to lecture him on the rules of law since the U.S. president has murdered hundreds of thousands of Iraqis. As Korshunov holds a gun on Alice's head to emphasize what is at stake if President Marshall refuses to give in to the demands, the president surrenders with the words: "Have you no honor?" His comment further underlines the different moral and ethical standards between the hero and the villain. Cornered, President Marshall realizes his family takes priority over national policies: "I'll do it. Just leave my family alone." His cabinet questions his actions, but his vice president refuses to sign a document which would temporarily remove the president from power while he is "under duress."

As Russian ultranationalist terrorist Korshunov threatens the president's wife, Grace Marshall (Wendy Crewson, back), and preteen daughter, Alice (Liesel Matthews), the American hero breaks the U.S. policy of no concessions to terrorists, but soon keeps his promise of being tough on terrorists. President Marshall sends Ivan Korshunov to his death with the words: "Get off my plane."

Profitable Action-Adventure Film: Weak Story, Strong Performance

Air Force One relies in its storyline on the power of the U.S. president as the target. The film's plot is simple, but Harrison Ford's strong performance as the president draws the attention away from the weak storyline and draws viewers in for an emotional journey during which they can fear for him and his family, and throughout the film take pride in his heroic actions. The Russian ultranationalist group sets a terrorist threat, but the film focuses on the threat to the hero's family rather than on the threat against the U.S. When the secretary of defense strongly supports the prevailing U.S. policy of no concessions to terrorists, it is he whom the film paints as cold because he would be willing to sacrifice the country's leader.

The film loyally follows action-adventure film traditions, including the typical physical one-on-one final confrontation. As General Radek is released, the film crosscuts between his release, the Russian president, and the events on Air Force One. Korshunov and President Marshall wrestle and use their fists when they fight on the parachute ramp of the plane's cargo area where Korshunov was threatening to push Marshall's wife out of the plane without a parachute. Marshall's determination and love for his family win the hero's love for Mother Russia. The hero breaks the villain's neck with a parachute string, reestablishing his authority when he pushes the villain out of the plane. Soon after, as the Russian president learns that Air Force One is again in American hands, the Russians shoot Radek dead right after he has left the prison gates.

A second confrontation follows the president's attempts to fly Air Force One, which now has no pilots. Previously the president had asked the plane to be shot at, since it was strong enough to survive the shots, which would hinder the terrorists' efforts. But by now Air Force One is in bad shape, and there is no way for the president to land the plane. As a rescue plane arrives to move everyone onto another plane, President Marshall is left to face Secret Agent Gibbs. A white and loyal sidekick takes the bullet Gibbs means for the president. The rescue plane can take only one more person on board. His family secure on the other plane, the hero struggles with Gibbs until he succeeds in leaving the traitor to face his death on the doomed plane. The president then grabs the wire that takes him to the rescue plane.

Similar to *Die Hard*, the news media play a central role in *Air Force One* when they reveal to the antagonist information that helps him in his fight against the protagonist. When the news media broadcast the vice president's words that President Marshall, who is not shown on television, is still the president of the U.S., the antagonist realizes that the president must be on board. Korshunov comprehends that he, after all, has the ultimate ace in his hands. He realizes that the man who has been killing his henchmen is the U.S. president. With this piece of information he is able to smoke the hero out of hiding and force him to comply with the group's demands.

The film portrays strong violence when the terrorists execute American hostages. Viewers know the characters and can identify with them and see their fear before the terrorists shoot them dead. For example, Korshunov executes Deputy Press Secretary Melanie Mitchell (Donna Bullock) in front of the president's family after having asked her questions about her life. She is afraid to die, and viewers can feel that fear.

Air Force One follows the 1990s film format of presenting terrorists as individuals who have individual deaths at the hero's hands. The six terrorists speak in Russian and English among one another, each dedicated to liberating General Radek. Although Korshunov does not reveal his group's exact goals, the film provides him with lines that tell of his family, his disagreement with U.S. policies, and his love for Mother Russia. His character is not developed, but the film provides a reason for his anger. It does not do so for Secret Agent Gibbs.

Although the film reflects in its female vice president the gains women had made in U.S. society in the 1990s, the film reaffirms patriarchal values. It is Vice President Bennett who first makes the decision to give in to the terrorists' demands. She does not have it in her to make the tough decision to remove President Marshall from power and to refuse to comply with the terrorists' demands, as the secretary of defense suggests. She undermines the U.S. policies. It is left to the male hero to correct her and his own mistake.

The female members of President Marshall's family, a wife and preteen daughter, exist to be saved by the heroic white male character. The film has a traditional 1990s family ending when the preteen daughter, who at the film's beginning is eager to grow up, returns to being daddy's little girl once again. At the early stages of the film Grace Marshall points out to her husband that their daughter "cannot stay your little girl forever." After Korshunov has shot the deputy press secretary in front of the First Lady and the daughter, he points out to Alice that her father is not really any different from him: "He kills in a tuxedo with a telephone and a smart bomb." Her response to that is: "You are a monster. My father is a great man. You are nothing like my father." Just as the preteen daughter in *Commando* jumped to her father's defense with her words, so too does this daughter. The terrorists in *Air Force One* attack the traditional family unit and the family members' love for each other but do not succeed in destroying them. The protagonist saves his wife and daughter, just as the heroes of *Patriot Games* and *True Lies* did. Similar to *Patriot Games,* it is the family that comes first. That is the hero's prodigal journey. A job is only a job, but a family is forever.

The film's end credits highlight the story's patriotic take on the ability of the highest office holder to defend the country and his family. The filmmakers "gratefully acknowledge the cooperation of the Department of Defense, the Department of the Air Force, the Department of the Army, the National Guard Bureau...." Special acknowledgments include the public affairs project officer at the Department of Defense, U.S. Air Force, and several other military and national guard offices and facilities. The film tells a powerfully emotional story, largely due to Harrison Ford's strong performance, but its superficial and simplified portrayal of international terrorism and American counterterrorism, not to mention the ineffectiveness of the Secret Service to protect the U.S. president, leaves a lot to wish for in American counterterrorism. It is interesting that *Air Force One* received such strong supporters when the film's underlying message actually undermines the official U.S. counterterrorism policies, structure and crisis response. All parts of the official U.S. counterterrorism structure are quite helpless in the film without the heroic U.S. president. He is the catalyst who can make a difference.

After the success of *Air Force One* only one more film that had international terrorism as its central theme entered the annual top fifty domestic box office before 9/11. In 1998 *The Siege* abandoned the easy genre traditions when it created a complex story of a terrorist threat in New York City whose roots were in U.S. policies in the Middle East. The film comes the closest of the sixteen films to acknowledging that international terrorism is more than a simple fight between the good (us) and bad (them). *The Siege* eerily predicted some of the events the U.S. experienced on September 11, 2001, and in its aftermath. The next chapter analyzes the film's content and similarities to 9/11.

Chapter 10

Predicting 9/11: Power of Belief

The Siege (1998)

In the late 1990s the State Department was highlighting religious extremist groups, including groups that drew from fundamentalist Islamic beliefs, as primary terrorist threats to the U.S. security. For example, al Qaeda was planning and executing anti–U.S. attacks. In August 1998 the U.S. got a powerful reminder of the network's reach when al Qaeda targeted the U.S. embassies in Tanzania and Kenya with coordinated bombings. By that time the terrorist organization had also already planted the seeds of the September 11, 2001, attacks. In the era of new terrorism, *True Lies* and *Executive Decision* did little for the public understanding of the threat of terrorists who aim at mass casualties and are capable of planning and carrying out detailed attacks. *The Siege,* which arrived in movie theaters in November 1998, directly tackled the topic. The film portrays international terrorism that is intertwined with U.S. policies, showing how changes in policy interests can make old friends turn into enemies. While the movie still touched on the religion of Islam only superficially, as the religion of the fictional terrorists, it expanded its storyline to address what happens to a nation when it is under a terrorist attack and its government takes extreme defensive action. In the film the enemy within, an extreme U.S. response to an international terrorist threat, poses a bigger threat to civil liberties and democratic society than the enemy from outside. This chapter discusses how *The Siege* portrays international terrorism that drew from fundamentalist views of Islam, and U.S. counterterrorism under a terrorist attack.

The Siege (1998: #48)

Distributor:	20th Century Fox
Production company:	Lynda Obst
Producer:	Lynda Obst and Edward Zwick
Director:	Edward Zwick
Screenplay:	Lawrence Wright and Menno Meyjes & Edward Zwick
Story:	Lawrence Wright
Executive producer:	Peter Schindler
MPAA rating:	R
Release date:	November 6, 1998[1]
DVD (WS) running time:	116 minutes
Box office:	$40,278,848, cumulative total: 40,981,289[2]

When 20th Century Fox released *The Siege* in movie theaters in November 1998, protesters challenged the film's plot device of Middle Eastern villains who are motivated by their Islamic faith. When the film was in production, Arab-American organizations criticized it for reinforcing U.S. stereotypes of Muslims and of Islam as a religion of terrorism. As a result of this criticism and a meeting with representatives of Arab-American organizations, the movie producers made some changes to the film, but did not change the script to replace the Muslim terrorists with domestic terrorists, as had been suggested.[3] The film's director, Edward Zwick, defended the film by stating that art should be provocative. Also, the film was already in its shooting stage, which would have made changes very costly. The studio, 20th Century Fox, further defended the film by releasing a statement declaring: "This movie is not an anti–Muslim but an anti-prejudice film, and shows the tragic consequences of racism."[4] The film's hero, FBI agent Anthony Hubbard, played by Denzel Washington, further promotes the view that the film is an anti-prejudice film when he, after a bombing which is attributed to terrorists possibly from the Middle East, describes Arab-Americans with the words: "They love this country as much as we do."

The Siege is an example of a film that responds to changes in the prevailing political environment. The movie draws its theme from the late 1990s terrorism threats when it brings Islamic radicals, former U.S. allies, to threaten New York City. Through the 1990s the State Department warned about radical religious movements. For example, the 1995 and 1996 reports point out that

> Terrorism by extremist individuals or groups claiming to act for religious motives continued to dominate international terrorism in 1995.[5]
>
> Terrorism by religious fanatics and groups manipulating religion, especially Islam, for political purposes continued to dominate international terrorism in 1996.[6]

However, audiences were not ready for a film which addressed the complexity of international terrorism and the fact that the country's own policies can come back to bite it. *The Siege* did poorly in the domestic box office when it was released in 1998, barely finishing in the annual top fifty with its #48 position and making just over $40 million. When reality imitated fiction on September 11, 2001, viewers found the film at rental stores. The VHS version of *The Siege* finished in the top 200 the week following the attacks and was still in the top 250 a week later. The movie's DVD version also attracted renters.[7]

The Siege opens with news footage of a bombed army barracks in Saudi Arabia, similar to the 1983 Beirut attack on a Marine barracks, which killed 241, and the June 1996 fuel truck bombing outside a U.S. housing facility near Dhahran, Saudi Arabia. The latter bombing killed 19 U.S. airmen and wounded about 500. Of the wounded, 240 were Americans. Several Islamic extremist groups, claiming to be Sunni or Shia, took responsibility for the attack.[8] The previous year another attack had killed seven, five of them Americans, and wounded 42 in another vehicle bomb attack in Saudi Arabia.[9] Bringing recent news headlines to the fictional feature film, *The Siege* introduces a fundamentalist Islamic group which is attacking the U.S. News media reports provide exposition revealing in the film that the suspect behind the bombing in Saudi Arabia is an Iraqi cleric, Sheik bin Talal (played by Ahmed Ben Larby), a fundamentalist Muslim. A news clip shows President Clinton stating that the act must not go unpunished.

The film introduces its plot immediately when it moves to show how, in a covert operation, a special U.S. military task force captures bin Talal. In retaliation and in their efforts to release the cleric, his Middle Eastern followers start setting off bombs in Manhattan. Small terrorist cells, from one to three members, act independently of each other in New York City.

Each cell takes action after the success or failure of another cell. The terrorists bomb a bus, a Broadway theater, and the FBI counterterrorism task force headquarters, killing hundreds of citizens. But they fail in the bombing of a school and in their final attack, the bombing of a citizens' march which is protesting martial law and the detainment of Arabs and Arab-Americans.

Beyond a White Hero

The Siege reflects a changing U.S. society. FBI agent Anthony "Hub" Hubbard is a strong African American hero who leads a joint FBI/NYPD counterterrorist force. He works with a strong white female, CIA operative Elise Kraft, played by Annette Bening. The name Elise Kraft is her operative alias. During the investigation she at first hides her real name, Sharon Bridger, as well as her own close connection to the suspected radical Muslim terrorists. In addition to the female sidekick, whose loyalties are questionable, Hubbard also has on his side Beirut-born FBI agent Haddad, played by Tony Shalhoub (later better known to TV audiences as neurotic detective Adrian Monk). Hollywood's answer to accusations of stereotyping certain groups as villains has been to add a sidekick from the same ethnic group as the villains.[10] Arab-American Haddad fills the role of the *good* Arab Muslim. He has adapted to the West. He practices his religion, Islam, only in one brief scene while other scenes show how he has become part of the mainstream American society. He plays American football with his teenage son, goes to a bar with his colleagues, and, against his religion, gets tipsy on alcohol.

The film provides its foreign terrorists with a backstory which draws on the first Persian Gulf War, and combines that with the 1980s U.S. experience with Afghan mujahideen fighters. Exposition reveals that the U.S. supported and financed the terrorist group's leader, Sheik Ahmed bin Talal, during a two-year U.S. operation to destabilize Iraqi leader Saddam Hussein. The radical cleric and his followers helped the U.S. effort and were trained by the CIA. However, the U.S. abandoned the group after the Persian Gulf War, which led to the slaughter of many of the group's members. The film's female sidekick, CIA agent Elise Kraft, was involved in the group's training and feels guilty about the shift in the U.S. policy interests which caused the group's abandonment.

The foreign terrorist villain most developed as a character in *The Siege* is Samir Nazhde, played by Sami Bouajila, a teacher of Arab studies at Brooklyn College. He was a U.S. ally, being part of the CIA covert operation in Iraq which was run by Elise Kraft. In her words, "He risked his life for us." Nazhde's backstory, as given in exposition, draws from real-life events, from the Palestinian uprising, the intifadah,[11] in the occupied areas in Israel during which he spent two years in jail. The script gives him a certain amount of sympathetic dialogue. Nazhde tells how his brother became a suicide bomber because the youth could no longer tolerate living in a camp. The brother was promised a life in paradise with seventy virgins and that his parents would be taken care of after his death. Bitterly, Samir Nazhde relates: "Living in a camp, my brother needs to believe it very much." And so the brother blew up a movie theater in Tel Aviv. It is exceptional for a Hollywood action or action-adventure film, especially for one that draws on Middle Eastern terrorism, to provide the film's antagonist with a backstory or any human feelings other than insanity or vengeance. Furthermore, the film also provides the villain's brother, a suicide bomber who is not even portrayed in the film, with a backstory, describing the despair of living in inhuman conditions, even if just briefly.

The Siege finds the biggest threat to the U.S. in a domestic source. The FBI, CIA, NYPD and U.S. Army all become involved in finding the terrorists and preventing future attacks. This follows a U.S. crisis response structure. The FBI is the lead federal agency when the U.S. is under a terrorist attack or threat on U.S. soil, its local Joint Operations Center and its local Special Agent in Charge taking the lead, as the film portrays. Following real-life models, the film depicts interagency cooperation which includes forces from the federal, state and local levels. The storyline portrays conflicts and distrust among these agencies' representatives, reflecting real-life trouble among the some fifty agencies involved in the country's counterterrorism efforts before 9/11. Overzealous General Devereaux, played by Bruce Willis, stands for the armed forces. He is the one who sets the film's events in motion when he takes matters in his own hands and arranges the kidnapping of bin Talal without the knowledge of the White House. That brings international terrorists to the U.S. to demand the release of their leader. At first even the FBI/NYPD counterterrorism task force does not know that the U.S. has the cleric, and is baffled by a faxed demand that says only "Release him." General Devereaux is a man who undermines the rule of law in the name of protecting his country, indifferent to whose rights he may be violating. The general further complicates Agent Hubbard's efforts to uphold the law when the country is under a terrorist threat by implementing martial law, on the directions from the White House. The film's hero has to fight on two fronts: he has to bring down the foreign terrorists as well as remove the domestic threat to civil society and the Constitution.

***The Siege* (1998, 20th Century Fox) both imitates and predicts reality. As fundamentalist Islamic terrorists arrive in New York City, a government response in the crisis situation limits civil liberties. In the film FBI agent Anthony "Hub" Hubbard (Denzel Washington), with an Arab-American FBI agent and a female CIA agent at his side, removes the fictional international terrorist threat to American security and prevents overzealous General Devereaux's (Bruce Willis) threat to the U.S. Constitution.**

THE SIEGE IMITATES AND PREDICTS REALITY

The Siege reflected real life in its plot, which relies on a form of terrorism that the U.S. foreign policy agenda and news headlines described on in the 1990s. The film's screenwriters did their homework well. The fictional foreign threat fits the State Department's definitions of international terrorism. Foreign nationals are threatening the security of the U.S. and U.S. citizens, and are crossing international borders to perform politically motivated attacks. Their political motivation is due to their past and present relationship with the U.S. Former friends turned foes, they are now in the U.S. to demand the release of their radical religious leader and to take revenge on the U.S.

The script makes international terrorism a complicated phenomenon of international relations that has historical similarities to world politics, as described in the State Department's *Patterns of Global Terrorism* publications. Several facts from the department's documents on international terrorism appear in the film. These include, for example, a $2 million reward for leads (the amount of the real reward money in 1998)[12] the cell structure of modern terrorist organizations, and the list the film gives as possible countries behind the fictional attacks: Libya, Iran, Iraq and Syria. Each of these countries is familiar from the State Department's list of the state sponsors of terrorism.

The terrorist group's backstory echoes the development of the U.S. relationship with the group that attacked the country on September 11, 2001. Osama bin Laden and his al Qaeda network grew out of the veterans of the Saudi Arabia and CIA-backed mujahideen fighters in Afghanistan, although, according to *The 9/11 Commission Report*, while the Saudi and U.S. aid to Afghan fighters was worth billions of dollars, Osama bin Laden and his group received little or no U.S. funding. Subsequent to the Soviet withdrawal from Afghanistan and the end of the Cold War, U.S. interests in the region waned to the level of indifference.[13] After the Soviet departure, Osama bin Laden's goal was to form a group of mujahideen fighters which would be ready to be deployed when needed. That opportunity came when Iraq invaded Kuwait.

Osama bin Laden's response to the Iraqi invasion was an offer to the Saudi monarchy to call for a jihad, and to deploy his mujahideen fighters to fight Iraq and defend Saudi Arabia. Saudi Arabia refused the offer and instead joined the U.S.-led international coalition.[14] In 1990, as part of the first Persian Gulf War, the George H. W. Bush administration brought U.S. troops as the first foreign military forces to Saudi Arabia, the holy land of Islam, and they never left. This was an insult to Islamic fundamentalists, including bin Laden. He made clear his opposition to U.S. forces in Saudi Arabia. An old ally was now turning on his old friend of circumstances. From bin Laden's viewpoint, the U.S. had betrayed him and his group. Consequently, the United States became a target of Osama bin Laden and his group's new jihad.[15]

Similar to real-life political developments, the film's terrorists feel that the U.S. broke its word to them when the country changed its policy interests. Their loyal American friend betrayed them, leaving them behind unprotected to be slaughtered. Now the group is going after its former friend. Further insult to the former allies is the U.S. kidnapping of their radical religious leader. As in real life, in the film's blowback situation the country's own policy is coming back to bite it. Furthermore, it was nothing new for real-life mujahideen fighters to take on a superpower. After years of real-world warfare, the Afghan and foreign mujahideen fighters had succeeded in driving the Soviet Union out of Afghanistan. For anti–American fundamentalist Islamic militants, the U.S. withdrawals from Lebanon and Somalia were examples of their success against the United States. When 20th Century Fox released *The Siege*, al Qaeda had already been directly targeting the U.S. for a few years, and had sown the seeds of the 9/11 attack plan.

The attacks that *The Siege* portrays in New York City are reminiscent of the terrorist acts and threats the U.S. experienced in the first part of the 1990s. Just as took place in 1993, the film's foreign antagonists bring terror into New York City. When fundamentalist Islamic terrorists bombed the World Trade Center on February 26, 1993, they killed six Americans and wounded a thousand. The goal of the bombing's mastermind, Ramzi Ahmad Yousef, had been to kill at least a quarter million people. Later that same year the FBI defused another threat in New York City. According to the State Department, the World Trade Center suspects had links to Islamic radicals whose targets in the summer of 1993 had included, for example, the

United Nations building and the Holland and Lincoln Tunnels. Their motivation to fight an urban "holy war" drew from the extremists' view that the U.S. is an enemy of Islam.[16] In the 1990s both domestic extremists and foreign Islamic extremists relied on the same terrorist methods and goals in the decade's terrorist media spectacles: bombings and mass casualties. In 1995 in Oklahoma City, a van bomb destroyed a federal building, killing 168 people and wounding over 500 in an attack by domestic right-wing extremists. Similarly, the film's foreign terrorists destroy a federal building, in this case the headquarters of the FBI Counterterrorism Task Force, killing some six hundred people.

While *The Siege* brings believable terrorist threats to the screen, it simplifies and stereotypes the threat by focusing on the terrorists' vengeful crusade against the United States. Real-life radical Islamic militants who target the U.S.— for example, Sunni Muslim extremist Osama bin Laden — also have political goals. The film skips this essential part of terrorism. More than pure vengeance motivates real-life terrorists. For example, in August 1996 bin Laden clearly stated that his organization aims to "drive U.S. forces from the Arabian Peninsula, overthrow the Government of Saudi Arabia, "liberate" Muslim holy sites in "Palestine," and support Islamic revolutionary groups around the world."[17]

The Siege relies on a traditional action-adventure genre ingredient when it portrays a vengeful villain. Vengeance has brought Samir Nazhde to the U.S. because the country threw him away when he and his group were no longer useful. While the film refers to the terrorists and the U.S. having shared same political goals in the past, it does not describe the fictional terrorists' current or long-term political goals. Their only goal is to gain the release of their religious leader. The film adds to the mix a touch of radical interpretations of Islam as the terrorist's motivation but does a poor job of portraying a religiously motivated extremist who would actually practice his religion. The movie does portray its terrorists drawing from their religion in one instant: when they are preparing for their bombings. *The Siege* portrays ritualistic self-purification as fasting, washing one's body, and using funeral shrouds. Shots of ritualistic hand-washing signify that another bomb attack is coming.

Supposedly for the film's sleeper-cell terrorist, Samir Nazhde, "belief is power," as he says to his CIA handler Elise Kraft. Earlier in the film Kraft has stated that she tends to be suspicious of all true believers. The film's good Arab-American, FBI agent Haddad, does not follow Islam fully in his everyday life. In other words, he is not a *true* believer of Islam, which makes him trustworthy to the white Americans. Significantly, the only time the film portrays Samir Nazhde, supposedly a "true believer," following his religion is when he is preparing for a suicide bombing near the film's climax. Elise Kraft is right: the supposed "true believer" is not trustworthy. However, the film fails to bring the theme of a fundamentalist Islamic terrorist to its closure. As a sleeper-cell member, Samir Nazhde is as deceitful as Elise Kraft, making love and consuming alcohol with her to throw the CIA off his track. But instead of portraying him as an Islamic fundamentalist, the film rather develops the main terrorist as a character who is motivated by his disillusionment at U.S. betrayal, his feeling of powerlessness, and his need for vengeance. An Islamic extremist, even if motivated by hatred rather than by a larger political goal, has certain guidelines he must follow even when hiding in a Western society as an undercover terrorist agent. For example, an al Qaeda manual gives instructions on how to do espionage, recommending "the covert search for and examination of the enemy's news and information for the purpose of using them when a plan is devised."[18] Spying on the enemy is done in the name of a war between Muslims and others. As a spy, a believer can follow in appearance those around him and combine his daily prayers. The manual continues: "It is noted, however, that it is forbidden to do the unlawful, such as drinking wine and fornicating. There is nothing that permits those."[19] While the radical Muslim terrorist angrily states in

The Siege that belief is power, the film's script does not make a fully developed effort to portray a fundamentalist Islamic terrorist for whom belief truly is power. The film terrorist's everyday actions ignore his beliefs. Prayers, even combined daily ones, are missing from his life, he sleeps with the enemy, and he consumes alcohol with her.

Although *The Siege* successfully avoids the use of the very traditional insane terrorist villain, its portrayal does not differ much from previous films on Arab terrorism. Islam is the religion of terrorism in the film, as it is in the other four films with Arab terrorists in this study. Hollywood portrayals of terrorism draw inspiration from the State Department's lists of foreign terrorist organizations and state sponsors of terrorism. But the State Department emphasizes in its annual reports that different nations and religious and ethnic groups should not be stereotyped due to the activities of small groups, and Hollywood is guilty of doing exactly that. The commercial film industry has produced repeated images of anti–U.S. Arab Muslims as well as of PIRA heroes and mad PIRA slinter group extremists. The main difference in the portrayal of Arabs in the films of the 1980s and 1990s is that the former only refer to Islam briefly, and not as the villains' motivation, while the latter use religion as the main motivation. The shift to focus on religion as a motivation reflects the development of concepts about international terrorism in U.S. foreign policy. Terrorism motivated by fundamentalist religious views emerged in the 1990s State Department reports as a primary threat to U.S. interests and citizens. Specifically, towards the end of the decade there were reports that detailed Osama bin Laden's fundamentalist Islamic network al Qaeda as a primary threat to the U.S., although the reports missed the magnitude of that threat. Similar to the State Department's reports, Hollywood films of the 1990s portrayed extremist Islamic terrorists who were threatening the U.S. mainland, while in the films of the 1980s the threat was outside the U.S. borders. Thus film plots followed the development of real-life international terrorism which was introduced to the U.S. as a real threat in 1993 when the World Trade Center was bombed, although the threat soon disappeared from news headlines. The three 1990s films, each distributed by a major U.S. studio, were imitating real-life international terrorism but ignoring the political aspects of religiously motivated terrorism. Furthermore, the films fail to depict Islam accurately and never actually portray characters acting realistically according to fundamentalist interpretations of their religion.

When Elise realizes in *The Siege* that Samir Nazhde alone comprises the last terrorist cell in New York City, Samir tells her: "You believe money is power. Belief is power." This brings to mind Osama bin Laden's February 1998 fatwa declaration which targeted the U.S. and also touched on the subject of money: "We — with Allah's help — call on every Muslim who believes in Allah and wishes to be rewarded to comply with Allah's order to kill the Americans and plunder their money wherever and whenever they find it."[20]

In the film the former CIA ally has become a terrorist on a suicide mission, having learned from the CIA how to make bombs. Samir continues: "Now you are to face the consequences of telling the world how to live." His act is pure vengeance; a retaliation that does not distinguish between civilians and military targets, just as bin Laden announced. And just as al Qaeda's and other extremists' attacks targeted other Muslims, for Samir a demonstration which has "Arabs and Jews side by side. Black and White. Christian and Muslim" is a perfect target for the whole world to hear his and his group's anger. However, while bin Laden declares his fundamentalist religious views, the film script does not articulate such views beyond the line "belief is power." Furthermore, bin Laden has been declaring a clear political goal: forcing the U.S. out of the Middle East. In addition to hoping to force the release of his group's religious leader, the film terrorist has an individual goal: to avenge past injustices.

The film's script development parallels the way the mainstream news media structure international terrorism. The news mentions religion when terrorists come from the Middle East and when that religion is Islam but otherwise rarely touches the topic, as should be the case, for example, in portrayals of Northern Ireland where religion is an important ingredient of the complex construction of the region's terrorism. Furthermore, the way the script fails to explain the group's political or social objectives also parallels news media portrayals of terrorism which focus on the act, not on the motivation or the political or social context of terrorism.[21] While *The Siege* continues action-adventure film traditions by not exploring the villain's larger political and social motivations, the news media have no excuse for their poor coverage of the phenomenon of terrorism.

Despite the film's shortcomings, the foreign threat scenario it brings to the big screen resembles the roots and actions of Osama bin Laden's al Qaeda. Actually, when simplifying the storyline to match the Hollywood film genre traditions, *The Siege* portrays a threat that is reminiscent of Osama bin Laden's image in the West. At first the threat was not realized or taken seriously in the West. The U.S. government only started to take notice of al Qaeda in the late 1990s. However, the group still had a hard time attracting the attention of the U.S. news media gatekeepers when its attacks were taking place outside U.S. borders. According to *The 9/11 Commission Report*, Osama bin Laden has been targeting the U.S. since 1992. Publicly he has announced the U.S. as his main target several times. First, in 1992 al Qaeda issued a fatwa, encouraging a jihad to drive the Western powers, in particular the U.S., from Islamic lands. In 1996 bin Laden himself urged Muslims to drive Americans out of Saudi Arabia. In 1998 he and Ayman al Zawahiri, a fugitive Egyptian physician, and three others, declared a fatwa against the United States in an Arabic newspaper published in London. *The 9/11 Commission Report* points out that only scholars of Islamic law can issue a fatwa as interpretations of the law.

The February 23, 1998, declaration, authored by Osama bin Laden and signed by the other four, was titled *Jihad Against Jews and Crusaders*. The group was making its case against the U.S., accusing the superpower of "occupying the lands of Islam in the holiest of places, the Arabian peninsula, plundering the riches, dictating to its rulers, humiliating its people, terrorizing its neighbors, and turning its bases in the peninsula into a spearhead through which to fight the neighboring Muslim peoples."[22] Furthermore, the declaration charged the U.S. of trying to "repeat the horrific massacres" that "the crusader–Zionist alliance" had committed in Iraq, having killed over a million, in bin Laden's view. Bin Laden continues: "if the Americans' aims behind these wars are religious and economic, the aim is also to serve the Jews' petty state and divert attention from its occupation of Jerusalem and murder of Muslims there."[23] In his opinion the U.S. has been eager to destroy Iraq and weaken several other countries in the region in order to support Israel. The statement further declares: "All these crimes and sins committed by the Americans are a clear declaration of war on Allah, his Messenger, and Muslims."[24] In bin Laden's interpretation, an individual Muslim's duty is to defend his belief and force away an enemy who attacks his religious being:

> On that basis, and in compliance with Allah's order, we issue the following fatwa to all Muslims: 'The ruling to kill the Americans and their allies — civilians and military — is an individual duty for every Muslim who can do it in any country in which it is possible to do it, in order to liberate the al-Aqsa Mosque and the holy mosque [Mecca] from their grip, and in order for their armies to move out of all the lands of Islam, defeated and unable to threaten any Muslim. This is in accordance with the words of Almighty Allah, "and fight the pagans all together as they fight you all together," and "fight them until there is no more tumult or oppression, and there prevail justice and faith in Allah."[25]

Three months later bin Laden reemphasized the group's message in an ABC-TV interview when he pointed out that "it was more important for Muslims to kill Americans than to kill other infidels."[26] Killing an American soldier was a religious duty. Soon bin Laden declared both American civilians and military personnel as his targets.[27]

Although the terrorist villains of *The Siege* cause human casualties in the hundreds, the film was a bit behind the times in depicting real-life terrorism goals, that is, mass casualties that would be counted in thousands. In the other two 1990s films that portray Middle Eastern–originated terrorism that is motivated by extreme religious views, *True Lies* (1994) and *Executive Decision* (1996), the fictional foreign terrorists aim at mass casualties, imitating al Qaeda's attack goals and aim to acquire WMD. For the Arab Muslim villains who in *True Lies* and *Executive Decision* come from undefined Middle Eastern countries, a male Arab Muslim's hatred of the U.S. is enough to motivate an attack on Americans. In *True Lies*, similarly to Osama bin Laden's statements, Aziz, the main villain, briefly states his opposition to U.S. presence in the Middle East and his goal to drive the U.S. out of there. However, a clear backstory and human feelings, other than insanity and unexplained rage, are missing in these two films. They follow the traditional simple action-adventure film portrayal of villains whose acts are motivated by madness rather than by political agendas and goals.

True Lies and *Executive Decision* highlight in their storylines the effectiveness of a special federal agency and a special military unit of U.S. counterterrorism. The movies heroically bring the film terrorists to Hollywood justice, that is, to their deaths, and not to justice in the United States as the State Department describes as one of the main goals of U.S. counterterrorism. In terms of historical developments, the films predicted a shift in U.S. policy: in 1998 President Clinton declared that the United States has a legal right to kill those it defines as terrorist leaders.[28] This was brought on by the simultaneous 1998 attacks on the U.S. embassies in Kenya and Tanzania, which the U.S. traced back to Osama bin Laden and his network. However, the administration's attempts to kill Osama bin Laden in the name of self-defense were futile.

The Enemy from Within

The Siege followed the U.S. counterterrorism structure, naming the agency in charge as the Federal Bureau of Investigation when investigating a terrorist threat on U.S. soil. In the film the FBI works in cooperation with the NYPD, the CIA, and the armed forces, the last having power-hungry General Devereaux lurking in the background. When Hubbard and Kraft, and Hubbard's multiracial task force, fail to capture the terrorists and prevent various bombings — of a bus, a Broadway theater, and the FBI counterterrorism headquarters — the U.S. army takes over. General Devereaux dictates the rules of martial law in New York City: "I am the law. Right here, right now, I am the law." While the president's chief of staff announces to the general that the president is ready to be presidential, which allows General Devereaux to make his move, the film simplifies the implementation of martial law. Interagency cooperation has taken shortcuts, and the overzealous general has been spying on the interagency efforts to prevent terrorist acts. As National Defense Fellow Jeffrey D. Brake discusses:

> Military involvement in direct law enforcement activities is normally prohibited by 18 U.S.C. Section 1385, unless otherwise specifically authorized under the Constitution or Act of Congress.[29] Better known as the *Posse Comitatus* Act, 18 U.S.C. Section 1385 prohibits the use of the military in activities such as:
>
> > Arrest; seizures of evidence; search of persons; search of a building; investigation of a crime; interviewing witnesses; pursuit of an escaped prisoner; search of an area for a suspect and other like activities.[30]

> The *Posse Comitatus* Act, however, has not precluded the military from providing logistical support, technical advice, facilities, training, and other forms of assistance to civilian law enforcement agencies even though that assistance may aid those activities.[31]

These activities are considered to be passive involvement and therefore not breaking the law. In the film the military is not providing support. Rather, it is competing with the civilian law enforcement structure. The film violates the strict guidelines the law provides on military involvement, even before the military marches in and starts to run the operation.[32] The film does follow the commander in chief's authority to order the deployment of the military if a terrorist attack or threat endangers the public, or threatens the country and government's survival in the U.S.[33] However, the film takes shortcuts, skipping the executive order from the president to the secretary of defense, and the latter's coordination with the attorney general.[34] In the film FBI agent Hubbard learns of the military deployment through TV news, while in real life the attorney general would be in contact with the FBI, which in return would notify the FBI's designated federal on-scene-commander (OSC) who manages the situation for the U.S. government.[35] The OSC temporarily gives authority to a military commander, but the OSC can reclaim authority if it is not during an assault phase and he sees that no military is needed.[36] In the film General Devereaux ignores the rule of law and takes over from the FBI as the ultimate authority.

Only four years after the film's release, reality borrowed from the film's shortcuts. After 9/11 the George W. Bush administration was contemplating deploying the U.S. military on U.S. soil to use it, for example, to arrest U.S. citizens who were suspected of having links to al Qaeda. In March 2009 *The New York Times* reported on a Department of Justice memo titled "Authority for Use of Military Force to Combat Terrorist Activities Within the United States" by Assistant Attorney General John Yoo and Department of Justice Special Counsel Robert Delahunty. The memo was dated October 23, 2001, and addressed to Alberto R. Gonzales, counsel to the president, and William J. Haynes II, general counsel at the Department of Defense. The memo makes for chilling reading. For example, it declared that the U.S. president has the sole authority to deploy the U.S. military on U.S. soil against the country's own citizens. The memo's interpretation ignored the Constitution and Congress, including the Posse Comitatus Act and the Fourth Amendment since, in the memo writers' view, the military would not be in a law enforcement role but doing a military operation.[37] The memo was not revoked until the final days of the Bush administration.

The interagency cooperation in *The Siege* is missing one aspect of possible national-level counterterrorism coordination: the use of the Domestic Emergency Support Team (DEST), which is a "rapidly deployable, interagency team of experts to advise and support the FBI crisis management effort."[38] The team can have experts, for example, from the Federal Emergency Management Agency, the Environmental Protection Agency, and the Departments of Defense, Energy, and Health and Human Services. The DEST team's role is to provide support and advice to the OSC.

The Siege rewrites U.S. laws and bumps up the volume to dramatize the role of the enemy from within. The script pushes the power-hungry general's role to the extreme, and has him run the operation, with the FBI, citizens and the whole city of New York completely at his mercy. In the movie the president's chief of staff notifies General Devereaux of the president's decision to deploy military forces in New York City. Just as *Executive Decision* did, *The Siege* leaves the president of the hook: neither film shows a U.S. president making a decision that could be harmful to American citizens, but only shows a president's representative doing that. The two films predicted the real-life response to 9/11: after President Bush had been whisked to safety, his representatives forwarded the order from the president to shoot down the hijacked United flight 93 which was fast approaching Washington, D.C.

In *The Siege* tanks roll into New York City in the name of security. Martial law cancels civil liberties when soldiers maintain security. The general's siege is more dangerous to citizens and civil society than the film's terrorist threat. Counterterrorism becomes warfare on the country's own soil. General Devereaux orders the internment of all young Arab-American males in New York, particularly in Brooklyn. The film portrays him as a sadist and extremist who does not protect the law but who relies on methods that are not unlike the terrorists' methods. He tortures an Arab prisoner who has no information to give. As the cutting of the suspect brings no results, a loud sound of a gunshot reveals his final destiny.

The military siege of New York City and General Devereaux's disregard for the country's laws leave it to agent Hubbard not only to save the U.S. from an international terrorist threat but, in particular, to save the American way of life, civil liberties and constitutional rights. Hubbard's primary antagonist is the U.S. military, personified in General Devereaux. International terrorism itself and the phenomenon's main proponent in the film, Samir Nazhde, are only secondary threats. Since Samir Nazhde personifies the foreign threat, the protagonist kills him at the film's end, just as the action-adventure and thriller genre traditions require. The patriotic white American general, who acted in the name of defending his country when he was treading on civil rights and the Constitution, is arrested when hero Hubbard reinstates the country's laws and Constitution.

Response to Terrorist Incidents

The Siege eerily predicted not only the arrival of an international terrorist media spectacle on U.S. soil but also some of the responses to terrorism witnessed in the U.S. after 9/11. For example, the U.S. government spied without warrants on U.S. citizens and residents on their phone calls, e-mail messages, library transactions and Internet habits. The George W. Bush administration indefinitely detained terror suspects in the U.S. Naval Base in Guantánamo Bay, Cuba. It also hid unreported and therefore officially nonexistent terror suspects, so-called ghost detainees, at secret locations, and used torture as a method of questioning. Also, press freedoms and freedom of expression were at stake in the name of defending the U.S. According to "Authority for Use of Military Force to Combat Terrorist Activities Within the United States," a Department of Justice memo by John Yoo and Robert Delahunty, issued in October 2001 and revoked in the last days of the Bush administration, "First Amendment speech and press rights may also be subordinated to the overriding need to wage war successfully."[39]

After 9/11 the United States witnessed politicians getting into the game of questionable political methods. For example, in the first years after 9/11, some politicians, media commentators and citizens hurled around terms such as "un-American" and "unpatriotic" to describe those who questioned some of the Bush administration's methods in fighting global terrorism, and its strict way of dividing the world into enemies and friends and leaving no ground between. *The Siege* too uses these propagandistic techniques which aim at undermining any opposition to extreme methods. For example, when Agent Hubbard questions General Devereaux's extreme counterterrorism methods and the implementation of martial law, which erode civil liberties and terrorize American citizens, the general angrily responds: "Are you questioning my patriotism?" When tactics which undermine the principles of democracy and freedom are hidden under the pretense of patriotism, all discussion can effectively be crushed. In the U.S. it was only towards the end of the Bush presidency that the mainstream media, public and politicians started to question the War on Terror, the torturing of terrorist suspects, and in particular, the U.S. invasion of Iraq, a country which had had nothing to do with the 9/11 attacks but which the administration had invaded as part of its War on Terror.

In Agent Hubbard's words in *The Siege*, the terrorists "have won" if our society fights terror with terror and takes steps that erode the rules of civil society. At the same time, the film's main terrorist, Samir Nazhde, reminds viewers of the reality of terrorism: "There will never be a last cell." The film terrorist succeeded in his mission when he created fear and chaos in society through his own and his group's actions, as well as through his target's countermeasures. But he lost when the film's U.S., through FBI agent Hubbard's actions, did not bring itself down to the same level with the terrorists.

While *The Siege* is quite critical of and analytical about the U.S. governmental and military role in counterterrorism when the country is under a terrorist threat on its own soil, the film also supports the prevailing social order. The film's hero, a special FBI agent, not only beats the terrorist threat but also the threat of the military general who has run amok. FBI agent Hubbard's work and words throughout the film support the view that terrorism is a matter of law enforcement; that is, a foreign terrorist threat on U.S. soil is a crime, not war. Therefore the cases of terrorism fall under the jurisdiction of the FBI, the agency which carries the primary responsibility of investigating terrorist acts and threats on U.S. soil, performing that task under the Justice Department. Hero Hubbard distrusts the CIA's involvement in the case, as well as that of the army. His suspicion is confirmed when he catches the army spying on his task force. This type of distrust was later echoed in *The 9/11 Commission Report*'s description of the problems in cooperation among the country's counterterrorist agencies in the pre–9/11 United States. While the U.S. Army has a major role in *The Siege*, the film denounces the view that terrorism is war. If that were the case, counterterrorism would fall under military purview.[40]

When addressing the film's international threat, the storyline explores how shifts in the country's foreign policy can work against its own security. In this particular film former U.S. allies enter the U.S. to attack the country on its own soil. The film brings to focus how extreme government responses to terrorism can be bigger threats to a democratic society than international terrorism. The film's conclusion deals with what happens to citizens and society when, in the name of defending the country, the U.S. government uses extreme actions which actually make American citizens become targets. Martial law limits civil liberties and makes innocent citizens terrorist suspects.

Agent Hubbard says at one point in the film that the terrorists "are attacking our way of life." However, the terrorist attacks per se are not the major threat, but how citizens and the government respond to the attacks. In the film the armed forces are the ultimate answer to U.S. security but also a threat to civil society bigger than terrorism. Hate crimes and government actions that undermine civil liberties and the Constitution are more effective in destabilizing a society than that society's external terrorist enemies.

The Siege clearly takes a much darker approach to international terrorism than any other film with terrorist themes that was in the annual top fifty domestic box office in the two decades prior to the September 11, 2001, attacks. The film largely relies on creating a mood and fear of terrorism before it focuses on the aftermath and social consequences of terrorist attacks. The movie avoids portraying explosives, bloody massacres and detailed killings of villains. It does show a bus explosion and some minor counterterrorism attacks in New York City. The film addresses the emotional impact of terrorist attacks when the camera pans to reveal the destruction and victims' anguish after an attack. The film's portrayal of violence is strong when viewers see the human toll of terrorist attacks, which makes audiences uncomfortable and goes against traditional action and action-adventure film traditions. Viewers are not able to escape the threat and acts of terrorism, murky U.S. policies that contributed to the threat, and the impact of the constant threat and fear on society and on some of the film's main characters. The movie offers its audiences uncomfortable glimpses of the reality of international terrorism and U.S. involvement in world politics.

In contrast to a more traditional Hollywood portrayal of terrorist villains, the film's foreign antagonists are not insane individuals but people who have clear plans of how to carry out their terror campaign. They present a threat to U.S. society that makes viewers squirm because the threat the film describes is believable. It is not entertaining when the threat invades the viewer's comfort zone. This was realized in a similar but even more horrifying form on September 11, 2001, when foreign terrorists killed some 3,000 people. The architects of the simultaneous 9/11 attacks had a long-term plan, trained and paid the terrorists who took part in the mission, and made practice runs of the final mission before the H-hour.

True to modern terrorism and the way it is communicated in our time, *The Siege*'s narrative depicts the news media as the public's main source of information about terrorism. The film further uses the news media for exposition, and even mentions news coverage as a specific goal of modern terrorism, as has been the case with modern international terrorism since its emergence in the late 1960s. When news helicopters arrive at a public bus which Arab terrorists on a suicide mission have taken over, the film's female CIA operative cries out: "They are not here to negotiate. They were waiting for the cameras. They want everyone watching." Just like their real-life counterparts, the film's terrorists seek media attention through their violent attacks.

Destiny of Minority Sidekicks and the Domestic Villain

Agent Hubbard's Arab-American sidekick, Agent Haddad, survives General Devereaux's attacks on the Arab-American community, although he refuses to be an Arab poster boy, in the character's own words a "sand nigger," to the U.S. government when his family is affected by martial law. The army takes his teenage son to a government internment camp with other young Arab males, poignantly predicting the ethnic profiling of suspected terrorists in the post–9/11 United States. When Agent Haddad goes to look for his son, he becomes disillusioned by extreme government actions. He resigns his job, yelling at his supervisor, Agent Hubbard, at the internment camp: "It's here where I belong." Through Haddad's eyes viewers can experience an innocent person's pain when his family becomes a target of ethnic profiling. However, while Agent Haddad questions how welcoming his adopted country is to his ethnic group, he eventually returns to fill his role as a loyal sidekick, as the action-adventure film traditions require (that is, if a film allows its sidekick to survive the film's events). Agent Haddad returns to help agent Hubbard to bring down General Devereaux.

Elise Kraft is a strong CIA agent but is compromised as a character. Kraft is Samir Nazhde's handler and has a sexual relationship with him in order to support him in his work and thus receive information. She is a tainted woman who sleeps around as an aid to her spy work. When she is trying to convince agent Hubbard that she is not hiding any information, she forcefully emphasizes her message by saying, "I'm not fucking with you." Agent Hubbard's terse response to her is, "How could you possibly remember who you are fucking?" Like the strong Russian female major in *The Jackal*, this strong woman also faces the fate of other sidekicks: death. As a strong and independent woman she is the new minority to die for the hero. Elise Kraft dies at the hands of the terrorist antagonist, her former lover, who has used her as a shield. Hubbard and Haddad both shoot at Samir Nazhde, who dies without getting a chance to set off the bomb attached to his body. Hubbard then rushes to help Kraft, who dies before his eyes. If there had been a budding romance between her and Hubbard, it never had a chance. He fails to save her, which is just as well because her character was built as tainted. She used all methods available to her. This deluded and flawed woman was not only sleeping with the enemy but also approved of and was part of questionable counterterrorism methods, such as torture of terrorist suspects. Limited by her lies and delusions, she has to pay the ultimate price. It is up to the honest hero Hubbard to uphold the law and stop the counterterrorism methods that undermine civil society.

The final confrontation is between Agent Hubbard and his white U.S. antagonist, General Devereaux, who has taken law into his own hands. Unlike foreign antagonists, the bad general's destiny is to stay alive and only get arrested. Hubbard's prodigal journey is his returned faith in U.S. society and law. A strong African American male hero saves the country. It is a job a strong woman in the 1990s was not yet capable of doing in Hollywood. Although the film's events are similar to the events of 9/11, it still offers a typical action-adventure film ending which is more utopian than what occurred in the post–9/11 social reality. As the genre traditions require, the film's conclusion reproduces and maintains the prevailing order that has been attacked. The film's ending even restores racial justice, rejecting the overzealous general's attack on civil liberties, including the civil liberties of ethnic minorities. In addition, the film offers a true Hollywood ending: the hero kills the foreign terrorist villain.

Towards 9/11

Despite its shortcomings, *The Siege* does succeed in developing concepts that other films and the mainstream news media had done poorly in the pre–9/11 United States. Terrorism and counterterrorism are not simple phenomena that exist in any particular moment in history. Rather, they develop and change over time as social, historical and political conditions change. Mujahideen fighters, whom President Reagan once saw as freedom fighters and whom he compared to the founding fathers of the United States, developed into a U.S. enemy several years later. Similar to the U.S. experience with mujahideen fighters, the film's terrorists react to U.S. actions and vice versa, the two parties having a long history with each other. Even the main terrorist, Samir Nazhde, has a more complicated storyline and personal motivation in the film than the more traditional insane killer who is far too familiar in Hollywood films on terrorism.

At the film's end the citizens of New York City, who are living under a terrorist threat and harsh U.S. counterterrorism measures, become part of the story when they react against government detention of Arab-Americans and the implementation of martial law. Different ethnic and religious groups unite to protest against terrorism and extreme government actions. In its imagery of the detention camp of Arabs in New York City and the mass public protest against it and martial law, *The Siege* does generate sympathy at the end for the Arab people and against the U.S. military in the person of General Devereaux who is responsible for the extreme measures. Interestingly, it was at that demonstration that Samir had intended to set off his bomb, implying how terrorists can take advantage of progressive forces and views in the U.S. His plan was not only to exploit the suffering of his own ethnic and religious group but also target those who were voicing their objection to that suffering. Their opposition to terrorism and also to extreme government actions that undermine civil rights posed a threat to Samir's group's terrorist goal of creating fear and chaos in society; in this case fear and chaos were caused by both terrorists and the country's own government in the name of security. The film only briefly touches on this important aspect of terrorism.

The portrayals of terrorism, and of citizen and government responses to terrorism that

The Siege brings to viewers come closer to reality than the depictions in the other annual top fifty box office films before 9/11. But even though the film draws from the long-term historical and political U.S. experiences with terrorism, which is exceptional for an action-adventure film, its portrayal of Arabs, and in particular, of fundamentalist Islamic terrorism, does not rise above stereotypical news media and earlier film images. Largely ignoring what fundamentalist Islamic terrorism is, as well as its long-term goals, the film offers viewers a misrepresentation of a religious and an ethnic group. In the film anyone who is an Arab is also a Muslim and becomes a suspect. There is no understanding in the film that, just like Christianity, Islam has no one single interpretation. The film does not separate Sunni or Shia, or extremist and moderate views within either sect. Furthermore, neither of the film's two major Arab characters, both of whom are Muslims, fully practices his religion. The cultural Other remains incomprehensible in this film. *The Siege* reinforces prejudice in the major ways in which it develops its plot. Despite the impressive impact of the mise-en-scène at the film's end of a citizens' march against terrorism and extreme methods of counterterrorism, the film fails in its attempt to be anti-prejudice, a film that shows "the tragic consequences of racism," as 20th Century Fox put it.

The film has a traditional Hollywood ending with the Third World terrorist, Samir, killed and the white U.S. threat to civil liberties, General Devereaux, arrested. However, the film's dark tone and portrayal of the threat of government responses to terrorism better describe terrorism and its threats to civil society than familiar questions from the news media, such as "Why do they hate us?" A better question is "What is the whole story?" Focus on hatred and on cultural, religious and ideological differences prevents us from seeing the big picture, and from understanding how current and future terrorist threats have developed and are developing. On September 11, 2001, a threat that had been brewing since the Soviet withdrawal from Afghanistan exploded in front of the world's news media, changing the U.S. and Western experience with international terrorism.

The 9/11 attacks were in the works for several years. Their political background and motivations grew out of historical and political developments and changes that took several decades, just as did the events that resulted in the terrorist attacks and threats in *The Siege*. We can understand the complexity of terrorism better, and also better protect the country and its citizens against terrorists, if we analyze the historical, political and social development of terrorism, and terrorists' motivation and goals. *The Siege* somewhat tried to do that but its attempt was not a big box office draw in the pre–9/11 America. The film barely reached the top fifty in its release year. The movie's storyline scratched the surface of the complexity of international terrorism, and did not provide viewers with easy answers. The other pre–9/11 film portrayals of international terrorism had left audiences unprepared for the reality of terrorists who are smart and committed, and who have detailed long-term plans to harm and kill Americans and others whom they consider their enemy.

On Tuesday morning, September 11, 2001, al Qaeda murdered some 3,000 real people, wounded others, and caused massive destruction in front of live television cameras. In reality the post–9/11 world proved to be more complicated than the world of *The Siege* and other Hollywood depictions. President George W. Bush announced two days after the September 11, 2001, attacks that the fight against international terrorism is "the first war of the 21st century. It will be the focus of my administration."[41] A few days later President Bush announced to the world: "Every nation in every region now has a decision to make. Either you are with us, or you are with the terrorists."[42] The U.S. War on Terror had just begun.

Conclusion: Patterns and Themes of the Hollywood Terrorist

Tuesday morning, September 11, 2001, changed the U.S. experience with terrorism. International terrorists hijacked four civilian airliners and turned them into missiles, killing and wounding thousands of people. On that day terrorists created a media spectacle larger than any Hollywood film had ever done, bringing destruction of human life and property for viewers to witness in real time around the world.

Hollywood uses fictional terrorist violence to scare, entertain and draw in paying viewers. For the real-life terrorist, violence is a political method that is about creating fear and chaos in society and about delivering those messages through news media to audiences. Through murder and destruction, terrorists gain recognition as oppositional forces in society. Hollywood easily resolves the problem of violent political threats by killing off its terrorist film villains — that is, until the next Hollywood terrorist appears on the screen. In real life, terrorists have also lost their lives and, as in films, new terrorists have emerged to claim the position of those who have perished, or those who have converted their violence to more traditional methods of international politics.

The commercial film industry and terrorists have been paying attention to each other. Hollywood creations have drawn ideas from televised real-life terrorist events and the U.S. Department of State's annual *Patterns of Global Terrorism* documents. Those responsible for the 9/11 terrorist attacks watched films about terrorist hijackings as part of their training. The federal government took notice of the country's creative minds in the immediate post–9/11 world when it asked for the entertainment industry's assistance in countering terrorism and discussing what possible targets terrorists might have in the U.S. To look for help in Hollywood was not a great leap; after all, Hollywood scriptwriters and producers have been "planning" elaborate anti–American terrorist attacks for decades, and the film industry has brought these fictional threatening and destructive images to worldwide audiences.

While the number of films on international terrorism is plentiful, not all of the movies have been popular among paying audiences. This study has analyzed how the U.S. commercial film industry has portrayed international terrorism in the films of the annual top fifty domestic box office from 1980 until September 11, 2001.

The Hollywood Terrorist versus the U.S. Department of State's Patterns of Global Terrorism Documents

Action-adventure films on international terrorism have kept up with the times and have updated fictional terrorist threats as real-life threats have changed in the U.S. foreign policy agenda. In the 1980s the popular Hollywood threat scenarios directly drew from the Reagan administration's agenda. The U.S. commercial film industry introduced terrorists of the communist Red Terror Network which had links to Latin America. Terrorists from the Middle East threatened American lives and interests in the region as terrorism originating in the Middle East started to raise its head as an anti–U.S. force, in particular since the 1983 bombings in Beirut, Lebanon.

Coming to the late 1980s and the turn of a new decade, the monster of communism disappeared and Hollywood discarded Cold War heroes and villains. The movie industry focused on urban threats of international terrorism on U.S. soil, bringing Western European villains from Germany, Northern Ireland and Britain, and also from the newly capitalist Russia. After the 1993 World Trade Center bombing by Islamic extremists, Hollywood reintroduced Middle Eastern terrorism, now as a threat by fundamentalist Islamic terrorists. This followed the latest forms of international terrorism, including the threat of weapons of mass destruction in terrorists' hands. Only one of the decade's films took the story away from a U.S.-focused script, while still portraying a story that was close to the country's political interests. In *Ronin* an undercover CIA agent in France tracks down a threat to the peace process in Northern Ireland.

The commercial film industry's worldview of international terrorism is quite narrow. The interconnected relationship between the mainstream media and government is reflected in news media and film portrayals of international terrorism. The U.S. mainstream news media focus on stories that are in American foreign policy interests. Hollywood has not looked much further. Screenwriters have their fictional terrorists borrow ideas from the latest terrorist news headlines as well as from the State Department's annual documents on global terrorism. However, while the State Department documents cover the whole world, both the mainstream news media and film industry find their villains and stories from regions that are somehow directly connected to the U.S. The mainstream news media constantly cover America's closest allies and main adversaries. These are also the stories that have been most popular among paying audiences in movie theaters.

In the time period from 1980 until September 11, 2001, Hollywood found most threats originating in the Middle East and the United Kingdom, both claiming five films of the sixteen movies that were among the most commercially successful films in the annual top fifty box office. The films that portrayed threats from the Middle East all had Arab Muslim villains: *Iron Eagle* (1986), *The Delta Force* (1986), *True Lies* (1994), *Executive Decision* (1996), and *The Siege* (1998). Hollywood used one British main villain in *Passenger 57* (1992). The four films that drew from the conflict in Northern Ireland introduced Northern Irish villains: *Patriot Games* (1992), *Blown Away* (1994), and *Ronin* (1998). *Blown Away* (1994) and *The Jackal* (1997) introduced Northern Irish heroes who had terrorist backgrounds.

The main threat arose in Latin America in two of the sixteen films, in *Commando* (1985) and *Die Hard 2: Die Harder* (1990). In these films the foreign antagonists had American military men as their accomplices. Steven E. de Souza was the screenwriter or co-screenwriter of both films.

Russia was the origin of the Hollywood terrorist in two films, *Invasion USA* (1985) and *Air Force One* (1997). In the 1980s Soviet Russia tried to harm and invade the U.S. with the assistance of Spanish-speaking Latin American associates in *Invasion USA*. A decade later, in the post–Cold War world, Russian nationalists were not welcoming capitalism, and took out their anger on the U.S. president in their effort to turn back time.

The last two of the sixteen films, the first and third installments of the *Die Hard* series, brought German brothers Hans and Simon Gruber onto U.S. soil. Both former left-wing terrorists, they came to the U.S. to look for their place in the capitalist world and their share of its profits in the new world order.

The Arab Hollywood Terrorist

While Arabs top the Hollywood list as the most popular screen terrorists, the actual number of films is low at five over the period of two decades. Two of the films, *Iron Eagle* and *The Delta Force*, are from 1986. Three of the films are from the 1990s, each distributed by a major Hollywood production and distribution company: *True Lies* (1994), *Executive Decision* (1996) and *The Siege* (1998).

The villains in *Iron Eagle* come from Bilyad, an obvious near-anagram for Libya, which was a 1980s adversary of the U.S. *The Delta Force* and *The Siege* refer to Palestine when bringing up their terrorists' background. They are also the only terrorists from the Middle East who are not insane or completely possessed by their hatred for the U.S. to the point of madness. However, both films fail to give a clear political motivation or goals for their terrorists. The Arab villains in *True Lies* and *Executive Decision* come from undefined countries, which not only trivializes terrorism by simply making any Arab the villain, but also stereotypes that ethnic group as all terrorists. In both films a male Arab Muslim's hatred of the U.S. is enough to motivate an attack on Americans. The terrorists want to kill Americans in large numbers but the films do not address what the villains aim to gain politically through these actions.

Each of the five films portrays the fictional Arab villains as Muslims, although only the films of the 1990s portray the religion of Islam, particularly fundamentalist interpretations of it which see the U.S. as an enemy of Islam, as a *motivating* force for the terrorists' acts. This development reflects the U.S. State Department's *Patterns of Global Terrorism* documents, which started to detail extremist religious views as a source of terrorist violence in the 1990s. The further the decade proceeded, the more information the State Department listed in particular on fundamentalist Islamic extremists as threats to the U.S., with a focus on Osama bin Laden's fundamentalist Sunni Islamic network, al Qaeda. While the Arab Muslim terrorist of Hollywood creations is incapable of having a clear political agenda for his vicious violent actions, Osama bin Laden has clearly stated his goals and motivations (also detailed in the State Department's annual documents). Bin Laden is against the U.S. and other Western influences in the Middle East, in particular in Saudi Arabia where the holy cities of Islam, Mecca and Medina are located. He has manifested the fact that he aims to drive foreign influences out of the Middle East and oust the Saudi ruling family from power, as well as other governments in the Middle East that in his view are influenced too much by the Western world. Additionally, bin Laden has stated the liberation of Palestine as one of his goals.[1] Furthermore, in the terrorist leader's view, the U.S. has declared a war on Islam, and therefore the duty of all Muslims is to kill Americans in order to wage a war against an enemy which should convert to Islam in order to purify itself from immorality and the lack of God's presence.[2] In bin Laden's own words in February 1998:

> First, for over seven years the United States has been occupying the lands of Islam in the holiest of places, the Arabian peninsula, plundering its riches, dictating to its rulers, humiliating its

people, terrorizing its neighbors, and turning its bases in the peninsula into a spearhead through which to fight the neighboring Muslim peoples.[3]

In the late 1990s it started to become clear to the State Department, as well as to the FBI and CIA, that Osama bin Laden was much more than just a financer of terrorism. In 1997 and 1998 several government agencies were working to bring bin Laden to justice in the U.S. In 1999 the FBI added him to its Ten Most Wanted Fugitives list in the aftermath of the 1998 bombings in Kenya and Tanzania against U.S. embassies. By that time al Qaeda's 9/11 attack plans had already been brewing for years.

In the 1990s Hollywood's fictional creations presented to the public terrorist attacks which resembled what al Qaeda was planning to do. In 1994 *True Lies* and in 1996 *Executive Decision* showed viewers international terrorists who aimed at mass casualties on U.S. soil. The first movie depicted nuclear fears while the second one told a story of a passenger plane, carrying a nerve toxin bomb, that the film's main villain was planning to crash in the U.S.

The film that comes the closest to the State Department's assessment of the main 1990s threats is *The Siege* (1998) which portrays events reminiscent of those perpetrated by al Qaeda. In the film, old U.S. allies turn on the U.S. because they feel betrayed by shifts in U.S. policy. Similarly, mujahideen fighters were allies when they and the U.S. had a common enemy in the Soviet Union in Afghanistan. The film's villains run a terrorist campaign in New York City which is similar to the 1993 plans of Islamic fundamentalists who attacked the World Trade Center, and also the plans of the group which was targeting New York City landmarks, the latter a plot which the FBI was able to preempt. The film also presents several pieces of factual information, such as rewards for information that leads to the capture of terrorists, and the cell structure of modern terrorist organizations.

The Northern Irish and British Hollywood Terrorist

Passenger 57 (1992) was the first of the sixteen films to bring a terrorist from the United Kingdom to threaten the United States. On the surface the British aristocratic terrorist has no counterpart in reality or in the State Department's documents. Scratching that image, the script gives the villain a terrorist past with links to real-life foreign terrorist organizations and state sponsors of terrorism. In addition to *Passenger 57*, Hollywood dug up terrorists in Northern Ireland. Actually, the second most covered form of international terrorism during the analysis period was terrorism originating in Northern Ireland. It was the topic of four films, each produced in the 1990s and distributed by a major studio or a minor major: *Patriot Games* (1992) by Paramount Pictures; *Blown Away* (1994) by Metro-Goldwyn-Mayer; *The Jackal* (1997) by Universal Pictures and Mutual Film Company; and *Ronin* (1998) by United Artists Pictures, part of Metro-Goldwyn-Mayer. In the films of the 1990s, the decade when the U.S. was actively involved in peace negotiations in Northern Ireland, the region's terrorism was the most attractive form of international terrorism among domestic viewers.

None of the four films portrays the most influential Northern Irish terrorist group, the Provisional Irish Republican Army (PIRA), in negative terms although the State Department categorized it as a terrorist group in the 1990s. Actually, PIRA terrorists either become heroes who have strong moral and ethical standards, as they do in *The Jackal* and *Blown Away*, although only the first film gives the PIRA a central role as the hero's background, while the second one just refers to the group between the lines. No PIRA terrorist is a threat to Americans. *Patriot Games*, *Blown Away* and *Ronin* all portray extremely violent villains who are members of PIRA splinter groups. As the PIRA did during the years of peace negotiations, these Hollywood productions denounce the fringe groups as too extreme. As is the case with the films which give no clear country of origin to their Arab villains, the lack of an organization name for the PIRA splinter groups simplifies terrorism when the films paint all splinter group terrorists with the same brush: the characters are overcome by their madness and/or the villain's personal vendetta against the hero. The films undermine the real-life splinter groups by misrepresenting their actions and motivations or, rather, by not assigning political or ideological motivations to the main villains.

In *The Jackal* an imprisoned PIRA terrorist comes to the rescue when the U.S. and Russia are seeking an international terrorist assassin known as the Jackal. In the 1970s and 1980s the real world was well aware of another Jackal, a Venezuelan called Ilich Ramírez Sánchez but better known to the world as Carlos the Jackal. France had captured this international terrorist assassin three years before the film was released. *The Jackal* is based on an earlier version of the film, 1973's *The Day of the Jackal*, itself based on Frederick Forsyth's 1971 novel about the attempt on French president Charles de Gaulle's life, one of many in the 1960s. Georges Henri Watin, the leader of the group that targeted de Gaulle in 1962, was known as the Jackal.

Other Hollywood Terrorists

Like the Middle East, Latin America is depicted as one-dimensional in Hollywood productions, following in the film traditions of stereotyping Latin Americans as greasers or criminals. In 1985 *Commando* brought U.S. policies in a fictional Central American country by the name of Val Verde to haunt a naturalized American colonel who is originally from the wrong side of the Iron Curtain, communist East Germany. A dictator whom the hero had helped to oust from power wants to replace the man the U.S. had helped to put in power. In the 1980s the U.S. was heavily involved in different parts of Latin America, supporting dictators whose interests coincided with the U.S. policy of rejecting leftist influences in the Americas. The film does not bring up the foreign villain's ideological background; it only presents him in a uniform as a cold man who hires former U.S. soldiers to go against their own country in his quest for power. Furthermore, the villain is willing to have a small girl, the hero's daughter, murdered in his pursuit for power.

Another film from the same year as *Commando*, the first film with international terrorist themes to break into the annual top fifty, was *Invasion USA*. When the Reagan administration emphasized the fear of communism and announced the Soviet Union to be the brains behind a worldwide communist Red Terror Network which threatened the U.S. and its interests around the world, in particular in Latin America, Hollywood imitated the fear on the big screen. In 1985 an American hero stopped a communist takeover in *Invasion USA*. Soviet Russians led terrorist attacks on innocent Americans with the aid of largely faceless Spanish-speaking accomplices, playing on the screen a Reaganite-era nightmare of a Soviet or Soviet-inspired attack on the U.S. from the south side of the border. The main villain came from Soviet Russia, the era's main U.S. adversary.

In the 1990s the communist fiend was largely buried in the grave of the Cold War. In *Die Hard 2: Die Harder* (1990) a former Central American ally in rejecting communism and his accomplices of the U.S. special forces are no longer heroes but need to be buried along with the Cold War. The film reflects the U.S. experience with Panama's General Manuel Noriega, a former anti-communist ally who was convicted of drug trafficking, racketeering and money laundering in the U.S. The U.S. captured him in January 1990 after a U.S. invasion of Panama.

Commando and *Die Hard 2: Die Harder* trivialize Latin American antagonists, depicting them as power-hungry and greedy men but only as the films' secondary villains. In both films current or former U.S. soldiers aid the films' ex-dictators, and in both films one is advanced to be the film's main villain. The use of Central American antagonists refers to real-life U.S. interests and involvement in the region in the 1970s and 1980s but does not address the actual threat of terrorism that American businesses and diplomats were facing in the region. This follows news media portrayals of terrorism against U.S. interests in Latin America, or rather, the lack of coverage of such terrorism. Similarly, in the two films the Latin American villains are not even important enough to rise to the main villain role, which is accorded to homegrown American villains. The characterization of these foreign villains from the south side of the border also replays old movie depictions of Latin America. According to Cortes, Hollywood has traditionally portrayed Latin American characters as dictators and, since the 1990s, as involved in drug cartels.[4] Neither film tries anything more complex in its depiction of Latin American characters.

After the end of the Cold War, communists of the old Soviet Union returned to make one more attempt to rescue their ideology in the most popular terrorist films among the North American theatergoers. In one of the most popular terrorist films ever, *Air Force One* (1997), Russian ultranationalists attack the U.S. president in their effort to stop capitalism invading the new Russia. But the new world order is in place, and the U.S. and Russia both support the new structures.

Hollywood films brought Euroterrorism across the Atlantic after the phenomenon had largely faded out in Europe. The Gruber brothers Hans and Simon, both former left-wing terrorists, are trying to make a life for themselves in a world where their ideology is old news. Originally from opposite sides of the Iron Curtain, Hans from West Germany and Simon from East Germany, the brothers use their old terror methods to claim a space in the new world order as master thieves. But their attempts to realize their capitalist dreams of prosperity die at the hands of police officer John McClane, for Hans in *Die Hard* (1988) and for Simon in *Die Hard with a Vengeance* (1995).

The end of the Cold War and the lack of one specific country as the ideological adversary of the United States forced Hollywood to update its offerings. As a result, the movie industry used its greatest variety of terrorists in the 1990s, but still focused only on a few regions, each relevant to immediate U.S. foreign policy interests. The film industry did not dare to try its luck with regions that the State Department had marked as threats to the U.S. but which the news media had not covered extensively, and which therefore were largely unknown to the public. For example, the State Department's list of state sponsors of terrorism has not changed much over the years. In the 1980s Libya, Iran, Syria and for a while also South Yemen were listed, as well as Cuba, and later also North Korea. From 1993 to 2001 the list was completely unchanged, consisting of Cuba, Iran, Iraq, Libya, North Korea, Sudan and Syria. While Hollywood films portrayed a variety of Middle Eastern threats, either directly or as links to different villains' pasts, North Korea and Sudan were missing from the films, just as they were missing from the mainstream news media portrayals of international terrorism before 9/11. Even the threat closest to the U.S., Cuba, only superficially figured in *Invasion USA*, as the likely country of origin of the Soviet Russian terrorist's Spanish-speaking accomplices.

The Hollywood Terrorist's Weapons

Hollywood's choice of weapons in terrorists' hands reflects the State Department data on the most used methods of terrorism. The films in which terrorists use or plan to use bombings, by far the most common terrorist method, are *Invasion USA*, *Die Hard*, *Die Hard 2: Die Harder*, *Die Hard with a Vengeance*, *Blown Away*, *Ronin* and *The Siege*. Suicide bombings, a method the U.S. started to experience in the Middle East in the 1980s, are depicted in two of the films of the 1990s, *Executive Decision* and *The Siege*. *Executive Decision* portrays a suicide bombing in Europe. Additionally, the film's Arab Muslim villain has a bigger suicide mission in mind, a plan which al Qaeda executed with a twist on 9/11. In the film the main terrorist plans to explode a bomb by crashing a passenger airliner in Washington, D.C. Five years later al Qaeda made planes crash into targets on U.S. soil, using the planes with their bellies full of fuel as bombs. In *The Siege*, terrorists perform suicide attacks in New York City, but on a smaller scale than what real-life terrorists with fundamentalist Islamic motivations had in mind in the 1990s.

While bombings are the weapon of choice for real-life terrorists, for Hollywood's traditional one-on-one confrontations bombings do not give much flexibility for extended physical confrontations between the hero and the villain. Unlike real-life terrorism, guns and assault weapons are the number one choice of the Hollywood terrorist. They can be found in regular use in *Invasion USA*, *Commando*, *The Delta Force*, the first three *Die Hard* films, *Passenger 57*, *Patriot Games*, *The Jackal*, *Ronin*, *Executive Decision*, *True Lies*, and *Air Force One*. Portable rocket launchers add to the weapons arsenal in *Invasion USA*, *The Delta Force*, and *Commando*. While hijackings are very rare in real life, four of the sixteen films portray a hijacking: *The Delta Force*, *Executive Decision*, *Passenger 57* and *Air Force One*. Additionally, *Die Hard 2: Die Harder* tells the story of the hijacking of an airport. *Iron Eagle* touches on the topic of flying, but in that film the terrorist villain takes an American hostage after shooting down his F-16 plane. The villain's method is the threat to execute the American hostage.

In the late 1990s the State Department warned that terrorist organizations, in particular al Qaeda, were trying to acquire weapons of mass destruction. Before the State Department warnings, Hollywood had already portrayed the threat on U.S. soil. In 1994 in *True Lies*, fundamentalist Islamic terrorists from the Middle East planned to use nuclear weapons against targets in the U.S. Two years later in *Executive Decision*, another set of fundamentalist Islamic terrorists from the Middle East tried to crash a hijacked plane which had a nerve toxin bomb on board. The villains of the two films reflected the fears of the 1990s when the State Department highlighted extreme religious views as a growing threat in the world.

The American Counterterrorism Hero

Before 9/11 there were some fifty different agencies involved in American counterterrorism efforts. In a crisis situation on U.S. soil the FBI, under the Justice Department, was the lead federal agency, and abroad, the State Department. But as *The 9/11 Commission Report* points out, the counterterrorism structure was slow to react to the events of September 11, 2001, when, for example, the order to shoot down United flight 93, which was threatening Washington, D.C., was never delivered to pilots. Furthermore, the cooperation between different agencies was not working as desired. The confusion over which agency was in charge is also reflected in the sixteen films. They portray law enforcement, the U.S. military, CIA and FBI agents, as well as agents of fictional federal agencies as the country's counterterrorist weapons. The films do to an extent hew to the separation between terrorism outside and inside the U.S. borders. Primarily the films have introduced the FBI in the lead and local law enforcement as helping when countering terrorist threats on U.S. soil, although not always effectively, especially if the film's hero is not from the FBI. When countering terrorism outside the U.S.

borders, Hollywood has not found the State Department sexy enough to handle the cases, so the films have brought in the CIA, and have also promoted fictional terrorist acts from crimes to warfare, which requires military firepower.

The heroes are all somehow linked to federal or local agencies, only three of them not directly on their payroll. Doug Masters in *Iron Eagle* is an Air Force colonel's son with access to an Air Force base and F-16 aircraft. By the film's end he also becomes part of the official power structure when he is accepted into the Air Force Academy. Declan Mulqueen in *The Jackal* is an imprisoned member of the PIRA who helps the FBI and the Russian police to catch an international terrorist. John Cutter in *Passenger 57* is a freshly hired airline counterterrorism security chief who is highly respected by the FBI. The heroes in *Commando* and *The Delta Force* represent the U.S. military. The protagonists of *Invasion USA*, *Patriot Games*, and *Ronin* are current or former members of the CIA. The hero of *The Siege* is from the FBI. *True Lies* gives its hero a federal agency as his background, but only a fictional one. Law enforcement is the hero's profession in the *Die Hard* films as well as in *Blown Away*. *Air Force One* portrays the ultimate attack against the American power structure when the film terrorists target the U.S. president. Holder of the highest office in the land, he also has a military background as a decorated hero of the Vietnam War.

Dr. Grant of *Executive Decision* has no military or law enforcement background, but he is connected to the official power structure. He is a civilian analyst in a think tank that is serving the federal government. In the film he works with a special military unit which is in charge of the killing of the film's terrorist villains. As a civilian, however, Dr. Grant's hands are clean of killing. Also, the hero of *Blown Away*, Jimmy Dove, who is leaving behind his terrorist past and hero's life, avoids killing his nemesis. A new emerging hero helps Dove to escape when the film's villain dies in an explosion the terrorist had set up himself. In addition, in *Ronin*, the film's undercover and shady CIA agent is saved by his French accomplice when the men together save the day and Vincent kills the mad Northern Irish terrorist.

While these films have largely supported the prevailing power structures by portraying heroic protagonists who are federal or local law enforcement officials or military representatives, the films have also shown their heroes dealing with moronic and inefficient government representatives. These are narrative methods to elevate the hero and his prowess as the only official representative who can save the U.S. The films emphasize that an individual American male hero can make a difference.

American Counterterrorism Policy in Films

The commercial film industry's fictional foreign terrorist has borrowed story ideas from the terrorist threats and the U.S. counterterrorism policy that the U.S. Department of State has detailed in the department's annual documents on global terrorism. However, the classical Hollywood narrative structure does not always easily swallow reality when creating film commodities whose goal is to make a profit at the box office. Hollywood screenwriters have not been ashamed to distort reality, both in the case of terrorism and U.S. counterterrorism, if the real story does not fit the business goals and traditionally profitable screenwriting formats.

The U.S. Department of State has been in charge of defining American counterterrorism since the 1970s. It details the four main parts of the U.S. counterterrorism policy as:

- **First**, make no concessions to terrorists and strike no deals.
- **Second**, bring terrorists to justice for their crimes.

- **Third,** isolate and apply pressure on states that sponsor terrorism to force them to change their behavior.
- **Fourth,** bolster the counterterrorist capabilities of those countries that work with the United States and require assistance.[5]

The action-adventure film format has clearly contradicted one of the policies in every film of the sixteen films: the bringing of terrorists to justice for their crimes. In Hollywood action-adventure film terms, justice translates into a one-on-one fight between the protagonist and the antagonist which ends in the killing of the villain at the hero's hands. This follows the traditional action-adventure film format. The villain's death is justified since his killer is usually an official representative of the prevailing power structure. The hero is protecting the way of life of all Americans. As Sobchack points out, traditionally adventure film heroes restore the prevailing power when they defeat a variety of threats to that structure.[6] In the late 1990s real life imitated Hollywood fiction when the U.S. borrowed from the traditional action-adventure film Hollywood ending. President Clinton gave an order which allowed the targeting and killing of Osama bin Laden, eventually even if bystanders might also be killed.

Hollywood occasionally pays attention to the other three counterterrorism parts. Several films have addressed the point of making no concessions to terrorists and striking no deals. The only film to clearly break that rule is *Air Force One* in which the U.S. president, in order to save his wife and daughter, gives in to the Russian terrorists' demands to have a terrorist leader released. The film depicts in an unflattering light the secretary of defense, who insists that the country should not change its policies even when the president and his family are at risk. Naturally President Marshall saves the situation and defeats the terrorists, and Russians kill the terrorist leader right after his release.

The third and fourth aspects of the U.S. counterterrorism policy have not attracted much attention from filmmakers. State sponsorship of terrorism does not translate well into stories on the big screen as they must reduce complex international relations into a story of an individual protagonist against an individual antagonist. *Iron Eagle* is rare in that it depicts a state sponsor of terrorism as the enemy, the main villain being a Libya-like country's minister of defense. While the film crudely distorted international terrorism and American counterterrorism in its heroic story of a male American teenager becoming a man when he rescues his father by bombing "Bilyad" to pieces, the film did follow the U.S. policy of not giving in to terrorist demands, and of isolating and applying pressure on the states which sponsor terrorism. Another 1986 film, *The Delta Force*, referred to Iran as the film terrorists' supporter but did not introduce the country as the film's main villain. While in the 1980s the U.S. largely interpreted terrorism as a problem of state sponsors, they were mostly missing in pre–9/11 films. Hollywood qualified state sponsors of terrorism for exposition, for example, Libya and Syria, when discussing terrorist villains' backgrounds and their past connections. In the 1980s and the 1990s state sponsorship was a bad film commodity because it did not easily translate into a heroic, filmic story of an American protagonist confronting a foreign terrorist villain.

Some of the sixteen films portray international cooperation but none of them shows efforts to bolster other countries' counterterrorism. Each film portrays crisis situations in which immediate action must be taken in order to counter and prevent terrorist threats or acts. While there is no time for international training in a crisis situation, several of the films show how the U.S. cooperates with other countries. For example, in *The Delta Force* the U.S. cooperated with Israel and Algeria. In the next decade's films the U.S. received information on suspected Arab Muslim terrorists from Israel. In the late 1990s Hollywood gave a nod to the fact that its foreign market, in particular in Europe, was important to its revenues. *The Jackal* and *Ronin* portrayed an international set of characters and locations. However, mostly the popular films on international terrorism pre–9/11 were stories about American heroes' efforts to save the country largely on their own, or with sidekicks.

The Hollywood Terrorist and the Action-Adventure Film Genre

The analyzed action-adventure films on international terrorism support the action-adventure film genre traditions by drawing on the successful formats of the past. These include the use of male, usually white, heroes against mad and primarily foreign villains, heroic one-on-one physical fights, and massive killings of Third World citizens. In addition, the films include heroes' prodigal journeys, romantic subplots, and sidekicks from minority groups.

As in news, also in drama a conflict is the essence of the story.[7] For example, international news is structured as "us versus them."[8] Hollywood's method to dramatize scripts that draw ideas from world politics is to reduce complex events of international relations to conflicts between two people.[9] Individual characters are Hollywood films' causal agents,[10] so each story needs a hero and a villain whom viewers can easily identify. To further dramatize a storyline, in each film it is the foreign villain who initiates the film's events, and therefore forces the protagonist to become involved.

Some of the films combine a foreign threat with a domestic villain. For example, both films that bring threats directly from Latin America, *Commando* and *Die Hard 2: Die Harder*, have the reason for the terrorists' actions in former Central American dictators. These men's American special forces supporters do the dirty work on U.S. soil. In *Commando* the U.S. involvement in a fictional Central American country, Val Verde, brings a former dictator and his American accomplices to force an American colonel to help him to return to power. In *Die Hard: Die Harder* the main villain is from the U.S., an anti-communist fighter who tries to secure freedom for a former U.S. ally. The two characters from Val Verde appear only in supporting roles to the two films' domestic villains.

In three films, *Patriot Games*, *Blown Away* and *Ronin*, the villains come from Northern Ireland, from groups that have left the PIRA because they want to use harsher, more violent methods. While part of the conflict in Northern Ireland draws from the centuries-old conflict between the Catholics and the Protestants, none of the four films that draw from the conflict in Northern Ireland, *The Jackal* in addition to the above three, brings that up. The other European terrorists come from Britain (*Passenger 57*), the Soviet Union (*Invasion USA*), Russia (*Air Force One*) and Germany (*Die Hard* and *Die Hard with a Vengeance*). In *The Jackal* Bruce Willis plays an American who is an international terrorist assassin for hire.

The terrorists of the five films with Middle Eastern background are all Muslims. The films mention religion only if the villain comes from the Middle East. The films of the 1980s only briefly refer to Islam while in the films of the 1990s each of the terrorists draws his motivation from Islam, supposedly from its extremist forms. Otherwise the films leave the political and social goals and context of the villains largely untouched, except for *The Siege*. But that film also largely draws the villain's motivation from vengeance with a touch of religious fundamentalism while not explaining the primary goal of the film's terrorists. Although the three 1990s films refer to Islam, particularly to fundamentalist Islamic views, and use the religion as terrorists' motivation, at the same time the films do a poor job of portraying any of the terrorists as characters who would actually act according to their religious views. This follows news media coverage of international terrorism which brings up the topic of religion when terrorists are motivated by their extremist interpretation of Islam. In contrast, mainstream news rarely touches on the topic if terrorism is motivated by extremist Christian views.

The depiction of villains in the 1990s films on Arab terrorism and on British and Northern Irish terrorism is similar. Madness and vengeance are the driving forces for the Arab villains in *True Lies* and *Executive Decision*, and also in the 1986 *Iron Eagle*, as well as for the British and Northern Irish antagonists in *Passenger 57*, *Blown Away*, *Patriot Games* and *Ronin*. Previous research has argued that Hollywood portrays Arabs as insane and blood-hungry villains due to their ethnicity and religion. While that type of a portrayal can be found in three of the five films on Arab terrorism, these character traits are not reserved only for Arab characters. Rather, insanity and brutality as the main villain's character traits follow the action-adventure film genre traditions. Villains are characters whose deaths have to be justified in the end. A villain's madness and brutality distances him from viewers to the point that the villain *deserves* his death, often a brutal one, at the film's end and at the hero's hands after a traditional one-on-one confrontation.

Hollywood writers have pushed the boundaries of international terrorism when portraying fictional international terrorists who largely draw their motivation from madness and an insane need for vengeance. As Pillar points out: "Terrorism is not a matter of momentary rage or impulse."[11] The National Foreign Assessment Center's 1979 report directly addressed the problem of including in the annual governmental data on international terrorism violence that is caused by insanity or by criminal activity that is motivated by search for personal gain. According to the center and its successor in the data collection, the State Department, terrorism is a *politically* motivated act. Acts caused and/or motivated by insanity or criminal activity are not acts of terrorism, and therefore their inclusion in any terrorism data would contaminate the data.

When the film industry mixes real-life international terrorism and traditional film formats in the portrayal of terrorist villains in its storylines, it produces pictures that producers and distributors claim to be terrorist films but which in most cases are not. The Hollywood terrorist does not have political motivations but is usually motivated by different levels of insanity or criminal activity. These are the driving forces for the foreign villains of *Invasion USA* (Soviet Russian), *Iron Eagle* (an Arab from "Bilyad"; a look-alike for Libyan leader Qadhafi), *Passenger 57* (British aristocrat), *Patriot Games* (Northern Irish extremist), *Blown Away* (Northern Irish extremist), *Ronin* (Northern Irish extremist), *Executive Decision* (Arab Muslim of an undefined country), *True Lies* (Arab Muslim of an undefined country). In *Commando* it is the domestic antagonist on the foreign villain's payroll who has a deep personal hatred and vendetta against the hero. In addition, the villains of *Die Hard* and *Die Hard with a Vengeance*, the Gruber brothers, are former terrorists turned common criminals. They only pretend to be terrorists, so the hero reacts to the crisis situations as if they were terrorist acts.

Eight of the films depict foreign villains who keep their sanity, and who are rational and systematic (if anti–American) in their actions. Such are the Palestinian antagonists of *The Delta Force* and *The Siege*. In *Commando* the film's Central American secondary antagonist is rational in his plans, but the movie's domestic main villain is a man whose actions are motivated by his insane personal vendetta against the hero. The films that portray international terrorists who are businesslike in their killings and actions are *Die Hard* (the German Hans Gruber) and *Die Hard 2: Die Harder* (General Ramon Esperanza of the fictional Central American country Val Verde and his domestic accomplice, the main antagonist, Colonel Stuart). In *The Jackal* the international terrorist assassin, originally from the U.S., is an effective killing machine. His composure only cracks briefly, during the film's final confrontation. Even Simon Gruber of *Die Hard with a Vengeance*, whom the film's police psychiatrist calls "nuts" with a megalomania personality, is very systematic and rational in his actions. Yet despite the other characters' descriptions of him, Simon Gruber does not act as a madman. *Air Force One* sets up two veterans of lost wars against each other, the Russian Ivan Korshunov, who is passionate about his country's great communist past but not insane, and U.S. president James Marshall, a defender of the new world order and his family.

While the action-adventure film genre's love for madmen undermines the films' claim to be terrorist films, each of the sixteen films does depict international terrorism, even if in disguise for a robbery, under the State Department's definitions. In each film the villain and his supporters commit premeditated acts and threaten noncombatants. Also, it is foreign nationals who threaten the U.S., in some cases with American assistance. However, most of the films are missing an essential part of terrorism — political motivation — and therefore undermine the films' terrorism theme. Rather, it is simplified into a fight between the hero and the villain. This follows the classical Hollywood cinema structure but reduces a large political phenomenon into an individual adversarial relationship. The reliance on the action-adventure genre tradition undermines the reality of international terrorism, its threats to any society, and how effectively to counter terrorism.

In some of the sixteen films the screenplay turns up the heat by introducing a previous adversarial relationship between the hero and the villain, as do *Invasion USA*, *Commando*, *Blown Away* and *The Jackal*. In *Die Hard with a Vengeance* the brother of Hans Gruber, whom John McClane killed in *Die Hard*, plays a cat-and-mouse game with the hero but has no real emotional attachment to the killing of his brother. In *The Siege* the hero's female sidekick supported the man, who turns out to be the main terrorist, when he was a U.S. ally, and is still sleeping with him in order to control him and receive information. The stakes are even higher when the terrorist poses a personal threat to the protagonist's family, as is the case in *Commando*, *Iron Eagle*, *Die Hard*, *Die Hard 2: Die Harder*, *Patriot Games*, *Blown Away*, *True Lies* and *Air Force One*. *Passenger 57* and *Executive Decision* use similar storylines when the film's hero shows romantic interest in the flight attendant who helps him, and therefore is concerned about her safety. Even in *Ronin*, which portrays a committed undercover CIA agent, the protagonist's interest in a female terrorist endangers his job. *The Delta Force* is the only film to focus on the job and keep emotions at bay, except for the moment when the unit loses one of its own.

The American Counterterrorism Hero and the Action-Adventure Film Genre

The heroes of the sixteen films are all male Western citizens. The only non–American hero is Mulqueen, a PIRA terrorist in prison in the U.S., whom *The Jackal* advances to the role of protagonist. Also, the hero of *Blown Away* is originally from Northern Ireland, but has lived in the U.S. for years and has become an American hero. Hollywood even promotes a man from the wrong side of the Iron Curtain, East Germany, to become the hero in *Commando*. The other heroes are "purebred" Americans, with all–American accents, which further contrasts the villains' accented English. Two of the sixteen films portray an African American hero, Anthony "Hub" Hubbard (Denzel Washington) in *The Siege* and John Cutter (Wesley Snipes) in *Passenger 57*. The other fourteen films portray white heroes.

The heroes' religious background is left ambiguous, though in several of the films the hero and other American characters use "Christ" and "Jesus Christ" in their dialogue, but that is the only clear reference to Christianity in the films. Religion only matters if the religion is Islam, even in the case when the character is a sidekick, as in *The Siege*. As discussed in the previous chapters, to portray the hero's sidekick from the same ethnic group, and in this case, also from the same religious group, as the villain, is a Hollywood attempt to avoid accusations of offering negative stereotypes of certain groups.

The American Counterterrorism Hero's Sidekicks

In three of the sixteen films the hero's sidekick is a woman. The first film to portray a female sidekick was *Commando*. It introduced Cindy, a mixed-race woman and the film's only sidekick. However, once the real violent action started between the hero and his adversaries, the muscled hero worked alone. *The Jackal* and *The Siege* both presented a strong female sidekick but balanced their presence with a male minority sidekick, an African American and Arab-American, respectively. *Passenger 57* and *Executive Decision* portrayed African American female flight attendants assisting the hero, but both characters represented the story's romantic interest rather than sidekick. Only *Invasion USA* was a film totally without a sidekick when the action started. That film made the terrorists kill off the hero's Native American friend at the end of the first act. As Parenti observed in the early 1990s, if a minority character appeared in a film, the character's purpose was often to give his or her life for the hero.[12] In *Invasion USA* the friend's death was the catalyst that motivated the hero to become involved in action.

As times change, also Hollywood changes. Minorities have become more visible in public life and the media, although they are still underrepresented in mainstream popular and news media portrayals in comparison to their percentage of the U.S. population. The growth of minority population has helped minority film characters to stay alive. In the eight films which portrayed a minority sidekick, he, and in *Commando*, she, survived. In the 1990s the only sidekicks to die were strong white women in law enforcement who entered the man's world and fully took part in the physical and intellectual action. They were the minority characters of 1990s action-adventure films. While in the past it was the role of the racial or ethnic minority sidekick to give his (rarely her) life for the hero, in the 1990s male minority sidekicks survived while the strong white women who professionally dared to enter the male hero's world as heroes in their own right died for the male hero and the U.S. In *The Jackal* and *The Siege* the strong female sidekicks die at the Hollywood terrorist's hands and therefore leave the man's world of action-adventure to male heroes. The women are sacrificial lambs who provide the final motivation for the hero to protect his society from the latest terrorist threat. The other female characters in popular 1990s action-adventure films, who on the surface were strong career women as wives and possible romantic interests, still filled the traditional role of women: they had to wait, admire and stay pretty while the male hero was saving the day. In the 1980s, flight attendant Cindy in *Commando* combined the two roles. Her actions were essential for the hero's success, but she stayed behind when Colonel Matrix actually encountered his main nemesis and his group. In return for that, Cindy stayed alive and had a promise of a possible romantic match.

While two African Americans star as heroes and six African Americans as sidekicks, the latter in *Iron Eagle*, *Die Hard*, *Die Hard 2: Die Harder*, *Die Hard with a Vengeance*, *Blown Away*, and *The Jackal*, Asian Americans and Latinos are missing in these roles. The Arab-American sidekick in *The Siege* partially evens the score between evil Arabs and good Arab-Americans, as does the secondary sidekick in *True Lies*, whose ethnicity could be traced to the Middle East due to the character's name, Faisil, and his appearance. However, these two characters cannot hide the fact that on film, Arabs and Muslims are seen as outsiders in American society. Even in *The Siege* all Arabs become suspects, including the sidekick's family, when one group targets New York City. The film's attempt to counter racism is not very effective when it does not provide character depth beyond its surface portrayal of Arabs and Islam.

In two of the films, *The Delta Force* and *Executive Decision*, the hero's sidekick is his whole multi-ethnic unit. In *Air Force One* the hero is a one-man fighting machine in the first part of the film until he gets help from the plane's hostages after he has released them.

Portrayals of Women and Family

During the Reagan presidency Hollywood's answer to the women's movement was to deny women and sexuality in action and action-adventure films, and to portray muscular one-man fighting machines. This largely applies to the analyzed films of the Reagan era. Previous research has argued that Hollywood awarded the hero with a wife and family in the 1990s to better match contemporary American society. Although that is partially true in the studied films, the complete absence of sons in the movies also points to the ideas of previous decades when female characters were in the films either to be protected by the hero, seduced by the hero, or to be seducers of the hero. As women started to appear in films in bigger numbers, there was no room for a son to compete with his father for women's attention. The only children present in the films are preteen or teenage daughters. The only son portrayed is actually the protagonist of one of the films, *Iron Eagle*, which tells the story of a teenage boy becoming a man when he saves his father. The film follows the Reaganite cinema approaches of a strong father-son relationship and male bonding.

The Hollywood message is that male characters, whether children or adults, do not need heroes, while female characters do. The terrorist film, like other action-adventure films, offers stories about men, as both the heroes and the terrorists are men. It is true that in the 1990s women repeatedly appeared in bigger roles, but their characters functioned to provide a home life which the terrorist was endangering. If the female was on the terrorist's side, she was a treacherous, attractive woman who threatened the hero due to her sexuality.

The films' women characters follow the traditional genre portrayals, drawing from women's role in war films and westerns. War films traditionally focus on men. If a woman appears in a war film, which is rare, she is a target of men's desire and therefore a threat to the male hero's mission. A woman would make a man vulnerable in war conditions because she would draw his focus away from the war.[13] This idea is illogical and devalues women. The Hollywood hero, supposedly a strong man, cannot control his desires, thus putting the blame for his dirty thoughts on the women. That approach supports patriarchal and conservative values which keep women at home as the weak and helpless gender which needs men to run society and their lives for them.

In Western films women have traditionally represented civilization, family and community.[14] The films that depict heroes who have families fall under this category. The first two *Die Hard* films, *Patriot Games*, *True Lies*, *Blown Away* and *Air Force One* portray women who have their own careers and children. Their role in the films is to stay put and be saved by the hero and remind him of the importance of family. Unlike in traditional westerns where the hero rides away into the sunset, these protagonists do stay with the women of their lives. In the third *Die Hard* film the hero's family loses to male comradeship. In *Iron Eagle* women and family signify home and community, ideals that they uphold while the hero does the man's job: fighting for his family. *Executive Decision* and *Passenger 57* are similar in their depiction of female flight attendants who are strong women and romantic targets. However, each flight attendant's primary role is still to be protected by the hero. They act according to the hero's instructions as they are not capable of saving themselves and others on their own. Only the hero is smart and strong enough to save the situation and everyone caught in it.

In *Invasion USA* the hero barely reacts to the film's female character. He is similar to a lonely rider who has no interest in or time for women but to rescue them. An interesting exception to the rule is *Commando*, also from the Reaganite cinema era. The film depicts a strong female sidekick from a minority group who is essential for the hero's rescue. It is the study's only film which allows a strong female character to stay alive, although she is still depicted as a screaming and scared woman, and does not fully take part in the rescue effort. In both *The Siege* and *The Jackal* the strong woman is a target of the hero's desire. She is killed so he can stay strong. In *Ronin* the hero's desire makes him weak and makes him compromise his job as an undercover agent, but in this film the threat the woman poses is removed by the woman's decision to leave the hero.

The Delta Force from the Reaganite cinema era is a pure war film in its portrayal of male comradeship. While the film does depict a strong female character as the person who communicates between the terrorists and the hostages onboard, she and the hero do not meet in the film. The protagonist and his unit never have to face the danger of a woman and their desire for her.

Portrayals of Romance

According to Maltby, almost nine out of ten Hollywood films have romance as a primary or secondary storyline.[15] This study supports Maltby's findings. Of the sixteen films, only one has absolutely no romantic development. *The Delta Force* focuses completely on male comradeship. The other fifteen films either hint at romance or have the hero becoming or being involved in a romantic relationship.

Invasion USA portrays a female journalist who constantly runs into Matt Hunter (Chuck Norris). As is traditional, Hunter saves his possible romantic interest but he does not drive off into the sunset with her or take the story in any way further. The primary story of *Iron Eagle* is on a father/mentor-son relationship, but the film also grants the heroic teenage son a girlfriend. However, the hero has to leave her behind when his father needs him. *Die Hard with a Vengeance* focuses on the relationship of a mismatched interracial male partnership, but cannot completely ignore the wife character in the first two films. This film allows hero John McClane to discuss his failed marriage and his attempt to try to make things better.

The other twelve films introduce a clear heterosexual romantic interest as a wife, colleague, or a female flight accomplice. In *The Siege* and *The Jackal* the female sidekicks give their lives for the counterterrorism fight. In the other ten films the hero patches up his marriage, stays in a happy marriage, or the film ends with a promise of a relationship between the hero and his romantic interest. Each of the films supports a heterosexual coupling.

In protecting its commodities and avoiding controversies, Hollywood has been quite careful with whom the industry allows to become romantically involved on the screen. Heterosexual couples are white married couples, as in *Die Hard*, *Die Hard 2: Die Harder*, *Patriot Games*, *Blown Away*, *True Lies* and *Air Force One*. The 1980s Reaganite cinema films that barely admitted the existence of women, *Invasion USA* and *Iron Eagle*, also portrayed a white female interest for the film's hero. The white heroes of *The Jackal* and *Ronin* also had romantic interest in white international females, but neither story ended happily. In *The Jackal* the Russian female major dies at the end of act two, motivating the hero and making him realize what the villain was planning to do. In *Ronin* the CIA agent could stay a strong spy only if the threat to his work, a Northern Irish woman, left him since he was not willing to give her up.

Two of the films, *Commando* and *Executive Decision*, tried audience reactions to interracial coupling when they brought together a white hero and minority female interest, with a promise of a romance at the end. *Passenger 57* was the only film to show an African American coupling, which took place between the hero and the film's flight attendant.

The Siege was the only film that was brave enough to pair minority men with a white woman. However, Elise Kraft, the CIA operative who was sleeping with an Arab Muslim enemy to obtain information, was an unsavory character whom the terrorist eventually killed before she had a chance to realize her possible romance with the film's upstanding African American hero. Before 9/11 Hollywood was not ready to test a real romance with sexual encounters, or with a promise of them, between an African American man, or any other minority man, and a white woman in action-adventure films. She could sleep with the enemy for pillow talk but she had to pay for it with her life. In the late 1990s Hollywood was still too afraid to test what kind of a commodity it would be to portray a white woman having a real romance based on love and mutual respect with a minority man.

Pre–9/11 Hollywood action-adventure heroes were strong heterosexual men. The only film to show a same-sex romantic moment was *The Jackal*. The international terrorist for hire, played by Bruce Willis, tenderly kissed a gay man whose apartment he needed for his assignment, only to shoot him later in cold blood when the man got in his way.

Screen Violence

Fifteen of the sixteen films are rated R. Only *Iron Eagle* has a PG-13 rating. In other words, the content of virtually all the films is not considered suitable for audiences younger than 17 years of age if not accompanied with an adult. In action-adventure films the main content concern is violence.

In this study the films with the highest body counts were the four films of the 1980s, *Invasion USA, Commando, Iron Eagle* and *The Delta Force*, as well as *True Lies*, from 1994. The terrorists killed several hundred Americans in *The Siege* but the movie did not actually show large numbers of deaths on the screen. Instead it focused on the aftermath of terrorist attacks and their impact on civil society.

The four 1980s films relied on massive firepower that destroyed the lives of large numbers of villains. In the 1990s the killings performed by the protagonist and the antagonist were quite even in numbers in the films that depicted German, Russian, British and Northern Irish threats, while *True Lies* with Arab villains presented a more traditional portrayal, that is, the killing of large numbers of Third World citizens. Austria's gift to the U.S. film industry and political life, Arnold Schwarzenegger, gave the villains no opportunity in *Commando* and *True Lies* to respond to his character's massive arsenal of knives, guns, automatic weapons and even rocket launchers. It was the hero who killed masses of his opponents while the villains only got a few, if any, shots in; they only threatened violence. Violence was most extreme in these films, yet it was not the terrorists but the films' American heroes who performed the killings. The Arab and Latin American villains served as props in these movies, only to be killed in a variety of creative ways by the hero. Similar to news media coverage of foreign countries, the further away the film villains are from the U.S., the more stereotypical their image is and the higher their body count. In contrast, Western and Soviet Russian and post–Cold War Russian antagonists were accorded individual deaths at the American hero's hands in both decades.

For example, in *Commando* only the main foreign villain of the Central American opponents warranted an individual death at the colonel's hands; domestic villains on former dictator Arius's payroll had individual encounters with the hero. The 1990s movies followed the format and focused on an individual fight between the hero and the villain, and the hero and the villain's individual accomplices, adding the number of recognizable villains whom the protagonist can kill in spectacular and entertaining ways. In the 1990s, and in particular with European villains, Hollywood heroes killed terrorists one by one, as if going through an obstacle course, until getting to the finishing line of the final one-on-one confrontation with the main villain. In video game style the protagonist would proceed through different difficulty levels, from weaker villains to the strongest villain by the film's end. The payoff was the killing of the main terrorist antagonist after a spectacular showcase of violence, and the saving of the country and the hero's family or his new possible romantic interest.

Malik discusses that racist language was developed to justify the killing of people of the less developed world when more developed countries were conquering those countries and their natural resources.[16] The British and other colonial masters relied on massive firepower that they used against natives who could not match the weaponry of the Western world. Similarly, in Hollywood action-adventure films about international terrorism the lives of Third World citizens have low value. The heroes of the films that portray Arab and Latin American villains in the 1980s, and Arab villains in *True Lies*, kill a much larger number of people than the heroes of the films in which the villains come from countries that are culturally and ideologically closer to the U.S. This even applies to main ideological antagonists, Soviet Russian villains of *Invasion USA* and the antagonists of the new capitalist Russia in *Air Force One*.

In cinematic terms, the films are full of weak violence, in other words, violence which is produced for special effects. Viewers have no emotional involvement with the targets of violence unless the victims are on the hero's side, and in that case they are presented with a background which creates audience identification and sympathy for them. Computerized special effects have helped movies to portray more spectacular acts of terrorism than what the real world offered before September 11, 2001. Exploding buildings, nuclear weapons, massive massacres, fires, airliner hijackings and bombings have entertained viewers worldwide. Just as news has to be visually interesting for television audiences in order for a story to be profitable,[17] commercially produced terrorist films have offered viewers spectacular visions of violence and threats of violence on the big screen, ending each story in the hero's killing spree when he has removed the global terrorist threat to the United States.

Some of the films do portray strong violence, touching on the finality of death or true consequences of violent action.[18] In each case the screen violence targets a close family member of the protagonist or humanizes some of the terrorists' victims with a backstory, as in, for example, *The Delta Force*. The pain of the Jewish families whose male family members the terrorists take away is shown in the tears of their wives and daughters. A shot of an elderly man's arm reveals tattooed numbers. This survivor of a Nazi death camp somberly accepts that he is again targeted because of his ethnicity and religion. The family-centered films *Patriot Games* and *Air Force One*, which both star Harrison Ford, portray the toll that sudden and unexpected violence takes on a family, especially when the target is the family's young daughter.

The majority of the sixteen films portray good violence, that is, violence that the prevailing power structure and its representatives practice. In the analyzed films, as discussed above, the heroes are overwhelmingly representatives of the U.S. military and federal and local power structures. Good violence that American protagonists practice by far exceeds bad violence which terrorist villains practice, and which society condemns as illegal. However, most of the villains' violence is rather a threat of violence, and in most cases a personal threat to the hero.

The Hollywood Terrorist and the Mainstream News Media

The skin color and national origin of the villain are the deciding factors for how many and how villains die in the sixteen films. Similar to news coverage of international events, the further away from the U.S. a country is in cultural, political and religious terms, the more stereotypical the images of the country's citizens are in the news media.[19] Also, the further away, the bigger the number of the people killed needs to be for a story to be covered. The film portrayals of this study largely follow the mainstream news media trends. Third World citizens die in large numbers in *Commando*, *Iron Eagle*, *The Delta Force* and *True Lies*. When a Western or Russian Hollywood terrorist targets American citizens on their own soil, the hero's firepower is reduced and the conflicts focus on one-on-one confrontations. Even in the middle of the massacres of the 1985 films *Invasion USA* and *Commando*, and the 1986 *The Delta Force*, the hero found individual encounters with Soviet Russian and American villains, respectively, in 1985, and with Palestinian terrorists in Lebanon in 1986.

The news media are central in modern international terrorism which relies on distributing messages of terrorist acts and threats to audiences via mass media. In the studied sixteen films only *The Siege* and *The Delta Force* portray the central role of the news media in terrorism in getting violent messages to the public. In addition, the Arab terrorist Aziz of *True Lies* videotapes messages to viewers, and in *Invasion USA* the anticommunist Matt Hunter sends a direct message to the Soviet Russian communist villain through TV news, telling him that it is time to die. In *The Siege* the terrorists wait for the television cameras to arrive before exploding a bus in a suicide bombing. Imitating the terrorists of the TWA Flight 847 hijacking, in *The Delta Force* the Hollywood terrorists hold a press conference.

Film scripts use the news media for providing exposition in *Die Hard 2: Die Harder*, *Die Hard with a Vengeance*, *Executive Decision*, *Air Force One*, *The Delta Force*, *Patriot Games*, *Ronin* and *The Siege*. In the films of the 1990s, the expanding role of CNN as a leading world news provider is shown when, for example, *Air Force One* and *Executive Decision* provide exposition through CNN reports. In *Blown Away* and *Air Force One* the Hollywood terrorist finds out the hero's location through television reports. In *Die Hard* the antagonist learns from TV news that his nemesis in the building is a hostage's husband. *Commando* and *Passenger 57* keep the news media completely out of action. Otherwise in Hollywood terms the news media are moronic. They either help the villain by providing him with essential information about the hero or his family, as in *Die Hard*, or they simply have no clue of what is going on, as is the case, for example, in *Iron Eagle*.

According to Hess, the American news media have certain locales they cover constantly, the specific locales being Russia and former Soviet Union, the UK, Israel, Japan, Germany, and the latest crisis areas.[20] Each of the films studied coincides with these categories, as each terrorist villain refers to a variety of crises of the 1980s or 1990s, from Soviet Russia and its influence in Latin America to Libya, Lebanon, and generally to the Middle East. Northern Irish terrorists, left-wing Euroterrorists and Russian nationalists complete the list. Japan, a constant presence in the financial news, appears as John McClane's wife's employer in *Die Hard*.

Steuter points out that each terrorist group has very different motives for its actions but once the media represent different groups as one big common phenomenon of terrorism, it becomes hard for the public to understand the complexities of terrorism.[21] A simplified and generalized view of the threat also makes it easier to accept militaristic responses to acts and threats of terrorism when the context and motivations of the phenomenon are missing. This is the case with the Hollywood terrorist. A film's theme, in other words, its underlying message, often emerges only after the film has been completed.[22] The repeated theme of the action-adventure films on international terrorism has been the use of effective and destructive power whose performers are individual heroic representatives of the prevailing power structure. Their use of deadly force overpowers international terrorists' skills and weaponry. The only justice Hollywood knew and offered before 9/11 was the killing of those who posed a threat to the U.S. The Hollywood terrorist's destiny was obvious: death at the hero's hands. The solution repeated an old news format when covering stories of public executions: crime does not pay.[23] The sixteen films' message is loud and clear: do not attack the U.S., or you will pay with your life.

Several researchers in the 1980s and 1990s argued that the American news media were portraying the United States as a victim and target of terrorism, ignoring the context of events.[24] U.S. actions and policies that could have brought on some of the threats the U.S. was facing rarely received coverage. In that news framing, the only solution for the United States was to defeat the enemy, relying on the use of excessive military force. The deaths in those attacks became a deterrent; that is, as in films, the U.S. would respond with a military strike against those who attack the country and its citizens. But as Taylor points out the difference between real wars and media wars,[25] pre–9/11 Hollywood depictions of international terrorism offered only sanitized versions of terrorism, and of the suffering of the targets of terrorism and the targets of U.S. heroes' violence.

The Hollywood Terrorist: A Commodity of the Major Hollywood Production and Distribution Companies

The major studios are cautious about new film ideas, and usually bring to the screen new content only after smaller companies have proved at the box office that a new idea can weather the storm. That is the case also with the topic of international terrorism. In the 1980s the majors sparingly invested in distributing films that portrayed international terrorism. In 1985, 20th Century Fox distributed *Commando*, and three years later it put out *Die Hard*. Tri-Star, a joint venture launched by Columbia, CBS, and HBO in 1982, distributed *Iron Eagle* in 1986. A year later Columbia and Tri-Star Pictures merged to create Columbia Pictures Entertainment, a company that Coca-Cola, which had purchased Columbia in 1982, sold to Sony in 1989. Cannon Group, a U.S.-based company of Israeli cousins Menahem Golan and Yoram Globus, distributed *Invasion USA* and *The Delta Force*, which the cousins also produced under the name Golan-Globus.

In the 1990s each of the films that appeared in the annual top fifty box office was distributed by a major studio, or a minor major (MGM). Overall, 20th Century Fox emerged as the winner. It was the main distributor of the pre–9/11 terrorist action fare that was popular among paying audiences. The company distributed six of the sixteen films: the two films starring Arnold Schwarzenegger, *Commando* and *True Lies*, the first three installments of the *Die Hard* series included in this study and each starring Bruce Willis as John McClane, and *The Siege*, which starred Denzel Washington as a rare African American hero.

Warner Bros. distributed two terrorist-inspired films, *Passenger 57*, which starred the first African American hero in Wesley Snipes, and *Executive Decision*. MGM released two movies, *Blown Away* (MGM) in 1994 and *Ronin* (UA, part of MGM) in 1998. Walt Disney

Pictures/Buena Vista International, part of the Walt Disney Company, was the only major that did not distribute any of the most commercially successful action-adventure films that portrayed international terrorism before 9/11. The other majors distributed one film each: Paramount Pictures released *Patriot Games* in 1992, Universal Pictures with Mutual Film Company distributed *The Jackal* in 1997, and Columbia Pictures (now under Sony) released *Air Force One* in 1997. DreamWorks, which was founded in 1994 by Steven Spielberg, Jeffrey Katzenberg and David Geffen, tried to enter the game with its first release, *The Peacemaker*, in September 1997, but the story's background in a complex situation in the former Yugoslavia failed to bring in big crowds.

The main producer of action fare was Silver Pictures. Joel Silver's first production under his Silver Pictures company was *Commando*. This producer of the *Lethal Weapon* series also produced *Executive Decision*, and the first two *Die Hard* films with Gordon Company. Golan-Globus produced two films. The rest of the ten films each had a separate production company.

The American Counterterrorism Hero: Bankable Stars

The budgets, according to available estimates in movie reviews, *Variety* and the Internet Movie Database, indicate that 1990s action-adventure film budgets took an enormous leap from the budgets of the 1980s films. While the films' running times did not change much, bigger stars, more action-filled stories, and special effects entered the screen. Only two films of the sixteen films run for less than 100 minutes, *Commando* at 90 minutes, and *Passenger 57* at 84 minutes. The rest of the films are right under or over two hours. The longest of the films is *True Lies*, at 141 minutes.

The emergence of the ultra–high-budget film did not guarantee success at the North American box office. For example, some of the films in the annual top fifty, such as *The Jackal* (1997: #34), *Ronin* (1998: #46) and *The Siege* (1998: #48), were disappointments because, as indicated by the available information on their box office success and budgets at Variety.com and the Internet Movie Database, their success at the domestic box office did not cover their production costs. Hollywood has had to rely on its different release windows, including DVD and, now disappearing, VCR releases, and the foreign market, in order to recoup different films' production costs and make a profit.

Producers of action-adventure films tend to hire recognizable actors as their stars in order to attract audiences. This study supports that argument. Only one of the analyzed films, *Iron Eagle*, starred a young actor, Jason Gedrick, who was unknown and untested before big audiences. However, his sidekick Louis Gossett, Jr. was a very familiar name to domestic audiences. Another untested hero, although familiar from television, was Bruce Willis when he played John McClane in the first *Die Hard* film. After that success, he became a bankable action-adventure hero. The other fourteen films each starred an actor who had previously been tested at the box office with a profitable return. In the 1990s, the heroes were all stars known worldwide as A-list actors.

Bruce Willis is the biggest name in the pre–9/11 action-adventure films on international terrorism. Not only does he play the hero of the *Die Hard* films, but he is also the antagonist in two films: an international terrorist assassin in *The Jackal* and the domestic threat to civil liberties in *The Siege*. Another recognizable antagonist is Tommy Lee Jones in *Blown Away*. Harrison Ford, Arnold Schwarzenegger and Chuck Norris each starred as the hero in two films. Norris was also one of the screenwriters of *Invasion USA*. The list of stars also includes Jeff Bridges, Robert De Niro, Richard Gere, Kurt Russell, Wesley Snipes and Denzel Washington.

With the exception of Tommy Lee Jones as a mad Northern Irish terrorist extremist in *Blown Away*, and Bruce Willis in *The Jackal*, the pre–9/11 Hollywood terrorist was not a bankable action-adventure American actor on whose star quality a studio would have relied. Dan Hedaya as the Latin American villain of *Commando* was a familiar face to domestic audiences in the 1980s, as were some of the British actors who portrayed villains in the 1980s and 1990s, but none of them was a major star at the production and release time of the movies in which they acted.

Eight of the sixteen films cast British actors as foreign terrorists. David Suchet starred as the main Arab villain in two films, *Iron Eagle* and *Executive Decision*. He is best known abroad and to smaller American audiences as Belgian detective Hercule Poirot in the popular television adaptations of Agatha Christie's Poirot books. Other British actors recognizable as villains to American audiences are Alan Rickman in *Die Hard* (now famous in Harry Potter films), Jeremy Irons in *Die Hard with a Vengeance*, Sean Bean in *Patriot Games*, Gary Oldman in *Air Force One*, Bruce Payne and his accomplice in the film, Elizabeth Hurley, in *Passenger 57*, and Art Malik, a Pakistani-born British actor, in *True Lies*. *Die Hard 2: Die Harder* introduced a well-known Italian actor, Franco Nero, as the film's Central American villain. *Ronin* brought to audiences a group of recognizable European actors including Jean Reno, Natascha McElhone, Stellan Skarsgård, Sean Bean, and Jonathan Pryce as the villain. *The Siege* introduced Sami Bouajila, a French actor, as the film's foreign villain. Interestingly enough, Hollywood hired for the role of its foreign villains only Western or Westernized actors if their looks fit the role, especially in the case of a Third World villain. That imitates an older Hollywood method of hiring white actors to play African Americans and Native Americans. The approach trivializes minorities when minority characters in films are not even played by actors from the region or ethnic groups that the films portray. On the other hand, an actor might refuse to play another negative Hollywood stereotype of his own people.

The only director to appear twice on the list is John McTiernan, who directed the first and third *Die Hard* films. John Frankenheimer, the director of *Ronin*, directed in 1977 one of the first feature films on modern international terrorism, *Black Sunday*. It explored the complexity of the phenomenon through the story of an Israeli agent in charge of defusing a Black September attack targeting the annual Super Bowl.

One screenwriter, Steven E. de Souza, wrote or co-wrote three 20th Century Fox screenplays: *Commando* and the first two *Die Hard* films. The two Golan-Globus films, *Invasion USA* and *The Delta Force*, also shared a writer, James Bruner. Four directors contributed to the their own film's script: Sidney J. Furie (*Iron Eagle*), Menahem Golan (*The Delta Force*), James Cameron (*True Lies*; the script was based on the French film *La Totale!*) and Edward Zwick (*The Siege*). In addition, six directors combined directing and producing duties, producing or co-producing the films they directed: Menahem Golan (*The Delta Force*), John McTiernan (*Die Hard with a Vengeance*), Michael Caton-Jones (*The Jackal*), James Cameron (*True Lies*), Wolfgang Petersen (*Air Force One*), and Edward Zwick (*The Siege*). Three directors, Golan, Cameron and Zwick, participated in both producing and writing. A rarer combination was a writer as an executive producer, which Kevin Elders did for *Iron Eagle*.

Commodifying Death and Threats in Film Titles

The commercial film industry not only commodified international terrorism as a film product before the 9/11 attacks, it also commodified death, violence and representatives of the prevailing power structure. The sixteen films' names draw from military, federal and law enforcement, as well as from security threats to the U.S. and the protagonist. *Commando, Iron Eagle, The Delta Force* and *The Siege* all display military themes. The first three titles refer to each film's hero character. The last one refers to the threat the U.S. military poses in the film to civil liberties in its response to an international terrorist threat on U.S. soil.

Three of the films draw their names from federal themes. *Executive Decision* and *Air Force One* directly refer to the highest office in the country, the first one referring to a president's command, and the second one to his official aircraft. *Patriot Games* finds its name in the classified "Patriot" folders at the CIA headquarters. In the film the hero relies on them to find out information that will help him to defeat the terrorist threat to his family.

True Lies refers to the protagonist's lies to hide his profession from his family. He has been working as a spy for seventeen years although the film's antagonist has no trouble finding out his identity and his location. Like *True Lies, Passenger 57* and *Ronin* refer to the protagonist. In *Passenger 57* the name simply refers to the protagonist's seat on the plane that British terrorists hijack. In *Ronin* the hero becomes a ronin as part of his covert operation — an undercover CIA agent pretends to be a former agent down on his luck whose services are for hire.

Each film of the *Die Hard* trilogy repeats the first film's name. The second film promises even more action and violence with the added "Die Harder," while the third one promises more deaths, this time with a vengeance. However, the person delivering the deaths in the films was not the Hollywood terrorist but the Hollywood hero.

The only films titled after the terrorist threat are *Invasion USA* and *Blown Away.* Both titles clearly spell out the threat to the U.S. and the hero.

Conclusion: Theorizing the Hollywood Terrorist

According to Antonio Gramsci, ideology is manifest in everyday life in any society. Political and economic activity as well as culture and cultural products reveal the prevailing values in society, values that different private and state sectors maintain and reproduce in order to keep the status quo.[26] Louis Althusser points out the media's central role in the process of maintaining the prevailing ideology in society. The mass media have power to influence, promote and spread certain views to the masses in society on a regular basis. The public receives from the media "daily doses of nationalism, chauvinism, liberalism, moralism, etc."[27] According to this study's results, the action-adventure films on international terrorism which were most popular at the North American box office before 9/11 offered audiences doses of the prevailing hegemony. At times Hollywood's fictional terrorism even told stories that the official state structure later played in real life, such as the bombing of Libya in response to Libya's involvement in anti–U.S. terrorist attacks, which took place soon after the release of *Iron Eagle.* The terrorist films that paying audiences preferred to see at movie theaters before September 11, 2001, depicted heroic official representatives of the prevailing power structure. Furthermore, the stories emphasized the role of *white* men, from police officers and federal agents to soldiers, as the defenders of the American way of life. Firepower in the heroes' hands overwhelmed international terrorists' attempts. Outside U.S. soil, the weapons of the U.S. military highlighted their effectiveness against foreign threats. The films promoted nationalism and patriarchal structures in an entertaining wrapping of images of intense action.

As Theodor Adorno and Max Horkheimer of the Frankfurt School have argued, all cultural products are produced for a profit. As a result of cultural products being commodified, culture is commercialized.[28] Commodified cultural products, such as Hollywood films, are like any other products in the mass market where the goal is to attract the largest number of paying consumers. As with news, audiences are most receptive to stories that support the prevailing values. The terrorist films that were most popular among pre–9/11 paying audiences heavily reflect in their content the U.S. Department of State's annual *Patterns of Global Terrorism* documents. The movies are ideological products which support the official pre–9/11 understanding of international terrorist threats. However, just like mainstream news, the analyzed films disproportionally focus on a few regions, nationalities and ethnic groups, and one religion, as the main threats. In contrast, the State Department warns against stereotyping any nationality or ethnic or religious group as terrorists on the basis of the actions of a small minority.

While commercial films have used threats that the U.S. Department of State has pointed out, the film industry has prioritized international terrorism as a commodity of the action-adventure film genre and its traditions, which has influenced the Hollywood depiction of international terrorism. Films have embraced previously proven action-adventure film narrative structures and traditions. But Hollywood also well knows that in order to stay in business, the industry must respond to changes in political conditions, public opinion and audience interests.[29] As social and political values and developments have changed society, also Hollywood has updated its versions of the Hollywood terrorist and the American counterterrorism hero. For example, the move from more conservative values under a Republican White House to a more centrist approach under a Democratic White House and the end of the Cold War shaped and updated the heroes and the category of international terrorists. American communist hunters turned from heroes into villains when the world changed, and female characters and helpless preteen and teenage daughters entered the hero's world. As the Cold War was drawing its last breath, terrorists from Europe started to arrive to threaten the U.S., soon to be accompanied by Middle Eastern terrorists who were motivated by their religion.

This study has found that the terrorist films that movie theater audiences preferred to see before the 9/11 terrorist attacks supported the prevailing hegemony, both political and social. Critical views are missing in the study's sixteen action-adventure films on international terrorism. In Hollywood, questioning the prevailing values on international terrorism has not been a successful commodity. This is similar to news production. Typically audiences are not receptive to news that questions government policies and decisions, but rather turn their anger on the messenger.[30] Hollywood has also produced films that have clearly conflicted with and undermined official U.S. views, such as *Missing* (1982) and *Salvador* (1986), which were critical of U.S. policies and actions in Latin America, but these films were not popular among paying audiences. Before 9/11 a fictional film with a critical or in-depth analysis of international terrorism was not a good commodity. This study's only film which clearly contradicted the U.S. State Department views was *The Jackal*, which starred a PIRA terrorist as the film's hero. In that film, the FBI deputy director even let the Northern Irish terrorist hero go free at the film's end. Furthermore, while four of the sixteen films found their theme in Northern Irish terrorism, none of the four films depicted the PIRA in negative terms. The films reserved that portrayal for the organization's violent splinter groups. Hollywood decision to give the PIRA understanding between the lines was not a groundbreaking choice, since the news media had already found the PIRA to be a lucrative news commodity.

According to Gramsci, both civil society and the state exercise power in society. It is the responsibility of civil society to create voluntary consent for the use of power as a legal method to support the prevailing ideology. When that has successfully been done, the state can legally enforce discipline — in other words, it can use power as a legal method to maintain the prevailing ideology.[31] In these sixteen films the state is enforcing discipline when its representatives kill the films' terrorists. Viewers' voluntary consent to the killings is further supported by the action and action-adventure film traditions which require the protagonist to kill the villain who poses a threat to innocent civilians. While some of the films portray different federal or local representatives as less than effective, even comical, the films repeatedly support the use of power, at times extreme methods of killing, by the protagonists.

The Siege was the only film to portray more realistic terrorism and effects of terrorism in more detail. Although the movie portrayed international terrorism, a larger threat than terrorism to civil society was posed by the state's response to a terrorist conflict situation. The state's actions, in the name of defending society, undermined civil rights and the country's Constitution. Through the actions of a power-greedy general and his twisted interpretation of ultra-patriotism, the film portrayed a branch of the U.S. military as a repressive state apparatus which tried to implement a new ideology in society by relying on the use of force without popular consent. The film's hero, an African American FBI agent in charge, was a representative of the old hegemony that had been attacked, both by the film's international terrorists and the army. At the film's end the hero successfully defeats the two anti-hegemonies and therefore reproduces the old prevailing hegemony, restoring status quo. The film's portrayal of a sinister U.S. response to a terrorist plot on its own soil left *The Siege* looking for viewers at the box office. In the immediate weeks following September 11, 2001, the day when reality imitated fiction, audiences in large numbers found the film at rental stores. The movie's events are reminiscent of the 9/11 attacks but with one important difference which gives audiences a major relief: the film restores status quo. In particular, *The Siege* offers a true action-adventure film ending which reality was incapable of delivering: the hero kills the foreign terrorist villain at the film's end. The protagonist also brought down the domestic threat to civil liberties, which ended the siege on New York City as well as on the country's Constitution and the rule of law.

If the world is continuously represented in a certain way, that repetition creates traditions as well as voluntary consent to approve the repeated worldview.[32] For example, in the post–9/11 world a war on Iraq, which was not behind the 9/11 attacks, was an easy sell since the threat of war had been present in American minds for over a decade when American leaders and the mainstream media had repeatedly described Iraq's dictator as a major threat to American security. The sixteen films also represent the world in a certain way, repeatedly telling a story of the international Hollywood terrorist who must die for his crimes. The movie depictions largely follow in their portrayals of international terrorism the U.S. State Department interpretations of the phenomenon, but with a focus on the threats the news media have covered. The films' alternative interpretations of international terrorism mainly draw from the traditions of the classical Hollywood narrative structure and the traditions of the action-adventure film genre. For example, not only are Arab terrorists portrayed as insane and/or vengeful villains, but Northern Irish villains as well. The portrayal draws from the genre traditions to write film villains in such terms that viewers accept them as antagonists and welcome their death at the hero's hands as necessary for the protagonist to be able to protect society. A villain who might evoke sympathy and even understanding for his motives is a bad commodity because it would be hard for an action-adventure film to qualify his death at the film's end.

The Terrorist Film Commodity

This study has indicated that profit-conscious Hollywood followed the U.S. foreign policy and domestic agendas in its movies on international terrorism before the 9/11 terrorist attacks. In the 1970s terrorism hardly touched the lives of Americans, and rarely made U.S. news headlines. As a result there were few Hollywood productions that used international terrorism as their central storyline. In the Reagan era Hollywood made international terrorism a profitable film product, truly succeeding in its efforts in 1988 with *Die Hard.* The movie's box office success far exceeded that of earlier films on international terrorism. Furthermore, the sequel to *Die Hard* was the first true blockbuster terrorist film which had a massive production budget and aimed at a worldwide financial success.

Although terrorist-themed films evolved during the conservative Reagan and Bush administrations of the 1980s and early 1990s, they did not reach their true financial peak until the 1990s, during the Clinton era. During that decade they became true blockbuster products to the point that only the majors and a minor major, MGM, distributed commercially successful films on international terrorism. The Hollywood terrorist also changed most dramatically during that decade to become a more successful commodity in the changed social and political environment in America. Post–Cold War villains arrived from the Middle East, Central America, Europe, and the U.S. to threaten the hero (now often a family man) whose comical approach drew from the film traditions of previous decades. While minorities started to appear in films in the 1990s in larger numbers, the hero was still almost always a white male representative of the official power structure, as well as a bankable movie star. The action-adventure film genre was patriarchal, centered on a white male hero. A woman was still to be protected by the male hero, or to be killed if she entered his world as a threat to his masculinity due to her intelligence and capabilities in the hero's profession. Furthermore, the analyzed films enforce a heterosexual coupling of a white man with a white or minority woman, or an African American man with an African American woman. The films stay away from mixing a respectable white woman with a minority man.

It is clear that terrorism was a profitable Hollywood commodity before 9/11. It was an entertaining but also a risky commodity. As publicly estimated, the budgets of the most expensive terrorist films in the 1990s grew to over $100 million. While the role of the foreign market has been emphasized since the mid–1990s, the pre–9/11 worldview of Hollywood films on international terrorism was narrow and centered on the U.S. *The Jackal* (1997) and *Ronin* (1998) were rare exceptions when they acknowledged in their content the changing film business and the importance of attracting foreign viewers. These films were set in Canada and Europe, and international cooperation was central to each film's storyline. The international locations existed for the advancement of the story rather than as exotic targets of the hero's violence. In contrast, the 1986 films *Iron Eagle* and *The Delta Force,* which were released in the aftermath of a series of anti–American attacks in Lebanon, stereotyped the Middle East as a region of violence. Foreign terrorists used some violence and threats of more violence against Americans, but the film terrorists and their foreign locations largely existed as targets of the American heroes' massive violence.

Just as different news outlets repeat the formats that sell well,[33] pre–9/11 terrorist films by different studios repeated formats that had been profitable in the past. It can be argued that the commercial profitability of international terrorism as a film product was closely tied to its ideological content. Film heroes from different military branches or federal or local law enforcement effectively protected Americans from the forms of international terrorism that were familiar to domestic viewers from news media headlines and from the State Department's annual documents.

As Gramsci points out, culture has a central role in the creation of consensus in society.[34] This study has indicated that commercially successful films on international terrorism reproduced prevailing structures and worldviews in the 1980s and 1990s. The MPAA's claim that it is a "little State Department" is not only true because the organization negotiates film trade policies on its own, but also from the perspective of Hollywood film content. The analyzed films' foreign policy largely supports the 1980s and 1990s U.S. foreign policy on international terrorism and the State Department's view of international terrorism, except in the case of bringing terrorists to justice. Ironically, the Hollywood policy of killing the Hollywood terrorist spread to reality already in the 1980s when the U.S. bombed Libya and targeted its leader, Qadhafi, after the U.S. had linked Libya to several anti–U.S. terrorist attacks that had killed American citizens. An American teenager in *Iron Eagle* did the same job on the screen three months before the federal government. Additionally, in the 1990s President Clinton approved the killing of Osama bin Laden even if innocent bystanders might be killed. The interrelationship between the state and culture is also reflected in production policies. Several of the analyzed films, as discussed in previous chapters, relied on the help of the U.S. military in their productions. The relationship between the commercial film industry and the federal government is not a one-way street. After 9/11 it was not only the U.S. military intelligence that asked for the film industry's help in determining what future attacks and methods terrorists might use; the White House, too, asked the movie industry to join the fight against terrorism.[35]

The Hollywood Terrorist and Real Terrorist: "There Will Never Be a Last Cell"

For Hollywood, international terrorism has been a film commodity whose costs have been rapidly rising since the early 1990s, that is, since the terrorist film became a product of the major studios. As new forms of international terrorism have emerged, and as social and cultural conditions have changed, the film industry has given the Hollywood terrorist and the American counterterrorism hero Hollywood makeovers in order to better attract audiences. The films that domestic audiences preferred before 9/11 did not leave much room for the Hollywood terrorist's anti-hegemonic stand. His political motivation and goals and his ideological views were largely missing in the films. Hollywood terrorism did not explain the phenomenon of terrorism or offer alternative interpretations of terrorism.

Over the years real-life terrorism and Hollywood terrorism have both competed for mass audiences in their productions of spectacular terrorist attacks. The commercial film industry and real-life international terrorism have been playing leapfrog with one another, in which real-life terrorism took the lead on September 11, 2001, when the media spectacle it created was bigger than any previous Hollywood creation. In the 1970s both Hollywood and international terrorists had made attempts to bring international terrorist spectacles onto U.S. soil, but with feeble results. In the 1980s Hollywood was trying to catch up with real-life terrorism. For example, commercial film productions vaguely rewrote real-life foreign threats, mainly Libya, and Hezbollah in Lebanon, as threats to Americans outside U.S. borders in *Iron Eagle* (1986) and *The Delta Force* (1986). In the 1980s Reaganite nightmares struck inside U.S. borders in *Invasion USA* and *Commando*. In the late 1980s and early 1990s European film terrorists arrived in the U.S., while in real life, fundamentalist Islamic extremists partially succeeded in waking up the U.S. and Hollywood to the threat of international terrorism on U.S. soil. Real-life terrorists caught news media and public attention with the first World Trade Center bombing in February 1993, and later that same year with a failed plot to bomb New York City landmarks. Hollywood's answer was to create even bigger threats on U.S. soil. The Hollywood terrorist surpassed his real-life counterpart in plotting anti–American activities

In the words of the fictional Samir Nazhde, the fundamentalist Islamic terrorist of *The Siege* (1998, 20th Century Fox): "There will never be a last cell." The 9/11 Memorial site retorts: "From the horrific attacks on New York, Shanksville and the Pentagon has grown a fierce resolve that terrorism may wound, but will never defeat us."

until the real-life terrorist shocked the world, including the Hollywood film industry and the Hollywood terrorist, on Tuesday morning, September 11, 2001. The Hollywood terrorist took cover as the commercial film industry shelved him and his menacing plans in the immediate post–9/11 months.

The attacks of September 11, 2001, were such a shock to the U.S. because the mainstream news media and commercial films had misrepresented terrorists as ineffective and insane individuals who were not capable of rational planning. Furthermore, in pre–9/11 commercial films the American counterterrorism hero effectively killed the Hollywood terrorist, and therefore removed the threat and restored the status quo. Unfortunately the real-life terrorists of the September 11, 2001, attacks had another story to tell. On that day al Qaeda attacked the U.S. military center, the world's economic center, and civilians in front of the world's leading media. Live images of the attacks immediately spread around the world. In contrast to popular media images of international terrorism, the real-life terrorists were effective in making long-term plans and choosing their targets according to strategic decisions. Audiences were unprepared for the reality of global terrorism.

The relationship between global terrorism and the U.S. government is like the action-adventure movie genre. The characters are predictable as are their actions. Each U.S. president represents the hero of the story as the president confronts the latest foreign terrorist villain. Any terrorist group that targets the U.S. and its population in any way will gain America's attention, assuming the role of the latest villain. When the U.S. defends itself by attacking and using violence, as any action-adventure hero should, the story reaches the climax of its classical Hollywood narrative structure. Through violent action the U.S. tries to resolve the conflict and restore the status quo. However, that will be the beginning of a new storyline: now the terrorist opponent has a conflict which he needs to resolve in order to restore the status quo from his perspective. It is circular motion. There seems to be no end to the genre. Reality and the Hollywood movie-making machine will continue to compete for the latest stories on the real-life and Hollywood terrorist and the American counterterrorism hero. As Samir Nazhde, the foreign terrorist of *The Siege*, reminded us in 1998: "There will never be a last cell." There will never be a last terrorist cell, and there will never be a last film cell. After a short self-imposed hiatus from terrorist spectacles in the aftermath of the 9/11 attacks, the commercial film industry returned to producing films which portray international terrorists who target and kill Americans. The story of and competition between the real-life terrorist and the Hollywood terrorist has continued after 9/11.

Chapter Notes

Introduction

1. "Altman Says Hollywood 'created atmosphere' for September 11" (2001, October 18). Guardian Unlimited citing *Hollywood Reporter,* http://www.guardian.co.uk/film/2001/oct/18/news2.

2. "Disaster Becomes a Disaster for Studios" (2001, September 13). From Studio Briefing, Internet Movie Database, http://entertaindom.imdb.de/news/ni0084096.

3. Video Software Dealers Association, 2001, September press release, http://www.vsda.org/news/press/press.phtml.

4. Hess, Stephen (1996). *International News and Foreign Correspondents.* Washington, D.C.: Brookings Institution; Rosenblum, Mort (1993). *Who Stole the News? Why We Can't Keep Up with What Happens in the World and What We Can Do about It.* New York: John Wiley & Sons; Seaton, Edward (1998, July 1; last updated 2002, August 28). The Diminishing Use of Foreign News Reporting. Delivered May 26, 1998, in Moscow, before the International Press Institute by Edward Seaton, editor-in-chief, *The Manhattan* (Kan.) *Mercury,* 1998–99 ASNE (American Society of Newspaper Editors) President, http://204.8.120.192/index.cfm?ID=627.

5. Maltby, Richard (2003). *Hollywood Cinema: An Introduction.* 2nd ed. Malden, Mass.: Blackwell Publishing.

6. Groves, Don (1999, December 16). "America's pics find foreign B.O. hit, miss puzzle." In *Variety*; Herman, Edward S., and Robert W. McChesney (1997). *The Global Media: The New Missionaries of Corporate Capitalism.* London & Washington: Cassell.

7. Hoffman, Bruce (1998). *Inside Terrorism.* New York: Columbia University Press; Trends in Terrorism. Report #2000/01 (1999, December 18). In *Perspectives.* Canadian Security Intelligence Service Publication.

8. Wieviorka, Michel (1995). "Terrorism in the Context of Academic Research." In Martha Crenshaw (Ed.) *Terrorism in Context.* University Park: Pennsylvania State University Press.

9. Combs, James E. (1990) *American Political Movies: An Annotated Filmography of Feature Films.* New York and London: Garland Publishing.

10. Hall, Stuart (1982). "The Discovery of 'Ideology': Return to the Repressed in Media Studies." In Gurevitch, Michael, Tony Bennett, James Curran, and Janet Woollacott (Eds.) *Culture, Society and the Media.* London: Methuen.

11. CNN (2001, September, 13). Coverage of the 9/11 terrorist attacks and their aftermath.

12. Nielsen EDI, http://www.acnielsenedi.com/about/about.html.

13. Box Office Data Sources. In Charts and Data, Variety.com, http://www.variety.com/index.asp?layout=chart_pass&charttype=chart_bo_details&dept=Film

14. Internet Movie Database, http://www.imdb.com.

15. *Halliwell's Film and Video Guide 2001* (2000). 16th ed. Revised and updated. John Walker (Ed.). New York: HarperResource.

16. Wasko, Janet (1994). *Hollywood in the Information Age: Beyond the Silver Screen.* Texas Film Studies Series. Ed. Thomas Schatz. Cambridge, U.K.: Polity Press, and University of Texas Prcss.

17. Variety.com, box office data: Top 250 films of the years 1980–2001.

18. Balio, Tino (1998). "A major presence in all of the world's important markets": The globalization of Hollywood in the 1990s." In Steve Neale and Murray Smith (Eds.) *Contemporary Hollywood Cinema.* London and New York: Routledge.

19. *Ibid.*

20. See U.S. Department of State, http://www.state.gov/s/ct/rls/crt/.

21. Falkenrath, Richard (2001). "Analytic Models and Policy Prescription." In *Studies in Conflict and Terrorism,* 24.

22. United States Department of State (1990, April). *Patterns of Global Terrorism: 1989.* Department of State Publication 9743. Office of the Secretary of State. Office of the Coordinator for Counter-Terrorism.

23. United States Department of State (1984, September). *Patterns of Global Terrorism: 1983*, preface to the report.

24. United States Department of State (1992, April). *Patterns of Global Terrorism: 1991.* Department of State Publication 9963. Office of the Secretary of State. Office of the Coordinator for Counter-terrorism, p. v.

25. This includes companies that are based in Hollywood but may have foreign ownership due to changed ownership structures over the years.

26. United States Department of State (2000, April). *Patterns of Global Terrorism 1999.* Department of State Publication 10687. Office of the Secretary of State. Office of the Coordinator for Counterterrorism, p. iii.

27. Falkenrath, Richard (2001). "Analytic Models and Policy Prescription." In *Studies in Conflict and Terrorism,* 24.

28. Reagan, Ronald (1982, April 10). National Security Decision Directive Number 30. Unclassified, Washington: The White House; Reagan, Ronald (1986, January 20). The National Program for Combatting Terrorism. National Security Decision Directive Number 207. Unclassified. Washington: The White House. Later presidents reconfirmed the federal structure of the State Department as the lead agency outside U.S. borders, and the FBI, under the Justice Department, as lead on U.S. soil when managing terrorist incidents.

29. Van Dijk, Teun A. (1988). *News As Discourse.* Hillsdale, N.J.: Lawrence Erlbaum Associates.

30. Hall, Stuart (1982). "The Discovery of 'Ideology':

Return to the Repressed in Media Studies." In Gurevitch, Michael, Tony Bennett, James Curran, and Janet Woollacott (Eds.) *Culture, Society and the Media.* London: Methuen.

31. *Ibid.*; Gitlin, Todd (1980). *The Whole World Is Watching: Mass Media in the Making and Unmaking of the New Left.* Berkeley: University of California Press; Steuter, Erin (1990). "Understanding the Media/Terrorism Relationship: An Analysis of Ideology and the News in *Time* Magazine." In *Political Communication and Persuasion*, Vol. 7.

32. Falkenrath, Richard (2001). "Analytic Models and Policy Prescription." In *Studies in Conflict and Terrorism,* 24.

33. Picard, Robert G. (1993). *Media Portrayals of Terrorism: Functions and Meaning of News Coverage.* Ames: Iowa State University Press; Nacos, Brigitte L. (1994). *Terrorism and the Media: From the Iran Hostage Crisis to the World Trade Center Bombing.* New York: Columbia University Press; Clutterbuck, Richard (1983). *The Media and Political Violence.* 2nd ed. London: Macmillan.

34. See, for example, Picard, Robert G. (1993). *Media Portrayals of Terrorism. Functions and Meaning of News Coverage.* Ames: Iowa State University Press; and Herman, Edward S., and Gerry O'Sullivan (1989). *The "Terrorism Industry": The Experts and Institutions That Shape Our View of Terror.* New York: Pantheon Books.

35. Gramsci, Antonio. *Selections from the Prison Notebooks* (2003). Quintin Hoare and Geoffrey Nowell Smith (Eds. and trans.). New York: International Publishers. (Original work in English published 1971); Gitlin, Todd (1980). *The Whole World Is Watching: Mass Media in the Making and Unmaking of the New Left.* Berkeley: University of California Press; McKinney, Devin (2000). "Violence: The Strong and the Weak." In Stephen Prince (Ed.) *Screening Violence.* New Brunswick, N.J.: Rutgers University Press.

36. Organization of the Islamic Conference, http://www.oic.oci.org/member_states.

37. Parenti, Michael (1992). *Make-Believe Media: The Politics of Entertainment.* New York: St. Martin's Press.

38. Maltby, Richard (2003). *Hollywood Cinema: An Introduction.* 2nd ed. Malden, Mass.: Blackwell Publishing.

Part I

1. CNN (2001, September 11–12, 20). Coverage of the 9/11 terrorist attacks and their aftermath.

2. CNN (2001, September 13). Coverage of the 9/11 terrorist attacks and their aftermath.

3. Anderson, Sean, and Stephen Sloan (1995). *Historical Dictionary of Terrorism.* Historical Dictionaries of Religions, Philosophies, and Movements, No. 4. Metuchen, N.J.: Scarecrow Press.

4. Crenshaw, Martha (1995). "Introduction." In Martha Crenshaw (Ed.) *Terrorism in Context.* University Park: Pennsylvania State University Press; Hoffman, Bruce (1998). *Inside Terrorism.* New York: Columbia University Press.

5. Crenshaw, Martha (1995). "Introduction." In Martha Crenshaw (Ed.) *Terrorism in Context.* University Park: Pennsylvania State University Press.

6. Hoffman, Bruce (1998). *Inside Terrorism.* New York: Columbia University Press, p. 31.

7. Central Intelligence Agency Directorate of Intelligence (1977, July). *International Terrorism in 1976.*

8. United States Department of State (1982, July). *Patterns of International Terrorism: 1981.* Office for Combatting Terrorism.

9. Rubenstein, Richard E. (1987). *Alchemists of Revolution: Terrorism in the Modern World.* New York: Basic Books.

10. Falkenrath, Richard (2001). "Analytic Models and Policy Prescription." In *Studies in Conflict and Terrorism,* 24.

11. Rubenstein, Richard E. (1987). *Alchemists of Revolution: Terrorism in the Modern World.* New York: Basic Books, p. 21.

12. Van Dijk, Teun A. (1998). *Ideology: A Multidisciplinary Approach.* Thousand Oaks, Ca.: SAGE Publications.

13. Lewis, Charles, and Mark Reading-Smith (2008, January 23). "Iraq: The War Card. Orchestrated Deception on the Path to War." The Center for Public Integrity, http://projects.publicintegrity.org/WarCard/Default.aspx?source=home&context=overview&id=945.

14. Ahmad, Eqbal (2004). "Terrorism: Theirs and Ours." In Russell D. Howard and Reid L. Sawyer (Eds.) *Terrorism and Counterterrorism: Understanding the New Security Environment. Readings & Interpretations.* Rev. and updated. Guilford, Conn.: McGraw-Hill/Dushkin. (Original transcript of a public talk 1998; original work published 2001).

15. *Ibid.*, p. 47.

16. *Ibid.*

17. Parks, W. Hays (2003, January 7). Lessons from the 1986 Libya Airstrike. In *New England Law Review.* Vol. 36, No. 4, pp. 755–766, http://www.nesl.edu/lawrev/vol36/4/parks.pdf.

18. Rubenstein, Richard E. (1987). *Alchemists of Revolution. Terrorism in the Modern World.* New York: Basic Books.

19. Hoffman, Bruce (1998). *Inside Terrorism.* New York: Columbia University Press, pp. 34–35.

20. Corum, James S. (2007). *Fighting the War on Terror: A Counterinsurgency Strategy.* St. Paul, Minn.: Zenith Press.

21. Pillar, Paul R. (2004). "The Dimensions of Terrorism and Counterterrorism." In Russell D. Howard and Reid L. Sawyer (Eds.) *Terrorism and Counterterrorism: Understanding the New Security Environment. Readings and Interpretations.* Rev. and updated. Guilford, Conn.: McGraw-Hill/Dushkin. (Original work published 2001).

22. Picard, Robert G. (1993). *Media Portrayals of Terrorism: Functions and Meaning of News Coverage.* Ames: Iowa State University Press; Stohl, Michael (1988). "Demystifying Terrorism: The Myths and Realities of Contemporary Political Terrorism." In Michael Stohl (Ed.) *The Politics of Terrorism.* 3rd ed. Rev. and expanded. New York and Basel: Marcel Dekker.

23. See "Categories of Terrorist Incidents" in United States Department of State (1982, July). *Patterns of International Terrorism: 1981.* Office for Combatting Terrorism, p. 22.

24. Hoffman, Bruce (1998). *Inside Terrorism.* New York: Columbia University Press, pp. 14–15.

25. Pillar, Paul R. (2004). "The Dimensions of Terrorism and Counterterrorism." In Russell D. Howard and Reid L. Sawyer (Eds.) *Terrorism and Counterterrorism: Understanding the New Security Environment. Readings and Interpretations.* Rev. and updated. Guilford, Conn.: McGraw-Hill/Dushkin. (Original work published 2001), p. 28; emphasis original.

26. *Ibid.*

27. Evans, Ernest (1979). *Calling a Truce to Terror: The American Response to International Terrorism.* Bernard K. Johnpoll (Ed.) Contributions in Political Science, Number 29. Westport, Conn.: Greenwood Press.

28. Herman, Edward S., and Gerry O'Sullivan (1989). *The "Terrorism Industry": The Experts and Institutions That Shape Our View of Terror.* New York: Pantheon Books.

29. Hoffman, Bruce (1998). *Inside Terrorism.* New York: Columbia University Press.

30. *Ibid.*, pp. 29–30.

31. Gramsci, Antonio. *Selections from the Prison Notebooks* (2003). Quintin Hoare and Geoffrey Nowell Smith (Eds. and trans.) New York: International Publishers. (Original work in English published 1971).

32. McNally, David (1997). "Language, History, and Class Struggle." In Ellen Meiksins Wood and John Bellamy Foster (Eds.) *In Defense of History: Marxism and the Postmodern Agenda.* New York: Monthly Review Press.

33. Gramsci, Antonio. *Selections from the Prison Notebooks* (2003). Quintin Hoare and Geoffrey Nowell Smith (Eds. and trans.) New York: International Publishers. (Original work in English published 1971).

34. Ahmad, Aijaz (1997). "Interview: Culture, Nationalism, and the Role of Intellectuals." In Ellen Meiksins Wood and John Bellamy Foster (Eds.) *In Defense of History. Marxism and the Postmodern Agenda.* New York: Monthly Review Press.

35. Malik, Kenan (1996). *The Meaning of Race: Race, History and Culture in Western Society.* Washington Square, N.Y.: New York University Press.

36. Laqueur, Walter (1987). *The Age of Terrorism.* Boston: Little, Brown.

37. Crenshaw, Martha (1995). "Introduction." In Martha Crenshaw (Ed.) *Terrorism in Context.* University Park: Pennsylvania State University Press.

38. Combs, Cindy C. (1997). *Terrorism in the Twenty-First Century.* Upper Saddle River, N.J.: Prentice Hall; Laqueur, Walter (1999). *The New Terrorism: Fanaticism and the Arms of Mass Destruction.* New York: Oxford University Press; Higonnet, Patrice (1997, April 5). "Remembering and Forgetting the French Revolution." In *Human Rights at Harvard: Interdisciplinary Faculty Perspectives on the Human Rights Movement. Second Symposium.* Harvard University, http://www.law.harvard.edu/programs/HRP/Publications/symposium2.html.

39. Best, Steven (1995). *The Politics of Historical Vision: Marx, Foucault, Habermas.* In Douglas Kellner (Ed.) Critical Perspectives: A Guilford Series. New York: Guilford Press; Malik, Kenan (1996). *The Meaning of Race: Race, History and Culture in Western Society.* New York: New York University Press; Higonnet, Patrice (1997, April 5). "Remembering and Forgetting the French Revolution." In *Human Rights at Harvard, Interdisciplinary Faculty Perspectives on the Human Rights Movement. Second Symposium.* Harvard University, http://www.law.harvard.edu/programs/HRP/Publications/symposium2.html.

40. Higonnet, Patrice L. R. (1998). *Goodness Beyond Virtue. Jacobins during the French Revolution.* Cambridge, Mass.: Harvard University Press; Higonnet, Patrice (1997, April 5). "Remembering and Forgetting the French Revolution." In *Human Rights at Harvard, Interdisciplinary Faculty Perspectives on the Human Rights Movement. Second Symposium.* Harvard University, http://www.law.harvard.edu/programs/HRP/Publications/symposium2.html.

41. Hoffman, Bruce (1998). *Inside Terrorism.* New York: Columbia University Press, p. 15; emphasis original.

42. *Ibid.*; Higonnet, Patrice (1997, April 5). "Remembering and Forgetting the French Revolution." In *Human Rights at Harvard, Interdisciplinary Faculty Perspectives on the Human Rights Movement. Second Symposium.* Harvard University, http://www.law.harvard.edu/programs/HRP/Publications/symposium2.html.

43. Laqueur, Walter (1987). *The Age of Terrorism.* Boston: Little, Brown, p. 11.

44. *Ibid.*; Combs, Cindy C. (1997). *Terrorism in the Twenty-first Century.* Upper Saddle River, N.J.: Prentice Hall.

45. Hoffman, Bruce (1998). *Inside Terrorism.* New York: Columbia University Press.

46. *Ibid.*, p. 16.

47. *Ibid.*, p. 17.

48. *Ibid.*

49. Miller, Martin A. (1995). "The Intellectual Origins of Modern Terrorism in Europe." In Martha Crenshaw (Ed.) *Terrorism in Context.* University Park: Pennsylvania State University Press.

50. Laqueur, Walter (1978). "Introductory Note. Part I: Tyrannicide." In Walter Laqueur (Ed.). *The Terrorism Reader: A Historical Anthology.* New York: New American Library.

51. United States Department of State (1989, March). *Patterns of Global Terrorism: 1988.* Department of State Publication 9705. Office of the Secretary of State. Ambassador-at-Large for Counter-terrorism, p. iii.

52. Karim, Karim H. (2000). *Islamic Peril. Media and Global Violence.* Montreal and New York: Black Rose Books, p. 75.

53. United States Department of State (1989, March). *Patterns of Global Terrorism: 1988.* Department of State Publication 9705. Office of the Secretary of State. Ambassador-at-Large for Counterterrorism, p. iii.

54. Miller, Martin A. (1995). The Intellectual Origins of Modern Terrorism in Europe. In Martha Crenshaw (Ed.) *Terrorism in Context.* University Park, Pa.: Pennsylvania State University Press.

55. Hoffman, Bruce (1998). *Inside Terrorism.* New York: Columbia University Press, p. 17.

56. *Ibid.*

57. *Ibid.*

58. *Ibid.*

59. *Ibid.*

60. *Ibid.*

61. *Ibid.*; Alleyne, Mark D. (1995). *International Power and International Communication.* New York: St. Martin's Press.

62. Johnson, Chalmers (1978). "Perspectives on Terrorism." In Walter Laqueur (Ed.) *The Terrorism Reader: A Historical Anthology.* New York: New American Library.

63. *Ibid.*

64. Anderson, Sean, and Stephen Sloan (1995). *Historical Dictionary of Terrorism.* In Historical Dictionaries of Religions, Philosophies, and Movements, No. 4. Metuchen, N.J.: Scarecrow Press.

65. *Ibid.*; Trends in Terrorism. Report # 2000/01 (1999, December 18). In *Perspectives.* Canadian Security Intelligence Service Publication; Hoffman, Bruce (1998). *Inside Terrorism.* New York: Columbia University Press.

66. Hoffman, Bruce (1998). *Inside Terrorism.* New York: Columbia University Press.

67. Wilkinson, Paul (1986). *Terrorism and the Liberal State.* 2nd ed. New York: New York University Press; Stohl, Michael (1988). "Terrorism: The Myths and Realities of Contemporary Political Terrorism." In Michael Stohl (Ed.) *The Politics of Terrorism.* 3rd ed. Rev. and expanded. New York: Marcel Dekker.

68. Hoffman, Bruce (1998). *Inside Terrorism.* New York: Columbia University Press.

69. Ahmad, Eqbal (2004). "Terrorism: Theirs and Ours." In Russell D. Howard and Reid L. Sawyer (Eds.) *Terrorism and Counterterrorism: Understanding the New Security Environment. Readings and Interpretations.* Rev. and updated. Guilford, Conn.: McGraw-Hill/Dushkin. (Original transcript of a public talk 1998; original work published 2001), p. 50.

70. Hoffman, Bruce (1998). *Inside Terrorism.* New York: Columbia University Press, Wilkinson, Paul (1986). *Terrorism and the Liberal State.* 2nd ed. New York: New York University Press.

71. Wilkinson, Paul (1986). *Terrorism and the Liberal State.* 2nd ed. New York: New York University Press.

72. Hoffman, Bruce (1998). *Inside Terrorism.* New York: Columbia University Press, p. 68, citing Schmid, Alex P., and Janny de Graaf (1982). *Violence as Communication: Insurgent Terrorism and the Western News Media.* Beverly Hills, Calif.: Sage, p. 32.

73. Anderson, Sean, and Stephen Sloan (1995). *Historical Dictionary of Terrorism.* In Historical Dictionaries of Religions, Philosophies, and Movements, No. 4. Metuchen, N.J.: Scarecrow Press.

74. Wardlaw, Grant (1989). *Political Terrorism. Theory,*

Tactics, and Counter-Measures. 2nd ed. Cambridge, U.K.: Cambridge University Press; Stohl, Michael (1988). "Demystifying Terrorism: The Myths and Realities of Contemporary Political Terrorism." In Michael Stohl (Ed.) *The Politics of Terrorism.* 3rd ed. Rev. and expanded. New York: Marcel Dekker; Evans, Ernest (1979). *Calling a Truce to Terror: The American Response to International Terrorism.* In Bernard K. Johnpoll (Ed.) Contributions in Political Science, Number 29. Westport, Conn.: Greenwood Press.

75. *Ibid.*; Wilkinson, Paul (1986). *Terrorism and the Liberal State.* 2nd ed. New York: New York University Press.

76. Weimann, Gabriel (1992). "Modern Terrorism, the Media and Public Opinion." In Stanley Rothman (Ed.) *The Mass Media in Liberal Democratic Societies.* In Morton A. Kaplan (Ed.) World Social Systems. General ed. New York: Paragon House, p. 103, citing Dobson and Payne (1977).

77. United States Department of State (1984, September). *Patterns of Global Terrorism: 1983.*

78. Falkenrath, Richard (2001). "Analytic Models and Policy Prescription." In *Studies in Conflict and Terrorism, 24.*

79. Hoffman, Bruce (1998). *Inside Terrorism.* New York: Columbia University Press, p. 131.

80. Central Intelligence Agency (1976, April). Research Study. International and Transnational Terrorism: Diagnosis and Prognosis." PR 76 10030, p. 5.

81. Deutch, John (1997). "Terrorism: Think Again." *Foreign Policy*, Fall.

82. Johnson, Chalmers (1978). "Perspectives on Terrorism." In Walter Laqueur (Ed.) *The Terrorism Reader: A Historical Anthology.* New York: New American Library, p. 280.

83. United States Department of State (1990, April). *Patterns of Global Terrorism: 1989.* Department of State Publication 9743. Office of the Secretary of State. Office of the Coordinator for Counter-terrorism.

84. Corum, James S. (2007). *Fighting the War on Terror: A Counterinsurgency Strategy.* St. Paul, Minn.: Zenith Press.

85. The Bush administration's post–9/11 methods contradicted the administration's view of extreme methods in the pre–9/11 era. For example, in April 2001 at the release of *Patterns of Global Terrorism 2000*, a member of the Bush administration, Acting Coordinator for Counterterrorism Edmund J. Hull, was asked to comment on a CIA official's statement that "every time Israel tortures someone — and the torture is continuing — she creates two terrorists, one the father ... and the other the brother." As a response, Mr. Hull drew a connection between human rights and counterterrorism: "I think there is a relationship. It is one of the reasons that when we do the training of foreign security officials in counterterrorism there is a very heavy dose of human rights training as we go through that process because you do have a problem if, in responding to terrorism, you use methods that alienate more and more of the population. So, in principle, we acknowledge that connection and we do what we can in our training to address that issue." Briefing upon the Release of the Report "Patterns of Global Terrorism 2000" (2001, April 30). Phillip T. Reeker, Acting Spokesman, and Edmund J. Hull, Acting Coordinator for Counterterrorism, Washington, D.C. http://www.state.gov/s/ct/rls/rm/2001/2571.htm.

86. Hoffman, Bruce (1998). *Inside Terrorism.* New York: Columbia University Press.

Chapter 1

1. "Al Qa'eda: Manual." In Walter Laqueur (Ed.) *Voices of Terror: Manifestos, Writings and Manuals of Al Qaeda, Hamas, and Other Terrorists from Around the World and throughout the Ages.* New York: Reed Press, 2004.

2. Wieviorka, Michel (1995). "Terrorism in the Context of Academic Research." In Martha Crenshaw (Ed.) *Terrorism in Context.* University Park: Pennsylvania State University Press.

3. Jenkins, Brian Michael (1998). "Foreword." In Ian O. Lasser, Bruce Hoffman, John Arquilla, David Ronfeldt, and Michele Zanini (Eds.) *Countering the New Terrorism.* Rand Corporation. http://www.rand.org/publications/MR/MR989; Jenkins, Brian (1985). "Will Terrorists Go Nuclear." *Orbis*, Autumn.

4. United States Department of State (1996, April). *Patterns of Global Terrorism 1995.* Department of State Publication 10321. Office of the Secretary of State. Office of the Coordinator for Counterterrorism.

5. Thussu, Daya Kishan (2000). *International Communication: Continuity and Change.* London: Arnold, co-published in the United States of America by Oxford University Press, New York.

6. Coca-Cola website, http://www.coca-cola.com/worldwide/flashindex1.html.

7. Gramsci, Antonio. *Selections from the Prison Notebooks* (2003). Quintin Hoare and Geoffrey Nowell Smith (Eds. and trans.). New York: International Publishers. (Original work in English published 1971).

8. Agger, Ben (1992). *Cultural Studies as Critical Theory.* London and Washington, D.C.: Falmer Press.

9. Williams, Raymond (1977). *Marxism and Literature.* New York: Oxford University Press.

10. Murdock, Graham, and Peter Golding (1997). "For a Political Economy of Mass Communications." In Peter Golding and Graham Murdock (Eds.) *The Political Economy of the Media I.* Cheltenham & Brookfield, Vt.: Edward Elgar. (Original work 1973, published in *Socialist Register*), pp. 3–4.

11. Tuchman, Gaye (1978). *Making the News: A Study in Construction of Reality.* London: Free Press.

12. Simon, Jeffrey D. (1994). *The Terrorist Trap: America's Experience with Terrorism.* Bloomington & Indianapolis: Indiana University Press.

13. Murdock, Graham, and Peter Golding (1997). "For a Political Economy of Mass Communications." In Peter Golding and Graham Murdock (Eds.) *The Political Economy of the Media I.* Cheltenham & Brookfield, Vt.: Edward Elgar. (Original work 1973, published in *Socialist Register*).

14. Gitlin, Todd (1980). *The Whole World Is Watching: Mass Media in the Making and Unmaking of the New Left.* Berkeley: University of California Press.

15. Ryan, Charlotte, Kevin M. Carragee, and Cassie Schwerner (1998). "Media, Movements, and the Quest for Social Justice." In *Journal of Applied Communication Research 26.*

16. Gitlin, Todd (1980). *The Whole World Is Watching: Mass Media in the Making and Unmaking of the New Left.* Berkeley: University of California Press.

17. Van Dijk, Teun A. (1988). *News As Discourse.* Hillsdale, N.J.: Lawrence Erlbaum Associates.

18. Van Zoonen, Liesbet (1996). "A Dance of Death: New Social Movements and Mass Media." In David D. Paletz (Ed.) *Political Communication in Action: States, Institutes, Movements, Audiences.* Cresskill, N.J.: Hampton Press.

19. Fishman, Mark (1980). *Manufacturing the News.* Austin: University of Texas Press, p. 11.

20. Fowler, Roger (1991). *Language in the News: Discourse and Ideology in the Press.* London and New York: Routledge.

21. Fishman, Mark (1980). *Manufacturing the News.* Austin: University of Texas Press.

22. Van Dijk, Teun A. (1988). *News as Discourse.* Hillsdale, N.J.: Lawrence Erlbaum Associates.

23. Bremen, L. Paul, III, (1987, June 25). "Terrorism and the Media." In *Department of State Bulletin,* (1987) September, Vol. 87. (Presentation before the International Association of Airline Security Officers on June 25, 1987), p. 74.

24. Fishman, Mark (1980). *Manufacturing the News.* Austin: University of Texas Press.

25. Krajicek, David J. (1998). *Scooped! Media Miss Real Story on Crime While Chasing Sex, Sleaze and Celebrities.* New York: Columbia University Press.

26. Murdock, Graham, and Peter Golding (1997). "For a Political Economy of Mass Communications." In Peter Golding and Graham Murdock (Eds.) *The Political Economy of the Media I.* Cheltenham & Brookfield, Vt.: Edward Elgar. (Original work 1973, published in *Socialist Register*), p. 25.

27. Gitlin, Todd (1980). *The Whole World Is Watching: Mass Media in the Making and Unmaking of the New Left.* Berkeley: University of California Press.

28. Krajicek, David J. (1998). *Scooped! Media Miss Real Story on Crime While Chasing Sex, Sleaze and Celebrities.* New York: Columbia University Press; Foucault, Michel (1977). *Discipline and Punish: The Birth of the Prison.* Trans. Alan Sheridan. New York: Pantheon Books.

29. Foucault, Michel (1977). *Discipline and Punish: The Birth of the Prison.* Trans. Alan Sheridan. New York: Pantheon Books.

30. Krajicek, David J. (1998). *Scooped! Media Miss Real Story on Crime While Chasing Sex, Sleaze and Celebrities.* New York: Columbia University Press, p. 7.

31. Laqueur, Walter (1978). "Terrorism: A Balance Sheet." In Walter Laqueur (Ed.) *The Terrorism Reader: A Historical Anthology.* New York: New American Library.

32. Hoffman, Bruce (1998). *Inside Terrorism.* New York: Columbia University Press, p. 142.

33. *Ibid.*, pp. 183–184; emphasis original.

34. Corum, James S. (2007). *Fighting the War on Terror: A Counterinsurgency Strategy.* St. Paul, Minn.: Zenith Press; Laqueur, Walter (1978). "Terrorism — A Balance Sheet." In Walter Laqueur (Ed.) *The Terrorism Reader: A Historical Anthology.* New York: New American Library.

35. Hoffman, Bruce (1998). *Inside Terrorism.* New York: Columbia University Press.

36. Corum, James S. (2007). *Fighting the War on Terror. A Counterinsurgency Strategy.* St. Paul, Minn.: Zenith Press.

37. Jenkins, Brian Michael (1998). "Foreword." In Ian O. Lasser, Bruce Hoffman, John Arquilla, David Ronfeldt, and Michele Zanini (Eds.) *Countering the New Terrorism.* Rand Corporation, http://www.rand.org/publications/MR/MR989; Jenkins, Brian (1985). "Will Terrorists Go Nuclear?" *Orbis,* Autumn; Stohl, Michael (1988). "Demystifying Terrorism: The Myths and Realities of Contemporary Political Terrorism." In Michael Stohl (Ed.) *The Politics of Terrorism.* 3rd ed. Rev. and expanded. New York and Basel: Marcel Dekker.

38. Hoffman, Bruce (1998). *Inside Terrorism.* New York: Columbia University Press, p. 131.

39. *Ibid.*

40. *Ibid.*

41. For more on the two perspectives, see, for example: Herman, Edward S., and Gerry O'Sullivan (1989). *The "Terrorism Industry": The Experts and Institutions That Shape Our View of Terror.* New York: Pantheon Books; Picard, Robert G. (1993). *Media Portrayals of Terrorism: Functions and Meaning of News Coverage.* Ames: Iowa State University Press; Perdue, William D. (1989) *Terrorism and the State: A Critique of Domination through Fear.* New York: Praeger; Steuter, Erin (1990). "Understanding the Media/Terrorism Relationship: An Analysis of Ideology and the News in *Time* Magazine." In *Political Communication and Persuasion,* Vol. 7; Dobkin, Bethami A. (1992). *Tales of Terror: Television News and the Construction of the Terrorist Threat.* New York: Praeger.

42. Dobkin, Bethami A. (1992). *Tales of Terror: Television News and the Construction of the Terrorist Threat.* New York: Praeger; Perdue, William D. (1989) *Terrorism and the State: A Critique of Domination through Fear.* New York: Praeger; Picard, Robert G. (1993). *Media Portrayals of Terrorism: Functions and Meaning of News Coverage.* Ames: Iowa State University Press; Terrel, Robert, and Kristina Ross (1991). "The Voluntary Guidelines' Threat to U.S. Press Freedom." In Yonah Alexander and Robert G. Picard (Eds.) *In the Camera's Eye: News Coverage of Terrorist Events.* New York: Brassey's.

43. See, for example, Chaliand, Gerard (1989). *Terrorism: From Popular Struggle to Media Spectacle.* London and Atlantic Highlands, N.J.: Saqi Books; Clutterbuck, Richard (1983). *The Media and Political Violence.* 2nd ed. London: Macmillan; Nacos, Brigitte L. (1994). *Terrorism and the Media: From the Iran Hostage Crisis to the World Trade Center Bombing.* New York: Columbia University Press; O'Heffernan, Patrick (1991). *Mass Media and American Foreign Policy: Insider Perspectives on Global Journalism and the Foreign Policy Process.* Norwood, N.J.: Ablex Publishing.

44. Cottle, Simon (1997). "Reporting the Troubles in Northern Ireland: Paradigms and Media Propaganda." In Celeste Michelle Condit (Ed.) Review and Criticism. In *Critical Studies in Mass Communication 14,* 1997; Curtis, Liz (1984). *Ireland the Propaganda War: The British Media and the "Battle for Hearts and Minds."* London and Sydney: Pluto Press.

45. Curtis, Liz (1984). *Ireland the Propaganda War: The British Media and the "Battle for Hearts and Minds."* London and Sydney: Pluto Press.

46. Pearl, Raphael F. (1997). "Terrorism, the Media, and the Government: Perspectives, Trends, and Options of Policymakers." In *International Affairs, Foreign Affairs and National Defense Division. Congressional Research Service,* http://205.177.54.21/mterror.htm.

47. See, for example, Herman, Edward S., and Noam Chomsky (1988). *Manufacturing Consent: The Political Economy of the Mass Media.* New York: Pantheon Books.

48. Altheide, David L. (1981). "Iran vs. U.S. TV News: The Hostage Story out of Context." In William C. Adams (Ed.). *Television Coverage of the Middle East.* Norwood, N.J.: Ablex.

49. Van Zoonen, Liesbet (1996). "A Dance of Death: New Social Movements and Mass Media." In David D. Paletz (Ed.) *Political Communication in Action: States, Institutes, Movements, Audiences.* Cresskill, N.J.: Hampton Press, p. 208.

50. "News judgment, professionalism are guides to crisis coverage" (1986, February 17) in *Broadcasting,* v110. Retrieved July 22, 2010, from Expanded Academic ASAP via Gale.

51. Crenshaw, Martha (2004). "The Logic of Terrorism; Terrorist Behavior as a Product of Strategic Choice." In Russell D. Howard and Reid L. Sawyer (Eds.) *Terrorism and Counterterrorism: Understanding the New Security Environment. Readings & Interpretations.* Rev. and updated. Guilford, Conn.: McGraw-Hill/Dushkin. (Original work published 1998).

52. Falkenrath, Richard (2001). "Analytic Models and Policy Prescription." In *Studies in Conflict and Terrorism* 24.

53. Hoffman, Bruce (1998). *Inside Terrorism.* New York: Columbia University Press, p. 149.

54. *Ibid.*

55. Kopel, David. Remarks at Cato Institute Conference on Terrorism. Cato Institute, http://www.cato.org/speeches/sp-dk101096.html; Dobkin, Bethami A. (1992). *Tales of Terror: Television News and the Construction of the Terrorist Threat.* New York: Praeger.

56. United States Department of Transportation. National Highway Traffic Safety Administration, 2001 (2002, December). *Traffic Safety Facts 2001. A Compilation of Motor Vehicle Crash Data from the Fatality Analysis Reporting System and the General Estimates System.* Washington, D.C. 20590. DOT HS 809 484. Traffic Safety Facts Annual Reports, http://www-nrd.nhtsa.dot.gov/cats/listpublications.aspx?Id=E&ShowBy=DocType.

57. Wieviorka, Michael (1993). *The Making of Terrorism.* Trans. David Gordon White. Chicago: University of Chicago Press.

58. Laqueur, Walter (1978). "Terrorism — A Balance Sheet." In Walter Laqueur (Ed.) *The Terrorism Reader. A Historical Anthology.* New York: New American Library, p. 262.

59. Hoffman, Bruce (1998). *Inside Terrorism.* New York: Columbia University Press, p. 140.

60. Picard, Robert G. (1993). *Media Portrayals of Terrorism: Functions and Meaning of News Coverage.* Ames: Iowa State University Press.

61. Gerbner, George, with the bibliographic assistance of Nancy Signorielli (1988). *Violence and Terrorism in the Mass Media.* Paris, France: UNESCO and Lanham, Md.: UNIPUB, citing Plaetz, Fozzard, and Ayunian, 1982.

62. *Ibid.*, citing a 1987 study by M. A. Milburn, C. Bowley, J. Fay-Dumaine, and D. A. Kennedy.

63. Falkenrath, Richard (2001). "Analytic Models and Policy Prescription." In *Studies in Conflict and Terrorism* 24.

64. For discussion on bad and good violence, see, for example, Frazer, Elizabeth, and Kimberly Hutchings (2008). "On Politics and Violence: Arendt contra Fanon" (2008). In *Contemporary Political Theory.* 7. doi:10.1057/palgrave.cpt.9300328, http://www.palgrave-journals.com/cpt/journal/v7/n1/full/9300328a.html.

65. Rosenblum, Mort (1993). *Who Stole the News? Why We Can't Keep Up with What Happens in the World and What We Can Do about It.* New York: John Wiley & Sons.

66. Altschull, J. Herbert (1984). *Agents of Power: The Role of the News Media in Human Affairs.* New York & London: Longman.

67. Dobkin, Bethami A. (1992). *Tales of Terror: Television News and the Construction of the Terrorist Threat.* New York: Praeger.

68. The Center for Defense Information (1995). *The CNN Effect* (1995). America's Defense Monitor, Washington, D.C.

69. Hess, Stephen (1996). *International News and Foreign Correspondents.* Washington, D.C.: Brookings Institution; Alleyne, Mark D. (1997). *News Revolution: Political and Economic Decision about Global Information.* New York: St. Martin's Press.

70. Seaton, Edward (1998, July 1; last updated 2002, August 28). "The Diminishing Use of Foreign News Reporting." Delivered May 26, 1998, in Moscow before the International Press Institute by Edward Seaton, editor-in-chief, The Manhattan (Kan.) *Mercury,* 1998–1999 ASNE (American Society of Newspaper Editors) President, http://asne.org/index.cfm?ID=627.

71. Hess, Stephen (1996). *International News and Foreign Correspondents.* Washington, D.C.: Brookings Institution.

72. Mowlana, Hamid (1997). *Global Information and World Communication: New Frontiers in International Relations.* 2nd ed. Thousand Oaks, Calif.: Sage.

73. Hess, Stephen (1996). *International News and Foreign Correspondents.* Washington, D.C.: Brookings Institution; Rosenblum, Mort (1993). *Who Stole the News? Why We Can't Keep Up with What Happens in the World and What We Can Do about It.* New York: John Wiley & Sons.

74. Surk and Schreck, Associated Press. (2009, January 24). "Al-Jazeera Drew U.S. Viewers on Web During Gaza War." http://www.nytimes.com/aponline/2009/01/24/world/AP-ML-Jazeeras-Breakthrough.html.

75. Hess, Stephen (1996). *International News and Foreign Correspondents.* Washington, D.C.: Brookings Institution.

76. Seib, Philip (1997). *Headline Diplomacy. How News Coverage Affects Foreign Policy.* Westport, Conn.: Praeger.

77. Taylor, Philip M. (1997). *Global Communications: International Affairs and the Media since 1945.* London and New York: Routledge; Carpenter, Ted Galen (1995). *The Captive Press. Foreign Policy Crises and the First Amendment.* Washington, D.C.: Cato Institute.

78. Taylor, Philip M. (1997). *Global Communications: International Affairs and the Media since 1945.* London and New York: Routledge.

79. Seib, Philip (1997). *Headline Diplomacy: How News Coverage Affects Foreign Policy.* Westport, Conn.: Praeger.

80. *Ibid.*; Carpenter, Ted Galen (1995). *The Captive Press: Foreign Policy Crises and the First Amendment.* Washington, D.C.: Cato Institute.

81. Carpenter, Ted Galen (1995). *The Captive Press: Foreign Policy Crises and the First Amendment.* Washington, D.C.: Cato Institute.

82. Seib, Philip (1997). *Headline Diplomacy: How News Coverage Affects Foreign Policy.* Westport, Conn.: Praeger.

83. O'Heffernan, Patrick (1991). *Mass Media and American Foreign Policy: Insider Perspectives on Global Journalism and the Foreign Policy Process.* Norwood, N.J.: Ablex Publishing.

84. Taylor, Philip M. (1997). *Global Communications, International Affairs and the Media since 1945.* London and New York: Routledge, citing on p. 92, Friedland, Lewis (1992). *Covering the World: International Television News Services.* New York: 20th Century Fund Press, pp. 7–8.

85. Taylor, Philip M. (1997). *Global Communications, International Affairs and the Media since 1945.* London and New York: Routledge, pp. 93–94.

86. *Ibid.*, p. 93, citing Stech, Frank J. (1994). "Winning CNN Wars." In *Parameters,* Autumn, p. 38.

87. Taylor, Philip M. (1997). *Global Communications, International Affairs and the Media since 1945.* London and New York: Routledge, pp. 92–94.

88. Hess, Stephen (1996). *International News and Foreign Correspondents.* Washington, D.C.: Brookings Institution.

89. Taylor, Philip M. (1997). *Global Communications, International Affairs and the Media since 1945.* London and New York: Routledge.

90. Seib, Philip (1997). *Headline Diplomacy. How News Coverage Affects Foreign Policy.* Westport, Conn.: Praeger.

91. Taylor, Philip M. (1997). *Global Communications, International Affairs and the Media since 1945.* London and New York: Routledge, p. 119.

92. Rosenblum, Mort (1993). *Who Stole the News? Why We Can't Keep Up with What Happens in the World and What We Can Do about It.* New York: John Wiley & Sons.

93. Carpenter, Ted Galen (1995). *The Captive Press: Foreign Policy Crises and the First Amendment.* Washington, D.C.: Cato Institute.

94. Corum, James S. (2007). *Fighting the War on Terror: A Counterinsurgency Strategy.* St. Paul, Minn.: Zenith Press.

95. Taylor, Philip M. (1997). *Global Communications, International Affairs and the Media since 1945.* London and New York: Routledge.

96. Carpenter, Ted Galen (1995). *The Captive Press: Foreign Policy Crises and the First Amendment.* Washington, D.C.: Cato Institute.

97. Taylor, Philip M. (1997). *Global Communications, International Affairs and the Media since 1945.* London and New York: Routledge.

98. *Ibid.*; Carpenter, Ted Galen (1995). *The Captive Press: Foreign Policy Crises and the First Amendment.* Washington, D.C.: Cato Institute.

99. Rosenblum, Mort (1993). *Who Stole the News? Why We Can't Keep Up with What Happens in the World and What We Can Do about It.* New York: John Wiley & Sons.

100. The Senate vote was 77–23: 48 Republicans and 29 Democrats voted "Yes"; 1 Republican, 21 Democrats, and 1 Independent voted "No." The House vote was 296–133: 215 Republicans and 81 Democrats voted "Yes"; 6 Republicans,

126 Democrats, and 1 Independent voted "No"; 2 Republicans and 1 Democrat did not vote, according to the *Washington Post's* U.S. Congress Votes Database at http://projects.washingtonpost.com/congress/107/senate/2/votes/237/ and at http://projects.washingtonpost.com/congress/107/house/2/votes/455/.

Chapter 2

1. United States Department of State (1982, July). *Patterns of International Terrorism: 1981.* Office for Combatting Terrorism.

2. Kraft, Michael B. "Introduction." In Evolution of U.S. Counterterrorism Laws, Policies, and Programs. In Alexander, Yonah, and Michael B. Kraft (Eds.) *Evolution of U.S. Counterterrorism Policy.* Volume I. Westport, Conn.: Praeger Security International.

3. Reagan, Ronald (1982, April 10). "Managing Terrorist Incidents." National Security Decision Directive Number 30. Washington: The White House. Unclassified, p. 2.

4. The list included kidnapping, barricade-hostage, bombing, armed attack, hijacking ("of air, sea, or land transport"), assassination ("includes assassination or attempt to assassinate where the victim was preselected by name"), sabotage, exotic pollution ("Use of exotic substances — atomic, chemical, or biological — to contaminate material"), bombing (minor), threat, theft or break-in, hoax, and other: ("Includes conspiracy, and other actions such as sniping, shootout with police, arms smuggling" and terrorist plots). United States Department of State (1982, July). *Patterns of International Terrorism: 1981.* Office for Combatting Terrorism, p. 2, and "Categories of Terrorist Incidents, p. 22 (unnumbered page in the document).

5. Sheridan, Brian, Assistant Secretary of Defense for Special Operations and Low-Intensity Conflict (2000, March 24). Statement before the Subcommittee on Emerging Threats and Capabilities of the Committee on Armed Services. United States Senate. 106th Congress. Department of Defense and Combatting Terrorism, p. 2.

6. Elcock, Ward (1999, July). Counter-Terrorism. Submission to the Special Committee of the Senate on Security and Intelligence. (Original submission June 24, 1998; revised July 1999).

7. Bureau of Public Affairs, United States Department of State (1981). International Terrorism, June 1981. In Gist series.

8. Bureau of Public Affairs. United States Department of State. (1984). International Terrorism, 1984, September. In Gist series.

9. U.S. Department of State (1983, September). *Patterns of Global Terrorism: 1982.*

10. Nash, Jay (1998). *Terrorism in the 20th Century: A Narrative Encyclopedia from the Anarchists through the Weathermen to the Unabomber.* New York: M. Evans.

11. U.S. State Department (1982, July). *Patterns of International Terrorism: 1981.* Office for Combatting Terrorism.

12. Bureau of Public Affairs, United States Department of State. (1981). International Terrorism, June 1981. In Gist series.

13. United States Department of State (1982, July). *Patterns of International Terrorism: 1981.* Office for Combatting Terrorism.

14. *The 9/11 Commission Report: Final Report on the National Commission on Terrorist Attacks upon the United States* (2004). Authorized edition. New York and London: W. W. Norton.

15. *Patterns of Global Terrorism: 1985* discusses in detail why Western Europe was experiencing a Middle Eastern spillover: Western European prisons had several dozen terrorists who were from the Middle East, so at times their group members would try to pressure Western European governments to release these prisoners; large Middle Eastern communities of expatriates and students could provide shelter, hiding places and potential recruits; several countries in the region were hosting exile groups that could attract state sponsors of terrorism to try to silence these opponents; personal freedoms in these free societies made it easy for terrorists to function in the region; Western Europe had few restrictions on travel across borders; the region had a large number of easily accessible targets; guest worker programs for those coming from the Middle East; violent attacks in otherwise peaceful Western Europe were guaranteed worldwide media coverage; and some of the countries in the region had given passive support to terrorist groups which could lead to concessions and deals in order to prevent attacks in these countries. United States Department of State (1986, October). *Patterns of Global Terrorism: 1985.* Office of the Ambassador at Large for Counter-Terrorism.

16. Evans, Ernest (1979). *Calling a Truce to Terror: The American Response to International Terrorism.* In Bernard K. Johnpoll (Ed.) Contributions in Political Science, Number 29. Westport, Conn.: Greenwood Press; Korn, David A. (1993). *Assassination in Khartoum.* Bloomington: Indiana University Press.

17. Combs, Cindy C. (1997). *Terrorism in the Twenty-first Century.* Upper Saddle River, N.J.: Prentice Hall.

18. Richard Nixon Library & Birthplace Foundation Research Center (1972, September 25). Memorandum Establishing a Cabinet Committee to Combat Terrorism. http://www.nixonlibraryfoundation.org/index.php?src=gendocs&link=papers_1972; Hoffman, Bruce (1998). *Inside Terrorism.* New York: Columbia University Press; Jenkins, Brian Michael (1998). "Foreword." In Ian O. Lasser, Bruce Hoffman, John Arquilla, David Ronfeldt and Michele Zanini (Eds.) *Countering the New Terrorism.* Rand Corporation, http://www.rand.org/publications/MR/MR989.

19. Kraft, Michael B. "Introduction." In Evolution of U.S. Counterterrorism Laws, Policies, and Programs. In Alexander, Yonah, and Michael B. Kraft (Eds.) *Evolution of U.S. Counterterrorism Policy.* Volume I. Westport, Conn.: Praeger Security International.

20. Alexander, Yonah (2007). "Introduction." In Alexander, Yonah, and Michael B. Kraft (Eds.) *Evolution of U.S. Counterterrorism Policy.* Volume I. Westport, Conn.: Praeger Security International.

21. Carter, Jimmy (Brzezinski, Zbigniew) (1977, June 2). Presidential Review Memorandum/NSC-30. Subject: Terrorism. Washington: The White House. Unclassified; Smith, G. Davidson (1990). *Combating Terrorism.* London: Routledge.

22. National Security Agency (declassified and approved for release by NSA on April 19, 2007 pursuant to E.O. 12958 as amended. MDR51909). "The First Round: NSA's Effort against International Terrorism in the 1970s." In Cryptologic Almanac 50th Anniversary Series; Associated Press (2009, February 2). "NSA Helped Uncover 1973 NYC Bombing Plot," http://www.nytimes.com/aponline/2009/02/02/us/AP-Mystery-Terrorist.html?_r=1.

23. Korn, David A (1993). *Assassination in Khartoum.* Bloomington: Indiana University Press.

24. *Ibid.*; Simon, Jeffrey David (2001). *The Terrorist Trap: America's Experience with Terrorism.* 2nd ed. Bloomington: Indiana University Press; Jenkins, Brian, Janera Johnson, and David Ronfeldt (1977, July). "Numbered Lives: Some Statistical Observations from 77 International Hostage Episodes." Santa Monica, Calif.: Rand Corporation. P-5905.

25. Simon, Jeffrey David (2001). *The Terrorist Trap: America's Experience with Terrorism.* 2nd ed. Bloomington: Indiana University Press, p. 109.

26. *Ibid.*

27. Bureau of Public Affairs, United States Department of State (1985). International Terrorism, August 1985. In Gist series.

28. Alexander, Yonah (2007) "Introduction." In Alexander, Yonah, and Michael B. Kraft (Eds.) *Evolution of U.S. Counterterrorism Policy.* Volume I. Westport, Conn.: Praeger Security International.

29. *Ibid.*, p. xxxviii.

30. Barker, Jonathan (2003). *The No-Nonsense Guide to Terrorism.* Oxford, U.K.: New Internationalist Publications.

31. Jimmy Carter Library & Museum. The Hostage Crisis in Iran. http://www.jimmycarterlibrary.org/documents/hostages.phtml.

32. Jimmy Carter Library & Museum. The Hostages and the Casualties. http://www.jimmycarterlibrary.org/documents/list_of_hostages.phtml. The list was adapted from information in *Free at Last* by Doyle McManus; the site lists the hostages and the six who succeeded to escape as:

The 52:
Thomas L. Ahern, Jr., 48, McLean, VA. Narcotics control officer.
Clair Cortland Barnes, 35, Falls Church, VA. Communications specialist.
William E. Belk, 44, West Columbia, SC. Communications and records officer.
Robert O. Blucker, 54, North Little Rock, AR. Economics officer specializing in oil.
Donald J. Cooke, 26, Memphis, TN. Vice consul.
William J. Daugherty, 33, Tulsa, OK. Third secretary of U.S. mission.
Lt. Cmdr. Robert Englemann, 34, Hurst, TX. Naval attaché.
Sgt. William Gallegos, 22, Pueblo, CO. Marine guard.
Bruce W. German, 44, Rockville, MD. Budget officer.
Duane L. Gillette, 24, Columbia, PA. Navy communications and intelligence specialist.
Alan B. Golancinksi, 30, Silver Spring, MD. Security officer.
John E. Graves, 53, Reston, VA. Public affairs officer.
Joseph M. Hall, 32, Elyria, OH. Military attaché with warrant officer rank.
Sgt. Kevin J. Hermening, 21, Oak Creek, WI. Marine guard.
Sgt. 1st Class Donald R. Hohman, 38, Frankfurt, West Germany. Army medic.
Col. Leland J. Holland, 53, Laurel, MD. Military attaché.
Michael Howland, 34, Alexandria, VA. Security aide, one of three held in Iranian Foreign Ministry.
Charles A. Jones, Jr., 40, Communications specialist and teletype operator. Only African American hostage not released in November 1979.
Malcolm Kalp, 42, Fairfax, VA. Position unknown.
Moorhead C. Kennedy Jr., 50, Washington, D.C. Economic and commercial officer.
William F. Keough, Jr., 50, Brookline, MA. Superintendent of American School in Islamabad, Pakistan, visiting Tehran at time of embassy seizure.
Cpl. Steven W. Kirtley, 22, Little Rock, AR. Marine guard.
Kathryn L. Koob, 42, Fairfax, VA. Embassy cultural officer; one of two women hostages.
Frederick Lee Kupke, 34, Francesville, IN. Communications officer and electronics specialist.
L. Bruce Laingen, 58, Bethesda, MD. Chargé d'affaires. One of three held in Iranian Foreign Ministry.
Steven Lauterbach, 29, North Dayton, OH. Administrative officer.
Gary E. Lee, 37, Falls Church, VA. Administrative officer.
Sgt. Paul Edward Lewis, 23, Homer, IL. Marine guard.
John W. Limbert, Jr., 37, Washington, D.C. Political officer.
Sgt. James M. Lopez, 22, Globe, AZ. Marine guard.
Sgt. John D. McKeel, Jr., 27, Balch Springs, TX. Marine guard.
Michael J. Metrinko, 34, Olyphant, PA. Political officer.
Jerry J. Miele, 42, Mt. Pleasant, PA. Communications officer.
Staff Sgt. Michael E. Moeller, 31, Quantico, VA. Head of Marine guard unit.
Bert C. Moore, 45, Mount Vernon, OH. Counselor for administration.
Richard H. Morefield, 51, San Diego, CA. U.S. Consul General in Tehran.
Capt. Paul M. Needham, Jr., 30, Bellevue, NE. Air Force logistics staff officer.
Robert C. Ode, 65, Sun City, AZ. Retired Foreign Service officer on temporary duty in Tehran.
Sgt. Gregory A. Persinger, 23, Seaford, DE. Marine guard.
Jerry Plotkin, 45, Sherman Oaks, CA. Private businessman visiting Tehran.
MSgt. Regis Ragan, 38, Johnstown, PA. Army noncom, assigned to defense attaché's officer.
Lt. Col. David M. Roeder, 41, Alexandria, VA. Deputy Air Force attaché.
Barry M. Rosen, 36, Brooklyn, NY. Press attaché.
William B. Royer, Jr., 49, Houston, TX. Assistant director of Iran-American Society.
Col. Thomas E. Schaefer, 50, Tacoma, WA. Air Force attaché.
Col. Charles W. Scott, 48, Stone Mountain, GA. Army officer, military attaché.
Cmdr. Donald A. Sharer, 40, Chesapeake, VA. Naval air attaché.
Sgt. Rodney V. (Rocky) Sickmann, 22, Krakow, MO. Marine Guard.
Staff Sgt. Joseph Subic, Jr., 23, Redford Township, MI. Military policeman (Army) on defense attaché's staff.
Elizabeth Ann Swift, 40, Washington, D.C. Chief of embassy's political section; one of two women hostages.
Victor L. Tomseth, 39, Springfield, OR. Senior political officer; one of three held in Iranian Foreign Ministry.
Phillip R. Ward, 40, Culpeper, VA. Administrative officer.

One hostage was freed July 11, 1980, because of an illness later diagnosed as multiple sclerosis:
Richard I. Queen, 28, New York, NY. Vice consul.

Six American diplomats avoided capture when the embassy was seized. For three months they were sheltered at the Canadian and Swedish embassies in Tehran. On Jan. 28, 1980, they fled Iran using Canadian passports:
Robert Anders, 34, Port Charlotte, FL. Consular officer.
Mark J. Lijek, 29, Falls Church, VA. Consular officer.
Cora A. Lijek, 25, Falls Church, VA. Consular assistant.
Henry L. Schatz, 31, Coeur d'Alene, ID. Agriculture attaché.
Joseph D. Stafford, 29, Crossville, TN. Consular officer.
Kathleen F. Stafford, 28, Crossville, TN. Consular assistant.

Thirteen women and African Americans among the Americans who were seized at the embassy were released on Nov. 19 and 20, 1979:
Kathy Gross, 22, Cambridge Springs, PA. Secretary.
Sgt. James Hughes, 30, Langley Air Force Base, VA. Air Force administrative manager.
Lillian Johnson, 32, Elmont, NY. Secretary.
Sgt. Ladell Maples, 23, Earle, AR. Marine guard.
Elizabeth Montagne, 42, Calumet City, IL. Secretary.
Sgt. William Quarles, 23, Washington, D.C. Marine guard.
Lloyd Rollins, 40, Alexandria, VA. Administrative officer.
Capt. Neal (Terry) Robinson, 30, Houston, TX. Administrative officer.
Terri Tedford, 24, South San Francisco, CA. Secretary.
Sgt. Joseph Vincent, 42, New Orleans, LA. Air Force administrative manager.
Sgt. David Walker, 25, Prairie View, TX. Marine guard.
Joan Walsh, 33, Ogden, UT. Secretary.
Cpl. Wesley Williams, 24, Albany, NY. Marine guard.

33. Jentleson, Bruce W. (2004). *American Foreign Policy: The Dynamics of Choice in the 21st Century.* 2nd ed. New York: W. W. Norton; "1981: Tehran Frees U.S. Hostages After 444 Days," BBC On This Day, 21 January. http://news.bbc.

co.uk/onthisday/hi/dates/stories/january/21/newsid_2506000/2506807.stm.

34. Anderson, Sean, and Stephen Sloan (1995). *Historical Dictionary of Terrorism.* In Historical Dictionaries of Religions, Philosophies, and Movements, No. 4. Metuchen, N.J.: Scarecrow Press; Wilkinson, Paul (1986). *Terrorism and the Liberal State.* 2nd ed. New York: New York University Press; Stohl, Michael (1988). "Demystifying Terrorism: The Myths and Realities of Contemporary Political Terrorism." In Michael Stohl (Ed.) *The Politics of Terrorism.* 3rd ed. Rev. and expanded. New York and Basel: Marcel Dekker; Stohl, Michael (1988). "National Interests and State Terrorism." In Michael Stohl (Ed.) *The Politics of Terrorism.* 3rd ed. Rev. and expanded. New York and Basel: Marcel Dekker.

35. Hoffman, Bruce (1998). *Inside Terrorism.* New York: Columbia University Press.

36. Palmer, William J. (1993). *The Films of the Eighties: A Social History.* Carbondale and Edwardsville: Southern Illinois University Press.

37. *The 9/11 Commission Report: Final Report on the National Commission on Terrorist Attacks upon the United States* (2004). Authorized edition. New York and London: W. W. Norton.

38. National Foreign Assessment Center. CIA. (1981, June). *Patterns of International Terrorism: 1980. A Research Paper.* PA81-10163U. United States Department of State (1982, July). *Patterns of International Terrorism: 1981.* Office for Combatting Terrorism.

39. Jentleson, Bruce W. (2004). *American Foreign Policy: The Dynamics of Choice in the 21st Century.* 2nd ed. New York: W. W. Norton.

40. *Ibid.*

41. Norwitz, Jeffrey H. (2004). Combating Terrorism: With a Helmet or a Badge? In Russell D. Howard and Reid L. Sawyer (Eds.) *Terrorism and Counterterrorism: Understanding the New Security Environment. Readings and Interpretations.* Rev. and updated. Guilford, Conn.: McGraw-Hill/Dushkin (original work published 2002), p. 475.

42. United States Department of State (1986, October). *Patterns of Global Terrorism: 1985.* Office of the Ambassador at Large for Counter-Terrorism; United States Department of State. (January, 1988). *Patterns of Global Terrorism: 1986.* Office of the Ambassador at Large for Counter-Terrorism.

43. *The 9/11 Commission Report: Final Report on the National Commission on Terrorist Attacks upon the United States* (2004). Authorized edition. New York and London: W. W. Norton, p. 99; footnote 96 on p. 478, citing http://www.reagan.utexas.edu/resource/speeches/1985/70885a.htm.

44. See, for example, the 1984 report: "The Soviet Union clearly supports international terrorism, although — in contrast to Iran, Syria, and Libya — we have no evidence of the Soviets directly planning or orchestrating terrorist acts by Middle Eastern, West European, or Latin American groups. However: The Soviets have a long history of maintaining relations with groups that participate in or are linked to terrorism. They provide political backing, funding, and, in some cases, conventional arms and military training. Moscow, at least indirectly, has given material support to groups that have committed terrorist acts, particularly in the Middle East and Latin America. The Soviets have trained personnel linked to or belonging to national liberation groups, and they openly sell large quantities of arms to Palestinian terrorists, states that support terrorism (with Libya a leading customer), and gray market arms dealers. Absence of end-user restrictions means that such weapons often make their way into the hands of terrorists. The Soviets also support certain Palestinian groups, East European states, South Yemen, and Cuba, all of whom support terrorist organizations or groups that commit terrorist acts. Bulgaria's state trading organization — KINTEX — and Czechoslovakia's comparable organization — OMNIPOL — are among the most prominent companies whose weapons eventually have appeared in terrorist hands. The East Europeans, almost certainly with Soviet knowledge and support, provide safe-haven, grant transit privileges, and allow the movement of weapons and bombs for terrorists such as Carlos, Abu Nidal, and others. In backing revolutionary causes against established governments, the Soviets seem to be largely indifferent to whether terrorist tactics are used. As long as groups committing terrorist acts are ideologically aligned with the Soviet Union and continue to attack non-Soviet and non–Bloc targets, the Soviets benefit from the disruptive and destabilizing effects of terrorism, which partly explains why they have not supported international efforts to combat it." United States Department of State (1985, November). *Patterns of Global Terrorism: 1984.* Office of the Ambassador-at-Large for Counter-Terrorism, pp. 4–5.

45. United States Department of State (1982, July). *Patterns of International Terrorism: 1981.* Office for Combatting Terrorism.

46. United States Department of State (1986, October). *Patterns of Global Terrorism: 1985.* Office of the Ambassador at Large for Counter-Terrorism; United States Department of State (1985, November). *Patterns of Global Terrorism: 1984.* Office of the Ambassador-at-Large for Counter-Terrorism.

47. In the aftermath of revelations of U.S. involvement in planning the assassination of Cuban president Fidel Castro and the role of intelligence services in the Watergate scandal, President Gerald Ford's Executive Order 11905 (1976) clarified American intelligence activities, prohibiting assassinations. President Carter's 1978 Executive Order 12036 updated Ford's order. In 1981 President Reagan issued Executive Order 12333, which reconfirmed the assassination ban and updated Carter's order. Bazan, Elizabeth B., Legislative Attorney, American Law Division. "Assassination Ban and E.O. 12333: A Brief Summary." In CRS Report for Congress. Received through the CRS Web. Order Code RS21037. Updated January 4, 2002. http://www.fas.org/irp/crs/RS21037.pdf.

48. Parks, W. Hays (2003, January 7). "Lessons from the 1986 Libya Airstrike." In *New England Law Review* 36:4, pp. 755–766, http://www.nesl.edu/lawrev/vol36/4/parks.pdf, p. 766 (12).

49. United States Department of State. (1988, January). *Patterns of Global Terrorism: 1986.* Office of the Ambassador at Large for Counter-Terrorism; *The 9/11 Commission Report: Final Report on the National Commission on Terrorist Attacks upon the United States* (2004). Authorized edition. New York: W. W. Norton; Chomsky, Noam (1988). *The Culture of Terrorism.* Boston, Mass.: South End Press.

50. President Reagan's approach to Latin America differed from his predecessor's. President Carter emphasized human rights as part of his administration's policies to the point that he had cut back U.S. support, for example, to Nicaragua, where the Somoza family's claim to power had resulted in an extensive amount of human rights violations. The Reagan administration's view was that U.S. support to authoritarian regimes was acceptable because they would mostly limit their repression "only" to the political sphere. The administration preferred these actions to communist totalitarian governments, which, in the administration's view, would also try to dominate the citizens' personal lives. This argument was also evident in the U.S. approach to Nicaragua, where the Reagan administration gave extensive support to the Contras, who were opposing the communist-nationalist Sandinistas' power. The latter had gained power in the country after the authoritarian Somoza regime. Nicaragua became a showcase of U.S. power. Military aid as well as assistance from the CIA flowed into the country. The new policy was also reflected in U.S. actions in El Salvador, where the military regime that the U.S. was supporting was killing large

numbers of its own citizens. But in this case Congress ignored the Reagan administration's objections and married the country's human rights conditions and U.S. aid as a package deal. Jentleson, Bruce W. (2004). *American Foreign Policy: The Dynamics of Choice in the 21st Century.* 2nd ed. New York: W. W. Norton.

51. *The 9/11 Commission Report: Final Report on the National Commission on Terrorist Attacks upon the United States* (2004). Authorized edition. New York: W. W. Norton.

52. Bureau of Public Affairs, United States Department of State (1985). International Terrorism, August 1985. In Gist series.

53. *The 9/11 Commission Report: Final Report on the National Commission on Terrorist Attacks upon the United States* (2004). Authorized edition. New York: W. W. Norton.

54. Norwitz, Jeffrey H. (2004). "Combating Terrorism: With a Helmet or a Badge?" In Russell D. Howard and Reid L. Sawyer (Eds.) *Terrorism and Counterterrorism: Understanding the New Security Environment. Readings & Interpretations.* Rev. and updated. Guilford, Conn.: McGraw-Hill/Dushkin. (Original work published 2002.)

55. *The 9/11 Commission Report: Final Report on the National Commission on Terrorist Attacks upon the United States* (2004). Authorized edition. New York: W. W. Norton.

56. During the first Reagan administration the presidential staff had been in charge of coordinating counterterrorism. In Reagan's second administration, "the coordination of counterterrorism was overseen by a high-level interagency committee chaired by the deputy national security adviser," *Ibid.*, p. 99.

57. *The 9/11 Commission Report: Final Report on the National Commission on Terrorist Attacks upon the United States* (2004). Authorized edition. New York: W. W. Norton.

58. United States Department of State (1990, April). *Patterns of Global Terrorism: 1989.* Department of State Publication 9743. Office of the Secretary of State. Office of the Coordinator for Counter-Terrorism; United States Department of State (1991, April). *Patterns of Global Terrorism: 1990.* Department of State Publication 9862. Office of the Secretary of State. Office of the Coordinator for Counterterrorism.

59. United States Department of State (1995, April). *Patterns of Global Terrorism 1994.* Department of State Publication 10239. Office of the Secretary of State. Office of the Coordinator for Counterterrorism, p. iii.

60. *The 9/11 Commission Report: Final Report on the National Commission on Terrorist Attacks upon the United States* (2004). Authorized edition. New York: W. W. Norton, p. 72.

61. *Ibid.*; United States Department of State (1994, April). *Patterns of Global Terrorism 1993.* Department of State Publication 10136. Office of the Secretary of State. Office of the Coordinator for Counterterrorism.

62. United States Department of State (1994, April). *Patterns of Global Terrorism 1993.* Department of State Publication 10136. Office of the Secretary of State. Office of the Coordinator for Counterterrorism, p. iii.

63. United States Department of State (1996, April). *Patterns of Global Terrorism 1995.* Department of State Publication 10321. Office of the Secretary of State. Office of the Coordinator for Counterterrorism.

64. *The 9/11 Commission Report: Final Report on the National Commission on Terrorist Attacks upon the United States* (2004). Authorized edition. New York: W. W. Norton.

65. *Ibid.*

66. Norwitz, Jeffrey H. (2004). "Combatting Terrorism: With a Helmet or a Badge?" In Russell D. Howard and Reid L. Sawyer (Eds.) *Terrorism and Counterterrorism: Understanding the New Security Environment. Readings and Interpretations.* Rev. and updated. Guilford, Conn.: McGraw-Hill/Dushkin. (Original work published 2002.)

67. *The 9/11 Commission Report: Final Report on the National Commission on Terrorist Attacks upon the United States* (2004). Authorized edition. New York: W. W. Norton.

68. Gordon, Philip (2001, November). "September 11 and American Foreign Policy." *Aspenia.* http://www.brook.edu/views/articles/gordon/2001aspenia.htm.

69. Holland, Jesse J., Associated Press Online. (2001, April 3). Terrorists Change U.S. Targets. Retrieved through LexisNexis Academic.

70. *The 9/11 Commission Report: Final Report on the National Commission on Terrorist Attacks upon the United States* (2004). Authorized edition. New York: W. W. Norton, p. 154.

71. *The 9/11 Commission Report: Final Report on the National Commission on Terrorist Attacks upon the United States* (2004). Authorized edition. New York: W. W. Norton.

72. American Airlines flight 11 hijackers: Mohamed Atta (pilot), Waleed al Shehri, Wail al Shehri, Satam al Suqami, and Abdulaziz al Omari. United Airlines flight 175 hijackers: Marwan al Shehhi (pilot), Fayez Banihammad, Ahmed al Ghamdi, Hamza al Ghamdi, and Mohand al Shehri. American Airlines flight 77 hijackers: Hani Hanjour (pilot), Nawah al Hazmi, Khalid al Mihdhar, Majed Moqed, and Salem al Hazmi. United Airlines flight 93 hijackers: Ziad Jarrah (pilot), Saeed al Ghamdi, Ahmad al Haznawi, and Ahmed al Nami. *The 9/11 Commission Report: Final Report on the National Commission on Terrorist Attacks upon the United States* (2004). Authorized edition. New York: W. W. Norton.

73. CNN coverage of the 9/11 attacks (2001, September 11–12 and 20).

74. CNN coverage of the 9/11 attacks (2001, September 13).

75. *The 9/11 Commission Report: Final Report on the National Commission on Terrorist Attacks upon the United States* (2004). Authorized edition. New York: W. W. Norton.

76. The State Department dropped in 1989 intra–Palestinian violence from international terrorist attack numbers. Accordingly, it changed the attack numbers in the future reports to reflect the revised data collection. The year 1987's attack numbers are from the revised data.

77. United States Department of State (1993, April). *Patterns of Global Terrorism 1992.* Department of State Publication 10054. Office of the Secretary of State. Office of the Coordinator for Counterterrorism.

78. United States Department of State. *Patterns of Global Terrorism* reports 1983–2001; United States Department of State (1983, September). *Patterns of International Terrorism: 1982;* United States Department of State. (1982, July). *Patterns of International Terrorism: 1981.* Office for Combatting Terrorism; Bureau of Public Affairs, United States Department of State. (1981). International Terrorism, June 1981. In Gist series.

79. Holland, Jesse J., Associated Press Online. (2001, April 3). Terrorists Change U.S. Targets. Retrieved through LexisNexis Academic.

80. Briefing upon the Release of the Report *Patterns of Global Terrorism 2000* (2001, April 30). Phillip T. Reeker, Acting Spokesman. Edmund J. Hull, Acting Coordinator for Counterterrorism. Washington, D.C., http://www.state.gov/s/ct/rls/rm/2001/2571.htm.

81. United States Department of State (2002, May). *Patterns of Global Terrorism 2001.* Department of State Publication 10940. Office of the Secretary of State. Office of the Coordinator for Counterterrorism, p. 139.

82. United States Department of State (1999, April). *Patterns of Global Terrorism 1998.* U.S. Department of State Publication 10610. Office of the Secretary of State. Office of the Coordinator for Counterterrorism.

83. Institute for Defense Analyses (1997). Federal Structures for Infrastructure Protection. Report to the President's Commission on Critical Infrastructure Protection, p. 6.

84. Pillar, Paul R. (2004). The Dimensions of Terrorism and Counterterrorism. In Russell D. Howard and Reid L. Sawyer (Eds.) *Terrorism and Counterterrorism: Understanding the New Security Environment. Readings and Interpretations.* Revised and Updated. Guilford, Conn.: McGraw-Hill/Dushkin. (Original work published 2001).

85. The first two reports issued by the State Department continued to call the annual reports *Patterns of International Terrorism.* The 1983 report replaced the word *international* with *global.*

86. United States Department of State (1993, April). *Patterns of Global Terrorism 1992.* Department of State Publication 10054. Office of the Secretary of State. Office of the Coordinator for Counterterrorism; Kraft, Michael B. "Introduction." In Evolution of U.S. Counterterrorism Laws, Policies, and Programs. In Alexander, Yonah (2007) Introduction. In Alexander, Yonah and Michael B. Kraft (Eds.) *Evolution of U.S. Counterterrorism Policy.* Volume I. Westport, Conn.: Praeger Security International.

87. See United States Department of State at http://www.state.gov/s/ct/rls/crt/.

88. "[W]e have chosen the definition commonly used by the US Government for the past 21 years [since 1968], which also is widely accepted and one which we have used in previous reports," United States Department of State (1990, April). *Patterns of Global Terrorism: 1989.* Department of State Publication 9743. Office of the Secretary of State. Office of the Coordinator for Counter-Terrorism. p. v.

89. United States Department of State (1983, September) *Patterns of International Terrorism: 1982,* prepage to the report. See also United States Department of State (1982, July). *Patterns of International Terrorism: 1981.* Office for Combatting Terrorism.

90. United States Department of State (1984, September). *Patterns of Global Terrorism: 1983,* prepage to the report.

91. United States Department of State (1991, April). *Patterns of Global Terrorism: 1990,* p. v.

92. United States Department of State (1993, April). *Patterns of Global Terrorism 1992,* p. v.

93. Pillar, Paul R. (2004). The Dimensions of Terrorism and Counterterrorism. In Russell D. Howard and Reid L. Sawyer (Eds.) *Terrorism and Counterterrorism: Understanding the New Security Environment. Readings and Interpretations.* Revised and Updated. Guilford, Conn.: McGraw-Hill/Dushkin. (Original work published 2001), p. 25.

94. See National Foreign Assessment Center, CIA (1978, August). *International Terrorism in 1977. A Research Paper.* P78-10255U, p. 5: "Although terrorism has risen from 1960s' levels, the 1970s seem to have produced a cyclical pattern in terms of overall numbers of incidents. Most terrorist campaigns do not appear to be sustainable for more than a few months, as governments adapt to terrorist tactics, group leaders are arrested, and logistic problems arise. In time, however, new terrorist recruits appear and develop new methods — thus the cycle continues." Also see National Foreign Assessment Center, CIA (1979, March). *International Terrorism in 1978. A Research Paper.* RP 79-10149.

95. United States Department of State (1990, April). *Patterns of Global Terrorism: 1989.* Department of State Publication 9743. Office of the Secretary of State. Office of the Coordinator for Counter-Terrorism.

96. Briefing upon the Release of the Report *Patterns of Global Terrorism 2000* (2001, April 30). Phillip T. Reeker, Acting Spokesman. Edmund J. Hull, Acting Coordinator for Counterterrorism. Washington, D.C., http://www.state.gov/s/ct/rls/rm/2001/2571.htm.

97. Since 1990 the reports have been submitted "in compliance with Title 22 of the United States Code, Section 2656f(a), which requires the Department of State to provide Congress with a full and complete annual report on terrorism for those countries and groups meeting the criteria of Section a (1) and (2) of the Act." U.S. Department of State (1992, April) *Patterns of Global Terrorism: 1991,* p. iv. In 1996 Congress added the requirement to report on other countries' level of cooperation with the U.S. in "apprehending, convicting, and punishing terrorists responsible for attacking US citizens or interests." Additionally, the annual reports were required to describe other countries' cooperation over the past five years in preventing future terrorist acts. U.S. Department of State (1997, April). *Patterns of Global Terrorism 1996,* online report.

98. The 1990 report further defined "noncombatant," as did also the future *Patterns of Global Terrorism* reports. The footnote clarifies: "For purposes of this definition, the term noncombatant is interpreted to include, in addition to civilians, military personnel who at the time of the incident are unarmed and/or not on duty. For example, in past reports we have listed as terrorist incidents the murders of the following military personnel: Col. James Rowe, killed in Manilla in April 1989; Capt. William Nordeen, US defense attaché, killed in Athens in June 1988; the two servicemen killed in the La Belle disco bombing in West Berlin in April 1986; and the four off-duty US Embassy Marine guards killed in a cafe in El Salvador in June 1985. We also consider as acts of terrorism attacks on military installations or on armed military personnel when a state of military hostilities does not exist at the site, such as bombings against US bases in Europe, the Philippines, or elsewhere." United States Department of State (1991, April). *Patterns of Global Terrorism: 1990.* Department of State Publication 9862. Office of the Secretary of State. Office of the Coordinator for Counterterrorism, p. iv.

99. United States Department of State (1988, August). *Patterns of Global Terrorism: 1987.* Department of State Publication 9661. Office of the Secretary of State. Ambassador-at-Large for Counter-Terrorism, pp. iv–v.

100. The data collection has been updated several times; see, for example, the 1980, 1983, and 1989 reports, and the 1993 report in which the State Department readjusted the reporting of Palestinian violence and applied the readjustment also to past reports. One of the major changes was done in the aftermath of the Lebanon bombings, which was reflected in the 1983 report:

"Nonterrorist hijackings, threats and hoaxes, arms smuggling, conspiracies, and events where the victim was a suspected terrorist — which were included routinely in statistics for previous years — have been excluded from the counts. The 'other' category now comprises incidents of sabotage, vandalism, theft, extortion, and harassment or intimidation. Terrorist assassinations are now indexed according to the method used — armed attack, bombing, and so forth. A new 'intent' variable allows for identification of assassinations and failed attempts and distinguishes them from executions and other forms of murder — something that was not possible under the old system." United States Department of State (1984, September). *Patterns of Global Terrorism: 1983,* p. 2, footnote 1. The department refined its data in the following year's report to make the data "more complete, accurate, and reliable. For example, political demonstrations; nonpolitical violence; conspiracies never activated; and nonviolent, unpremeditated, or defensive attacks are no longer coded as terrorism." United States Department of State (1985, November). *Patterns of Global Terrorism: 1984.* Office of the Ambassador-at-Large for Counter-Terrorism, p. 2, footnote 2. In addition, it added Palestinian attacks in Israel and the occupied territories against civilian Israeli targets in the data, and included greater detail in the coding in insurgent attacks in Africa, Asia and Latin America.

101. National Foreign Assessment Center, CIA (1980, April). *International Terrorism in 1979. Research Paper.* PA 80-10072U, p. 13.

102. United States Department of State (1984, September). *Patterns of Global Terrorism: 1983.*

103. Falkenrath, Richard (2001). "Analytic Models and Policy Prescription." In *Studies in Conflict and Terrorism, 24.*

104. Jentleson, Bruce W. (2004). *American Foreign Policy: The Dynamics of Choice in the 21st Century.* 2nd edition. New York and London: W. W. Norton, p. 68.

105. United States Department of State (1988, August). *Patterns of Global Terrorism: 1987.* Department of State Publication 9661. Office of the Secretary of State. Ambassador-at-Large for Counter-Terrorism, pp. iii–iv.

106. United States Department of State (2000, April). *Patterns of Global Terrorism 1999.* Department of State Publication 10687. Office of the Secretary of State. Office of the Coordinator for Counterterrorism, p. iii.

107. *Ibid.*

108. United States Department of State (2002, May). *Patterns of Global Terrorism 2001.* Department of State Publication 10940. Office of the Secretary of State. Office of the Coordinator for Counterterrorism, p. 140.

109. *Ibid.*, p. xiii.

110. *Ibid.*, p. 140.

111. United States Department of State (2000, April). *Patterns of Global Terrorism 1999.* Department of State Publication 10687. Office of the Secretary of State. Office of the Coordinator for Counterterrorism, p. iv.

112. *Ibid.*

113. United States Department of State (1988, August). *Patterns of Global Terrorism: 1987.* Department of State Publication 9661. Office of the Secretary of State. Ambassador-at-Large for Counter-Terrorism, p. 38, footnote.

114. Kraft, Michael B. "Introduction." In Evolution of U.S. Counterterrorism Laws, Policies, and Programs. In Alexander, Yonah (2007) Introduction. In Alexander, Yonah, and Michael B. Kraft (Eds.) *Evolution of U.S. Counterterrorism Policy.* Volume I. Westport, Conn.: Praeger Security International.

115. United States Department of State (1990, April). *Patterns of Global Terrorism: 1989.* Department of State Publication 9743. Office of the Secretary of State. Office of the Coordinator for Counter-Terrorism, p. 43.

116. United States Department of State. (1988, January). *Patterns of Global Terrorism: 1986.* Office of the Ambassador at Large for Counter-Terrorism, p. 5.

117. The State Department added Sudan to the list of the states that sponsor terrorism in 1993. According to the 1995 report, Sudan emerged in 1995 as a center of international terrorist activities. It was supporting oppositional groups in its neighboring countries. Furthermore, it was suspected of being behind the assassination attempt of Egyptian President Hosni Mubarak. The 1995 report stated that "Sudan continues to harbor Usama Bin Ladin, a major financier of terrorism, and members of some of the world's most violent groups like the IG, ANO, Lebanese Hizballah and HAMAS." United States Department of State (1996, April). *Patterns of Global Terrorism 1995.* Department of State Publication 10321. Office of the Secretary of State. Office of the Coordinator for Counterterrorism, p. 24.

118. United States Department of State (1996, April). *Patterns of Global Terrorism 1995.* Department of State Publication 10321. Office of the Secretary of State. Office of the Coordinator for Counterterrorism.

119. United States Department of State (1990, April). *Patterns of Global Terrorism: 1989.* Department of State Publication 9743. Office of the Secretary of State. Office of the Coordinator for Counter-Terrorism.

120. United States Department of State (2000, April). *Patterns of Global Terrorism 1999.* Department of State Publication 10687. Office of the Secretary of State. Office of the Coordinator for Counterterrorism.

121. United States Department of State (1999, April). *Patterns of Global Terrorism 1998.* U.S. Department of State Publication 10610. Office of the Secretary of State. Office of the Coordinator for Counterterrorism.

122. See United States Department of State (1988, August). *Patterns of Global Terrorism: 1987.* Department of State Publication 9661. Office of the Secretary of State. Ambassador-at-Large for Counter-Terrorism, p. 41.

123. "[P]ursuant to section 219 of the Immigration and Nationality Act, as amended by the Antiterrorism and Effective Death Penalty Act of 1996," United States Department of State (2000, April). *Patterns of Global Terrorism 1999.* Department of State Publication 10687. Office of the Secretary of State. Office of the Coordinator for Counterterrorism.

124. United States Department of State (2000, April). *Patterns of Global Terrorism 1999.* Department of State Publication 10687. Office of the Secretary of State. Office of the Coordinator for Counterterrorism, p. v.

125. Kraft, Michael B. "Introduction." In Evolution of U.S. Counterterrorism Laws, Policies, and Programs. In Alexander, Yonah (2007) Introduction. In Alexander, Yonah, and Michael B. Kraft (Eds.) *Evolution of U.S. Counterterrorism Policy.* Volume I. Westport, Conn.: Praeger Security International.

126. In the aftermath of the 1993 World Trade Center bombing, INS Commissioner Doris Meissner had provided the State Department's Consular Affairs Bureau with funding which had allowed it to automate its terrorist watch list. The list, which the State Department had started to deal with terrorism concerning visa applications and entrance into the U.S., had not been effective. For example, while entry port inspectors may have had a copy of the list, the inspectors did not necessarily have information about the list's purpose. They did not know who they should have been preventing from entering the U.S. The INS tried to establish a system that would verify if foreign students stayed in the country for the purpose stated in the visa. That did not succeed and neither did the INS's effort to track foreign travelers' entry to and exit from the U.S. After 9/11 some of these methods were implemented. *The 9/11 Commission Report: Final Report on the National Commission on Terrorist Attacks upon the United States* (2004). Authorized edition. New York and London: W. W. Norton.

127. United States Department of State (1998, April). *Patterns of Global Terrorism 1997.* Department of State Publication 10535. Office of the Secretary of State. Office of the Coordinator for Counterterrorism; United States Department of State (1997, April). *Patterns of Global Terrorism 1996.* Department of State Publication 10433. Office of the Secretary of State. Office of the Coordinator for Counterterrorism.

128. Briefing upon the Release of the Report *Patterns of Global Terrorism 2000* (2001, April 30). Phillip T. Reeker, Acting Spokesman. Edmund J. Hull, Acting Coordinator for Counterterrorism. Washington, D.C., http://www.state.gov/s/ct/rls/rm/2001/2571.htm.

129. *Ibid.*

130. Bureau of Public Affairs, United States Department of State (1985). International Terrorism, August 1985. In Gist series; United States Department of State (2002, May). *Patterns of Global Terrorism 2001.* Department of State Publication 10940. Office of the Secretary of State. Office of the Coordinator for Counterterrorism.

131. United States Department of State (1991, April). *Patterns of Global Terrorism: 1990.* Department of State Publication 9862. Office of the Secretary of State. Office of the Coordinator for Counterterrorism.

132. United States Department of State (2000, April). *Patterns of Global Terrorism 1999.* Department of State Publication 10687. Office of the Secretary of State. Office of the Coordinator for Counterterrorism.

133. United States Department of State (1995, April). *Patterns of Global Terrorism 1994*. Department of State Publication 10239. Office of the Secretary of State. Office of the Coordinator for Counterterrorism, p. v.

134. House of Representatives (2004, August 19). Diplomacy in the Age of Terrorism: What Is the State Department's Strategy? Hearing before the Committee on International Relations, 108th Congress, 2nd Session. Serial No. 108-152. 95-542PDF 2005, http://commdocs.house.gov/committees/intlrel/hfa95542.000/hfa95542_0f.htm.

135. See http://www.rewardsforjustice.net for details about the Rewards for Justice Program.

136. United States Department of State (2002, May). *Patterns of Global Terrorism 2001*. Department of State Publication 10940. Office of the Secretary of State. Office of the Coordinator for Counterterrorism, p. 142.

137. *The 9/11 Commission Report: Final Report on the National Commission on Terrorist Attacks upon the United States* (2004). Authorized edition. New York and London: W. W. Norton.

138. *Ibid.*; Federal Bureau of Investigation. FBI History, http://www.fbi.gov/libref/historic/history/text.htm.

139. Federal Bureau of Investigation. Terrorism 2001/2002, http://www.fbi.gov/publications/terror/terror2002_2001.htm.

140. Federal Bureau of Investigation. Terrorism 2000/2001, http://www.fbi.gov/publications/terror/terror2000_2001.htm.

141. The FBI further defines one more form of terrorism, special interests terrorism, in which "extremist special interest groups seek to resolve specific issues, rather than effect widespread political change. Special interest extremists continue to conduct acts of politically motivated violence to force segments of society, including the general public, to change attitudes about issued considered important to their causes. These groups occupy the extreme fringes of animal rights, pro-life, environmental, anti-nuclear, and other movements." Federal Bureau of Investigation (2002, February 12). The Threat of Eco-Terrorism. Testimony of James F. Jarboe, Domestic Terrorism Section Chief, Counterterrorism Division, FBI Before the House Resources Committee, Subcommittee on Forests and Forest Health, http://.www.fbi.gov/congress/congress02/jarboe021202.htm.

142. Federal Bureau of Investigation. U.S. Department of Justice (1998). *Terrorism in the United States 1998*. Counterterrorism Threat Assessment and Warning Unit. National Security Division, p. ii.

143. Federal Bureau of Investigation (2002, February 6) The Terrorist Threat Confronting the United States. Testimony of Dale L. Watson, Executive Assistant Director, Counterterrorism/Counterintelligence Division, FBI Before the Senate Select Committee on Intelligence, http://www.fbi.gov/congress/congress02/watson020602.htm; Federal Bureau of Investigation. Investigative Programs Counterintelligence Division. History and Evolution, http://www.fbi.gov/hq/ci/cihistory.htm; *The 9/11 Commission Report: Final Report on the National Commission on Terrorist Attacks upon the United States* (2004). Authorized edition. New York and London: W. W. Norton.

144. Federal Bureau of Investigation. U.S. Department of Justice (1998). *Terrorism in the United States 1998*. Counterterrorism Threat Assessment and Warning Unit. National Security Division, p. ii.

145. *Ibid.*

146. *The 9/11 Commission Report: Final Report on the National Commission on Terrorist Attacks upon the United States* (2004). Authorized edition. New York and London: W. W. Norton.

147. *Ibid.*

148. Federal Bureau of Investigation. Today's FBI: Investigative Programs. http://www.fbi.gov/facts_and_figures/investigative_programs.htm#counterterrorism.

149. Federal Bureau of Investigation. Your Local FBI Office, http://www.fbi.gov/contact/fo/fo.htm.

150. *The 9/11 Commission Report: Final Report on the National Commission on Terrorist Attacks upon the United States* (2004). Authorized edition. New York and London: W. W. Norton.

151. *Ibid.*

152. *Ibid.*

153. Federal Bureau of Investigation. Today's FBI: International Offices/FBI Budget, http://www.fbi.gov/facts_and_figures/international_budget.htm.

154. Federal Bureau of Investigation. Legal Attaché Offices, http://www.fbi.gov/contact/legat/legat.htm.

155. *The 9/11 Commission Report: Final Report on the National Commission on Terrorist Attacks upon the United States* (2004). Authorized edition. New York and London: W. W. Norton, p. 92.

156. Federal Bureau of Investigation. Today's FBI: Investigative Programs. http://www.fbi.gov/facts_and_figures/investigative_programs.htm#counterterrorism.

157. *The 9/11 Commission Report: Final Report on the National Commission on Terrorist Attacks upon the United States* (2004). Authorized edition. New York and London: W. W. Norton.

158. Sheridan, Brian, Assistant Secretary of Defense for Special Operations and Low-Intensity Conflict (2000, March 24). Statement Before the Subcommittee on Emerging Threats and Capabilities of the Committee on Armed Services. United States Senate. 106th Congress. Department of Defense and Combating Terrorism.

159. Brake, Jeffrey D. National Defense Fellow. Foreign Affairs, Defense, and Trade Division (2001, April 19) "Terrorism and the Military's Role in Domestic Crisis Management: Background and Issues for Congress." In CRS Report for Congress. Received through the CRS Web. Order Code RL30938. In Richelson, Jeffrey and Michael L. Evans (Eds.) *The September 11th Sourcebooks. Volume I: Terrorism and U.S. Policy*. The National Security Archive. The George Washington University. National Security Archive Electronic Briefing Book No. 55. September 21, 2001, http://www.gwu.edu/~nsarchiv/NSAEBB/NSAEBB55/index1.html.

160. Departments of the Army and the Air Force (1990). *Military Operations in Low Intensity Conflict. Field Manual 100-20/Air Force Pamphlet 3-20*. Washington, D.C.: Headquarters, Departments of the Army and the Air Force, p. 3-1.

161. Holmes, H. Allen, Assistant Secretary of Defense for Special Operations and Low Intensity Conflict (1994, June 15). *Department of Defense INSTRUCTION*. Number 2000.14. SUBJECT: DoD Combating Terrorism Program Procedures, p. 2.

162. *Ibid.*

163. *The 9/11 Commission Report: Final Report on the National Commission on Terrorist Attacks upon the United States* (2004). Authorized edition. New York and London: W. W. Norton.

164. *Ibid.*; Stoffa, Adam Paul (2005). "Special Forces, Counterterrorism, and the Law of Armed Conflict." In *Studies in Conflict and Terrorism*, Vol. 18.

165. Stoffa, Adam Paul (2005). "Special Forces, Counterterrorism, and the Law of Armed Conflict." In *Studies in Conflict and Terrorism*, Vol. 18.

166. *The 9/11 Commission Report: Final Report on the National Commission on Terrorist Attacks upon the United States* (2004). Authorized edition. New York and London: W. W. Norton; Hoffman, Bruce (1998). *Inside Terrorism*. New York: Columbia University Press.

167. Stoffa, Adam Paul (2005). "Special Forces, Counter-

terrorism, and the Law of Armed Conflict." In *Studies in Conflict and Terrorism*, Vol. 18, pp. 49–50.

168. Howard, Russell D. (2004). Understanding Al Qaeda's Application of the New Terrorism: The Key to Victory in the Current Campaign. In Russell D. Howard and Reid L. Sawyer, *Terrorism and Counterterrorism: Understanding the New Security Environment. Readings & Interpretations.* Revised and Updated. Guilford, Conn.: McGraw-Hill/ Dushkin. (Original work published 2003).

169. *Ibid.*, p. 76.

170. United States Special Operations Command, http:// www.socom.mil.

171. Medd, Roger, and Frank Goldstein (1997). "International Terrorism on the Eve of a New Millennium." In *Studies in Conflict & Terrorism*, Vol. 20.

172. *Ibid.*, pp. 306–307.

173. Stoffa, Adam Paul (2005). "Special Forces, Counterterrorism, and the Law of Armed Conflict." In *Studies in Conflict and Terrorism*, Vol. 18.

174. *The 9/11 Commission Report: Final Report on the National Commission on Terrorist Attacks upon the United States* (2004). Authorized edition. New York and London: W. W. Norton, p. 97.

175. *The 9/11 Commission Report: Final Report on the National Commission on Terrorist Attacks upon the United States* (2004). Authorized edition. New York and London: W. W. Norton.

176. *Ibid.*, p. 86.

177. Deutch, John (1997, Fall). "Terrorism. Think Again." *Foreign Policy.*

178. *The 9/11 Commission Report: Final Report on the National Commission on Terrorist Attacks upon the United States* (2004). Authorized edition. New York and London: W. W. Norton, p. 87.

179. *The 9/11 Commission Report: Final Report on the National Commission on Terrorist Attacks upon the United States* (2004). Authorized edition. New York and London: W. W. Norton.

180. *Ibid.*, p. 85.

181. *Ibid.*, p. 87.

182. National Foreign Assessment Center. CIA. (1981, June). *Patterns of International Terrorism: 1980. A Research Paper.* PA81-10163U, p. ii.

183. The Central Intelligence Agency (posted 2007, April 6; last updated 2007, November 16). CIA & the War on Terrorism. Terrorism FAQs, https://www.cia.gov/news-information/cia-the-war-on-terrorism/terrorism-faqs.html.

184. Deutch, John (1997, Fall). "Terrorism." Think Again. *Foreign Policy.*

185. *The 9/11 Commission Report: Final Report on the National Commission on Terrorist Attacks upon the United States* (2004). Authorized edition. New York and London: W. W. Norton, p. 86.

186. *The 9/11 Commission Report: Final Report on the National Commission on Terrorist Attacks upon the United States* (2004). Authorized edition. New York and London: W. W. Norton.

187. *Ibid.*; Jentleson, Bruce W. (2004). *American Foreign Policy: The Dynamics of Choice in the 21st Century.* 2nd edition. New York and London: W. W. Norton.

188. *The 9/11 Commission Report: Final Report on the National Commission on Terrorist Attacks upon the United States* (2004). Authorized edition. New York and London: W. W. Norton.

189. *Ibid.*

190. Taylor, Philip M. (1997). *Global Communications, International Affairs and the Media since 1945.* London and New York: Routledge, pp. 93–94, citing Friedland, Lewis (1992). *Covering the World: International Television News Services.* New York: 20th Century Fund Press, pp. 7–8.

191. *The 9/11 Commission Report: Final Report on the National Commission on Terrorist Attacks upon the United States* (2004). Authorized edition. New York and London: W. W. Norton.

192. Holland, Jesse J., Associated Press Online. (2001, April 3). Terrorists Change U.S. Targets. Retrieved through LexisNexis Academic.

193. Evans, Harold (2001, November/December). "What We Knew: Warning given ... story missed." In *Columbia Journalism Review*. Special 40th Anniversary Issue: Before and After.

194. Holland, Jesse J., Associated Press Online. (2001, April 3). Terrorists Change U.S. Targets. Retrieved through LexisNexis Academic.

195. Department of Homeland Security. Strategic Plan — Securing Our Homeland, http://www.dhs.gov/x about/strategicplan/index.shtml.

196. National Counterterrorism Center, http://www.nctc.gov/about_us/about/nctc.html.

197. Thomas, Gary (2007, May 7). Protecting America from Terrorism. National Counterterrorism Center, Washington D.C., http://www.nctc.gov/press_room/interviews/ VOA+Protecting+America+from+Terrorism.pdf.

198. Pillar, Paul R. (2004). The Dimensions of Terrorism and Counterterrorism. In Russell D. Howard and Reid L. Sawyer (Eds.) *Terrorism and Counterterrorism: Understanding the New Security Environment. Readings and Interpretations.* Revised and Updated. Guilford, Conn.: McGraw-Hill/ Dushkin. (Original work published 2001), pp. 34–35.

199. Pillar, Paul R. (2004). The Dimensions of Terrorism and Counterterrorism. In Russell D. Howard and Reid L. Sawyer (Eds.) *Terrorism and Counterterrorism: Understanding the New Security Environment. Readings and Interpretations.* Revised and Updated. Guilford, Conn.: McGraw-Hill/ Dushkin. (Original work published 2001).

200. United States Department of State (2002, May). *Patterns of Global Terrorism 2001.* Department of State Publication 10940. Office of the Secretary of State. Office of the Coordinator for Counterterrorism, p. 63.

201. Bart, Peter (2001, October 17). "H'wood enlists in war: Net, studios answer call to arms in fight against terrorism." *Variety*.com, http://www.variety.com; Brodesser, Claude (2001, October 7). "Feds seek H'wood's help: Helmers, scribes probe terrorism at U.S. Army's request." In *Variety*.com, http://www.variety.com.

202. The United Service Organizations, http://www.uso.org.

203. Schodolski, Vincent J. (2001, November 12). "Administration drafts Hollywood effort." *Chicago Tribune*, p. 6.

204. Suid, Lawrence H. (2002). *Guts and Glory: The Making of the American Military Image in Film.* Revised and Expanded Edition. Lexington: University Press of Kentucky.

205. Grossberg, Josh (2001, September 27). Rated "T" for Terrorism. In *E! Online News*, http://www.eonline.com/ News/Items/0,1,8888,00.html.

206. Wasko, Janet (1994). *Hollywood in the Information Age: Beyond the Silver Screen.* Texas Film Studies series. Thomas Schatz (Ed.). Cambridge, U.K.: Polity Press; Guback, Thomas H. (1985). "Hollywood's International Market." In Tino Balio, *The American Film Industry.* Rev. ed. Madison: University of Wisconsin Press. (Original work published 1976.)

Chapter 3

1. *The 9/11 Commission Report: Final Report on the National Commission on Terrorist Attacks upon the United States* (2004). Authorized edition. New York and London: W. W. Norton.

2. "Disaster Becomes a Disaster for Studios" (2001,

September 13). From Studio Briefing. IMDB citing *Wall Street Journal* (2001, September 13), http://entertaindom.imdb.de/news/ni0084096.

3. Grossberg, Josh (2001, September 27). "Rated 'T' for Terrorism." In *E! Online News,* http:// www.eonline.com/News/Items/0,1,8888,00.html.

4. Thussu, Daya Kishan (2000). *International Communication. Continuity and Change.* London: Arnold, and New York: Oxford University Press; MPAA, www.mpaa.org/about/content.htm.

5. Gregg, Robert W. (1998). *International Relations on Film.* Boulder, Colo.: Lynne Rienner Publishers.

6. Parenti, Michael (1992). *Make-Believe Media: The Politics of Entertainment.* New York: St. Martin's Press.

7. *Ibid.*; Welsh, James M. (2000). "Action Films: The Serious, the Ironic, the Post-Modern." In Wheeler Winston Dixon (Ed.) *Film Genre 2000: New Critical Essays.* Albany: State University of New York Press; Schatz, Thomas (1994). "Genre." In Gary Crowdus (Ed.) *A Political Companion to American Film.* Chicago: Lake View Press.

8. For further discussion, see, for example, Combs, James E. (1990). *American Political Movies: An Annotated Filmography of Feature Films.* New York and London: Garland Publishing; Parenti, Michael (1992). *Make-Believe Media: The Politics of Entertainment.* New York: St. Martin's Press; Kellner, Douglas (1995). *Media Culture: Cultural Studies, Identity and Politics between the Modern and the Postmodern.* London and New York: Routledge.

9. Balio, Tino (1998). "'A Major Presence in All of the World's Important Markets': The Globalization of Hollywood in the 1990s." In Steve Neale and Murray Smith (Eds.) *Contemporary Hollywood Cinema.* London and New York: Routledge.

10. Falkenrath, Richard (2001). "Analytic Models and Policy Prescription." In *Studies in Conflict and Terrorism,* 24.

11. Gregg, Robert W. (1998). *International Relations on Film.* Boulder: Lynne Rienner Publishers.

12. Parenti, Michael (1992). *Make-Believe Media: The Politics of Entertainment.* New York: St. Martin's Press; Woll, Allen L. (1993). "Hollywood Views the Mexican-American: From *The Greaser's Revenge* to *The Milagro Beanfield War.*" In Robert Brent Toplin (Ed.) *Hollywood as Mirror: Changing View of "Outsiders" and "Enemies" in American Movies.* In Contributions to the Study of Popular Culture, Number 38. Westport, Conn.: Greenwood Press; Cortes, Carlos E. (1993). "Them and Us: Immigration as Societal Barometer and Social Educator in American Film." In Robert Brent Toplin (Ed.) *Hollywood as Mirror: Changing View of "Outsiders" and Enemies" in American Movies.* Westport, Conn.: Greenwood Press.

13. See, for example, Parenti, Michael (1992). *Make-Believe Media: The Politics of Entertainment.* New York: St. Martin's Press; Crowdus, Gary (1994). "Introduction." *The Political Companion to American Film.* Chicago: Lake View Press; Gregg, Robert W. (1998). *International Relations on Film.* Boulder, Colo.: Lynne Rienner Publishers.

14. Hess, Stephen (1996). *International News and Foreign Correspondents.* Washington, D.C.: Brookings Institution; Rosenblum, Mort (1993). *Who Stole the News?: Why We Can't Keep Up with What Happens in the World and What We Can Do about It.* New York: John Wiley & Sons.

15. The Pew Research Center for the People and the Press (2002, June 9). "Public's News Habits Little Changed by September 11: Americans Lack Background to Follow International News," In Survey Reports. http://people-press.org/reports/display.php3?ReportID=156.

16. Groves, Don (1999, December 16). "America's pics find foreign B.O. hit, miss puzzle." In *Variety.*

17. Theatrical Market Statistics 2008, MPAA, http://www.mpaa.org/researchStatistics.asp.

18. Dixon, Wheeler Winston. "Introduction: The New Genre Cinema." In Wheeler Winston Dixon (Ed.) *Film Genre 2000: New Critical Essays.* Albany: State University of New York Press; Crowdus, Gary (1994). "Introduction." *The Political Companion to American Film.* Chicago: Lake View Press; Variety.com box-office data.

19. Combs, James E. (1990). *American Political Movies: An Annotated Filmography of Feature Films.* New York and London: Garland Publishing.

20. Wasko, Janet (1994). *Hollywood in the Information Age: Beyond the Silver Screen.* Texas Film Studies Series. Thomas Schatz (Ed.). Great Britain: Polity Press, and Austin: University of Texas Press; Geuens, Jean-Pierre (2000). *Film Production Theory.* In Wheeler Winston Dixon (Ed.) The SUNY Series Cultural Studies in Cinema/Video. Albany: State University of New York Press.

21. Wasko, Janet (1994). *Hollywood in the Information Age: Beyond the Silver Screen.* Texas Film Studies Series. Thomas Schatz (Ed.). Great Britain: Polity Press, and Austin: University of Texas Press.

22. Maltby, Barbara (1998). "The Homogenization of Hollywood." In Nancy J. Woodhull and Robert W. Snyder (Eds.) *Media Mergers.* New Brunswick, N.J.: Transaction Publishers. (Original work published in *Media Studies Journal,* Spring/Summer 1996.)

23. Wasko, Janet (1994). *Hollywood in the Information Age: Beyond the Silver Screen.* Texas Film Studies Series. Thomas Schatz (Ed.). Great Britain: Polity Press, and University of Texas Press.

24. Adorno, Theodor, and Max Horkheimer (1989). "Selections from 'The Culture Industry: Enlightenment as Mass Deception.'" In *Dialectic of Enlightenment.* In Roger S. Gottlieb (Ed.) *An Anthology of Western Marxism: From Lukacs and Gramsci to Socialist-Feminism.* New York and Oxford: Oxford University Press. (Original work published 1972).

25. Bordwell, David, and Kristin Thompson (2004). *Film Art: An Introduction.* 7th ed. Boston: McGraw-Hill.

26. Donahue, Mary Suzanne (1987). *American Film Distribution: The Changing Marketplace.* In Diane M. Kirkpatrick (Ed.) Studies in Cinema, No. 40. Ann Arbor, Mich.: UMI Research Press.

27. Motion Picture Association of America, http://www.mpaa.org/about/content.htm; Thussu, Daya Kishan (2000). *International Communication: Continuity and Change.* London: Arnold, and New York: Oxford University Press.

28. Miller, Toby, Nitin Govil, John McMurria, and Richard Maxwell (2001). *Global Hollywood.* London: BFI Publishing, p. 3.

29. Maltby, Richard (2003). *Hollywood Cinema: An Introduction.* 2nd ed. Malden, Mass.: Blackwell Publishing.

30. Wasko, Janet (2003). *How Hollywood Works.* Thousand Oaks, Calif.: Sage Publications, p. 2.

31. The MPAA, which represents the major studios, was founded in 1922 to prevent outside efforts to regulate the industry. Belton, John (1996). "The Production Code." In John Bolton (Ed.) *Movies and Mass Culture.* In Charles Affron, Mirella Affron, and Robert Lyons (Eds.) Rutgers Depth of Field Series. New Brunswick, N.J.: Rutgers University Press.

32. Motion Picture Association of America, http://www.mpaa.org/anti-piracy/content.htm.

33. Wasko, Janet (2003). *How Hollywood Works.* Thousand Oaks, Calif.: Sage Publications.

34. Bordwell, David, and Kristin Thompson (2004). *Film Art: An Introduction.* 7th ed. Boston: McGraw-Hill.

35. Wasko, Janet (1994). *Hollywood in the Information Age: Beyond the Silver Screen.* Texas Film Studies Series. Thomas Schatz (Ed.). Great Britain: Polity Press, and Austin: University of Texas Press, p. 33.

36. Maltby, Barbara (1998). "The Homogenization of Hollywood." In Nancy J. Woodhull and Robert W. Snyder

(Eds.) *Media Mergers.* New Brunswick, N.J.: Transaction Publishers. (Original work published in *Media Studies Journal,* Spring/Summer 1996.)

37. Wasko, Janet (2003). *How Hollywood Works.* Thousand Oaks, Calif.: Sage Publications, p. 37.

38. Wasko, Janet (2003). *How Hollywood Works.* Thousand Oaks, Calif.: Sage Publications.

39. Bordwell, David (1986). "Classical Hollywood Cinema: Narrational Principles and Procedures." In Philip Rosen (Ed.) *Narrative, Apparatus, Ideology: A Film Theory Reader.* New York: Columbia University Press.

40. Wasko, Janet (2003). *How Hollywood Works.* Thousand Oaks, Calif.: Sage Publications.

41. *Ibid.*, p. 84.

42. Donahue, Mary Suzanne (1987). *American Film Distribution: The Changing Marketplace.* In Diane M. Kirkpatrick (Ed.) Studies in Cinema, No. 40. Ann Arbor, Mich.: UMI Research Press.

43. Bordwell, David, and Kristin Thompson (2008). *Film Art: An Introduction.* 8th ed. Boston: McGraw-Hill, p. 34.

44. Wasko, Janet (2003). *How Hollywood Works.* Thousand Oaks, Calif.: Sage Publications, pp. 61–78.

45. Bordwell, David, and Kristin Thompson (2008). *Film Art: An Introduction.* 8th ed. Boston: McGraw-Hill.

46. Scott, citing the Motion Picture Association of America and the National Association of Theater Owners, finds the following figures for the majors' share of the gross domestic box office: 1980, 91%; 1985, 77%; 1990, 80%; 1995, 86%; 2000, 83%. Scott, Allen J. (2005). *On Hollywood: The Place. The Industry.* Princeton, N.J.: Princeton University Press, p. 142.

47. *Ibid.*

48. Vivendi Universal press release, www.vivendiuniversal.com/vu/en/press_2003/20031008_General_Electric_and_Vivendi_Universal_Sign_Agreement_To_Merge_NBC_and_Vive.cfm.

49. Vivendi. Company History, http://www.vivendi.com/vivendi/Company-history; NBC Universal. Company Overview, http://www.nbcuni.com/About_NBC_Universal/Company_Overview/; NBC Europe (2004, May 12). "NBC and Vivendi Universal Entertainment unite to create NBC Universal," http://www.cnbc.com/id/18037310; msn.money (2009, February 12). "Joseph Cates Named Senior Vice President Technology, Universal Pictures," http://news.moneycentral.msn.com/ticker/article.aspx?symbol=US:GE&feed=PR&date=20090212&id=9605977.

50. Tom Cruise and Paula Wagner, in partnership with MGM, formed United Artists Entertainment LLC (http://www.unitedartists.com) as a new entity in November 2006. Cruise and Wagner have control over which films to produce, with minor limitations. MGM is in charge of the UA movies' worldwide marketing and distribution. MGM and its partners finance the production and development of the UA films; "MGM Partners with Tom Cruise and Paula Wagner; Paula Wagner to Serve as CEO of the New UA" (2007, September 16). Press release. United Artists, http://www.unitedartists.com/popups/pr/release_08.html. Wagner left her CEO position in August 2008.

51. In 2004 an investor consortium bought MGM, whose main owner had been Kirk Kerkorian. According to the official MGM website (March 2009), "MGM is owned by an investor consortium comprised of Providence Equity Partners, TPG [Texas Pacific Group], Sony Corporation of America, Comcast Corporation, DLJ Merchant Banking Partners and Quadrangle Group," http://www.mgm.com/corp_main.php.

52. Wasko, Janet (2003). *How Hollywood Works.* Thousand Oaks, Calif.: Sage Publications.

53. Hoovers.com. DreamWorks SKG DreamWorks Company Description, http://www.hoovers.com/dreamworks/--ID__42800--/free-co-profile.xhtml; Cieply, Michael (2008, October 5). "DreamWorks Executives Sever Ties with Paramount to Form a New Company." *New York Times,* http://www.nytimes.com/2008/10/06/business/media/06dreamworks.html; Associated Press (2009, February 9). "Walt Disney Studios, Dreamworks Reach Deal." *Los Angeles Times.*

54. Donahue, Mary Suzanne (1987). *American Film Distribution: The Changing Marketplace.* In Diane M. Kirkpatrick (Ed.) Studies in Cinema, No. 40. Ann Arbor, Mich.: UMI Research Press.

55. Wasko, Janet (2003). *How Hollywood Works.* Thousand Oaks, Calif.: Sage Publications.

56. Bordwell, David, and Kristin Thompson (2004). *Film Art: An Introduction.* 7th ed. Boston: McGraw-Hill.

57. *Ibid.*

58. *Ibid.*, p. 9.

59. Wasko, Janet (1994). *Hollywood in the Information Age: Beyond the Silver Screen.* Texas Film Studies Series. Thomas Schatz (Ed.). Great Britain: Polity Press, and Austin: University of Texas Press.

60. Gomery, Douglas (2000). "The Hollywood Film Industry: Theatrical Exhibition, Pay TV, and Home Video." In Benjamin M. Compaine and Douglas Gomery, *Who Owns the Media? Competition and Concentration in the Mass Media Industry.* 3rd edition. Mahwah, N.J.: Lawrence Erlbaum Associates, p. 360.

61. *Ibid.*

62. Wasko, Janet (2003). *How Hollywood Works.* Thousand Oaks, Calif.: Sage Publications.

63. Groves, Don (1999, December 16). "America's pics find foreign B.O. hit, miss puzzle." In *Variety*; Klady, Leonard (1996, November 25–December 1). "Why megaflicks click." In *Variety.*

64. Guback, Thomas H. (1985). "Hollywood's International Market." In Tino Balio, *The American Film Industry.* Rev. ed. Madison: University of Wisconsin Press. (Original work published 1976), p. 485.

65. Geuens, Jean-Pierre (2000). *Film Production Theory.* In Wheeler Winston Dixon (Ed.) The SUNY Series Cultural Studies in Cinema/Video. Albany: State University of New York Press; Thompson, Kristin, and David Bordwell (2003). *Film History: An Introduction.* 2nd ed. New York: McGraw-Hill.

66. *Ibid.*; Bordwell, David, and Kristin Thompson (2004). *Film Art: An Introduction.* 7th ed. Boston: McGraw-Hill.

67. Guback, Thomas H. (1985). "Hollywood's International Market." In Tino Balio, *The American Film Industry.* Rev. ed. Madison: The University of Wisconsin Press. (Original work published 1976).

68. *Ibid.*

69. Trumpbour, John (2002). *Selling Hollywood to the World: U.S. and European Struggles for Mastery of the Global Film Industry, 1920–1950.* Cambridge, U.K.: Cambridge University Press.

70. Guback, Thomas H. (1985). "Hollywood's International Market." In Tino Balio, *The American Film Industry.* Rev. ed. Madison: University of Wisconsin Press. (Original work published 1976), p. 473 citing *Motion Picture Letter 3* (1944, September) and *Motion Picture Letter 4* (1945, February). Issued by the Public Information Committee of the Motion Picture Industry.

71. Trumpbour, John (2002). *Selling Hollywood to the World: U.S. and European Struggles for Mastery of the Global Film Industry, 1920–1950.* Cambridge, U.K.: Cambridge University Press.

72. Jarvie, Ian C. (1998). "Free Trade as Cultural Threat: American film and TV exports in the post-war period." In Geoffrey Nowell-Smith and Steven Ricci (Eds.) *Hollywood and Europe. Economics, Culture, National Identity 1945–95.* London: BFI Publishing, pp. 34–46.

73. Donahue, Mary Suzanne (1987). *American Film Distribution: The Changing Marketplace.* In Diane M. Kirkpatrick (Ed.) Studies in Cinema, No. 40. Ann Arbor, Mich.: UMI Research Press.

74. Guback, Thomas H. (1985). "Hollywood's International Market." In Tino Balio, *The American Film Industry.* Rev. ed. Madison: University of Wisconsin Press. (Original work published 1976.)

75. *Ibid.*; Donahue, Mary Suzanne (1987). *American Film Distribution: The Changing Marketplace.* In Diane M. Kirkpatrick (Ed.) Studies in Cinema, No. 40. Ann Arbor, Mich.: UMI Research Press; MPAA, www.mpaa.org/about/content.htm.

76. Guback, Thomas H. (1985). "Hollywood's International Market." In Tino Balio, *The American Film Industry.* Rev. ed. Madison: University of Wisconsin Press. (Original work published 1976.)

77. Trumpbour, John (2002). *Selling Hollywood to the World: U.S. and European Struggles for Mastery of the Global Film Industry, 1920–1950.* Cambridge, U.K.: Cambridge University Press.

78. *Ibid.*, p. 471 citing Valenti, Jack. "The 'Foreign Service' of the Motion Picture Association of America" (1968, March). In *Journal of the Producers Guild of America* 10, p. 22.

79. Motion Picture Association of America, http://www.mpaa.org/about/content.htm.

80. Guback, Thomas H. (1985). "Hollywood's International Market." In Tino Balio, *The American Film Industry.* Rev. ed. Madison: University of Wisconsin Press. (Original work published 1976), p. 473 citing Johnston, Eric. "Messengers from a Free Country." In Motion Picture Association of America. According to Guback (1985, p. 473), the article was also published in *Saturday Review of Literature* 33 (1950, March), pp. 9–12.

81. Wasko, Janet (1994). *Hollywood in the Information Age: Beyond the Silver Screen.* Texas Film Studies Series. Thomas Schatz (Ed.). Great Britain: Polity Press, and Austin: University of Texas Press.

82. Steinbock, Dan (1995). *Triumph and Erosion in the American Media and Entertainment Industries.* Westport, Conn.: Quorum Books.

83. Wasko, Janet (2003). *How Hollywood Works.* Thousand Oaks, Calif.: Sage Publications, p. 59.

84. Balio, Tino (1998). "'A major Presence in All of the World's Important Markets': The Globalization of Hollywood in the 1990s." In Steve Neale and Murray Smith (Eds.). *Contemporary Hollywood Cinema.* London and New York: Routledge, p. 58.

85. Murdock, Graham, and Peter Golding (1997). "For a Political Economy of Mass Communications." In Peter Golding and Graham Murdock (Eds.) *The Political Economy of the Media I.* Cheltenham & Brookfield, Vt.: Edward Elgar. (Original work published 1973 in *Socialist Register*), p. 11; Mosco, Vincent (1996). *The Political Economy of Communication: Rethinking and Renewal.* Thousand Oaks, Calif.: Sage Publications.

86. Balio, Tino (1998). "'A Major Presence in All of the World's Important Markets': The Globalization of Hollywood in the 1990s." In Steve Neale and Murray Smith (Eds.). *Contemporary Hollywood Cinema.* London and New York: Routledge.

87. *Ibid.*

88. *Ibid.*

89. *Ibid.*

90. *Ibid.*

91. Wasko, Janet (2003). *How Hollywood Works.* Thousand Oaks, Calif.: Sage Publications; Balio, Tino (1998). "'A Major Presence in All of the World's Important Markets': The Globalization of Hollywood in the 1990s." In Steve Neale and Murray Smith (Eds.). *Contemporary Hollywood Cinema.* London and New York: Routledge.

92. Wasko, Janet (2003). *How Hollywood Works.* Thousand Oaks, Calif.: Sage Publications, p. 189.

93. Balio, Tino (1998). "'A Major Presence in All of the World's Important Markets': The Globalization of Hollywood in the 1990s." In Steve Neale and Murray Smith (Eds.) *Contemporary Hollywood Cinema* (pp. 58–73). London and New York: Routledge; Bart, Peter. (1994, March 14–20). "Numbing numbers." In *Variety.*

94. Wasko, Janet (1994). *Hollywood in the Information Age: Beyond the Silver Screen.* Texas Film Studies Series. Thomas Schatz (Ed.). Great Britain: Polity Press, and Austin: University of Texas Press; Dixon, Wheeler Winston. "Introduction: The New Genre Cinema." In Wheeler Winston Dixon (Ed.) *Film Genre 2000: New Critical Essays.* Albany: State University of New York Press.

95. Motion Picture Association of America, http://www.mpaa.org/anti-piracy/content.htm.

96. *Ibid.*, emphasis original.

97. Balio, Tino (1998). "'A Major Presence in All of the World's Important Markets': The Globalization of Hollywood in the 1990s." In Steve Neale and Murray Smith (Eds.). *Contemporary Hollywood Cinema.* London and New York: Routledge.

98. Miller, Toby, Nitin Govil, John McMurria, and Richard Maxwell (2001). *Global Hollywood.* London: BFI Publishing.

99. Maltby, Barbara (1998). "The Homogenization of Hollywood." In Nancy J. Woodhull and Robert W. Snyder (Eds.) *Media Mergers.* New Brunswick, N.J.: Transaction Publishers. (Original work published in *Media Studies Journal,* Spring/Summer 1996.)

100. Maltby, Richard (1995). *Hollywood Cinema: An Introduction.* Cambridge, Mass.: Blackwell Publishers, p. 40.

101. Miller, Toby, Nitin Govil, John McMurria, and Richard Maxwell (2001). *Global Hollywood.* London: BFI Publishing.

102. Wasko, Janet (1994). *Hollywood in the Information Age: Beyond the Silver Screen.* Texas Film Studies Series. Thomas Schatz (Ed.). Great Britain: Polity Press, and Austin: University of Texas Press.

103. Groves, Don (1999, December 16). "America's Pics Find Foreign B.O. Hit, Miss Puzzle." In *Variety.*

104. Welsh, James M. (2000). "Action Films: The Serious, the Ironic, the Post-Modern." In Wheeler Winston Dixon (Ed.) *Film Genre 2000: New Critical Essays.* Albany: State University of New York Press.

105. Groves, Don (1999, December 16). "America's Pics Find Foreign B.O. Hit, Miss Puzzle." In *Variety.*

106. Welsh, James M. (2000). "Action Films: The Serious, the Ironic, the Post-Modern." In Wheeler Winston Dixon (Ed.) *Film Genre 2000: New Critical Essays.* Albany: State University of New York Press.

107. *Ibid.*

108. Herman, Edward S., and Robert W. McChesney (1997). *The Global Media. The New Missionaries of Corporate Capitalism.* London and Washington: Cassell, p. 45.

109. Belton, John (2009). *American Cinema/American Culture.* 3rd ed. Boston: McGraw-Hill Higher Education.

110. Wasko, Janet (1994). *Hollywood in the Information Age: Beyond the Silver Screen.* Texas Film Studies Series. Thomas Schatz (Ed.). Great Britain: Polity Press, and Austin: University of Texas Press.

111. Guback, Thomas H. (1985). "Hollywood's International Market." In Tino Balio, *The American Film Industry.* Rev. ed. Madison: University of Wisconsin Press. (Original work published 1976), p. 463.

112. Adorno, Theodor, and Max Horkheimer (1989). "Selections from 'The Culture Industry: Enlightenment as Mass Deception.'" In *Dialectic of Enlightenment.* In Roger S. Gottlieb (Ed.) *An Anthology of Western Marxism: From Lukacs and Gramsci to Socialist-Feminism.* New York and Oxford: Oxford University Press. (Original work published 1972.)

113. See, for example, Crowdus, Gary (1994). "Introduction." *The Political Companion to American Film.* Chicago: Lake View Press; Combs, James E. (1990). *American Political Movies: An Annotated Filmography of Feature Films.* New York and London: Garland Publishing.

114. Adorno, Theodor, and Max Horkheimer (1989). "Selections from 'The Culture Industry: Enlightenment as Mass Deception.'" In *Dialectic of Enlightenment.* In Roger S. Gottlieb (Ed.) *An Anthology of Western Marxism: From Lukacs and Gramsci to Socialist-Feminism.* New York and Oxford: Oxford University Press. (Original work published 1972), p. 183.

115. Belton, John (1994). *American Cinema/American Culture.* New York: McGraw-Hill.

116. *Ibid.*, p. 115.

117. Neale, Steve (2000). *Genre and Hollywood.* London and New York: Routledge.

118. Maltby, Richard (1995). *Hollywood Cinema: An Introduction.* Cambridge, Mass.: Blackwell Publishers.

119. *Ibid.*, p. 110: The Motion Picture Research Bureau's survey, authored by Leo Handel, listed eighteen different types of movies in 1942: comedies (sophisticated, slapstick, family life, musical and "just" comedies); war pictures; mystery/horror pictures; historicals/biographies; fantasies; western pictures; gangster and G-men pictures; serious dramas; love stories and romantic pictures; socially significant pictures; adventure and action pictures; musicals (serious); child star pictures; and (wild) animal pictures.

120. Maltby, Richard (1995). *Hollywood Cinema: An Introduction.* Cambridge, Mass.: Blackwell Publishers.

121. Maltby, Richard (2003). *Hollywood Cinema. An Introduction.* 2nd ed. Malden, Mass.: Blackwell Publishing, p. 17.

122. Armer, Alan A. (1993). *Writing the Screenplay: TV and Film.* 2nd ed. Belmont, Calif.: Wadsworth.

123. Maltby, Richard (1995). *Hollywood Cinema: An Introduction.* Cambridge, Mass.: Blackwell Publishers.

124. Cawelti, John G. (1993). "Who Is Running This Show?: Ideology, Formula, and Hegemony in American Film and Television." In James Combs (Ed.) *Movies and Politics: The Dynamic Relationship.* New York & London: Garland Publishing.

125. Belton, John (1994). *American Cinema/American Culture.* New York: McGraw-Hill.

126. Maltby, Richard (1995). *Hollywood Cinema: An Introduction.* Cambridge, Mass.: Blackwell Publishers.

127. Belton, John (1994). *American Cinema/American Culture.* New York: McGraw-Hill.

128. *Ibid.*

129. Bordwell, David, and Kristin Thompson (2004). *Film Art: An Introduction.* 7th ed. Boston: McGraw-Hill.

130. Belton, John (1994). *American Cinema/American Culture.* New York: McGraw-Hill.

131. Bordwell, David, and Kristin Thompson (2004). *Film Art: An Introduction.* 7th ed. Boston: McGraw-Hill.

132. Armer, Alan A. (1993). *Writing the Screenplay: TV and Film.* 2nd ed. Belmont, Calif.: Wadsworth.

133. *Ibid.*, p. 6.

134. Belton, John (1996). "Introduction." In John Belton (Ed.). *Movies and Mass Culture.* In Charles Affron, Mirella Affron, and Robert Lyons (Eds.) Rutgers Depth of Field Series. New Brunswick, N.J.: Rutgers University Press, p. 12, emphasis original.

135. Armer, Alan A. (1993). *Writing the Screenplay: TV and Film.* 2nd ed. Belmont, Calif.: Wadsworth.

136. Bordwell, David, and Kristin Thompson (2004). *Film Art. An Introduction.* 7th ed. Boston: McGraw-Hill.

137. Armer, Alan A. (1993). *Writing the Screenplay: TV and Film.* 2nd ed. Belmont, Calif.: Wadsworth, p. 8.

138. Lesage, Julia (1999, Spring Quarter). Graduate Course on Dramatic Screenwriting. Department of English, University of Oregon; Ferguson, Larry (2000, April). Advanced Screenwriting Workshop. Department of English, University of Oregon.

139. Ferguson, Larry (2000, April). Advanced Screenwriting Workshop. Department of English, University of Oregon.

140. Armer, Alan A. (1993). *Writing the Screenplay: TV and Film.* 2nd ed. Belmont, Calif.: Wadsworth.

141. Ferguson, Larry (2000, April). Advanced Screenwriting Workshop. Department of English, University of Oregon; Armer, Alan A. (1993). *Writing the Screenplay: TV and Film.* 2nd ed. Belmont, Calif.: Wadsworth; Miller, William (1998). *Screenwriting for Film and Television.* Boston: Allyn and Bacon; Lesage, Julia (1999, Spring Quarter). Graduate Course on Dramatic Screenwriting. Department of English, University of Oregon.

142. Armer, Alan A. (1993). *Writing the Screenplay: TV and Film.* 2nd ed. Belmont, Calif.: Wadsworth.

143. *Ibid.*; Miller, William (1998). *Screenwriting for Film and Television.* Boston: Allyn and Bacon.

144. Armer, Alan A. (1993). *Writing the Screenplay: TV and Film.* 2nd ed. Belmont, Calif.: Wadsworth; Ferguson, Larry (2000, April). Advanced Screenwriting Workshop. Department of English, University of Oregon.

145. Armer, Alan A. (1993). *Writing the Screenplay: TV and Film.* 2nd ed. Belmont, Calif.: Wadsworth.

146. *Ibid.*; Ferguson, Larry (2000, April). Advanced Screenwriting Workshop. Department of English, University of Oregon; Miller, William (1998). *Screenwriting for Film and Television.* Boston: Allyn and Bacon; Lesage, Julia (1999, Spring Quarter). Graduate Course on Dramatic Screenwriting. Department of English, University of Oregon.

147. Ferguson, Larry (2000, April). Advanced Screenwriting Workshop. Department of English, University of Oregon; Ferguson, Larry (2000, April). Personal Interview. University of Oregon, Eugene, OR.

148. Armer, Alan A. (1993). *Writing the Screenplay: TV and Film.* 2nd ed. Belmont, Calif.: Wadsworth, p. 41.

149. *Ibid.*, p. 54; emphasis original.

150. Armer, Alan A. (1993). *Writing the Screenplay: TV and Film.* 2nd ed. Belmont, Calif.: Wadsworth.

151. Bordwell, David, and Kristin Thompson (2004). *Film Art: An Introduction.* 7th ed. Boston: McGraw-Hill.

152. Wasko, Janet (1994). *Hollywood in the Information Age: Beyond the Silver Screen.* Texas Film Studies Series. Thomas Schatz (Ed.). Great Britain: Polity Press, and Austin: University of Texas Press.

153. Neale, Steve (2000). *Genre and Hollywood.* London and New York: Routledge, p. 52.

154. Neale, Steve (2000). *Genre and Hollywood.* London and New York: Routledge.

155. *Ibid.*

156. Sobchack, Thomas (1988). "The Adventure Film." In Wes D. Gehring (Ed.) *Handbook of American Film Genres.* New York: Westport, Conn.: Greenwood Press, p. 9.

157. *Ibid.*, p. 13.

158. Sobchack, Thomas (1988). "The Adventure Film." In Wes D. Gehring (Ed.) *Handbook of American Film Genres.* New York: Westport, Conn.: Greenwood Press.

159. *Ibid.*, p. 12.

160. *Ibid.*, p. 13.

161. Sobchack, Thomas (1988). "The Adventure Film."

In Wes D. Gehring (Ed.) *Handbook of American Film Genres.* New York: Westport, Conn.: Greenwood Press.

162. *Ibid.*, p. 14.

163. Belton, John (1994). *American Cinema/American Culture.* New York: McGraw-Hill, p. 165.

164. *Ibid.*, p. 154.

165. *Ibid.*, p. 165.

166. *Ibid.*, p. 168.

167. Parenti, Michael (1992). *Make-Believe Media: The Politics of Entertainment.* New York: St. Martin's Press.

168. Belton, John (1994). *American Cinema/American Culture.* New York: McGraw-Hill.

169. *Ibid.*

170. Parenti, Michael (1992). *Make-Believe Media: The Politics of Entertainment.* New York: St. Martin's Press.

171. Belton, John (1994). *American Cinema/American Culture.* New York: McGraw-Hill.

172. Neale, Steve (2000). *Genre and Hollywood.* London and New York: Routledge.

173. Welsh, James M. (2000). "Action Films: The Serious, the Ironic, the Post-Modern." In Wheeler Winston Dixon (Ed.) *Film Genre 2000: New Critical Essays.* Albany: State University of New York Press.

174. *Ibid.*, p. 169.

175. *Ibid.*, p. 170.

176. Parenti, Michael (1992). *Make-Believe Media: The Politics of Entertainment.* New York: St. Martin's Press.

177. Slocum, J. David (2001). "Introduction: Violence and American Cinema. Notes for an Investigation." In J. David Slocum (Ed.) *Violence and American Cinema.* AFI Film Readers series. New York: Routledge, p. 4.

178. Parenti, Michael (1992). *Make-Believe Media: The Politics of Entertainment.* New York: St. Martin's Press.

179. *Ibid.*

180. Sobchack, Thomas (1988). "The Adventure Film." In Wes D. Gehring (Ed.) *Handbook of American Film Genres.* New York: Westport, Conn.: Greenwood Press, pp. 16–17.

181. Lowry, Brian (1994, July 11). *True Lies.* Review. In *Variety.* Variety.com; *True Lies* box-office information, the top 250 box-office films of 1994, variety.com.

182. Dixon, Wheeler Winston. "Introduction: The New Genre Cinema." In Wheeler Winston Dixon (Ed.) *Film Genre 2000: New Critical Essays.* Albany: State University of New York Press.

183. King, Cynthia (2000). "Effects of Humorous Heroes and Villains in Violent Action Films." In *Journal of Communication,* Winter; Welsh, James M. (2000). "Action Films: The Serious, the Ironic, the Post-Modern." In Wheeler Winston Dixon (Ed.) *Film Genre 2000: New Critical Essays.* Albany: State University of New York Press.

184. Maltby, Richard (2003). *Hollywood Cinema. An Introduction.* 2nd ed. Malden, Mass.: Blackwell Publishing; Gallagher, Mark (2000). Action Figures: Spectacular Masculinity in the Contemporary Action Film and the Contemporary American Novel. Ph.D. dissertation. Department of English, University of Oregon.

185. Parenti, Michael (1992). *Make-Believe Media: The Politics of Entertainment.* New York: St. Martin's Press.

186. *Ibid.*

187. Shaheen, Jack. G. (2001). *Reel Bad Arabs: How Hollywood Vilifies People.* New York & Northampton: Olive Branch Press.

188. Gregg, Robert W. (1998). *International Relations on Film.* Boulder, Colo.: Lynne Rienner Publishers.

189. Parenti, Michael (1992). *Make-Believe Media: The Politics of Entertainment.* New York: St. Martin's Press.

190. Crowdus, Gary (1994). "Introduction." *The Political Companion to American Film.* Chicago: Lake View Press.

191. Schiller, Herbert (1973). *The Mind Managers.* Boston: Beacon Press.

192. Crowdus, Gary (1994). "Introduction." *The Political Companion to American Film.* Chicago: Lake View Press.

193. Ruiz, Raul (1995). *Poetics of Cinema.* Paris: Editions Dis Voir. Translated by Brian Holmes.

194. Schatz, Thomas (1981). *Hollywood Genres: Formulas, Filmmaking, and the Studio System.* Philadelphia: Temple University Press, p. 261.

195. Hall, Stuart (1982). "The Discovery of 'Ideology': Return to the Repressed in Media Studies." In Michael Gurevitch, Tony Bennett, James Curran, and Janet Woollacott (Eds.). *Culture, Society and the Media.* London: Methuen.

196. Schatz, Thomas (1994). "Genre." In Gary Crowdus (Ed.) *A Political Companion to American Film.* Chicago: Lake View Press.

197. Parenti, Michael (1992). *Make-Believe Media: The Politics of Entertainment.* New York: St. Martin's Press.

198. Gregg, Robert W. (1998). *International Relations on Film.* Boulder, Colo.: Lynne Rienner Publishers.

199. *Ibid.*, p. 11.

200. Gregg, Robert W. (1998). *International Relations on Film.* Boulder, Colo.: Lynne Rienner Publishers.

201. Lorence, James J. (1993). "The 'Foreign Policy of Hollywood': Interventionist Sentiment in the American Film, 1938–1941." In Robert Brent Toplin (Ed.) *Hollywood as Mirror: Changing View of "Outsiders" and Enemies" in American Movies.* In Contributions to the Study of Popular Culture, Number 38. Westport, Conn.: Greenwood Press.

202. Slocum, J. David. (2001). "Introduction: Violence and American Cinema. Notes for an Investigation." In J. David Slocum (Ed.) *Violence and American Cinema.* In AFI Film Readers series. New York: Routledge, p. 6.

203. Belton, John (1994). *American Cinema/American Culture.* New York: McGraw-Hill.

204. Parenti, Michael (1992). *Make-Believe Media: The Politics of Entertainment.* New York: St. Martin's Press.

205. Leab, Daniel J. (1993). "Hollywood and the Cold War, 1945–1961." In Robert Bret Toplin (Ed.) *Hollywood as Mirror: Changing View of "Outsiders" and "Enemies" in American Movies.* In Contributions to the Study of Popular Culture, Number 38. Westport, Conn.: Greenwood Press.

206. Lenihan, John H. (1993). "Hollywood Laughs at the Cold War, 1947–1961." In Robert Brent Toplin (Ed.) *Hollywood as Mirror: Changing View of "Outsiders" and "Enemies" in American Movies.* Westport, Conn.: Greenwood Press.

207. Parenti, Michael (1992). *Make-Believe Media: The Politics of Entertainment.* New York: St. Martin's Press.

208. Combs, James E. (1990). *American Political Movies: An Annotated Filmography of Feature Films.* New York and London. Garland Publishing.

209. Belton, John (1994). *American Cinema/American Culture.* New York: McGraw-Hill.

210. Slocum, J. David. (2001). "Introduction: Violence and American Cinema. Notes for an Investigation." In J. David Slocum (Ed.) *Violence and American Cinema.* In AFI Film Readers series. New York: Routledge.

211. Belton, John (1994). *American Cinema/American Culture.* New York: McGraw-Hill, pp. 280, 281.

212. *Ibid.*, pp. 294, 295.

213. *Ibid.*, p. 296.

214. Maltby, Richard (2003). *Hollywood Cinema: An Introduction.* 2nd ed. Malden, Mass.: Blackwell Publishing.

215. Combs, James E. (1990). *American Political Movies: An Annotated Filmography of Feature Films.* New York and London: Garland Publishing.

216. *Ibid.*

217. Kellner, Douglas (1995). *Media Culture: Cultural Studies, Identity and Politics between the Modern and the Postmodern.* London and New York: Routledge.

218. Mitchell, Lee Clark (2001). "Violence in the Film Western." In J. David Slocum (Ed.) *Violence and Ameri-*

can Cinema. In AFI Film Readers series. New York: Routledge.

219. Slocum, J. David. (2001). "Introduction: Violence and American Cinema. Notes for an Investigation." In J. David Slocum (Ed.) *Violence and American Cinema.* In AFI Film Readers series. New York: Routledge, p. 4.

220. Belton, John (1994). *American Cinema/American Culture.* New York: McGraw-Hill.

221. Parenti, Michael (1992). *Make-Believe Media: The Politics of Entertainment.* New York: St. Martin's Press.

222. Combs, James E. (1990) *American Political Movies: An Annotated Filmography of Feature Films.* New York and London: Garland Publishing; Chomsky, Noam (1988). *The Culture of Terrorism.* Boston: South End Press.

223. Palmer, William J. (1993). *The Films of the Eighties: A Social History.* Carbondale: Southern Illinois University Press; Baczkowski, Ronald F., U.S. Multinational Forces. "Tactical Lessons for Peacekeeping: U.S. Multinational Forces in Beirut 1982–1984," http://www.fas.org/man/dod_101/ops/docs/baczkow.htm (also available at http://www.globalsecurity.org/military/library/report/1995/BRF.htm).

224. Slocum, J. David (2001). "Introduction: Violence and American Cinema. Notes for an Investigation." In J. David Slocum (Ed.) *Violence and American Cinema.* In AFI Film Readers series. New York: Routledge.

225. Jeffords, Susan (1994). *Hard Bodies: Hollywood Masculinity in the Reagan Era.* New Brunswick, N.J.: Rutgers University Press, p. 25.

226. Jeffords, Susan (1994). *Hard Bodies: Hollywood Masculinity in the Reagan Era.* New Brunswick, N.J.: Rutgers University Press.

227. Belton, John (1994). *American Cinema/American Culture.* New York: McGraw-Hill, p. 316.

228. *Ibid.*, pp. 327–328.

229. Combs, James E. (1990). *American Political Movies: An Annotated Filmography of Feature Films.* New York and London: Garland Publishing; Kellner, Douglas (1995). *Media Culture. Cultural Studies, Identity and Politics between the Modern and the Postmodern.* London and New York: Routledge.

230. Parenti, Michael (1992). *Make-Believe Media: The Politics of Entertainment.* New York: St. Martin's Press.

231. Palmer, William J. (1993). *The Films of the Eighties: A Social History.* Carbondale: Southern Illinois University Press.

232. *Ibid.*; Prince, Stephen (2000). "Political Film in the Nineties." In Wheeler Winston Dixon (Ed.) *Film Genre 2000: New Critical Essays.* Albany: State University of New York Press.

233. Gregg, Robert W. (1998). *International Relations on Film.* Boulder, Colo.: Lynne Rienner Publishers.

234. *Ibid.*

235. Swanson Goldberg, Elizabeth (2001). "Splitting Difference: Global Identity Politics and the Representation of Torture in the Counterhistorical Dramatic Film." In J. David Slocum (Ed.) *Violence and American Cinema.* In AFI Film Readers series. New York: Routledge.

236. Parenti, Michael (1992). *Make-Believe Media: The Politics of Entertainment.* New York: St. Martin's Press, pp. 31–32.

237. Malik, Kenan (1996). *The Meaning of Race: Race, History and Culture in Western Society.* Washington Square, N.Y.: New York University Press.

238. Kellner, Douglas (1995). *Media Culture: Cultural Studies, Identity and Politics between the Modern and the Postmodern.* London and New York: Routledge.

239. Dixon, Wheeler Winston. "Introduction: The New Genre Cinema." In Wheeler Winston Dixon (Ed.) *Film Genre 2000: New Critical Essays.* Albany: State University of New York Press.

240. Groves, Don (1999, December 16). "America's pics find foreign B.O. hit, miss puzzle." In *Variety.*

241. Dixon, Wheeler Winston. "Introduction: The New Genre Cinema." In Wheeler Winston Dixon (Ed.) *Film Genre 2000: New Critical Essays.* Albany: State University of New York Press.

242. Buckland, Warren (1998). "A Close Encounter with *Raiders of the Lost Ark*: Notes on Narrative Aspects of the New Hollywood Blockbuster." In Steven Neale and Murray Smith. *Contemporary Hollywood Cinema.* London and New York: Routledge.

243. Dixon, Wheeler Winston. "Introduction: The New Genre Cinema." In Wheeler Winston Dixon (Ed.) *Film Genre 2000: New Critical Essays.* Albany: State University of New York Press.

244. Desser, David M. (2000). "The Martial Arts Film in the 1990s." In Wheeler Winston Dixon (Ed.) *Film Genre 2000: New Critical Essays.* Albany: State University of New York Press, p. 103.

245. Gallagher, Mark (2000). Action Figures: Spectacular Masculinity in the Contemporary Action Film and the Contemporary American Novel. Ph.D. dissertation. Department of English, University of Oregon.

246. *Ibid.*

247. See, for example, CNN and CBS news broadcasts on April 19, 1995.

248. Gregg, Robert W. (1998). *International Relations on Film.* Boulder, Colo.: Lynne Rienner Publishers.

249. *Ibid.*

250. Trumpbour, John (2002). *Selling Hollywood to the World: U.S. and European Struggles for Mastery of the Global Film Industry, 1920–1950.* Cambridge, U.K.: Cambridge University Press, pp. 70, 302, citing H. S. Villard, Office of the Economic Adviser, Department of State, cited in Foreign Restrictions on American Films (1929, March 25), U.S. NA RG59, 800.4061, Motion Pictures/41/2, 1910–29.

251. Trumpbour, John (2002). *Selling Hollywood to the World: U.S. and European Struggles for Mastery of the Global Film Industry, 1920–1950.* Cambridge, U.K.: Cambridge University Press.

252. Woll, Allen L. (1993). "Hollywood Views the Mexican-American: From *The Greaser's Revenge* to *The Milagro Beanfield War.*" In Robert Brent Toplin (Ed.) *Hollywood as Mirror: Changing View of "Outsiders" and "Enemies" in American Movies.* In Contributions to the Study of Popular Culture, Number 38. Westport, Conn.: Greenwood Press.

253. Cortes, Carlos E. (1993). "Them and Us: Immigration as Societal Barometer and Social Educator in American Film." In Robert Brent Toplin (Ed.) *Hollywood as Mirror: Changing View of "Outsiders" and Enemies" in American Movies.* Westport, Conn.: Greenwood Press.

254. Campbell, Edward D. C., Jr. (1993). "Film as Politics/Film as Business: The Blaxploitation of the Plantation." In Robert Brent Toplin (Ed.) *Hollywood as Mirror: Changing View of "Outsiders" and Enemies" in American Movies.* Westport, Conn.: Greenwood Press.

255. Van Deburg, William L. "Popular Culture Prophesy: Black American Slavery in Film." In Robert Brent Toplin (Ed.) *Hollywood as Mirror: Changing View of "Outsiders" and Enemies" in American Movies.* Westport, Conn.: Greenwood Press.

256. Campbell, Edward D. C., Jr. (1993). "Film as Politics/Film as Business: The Blaxploitation of the Plantation." In Robert Brent Toplin (Ed.) *Hollywood as Mirror: Changing View of "Outsiders" and Enemies" in American Movies.* Westport, Conn.: Greenwood Press.

257. Belton, John (1994). *American Cinema/American Culture.* New York: McGraw-Hill.

258. Long, Tom (2003, February 23). "Diversity in Entertainment: Minorities' music muscle loses punch at box

office: commercial clout, image, racism limit ethnic starring roles." *Detroit News*, http://www.detnews.com/2004/entertainment/0402/26/a01-71699.htm.

259. *Ibid.*

260. *Ibid.*

261. Belton, John (1994). *American Cinema/American Culture*. New York: McGraw-Hill.

262. Cortes, Carlos E. (1993). "Them and Us: Immigration as Societal Barometer and Social Educator in American Film." In Robert Brent Toplin (Ed.) *Hollywood as Mirror: Changing View of "Outsiders" and Enemies" in American Movies*. Westport, Conn.: Greenwood Press.

263. Shaheen, Jack G. (2001). *Reel Bad Arabs: How Hollywood Vilifies People*. New York and Northampton: Olive Branch Press.

264. Gregg, Robert W. (1998). *International Relations on Film*. Boulder, Colo.: Lynne Rienner Publishers, p. 61.

265. Shaheen, Jack G. (2001). *Reel Bad Arabs: How Hollywood Vilifies People*. New York and Northampton: Olive Branch Press, p. 2.

266. Pew Forum on Religion & Public Life. Pew Research Center (2011, January 27). "The Future of the Global Muslim Population," http://pewforum.org/The-Future-of-the-Global-Muslim-Population.aspx.

267. Karim, Karim H. (2000). *Islamic Peril: Media and Global Violence*. Montreal, New York, London: Black Rose Books.

268. Organization of the Islamic Conference, http://www.oic.oci.org/member_states.

269. Lyman, Rick (2001, October 3). "Bad Guys for Bad Times: Hollywood Struggles to Create Villains for a New Climate." *The New York Times*, p. E1.

270. Parenti, Michael (1992). *Make-Believe Media: The Politics of Entertainment*. New York: St. Martin's Press.

271. Lyman, Rick (2001, October 3). "Bad Guys for Bad Times. Hollywood Struggles to Create Villains for a New Climate." *The New York Times*, p. E1.

272. *Ibid.*

273. Federal Communications Commission (1996, last reviewed/updated 2003, June 13). Excerpts from V-Chip Legislation, www.fcc.gov/vchip/legislation.html.

274. Prince, Stephen (2000). "Graphic Violence in the Cinema: Origins, Aesthetic Design, and Social Effects." In Stephen Prince (Ed.) *Screening Violence*. New Brunswick, N.J.: Rutgers University Press; Felson, 2000.

275. *Ibid.*, p. 32.

276. French, Philip (1968). "Violence in the Cinema." In Otto N. Larsen (Ed.), *Violence and the Mass Media*. New York: Harper and Row.

277. Belton, John (1996). "Introduction." In John Belton (Ed.). *Movies and Mass Culture*. In Charles Affron, Mirella Affron, and Robert Lyons (Eds.) Rutgers Depth of Field Series. New Brunswick, N.J.: Rutgers University Press.

278. Prince, Stephen (2000). "Graphic Violence in the Cinema: Origins, Aesthetic Design, and Social Effects." In Stephen Prince (Ed.) *Screening Violence*. New Brunswick, N.J.: Rutgers University Press.

279. Belton, John (1996). "Introduction." In John Belton (Ed.). *Movies and Mass Culture*. In Charles Affron, Mirella Affron, and Robert Lyons (Eds.) Rutgers Depth of Field Series. New Brunswick, N.J.: Rutgers University Press, p. 136.

280. *Ibid.*

281. Prince, Stephen (2000). "Graphic Violence in the Cinema: Origins, Aesthetic Design, and Social Effects." In Stephen Prince (Ed.) *Screening Violence*. New Brunswick, N.J.: Rutgers University Press; Belton, John (1996). "Introduction." In John Belton (Ed.). *Movies and Mass Culture*. In Charles Affron, Mirella Affron, and Robert Lyons (Eds.) Rutgers Depth of Field Series. New Brunswick, N.J.: Rutgers University Press.

282. Prince, Stephen (2000). "Graphic Violence in the Cinema: Origins, Aesthetic Design, and Social Effects." In Stephen Prince (Ed.) *Screening Violence*. New Brunswick, N.J.: Rutgers University Press, p. 3.

283. Belton, John (1996). "Introduction." In John Belton (Ed.). *Movies and Mass Culture*. In Charles Affron, Mirella Affron, and Robert Lyons (Eds.) Rutgers Depth of Field Series. New Brunswick, N.J.: Rutgers University Press, pp. 138–149; reprint of the Production Code.

284. Prince, Stephen (2000). "Graphic Violence in the Cinema: Origins, Aesthetic Design, and Social Effects." In Stephen Prince (Ed.) *Screening Violence*. New Brunswick, N.J.: Rutgers University Press, p. 2.

285. Prince, Stephen (2000). "Graphic Violence in the Cinema: Origins, Aesthetic Design, and Social Effects." In Stephen Prince (Ed.) *Screening Violence*. New Brunswick, N.J.: Rutgers University Press.

286. Belton, John (1996). "Introduction." In John Belton (Ed.). *Movies and Mass Culture*. In Charles Affron, Mirella Affron, and Robert Lyons (Eds.) Rutgers Depth of Field Series. New Brunswick, N.J.: Rutgers University Press.

287. Prince, Stephen (2000). "Graphic Violence in the Cinema: Origins, Aesthetic Design, and Social Effects." In Stephen Prince (Ed.) *Screening Violence*. New Brunswick, N.J.: Rutgers University Press.

288. Belton, John (1996). "The Production Code." In John Bolton (Ed.) *Movies and Mass Culture*. In Charles Affron, Mirella Affron, and Robert Lyons (Eds.) Rutgers Depth of Field Series. New Brinswick, New Jersey: Rutgers University Press.

289. *Ibid.*

290. Prince, Stephen (2000). "Graphic Violence in the Cinema: Origins, Aesthetic Design, and Social Effects." In Stephen Prince (Ed.) *Screening Violence*. New Brunswick, N.J.: Rutgers University Press.

291. Belton, John (1996). "The Production Code." In John Bolton (Ed.) *Movies and Mass Culture*. In Charles Affron, Mirella Affron, and Robert Lyons (Eds.) Rutgers Depth of Field Series. New Brunswick, N.J.: Rutgers University Press, p. 137, emphasis original. The Production Code explicitly forbade the use of vulgar expressions: "V. PROFANITY Pointed profanity (this includes the words, God, Lord, Jesus, Christ — unless used reverently — Hell, S.O.B., damn, Gawd), or every other profane or vulgar expression however used, is forbidden." *Ibid.*, p. 140.

292. Prince, Stephen (2000). "Graphic Violence in the Cinema: Origins, Aesthetic Design, and Social Effects." In Stephen Prince (Ed.) *Screening Violence*. New Brunswick, N.J.: Rutgers University Press, p. 6.

293. Belton, John (1996). "Introduction." In John Belton (Ed.). *Movies and Mass Culture*. In Charles Affron, Mirella Affron, and Robert Lyons (Eds.) Rutgers Depth of Field Series. New Brunswick, N.J.: Rutgers University Press.

294. Prince, Stephen (2000). "Graphic Violence in the Cinema: Origins, Aesthetic Design, and Social Effects." In Stephen Prince (Ed.) *Screening Violence*. New Brunswick, N.J.: Rutgers University Press.

295. Belton, John (1996). "Introduction." In John Belton (Ed.). *Movies and Mass Culture*. In Charles Affron, Mirella Affron, and Robert Lyons (Eds.) Rutgers Depth of Field Series. New Brunswick, N.J.: Rutgers University Press, pp. 136–137.

296. *Ibid.*, p. 138.

297. Motion Picture Association of America. What Do the Ratings Mean? http://www.mpaa.org/FlmRat_Ratings.asp.

298. Prince, Stephen (2000). "Graphic Violence in the Cinema: Origins, Aesthetic Design, and Social Effects." In Stephen Prince (Ed.) *Screening Violence*. New Brunswick, N.J.: Rutgers University Press.

299. *Ibid.*

300. Valenti, Jack (1968; reprint, 2000). Statement by Jack Valenti, MPAA President, before the National Commission on the Causes and Prevention of Violence. In Stephen Prince (Ed.) *Screening Violence.* New Brunswick, N.J.: Rutgers University Press, p. 63.

301. Prince, Stephen (2000). "Graphic Violence in the Cinema: Origins, Aesthetic Design, and Social Effects." In Stephen Prince (Ed.) *Screening Violence.* New Brunswick, N.J.: Rutgers University Press, p. 10.

302. *Ibid.*, p. 15.

303. Prince, Stephen (2000). "Graphic Violence in the Cinema: Origins, Aesthetic Design, and Social Effects." In Stephen Prince (Ed.) *Screening Violence.* New Brunswick, N.J.: Rutgers University Press.

304. McKinney, Devin (2000). "Violence: The Strong and the Weak." In Stephen Prince (Ed.) *Screening Violence.* New Brunswick, N.J.: Rutgers University Press, p. 102.

305. Prince, Stephen (2000). "Graphic Violence in the Cinema: Origins, Aesthetic Design, and Social Effects." In Stephen Prince (Ed.) *Screening Violence.* New Brunswick, N.J.: Rutgers University Press.

306. *Ibid.*, p. 8, citing Wood, Peter (1980, July 20). "How a Film Changes from an 'X' to an 'R.'" *The New York Times*, section C.

307. Maltby, Richard (1995). *Hollywood Cinema: An Introduction.* Cambridge, Mass.: Blackwell Publishers.

308. McKinney, Devin (2000). "Violence: The Strong and the Weak." In Stephen Prince (Ed.) *Screening Violence.* New Brunswick, N.J.: Rutgers University Press.

309. A film about a Provisional Irish Republican Army (PIRA) terrorist and his promise to a dying kidnapped British soldier to look after his girlfriend.

310. McKinney, Devin (2000). "Violence: The Strong and the Weak." In Stephen Prince (Ed.) *Screening Violence.* New Brunswick, N.J.: Rutgers University Press, p. 100.

311. *Ibid.*, p. 108.

312. *Ibid.*

313. Prince, Stephen (2000). "Graphic Violence in the Cinema: Origins, Aesthetic Design, and Social Effects." In Stephen Prince (Ed.) *Screening Violence.* New Brunswick, N.J.: Rutgers University Press.

314. Sobchack, Vivian C. (2000). "The Violent Dance: A Personal Memoir of Death in the Movies." In Stephen Prince (Ed.) *Screening Violence.* New Brunswick, N.J.: Rutgers University Press.

315. Prince, Stephen (2000). "Graphic Violence in the Cinema: Origins, Aesthetic Design, and Social Effects." In Stephen Prince (Ed.) *Screening Violence.* New Brunswick, N.J.: Rutgers University Press.

316. *Ibid.*, p. 34.

Part II

1. Jeffords, Susan (1994). *Hard Bodies: Hollywood Masculinity in the Reagan Era.* New Brunswick, N.J.: Rutgers University Press; Belton, John (1994). *American Cinema/American Culture.* New York: McGraw-Hill; Balio, Tino (1998). "'A Major Presence in All of the World's Important Markets': The Globalization of Hollywood in the 1990s." In Steve Neale and Murray Smith (Eds.). *Contemporary Hollywood Cinema.* London and New York: Routledge.

2. Falk, Richard (1991). "The Terrorist Foundations of Recent U.S. Foreign Policy." In Alexander George (Ed.) *Western State Terrorism.* New York: Routledge.

3. Jentleson, Bruce W. (2004). *American Foreign Policy: The Dynamics of Choice in the 21st Century.* 2nd ed. New York and London: W. W. Norton.

4. Falk, Richard (1991). "The Terrorist Foundations of Recent US Foreign Policy." In Alexander George (Ed.) *Western State Terrorism.* New York: Routledge, p. 114.

5. Norwitz, Jeffrey H. (2004). "Combating Terrorism: With a Helmet or a Badge?" In Russell D. Howard and Reid L. Sawyer (Eds.) *Terrorism and Counterterrorism: Understanding the New Security Environment. Readings and Interpretations.* Rev. and updated ed. Guilford, Conn.: McGraw-Hill/Dushkin. (Original work published 2002.)

6. Bureau of Public Affairs, U.S. Department of State (1985). International Terrorism, August 1985, In Gist series; United States Department of State (1985, November). *Patterns of Global Terrorism: 1984.* Office of the Ambassador-at-Large for Counter-Terrorism.

7. Hoffman, Bruce (1998). *Inside Terrorism.* New York: Columbia University Press.

8. Jentleson, Bruce W. (2004). *American Foreign Policy: The Dynamics of Choice in the 21st Century.* 2nd ed. New York and London: W. W. Norton.

9. Richardson, Louise (2004). "Global Rebels: Terrorist Organizations as Trans-National Actors." In Russell D. Howard and Reid L. Sawyer (Eds.) *Terrorism and Counterterrorism: Understanding the New Security Environment. Readings and Interpretations.* Rev. and updated ed. Guilford, Conn.: McGraw-Hill/Dushkin. (Original published in *Harvard International Review*, Fall 1998.)

10. Rubenstein, Richard E. (1987). *Alchemists of Revolution: Terrorism in the Modern World.* New York: Basic Books.

11. Paletz, David L., and Laura L. Tawney (1992). "Broadcast Organizations' Perspectives." In David L. Paletz and Alex P. Schmidt, *Terrorism and the Media.* Newbury Park, Calif.: Sage Publications.

12. Bureau of Public Affairs, U.S. Department of State (1985). International Terrorism, August 1985, In Gist series.

13. United States Department of State. (1988, January). *Patterns of Global Terrorism: 1986.* Office of the Ambassador at Large for Counter-Terrorism, p. 5.

14. *Ibid.*, p. 11.

15. Herman, Edward S. (1982). *The Real Terror Network: Terrorism in Fact and Propaganda.* Boston: South End Press, p. 47.

16. *Ibid.*, p. 13.

17. United States Department of State (1985, November). *Patterns of Global Terrorism: 1984.* Office of the Ambassador-at-Large for Counter-Terrorism.

18. United States Department of State. (1988, January). *Patterns of Global Terrorism: 1986.* Office of the Ambassador at Large for Counter-Terrorism.

19. United States Department of State (1985, November). *Patterns of Global Terrorism: 1984.* Office of the Ambassador-at-Large for Counter-Terrorism, p. 4.

20. Wilkinson, Paul (1986). *Terrorism and the Liberal State.* 2nd ed. New York: New York University Press; Peleg, Ilan (1988). "Terrorism in the Middle East: The Case of the Arab-Israeli Conflict." In Michael Stohl (Ed.) *The Politics of Terrorism.* 3rd ed. Revised and Expanded. New York: Marcel Dekker; Hoffman, Bruce (1998). *Inside Terrorism.* New York: Columbia University Press.

21. Wilkinson, Paul (1986). *Terrorism and the Liberal State.* 2nd ed. New York: New York University Press; Hoffman, Bruce (1998). *Inside Terrorism.* New York: Columbia University Press; United States Department of State (1990, April). *Patterns of Global Terrorism: 1989.* Department of State Publication 9743. Office of the Secretary of State. Office of the Coordinator for Counter-Terrorism.

22. United States Department of State (1990, April). *Patterns of Global Terrorism: 1989.* Department of State Publication 9743. Office of the Secretary of State. Office of the Coordinator for Counter-Terrorism; United States Department of State (1996, April). *Patterns of Global Terrorism*

1995. Department of State Publication 10321. Office of the Secretary of State. Office of the Coordinator for Counterterrorism; United States Department of State (1997, April). *Patterns of Global Terrorism 1996*. Department of State Publication 10433. Office of the Secretary of State. Office of the Coordinator for Counterterrorism.

23. United States Department of State (1986, October). *Patterns of Global Terrorism: 1985*. Office of the Ambassador at Large for Counter-Terrorism.

24. *Ibid*., pp. 12–14.

25. United States Department of State. (1988, January). *Patterns of Global Terrorism: 1986*. Office of the Ambassador at Large for Counter-Terrorism.

26. United States Department of State (1986, October). *Patterns of Global Terrorism: 1985*. Office of the Ambassador at Large for Counter-Terrorism.

27. Bureau of Public Affairs, U.S. Department of State (1985, August). International Terrorism, In Gist series.

28. United States Department of State. (1988, January). *Patterns of Global Terrorism: 1986*. Office of the Ambassador at Large for Counter-Terrorism.

29. Norwitz, Jeffrey H. (2004). "Combating Terrorism: With a Helmet or a Badge?" In Russell D. Howard and Reid L. Sawyer (Eds.) *Terrorism and Counterterrorism: Understanding the New Security Environment. Readings and Interpretations*. Rev. and updated ed. Guilford, Conn.: McGraw-Hill/Dushkin. (Original work published 2002.)

30. *The 9/11 Commission Report: Final Report on the National Commission on Terrorist Attacks upon the United States* (2004). Authorized edition. New York and London: W. W. Norton, p. 99.

31. *Ibid*.

Chapter 4

1. United States Department of State (1986, October). *Patterns of Global Terrorism: 1985*. Office of the Ambassador at Large for Counter-Terrorism.

2. Jentleson, Bruce W. (2004). *American Foreign Policy: The Dynamics of Choice in the 21st Century*. 2nd ed. New York and London: W. W. Norton, pp. 176–177.

3. *The 9/11 Commission Report: Final Report on the National Commission on Terrorist Attacks upon the United States* (2004). Authorized edition. New York and London: W. W. Norton, p. 99.

4. Golan-Globus was part of the Cannon Group, an independent company of Israeli cousins Menahem Golan and Yoram Globus. The company actively produced action films, especially in the 1980s. Its other films include *Missing in Action* (1984), *American Ninja* (1985), *Cobra* (1986), and *The Delta Force* (1986).

5. Baseline Data-On-Demand information service on *Invasion USA* through variety.com, http://www.variety.com/profiles/Film/main/77849/Invasion+U.S.A..html?dataSet=1&query=invasion+usa.

6. Top 250 films of 1985, http://www.variety.com.

7. United States Department of State (1982, July). *Patterns of International Terrorism: 1981*. Office for Combatting Terrorism.

8. *Ibid*.; United States Department of State (1985, November). *Patterns of Global Terrorism: 1984*. Office of the Ambassador-at-Large for Counter-Terrorism; United States Department of State (1986, October). *Patterns of Global Terrorism: 1985*. Office of the Ambassador at Large for Counter-Terrorism.

9. United States Department of State (1982, July). *Patterns of International Terrorism: 1981*. Office for Combatting Terrorism.

10. United States Department of State (1985, November). *Patterns of Global Terrorism: 1984*. Office of the Ambassador-at-Large for Counter-Terrorism; United States Department of State (1986, October). *Patterns of Global Terrorism: 1985*. Office of the Ambassador at Large for Counter-Terrorism.

11. Belton, John (1994). *American Cinema/American Culture*. New York: McGraw-Hill.

12. Sobchack, Thomas (1988). "The Adventure Film." In Wes D. Gehring (Ed.) *Handbook of American Film Genres*. Westport, Conn.: Greenwood Press.

13. Baseline Data-On-Demand information service on *Commando* through variety.com, http://www.variety.com/profiles/Film/main/25660/Commando.html?dataSet=1&query=commando.

14. Top 250 films of 1985, http://www.variety.com.

15. Screenwriter Steven E. de Souza brought back the fictional Val Verde as a Central American country with close links to 1980s U.S. policies and action in *Die Hard 2: Die Harder* (1990).

16. United States Department of State (1991, April). *Patterns of Global Terrorism: 1990*. Department of State Publication 9862. Office of the Secretary of State. Office of the Coordinator for Counterterrorism. p. iv.

17. See Jeffords, Susan (1994). *Hard Bodies: Hollywood Masculinity in the Reagan Era*. New Brunswick, N.J.: Rutgers University Press.

18. Ruiz, Raul (1995). *Poetics of Cinema*. Paris: Editions Dis Voir. Translated by Brian Holmes.

Chapter 5

1. United States Department of State (1986, October). *Patterns of Global Terrorism: 1985*. Office of the Ambassador at Large for Counter-Terrorism.

2. Top 250 films of 1986 at variety.com. According to Baseline Data-On-Demand information service, *Iron Eagle* earned a cumulative box-office of $21,549,867.00, http://www.variety.com/profiles/Film/main/27876/Iron+Eagle.html?dataSet=1&query=iron+eagle.

3. United States Department of State (1985, November). *Patterns of Global Terrorism: 1984*. Office of the Ambassador-at-Large for Counter-Terrorism; United States Department of State (1986, October). *Patterns of Global Terrorism: 1985*. Office of the Ambassador at Large for Counter-Terrorism.

4. United States Department of State. (1988, January). *Patterns of Global Terrorism: 1986*. Office of the Ambassador at Large for Counter-Terrorism.

5. *Ibid*.

6. Parks, W. Hays (2003, January 7) "Lessons from the 1986 Libya Airstrike." In *New England Law Review* 36: 4, pp. 755–766, http://www.nesl.edu/lawrev/vol36/4/parks.pdf

7. Gulf of Sidra Incident. Letter to Congress, March 26, 1986(1) (1986 June). U.S. Department of State Bulletin, http://findarticles.com/p/articles/mi_m1079/is_v86/ai_4323912

8. U.S. response to Libyan attack (1986, May). U.S. Letter to Security Council, Mar. 25, 1986. U.S. Department of State Bulletin. http://findarticles.com/p/articles/mi_m1079/is_v86/ai_4223481

9. Parks, W. Hays (2003, January 7). "Lessons from the 1986 Libya Airstrike." In *New England Law Review*. 1/7/2003, Vol. 36: 4. 755–766, http://www.nesl.edu/lawrev/vol36/4/parks.pdf.

10. Significant Terrorist Incidents, 1961–2003: A Brief Chronology (2004, March). Office of the Historian. Bureau of Public Affairs. U.S. Department of State, http://www.state.gov/r/pa/ho/pubs/fs/5902.htm.

11. United States Department of State. (1988, January). *Patterns of Global Terrorism: 1986*. Office of the Ambassador at Large for Counter-Terrorism.

12. Parks, W. Hays (2003, January 7) "Lessons from the

1986 Libya Airstrike." In *New England Law Review.* 1/7/2003, Vol. 36: 4: 760, http://www.nesl.edu/lawrev/vol36/4/parks.pdf.

13. *Ibid.*, p. 766.

14. United States Department of State. (1988, January). *Patterns of Global Terrorism: 1986.* Office of the Ambassador at Large for Counter-Terrorism.

15. Parenti, Michael (1992). *Make-Believe Media: The Politics of Entertainment.* New York: St. Martin's Press.

16. Gregg, Robert W. (1998). *International Relations on Film.* Boulder, Colo.: Lynne Rienner Publishers.

17. For further discussion on the portrayal of a strong self-made man who pushes everything aside, and which can contradict with other cultures' values, see Ruiz, Raul (1995). *Poetics of Cinema.* Paris: Editions Dis Voir. Translated by Brian Holmes.

18. Baseline Data-On-Demand information service on *The Delta Force* through variety.com, http://www.variety.com/profiles/Film/main/83953/The+Delta+Force.html?dataSet=1&query=the+delta+force.

19. The top 250 films of 1986, variety.com. According to Baseline Data-On-Demand information service, *The Delta Force* earned a cumulative box-office of $15,885,415.00, http://www.variety.com/profiles/Film/main/83953/The+Delta+Force.html?dataSet=1&query=the+delta+force.

20. United States Department of State (1986, October). *Patterns of Global Terrorism: 1985.* Office of the Ambassador at Large for Counter-Terrorism.

21. Belton, John (1994). *American Cinema/American Culture.* New York: McGraw-Hill, p. 316.

22. "A Nation Challenged: The Hunted; The 22 Most Wanted Suspects, in a Five-Act Drama of Global Terror" (2001, October 14). New York Times, http://query.nytimes.com/gst/fullpage.html?res=9505E0D6103FF937A25753C1A9679C8B63#.

23. United States Department of State (1983, September). *Patterns of International Terrorism: 1982.*

24. Significant Terrorist Incidents, 1961–2003: A Brief Chronology (2004, March). Office of the Historian. Bureau of Public Affairs. U.S. Department of State, http://www.state.gov/r/pa/ho/pubs/fs/5902.htm; United States Department of State (1984, September). *Patterns of Global Terrorism: 1983;* United States Department of State (1990, April). *Patterns of Global Terrorism: 1989.* Department of State Publication 9743. Office of the Secretary of State. Office of the Coordinator for Counter-Terrorism.

25. United States Department of State (1984, September). *Patterns of Global Terrorism: 1983.*

26. See, for example, United States Department of State (1990, April). *Patterns of Global Terrorism: 1989.* Department of State Publication 9743. Office of the Secretary of State. Office of the Coordinator for Counter-Terrorism, and United States Department of State (1996, April). *Patterns of Global Terrorism 1995.* Department of State Publication 10321. Office of the Secretary of State. Office of the Coordinator for Counterterrorism.

27. Jentleson, Bruce W. (2004). *American Foreign Policy: The Dynamics of Choice in the 21st Century.* 2nd ed. New York and London: W. W. Norton, p. 178.

28. Jentleson, Bruce W. (2004). *American Foreign Policy: The Dynamics of Choice in the 21st Century.* 2nd ed. New York and London: W. W. Norton.

29. United States Department of State (1985, November). *Patterns of Global Terrorism: 1984.* Office of the Ambassador-at-Large for Counter-Terrorism, p. 4.

30. Significant Terrorist Incidents, 1961–2003: A Brief Chronology (2004, March). Office of the Historian. Bureau of Public Affairs. U.S. Department of State, http://www.state.gov/r/pa/ho/pubs/fs/5902.htm; Anderson, Sean, and Stephen Sloan (1995). *Historical Dictionary of Terrorism.* In Historical Dictionaries of Religions, Philosophies, and Movements, No. 4. Metuchen, N.J.: Scarecrow Press.

31. United States Department of State. (1988, January). *Patterns of Global Terrorism: 1986.* Office of the Ambassador at Large for Counter-Terrorism.

32. *Ibid.*; United States Department of State (1988, August). *Patterns of Global Terrorism: 1987.* Department of State Publication 9661. Office of the Secretary of State. Ambassador-at-Large for Counter-Terrorism; United States Department of State (1996, April). *Patterns of Global Terrorism 1995.* Department of State Publication 10321. Office of the Secretary of State. Office of the Coordinator for Counterterrorism.

33. United States Department of State (1985, November). *Patterns of Global Terrorism: 1984.* Office of the Ambassador-at-Large for Counter-Terrorism, p. 11.

34. United States Department of State (1988, August). *Patterns of Global Terrorism: 1987.* Department of State Publication 9661. Office of the Secretary of State. Ambassador-at-Large for Counter-Terrorism.

35. *Ibid.*; United States Department of State (2001, April). *Patterns of Global Terrorism 2000.* Department of State Publication 10822. Office of the Secretary of State. Office of the Coordinator for Counterterrorism.

36. United States Department of State. (1988, January). *Patterns of Global Terrorism: 1986.* Office of the Ambassador at Large for Counter-Terrorism.

37. United States Department of State (2002, May). *Patterns of Global Terrorism 2001.* Department of State Publication 10940. Office of the Secretary of State. Office of the Coordinator for Counterterrorism, p. 143.

38. United States Department of State (1986, October). *Patterns of Global Terrorism: 1985.* Office of the Ambassador at Large for Counter-Terrorism; Bureau of Public Affairs, U.S. Department of State (1985). International Terrorism, August 1985, in Gist series.

39. United States Department of State (1986, October). *Patterns of Global Terrorism: 1985.* Office of the Ambassador at Large for Counter-Terrorism.

40. Weimann, Gabriel, and Conrad Winn (1994). *The Theater of Terror: Mass Media and International Terrorism.* New York and London: Longman.

41. See United States Department of State (1986, October). *Patterns of Global Terrorism: 1985.* Office of the Ambassador at Large for Counter-Terrorism; and Significant Terrorist Incidents, 1961–2003: A Brief Chronology (2004, March). Office of the Historian. Bureau of Public Affairs. U.S. Department of State, http://www.state.gov/r/pa/ho/pubs/fs/5902.htm.

42. United States Department of State (1986, October). *Patterns of Global Terrorism: 1985.* Office of the Ambassador at Large for Counter-Terrorism; BBC (1985). "1985: Beirut Ordeal Ends for U.S. Hostages." In "On This Day," June 30, http://news.bbc.co.uk/onthisday/hi/dates/stories/june/30/newsid_2527000/2527337.stm.

43. Significant Terrorist Incidents, 1961–2003: A Brief Chronology (2004, March). Office of the Historian. Bureau of Public Affairs. U.S. Department of State, http://www.state.gov/r/pa/ho/pubs/fs/5902.htm; Weimann, Gabriel, and Conrad Winn (1994). *The Theater of Terror: Mass Media and International Terrorism.* New York and London: Longman; Hoffman, Bruce (1998). *Inside Terrorism.* New York: Columbia University Press.

44. Weimann, Gabriel, and Conrad Winn (1994). *The Theater of Terror: Mass Media and International Terrorism.* New York and London: Longman.

45. Bayot, Jennifer (2005, February 24). "Uli Derickson, 60, Flight Attendant Who Helped Airline Hostages, Dies." New York Times, http://www.nytimes.com/2005/02/24/national/24derickson.html.

46. According to Parks, "Classic examples are the July 4, 1976, Israeli rescue of the passengers and crew of Air France flight 139 in Entebbe, Uganda, and a mission by the West German Federal Border Guard Group 9 Special (GSG9) on October 18, 1977, in Mogadishu, Somalia, when the unit rescued the passengers and crew of Lufthansa flight 181 that had been hijacked by four Palestinian terrorists. *See generally* YESHAYAHU BEN-PORAT, ET AL., ENTEBBE RESCUE (1976); SEE ALSO ROLF TOPHOVEN, GSG9: GERMAN RESPONSE TO TERRORISM 66–73 (2d ed., 1985); LEROY THOMPSON, THE RESCUERS 23–28, 30–33 (1986); BARRY DAVIES, FIRE MAGIC (1994); and Sofaer, *supra* note 18, at 107." In Parks, W. Hays (2003, January 7) "Lessons from the 1986 Libya Airstrike." In *New England Law Review* 36: 4, pp. 755–766, p. 759, footnote 21, http://www.nesl.edu/lawrev/vol36/4/parks.pdf.

47. *Ibid.*, pp. 759–760.

48. Thurber, Jon, "Uli Derickson, Brave Flight Attendant." *Seattle Times* (2005, February 27), http://seattletimes.nwsource.com/html/nationworld/2002191381_dericksonobit27.html, *Los Angeles Times* reprint.

49. Hoffman, Bruce (1998). *Inside Terrorism.* New York: Columbia University Press.

50. Significant Terrorist Incidents, 1961–2003: A Brief Chronology (2004, March). Office of the Historian. Bureau of Public Affairs. U.S. Department of State, http://www.state.gov/r/pa/ho/pubs/fs/5902.htm.

51. O'Heffernan, Patrick (1991). *Mass Media and American Foreign Policy: Insider Perspectives on Global Journalism and the Foreign Policy Process.* Norwood, N.J.: Ablex Publishing.

52. Howard, Russell D. (2004). "Understanding Al Qaeda's Application of the New Terrorism: The Key to Victory in the Current Campaign." In Russell D. Howard and Reid L. Sawyer, *Terrorism and Counterterrorism: Understanding the New Security Environment. Readings & Interpretations.* Rev. and updated. Guilford, Conn.: McGraw-Hill/Dushkin. (Original work published 2003), p. 76.

53. See Parenti, Michael (1992). *Make-Believe Media: The Politics of Entertainment.* New York: St. Martin's Press.

Part III

1. United States Department of State (1988, August). *Patterns of Global Terrorism: 1987.* Department of State Publication 9661. Office of the Secretary of State. Ambassador-at-Large for Counter-Terrorism, p. iii.

2. United States Department of State (1988, August). *Patterns of Global Terrorism: 1987.* Department of State Publication 9661. Office of the Secretary of State. Ambassador-at-Large for Counter-Terrorism.

3. United States Department of State (1993, April). *Patterns of Global Terrorism 1992.* Department of State Publication 10054. Office of the Secretary of State. Office of the Coordinator for Counterterrorism.

4. United States Department of State (1994, April). *Patterns of Global Terrorism 1993.* Department of State Publication 10136. Office of the Secretary of State. Office of the Coordinator for Counterterrorism.

5. Variety box office data on the top 250 films of 1988, http://www.variety.com.

6. United States Department of State (1993, April). *Patterns of Global Terrorism 1992.* Department of State Publication 10054. Office of the Secretary of State. Office of the Coordinator for Counterterrorism, p. iv.

7. United States Department of State (1995, April). *Patterns of Global Terrorism 1994.* Department of State Publication 10239. Office of the Secretary of State. Office of the Coordinator for Counterterrorism.

8. United States Department of State (1993, April). *Patterns of Global Terrorism 1992.* Department of State Publication 10054. Office of the Secretary of State. Office of the Coordinator for Counterterrorism, p. iii.

9. *The 9/11 Commission Report: Final Report on the National Commission on Terrorist Attacks upon the United States* (2004). Authorized edition. New York and London: W. W. Norton.

10. Malik, Kenan (1996). *The Meaning of Race: Race, History and Culture in Western Society.* New York: New York University Press.

11. United States Department of State (1990, April). *Patterns of Global Terrorism: 1989.* Department of State Publication 9743. Office of the Secretary of State. Office of the Coordinator for Counter-Terrorism, p. 46.

12. United States Department of State (1991, April). *Patterns of Global Terrorism: 1990.* Department of State Publication 9862. Office of the Secretary of State. Office of the Coordinator for Counterterrorism.

13. Jentleson, Bruce W. (2004). *American Foreign Policy: The Dynamics of Choice in the 21st Century.* 2nd ed. New York and London: W. W. Norton.

14. Kellner, Douglas (1995). *Media Culture. Cultural Studies, Identity and Politics between the Modern and the Postmodern.* London and New York: Routledge.

15. *The 9/11 Commission Report: Final Report on the National Commission on Terrorist Attacks upon the United States* (2004). Authorized edition. New York and London: W. W. Norton.

16. Ahmad, Eqbal (2004). "Terrorism: Theirs and Ours." In Russell D. Howard and Reid L. Sawyer (Eds.) *Terrorism and Counterterrorism: Understanding the New Security Environment. Readings & Interpretations.* Rev. and updated. Guilford, Conn.: McGraw-Hill/Dushkin, pp. 46–52. (Original transcript of a public talk 1998; original work published 2001.)

17. *Ibid.*

18. *The 9/11 Commission Report: Final Report on the National Commission on Terrorist Attacks upon the United States* (2004). Authorized edition. New York and London: W. W. Norton.

19. United States Department of State (1992, April). *Patterns of Global Terrorism: 1991.* Department of State Publication 9963. Office of the Secretary of State. Office of the Coordinator for Counterterrorism.

20. United States Department of State (1993, April). *Patterns of Global Terrorism 1992.* Department of State Publication 10054. Office of the Secretary of State. Office of the Coordinator for Counterterrorism; United States Department of State (1994, April). *Patterns of Global Terrorism 1993.* Department of State Publication 10136. Office of the Secretary of State. Office of the Coordinator for Counterterrorism.

21. United States Department of State (1996, April). *Patterns of Global Terrorism 1995.* Department of State Publication 10321. Office of the Secretary of State. Office of the Coordinator for Counterterrorism, p. iii.

22. Jentleson, Bruce W. (2004). *American Foreign Policy. The Dynamics of Choice in the 21st Century.* 2nd ed. New York and London. W. W. Norton, p. 177.

23. Ahmad, Eqbal (2004). "Terrorism: Theirs and Ours." In Russell D. Howard and Reid L. Sawyer (Eds.) *Terrorism and Counterterrorism: Understanding the New Security Environment. Readings & Interpretations.* Rev. and updated. Guilford, Conn.: McGraw-Hill/Dushkin, p. 51. Italics original. (Original transcript of a public talk 1998; original work published 2001.)

24. *Ibid.*

25. Ahmad, Eqbal (2004). "Terrorism: Theirs and Ours. In Russell D. Howard and Reid L. Sawyer (Eds.) *Terrorism and Counterterrorism: Understanding the New Security Environment. Readings & Interpretations.* Rev. and updated. Guil-

ford, Conn.: McGraw-Hill/Dushkin. (Original transcript of a public talk 1998; original work published 2001.)

26. Ahmad, Eqbal (2004). "Terrorism: Theirs and Ours. In Russell D. Howard and Reid L. Sawyer (Eds.) *Terrorism and Counterterrorism: Understanding the New Security Environment. Readings & Interpretations.* Rev. and updated. Guilford, Conn.: McGraw-Hill/Dushkin, p. 48. (Original transcript of a public talk 1998; original work published 2001.)

27. *Ibid.*

28. United States Department of State (1996, April). *Patterns of Global Terrorism 1995.* Department of State Publication 10321. Office of the Secretary of State. Office of the Coordinator for Counterterrorism.

29. United States Department of State (1994, April). *Patterns of Global Terrorism 1993.* Department of State Publication 10136. Office of the Secretary of State. Office of the Coordinator for Counterterrorism.

30. *Ibid.*, p. 1.

31. United States Department of State (1998, April). *Patterns of Global Terrorism 1997.* Department of State Publication 10535. Office of the Secretary of State. Office of the Coordinator for Counterterrorism.

32. United States Department of State (1994, April). *Patterns of Global Terrorism 1993.* Department of State Publication 10136. Office of the Secretary of State. Office of the Coordinator for Counterterrorism; United States Department of State (1995, April). *Patterns of Global Terrorism 1994.* Department of State Publication 10239. Office of the Secretary of State. Office of the Coordinator for Counterterrorism; United States Department of State (1996, April). *Patterns of Global Terrorism 1995.* Department of State Publication 10321. Office of the Secretary of State. Office of the Coordinator for Counterterrorism.

33. *The 9/11 Commission Report: Final Report on the National Commission on Terrorist Attacks upon the United States* (2004). Authorized edition. New York and London: W. W. Norton.

34. United States Department of State (1994, April). *Patterns of Global Terrorism 1993.* Department of State Publication 10136. Office of the Secretary of State. Office of the Coordinator for Counterterrorism.

35. United States Department of State (2001, April). *Patterns of Global Terrorism 2000.* Department of State Publication 10822. Office of the Secretary of State. Office of the Coordinator for Counterterrorism.

36. See, for example, CNN and CBS news broadcasts on April 19, 1995.

37. *The 9/11 Commission Report: Final Report on the National Commission on Terrorist Attacks upon the United States* (2004). Authorized edition. New York and London: W. W. Norton, p. 101.

38. United States Department of State (1996, April). *Patterns of Global Terrorism 1995.* Department of State Publication 10321. Office of the Secretary of State. Office of the Coordinator for Counterterrorism.

39. United States Department of State (2002, May). *Patterns of Global Terrorism 2001.* Department of State Publication 10940. Office of the Secretary of State. Office of the Coordinator for Counterterrorism.

40. United States Department of State (1996, April). *Patterns of Global Terrorism 1995.* Department of State Publication 10321. Office of the Secretary of State. Office of the Coordinator for Counterterrorism.

41. United States Department of State (1999, April). *Patterns of Global Terrorism 1998.* U.S. Department of State Publication 10610. Office of the Secretary of State. Office of the Coordinator for Counterterrorism.

42. *Ibid.*, p. 6.

43. President Clinton, speech at the United Nations, September 21, 1998, http://www.state.gov/www/global/terrorism/980921_pres_terror.html.

44. Richter, Paul (1998, October 29). "White House Justifies Option of Lethal Force." *Los Angeles Times.* Reprinted in *The Register Guard* (1998, October 29).

45. Medd, Roger, and Frank Goldstein (1997). "International Terrorism on the Eve of a New Millennium." In *Studies in Conflict & Terrorism,* Vol. 20; Berkowitz, Bruce. "National Security: Is Assassination an Option?" In *Hoover Digest* 2002, No. 1. Research and Opinion on Public Policy, http://www.hoover.org/publications/digest/4477731.html; CNN (2002, November 4). U.S. policy on assassinations. In CNN.Com/Law Center, http://archives.cnn.com/2002/LAW/11/04/us.assassination.policy.

46. CNN (2002, November 4). U.S. policy on assassinations. In CNN.Com/Law Center, http://archives.cnn.com/2002/LAW/11/04/us.assassination.policy.

47. Berkowitz, Bruce. "National Security: Is Assassination an Option?" In *Hoover Digest* 2002, No. 1. Research and Opinion on Public Policy, http://www.hoover.org/publications/digest/4477731.html.

48. United States Department of State (2000, April). *Patterns of Global Terrorism 1999.* Department of State Publication 10687. Office of the Secretary of State. Office of the Coordinator for Counterterrorism, p. iii.

49. *Ibid.*

50. United States Department of State (2001, April). *Patterns of Global Terrorism 2000.* Department of State Publication 10822. Office of the Secretary of State. Office of the Coordinator for Counterterrorism.

51. *The 9/11 Commission Report: Final Report on the National Commission on Terrorist Attacks upon the United States* (2004). Authorized edition. New York and London: W. W. Norton.

52. *Ibid.*, p. 47, citing text of World Islamic Front's Statement Urging Jihad Against Jews and Crusaders (1998, February 23). In *Al Quds al Arabi.* (Foreign Broadcast Information Service transl.), signed by Usama bin Laden, Ayman al Zawahiri and three others.

53. *Ibid.*, p. 47 citing PBS *Frontline* broadcast (1998, May). Hunting Bin Ladin, http://www.pbs.org/wgbh/pages/frontline/shows/binladen/who/interview.html.

54. United States Department of State (1998, April). *Patterns of Global Terrorism 1997.* Department of State Publication 10535. Office of the Secretary of State. Office of the Coordinator for Counterterrorism.

55. *The 9/11 Commission Report: Final Report on the National Commission on Terrorist Attacks upon the United States* (2004). Authorized edition. New York and London: W. W. Norton.

56. Bin Laden, Osama. "Jihad against Jews and Crusaders." In Walter Laqueur (Ed.) *Voices of Terror: Manifestos, Writings and Manuals of Al Qaeda, Hamas, and Other Terrorists from around the World and throughout the Ages.* New York: Reed Press, 2004, p. 411.

57. *Ibid.*

58. *Ibid.*

59. *Ibid.*

60. United States Department of State (1999, April). *Patterns of Global Terrorism 1998.* U.S. Department of State Publication 10610. Office of the Secretary of State. Office of the Coordinator for Counterterrorism.

61. *The 9/11 Commission Report: Final Report on the National Commission on Terrorist Attacks upon the United States* (2004). Authorized edition. New York and London: W. W. Norton, p. 51.

62. United States Department of State (1994, April). *Patterns of Global Terrorism 1993.* Department of State Publication 10136. Office of the Secretary of State. Office of the Coordinator for Counterterrorism, p. 4.

63. *Ibid.*, italics original.

64. United States Department of State (1996, April). *Patterns of Global Terrorism 1995.* Department of State Publication 10321. Office of the Secretary of State. Office of the Coordinator for Counterterrorism.

65. U.S. Department of State (1996, July 18). Terrorism/ Usama bin Ladin: Who's Chasing Whom? (C). Top Secret. Unclassified, 2005, July 21.

66. *The 9/11 Commission Report: Final Report on the National Commission on Terrorist Attacks upon the United States* (2004). Authorized edition. New York and London: W. W. Norton, p. 109.

67. *Ibid.*, p. 111.

68. United States Department of State (2000, April). *Patterns of Global Terrorism 1999.* Department of State Publication 10687. Office of the Secretary of State. Office of the Coordinator for Counterterrorism.

69. United States Department of State (2001, April). *Patterns of Global Terrorism 2000.* Department of State Publication 10822. Office of the Secretary of State. Office of the Coordinator for Counterterrorism.

70. *Ibid.*, p. iii.

71. United States Department of State (2000, April). *Patterns of Global Terrorism 1999.* Department of State Publication 10687. Office of the Secretary of State. Office of the Coordinator for Counterterrorism, online version, italics original.

72. *The 9/11 Commission Report: Final Report on the National Commission on Terrorist Attacks upon the United States* (2004). Authorized edition. New York and London: W. W. Norton.

73. United States Department of State (2000, April). *Patterns of Global Terrorism 1999.* Department of State Publication 10687. Office of the Secretary of State. Office of the Coordinator for Counterterrorism.

74. *The 9/11 Commission Report: Final Report on the National Commission on Terrorist Attacks upon the United States* (2004). Authorized edition. New York and London: W. W. Norton.

75. *Ibid.*, p. 128.

76. "Bin Ladin Determined to Strike in U.S." Presidential Daily Brief (2001, August 6), p. 2. Declassified and approved for release 2004, April 10.

77. See, for example, Wright, Robin (2004, April 1). "Top Focus before 9/11 Wasn't on Terrorism," p. A01. Report contributions from staff researcher Lucy Shackelford and staff writer Mark Stencel.

78. Howard, Russell D. (2004). "Understanding Al Qaeda's Application of the New Terrorism: The Key to Victory in the Current Campaign." In Russell D. Howard and Reid L. Sawyer, *Terrorism and Counterterrorism: Understanding the New Security Environment. Readings & Interpretations.* Rev. and updated. Guilford, Conn.: McGraw-Hill/Dushkin. (Original work published 2003.)

79. *Ibid.*

80. Howard, Russell D. (2004). "Understanding Al Qaeda's Application of the New Terrorism: The Key to Victory in the Current Campaign. In Russell D. Howard and Reid L. Sawyer, *Terrorism and Counterterrorism: Understanding the New Security Environment. Readings & Interpretations.* Rev. and updated. Guilford, Conn.: McGraw-Hill/Dushkin. (Original work published 2003.)

81. *The 9/11 Commission Report: Final Report on the National Commission on Terrorist Attacks upon the United States* (2004). Authorized edition. New York and London: W. W. Norton, p. 171.

82. *Ibid.*, p. 87.

83. United States Department of State (2001, April). *Patterns of Global Terrorism 2000.* Department of State Publication 10822. Office of the Secretary of State. Office of the Coordinator for Counterterrorism, p. 36, italics original.

84. United States Department of State (1996, April). *Patterns of Global Terrorism 1995.* Department of State Publication 10321. Office of the Secretary of State. Office of the Coordinator for Counterterrorism.

85. United States Department of State (2000, April). *Patterns of Global Terrorism 1999.* Department of State Publication 10687. Office of the Secretary of State. Office of the Coordinator for Counterterrorism, p. 36, italics original.

86. United States Department of State (2001, April). *Patterns of Global Terrorism 2000.* Department of State Publication 10822. Office of the Secretary of State. Office of the Coordinator for Counterterrorism, p. 34, italics original.

87. United States Department of State (2000, April). *Patterns of Global Terrorism 1999.* Department of State Publication 10687. Office of the Secretary of State. Office of the Coordinator for Counterterrorism.

88. Howard, Russell D. (2004). "Understanding Al Qaeda's Application of the New Terrorism: The Key to Victory in the Current Campaign." In Russell D. Howard and Reid L. Sawyer, *Terrorism and Counterterrorism: Understanding the New Security Environment. Readings & Interpretations.* Rev. and updated. Guilford, Conn.: McGraw-Hill/Dushkin. (Original work published 2003.)

89. *The 9/11 Commission Report: Final Report on the National Commission on Terrorist Attacks upon the United States* (2004). Authorized edition. New York and London: W. W. Norton.

90. Fox News (2001, September 21).

91. Video Software Dealers Association (VSDA) (2001, September). Press release, http://www.vsda.org/news/press/press.phtml.

92. Grossberg, Josh (2001, September 27). "Rated 'T' for Terrorism." In *E! Online News*, http://www.eonline.com/News/Items/0,1,8888,00.html.

93. *Collateral Damage* (2002). Baseline Data-on-Demand information service through variety.com, http://www.variety.com/profiles/Film/main/25637/Collateral+Damage.html?dataSet=1&query=collateral+damage.

94. Evans, Harold (2001, November/December). "What We Knew: Warning given ... story missed." In *Columbia Journalism Review*. Special: 40th Anniversary Issue. Before and After.

95. *Ibid.*, p. 14, emphasis original.

Chapter 6

1. The film was released a few days earlier in bigger markets, on July 13, 1988, in Philadelphia, Boston, and Washington, D.C., and in New York City on July 15, 1988, Baseline Data-on-Demand information service on *Die Hard* through variety.com, http://www.variety.com/profiles/Film/main/26113/Die+Hard.html?dataSet=1&query=die+hard.

2. The top 250 films of 1988, variety.com. According to Baseline Data-On-Demand information service on *Die Hard* through variety.com, the cumulative box office take was $80,707,729.00, http://www.variety.com/profiles/Film/main/26113/Die+Hard.html?dataSet=1&query=die+hard.

3. The film was released in New York City a day earlier, on July 3, 1990. *Die Hard 2: Die Harder* Baseline Date-on-Demand information service through variety.com, http://www.variety.com/profiles/Film/main/26114/Die+Hard+2%3a+Die+Harder.html?dataSet=1&query=die+hard.

4. The top 250 films of 1990, variety.com. According to Baseline Data-On-Demand information service on *Die Hard 2: Die Harder* through variety.com, the cumulative

box-office was $115,288,665.00, http://www.variety.com/profiles/Film/main/26114/Die+Hard+2%3a+Die+Harder.html?dataSet=1&query=die+hard.

5. Certain original characters by Roderick Thorp.

6. Baseline Data-on-Demand information service on *Die Hard with a Vengeance* through variety.com, http://www.variety.com/profiles/Film/main/26116/Die+Hard+With+A+Vengeance.html?dataSet=1&query=die+hard.

7. The top 250 films of 1995, variety.com. According to Baseline Data-On-Demand information service on *Die Hard with a Vengeance* through variety.com, the cumulative box office was $99,490,977.00, http://www.variety.com/profiles/Film/main/26116/Die+Hard+With+A+Vengeance.html?dataSet=1&query=die+hard.

8. *Backstory: Die Hard* (2001). Prometheus Entertainment in association with Van Ness, Inc., FoxStar Productions, Fox Television Studios and American Movie Classics (AMC).

9. King, Cynthia (2000, Winter). "Effects of Humorous Heroes and Villains in Violent Action Films." In *Journal of Communication.*

10. InstantCast.com information on Jonathan Hensleigh, http://www.instantcast.com/AllStars/Jonathan_Hensleigh/Article; CelebCards.com information on *Die Hard with a Vengeance,* http://www.celebcards.com/movies/die_hard_with_a_vengeance.

11. *Backstory: Die Hard* (2001). Prometheus Entertainment in association with Van Ness Inc., FoxStar Productions, Fox Television Studios and American Movie Classics (AMC).

12. One of the film's writers, Steven E. de Souza, was also one of the writers of *Commando* (1985), which also introduces a fictional Central American country named Val Verde.

13. Grimmett, Richard F., and Sullivan, Mark P., "United States Army School of the Americas: Background and Congressional Concerns." Globalsecurity.org, http://www.globalsecurity.org/intell/library/reports/crs/soa.htm.

14. United States Department of State (1988, August). *Patterns of Global Terrorism: 1987.* Department of State Publication 9661. Office of the Secretary of State. Ambassador-at-Large for Counter-Terrorism; United States Department of State (1989, March). *Patterns of Global Terrorism: 1988.* Department of State Publication 9705. Office of the Secretary of State. Ambassador-at-Large for Counterterrorism; United States Department of State (1990, April). *Patterns of Global Terrorism: 1989.* Department of State Publication 9743. Office of the Secretary of State. Office of the Coordinator for Counter-Terrorism; BBC (2007, September 10, last updated), Q&A: Noriega extradition, http://news.bbc.co.uk/1/hi/world/americas/6983752.stm; United States Department of State web site on Panama, http://www.state.gov/r/pa/ei/bgn/2030.htm; Westcott, Kathryn (2007, September 6, last updated). "Is Noriega Too Hot to Handle?" BBC News, http://news.bbc.co.uk/2/hi/americas/6965870.stm.

15. United States Department of State web site on Panama, http://www.state.gov/r/pa/ei/bgn/2030.htm.

16. BBC (2007, September 10, last updated), "Q&A: Noriega Extradition," http://news.bbc.co.uk/1/hi/world/americas/6983752.stm.

17. *Ibid.*

18. Parenti, Michael (1992). *Make-Believe Media: The Politics of Entertainment.* New York: St. Martin's Press.

19. Ruiz, Raul (1995). *Poetics of Cinema.* Paris: Editions Dis Voir. Translated by Brian Holmes.

20. Armer, Alan A. (1993). *Writing the Screenplay: TV and Film.* 2nd ed. Belmont, Calif.: Wadsworth.

Chapter 7

1. *Passenger 57,* Variety.com, Baseline Data-on-Demand information service through variety/com, http://www.variety.com/profiles/Film/main/29727/Passenger+57.html?dataSet=1&query=passenger+57

2. Top 250 films of 1992, variety.com; according to Baseline Data-on-Demand information service on *Passenger 57* through variety.com, the cumulative box office was $42,874,833.00.

3. United States Department of State (1991, April). *Patterns of Global Terrorism: 1990.* Department of State Publication 9862. Office of the Secretary of State. Office of the Coordinator for Counterterrorism.

4. Howard, Russell D. (2004). Understanding Al Qaeda's Application of the New Terrorism — The Key to Victory in the Current Campaign. In Colonel Russell D. Howard & Major Reid L. Sawyer *Terrorism and Counterterrorism: Understanding the New Security Environment. Readings & Interpretations.* Revised and Updated. USA: McGraw-Hill/Dushkin. (Original work published 2003).

5. *The 9/11 Commission Report: Final Report on the National Commission on Terrorist Attacks upon the United States* (2004). Authorized edition. New York and London: W. W. Norton.

6. United States Department of State (1984, September). *Patterns of Global Terrorism: 1983,* p. 5.

7. United States Department of State (1993, April). *Patterns of Global Terrorism 1992.* Department of State Publication 10054. Office of the Secretary of State. Office of the Coordinator for Counterterrorism, pp. 8–9.

8. The Department of State has described the PIRA as a Marxist organization. See, for example, United States Department of State (1991, April). *Patterns of Global Terrorism: 1990.* Department of State Publication 9862. Office of the Secretary of State. Office of the Coordinator for Counterterrorism.

9. United States Department of State (2001, April). *Patterns of Global Terrorism 2000.* Department of State Publication 10822. Office of the Secretary of State. Office of the Coordinator for Counterterrorism, p. 75.

10. United States Department of State (1983, September). *Patterns of International Terrorism: 1982;* United States Department of State (1984, September). *Patterns of Global Terrorism: 1983;* United States Department of State (1985, November). *Patterns of Global Terrorism: 1984.* Office of the Ambassador-at-Large for Counter-Terrorism; United States Department of State. (January, 1988). *Patterns of Global Terrorism: 1986.* Office of the Ambassador at Large for Counter-Terrorism.

11. MI5, the U.K. Security Service. Provisional Irish Republican Army, http://www.mi5.gov.uk/output/provisional-irish-republican-army.html

12. United States Department of State (1992, April). *Patterns of Global Terrorism: 1991.* Department of State Publication 9963. Office of the Secretary of State. Office of the Coordinator for Counterterrorism.

13. United States Department of State (1988, August). *Patterns of Global Terrorism: 1987.* Department of State Publication 9661. Office of the Secretary of State. Ambassador-at-Large for Counter-Terrorism; United States Department of State (1992, April). *Patterns of Global Terrorism: 1991.* Department of State Publication 9963. Office of the Secretary of State. Office of the Coordinator for Counterterrorism; United States Department of State (2001, April). *Patterns of Global Terrorism 2000.* Department of State Publication 10822. Office of the Secretary of State. Office of the Coordinator for Counterterrorism.

14. United States Department of State (1992, April). *Patterns of Global Terrorism: 1991.* Department of State Publication 9963. Office of the Secretary of State. Office of the Coordinator for Counterterrorism, p. 61.

15. United States Department of State (1992, April). *Patterns of Global Terrorism: 1991.* Department of State Publi-

cation 9963. Office of the Secretary of State. Office of the Coordinator for Counterterrorism.

16. *Ibid.*, United States Department of State (1993, April). *Patterns of Global Terrorism 1992.* Department of State Publication 10054. Office of the Secretary of State. Office of the Coordinator for Counterterrorism.

17. United States Department of State (1995, April). *Patterns of Global Terrorism 1994.* Department of State Publication 10239. Office of the Secretary of State. Office of the Coordinator for Counterterrorism.

18. United States Department of State (2001, April). *Patterns of Global Terrorism 2000.* Department of State Publication 10822. Office of the Secretary of State. Office of the Coordinator for Counterterrorism.

19. United States Department of State (1997, April). *Patterns of Global Terrorism 1996.* Department of State Publication 10433. Office of the Secretary of State. Office of the Coordinator for Counterterrorism.

20. United States Department of State (1998, April). *Patterns of Global Terrorism 1997.* Department of State Publication 10535. Office of the Secretary of State. Office of the Coordinator for Counterterrorism.

21. BBC (2007, January 2). The Troubles, 1963 to 1985. Recent History. Northern Ireland: The Troubles. BBC History, http://www.bbc.co.uk/history/recent/troubles/the_troubles_article_01.shtml, pp. 1–8; Central Intelligence Agency (2008 December 18). Ireland. In the World Factbook, https://www.cia.gov/library/publications/the-world-factbook/geos/ei.html; BBC (2004 December 9). The Good Friday Agreement in full, http://news.bbc.co.uk/1/hi/northern_ireland/4079267.stm.

22. *Ibid.*

23. United States Department of State (2000, April). *Patterns of Global Terrorism 1999.* Department of State Publication 10687. Office of the Secretary of State. Office of the Coordinator for Counterterrorism, p. 23.

24. MI5, the U.K. Security Service. Provisional Irish Republican Army, http://www.mi5.gov.uk/output/provisional-irish-republican-army.html.

25. *Ibid.*

26. For German and part-German ancestry the figures were in 1990 almost 58 million (23.3 percent), and in 2000 almost 43 million (15.2 percent). For the third largest European ancestry, English ancestry, the numbers were in 1990 almost 33 million (13.1 percent), and in 2000 24.5 million (8.7 percent). African American ancestry was third largest, with almost 24 million in 1990 (9.5 percent), and almost 25 million in 2000 (8.8 percent), Brittingham, Angela, and G. Patricia de la Cruz, U.S. Census Bureau (2004 June). Ancestry 2000. In Census 2000 Brief. United States Census 2000. Census 2000 Briefs and Special Reports. C2KBR-35, http://www.census.gov/population/www/cen2000/briefs/index.html.

27. Baseline Data-On-Demand information service on *Patriot Games* through variety.com, http://www.variety.com/profiles/Film/main/29746/Patriot+Games.html?dataSet=1&query=PATRIOT+GAMES

28. The top 250 films of 1992, variety.com; Baseline Data-On-Demand information service on *Patriot Games* through variety.com gives the cumulative box office number as $82,690,527.00, http://www.variety.com/profiles/Film/main/29746/Patriot+Games.html?dataSet=1&query=PATRIOT+GAMES

29. United States Department of State (2002, May). *Patterns of Global Terrorism 2001.* Department of State Publication 10940. Office of the Secretary of State. Office of the Coordinator for Counterterrorism, p. 63.

30. United States Department of State (1995, April). *Patterns of Global Terrorism 1994.* Department of State Publication 10239. Office of the Secretary of State. Office of the Coordinator for Counterterrorism, p. iv.

31. Baseline Data-on-Demand information service on *Blown Away* through variety.com, http://www.variety.com/profiles/Film/main/25059/Blown+Away.html?dataSet=1&query=blown+away

32. The top 250 films of 1994, variety.com; according to the Baseline Data-on-Demand information service on *Blown Away* through variety.com, the cumulative box office was $30,059,999.00, http://www.variety.com/profiles/Film/main/25059/Blown+Away.html?dataSet=1&query=blown+away.

33. The organization has also used the People's Liberation Army (PLA), People's Republican Army (PRA), and Catholic Reaction Force (CRF), as its names, GlobalSecurity.org Irish National Liberation Army (INLA), People's Liberation Army (PLA), People's Republican Army (PRA), Catholic Reaction Force (CRF). In Military, http://www.globalsecurity.org/military/world/para/inla.htm.

34. United States Department of State (1997, April). *Patterns of Global Terrorism 1996.* Department of State Publication 10433. Office of the Secretary of State. Office of the Coordinator for Counterterrorism.

35. *Ibid.*

36. Hoffman, Bruce (1998). *Inside Terrorism.* New York: Columbia University Press.

37. Baseline Data-On-Demand information service on *The Jackal* through variety.com, http://www.variety.com/profiles/Film/main/27919/The+Jackal.html?dataSet=1&query=THE+JACKAL.

38. Box office information on the Top 250 films of 1997, variety.com; according to the Baseline Data-On-Demand information service on *The Jackal* through variety.com, the film's cumulative box-office was $54,910,560.00, http://www.variety.com/profiles/Film/main/27919/The+Jackal.html?dataSet=1&query=THE+JACKAL.

39. Reuters (1990, May 7). "'Jackal' Tells of Plan to Kidnap de Gaulle." In NYTimes.com, http://query.nytimes.com/gst/fullpage.html?res=9C0CE1DC173CF934A35756C0A966958260.

40. Baseline Data-On-Demand information service on *The Jackal* through variety.com, http://www.variety.com/profiles/Film/main/27919/The+Jackal.html?dataSet=1&query=THE+JACKAL.

41. Central Intelligence Agency (1976, April). Research Study. *International and Transnational Terrorism: Diagnosis and Prognosis.* PR 76 10030.

42. Carvajal, Doreen (published: 2007, May 5). "Carlos the Jackal to Be Tried for Role in 4 Bombing Attacks in '80s." In NYTimes.com, http://www.nytimes.com/2007/05/05/world/europe/05jackal.html?_r=1; NYTimes.com (published: 2001, October 13). "'Jackal' to Marry Lawyer," http://query.nytimes.com/gst/fullpage.html?res=9E03EFDB123FF930A25753C1A9679C8B63; NYTimes.com (published: 1999, September 16). "France Is Pressed on Treatment of 'Carlos,'" http://query.nytimes.com/gst/fullpage.html?res=9F03E0DC143CF935A2575AC0A96F958260; Whitney, Craig R. (published: 1998, November 15). "Jailed Carlos, The Terrorist, Is Continuing Hunger Strike." In NYTimes.com, http://query.nytimes.com/gst/fullpage.html?res=9A05E0D71331F936A25752C1A96E958260.

43. United States Department of State (1989, March). *Patterns of Global Terrorism: 1988.* Department of State Publication 9705. Office of the Secretary of State. Ambassador-at-Large for Counterterrorism, p. 3.

44. United States Department of State (1988, August). *Patterns of Global Terrorism: 1987.* Department of State Publication 9661. Office of the Secretary of State. Ambassador-at-Large for Counter-Terrorism; United States Department of State (2001, April). *Patterns of Global Terrorism 2000.* Department of State Publication 10822. Office of the Secretary of State. Office of the Coordinator for Counterterrorism.

45. United States Department of State (1993, April). *Patterns of Global Terrorism 1992.* Department of State Publication 10054. Office of the Secretary of State. Office of the Coordinator for Counterterrorism, p. v.

46. United States Department of State (1993, April). *Patterns of Global Terrorism 1992.* Department of State Publication 10054. Office of the Secretary of State. Office of the Coordinator for Counterterrorism, p. iii.

47. Parenti, Michael (1992). *Make-Believe Media: The Politics of Entertainment.* New York: St. Martin's Press.

48. Baseline Data-on-Demand information service on *Ronin* through variety.com, http://www.variety.com/profiles/Film/main/30365/Ronin.html?dataSet=1&query=RONIN.

49. According to the Baseline Data-on-Demand information service on *Ronin* through variety.com, the cumulative box office was $41,609,593.00, *Ibid.*

50. United States Department of State (1996, April). *Patterns of Global Terrorism 1995.* Department of State Publication 10321. Office of the Secretary of State. Office of the Coordinator for Counterterrorism.

51. *The 9/11 Commission Report: Final Report on the National Commission on Terrorist Attacks upon the United States* (2004). Authorized edition. New York and London: W. W. Norton, p. 113.

52. United States Department of State (1999, April). *Patterns of Global Terrorism 1998.* U.S. Department of State Publication 10610. Office of the Secretary of State. Office of the Coordinator for Counterterrorism, downloaded from the United States Department of State counterterrorism releases website http://www.state.gov/global/terrorism/annual_reports.html; website no longer available. The latest annual reports are available at http://www.state.gov/s/ct/rls/index.htm.

53. United States Department of State (April 2006). *Country Reports on Terrorism 2005.* Office of the Coordinator for Counterterrorism.

54. United States Department of State (1993, April). *Patterns of Global Terrorism 1992.* Department of State Publication 10054. Office of the Secretary of State. Office of the Coordinator for Counterterrorism.

Chapter 8

1. *The 9/11 Commission Report: Final Report on the National Commission on Terrorist Attacks upon the United States* (2004). Authorized edition. New York and London: W. W. Norton, p. 49.

2. Blanchard, Christopher M. (updated 2006, December 11). Islam: Sunnis and Shiites. In CRS Report for Congress. Order Code RS21745. The report was originally written by Febe Armanios, and updated for the 110th Congress.

3. *The 9/11 Commission Report: Final Report on the National Commission on Terrorist Attacks upon the United States* (2004). Authorized edition. New York and London: W. W. Norton, p. 50.

4. Blanchard, Christopher M. (updated 2006, December 11). Islam: Sunnis and Shiites. In CRS Report for Congress. Order Code RS21745. The report was originally written by Febe Armanios, and updated for the 110th Congress, p. 2.

5. *The 9/11 Commission Report: Final Report on the National Commission on Terrorist Attacks upon the United States* (2004). Authorized edition. New York and London: W. W. Norton, p. 50.

6. See, for example, United States Department of State (1999, April). *Patterns of Global Terrorism 1998.* U.S. Department of State Publication 10610. Office of the Secretary of State. Office of the Coordinator for Counterterrorism; United States Department of State (2000, April). *Patterns of Global Terrorism 1999.* Department of State Publication 10687. Office of the Secretary of State. Office of the Coordinator for Counterterrorism.

7. Blanchard, Christopher M. (updated 2006, December 11). Islam: Sunnis and Shiites. In CRS Report for Congress. Order Code RS21745. The report was originally written by Febe Armanios, and updated for the 110th Congress, p. 3.

8. Data-On-Demand by Baseline information service on *True Lies* through variety.com, http://www.variety.com/profiles/Film/main/31660/True+Lies.html?dataSet=1&query=true+lies.

9. The top 250 films of 1994, variety.com. According to Baseline Data-On-Demand information service on *True Lies* at Variety.com, the box office was $146,273,950.00. http://www.variety.com/profiles/Film/main/31660/True+Lies.html?dataSet=1&query=true+lies.

10. Data-On-Demand by Baseline information service on *True Lies* through variety.com, http://www.variety.com/profiles/Film/main/31660/True+Lies.html?dataSet=1&query=true+lies.

11. Lowry, Brian. *True Lies* film review. *Variety,* July 11, 1994; *Variety* box office information for 1994.

12. Shaheen, Jack. G. (2001). *Reel Bad Arabs: How Hollywood Vilifies People.* New York & Northampton: Olive Branch Press.

13. Ahmad, Eqbal (2004). "Terrorism: Theirs and Ours." In Russell D. Howard and Reid L. Sawyer (Eds.) *Terrorism and Counterterrorism: Understanding the New Security Environment. Readings & Interpretations.* Rev. and updated. Guilford, Conn.: McGraw-Hill/Dushkin. (Original transcript of a public talk 1998; original work published 2001.)

14. Belton, John (1994). *American Cinema/American Culture.* New York: McGraw-Hill.

15. Howard, Russell D. (2004). "Understanding Al Qaeda's Application of the New Terrorism: The Key to Victory in the Current Campaign." In Russell D. Howard and Reid L. Sawyer, *Terrorism and Counterterrorism: Understanding the New Security Environment. Readings & Interpretations.* Rev. and updated. Guilford, Conn.: McGraw-Hill/Dushkin. (Original work published 2003.)

16. United States Department of State (1993, April). *Patterns of Global Terrorism 1992.* Department of State Publication 10054. Office of the Secretary of State. Office of the Coordinator for Counterterrorism.

17. Parenti, Michael (1992). *Make-Believe Media: The Politics of Entertainment.* New York: St. Martin's Press; Welsh, James M. (2000). "Action Films: The Serious, the Ironic, the Post-Modern." In Wheeler Winston Dixon (Ed.) *Film Genre 2000: New Critical Essays.* Albany: State University of New York Press; Combs, James E. (1990). *American Political Movies: An Annotated Filmography of Feature Films.* New York and London: Garland Publishing.

18. Crowdus, Gary (1994). "Introduction." *The Political Companion to American Film.* Chicago, Ill.: Lake View Press.

19. Baseline Data-On-Demand information service on *Executive Decision* through variety.com, http://www.variety.com/profiles/Film/main/26499/Executive+Decision.html?dataSet=1&query=executive+decision.

20. The top 250 films of 1996, variety.com; according to Baseline Data-On-Demand information service on *Executive Decision* through variety.com, the box-office was $55,719,707.00. http://www.variety.com/profiles/Film/main/26499/Executive+Decision.html?dataSet=1&query=executive+decision.

21. The film was a bit behind the times in using the acronym ARPA for the Advanced Projects Research Agency. Very likely, the shooting of the scene had been done long before, but a few weeks before the film was released, on February 10, 1996, the agency changed its name to DARPA, the Defense Advanced Research Projects Agency. See DARPA website, http://www.darpa.mil/body/arpa_darpa.html.

22. Sobchack, Thomas (1988). "The Adventure Film." In Wes D. Gehring (Ed.) *Handbook of American Film Genres.* Westport, Conn.: Greenwood Press.

23. Belton, John (1994). *American Cinema/American Culture.* New York: McGraw-Hill.

24. Shaheen, Jack G. (2001). *Reel Bad Arabs: How Hollywood Vilifies People.* New York & Northampton: Olive Branch Press.

25. Parenti, Michael (1992). *Make-Believe Media: The Politics of Entertainment.* New York: St. Martin's Press.

26. *The 9/11 Commission Report: Final Report on the National Commission on Terrorist Attacks upon the United States* (2004). Authorized edition. New York and London: W. W. Norton. See pages 40–46 for details.

27. Brake, Jeffrey D. National Defense Fellow. Foreign Affairs, Defense, and Trade Division (2001, April 19) Terrorism and the Military's Role in Domestic Crisis Management: Background and Issues for Congress. In CRS Report for Congress. Received through the CRS Web. Order Code RL30938. In Richelson, Jeffrey and Michael L. Evans (Eds.) The September 11th Sourcebooks. Volume I: Terrorism and U.S. Policy. The National Security Archive. The George Washington University. National Security Archive Electronic Briefing Book No. 55, September 21, 2001, http://www.gwu.edu/~nsarchiv/NSAEBB/NSAEBB55/index1.html.

28. Suid, Lawrence H. (2002). *Guts & Glory. The Making of the American Military Image in Film.* Rev. and Expanded Edition. Lexington: University Press of Kentucky.

29. United States Department of State (1995, April). *Patterns of Global Terrorism 1994.* Department of State Publication 10239. Office of the Secretary of State. Office of the Coordinator for Counterterrorism, p. vi.

Chapter 9

1. Baseline-Data-on-Demand information service on *Air Force One* through variety.com, http://www.variety.com/profiles/Film/main/24369/Air+Force+One.html?dataSet=1&query=air+force+one.

2. Top 250 films of 1997, variety.com; according to Baseline-Data-on-Demand service on *Air Force One* through variety.com, the cumulative box office was $172,650,002.00, http://www.variety.com/profiles/Film/main/24369/Air+Force+One.html?dataSet=1&query=air+force+one.

3. United States Department of State (1996, April). *Patterns of Global Terrorism 1995.* Department of State Publication 10321. Office of the Secretary of State. Office of the Coordinator for Counterterrorism, p. 5.

4. United States Department of State (1997, April). *Patterns of Global Terrorism 1996.* Department of State Publication 10433. Office of the Secretary of State. Office of the Coordinator for Counterterrorism, no page numbers on the report's online version.

5. United States Department of State (1997, April). *Patterns of Global Terrorism 1996.* Department of State Publication 10433. Office of the Secretary of State. Office of the Coordinator for Counterterrorism; United States Department of State (1998, April). *Patterns of Global Terrorism 1997.* Department of State Publication 10535. Office of the Secretary of State. Office of the Coordinator for Counterterrorism; United States Department of State (1999, April). *Patterns of Global Terrorism 1998.* U.S. Department of State Publication 10610. Office of the Secretary of State. Office of the Coordinator for Counterterrorism; United States Department of State (2000, April). *Patterns of Global Terrorism 1999.* Department of State Publication 10687. Office of the Secretary of State. Office of the Coordinator for Counterterrorism.

6. United States Department of State (1989, March). *Patterns of Global Terrorism: 1988.* Department of State Publication 9705. Office of the Secretary of State. Ambassador-at-Large for Counterterrorism.

7. Bureau of Public Affairs, United States Department of State (1985). International Terrorism, August 1985. In Gist series.

Chapter 10

1. The film was first shown at the San Sebastian International Film Festival September 17–26, 1998, Baseline Data-On-Demand information service on *The Siege* through variety.com, http://www.variety.com/profiles/Film/main/30712/The+Siege.html?dataSet=1&query=the+siege.

2. The top 250 films of 1998, variety.com; according to Baseline Data-On-Demand information service on *The Siege* at variety.com, the cumulative box office was $40,932,372.00, http://www.variety.com/profiles/Film/main/30712/The+Siege.html?dataSet=1&query=the+siege.

3. Bay, Willow (November 10, 1998). "Director Ed Zwick defends 'The Siege.'" In CNN online SHOWBIZ, http://www.cnn.com/SHOWBIZ/movies/9811/10/siege/index.html.

4. Worsdale, Andrew (1999, January 12). "A Siege on Islamic Sensibilities." In Mail & Guardian online, ZA@Play — Movies, http://www.mg.co.za/mg/art/film/9901/990112-siege.html.

5. United States Department of State (1996, April). *Patterns of Global Terrorism 1995.* Department of State Publication 10321. Office of the Secretary of State. Office of the Coordinator for Counterterrorism, p. iii.

6. United States Department of State (1997, April). *Patterns of Global Terrorism 1996.* Department of State Publication 10433. Office of the Secretary of State. Office of the Coordinator for Counterterrorism, from the report's online version which has no page numbers.

7. Video Software Dealers Association, 2001, September press release, http://www.vsda.org/news/press/press.phtml; The Video Software Dealers Association website now takes to the Entertainment Merchant Association; the original press release is no longer available.

8. United States Department of State (1997, April). *Patterns of Global Terrorism 1996.* Department of State Publication 10433. Office of the Secretary of State. Office of the Coordinator for Counterterrorism.

9. United States Department of State (1996, April). *Patterns of Global Terrorism 1995.* Department of State Publication 10321. Office of the Secretary of State. Office of the Coordinator for Counterterrorism.

10. Lyman, Rick (2001, October 3). "Bad Guys for Bad Times. Hollywood Struggles to Create Villains for a New Climate." In *The New York Times*; Parenti, Michael (1992). *Make-Believe Media: The Politics of Entertainment.* New York: St. Martin's Press.

11. For a description of intifadah, see, for example, United States Department of State (1993, April). *Patterns of Global Terrorism 1992.* Department of State Publication 10054. Office of the Secretary of State. Office of the Coordinator for Counterterrorism.

12. In 1999 the reward was moved up to $5 million, and after 2001 to $25, and more on the permission of the Secretary of State.

13. Jentleson, Bruce W. (2004). *American Foreign Policy. The Dynamics of Choice in the 21st Century.* 2nd edition. New York and London: W. W. Norton; *The 9/11 Commission Report: Final Report on the National Commission on Terrorist Attacks upon the United States* (2004). Authorized edition. New York and London: W. W. Norton.

14. *The 9/11 Commission Report: Final Report on the National Commission on Terrorist Attacks upon the United States* (2004). Authorized edition. New York and London: W. W. Norton.

15. Ahmad, Eqbal (2004). "Terrorism: Theirs & Ours." In Colonel Russell D. Howard & Major Reid L. Sawyer (Eds.) *Terrorism and Counterterrorism: Understanding the New Security Environment. Readings & Interpretations.* Revised and Updated. USA: McGraw-Hill/Dushkin. (Original transcript of a public talk 1998; original work published 2001), p. 51.

16. United States Department of State (1995, April). *Patterns of Global Terrorism 1994.* Department of State Publication 10239. Office of the Secretary of State. Office of the Coordinator for Counterterrorism; United States Department of State (1996, April). *Patterns of Global Terrorism 1995.* Department of State Publication 10321. Office of the Secretary of State. Office of the Coordinator for Counterterrorism; *The 9/11 Commission Report: Final Report on the National Commission on Terrorist Attacks upon the United States* (2004). Authorized edition. New York and London: W. W. Norton.

17. United States Department of State (1998, April). *Patterns of Global Terrorism 1997.* Department of State Publication 10535. Office of the Secretary of State. Office of the Coordinator for Counterterrorism, accessed online, no report page number available.

18. "Al Qa'eda: Manual." In Walter Laqueur (Ed.) *Voices of Terror. Manifestos, Writings and Manuals of Al Qaeda, Hamas, and Other Terrorists from Around the World and Throughout the Ages.* New York: Reed Press, 2004, p. 404.

19. *Ibid.*, p. 406.

20. Bin Laden, Osama. "Jihad Against Jews and Crusaders." In Walter Laqueur (Ed.) *Voices of Terror. Manifestos, Writings and Manuals of Al Qaeda, Hamas, and Other Terrorists from Around the World and Throughout the Ages.* New York: Reed Press, 2004, p. 412.

21. For news media portrayals of terrorism in different decades, see, for example, Falkenrath, Richard (2001). "Analytic Models and Policy Prescription." In *Studies in Conflict and Terrorism,* 24; Picard, Robert G. (1993). *Media Portrayals of Terrorism. Functions and Meaning of News Coverage.* Ames, Iowa: Iowa State University Press; and Herman, Edward S. & Gerry O'Sullivan (1989). *The "Terrorism Industry." The Experts and Institutions That Shape Our View of Terror.* New York: Pantheon Books.

22. Bin Laden, Osama. "Jihad Against Jews and Crusaders." In Walter Laqueur (Ed.) *Voices of Terror. Manifestos, Writings and Manuals of Al Qaeda, Hamas, and Other Terrorists from Around the World and Throughout the Ages.* New York: Reed Press, 2004, p. 411.

23. *Ibid.*

24. *Ibid.*

25. *Ibid.*, pp. 411–412.

26. *The 9/11 Commission Report: Final Report on the National Commission on Terrorist Attacks upon the United States* (2004). Authorized edition. New York and London: W. W. Norton, p. 47.

27. *Ibid.*, p. 47 citing: "Hunting Bin Ladin" (1998, May). PBS *Frontline* broadcast, http://www.pbs.org/wgbh/pages/frontline/shows/binladen/who/interview.html.

28. Richter, Paul (1998, October 29). "White House Justifies Option of Lethal Force." In *The Los Angeles Times.* Syndicated, printed in *The Register Guard* (1998, October 29).

29. Brake, Jeffrey D. National Defense Fellow. Foreign Affairs, Defense, and Trade Division (2001, April 19) Terrorism and the Military's Role in Domestic Crisis Management: Background and Issues for Congress. In CRS Report for Congress. Received through the CRS Web. Order Code RL30938. In Richelson, Jeffrey and Michael L. Evans (Eds.) The September 11th Sourcebooks. Volume I: Terrorism and U.S. Policy. The National Security Archive. The George Washington University. National Security Archive Electronic Briefing Book No. 55.September 21, 2001, http://www.gwu.edu/~nsarchiv/NSAEBB/NSAEBB55/index1.html, p. CRS-12, footnote #30: "For a comprehensive discussion of the Posse Comitatus Act see Charles Doyle, *The Posse-Comitatus Act & Related Matters: The Use of the Military to Execute Civilian Law,* CRS Report 95-964, June 1, 2000."

30. *Ibid.*, footnote #31: "Department of Justice facsimile, *Posse Comitatus,* March 27, 2000."

31. Brake, Jeffrey D. National Defense Fellow. Foreign Affairs, Defense, and Trade Division (2001, April 19) Terrorism and the Military's Role in Domestic Crisis Management: Background and Issues for Congress. In CRS Report for Congress. Received through the CRS Web. Order Code RL30938. In Richelson, Jeffrey and Michael L. Evans (Eds.) The September 11th Sourcebooks. Volume I: Terrorism and U.S. Policy. The National Security Archive. The George Washington University. National Security Archive Electronic Briefing Book No. 55.September 21, 2001, http://www.gwu.edu/~nsarchiv/NSAEBB/NSAEBB55/index1.html.

32. For details, see above.

33. *Ibid.*

34. *Ibid.*

35. *Ibid.*

36. *Ibid.*

37. For more details, see Yoo, John and Robert Delahunty (2001, October 23). Authority for Use of Military Force To Combat Terrorist Activities <u>Within the United States</u>. Memorandum for Alberto R. Gonzales, Counsel to the President, and William J. Haynes, II, General Counsel, Department of Defense. Office of the Deputy Assistant Attorney General. Office of Legal Counsel. U.S. Department of Justice. Washington, D.C. 20530.

38. Brake, Jeffrey D. National Defense Fellow. Foreign Affairs, Defense, and Trade Division (2001, April 19) Terrorism and the Military's Role in Domestic Crisis Management: Background and Issues for Congress. In CRS Report for Congress. Received through the CRS Web. Order Code RL30938. In Richelson, Jeffrey and Michael L. Evans (Eds.) The September 11th Sourcebooks. Volume I: Terrorism and U.S. Policy. The National Security Archive. The George Washington University. National Security Archive Electronic Briefing Book No., p. 10. 55.September 21, 2001, http://www.gwu.edu/~nsarchiv/NSAEBB/NSAEBB55/index1.html.

39. Yoo, John and Robert Delahunty (2001, October 23). Authority for Use of Military Force to Combat Terrorist Activities <u>Within the United States</u>. Memorandum for Alberto R. Gonzales, Counsel to the President, and William J. Haynes, II, General Counsel, Department of Defense. Office of the Deputy Assistant Attorney General. Office of Legal Counsel. U.S. Department of Justice. Washington, D.C. 20530, p. 24.

40. Pillar, Paul R. (2004). "The Dimensions of Terrorism and Counterterrorism." In Colonel Russell D. Howard & Major Reid L. Sawyer (Eds.) *Terrorism and Counterterrorism: Understanding the New Security Environment. Readings and Interpretations.* Revised and Updated (pp. 24–45). USA: McGraw-Hill/Dushkin. (Original work published 2001).

41. CNN (2001, September 13). Coverage of the 9/11 terrorist attacks and their aftermath.

42. United States Department of State (2002, May). *Patterns of Global Terrorism 2001.* Department of State Publication 10940. Office of the Secretary of State. Office of the Coordinator for Counterterrorism, p. 63.

Conclusion

1. Bin Laden, Osama. "Jihad Against Jews and Crusaders." In Walter Laqueur (Ed.) *Voices of Terror. Manifestos, Writings and Manuals of Al Qaeda, Hamas, and Other Terrorists from Around the World and Throughout the Ages.* New York: Reed Press, 2004; United States Department of State

(1999, April). *Patterns of Global Terrorism 1998*. U.S. Department of State Publication 10610. Office of the Secretary of State. Office of the Coordinator for Counterterrorism; *The 9/11 Commission Report: Final Report on the National Commission on Terrorist Attacks upon the United States* (2004). Authorized edition. New York and London: W. W. Norton.

2. *The 9/11 Commission Report: Final Report on the National Commission on Terrorist Attacks upon the United States* (2004). Authorized edition. New York and London: W. W. Norton.

3. Bin Laden, Osama. "Jihad Against Jews and Crusaders." In Walter Laqueur (Ed.) *Voices of Terror. Manifestos, Writings and Manuals of Al Qaeda, Hamas, and Other Terrorists from Around the World and Throughout the Ages*. New York: Reed Press, 2004, p. 411.

4. Cortes, Carlos E. (1993). "Them and Us: Immigration as Societal Barometer and Social Educator in American Film." In Robert Brent Toplin (Ed.) *Hollywood as Mirror: Changing View of "Outsiders" and Enemies" in American Movies*. Westport, Connecticut and London: Greenwood Press.

5. United States Department of State (2000, April). *Patterns of Global Terrorism 1999*. Department of State Publication 10687. Office of the Secretary of State. Office of the Coordinator for Counterterrorism, p. iii.

6. Sobchack, Thomas (1988). "The Adventure Film." In Wes D. Gehring (Ed.) *Handbook of American Film Genres*. *New* York: Westport, Connecticut; and London: Greenwood Press.

7. Armer, Alan A. (1993). *Writing the Screenplay: TV and Film*. 2nd ed. Belmont, Calif.: Wadsworth.

8. Altschull, J. Herbert (1984). *Agents of Power. The Role of the News Media in Human Affairs*. New York & London: Longman.

9. Gregg, Robert W. (1998). *International Relations on Film*. Boulder, Colo.: Lynne Rienner Publishers.

10. Bordwell, David & Kristin Thompson (2004). *Film Art. An Introduction*. 7th ed. Boston: McGraw-Hill.

11. Pillar, Paul R. (2004). "The Dimensions of Terrorism and Counterterrorism." In Colonel Russell D. Howard & Major Reid L. Sawyer (Eds.) *Terrorism and Counterterrorism: Understanding the New Security Environment. Readings and Interpretations. Revised and Updated*. USA: McGraw-Hill/ Dushkin. (Original work published 2001), p. 25.

12. Parenti, Michael (1992). *Make-Believe Media: The Politics of Entertainment*. New York: St. Martin's Press.

13. Belton, John (1994). *American Cinema/American Culture*. New York: McGraw-Hill; Sobchack, Thomas (1988). "The Adventure Film." In Wes D. Gehring (Ed.) *Handbook of American Film Genres*. New York: Westport, Connecticut; and London: Greenwood Press.

14. Belton, John (1994). *American Cinema/American Culture*. New York: McGraw-Hill.

15. Maltby, Richard (2003). *Hollywood Cinema. An Introduction*. 2nd ed. Malden, Mass.: Blackwell Publishing.

16. Malik, Kenan (1996). *The Meaning of Race. Race, History and Culture in Western Society*. Washington Square, N.Y.: New York University Press.

17. Rosenblum, Mort (1993). *Who Stole the News? Why We Can't Keep Up with What Happens in the World and What We Can Do about It*. New York, Chichester, Brisbane, Toronto & Singapore: John Wiley & Sons.

18. McKinney, Devin (2000). "Violence: The Strong and the Weak." In Stephen Prince (Ed.) *Screening Violence*. New Brunswick, N.J.: Rutgers University Press.

19. Hess, Stephen (1996). *International News and Foreign Correspondents*. Washington D.C.: Brookings Institution.

20. *Ibid.*

21. Steuter, Erin (1990). "Understanding the Media/Terrorism Relationship: An Analysis of Ideology and the News in *Time* Magazine." In *Political Communication and Persuasion*, Vol. 7.

22. Armer, Alan A. (1993). *Writing the Screenplay: TV and Film*. 2nd ed. Belmont, Calif.: Wadsworth.

23. Foucault, Michel (1977). *Discipline and Punish. The Birth of the Prison*. Trans. by Alan Sheridan. New York: Pantheon Books.

24. See, for example, Herman, Edward S. & Gerry O'Sullivan (1989). *The "Terrorism Industry." The Experts and Institutions That Shape Our View of Terror*. New York: Pantheon Books; Dobkin, Bethami A. (1992). *Tales of Terror: Television News and the Construction of the Terrorist Threat*. New York: Praeger; and Steuter, Erin (1990). "Understanding the Media/Terrorism Relationship: An Analysis of Ideology and the News in *Time* Magazine." In *Political Communication and Persuasion*, Vol. 7.

25. Taylor, Philip M. (1997). *Global Communications. International Affairs and the Media since 1945*. London and New York: Routledge.

26. Gramsci, Antonio. *Selections from the Prison Notebooks* (2003). Quintin Hoare & Geoffrey Nowell Smith (Eds. and trans.). New York: International Publishers. (Original work in English published 1971).

27. Althusser, Louis (1971). "Ideology and Ideological Apparatuses." In *Lenin and Philosophy and Other Essays* (Ben Brewster transl.). New York: Monthly Review Press, p. 157.

28. Adorno, Theodor and Max Horkheimer (1989). "Selections from 'The Culture Industry: Enlightenment as Mass Deception.'" In *Dialectic of Enlightenment*. In Roger S. Gottlieb (Ed.) *An Anthology of Western Marxism. From Lukacs and Gramsci to Socialist-Feminism*. New York and Oxford: Oxford University Press. (Original work published 1972).

29. Combs, James E. (1990) *American Political Movies. An Annotated Filmography of Feature Films*. New York and London: Garland Publishing.

30. Rosenblum, Mort (1993). *Who Stole the News? Why We Can't Keep Up with What Happens in the World and What We Can Do about It*. New York, Chichester, Brisbane, Toronto & Singapore: John Wiley & Sons.

31. Gramsci, Antonio. *Selections from the Prison Notebooks* (2003). Quintin Hoare & Geoffrey Nowell Smith (Eds. and trans.). New York: International Publishers. (Original work in English published 1971).

32. *Ibid.*

33. Fishman, Mark (1980). *Manufacturing the News*. Austin and London: University of Texas Press.

34. Gramsci, Antonio. *Selections from the Prison Notebooks* (2003). Quintin Hoare & Geoffrey Nowell Smith (Eds. and trans.). New York: International Publishers. (Original work in English published 1971).

35. Bart, Peter (2001, October 17). "H'wood enlists in war. Net, studios answer call to arms in fight against terrorism." In Variety.com, http://www.variety.com.

Bibliography

Primary Films

Air Force One (1997). Distributor: Columbia Pictures (Sony). Production companies: Beacon Pictures, Radiant Productions, and Columbia Pictures.

Blown Away (1994). Distributor: Metro-Goldwyn-Mayer. Production company: Trilogy Entertainment Group.

Commando (1985). Distributor: 20th Century Fox. Production company: Silver Pictures

The Delta Force (1986). Distributor: Cannon Group. Production company: Golan-Globus.

Die Hard (1988). Distributor: 20th Century Fox. Production company: Gordon Company/Silver Pictures.

Die Hard 2: Die Harder (1990). Distributor: 20th Century Fox. Production company: Gordon Company/Silver Pictures.

Die Hard with a Vengeance (1995). Distributor: 20th Century Fox. Production company: Cinergi.

Executive Decision (1996). Distributor: Warner Bros. Production company: Silver Pictures.

Invasion USA (1985). Distributor: Cannon Group. Production company: Golan-Globus.

Iron Eagle (1986). Distributor: Tri-Star Pictures. Production company: Falcons Flight, Inc.

The Jackal (1997). Distributors: Universal Pictures and Mutual Film Company. Production company: Alphaville.

Passenger 57 (1992). Distributor: Warner Bros. Pictures. Production company: Lee Rich Productions.

Patriot Games (1992). Distributor: Paramount Pictures. Production company: Mace Neufeld and Robert Rehme Productions.

Ronin (1998). Distributor: United Artists Pictures. Production Company: FGM Entertainment.

The Siege (1998). Distributor: 20th Century Fox. Production company: Lynda Obst.

True Lies (1994). Distributor: 20th Century Fox. Production company: Lightstorm Entertainment.

U.S. Government Documents

Baczkowski, Major Ronald F., U.S. Multinational Forces, Tactical Lessons for Peacekeeping: U.S. Multinational Forces in Beirut 1982–1984. http://www.fas.org/man/dod_101/ops/docs/baczkow.htm (also available at http://www.globalsecurity.org/military/library/report/1995/BRF.htm).

Bazan, Elizabeth B. "Assassination Ban and E.O. 12333: A Brief Summary." In CRS Report for Congress. Received through the CRS Web. Order Code RS21037. Updated January 4, 2002. http://www.fas.org/irp/crs/RS21037.pdf.

Blanchard, Christopher M. (updated 2006, December 11). "Islam: Sunnis and Shiites." In CRS Report for Congress. Order Code RS21745. The report was originally written by Febe Armanios, and updated for the 110th Congress.

Brake, Jeffrey D. (2001, April 19). "Terrorism and the Military's Role in Domestic Crisis Management: Background and Issues for Congress." In CRS Report for Congress. Received through the CRS Web. Order Code RL30938. In Richelson, Jeffrey and Michael L. Evans, eds. *The September 11th Sourcebooks. Volume I: Terrorism and U.S. Policy.* The National Security Archive. The George Washington University. National Security Archive Electronic Briefing Book No. 55. September 21, 2001. http://www.gwu.edu/~nsarchiv/NSAEBB/NSAEBB55/index1.html.

Bremen, L. Paul, III (1987, June 25). Terrorism and the Media. In *Department of State Bulletin,* (1987) September, Vol. 87. (Presentation before the International Association of Airline Security Officers on June 25, 1987.)

Briefing upon the Release of the Report *Patterns of Global Terrorism 2000* (2001, April 30). Phillip T. Reeker, Acting Spokesman. Edmund J. Hull, Acting Coordinator for Counterterrorism, Washington, D.C., http://www.state.gov/s/ct/rls/rm/2001/2571.htm.

Brittingham, Angela, and G. Patricia de la Cruz (2004, June). "Ancestry 2000." In Census 2000 Brief. United States Census 2000. Census 2000 Briefs and Special Reports. C2KBR-35, http://www.census.gov/population/www/cen2000/briefs/index.html.

Bureau of Public Affairs, United States Department of State (1981). International Terrorism, June 1981. In Gist series.

Bureau of Public Affairs. United States Department of State (1984). International Terrorism, September 1984. In Gist series

Bureau of Public Affairs, United States Department of State (1985). International Terrorism, August 1985. In Gist series.

Bureau of Public Affairs. United States Department of State. Office of the Historian (2004, March). "Significant Terrorist Incidents, 1961–2003: A Brief Chronology." http://www.state.gov/r/pa/ho/pubs/fs/5902.htm.

Carter, Jimmy (Brzezinski, Zbigniew) (1977, June 2). Presidential Review Memorandum/NSC 30. Subject: Terrorism. Washington, D.C.: The White House, Unclassified.

Central Intelligence Agency (2008, December 18). "Ireland." In the World Factbook, https://www.cia.gov/library/publications/the-world-factbook/geos/ei.html.

Central Intelligence Agency (posted 2007, April 6; last updated 2007, November 16). *CIA & the War on Terrorism.* "Terrorism FAQs." https://www.cia.gov/news-information/cia-the-war-on-terrorism/terrorism-faqs.html.

Central Intelligence Agency (1976, April). "Research Study.

International and Transnational Terrorism: Diagnosis and Prognosis." PR 76 10030.

Central Intelligence Agency. Directorate of Intelligence (1977, July). *International Terrorism in 1976*. Washington, D.C.: Central Intelligence Agency.

Clinton, William (1998, September 21). "Remarks by the President to the Opening Session of the 53rd United Nations General Assembly." http://www.state.gov/www/global/terrorism/980921_pres_terror.html.

Defense Advanced Research Projects Agency (DARPA). http://www.darpa.mil/body/arpa_darpa.html.

Departments of the Army and the Air Force (1990). *Military Operations in Low Intensity Conflict. Field Manual 100-20/Air Force Pamphlet 3-20*. Washington, D.C.: Headquarters, Departments of the Army and the Air Force.

Department of Homeland Security. "Strategic Plan — Securing Our Homeland." http://www.dhs.gov/xabout/strategicplan/index.shtml.

Elcock, Ward (original submission 1998, June 24; revised 1999, July). Counter-Terrorism. Submission to the Special Committee of the Senate on Security and Intelligence.

Federal Bureau of Investigation. FBI History, http://www.fbi.gov/libref/historic/history/text.htm.

Federal Bureau of Investigation. "Legal Attaché Offices." http://www.fbi.gov/contact/legat/legat.htm.

Federal Bureau of Investigation. "Terrorism 2000/2001." http://www.fbi.gov/publications/terror/terror2000_2001.htm.

Federal Bureau of Investigation. "Terrorism 2001/2002." http://www.fbi.gov/publications/terror/terror2002_2001.htm.

Federal Bureau of Investigation (2002, February 6). "The Terrorist Threat Confronting the United States." Testimony of Dale L. Watson, Executive Assistant Director, Counterterrorism/Counterintelligence Division, FBI, before the Senate Select Committee on Intelligence. http://www.fbi.gov/congress/congress02/watson020602.htm.

Federal Bureau of Investigation (2002, February 12). "The Threat of Eco-Terrorism." Testimony of James F. Jarboe, Domestic Terrorism Section Chief, Counterterrorism Division, FBI, Before the House Resources Committee, Subcommittee on Forests and Forest Health. http://www.fbi.gov/congress/congress02/jarboe021202.htm.

Federal Bureau of Investigation. "Today's FBI: International Offices/FBI Budget." http://www.fbi.gov/facts_and_figures/international_budget.htm.

Federal Bureau of Investigation. "Today's FBI: Investigative Programs." http://www.fbi.gov/facts_and_figures/investigative_programs.htm#counterterrorism.

Federal Bureau of Investigation. "Investigative Programs Counterintelligence Division. History and Evolution." http://www.fbi.gov/hq/ci/cihistory.htm.

Federal Bureau of Investigation. U.S. Department of Justice (1998). *Terrorism in the United States 1998*. Counterterrorism Threat Assessment and Warning Unit. National Security Division.

Federal Bureau of Investigation. "Your Local FBI Office." http://www.fbi.gov/contact/fo/fo.htm.

Federal Communications Commission (1996; last reviewed/updated 2003, June 13). "Excerpts from V-Chip Legislation." http://www.fcc.gov/vchip/legislation.html.

Holmes, H. Allen (1994, June 15). *Department of Defense INSTRUCTION*. Number 2000.14. SUBJECT: DoD Combating Terrorism Program Procedures.

Institute for Defense Analyses (1997). "Federal Structures for Infrastructure Protection. Report to the President's Commission on Critical Infrastructure Protection."

National Counterterrorism Center, http://www.nctc.gov/about_us/about/nctc.html.

National Commission on Terrorist Attacks upon the United States (2004). *The 9/11 Commission Report: Final Report on the National Commission on Terrorist Attacks upon the United States* Authorized edition. New York: W. W. Norton.

National Foreign Assessment Center, CIA (1978, August). *International Terrorism In 1977: A Research Paper*. P78-10255U.

National Foreign Assessment Center, CIA (1979, March). *International Terrorism in 1978: A Research Paper*. RP 79-10149.

National Foreign Assessment Center, CIA (1980, April). *International Terrorism in 1979: Research Paper*. PA 80-10072U.

National Foreign Assessment Center. CIA. (1981, June). *Patterns of International Terrorism: 1980: A Research Paper*. PA81-10163U.

National Security Agency (declassified and approved for release by NSA on April 19, 2007, pursuant to E.O. 12958 as amended. MDR51909). "The First Round: NSA's Effort against International Terrorism in the 1970s." In Cryptologic Almanac 50th Anniversary Series.

Presidential Daily Brief (2001, August 6). "Bin Ladin Determined to Strike in US," p. 2. Declassified and approved for release 2004, April 10, p. 2.

Reagan, Ronald (1982, April 10). Managing Terrorist Incidents. National Security Decision Directive Number 30. Unclassified. Washington, D.C.: The White House.

Reagan, Ronald (1982, April 10). National Security Decision Directive Number 30. Unclassified, Washington, D.C.: The White House.

Reagan, Ronald (1986, January 20). The National Program for Combatting Terrorism. National Security Decision Directive Number 207. Unclassified. Washington, D.C.: The White House.

Rewards for Justice. http://www.rewardsforjustice.net.

Sheridan Brian (2000, March 24). Statement Before the Subcommittee on Emerging Threats and Capabilities of the Committee on Armed Services. United States Senate. 106th Congress. Department of Defense and Combating Terrorism.

Thomas, Gary (2007, May 7). "Protecting America from Terrorism." National Counterterrorism Center, Washington, D.C., http://www.nctc.gov/press_room/interviews/VOA+Protecting+America+from+Terrorism.pdf.

United Service Organizations. http://www.uso.org.

United States Department of State. http://www.state.gov/s/ct/rls/crt/.

United States Department of State Counterterrorism Releases. http://www.state.gov/global/terrorism/annual_reports.html.

United States Department of State (2006, April). *Country Reports on Terrorism 2005*. Office of the Coordinator for Counterterrorism.

United States Department of State (1982, July). *Patterns of International Terrorism: 1981*. Office for Combatting Terrorism.

United States Department of State (1983, September). *Patterns of International Terrorism: 1982*.

United States Department of State (1984, September). *Patterns of Global Terrorism: 1983*.

United States Department of State. Office of the Ambassador-at-Large for Counter-Terrorism (1985, November). *Patterns of Global Terrorism: 1984*.

United States Department of State. Office of the Ambassador at Large for Counter-Terrorism (1986, October). *Patterns of Global Terrorism: 1985*.

United States Department of State. Office of the Ambassador at Large for Counter-Terrorism (1988, January). *Patterns of Global Terrorism: 1986*.

United States Department of State. Office of the Secretary

of State. Ambassador-at-Large for Counter-Terrorism (1988, August). *Patterns of Global Terrorism: 1987*. Department of State Publication 9661.

United States Department of State. Office of the Secretary of State. Ambassador-at-Large for Counterterrorism (1989, March). *Patterns of Global Terrorism: 1988*. Department of State Publication 9705.

United States Department of State. Office of the Secretary of State. Office of the Coordinator for Counter-Terrorism (1990, April). *Patterns of Global Terrorism: 1989*. Department of State Publication 9743.

United States Department of State. Office of the Secretary of State. Office of the Coordinator for Counterterrorism (1991, April). *Patterns of Global Terrorism: 1990*. Department of State Publication 9862.

United States Department of State. Office of the Secretary of State. Office of the Coordinator for Counterterrorism (1992, April). *Patterns of Global Terrorism: 1991*. Department of State Publication 9963.

United States Department of State. Office of the Secretary of State. Office of the Coordinator for Counterterrorism (1993, April). *Patterns of Global Terrorism 1992*. Department of State Publication 10054.

United States Department of State. Office of the Secretary of State. Office of the Coordinator for Counterterrorism (1994, April). *Patterns of Global Terrorism 1993*. Department of State Publication 10136.

United States Department of State. Office of the Secretary of State. Office of the Coordinator for Counterterrorism (1995, April). *Patterns of Global Terrorism 1994*. Department of State Publication 10239.

United States Department of State. Office of the Secretary of State. Office of the Coordinator for Counterterrorism (1996, April). *Patterns of Global Terrorism 1995*. Department of State Publication 10321.

United States Department of State. Office of the Secretary of State. Office of the Coordinator for Counterterrorism (1997, April). *Patterns of Global Terrorism 1996*. Department of State Publication 10433.

United States Department of State. Office of the Secretary of State. Office of the Coordinator for Counterterrorism (1998, April). *Patterns of Global Terrorism 1997*. Department of State Publication 10535.

United States Department of State. Office of the Secretary of State. Office of the Coordinator for Counterterrorism (1999, April). *Patterns of Global Terrorism 1998*. U.S. Department of State Publication 10610.

United States Department of State. Office of the Secretary of State. Office of the Coordinator for Counterterrorism (2000, April). *Patterns of Global Terrorism 1999*. Department of State Publication 10687.

United States Department of State. Office of the Secretary of State. Office of the Coordinator for Counterterrorism (2001, April). *Patterns of Global Terrorism 2000*. Department of State Publication 10822.

United States Department of State. Office of the Secretary of State. Office of the Coordinator for Counterterrorism (2002, May). *Patterns of Global Terrorism 2001*. Department of State Publication 10940.

United States Department of State (1996, July 18; unclassified 2005, July 21). "Terrorism/Usama bin Ladin: Who's Chasing Whom?" (C). Top Secret.

United States Department of State Bulletin (1986, June). Gulf of Sidra incident. Letter to the Congress, March 26, 1986(1), http://findarticles.com/p/articles/mi_m1079/is_v86/ai_4323912.

United States Department of State Bulletin (1986, May). U.S. response to Libyan attack. U.S. Letter to Security Council, March 25, 1986, http://findarticles.com/p/articles/mi_m1079/is_v86/ai_4223481.

United States Department of State. Bureau of Western Hemisphere Affairs. "Background Note: Panama." http://www.state.gov/r/pa/ei/bgn/2030.htm.

United States Department of Transportation. National Highway Traffic Safety Administration (2002, December). *Traffic Safety Facts 2001. A Compilation of Motor Vehicle Crash Data from the Fatality Analysis Reporting System and the General Estimates System*. Washington, D.C. 20590. DOT HS 809 484. Traffic Safety Facts Annual Reports, http://www-nrd.nhtsa.dot.gov/cats/listpublications.aspx?Id=EandShowBy=DocType.

United States Special Operations Command. http://www.socom.mil.

Yoo, John, and Robert Delahunty (2001, October 23). Authority for Use of Military Force to Combat Terrorist Activities Within the United States. Memorandum for Alberto R. Gonzales, Counsel to the President, and William J. Haynes, II, General Counsel, Department of Defense. Office of the Deputy Assistant Attorney General. Office of Legal Counsel. U.S. Department of Justice. Washington, D.C. 20530.

Print and Online Sources

Adorno, Theodor, and Max Horkheimer (1989). Selections from "The Culture Industry: Enlightenment as Mass Deception." In *Dialectic of Enlightenment*. In Roger S. Gottlieb, ed. *An Anthology of Western Marxism: From Lukacs and Gramsci to Socialist-Feminism*. New York and Oxford: Oxford University Press. (Original work published 1972).

Agger, Ben (1992). *Cultural Studies as Critical Theory*. London and Washington, D.C.: Falmer Press.

Altheide, David L. (1981). "Iran vs. U.S. TV News: The Hostage Story out of Context." In William C. Adams, ed. *Television Coverage of the Middle East*. Norwood, N.J.: Ablex.

Ahmad, Aijaz (1997). "Interview: Culture, Nationalism, and the Role of Intellectuals." In Ellen Meiksins Wood and John Bellamy Foster, eds. *In Defense of History: Marxism and the Postmodern Agenda*. New York: Monthly Review Press.

Ahmad, Eqbal (2004). "Terrorism: Theirs and Ours." In Russell D. Howard and Reid L. Sawyer, eds. *Terrorism and Counterterrorism. Understanding the New Security Environment: Readings and Interpretations*. Revised and updated. Guilford, Conn.: McGraw-Hill/Dushkin. (Original transcript of a public talk 1998; original work published 2001)

Alexander, Yonah (2007) Introduction. In Yonah Alexander and Michael B. Kraft, eds. *Evolution of U.S. Counterterrorism Policy*. Volume I. Westport, Conn.: Praeger Security International.

Alleyne, Mark D. (1995). *International Power and International Communication*. New York: St. Martin's Press.

Alleyne, Mark D. (1997). *News Revolution: Political and Economic Decision about Global Information*. New York: St. Martin's Press.

Al Qa'eda: Manual. In Walter Laqueur, ed. *Voices of Terror: Manifestos, Writings and Manuals of Al Qaeda, Hamas, and Other Terrorists from around the World and throughout the Ages*. New York: Reed Press, 2004.

Althusser, Louis (1971). "Ideology and Ideological Apparatuses." In *Lenin and Philosophy and Other Essays* (Ben Brewster transl.). New York: Monthly Review Press.

"Altman Says Hollywood 'Created Atmosphere' for September 11" (2001, October 18). Guardian Unlimited citing *Hollywood Reporter*, http://www.guardian.co.uk/film/2001/oct/18/news2.

Altschull, J. Herbert (1984). *Agents of Power: The Role of the*

News Media in Human Affairs. New York and London: Longman.

Anderson, Sean, and Stephen Sloan (1995). *Historical Dictionary of Terrorism.* No. 4 in Historical Dictionaries of Religions, Philosophies, and Movements series. Metuchen, N.J., and London: Scarecrow Press.

Armer, Alan A. (1993). *Writing the Screenplay: TV and Film.* 2nd ed. Belmont, Calif.: Wadsworth.

Associated Press. (2009, January 24). "Al-Jazeera Drew U.S. Viewers on Web During Gaza War." NYTimes.com. http://www.nytimes.com/aponline/2009/01/24/world/AP-ML-Jazeeras-Breakthrough.html.

Associated Press (2009, February 2). "NSA Helped Uncover 1973 NYC Bombing Plot." NYTimes.com. http://www.nytimes.com/aponline/2009/02/02/us/AP-Mystery-Terrorist.html?_r=1.

Backstory: Die Hard (2001). Prometheus Entertainment in association with Van Ness Inc., FoxStar Productions, Fox Television Studios and American Movie Classics (AMC).

Balio, Tino (1998). "A Major Presence in All of the World's Important Markets. The Globalization of Hollywood in the 1990s." In Steve Neale and Murray Smith, eds. *Contemporary Hollywood Cinema.* London and New York: Routledge.

Barker, Jonathan (2003). *The No-Nonsense Guide to Terrorism.* Oxford, U.K.: New Internationalist Publications.

Bart, Peter (2001, October 17). "H'wood Enlists in War. Net, Studios Answer Call to Arms in Fight against Terrorism." In *Variety.com*, http://www.variety.com.

Bart, Peter. (1994, March 14–20). "Numbing Numbers." In *Variety.*

Bay, Willow (November 10, 1998). Director Ed Zwick defends "The Siege." CNN.com. http://www.cnn.com/SHOWBIZ/movies/9811/10/siege/index.html.

Bayot, Jennifer (2005, February, 24). "Uli Derickson, 60, Flight Attendant Who Helped Airline Hostages, Dies." NYTimes.com. http://www.nytimes.com/2005/02/24/national/24derickson.html.

BBC (1985). "1985: Beirut ordeal ends for U.S. hostages." In On This Day, June 30, http://news.bbc.co.uk/onthisday/hi/dates/stories/june/30/newsid_2527000/2527337.stm.

BBC (1981) "Tehran frees U.S. hostages after 444 days." In On This Day, January 21, http://news.bbc.co.uk/onthisday/hi/dates/stories/january/21/newsid_2506000/2506807.stm.

BBC (2004, December 9). "The Good Friday Agreement in Full." http://news.bbc.co.uk/1/hi/northern_ireland/4079267.stm.

BBC (2007, September 10, last updated). "Q and A: Noriega Extradition." http://news.bbc.co.uk/1/hi/world/americas/6983752.stm

BBC (2007, January 2). "The Troubles, 1963 to 1985. Recent History." *Northern Ireland: The Troubles.* BBC History. http://www.bbc.co.uk/history/recent/troubles/the_troubles_article_01.shtml.

Belton, John (1994). *American Cinema / American Culture.* New York: McGraw-Hill.

Belton, John (2009). *American Cinema / American Culture.* Third edition. Boston: McGraw-Hill Higher Education.

Belton, John (1996). Introduction. In John Belton, ed. *Movies and Mass Culture.* In Charles Affron, Mirella Affron, and Robert Lyons, eds. Rutgers Depth of Field series. New Brunswick, N.J.: Rutgers University Press.

Belton, John (1996). "The Production Code." In John Belton, ed. *Movies and Mass Culture.* In Charles Affron, Mirella Affron and Robert Lyons, eds. Rutgers Depth of Field series. New Brunswick, N.J.: Rutgers University Press.

Berkowitz, Bruce. "National Security: Is Assassination an Option?" *Hoover Digest*, 2002, No. 1. Research and Opinion on Public Policy, http://www.hoover.org/publications/digest/4477731.html.

Best, Steven (1995). *The Politics of Historical Vision: Marx, Foucault, Habermas.* In Douglas Kellner, ed. Critical Perspectives: A Guilford Series. New York and London: Guilford Press.

Bin Laden, Osama. "Jihad Against Jews and Crusaders." In Walter Laqueur, ed. *Voices of Terror: Manifestos, Writings and Manuals of Al Qaeda, Hamas, and Other Terrorists from around the World and throughout the Ages.* New York: Reed Press, 2004.

Box Office Data Sources. In Charts and Data, Variety.com, http://www.variety.com/index.asp?layout=chart_passand charttype=chart_bo_detailsanddept=Film.

Bordwell, David (1986). "Classical Hollywood Cinema: Narrational Principles and Procedures." In Philip Rosen, ed. *Narrative, Apparatus, Ideology: A Film Theory Reader.* New York: Columbia University Press.

Bordwell, David, and Kristin Thompson (2004). *Film Art: An Introduction.* 7th ed. Boston: McGraw-Hill.

Bordwell, David, and Kristin Thompson (2008). *Film Art: An Introduction.* 8th ed. Boston: McGraw-Hill.

Brodesser, Claude (2001, October 7). "Feds seek H'wood's help. Helmers, Scribes Probe Terrorism at U.S. Army's Request." In *Variety.com*, http://www.variety.com.

Buckland, Warren (1998). "A Close Encounter with *Raiders of the Lost Ark*: Notes on Narrative Aspects of the New Hollywood Blockbuster." In Steven Neale and Murray Smith, eds. *Contemporary Hollywood Cinema.* London and New York: Routledge.

Campbell, Edward D. C., Jr. (1993). "Film as Politics/Film as Business: The Blaxploitation of the Plantation." In Robert Brent Toplin, ed. *Hollywood as Mirror: Changing View of "Outsiders" and Enemies" in American Movies.* Westport, Conn.: Greenwood Press.

Carpenter, Ted Galen (1995). *The Captive Press: Foreign Policy Crises and the First Amendment.* Washington, D.C.: Cato Institute.

Carvajal, Doreen (2007, May 5). "Carlos the Jackal to Be Tried for Role in 4 Bombing Attacks in '80s." NYTimes.com, http://www.nytimes.com/2007/05/05/world/europe/05jackal.html?_r=1.

Cawelti, John G. (1993). "Who Is Running This Show? Ideology, Formula, and Hegemony in American Film and Television." In James Combs, ed. *Movies and Politics: The Dynamic Relationship.* New York and London: Garland Publishing.

CelebCards.com information on *Die Hard with a Vengeance*, http://www.celebcards.com/movies/die_hard_with_a_vengeance.

The Center for Defense Information (1995). *The CNN Effect.* Washington, D.C.: America's Defense Monitor.

Chaliand, Gerard (1987). *Terrorism: From Popular Struggle to Media Spectacle.* London: Saqi Books.

Chomsky, Noam (1988). *The Culture of Terrorism.* Boston, Mass.: South End Press.

Cieply, Michael (2008, October 5). "DreamWorks Executives Sever Ties With Paramount to Form a New Company. NYT.com, http://www.nytimes.com/2008/10/06/business/media/06dreamworks.html.

Clutterbuck, Richard (1983). *The Media and Political Violence.* 2nd ed. London: Macmillan.

CNN coverage of the 9/11 attacks (2001, September 11–12, 20).

CNN coverage of the 9/11 attacks (2001, September, 13).

CNN (2002, November 4). U.S. policy on assassinations. CNN.Com/Law Center, http://archives.cnn.com/2002/LAW/11/04/us.assassination.policy.

Coca-Cola. http://www.coca-cola.com/worldwide/flasindex1.html.

Combs, Cindy C. (1997). *Terrorism in the Twenty-First Century.* Upper Saddle River, N.J.: Prentice Hall.

Combs, James E. (1990) *American Political Movies: An Annotated Filmography of Feature Films.* New York and London: Garland Publishing.

Cortes, Carlos E. (1993). "Them and Us: Immigration as Societal Barometer and Social Educator in American Film." In Robert Brent Toplin, ed. *Hollywood as Mirror: Changing View of "Outsiders" and Enemies" in American Movies.* No. 38 in Contributions to the Study of Popular Culture series. Westport, Conn.: Greenwood Press.

Corum, James S. (2007). *Fighting the War on Terror: A Counterinsurgency Strategy.* St. Paul, Minn.: Zenith Press.

Cottle, Simon (1997). "Reporting the Troubles in Northern Ireland: Paradigms and Media Propaganda." In Celeste Michelle Condit, ed. Review and Criticism. In *Critical Studies in Mass Communication 14,* 1997.

Crenshaw, Martha (1995). Introduction. In Martha Crenshaw, ed. *Terrorism in Context.* University Park: Pennsylvania State University.

Crenshaw, Martha (2004). "The Logic of Terrorism: Terrorist Behavior as a Product of Strategic Choice." In Russell D. Howard and Reid L. Sawyer, eds. *Terrorism and Counterterrorism. Understanding the New Security Environment: Readings and Interpretations.* Revised and updated. Guilford, Conn.: McGraw-Hill/Dushkin. (Original work published 1998).

Crowdus, Gary (1994). Introduction. *The Political Companion to American Film.* Chicago, Ill.: Lake View Press.

Curtis, Liz (1984). *Ireland: The Propaganda War: The British Media and the "Battle for Hearts and Minds."* London and Sydney: Pluto Press.

Desser, David M. (2000). "The Martial Arts Film in the 1990s." In Wheeler Winston Dixon, ed. *Film Genre 2000: New Critical Essays.* Albany: State University of New York Press.

Deutch, John (1997, Fall). "Terrorism: Think Again." *Foreign Policy.*

Disaster Becomes a Disaster for Studios (2001, September 13). From Studio Briefing, Internet Movie Database, http://entertaindom.imdb.de/news/ni0084096.

Dixon, Wheeler Winston. "Introduction: The New Genre Cinema." In Wheeler Winston Dixon, ed. *Film Genre 2000: New Critical Essays.* Albany: State University of New York Press.

Dobkin, Bethami A. (1992). *Tales of Terror: Television News and the Construction of the Terrorist Threat.* New York: Praeger.

Donahue, Mary Suzanne (1987). *American Film Distribution. The Changing Marketplace.* No. 40 in Diane M. Kirkpatrick, ed. Studies in Cinema. Ann Arbor, Mich.: UMI Research Press.

Evans, Ernest (1979). *Calling a Truce to Terror: The American Response to International Terrorism.* In Bernard K. Johnpoll, ed., No. 29 in Contributions in Political Science series. Westport, Conn.: Greenwood Press.

Evans, Harold (2001, November/December). "What we knew: Warning given ... story missed." *Columbia Journalism Review.* Special: 40th Anniversary Issue. Before and After.

Falk, Richard (1991). "The Terrorist Foundations of Recent U.S. Foreign Policy." In Alexander George, ed. *Western State Terrorism.* New York: Routledge.

Falkenrath, Richard (2001). "Analytic Models and Policy Prescription." In *Studies in Conflict and Terrorism* 24.

Ferguson, Larry (2000, April). Advanced Screenwriting Workshop. Department of English, University of Oregon, Eugene, OR.

Ferguson, Larry (2000, April). Personal Interview. University of Oregon, Eugene, OR.

Fishman, Mark (1980). *Manufacturing the News.* Austin and London: University of Texas Press.

Foucault, Michel (1977). *Discipline and Punish: The Birth of the Prison.* Trans. by Alan Sheridan. New York: Pantheon Books.

Fowler, Roger (1991). *Language in the News: Discourse and Ideology in the Press.* London and New York: Routledge.

Fox News (2001, September 21). Foxnews Cable Channel.

"France Is Pressed on Treatment of 'Carlos.'" NYTimes.com (1999, September 16). http://query.nytimes.com/gst/fullpage.html?res=9F03E0DC143CF935A2575AC0A96F958260.

Frazer, Elizabeth, and Kimberly Hutchings (2008). "On Politics and Violence: Arendt Contra Fanon" (2008). In *Contemporary Political Theory* 7. doi:10.1057/palgrave.cpt.9300328, http://www.palgrave-journals.com/cpt/journal/v7/n1/full/9300328a.html.

French, Philip (1968). "Violence in the Cinema." In Otton N. Larsen. *Violence and the Mass Media.* New York: Harper and Row.

Gallagher, Mark (2000). "Action Figures: Spectacular Masculinity in the Contemporary Action Film and the Contemporary American Novel." Ph.D. Dissertation. Department of English, University of Oregon.

Gerbner, George, with the bibliographic assistance of Nancy Signorielli (1988). *Violence and Terrorism in the Mass Media.* Paris: UNESCO and Lanham, Md.: UNIPUB, citing Plaetz, Fozzard and Ayunian, 1982.

Geuens, Jean-Pierre (2000). *Film Production Theory.* In Wheeler Winston Dixon, ed. The SUNY Series Cultural Studies in Cinema/Video. Albany: State University of New York Press.

Gitlin, Todd (1980). *The Whole World Is Watching: Mass Media in the Making and Unmaking of the New Left.* Berkeley: University of California Press.

GlobalSecurity.org. Military: Irish National Liberation Army (INLA), People's Liberation Army (PLA), People's Republican Army (PRA), Catholic Reaction Force (CRF). http://www.globalsecurity.org/military/world/para/inla.htm.

Gomery, Douglas (2000). "The Hollywood Film Industry: Theatrical Exhibition, Pay TV, and Home Video." In Benjamin M. Compaine and Douglas Gomery, *Who Owns the Media? Competition and Concentration in the Mass Media Industry.* 3rd edition. Mahwah, N.J.: Lawrence Erlbaum Associates.

Gordon, Philip (2001, November). "September 11 and American Foreign Policy." In *Aspenia.* http://www.brook.edu/views/articles/gordon/2001aspenia.htm.

Gramsci, Antonio. (2003). *Selections from the Prison Notebooks.* Quintin Hoare and Geoffrey Nowell Smith (Eds. and trans.) New York: International Publishers. (Original work in English published 1971).

Gregg, Robert W. (1998). *International Relations on Film.* Boulder: Lynne Rienner Publishers.

Grimmett, Richard F., and Sullivan, Mark P. "United States Army School of the Americas: Background and Congressional Concerns." Globalsecurity.org, http://www.globalsecurity.org/intell/library/reports/crs/soa.htm.

Grossberg, Josh (2001, September 27). "Rated 'T' for Terrorism." In *Eonline News,* http://www.eonline.com/News/Items/0,1,8888,00.html.

Groves, Don (1999, December 16). America's Pics Find Foreign B.O. Hit, Miss Puzzle." *Variety.*

Guback, Thomas H. (1985). "Hollywood's International Market." In Tino Balio, ed. *The American Film Industry.* Revised edition. Madison: University of Wisconsin Press. (Original work published 1976.)

Hall, Stuart (1982). "The Discovery of 'Ideology': Return to the Repressed in Media Studies." In Gurevitch, Michael,

Tony Bennett, James Curran, and Janet Woollacott, eds. *Culture, Society and the Media*. London: Methuen.

Halliwell's Film and Video Guide 2001 (2000). 16th ed. Revised and updated. John Walker, ed. New York: HarperResource.

Herman, Edward S. (1982). *The Real Terror Network: Terrorism in Fact and Propaganda*. Boston: South End Press.

Herman, Edward S., and Noam Chomsky (1988). *Manufacturing Consent: The Political Economy of the Mass Media*. New York: Pantheon Books.

Herman, Edward S., and Robert W. McChesney (1997). *The Global Media: The New Missionaries of Corporate Capitalism*. London and Washington: Cassell.

Herman, Edward S., and Gerry O'Sullivan (1989). *The "Terrorism Industry": The Experts and Institutions That Shape Our View of Terror*. New York: Pantheon Books.

Hess, Stephen (1996). *International News and Foreign Correspondents*. Washington, D.C.: Brookings Institution.

Higonnet, Patrice L. R. (1998). *Goodness beyond Virtue: Jacobins during the French Revolution*. Harvard University Press.

Higonnet, Patrice (1997, April 5). "Remembering and Forgetting the French Revolution." In *Human Rights at Harvard: Interdisciplinary Faculty Perspectives on the Human Rights Movement*. Second Symposium. Harvard University. http://www.law.harvard.edu/programs/HRP/Publications/symposium2.html.

Hoffman, Bruce (1998). *Inside Terrorism*. New York: Columbia University Press.

Holland, Jesse J., Associated Press Online. (2001, April 3). "Terrorists Change U.S. Targets." Retrieved through LexisNexis Academic.

Hoovers.com. DreamWorks SKG, DreamWorks Company Description, http://www.hoovers.com/dreamworks/—ID__42800—/free-co-profile.xhtml.

Howard, Russell D. (2004). "Understanding Al Qaeda's Application of the New Terrorism: The Key to Victory in the Current Campaign." In Russell D. Howard and Reid L. Sawyer, *Terrorism and Counterterrorism. Understanding the New Security Environment: Readings and Interpretations*. Revised and Updated. Guilford, Conn.: McGraw-Hill/Dushkin. (Original work published 2003).

"'Jackal' to Marry Lawyer." NYTimes.com (2001, October 13). http://query.nytimes.com/gst/fullpage.html?res=9E03EFDB123FF930A25753C1A9679C8B63.

Jarvie, Ian C. (1998). "Free Trade as Cultural Threat: American film and TV exports in the post-war period." In Geoffrey Nowell-Smith and Steven Ricci, eds. *Hollywood and Europe: Economics, Culture, National Identity 1945–95*. London: BFI Publishing, pp. 34–46.

Jeffords, Susan (1994). *Hard Bodies: Hollywood Masculinity in the Reagan Era*. New Brunswick, N.J.: Rutgers University Press.

Jenkins, Brian (1985, Autumn). "Will Terrorists Go Nuclear?" *Orbis*.

Jenkins, Brian Michael (1998). Foreword. In Ian O. Lasser, Bruce Hoffman, John Arquilla, David Ronfeldt and Michele Zanini, eds. *Countering the New Terrorism*. Rand, http://www.rand.org/publications/MR/MR989.

Jenkins, Brian, Janera Johnson, and David Ronfeldt (1977, July). "Numbered Lives: Some Statistical Observations from 77 International Hostage Episodes." Santa Monica, Calif.: The Rand Corporation. P-5905.

Jentleson, Bruce W. (2004). *American Foreign Policy: The Dynamics of Choice in the 21st Century*. 2nd edition. New York and London: W. W. Norton.

Jimmy Carter Library and Museum. The Hostages and the Casualties, http://www.jimmycarterlibrary.org/documents/list_of_hostages.phtml.

Jimmy Carter Library and Museum. The Hostage Crisis in Iran, http://www.jimmycarterlibrary.org/documents/hostages.phtml.

Johnson, Chalmers (1978). "Perspectives on Terrorism." In Walter Laqueur, ed. *The Terrorism Reader: A Historical Anthology*. New York: New American Library.

Jonathan Hensleigh. InstantCast.com. http://www.instantcast.com/AllStars/Jonathan_Hensleigh/Article.

Karim, Karim H. (2000). *Islamic Peril: Media and Global Violence*. Montreal, New York, London: Black Rose Books.

Kellner, Douglas (1995). *Media Culture: Cultural Studies, Identity and Politics between the Modern and the Postmodern*. London and New York: Routledge.

King, Cynthia (2000, Winter). "Effects of Humorous Heroes and Villains in Violent Action Films." *Journal of Communication*.

Klady, Leonard (1996, November 25–December 1). "Why mega-flicks click." *Variety*.

Kopel, David. Remarks at Cato Institute Conference on Terrorism. Cato Institute. http://www.cato.org/speeches/sp-dk101096.html.

Korn, David A. (1993). *Assassination in Khartoum*. Bloomington: Indiana University Press.

Kraft, Michael B. Introduction. In "Evolution of U.S. Counterterrorism Laws, Policies, and Programs." In Alexander, Yonah, and Michael B. Kraft, eds. *Evolution of U.S. Counterterrorism Policy*. Volume I. Westport, Conn.: Praeger Security International.

Krajicek, David J. (1998). *Scooped! Media Miss Real Story on Crime While Chasing Sex, Sleaze and Celebrities*. New York: Columbia University Press.

Laqueur, Walter (1987). *The Age of Terrorism*. Boston: Little, Brown.

Laqueur, Walter (1978). Introductory Note. Part I: Tyrannicide. In Walter Laqueur, ed. *The Terrorism Reader: A Historical Anthology*. New York: New American Library.

Laqueur, Walter (1999). *The New Terrorism: Fanaticism and the Arms of Mass Destruction*. New York and Oxford: Oxford University Press.

Laqueur, Walter (1978). "Terrorism: A Balance Sheet." In Walter Laqueur, ed. *The Terrorism Reader: A Historical Anthology*. New York: New American Library.

Leab, Daniel J. (1993). "Hollywood and the Cold War, 1945–1961." In Robert Bret Toplin, ed. *Hollywood as Mirror: Changing View of "Outsiders" and "Enemies" in American Movies*. No. 38 in Contributions to the Study of Popular Culture series. Westport, Conn.: Greenwood Press.

Lesage, Julia (1999, Spring Quarter). Graduate Course on Dramatic Screenwriting. Department of English, University of Oregon.

Lenihan, John H. (1993). "Hollywood Laughs at the Cold War, 1947–1961." In Robert Brent Toplin, ed. *Hollywood as Mirror: Changing View of "Outsiders" and "Enemies" in American Movies*. Westport, Conn.: Greenwood Press.

Lewis, Charles, and Mark Reading-Smith (2008, January 23). "Iraq: The War Card. Orchestrated Deception on the Path to War." The Center for Public Integrity. http://projects.publicintegrity.org/WarCard/Default.aspx?source=homeandcontext=overviewandid=945.

Long, Tom (2003, February 23). "Diversity in Entertainment: Minorities' Music Muscle Loses Punch at Box Office." Detnews.com. http://www.detnews.com/2004/entertainment/0402/26/a01-71699.htm.

Lorence, James J. (1993). "The 'Foreign Policy of Hollywood': Interventionist Sentiment in the American Film, 1938–1941." In Robert Brent Toplin, ed. *Hollywood as Mirror: Changing View of "Outsiders" and Enemies" in American Movies*. No. 38 in Contributions to the Study of Popular Culture. Westport, Conn.: Greenwood Press.

Lowry, Brian (1994, July 11). *True Lies*. Review. *Variety*.

Lyman, Rick (2001, October 3). "Bad Guys for Bad Times: Hollywood Struggles to Create Villains for a New Climate." *New York Times.*

Malik, Kenan (1996). *The Meaning of Race: Race, History and Culture in Western Society.* New York: New York University Press.

Maltby, Barbara (1998). "The Homogenization of Hollywood." In Nancy J. Woodhull and Robert W. Snyder, eds. *Media Mergers.* New Brunswick, N.J.: Transaction Publishers. (Original work published in *Media Studies Journal,* Spring/Summer 1996).

Maltby, Richard (1995). *Hollywood Cinema: An Introduction.* Cambridge, Mass.: Blackwell Publishers.

Maltby, Richard (2003). *Hollywood Cinema: An Introduction.* 2nd ed. Malden, Mass.: Blackwell Publishing.

McKinney, Devin (2000). "Violence: The Strong and the Weak." In Stephen Prince, ed. *Screening Violence.* New Brunswick, N.J.: Rutgers University Press.

McNally, David (1997). "Language, History, and Class Struggle." In Ellen Meiksins Wood and John Bellamy Foster, eds. *In Defense of History: Marxism and the Postmodern Agenda.* New York: Monthly Review Press.

Medd, Roger, and Frank Goldstein (1997). "International Terrorism on the Eve of a New Millennium." In *Studies in Conflict and Terrorism,* Vol. 20.

Metro-Goldwyn-Mayer (2009, March), http://www.mgm.com/corp_main.php.

MI5, the U.K. Security Service. "Provisional Irish Republican Army." http://www.mi5.gov.uk/output/provisional-irish-republican-army.html.

Miller, Martin A. (1995). "The Intellectual Origins of Modern Terrorism in Europe." In Martha Crenshaw, ed. *Terrorism in Context.* University Park: Pennsylvania State University Press.

Miller, Toby, Nitin Govil, John McMurria and Richard Maxwell (2001). *Global Hollywood.* London: BFI Publishing.

Miller, William (1998). *Screenwriting for Film and Television.* Boston: Allyn and Bacon.

Mitchell, Lee Clark (2001). "Violence in the Film Western." In J. David Slocum, ed. *Violence and American Cinema.* AFI Film Readers series. New York: Routledge.

Mosco, Vincent (1996). *The Political Economy of Communication: Rethinking and Renewal.* Thousand Oaks, Calif.: Sage Publications.

Motion Picture Association of America, http://www.mpaa.org/about/content.htm.

Motion Picture Association of America, http://www.mpaa.org/anti piracy/content.htm.

Motion Picture Association of America. "What Do the Ratings Mean?" http://www.mpaa.org/FlmRat_Ratings.asp.

Mowlana, Hamid (1997). *Global Information and World Communication: New Frontiers in International Relations.* 2nd ed. Thousand Oaks, Calif.: Sage.

MSN.Money (2009, February 12). "Joseph Cates Named Senior Vice President Technology, Universal Pictures." http://news.moneycentral.msn.com/ticker/article.aspx?symbol=US:GEandfeed=PRanddate=20090212andid=9605977.

Murdock, Graham, and Peter Golding (1997). "For a Political Economy of Mass Communications." In Peter Golding and Graham Murdock, eds. *The Political Economy of the Media I.* Cheltenham and Brookfield, Vt.: Edward Elgar. (Original work published in *Socialist Register,* 1973).

Nacos, Brigitte L. (1994). *Terrorism and the Media: From the Iran Hostage Crisis to the World Trade Center Bombing.* New York: Columbia University Press.

Nash, Jay (1998). *Terrorism in the 20th Century: A Narrative Encyclopedia from the Anarchists, through the Weathermen, to the Unabomber.* New York: M. Evans.

"A Nation Challenged: The Hunted; The 22 Most Wanted Suspects, in a Five-Act Drama of Global Terror." (2001, October 14). NYTimes.com, http://query.nytimes.com/gst/fullpage.html?res=9505E0D6103FF937A25753C1A9679C8B63#.

NBC Europe (2004, May 12). "NBC and Vivendi Universal Entertainment unite to create NBC Universal." http://www.cnbc.com/id/18037310.

NBC Universal. "Company Overview." http://www.nbcuni.com/About_NBC_Universal/Company_Overview.

Neale, Steve (2000). *Genre and Hollywood.* London and New York: Routledge.

"News judgment, professionalism are guides to crisis coverage" (1986, February 17) in *Broadcasting,* v110. Retrieved July 22, 2010, from Expanded Academic ASAP via Gale.

Nielsen EDI. http://www.acnielsenedi.com/about/about.html.

Norwitz, Jeffrey H. (2004). "Combating Terrorism: With a Helmet or a Badge?" In Russell D. Howard and Reid L. Sawyer, eds. *Terrorism and Counterterrorism. Understanding the New Security Environment: Readings and Interpretations.* Revised and Updated. Guilford, Conn.: McGraw-Hill/Dushkin. Original work published 2002).

O'Heffernan, Patrick (1991). *Mass Media and American Foreign Policy: Insider Perspectives on Global Journalism and the Foreign Policy Process.* Norwood: Ablex Publishing.

Organization of the Islamic Conference. http://www.oic.oci.org/member_states.

Paletz, David L., and Laura L. Tawney (1992). "Broadcast Organizations' Perspectives." In David L. Paletz and Alex P. Schmidt, *Terrorism and the Media.* Newbury Park, Calif.: Sage Publications.

Palmer, William J. (1993). *The Films of the Eighties: A Social History.* Carbondale: Southern Illinois University Press.

Parenti, Michael (1992). *Make-Believe Media: The Politics of Entertainment.* New York: St. Martin's Press.

Parks, W. Hays (2003, January 7). "Lessons from the 1986 Libya Airstrike." *New England Law Review 36*(4):755–766, http://www.nesl.edu/lawrev/vol36/4/parks.pdf.

Pearl, Raphael F. (1997). "Terrorism, the Media, and the Government: Perspectives, Trends, and Options of Policymakers." In *International Affairs, Foreign Affairs and National Defense Division. Congressional Research Service.* http://205.177.54.21/mterror.htm.

Peleg, Ilan (1988). "Terrorism in the Middle East: The Case of the Arab-Israeli Conflict." In Michael Stohl, ed. *The Politics of Terrorism.* 3rd ed. Revised and Expanded. New York and Basel: Marcel Dekker.

Perdue, William D. (1989) *Terrorism and the State: A Critique of Domination through Fear.* New York: Praeger Publishers.

The Pew Research Center for the People and the Press (2002, June 9). "Public's News Habits Little Changed by September 11; Americans Lack Background to Follow International News," http://people-press.org/reports/display.php3?ReportID=156.

Picard, Robert G. (1993). *Media Portrayals of Terrorism: Functions and Meaning of News Coverage.* Ames: Iowa State University Press.

Pillar, Paul R. (2004). "The Dimensions of Terrorism and Counterterrorism." In Russell D. Howard and Reid L. Sawyer, eds. *Terrorism and Counterterrorism. Understanding the New Security Environment: Readings and Interpretations.* Revised and Updated. Guilford, Conn.: McGraw-Hill/Dushkin. (Original work published 2001).

Prince, Stephen (2000). "Graphic Violence in the Cinema: Origins, Aesthetic Design, and Social Effects." In Stephen Prince, ed. *Screening Violence.* New Brunswick, N.J.: Rutgers University Press.

Prince, Stephen (2000). "Political Film in the Nineties." In

Wheeler Winston Dixon, ed. *Film Genre 2000: New Critical Essays.* Albany: State University of New York Press.

Reuters (1990, May 7). "'Jackal' Tells of Plan To Kidnap de Gaulle." NYTimes.com, http://query.nytimes.com/gst/fullpage.html?res=9C0CE1DC173CF934A35756C0A966958260.

Richard Nixon Library and Birthplace Foundation Research Center (1972, September 25). "Memorandum Establishing a Cabinet Committee to Combat Terrorism." http://www.nixonlibraryfoundation.org/index.php?src=gendocsand link=papers_1972.

Richardson, Louise (2004). "Global Rebels: Terrorist Organizations as Trans-National Actors." In Russell D. Howard and Reid L. Sawyer, eds. *Terrorism and Counterterrorism. Understanding the New Security Environment: Readings and Interpretations.* Revised and Updated. Guilford, Conn.: McGraw-Hill/Dushkin. (Original published [1998] in *Harvard International Review,* Fall).

Richter, Paul (1998, October 29). "White House Justifies Option of Lethal Force." *The Register Guard.*

Rosenblum, Mort (1993). *Who Stole the News? Why We Can't Keep Up with What Happens in the World and What We Can Do about It.* New York: John Wiley and Sons.

Rubenstein, Richard E. (1987). *Alchemists of Revolution: Terrorism in the Modern World.* New York: Basic Books.

Ruiz, Raul (1995). *Poetics of Cinema.* Translated by Brian Holmes. Paris: Editions Dis Voir.

Ryan, Charlotte, Kevin M. Carragee, and Cassie Schwerner (1998). "Media, Movements, and the Quest for Social Justice." *Journal of Applied Communication Research 26.*

Schatz, Thomas (1994). "Genre." In Gary Crowdus, ed. *A Political Companion to American Film.* Chicago, Ill.: Lake View Press.

Schatz, Thomas (1981). *Hollywood Genres: Formulas, Filmmaking, and the Studio System.* Philadelphia: Temple University Press.

Schiller, Herbert (1973). *The Mind Managers.* Boston: Beacon Press.

Schodolski, Vincent J. (2001, November 12) "Administration Drafts Hollywood Effort." *Chicago Tribune.*

Scott, Allen J. (2005). *On Hollywood: The Place, the Industry.* Princeton, N.J.: Princeton University Press.

Seaton, Edward (1998, July 1; last updated 2002, August 28). "The Diminishing Use of Foreign News Reporting." Speech delivered May 26, 1998, in Moscow, before the International Press Institute by Edward Seaton, editor-in-chief, The Manhattan (Kan.) *Mercury,* 1998–99 American Society of Newspaper Editors President, http://asne.org/index.cfm?ID=627.

Seib, Philip. *Headline Diplomacy: How News Coverage Affects Foreign Policy.* Westport, Conn.: Praeger, 1997.

Shaheen, Jack G. (2001). *Reel Bad Arabs: How Hollywood Vilifies People.* New York and Northampton: Olive Branch Press.

Simon, Jeffrey D. (1994). *The Terrorist Trap: America's Experience with Terrorism.* Bloomington and Indianapolis: Indiana University Press.

Simon, Jeffrey David (2001). *The Terrorist Trap: America's Experience with Terrorism.* 2nd ed. Bloomington: Indiana University Press.

Slocum, J. David. (2001). "Introduction: Violence and American Cinema." Notes for an Investigation. In J. David Slocum, ed. *Violence and American Cinema.* AFI Film Readers series. New York: Routledge.

Smith, G. Davidson (1990). *Combating Terrorism.* London: Routledge.

Sobchack, Thomas (1988). "The Adventure Film." In Wes D. Gehring, ed. *Handbook of American Film Genres.* Westport, Conn.: Greenwood Press.

Sobchack, Vivian C. (2000). "The Violent Dance: A Personal Memoir of Death in the Movies." In Stephen Prince (2000) *Screening Violence.* New Brunswick, N.J.: Rutgers University Press.

Steinbock, Dan (1995). *Triumph and Erosion in the American Media and Entertainment Industries.* Westport, Conn.: Quorum Books.

Steuter, Erin (1990). "Understanding the Media/Terrorism Relationship: An Analysis of Ideology and the News in *Time* Magazine." In *Political Communication and Persuasion 7.*

Stoffa, Adam Paul (2005). "Special Forces, Counterterrorism, and the Law of Armed Conflict." In *Studies in Conflict and Terrorism* no. 18.

Stohl, Michael (1988). "Demystifying Terrorism: The Myths and Realities of Contemporary Political Terrorism." In Michael Stohl, ed. *The Politics of Terrorism.* 3rd ed. Revised and Expanded. New York and Basel: Marcel Dekker.

Stohl, Michael (1988). "National Interests and State Terrorism." In Michael Stohl, ed. *The Politics of Terrorism.* 3rd ed. Revised and Expanded. New York and Basel: Marcel Dekker.

Suid, Lawrence H. (2002). *Guts and Glory: The Making of the American Military Image in Film.* Revised and Expanded Edition. Lexington: University Press of Kentucky.

Swanson Goldberg, Elizabeth (2001). "Splitting Difference: Global Identity Politics and the Representation of Torture in the Counterhistorical Dramatic Film." In J. David Slocum, ed. *Violence and American Cinema.* New York: Routledge, 2001.

Taylor, Philip M. (1997). *Global Communications: International Affairs and the Media since 1945.* London and New York: Routledge.

Terrel, Robert, and Kristina Ross (1991). "The Voluntary Guidelines' Threat to U.S. Press Freedom." In Yonah Alexander and Robert G. Picard, eds. *In the Camera's Eye: News Coverage of Terrorist Events.* New York: Brassey's.

Thompson, Kristin, and David Bordwell. *Film History: An Introduction.* 2nd ed. New York: McGraw-Hill: 2003.

Thurber, Jon. (2005, February 27). "Uli Derickson, Brave Flight Attendant." *Seattle Times.* http://seattletimes.nwsource.com/html/nationworld/2002191381_derickson obit27.html.

Thussu, Daya Kishan (2000). *International Communication: Continuity and Change.* London: Arnold, co-published in the United States of America by Oxford University Press, New York.

Trends in Terrorism. Report # 2000/01 (1999, December 18). In *Perspectives.* Canadian Security Intelligence Service Publication.

Trumpbour, John (2002). *Selling Hollywood to the World: U.S. and European Struggles for Mastery of the Global Film Industry, 1920–1950.* Cambridge, U.K.: Cambridge University Press.

Tuchman, Gaye (1978). *Making the News: A Study in Construction of Reality.* London: Free Press.

United Artists. http://www.unitedartists.com.

United Artists (2007, September 16). "MGM Partners with Tom Cruise and Paula Wagner; Paula Wagner to Serve as CEO of the New UA." http://www.unitedartists.com/popups/pr/release_08.html.

Valenti, Jack (1968, reprint 2000). "Statement by Jack Valenti, MPAA President, before the National Commission on the Causes and Prevention of Violence." In Stephen Prince, ed. *Screening Violence.* New Brunswick, N.J.: Rutgers University Press.

Van Deburg, William L. "Popular Culture Prophesy: Black American Slavery in Film." In Robert Brent Toplin, ed. *Hollywood as Mirror: Changing View of "Outsiders" and Enemies" in American Movies.* Westport, Conn.: Greenwood Press.

Van Dijk, Teun A. (1998). *Ideology. A Multidisciplinary Approach.* Thousand Oaks, Calif.: Sage Publications.

Van Dijk, Teun A. (1988). *News as Discourse.* Hillsdale, N.J.: Lawrence Erlbaum Associates.

Van Zoonen, Liesbet (1996). "A Dance of Death: New Social Movements and Mass Media." In David D. Paletz, ed. *Political Communication in Action: States, Institutes, Movements, Audiences.* Cresskill, N.J.: Hampton Press.

Variety.com, box office data: Top 250 films of the years 1980–2001.

Video Software Dealers Association (2001, September). Press Release. http://www.vsda.org/news/press/press.phtml.

Vivendi. "Company History." http://www.vivendi.com/vivendi/Company-history.

Vivendi Universal. Press Release. http://www.vivendiuniversal.com/vu/en/press_2003/20031008_General_Electric_and_Vivendi_Universal_Sign_Agreement_To_Merge_NBC_and_Vive.cfm.

"Walt Disney Studios, DreamWorks reach deal." Associated Press through the *Los Angeles Times,* Business (2009, February 9).

Wardlaw, Grant (1989). *Political Terrorism: Theory, Tactics, and Counter-Measures.* 2nd ed. Cambridge, U.K.: Cambridge University Press.

The Washington Post. The U.S. Congress Votes Database at http://projects.washingtonpost.com/congress/107/senate/2/votes/237, and at http://projects.washingtonpost.com/congress/107/house/2/votes/455.

Wasko, Janet (1994). *Hollywood in the Information Age: Beyond the Silver Screen.* Texas Film Studies series. Ed. Thomas Schatz. Cambridge, U.K.: Polity Press.

Wasko, Janet (2003). *How Hollywood Works.* Thousand Oaks, Calif.: Sage Publications.

Weimann, Gabriel (1992). "Modern Terrorism, the Media and Public Opinion." In Stanley Rothman, ed. *The Mass Media in Liberal Democratic Societies.* In Morton A. Kaplan, Ed. World Social Systems series. New York: Paragon House.

Weimann, Gabriel, and Conrad Winn (1994). *The Theater of Terror: Mass Media and International Terrorism.* New York and London: Longman.

Welsh, James M. (2000). "Action Films: The Serious, the Ironic, the Post-Modern." In Wheeler Winston Dixon, ed. *Film Genre 2000: New Critical Essays.* Albany: State University of New York Press.

Westcott, Kathryn (2007, September 6, last updated). "Is Noriega Too Hot to Handle?" BBC News, http://news.bbc.co.uk/2/hi/americas/6965870.stm.

Whitney, Craig R. (1998, November 15). "Jailed Carlos, the Terrorist, Is Continuing Hunger Strike." New York Times. http://query.nytimes.com/gst/fullpage.html?res=9A05E0D71331F936A25752C1A96E958260.

Wieviorka, Michael (1993). *The Making of Terrorism.* Trans. David Gordon White. Chicago: University of Chicago Press.

Wieviorka, Michael (1995). "Terrorism in the Context of Academic Research." In Martha Crenshaw, ed. *Terrorism in Context.* University Park: Pennsylvania State University Press.

Wilkinson, Paul (1986). *Terrorism and the Liberal State.* 2nd ed. New York: New York University Press.

Williams, Raymond (1977). *Marxism and Literature.* New York: Oxford University Press.

Woll, Allen L. (1993). "Hollywood Views the Mexican-American: From *The Greaser's Revenge* to *The Milagro Beanfield War.*" In Robert Brent Toplin, ed. *Hollywood as Mirror: Changing View of "Outsiders" and "Enemies" in American Movies.* In Contributions to the Study of Popular Culture, Number 38. Westport, Conn.: Greenwood Press.

Worsdale, Andrew (1999, January 12). "A Siege on Islamic Sensibilities." *Mail and Guardian* Online. http://www.mg.co.za/mg/art/film/9901/990112-siege.html.

Wright, Robin (2004, April 1). "Top Focus before 9/11 Wasn't on Terrorism" A01. Report contributions from staff researcher Lucy Shackelford and staff writer Mark Stencel.

Index

Numbers in ***bold italics*** indicate pages with photographs.